TIM MACKINTOSH-SMIT[illegible]
whose previous publications [illegible] *Yemen* and *Landfalls*. In 2011, he was named by *Newsweek* as one of the twelve finest travel writers of the past hundred years. He has lived in the Arab world for over three decades, and is a Fellow of the Royal Asiatic Society and a Senior Fellow of the Library of Arabic Literature.

Further praise for *Arabs*:

'This astounding book portrays grand personalities, national journeys and thrilling adventures . . . A thoroughly remarkable achievement, unlike any other such history.' Steve Donoghue, *The National*

'This brilliant and fascinating history book will change the way we analyze the happenings in the Arab world.' *Washington Book Review*

'A true insight into the essence of Arab existence.' HRH Prince El Hassan bin Talal of Jordan

'A wonderful new book . . . Mackintosh-Smith combines deep learning with penetrating insights delivered with dazzling turns of phrase and illuminating comparisons.' Ian Black, *Observer*

'Mackintosh-Smith is ideally positioned to make the tangled past vividly present. . . . He handles his complex account with great aplomb.' Eric Ormsby, *Wall Street Journal*

'A long time in the making, Mackintosh-Smith's erudite study was worth the wait.' Justin Marozzi, *Evening Standard*

'A dazzling achievement, born of a historian's passionate affection for his subject . . . I have never felt so transported, so entertained and so immersed.' Barnaby Rogerson, *History Today*

'An accessible and readable account of a complex and long history.' Seth J. Frantzman, *Jerusalem Post*

'Extraordinary.' Shiraz Maher, *New Statesman*

'Elegant and provocative . . . It is tempting to reduce events to a few stereotypes. Mackintosh-Smith is far too keen an observer of all that surrounds him to give in to such enticement.' Lawrence Rosen, author of *Islam and the Rule of Justice*

OTHER WORKS BY THE AUTHOR

Travel/History

Yemen: Travels in Dictionary Land (1997)

Travels with a Tangerine: A Journey in the Footnotes of Ibn Battutah (2001)

The Hall of a Thousand Columns: Hindustan to Malabar with Ibn Battutah (2005)

Landfalls: On the Edge of Islam with Ibn Battutah (2010)

Editions/Translations

The Travels of Ibn Battutah (2002)

Two Arabic Travel Books (with James E. Montgomery; 2014)

Kitab al-Ifadah (Abd al-Latif al-Baghdadi's description of Egypt; forthcoming)

Fiction

Bloodstone (2017)

ARABS

A 3,000-YEAR HISTORY OF PEOPLES, TRIBES AND EMPIRES

TIM MACKINTOSH-SMITH

YALE UNIVERSITY PRESS
NEW HAVEN AND LONDON

First published in paperback in 2019

For information about this and other Yale University Press publications, please contact:
U.S. Office: sales.press@yale.edu yalebooks.com
Europe Office: sales@yaleup.co.uk yalebooks.co.uk

Set in Fournier MT by IDSUK (DataConnection) Ltd
Printed and bound by CPI Group (UK) Ltd, Croydon, CR0 4YY

Library of Congress Control Number: 2018968579

ISBN 978-0-300-18028-2 (hbk)
ISBN 978-0-300-25163-0 (pbk)

A catalogue record for this book is available from the British Library.

10 9 8 7 6 5 4 3 2 1

Sha'b: . . . Collection, or union; and also separation, division, or disunion . . . A nation, people, race, or family of mankind . . .
Edward William Lane, *An Arabic-English Lexicon*

And if your Lord had so willed, He could surely have made mankind one community. But they will not cease to disagree.
Qur'an 11:118

Thus we had upwards of 1,400 separate tribal 'governments' in the two [Hadhrami] states. There were also several hundred autonomous towns of unarmed men . . . Altogether I calculated there were about 2,000 separate 'governments' in the Hadhramaut.
Harold Ingrams, *Arabia and the Isles*

In memory of a unified Yemen (1990–2014)
and of Ali Husayn Ash'ab (1998–2016)
and all the others who died with it.

CONTENTS

CONTENTS

ILLUSTRATIONS AND MAPS

ILLUSTRATIONS

MAPS

FOREWORD

THE WHEEL AND THE HOURGLASS

لا أَحْسِبُ الدهْرَ يُبْلي جِدَّةً أبداً   ولا تُقَسِّمُ شعبًا واحدًا شُعَبُ

I did not think that time would ever wear out what was new,
or that its changes would divide a people who were one.
Dhu 'l-Rummah

Twenty-seven years ago I began work on my first book, an exploration of the land and history of Yemen, the country in which I was living, and where I still live now. The two former parts of the country had been unified not long before, in May 1990, just ahead of German unification. Walls were coming down, iron curtains parting, and a line in the wilderness was being erased. In Yemen, it was a time of optimism. Admittedly, there was a short war of attempted secession in 1994, in which the former regime in the south shot almost as many Scud missiles at us in San'a as Saddam Husayn had launched at Israel three years earlier; in response, our rulers in the north inflicted a horde of straggle-bearded islamists on Aden who trashed, *inter alia*, the only brewery in Arabia. But the unified Yemen survived. Bygones, it seemed, became bygones.

That first book of mine was a homage to a land that had held on to much from its past, to its millennial cultural unity. Between the lines, the book was also homage to its renewed political unity. Yemen had been a unified state in earlier periods: in pre-Islamic times, briefly in the fourteenth century, briefly again in the seventeenth. To many Yemenis, as to me, that unity seemed, still seems, to be somehow right and proper, something natural. It seemed right at least as long ago as the fourteenth century: 'If Yemen were to be united under one ruler,' wrote an observer in Egypt, 'its importance would increase and its position among the eminent nations would be strengthened'.

In fact, for more than nine-tenths of its known history, Yemen has not been unified; far from it. Now, as I write, it appears to be falling apart again. So too, seemingly, are Iraq and Libya; Syria may hold together, just, under brute force; Egypt's integrity looks safe, but its society is deeply riven. These five countries contain half the population of the Arabic-speaking world. According to a recent United Nations report, that 'world' is home to 5 per cent of humanity, but generates 58 per cent of the earth's refugees and 68 per cent of its 'battle-related deaths' . . . Sometimes it seems that only one thing unites Arabs, and that is their inability to get along with each other. Why this disunity? Why this extraordinary level of self-harm?

'The absence of democracy and its institutions,' Westerners (shorthand but useful) would say. They may have a point; but recent foreign interventions allegedly aiming to promote democracy appear only to have added to the mayhem. And when there *are* free and fair elections, the islamists tend to win them; the elections are annulled in a military coup, and the Westerners go strangely silent. Mouths and money do not go together, it seems.

'The failure of Islam to unify itself,' the islamists (again, shorthand) would say. But that unity has itself been a mirage almost from the Islamic year dot. Battles over authority and legitimacy have been fought within the community of Muslims, with words and other weapons, since the fourth decade of the Islamic era.

'The legacy of imperialism,' Arab nationalists (there are still a few left) would say. But nearly every attempt at unity in the post-imperial age has failed, usually because of inter-Arab suspicions and squabbles. One Arab commentator, in a post-mortem on the 1948 Arab-Israeli war, wrote that 'The Arabs would have won the battle for Palestine had there not been something false and rotten in themselves'. That 'something' was mutual distrust, resentment and fear. It was the rottenness of bad blood, and it has bubbled up time and again through Arab history.

Of course, disunity is hardly an Arab monopoly. Much of the map of Europe was a crazy paving of statelets well into the modern age. That German reunification of 1990, itself part of a contrary process that fragmented the Soviet Union, was a return to a unity that was then a mere two lifetimes old. During those lifetimes, Europe had been the epicentre of wars that blasted apart the Ottoman and Austro-Hungarian empires and led to the gentler meltdown of the British empire – but out of which came the United Nations and the European Union (those well-known bastions of unanimity). All the world's a crucible in which once-stable compounds are continually breaking down and new ones forming. If there were no such change, there would be no history. Union and division are part of the same process. Hence the first epigraph to this book, from Lane's *Arabic-English Lexicon*:

> Sha'b: . . . Collection, or union; and also separation, division, or disunion . . . A nation, people, race, or family of mankind . . .

(Things become slightly clearer when we see how this apparent contradiction in terms works: as well as a 'people' and all these other things, a *sha'b* is also a cranial suture, the place where the bones of the skull both meet and are separated; the bones themselves are called *qabilah*s, otherwise meaning 'tribes' . . . It is as if the human head, with its 'peoples' and 'tribes', provides an Arabic anatomy of humankind itself.)

And yet the Arabs always seem a special case. Don't we, and they themselves, usually call them just that – 'the' Arabs, as if they were a discrete and clearly identifiable body of people? If they are, then who are they? And why do they seem so particularly fissile, so reactive? Should there not be at least an Arab Union, or even a United Arabian States? . . . Come to think of it, there *was* a United Arab States (UAS), forgotten by most histories: it was a confederation formed of the United Arab Republic (UAR) – itself a political union of Egypt and Syria in the brief heyday of pan-Arabism – joined by the then Kingdom of North Yemen. The UAS and UAR lasted all of forty-four months, from 1958 to 1961.

There is no reason why political unity should be a good thing *per se*. But I believe there is a case for claiming that unity in at least a general sense – that of harmony, the absence of strife, peaceful coexistence and cooperation – is better for human society than fragmentation and violent competition.

On a small planet with too many people and too few resources, and particularly in crowded countries like Syria, Egypt and Yemen, it seems to hold out the only hope.

Unless we kill each other and start all over again.

Histories of Arabs tend to begin with Islam; perhaps with a prefatory nod to what came before. Islam certainly furnishes an identifiable body of people, unified for a great moment in history. But it was a unity that was apparent, not real. According to traditional accounts, the tribes of Arabia came together in 630–1, the Year of Delegations, when tribal representatives visited the Prophet Muhammad and paid allegiance to him and the state he had founded. Within two years, on the death of Muhammad, most of those tribes had gone back to their old independences and old squabbles. At first the splits were patched up, and the extraordinary conquests that took Arabs out of Arabia forged among them an esprit de corps that seemed miraculous – indeed, God-given. But the underlying tribal divisions were never healed. Within 300 years united Arab rule was only an elaborately cherished memory, and for the next thousand years or so Arabs, with few exceptions, were themselves divided and ruled by Turks, Persians, Berbers, Europeans and others. Their own empire had been amputated; the pain would subside in time, but the memory of it would remain, like that of a phantom limb.

The historiographical upshot of this is that political histories of Arabs by modern writers nearly always turn, when they reach about AD 900, into histories of Arabic culture, then – while Arabs themselves all but disappear from the picture – morph into histories of other peoples' empires. Part of the problem is the word 'Arab' itself. Like any name, it is not identical with the thing it denotes, but is a label placed on that thing. Labels are useful but confusing. They can cover up a multitude of differences and can hold splits together; they can tell lies. In time, a label fades and gets over-written, while its original meaning – if it ever had just the one – is forgotten. In reality, we are all like old-fashioned travelling trunks, covered with many labels, geographical, genetic, linguistic and so on (*inter alia*, I am British/English/Scottish/Anglo-Saxon/Celtic/European/Indo-European/Yemeni/Arabian/Arab(ic) . . .); few sections of humanity are as belabelled as the long-travelled people known as Arabs. But, in the end, most of us get stuck with just one label, and adhere to it, as it does to us. The broader it is, the harder it sticks.

'Arab' is a label that is very broad, very sticky (it has been around for almost 3,000 years), and yet very slippery. It has signified different things to different people at different times. The meaning has shape-shifted, expired and resurrected so often that it is misleading to talk about 'the' Arabs, and that is why this book does not. To do so would be to try to pin down Proteus. All one can say is that, for more of known history than not, the word has tended to mean tribal groups who live beyond the reach of settled society. That is probably what Arabs were during much of the long period up to Islam; it is certainly what they were throughout most of the second AD millennium. During both periods, there is good reason for transliterating them as a common noun, in italics, not as a 'proper' people: as *'arab*, not 'Arabs'. What is surprising is that those peripheral, mobile, numerically insignificant people – people without a capital letter, let alone a capital city – have been so central to an identity. From Greek city-states in the fifth century BC, through imperial China, to recently colonial Europe, societies have defined and simplified themselves in contradistinction to the nomad, the 'uncivilized', the 'barbarian'. Arabs, however, take not only their name but also their only consistent defining feature, their language, from the epitome of nomadism and footlooseness, those tribal *'arab*.

The people we know today as Arabs are an ethnic compound. The two main founding elements, nomadic or semi-nomadic *'arab* tribes and settled South Arabian peoples, may both have originated in the Fertile Crescent to the north of Arabia in prehistoric times; their languages descended from the same old 'Semitic' family. But over time their tongues had forked and split, and so too had their lifestyles: the South Arabians had developed settled societies based on irrigation systems and agriculture (they may well have inherited these systems from older, indigenous peoples already established in the Arabian south, with whom they intermingled); *'arab*, in contrast, practised pastoral transhumance, their wanderings directed by wells, rains and raids. Mutual interests, both commercial and political, meant that these two founding elements began to come together in the centuries before Islam. In early Islamic times, the shared experience of empire-building made the compound more cohesive for a time – but also more complex, as peoples from beyond the Arabian Peninsula were assimilated to the mix. Throughout this long process, tribal *'arab* were part of – indeed, at the heart of – Arabs in the wider sense; they still are, despite their tiny numbers. But they themselves have always complicated Arab history from the inside. For the tensions between the settled and unsettled elements of the compound have generated great strengths, but also fatal instabilities. We will examine these strengths and weaknesses in the coming chapters.

One force above all has brought the compound together, and held it together: language – not everyday speech, but the rich, strange, subtle, suavely hypnotic, magically persuasive, maddeningly difficult 'high' Arabic language that evolved on the tongues of tribal soothsayers and poets – has long, perhaps always, been the catalyst of a larger Arab identity. Shared language is important to any ethnic identity. It is an attempt to reverse the divinely inflicted disunity of Babel, that babble of misunderstanding that prevents people from coming together. For Arabs, it has acted not just as an ethnic marker, but as the ethnic genius: 'It is said,' goes an adage that was already old in the ninth century AD, 'that wisdom descended from the heavens on three organs of the people of the earth: the brains of the Greeks, the hands of the Chinese, and the tongues of the Arabs.'

For this reason, while history is often seen as a succession of men of action, Arab history is as much, or even more, a series of men (and some women) of words – poets, preachers, orators, authors; notably, the author (or, for Muslims, the transmitter) of the first Arabic book, the Qur'an. They and the words they have used will be prominent in this book. They are the ones who have formed identity, forged unity and forced the march of history. From time to time, therefore, for a page or two, we will take stock of how language has impelled progress, and at times impeded it. Progress and regress continue. Recent events, not least the 'Arab Spring' and its messy aftermath, have shown how words – slogans, chants, propaganda, mis- and disinformation, the old mesmerizing magic both white and black – still shape the course of the Arab world.

Or, rather, the Arab*ic* world, the Arabosphere. Language is still its defining feature and its genius, and 'the Arabs' are really arabophones. To call everyone from the Strait of Gibraltar to the Strait of Hormuz 'the Arabs' would be like calling all North Americans, South Africans, Australasians, Irish and British, regardless of origin, 'the English' – or even 'the Angles', another group of wandering clans whose language was to end up as the tide-wrack of a long-ebbed empire.

To explore the origins of the shared identity that – despite everything – has led Arabs to chase the mirage of unity, we must therefore listen to their language. We must also go back way beyond Islam. The pre-Islamic past is certainly less well known and much less knowable. But in terms of written history it is as long as the period since that fateful Islamic eruption from Arabia. The first known ancient inscription mentioning Arabs dates from 853 BC; I am writing the first draft of these words in AD 2017; according to tradition, the boy Muhammad was first recognized as a prophet in AD 582 – the precise mid-point between that inscription and now.

Islam began with such a flash that it tends to blind us to what was there before. Equally, the flash has cast its own powerful illumination over all subsequent history, throwing much into shadow. We need to look at the whole historical picture, and in a more even light; to give a stereoscopic view, one that sees what has happened since the Islamic year zero as only half of a panorama that goes back at least as far again.

What did begin with Islam, and gives the impression that a unified Arab narrative begins then too, was Arabic information technology – in other words, new ways to use and control language, and thus to shape identity. Before Islam, literature, culture, history, identity were largely oral. From Islam onwards, new technologies have underlain most of the major developments in Arab history. We will look more closely at them as they crop up over time; for now, a summary will give an idea of just how important they are to the story. In the early seventh century, the first, belated, Arabic book appeared – the Qur'an: overnight, in the terms of our 3,000-year timescale, it made a language and the various people who used it legible, visible. Suddenly they were there on their own page, in black and white. They already had a past; now they entered their historic present, and with an energy that won them a vast empire.

In about 700, a snap decision to ditch the inherited Greek and Persian languages of imperial administration in favour of Arabic also arabicized that whole empire and its peoples with amazing speed: Arabic became the new Latin. In the later eighth century, Arab paper-making stole a long march on a Europe still wrapped up in an age of parchment, and released an outpouring of Arabic words and ideas. Seven centuries later, with printing, Europe stole its own march; cursive Arabic script never worked happily as moveable type, and typeset Arabic was long viewed in its homeland rather as tinned spaghetti is in Italy. When at long last, in the nineteenth century, Arabic presses did grind slowly into action, so too did an Arab renaissance, the *Nahdah* or 'awakening'. Another hundred years on, and a new and thrilling pan-Arab nationalism was broadcast by the border-defying transistor radio. A generation later, Arabic typesetters finally found the antidote to the cursive curse – word-processing; at the same time satellite TV took off, and the words flew further and faster. Most recently, the social media of the early twenty-first century began to subvert old rhetorics and air alternative truths . . . until the reactionaries got on to Facebook too. Now digital dinosaurs do their best to dominate media and minds.

And yet the pre-Islamic half of history had its social media, its dominating voices; words flew then, too. Most of them flew away on the wind. But some were caught – on stones, in memories – and we can and must still try to listen to them.

A distinguished historian who begins in the middle, with Islam, is Albert Hourani. He draws the reader into his subject with a portrait of the great fourteenth-century Arab historian, Ibn Khaldun. After decades lived in the thick of intrigues and warring factions, Ibn Khaldun took himself off to a fortified village in rural Algeria and went into a period of intense intellectual retreat. He looked hard at what was going on around him and, with 'words and ideas pouring into my head like cream into a churn' as he put it (lucky man!), came up with a model for the rise and fall of dynasties. In short, the model explains how a nomad tribe can be united by what he calls *'asabiyyah*, literally something like 'bindedness' but often translated as 'group solidarity', and thus gain in military strength. The tribe takes over the rule of a settled state by force, and its leaders become a new dynasty: the once peripheral and footloose become the central and settled. In time, however – usually three generations – the energy of the dynasty is sapped by easy living, and the dynasty falls to a new one that still enjoys the old nomad vitality. ('Clogs to clogs,' as they used to say in Lancashire of a parallel kind of social mobility, 'is only three generations.')

Hourani was an academic, a library man writing from the purlieus of St Antony's College, Oxford. With his academic eye, he viewed Ibn Khaldun as a figure who represented an age and a culture. Rereading both authors in my tower-house in Yemen, I had a realization: here, in the thick of it, kept awake by mortars and missiles (my third major conflict) and bombarded by slogans and sermons and poems – political, not lyrical, poems – all day, I saw Ibn Khaldun as a fellow observer, sitting in his isolated redoubt in Algeria as I sit here in San'a, while tribes and dynasties make war and deals and plots and more war around us, both of us forming our philosophy of history from direct experience. While Hourani used Ibn Khaldun as a literary device, I find myself unintentionally impersonating him. In other words, I am experiencing history *in situ*. Its detritus lies beneath me, for my little tower stands on the tail-end of a ruin-mound built up of bits of pre-Islamic San'a – one of the great cities of Saba, or Sheba – as well as of the Abbasid governor's palace and God knows what else. *In situ*, and in real time: the raw materials of history are there, outside my window. (A group of small children has just gone past, shouting 'Death to America!' They are accompanied by the rat-tat-tats of drumbeats and firecrackers, and are followed by a red box, born aloft, containing yet another martyr. The box is pitifully small.)

The raw materials these days seem to be mostly steel and lead. Stuck recently with a flat battery and a kind fellow motorist but no jump-leads, we had a simultaneous lateral thought – and stopped a couple of tribesmen. We borrowed their AK47 assault rifles, and used them to join the batteries. The car started first go. Only connect! 'So they do have positive benefits,' I said brightly, handing the guns back. 'Their benefit,' one of the tribesmen replied, 'is killing.'

What can one say? In my first book I wrote that, in Yemen, I felt like both the guest at the feast and the fly on the wall. Nowadays I feel more like the skeleton at the feast and the fly in the soup. But one has to try to make light of it. Seeing the land I live in and love falling apart is like watching an old and dear friend losing his mind and committing slow, considered suicide.

I find that Ibn Khaldun's model, his elegant paradigm, still works. But I believe it can be further tuned in ways that make its workings clearer still, and more clearly applicable over the three millennia or so of recorded Arab history. The most important feature is still *'asabiyyah*, that collective potential energy that catalyses a short-lived unity:

'asabiyyah, in time, builds the momentum for

. . . a successful raid, conquest or, *mutatis mutandis*, coup d'état;

. . . as a result of the raid/conquest/coup, and of the group's resulting monopoly of resources (camels, taxes, oil and gas), the group prospers;

. . . either the resources are not enough for the group as it increases in size, and/or its leaders fall out over the division of wealth, so . . . unity fragments.

Eventually a new *'asabiyyah* will form, and the process will repeat itself.

I find also that Ibn Khaldun was right to see 'nomads' as the reservoir of change, and I believe – strange though it sounds – that in a sense this is still true today, even though the number of Arabs who actually live from nomadism is now infinitesimally small. Ibn Khaldun's two basic systems of human society are still in place:

hadari, or 'settled', political society, a (relatively) static system characterized by the related word *hadarah* – often translated as 'civilization', in the sense of people living together in a settlement, a town (Latin *civitas*, Greek *polis*); and

badawi, or 'bedouin', apolitical society, a dynamic system in which people live beyond the civil polity, and in which the basic 'institution' is that of the *ghazw* or raid (or conquest or coup d'état).

My point is that, while actual Bedouin are now a dying breed, there are still plenty of major players in the Arab game whose actions accord perfectly with that second, 'bedouin' system. The two systems, settled 'peoples' and bedouin 'tribes', are mentioned in a famous verse of the Qur'an, from which I take part of the subtitle of this book:

> O mankind, We have created you from male and female, and made you into peoples and tribes, that you may know one another.

The duality has been in place since the beginning of recorded Arab time, and it has not always been a question of opposition. That first mention of Arabs in 853 BC concerns the employment by the Assyrian state of a transport contractor, a certain Gindibu ('Locust'), an Arab chieftain who owned vast herds of camels: settled and bedouin societies benefited mutually. Moving to the mid-point in Arab history, part of the Prophet Muhammad's success was due to his combining elements of both the settled and bedouin systems to set up the original Islamic state. In recent times, the almost total failure of the popular democratic revolutions of 2011 has been bound up with a reassertion of the 'bedouin' system over the settled. The Yemen I see outside my window, for example, was considered until the summer of 2014 to be a success story of the Arab Spring, of the aspiration to build a settled, civil society. Since then, the northern part of the country has been seized in an armed raid – the resurgence of an old faction that had ruled for a thousand years – a civil war has raged, and the neighbouring states (all ruled by what Ibn Khaldun would class as 'Bedouin' dynasties) have weighed in. History, as I said, in real time. Wars are the worst of history, and civil wars are the worst of wars: they are waged not just within, but *against* civil society. Ibn Khaldun had no doubt who the main culprits were: 'civilization', he wrote, 'always collapsed in places where the Bedouins took over'.

Nowadays, it is not that actual nomads on camels undermine state institutions, hijack democratic uprisings or ignite civil conflict. But it does seem clear that the central nomad institution – the raid, the *ghazw* – is still very much alive. That, perhaps, is why the image of camel-borne regime loyalists causing mayhem among the Tahrir Square protesters in Cairo in 2011 was so potent. Elsewhere, the latest Toyota pick-ups mounted with heavy-calibre machine-guns are potent enough.

'Raiding' is a loaded word, of course; it smacks of the piratical, the barbarian, the uncivilized in its pejorative sense. But raiding is also an established institution, in that it is a long-accepted means for the redistribution, sometimes more equitable, of wealth. The means by which it is pursued may not be regarded as acceptable in some peoples' ethical systems, but, looked at coldly, they are rational: you have a surplus, I have a deficit, therefore I will take your surplus. It is important to remember that different cultures have different rationalities; even cannibals, as cultural commentators from Montaigne to Marshall Sahlins have explained, have their own rationalities. People may be essentially the same the world over, but they go about being the same in different ways.

For much of Arab history, two rationalities have coexisted, those of the 'settled' and of the 'bedouin', the peoples and the tribes, seemingly in perpetual duality, clashing yet embracing, loving and hating, yin and yang.

But which rationality is the more 'Arab'? Herein is a great dilemma of Arab identity: the term 'Arab', as I have said, has most often been applied to tribal groups who live outside settled society, beyond the pale and the politics of civil institutions. In one sense, therefore, the more Arabs submit to civil society, the less 'Arab' they become; they lose something of their ethos. In a globalized, urbanizing world of blurring identities, the prospect of losing that ancient aspect of arabness, of becoming part of the global blur, is painful.

There is more to the story than peoples and tribes. Draw back, look at the bigger picture on the map and over time, and it becomes clear that the cycle of unification and fragmentation sketched out above has been in motion within a context of empires – Assyrian, Roman, Persian, Byzantine, Ottoman, British, American. It is a cycle that has teeth, but is not necessarily vicious: sometimes the teeth have meshed with imperial interests at the points of contact – the two Fertile Crescents (more on them later), Egypt and Iran; at other times they have clashed. In both cases there is friction, heat, conflagration: the cycle is a wheel of fire, both creative and destructive, melding, melting and remoulding Arab identities over 3,000 years.

In telling the Arab story, this book will look more at that seemingly eternal and often tragic round of unity and fragmentation, and also at that force that feeds the fire, fuels revolutions and has, more than anything, defined Arabs across a history of shifting and regrouping identities: the Arabic language. Language is what ties together all those key historical developments based on information technology, from the word of God captured in writing, to word-processing, and on to mind-processing by newly reactionary regimes. Language is the thread that all would-be Arab leaders have tried to grasp: their aim has always been to create *'asabiyyah*, that 'bindedness' or unanimity – to 'gather the word' of their peoples and tribes, as Arabic also puts it.

This is a history of Arabs, not of Arabic. But to follow the linguistic thread through it is to explore the deepest strand of 'being Arab' in all its different senses. That thread is the only bond that has ever been able to keep Arabs together, to give them identity and unity; even the unity brought about by Islam was based, ultimately, on words. For modern Europeans and their heirs, as Thomas Carlyle pointed out, gunpowder, printing and

Protestantism underlay power; for Arabs and theirs, it has been words, rhymes and rhetoric.

The problem is that words can blow apart as well as bring together. That is what is happening now, both where I live and in many other Arab lands, and it is why unity remains a mirage. How all this has come about, over the entire known Arab timescale of nearly three millennia, is the subject of this book.

One last word of my own before the gathering of the Arab word. As well as listening to people and their voices, we will occasionally examine things. What might be called *tangibilia* are a good way of getting a grasp on the past; they can act as metaphors for time or times, handles on complexity. They can be as big as a whole building assembled from fragments – a mosque that salvages both pagan and Christian materials – or as small as an Arabic coin minted by King Offa in the English Midlands; they can be charged with enigma, like a talisman with Allah on one side and Krishna on the other, or loaded with irony, like a Colt revolver inscribed by a Cold War president of the United States. They are rather like what Jorge Luis Borges, minting a new meaning for an old Arabic coinage, called 'the Zahir': a visible and haunting object that takes on different shapes in different places and ages.

Other, more literary metaphors are useful too for the story to come. The wheel of fire is one; the allusion to legendary sufferings – of Ixion, subverter of divine order, of King Lear, tragic divider of his own realm, both of them 'bound / Upon a wheel of fire' – is not coincidental. Wheels, moreover, are good vehicles for histories: they travel along an ever-extending line – time – yet their own motion is cyclical; they combine the constant and the variable. But, for Arab history, they are not the only image to keep in mind.

In my first book I wrote that, in Yemen, the past is ever present. I didn't realize at the time that Harold Ingrams, the imperial administrator and Arabian traveller, had also written in his Yemen book, 'This is a country where the past is ever present'.

A generation and a revolution or two separated our statements, but the past we wrote about was the same, still present. It is present now, another generation and a few more revolutions on. And it is not only the Yemeni past as seen by British observers that is inescapable. Near the beginning of his sprawling book on *Stasis and Change*, the Syrian poet and critic Adonis writes of the tendency across the Arabic world 'to make the past ever present'. This ever-present past was what led that astute observer, Jan Morris, to call the Kingdom of Saudi Arabia 'an antique autocracy' in 1955, only two years after its founding autocrat had died.

We must all be stating the blinding obvious. What only becomes obvious with time is how that ever-present past also contains the future – contains in both senses: comprises, but also confines. An ever-present past can have positive effects, for it keeps societies rooted in themselves. Equally, it can entrap those same societies and stifle their futures. It can be an incubus, an undead weight. The recent and obvious example is that of the Arab Spring, the rolling revolution that began in 2011 and gave expression to a younger generation's aspirations – only to be smothered, almost everywhere, by the reactionary forces of the Arab past.

Exploring Arab history thus means stepping now and again off the time-line; looking ahead as well as back. 'Time present and time past,' as Eliot knew,

> Are both perhaps present in time future,
> And time future contained in time past.

This complexity is the bane of all historians, but maybe most of all for historians of Arabs: years and pages turn in sequence; but not necessarily action and reaction, cause and effect. Causes, factors, tragic flaws may remain latent for centuries, even millennia, until they work themselves out, if they ever do. An extreme though trifling instance is one in which, in the mid-twentieth century, a village *shaykh* (chief) demanded that the British colonial authorities in Aden should pay for an old well to be dug out and reinstated. His argument was that the well had been filled in by a Roman expeditionary force in 26 BC, and that the Romans and the British were both species of 'Frank' – that is, European. A more serious instance is that concerning the transfer and nature of power in the post-Muhammadan state: the problem has boiled up intermittently but bloodily over the past 1,400 years. Clearly, the wheel alone, trundling steadily along its time-line, is not always enough. We need another image, repetitious yet arbitrary.

As often, poets have the answer. The Syrian poet Nizar Qabbani saw the ever-present Arab past as

the hourglass that swallows you
Night and day.

That past is the sand in the bottom of the glass, waiting for the next turn of events. Qabbani knew that history is no mere timepiece or pastime, but a player in its own right, often malevolent. It is the hourglass, squatting there, marking time, not measuring it – until it is turned once more, and then you see the grains are human lives, or human deaths, for the people are both the quicksand and its victims.

You can count the grains: 6,660 civilians killed by the war in my adoptive land; at least 50,000 dead combatants, many of them no more than boys; perhaps 85,000 younger children, infants under five, starved quietly to death by war's old ally, poverty. These are the stark statistics – so far – from the UN, ACLED and Save the Children, as I let go of this book at the end of 2018. Would those who turned the hourglass have done so if they'd known, or even if they could have guessed?

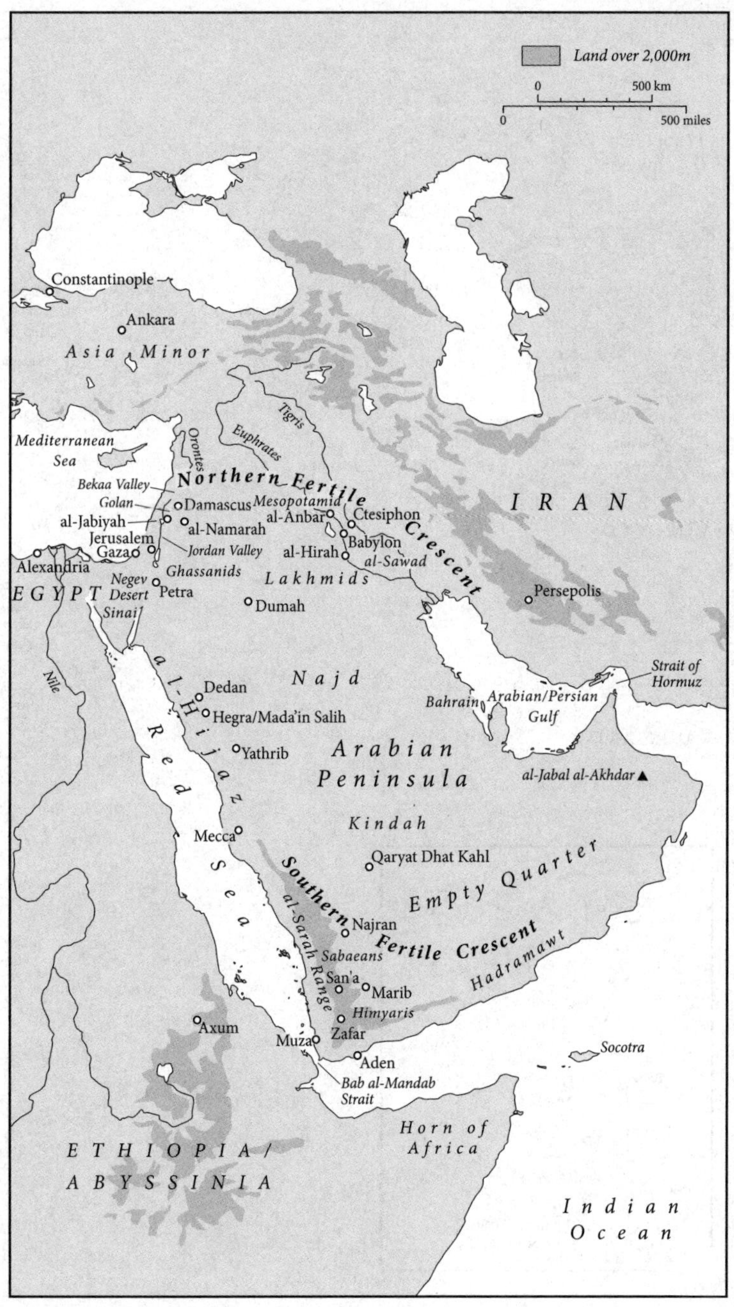

1 The Arabian Peninsula and adjoining regions before Islam.

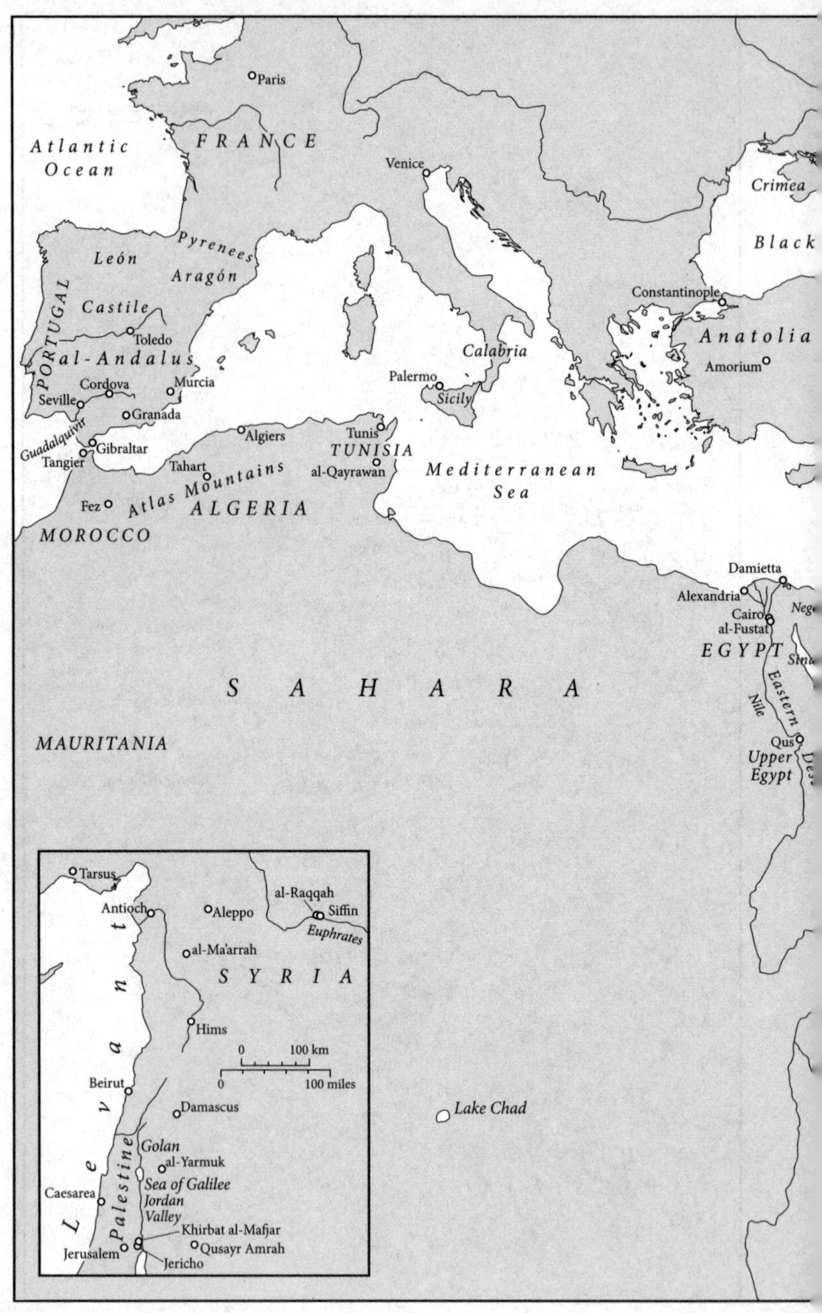

2 The Arab empire.

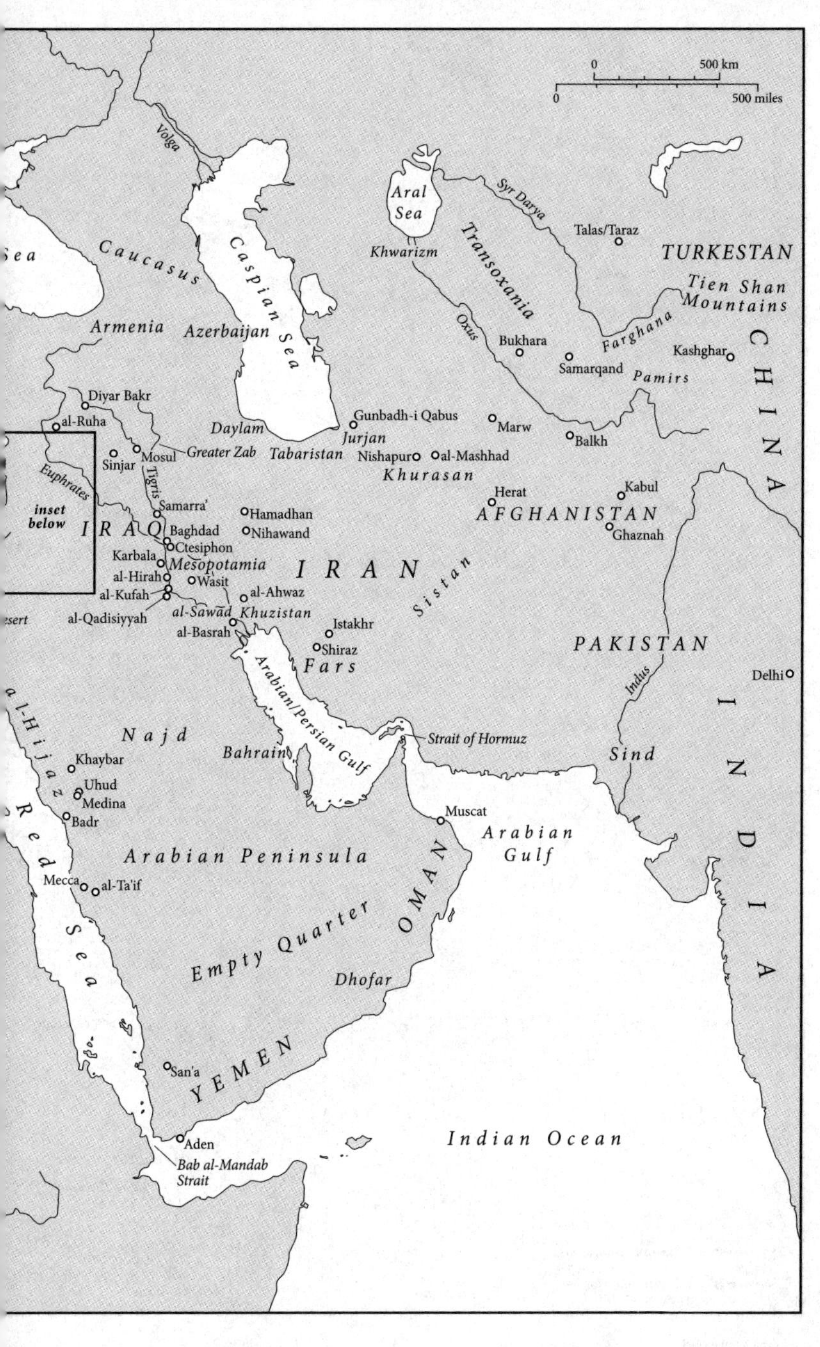

0
500 km
0
500 miles
Volga
Aral Sea
Syr Darya
Talas/Taraz
TURKESTAN
Tien Shan Mountains
Caucasus
Caspian Sea
Khwarizm
Transoxania
Armenia
Azerbaijan
Oxus
Farghana
Bukhara
Samarqand
Kashghar
Pamirs
CHINA
Diyar Bakr
al-Ruha
Daylam
Gunbadh-i Qabus
Jurjan
Marw
Balkh
Sinjar
Mosul
Greater Zab
Tabaristan
Nishapur
al-Mashhad
Euphrates
Tigris
Khurasan
inset below
Samarra'
Herat
Kabul
IRAQ
Hamadhan
Nihawand
AFGHANISTAN
Ghaznah
Baghdad
Ctesiphon
Karbala
Mesopotamia
IRAN
al-Hirah
Wasit
al-Kufah
al-Ahwaz
Sistan
al-Qadisiyyah
al-Sawad
Khuzistan
al-Basrah
Istakhr
Shiraz
Fars
PAKISTAN
Delhi
Arabian/Persian Gulf
Indus
al-Hijaz
Najd
Strait of Hormuz
Bahrain
Sind
Khaybar
Uhud
Medina
Badr
Muscat
Arabian Gulf
Red Sea
Arabian Peninsula
OMAN
INDIA
Mecca
al-Ta'if
Empty Quarter
Dhofar
San'a
YEMEN
Aden
Bab al-Mandab Strait
Indian Ocean

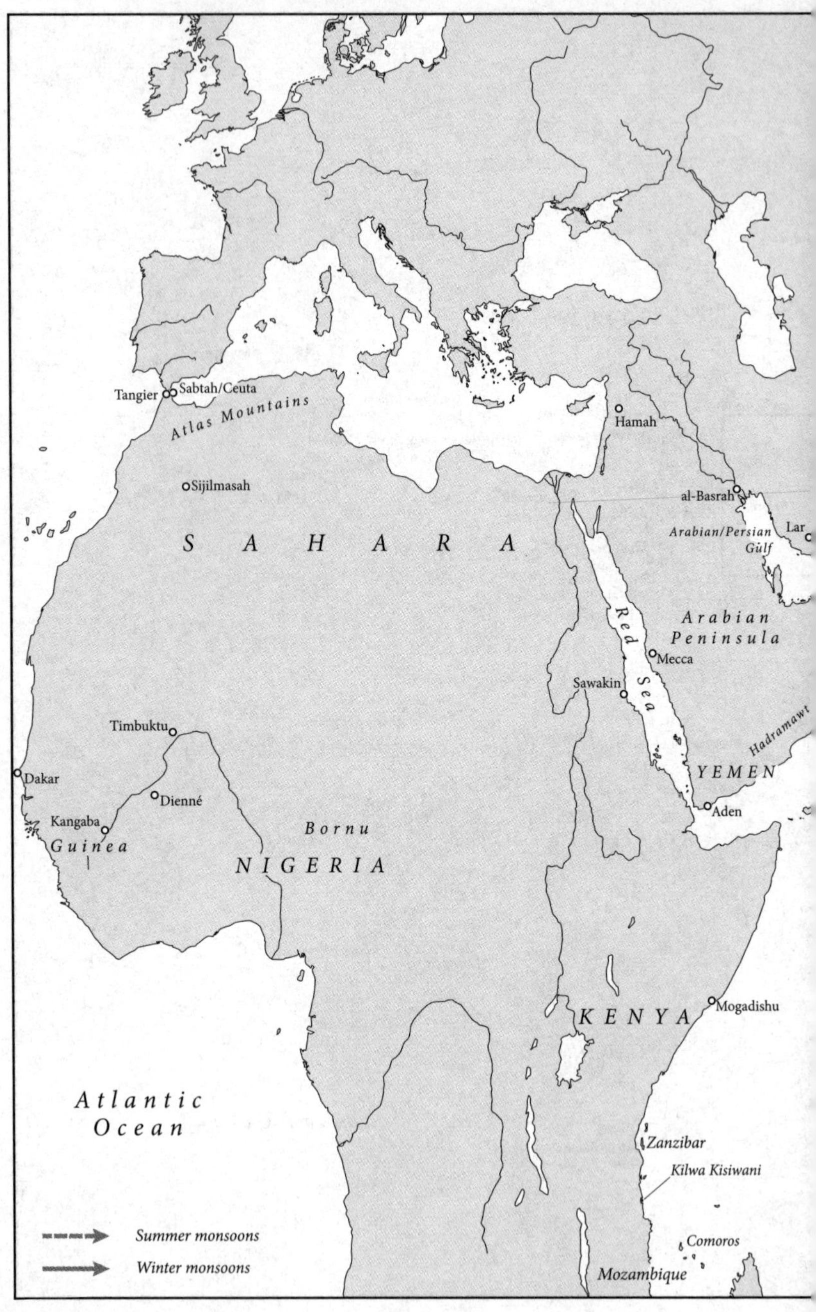

3 Arabs abroad.

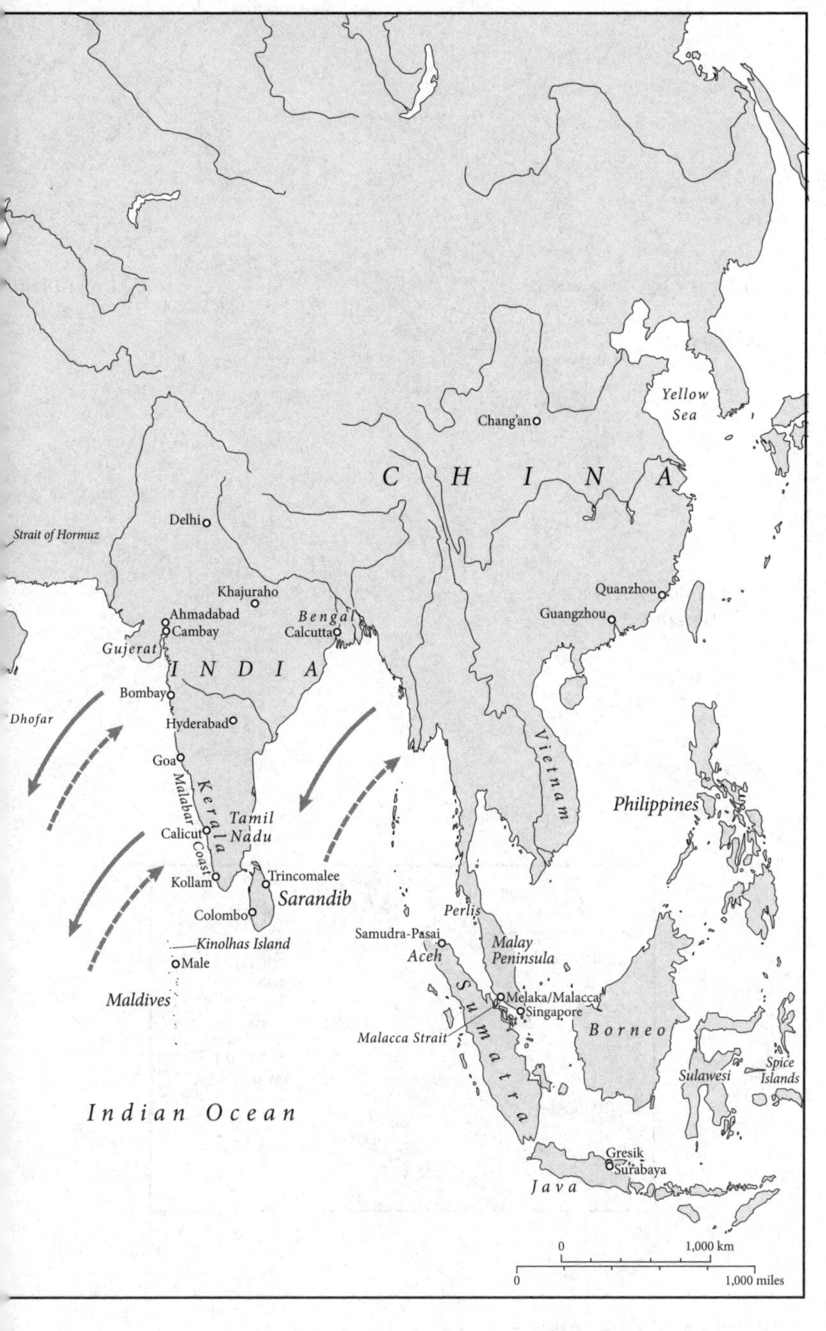
Yellow Sea
Chang'an
C H I N A
Delhi
Strait of Hormuz
Khajuraho
Quanzhou
Guangzhou
Ahmadabad
Cambay
Bengal
Calcutta
Gujerat
I N D I A
Bombay
Dhofar
Hyderabad
Goa
Malabar Coast
Kerala
Tamil Nadu
Calicut
Kollam
Trincomalee
Sarandib
Colombo
Vietnam
Philippines
Perlis
Samudra-Pasai
Aceh
Malay Peninsula
Kinolhas Island
Male
Maldives
Melaka/Malacca
Singapore
Malacca Strait
Sumatra
Borneo
Sulawesi
Spice Islands
Indian Ocean
Gresik
Surabaya
Java
0
1,000 km
0
1,000 miles

Atlantic
Ocean
Strait of Gibraltar
Algiers
Tunis
Mediterranean
Sea
TUNISIA
Rif Mountains
Atlas Mountains
ALGERIA
Casablanca
MOROCCO
LIBYA
SAHARA
Spanish Sahara/
Western Sahara
MAURITANIA
TUNISIA
SYRIA
LEBANON
West Bank
PALESTINE
IRAQ
ISRAEL
JORDAN
MOROCCO
KUWAIT
ALGERIA
LIBYA
EGYPT
BAHRAIN
QATAR
Western Sahara
SAUDI
ARABIA
UAE
OMAN
MAURITANIA
SUDAN
YEMEN

4 The Arabic world in recent centuries.

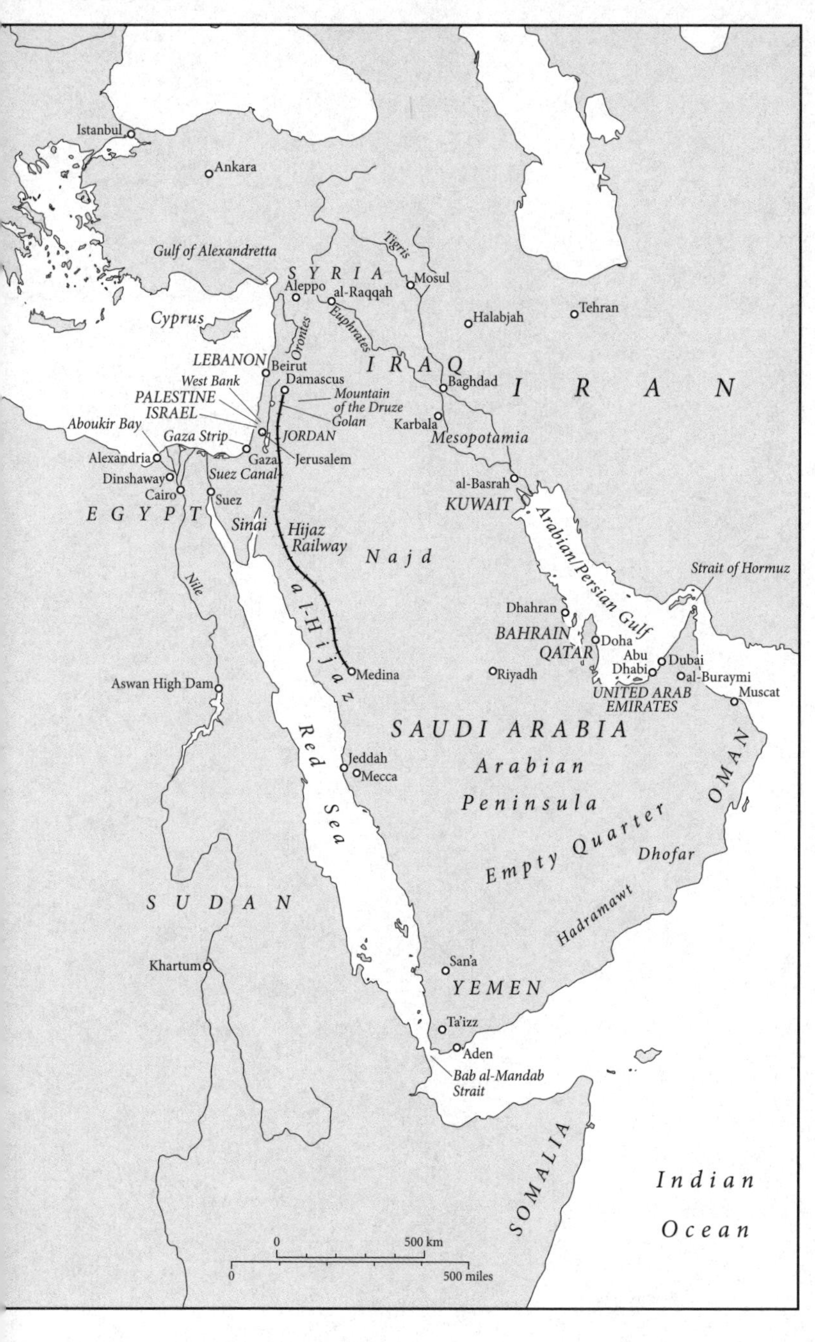

Istanbul
Ankara
Gulf of Alexandretta
SYRIA
Aleppo
al-Raqqah
Tigris
Mosul
Tehran
Halabjah
Cyprus
Orontes
Euphrates
LEBANON
Beirut
IRAQ
Damascus
Baghdad
IRAN
West Bank
PALESTINE
ISRAEL
Mountain of the Druze
Golan
Karbala
Aboukir Bay
Gaza Strip
JORDAN
Mesopotamia
Alexandria
Gaza
Jerusalem
Dinshaway
Suez Canal
al-Basrah
Cairo
Suez
KUWAIT
EGYPT
Sinai
Hijaz Railway
Najd
Arabian/Persian Gulf
Strait of Hormuz
Nile
Dhahran
al-Hijaz
BAHRAIN
Doha
QATAR
Abu Dhabi
Dubai
Medina
Riyadh
al-Buraymi
Aswan High Dam
UNITED ARAB EMIRATES
Muscat
Red Sea
SAUDI ARABIA
Jeddah
Mecca
Arabian Peninsula
OMAN
Empty Quarter
Dhofar
SUDAN
Hadramawt
San'a
Khartum
YEMEN
Ta'izz
Aden
Bab al-Mandab Strait
SOMALIA
Indian Ocean
0
500 km
0
500 miles

INTRODUCTION

GATHERING THE WORD

'The main function of a paramount shaykh is to gather the word of all.'
Paul Dresch, *Tribes, Government and History in Yemen*

ORATORS AND PREDATORS

Before sunrise on a winter's day early in the year 630, a captive in the Arabian town of Yathrib looked on as the men of the place gathered in the courtyard outside his cell. He could make out little between the few splashes of lamp-light. But when their leader arrived – it had to be him, for the whispering had stopped – and the men drew themselves up in rows, the captive sensed something momentous was about to happen. A thought came, colder than dawn: 'I believe they mean to kill me . . .'

It would not have been surprising. For several years the men of Yathrib had been raiding the rich trading caravans of the prisoner's own people; he himself had led a number of counter-raids. Many had died, and there was blood between them. Although a treaty earlier in the year had halted the skirmishing, it had recently been broken by allies of the captive's tribe. But in truth there was no knowing what the Yathrib men would do: they were a break-away group that crossed tribal boundaries and was led by a maverick but charismatic seer – a cousin, in fact, of the captive – and their actions were unknowable.

What happened next amazed the prisoner. The seer stood alone in front of the rows, chanted some of the strange incantations for which he was famous, bowed, and then prostrated himself. The ranks of men behind him copied his movements. It looked something like the worship of the Christians that the captive had witnessed on his trading trips to Syria. But these men were so precise, so drilled in their motions that they moved as a single body. As the prisoner watched, he uttered an oath on the old high deity of his tribe:

> By Allah! Never have I seen the discipline I've seen this day, and in men who have come from here, there and everywhere . . . No, not among the noble Persians, nor the Byzantines with their braided locks!

The captive was a clan chief of Mecca called Abu Sufyan. His maverick cousin was called Muhammad, and for a few years his captors had been calling themselves 'Muslims'.

What surprised Abu Sufyan so much was the unity of these men of Yathrib (or Madinat Rasul Allah, 'the City of Allah's Messenger' – al-Madinah or Medina for short – as they were starting to call it, in honour of their leader). This was a body of people of diverse origins, united neither by blood nor even, as was the case in most tribal groupings, by the pretence of a blood relationship. Some of them in fact were from his own tribe of Quraysh, which over the last five generations had split into competing clans. Most of them, however, were from tribes that had settled here in Yathrib long ago but came originally from South Arabia – al-Yaman, 'the South', a land of mountains and gorges, forests and fields, distant and different in its tongues and manners. There were even a few Jewish Arabians in the bowing ranks. Yet here they all were, moving, responding as one body. Muhammad had achieved, with spectacular success, what all would-be Arab leaders had always tried to do: he had 'gathered the word' of the people – he had achieved unanimity, and silenced all dissent.

Abu Sufyan's comparison with the Byzantines and the Persians is revealing. As an experienced merchant in the international trade, he was no stranger to the peninsula's warring imperial neighbours. But he knew that, for all their own claims of internal unity, those empires were themselves split by political disagreements and sectarian disputes. Here before him, in the heart of eternally squabbling Arabia, was a paradigm of unity – of unanimity, the gathered word – that put those imperial pretensions to shame.

It was too good to last. Within less than three decades, Abu Sufyan's son would be bloodily at war with Muhammad's son-in-law over the question of authority – control of people and of an income that would have made the rich old merchant's head dizzy. In a sense, that same conflict continues today, with exponentially enlarged figures and ramifications, often simplified with a sectarian gloss as a conflict between Sunnah and Shi'ah but in reality still to do not with dogma but with earthly powers: power over wealth, power over people, power over power.

For the moment, however, Muhammad had found the two keys to unity. The immediate key, as those disciplined ranks of worshippers showed, was a shared allegiance to a single deity. Despite the Christian-looking form of prayer with its prostrations, the deity was not so much like that of the Byzantines and Ethiopians with their interminable wranglings over the divine nature. Nor was He quite like that of the Jews; He might have been, had events turned out differently; but most of the Jews of Yathrib had rejected Muhammad's overtures in his early days in the town. Instead, He took His name from that of the cultic high god of Muhammad's own ancestral town of Mecca, one of the last great bastions of polytheism in a largely christianized or judaized Near East. As for His nature – a severely minimal nature, stripped of attributes, about which wranglings need not arise – it was as simple and self-contained as the desert stones the bedouins would come across and set up as their gods, or even more so. Indeed, this deity was unimaginable, except by reflex, through His creation and through His word as revealed to His prophet. That word inculcated a shared allegiance to the deity by daily prayers. It also forged a wider, deeper unity, expressed not in kinship but in worship.

The other key to unity, the ultimate one, unlocked that first key. It was Muhammad's power over language – not the language of everyday speech, but the special oracular tongue, the high Arabic with which daemons and familiar spirits inspired the traditional Arabian seers; except that in Muhammad's case, the tongue was inspired, via an angel, by that same abstract God who had chosen Muhammad as His 'noble messenger'. Muhammad had received the word of God and gathered the word of man. Yet He knew that the unity he had brought about was itself unique, and doomed. Whether or not it is true that he said, 'This community will split into seventy-three sects', he knew from his Qur'an, the collection of recitations sent down from God and passed on by him, that the reality was disunity:

By the night as it envelops,
By the day as it dawns bright,
By Him Who created male and female,
I tell you that your efforts lead to different ends.

He was also aware of a paradox. The oracular message that, in his mouth, had become divine, was aimed especially at the people who would best understand it – the many people across the peninsula who knew, or at least could be moved by, the high Arabic of divination and poetry; in other words, most tribal Arabs. That may sound like an obvious point, but it is one that the Qur'an makes, self-referentially, time and again. For example,

> We have sent it down as an Arabic Qur'an in order that you may understand.

And yet the only people referred to as Arabs in the Qur'an – those who might be expected to be most moved by the message, and in whom it might produce some spiritual benefit – were the least likely to heed it:

> The *a'rab* are the worst in unbelief and hypocrisy, and the least likely to know the laws which Allah has sent down to His messenger.

Divine words, then, falling on closed ears. Admittedly,

> Of the *a'rab* there are some who believe in Allah and the Last Day.

Admittedly, too, the form *a'rab* (a plural, while *'arab* is a collective . . . a quibbling difference) is often taken to refer to the outright nomads who lived on the margins of Muhammad's own environment of settled traders. But still, it was the raiding ethos of those very nomads on which the military success of the new community depended and which, in time, would give the community its edge over the ageing empires that surrounded it. The nomads and their predatory skills *had* to be incorporated into the community of believers.

The oldest Arabic book, the Qur'an, thus seems to be saying that there are two connotations of arabness – the eloquence of the high Arabic language, and the turbulence of the people among whom that language developed; that Arabs can be orators, but also predators. Looking at Arab history before and since Muhammad, this makes sense. A potent mixture of rhetoric and raiding has powered the cycle of unification and fragmentation, and still does.

True and lasting unity, as Muhammad knew, was impossible without one great principle, that of absolute equality under God. Among the fractious tribes and clans of Arabia, becoming part of a larger unity meant ceding power; to cede power to anyone stronger than you – other than the all-powerful God – was to admit defeat. But even with God in charge, that principle of equality, one of the eternal underpinnings of Islam, has always been elusive on earth. So, therefore, has unity: it remains a shimmering mirage on the horizon, while along the way the word is gathered at times by leaders with voices that are eloquent, persuasive or simply loud; they impose a perilous unison, then, inevitably it seems, it collapses in a din of competing rhetorics. Harmony – the coming together of diverse voices, in which all have an equal right to speak and an equal duty to listen – has seldom been heard.

But – you see how easy it is? – with Muhammad, Abu Sufyan and Islam, I too have started in the middle. It is an (probably the) illuminating 'moment' of Arab history, if such things can be said to exist; it sheds light on what came before, and what would come after. Medina, too, is in another middle: it mediates between the nomadic Arabia of the north and east and the more settled Arabia of the south and west; between *'arab* tribes and South Arabian peoples – the two main elements that were coming tentatively together in a single 'Arab' whole. And yet Medina was far from being the only mid-point in Arabia. And Muhammad, if he was the greatest gatherer of the word, was not the first. To go back and search instead for the beginnings of the long quest for unity will be, in part, to 'de-islamize' the history of Arabs, to fix a spotlight on the people, rather than to see them only against the rich and distracting background of what Islam has become. It is also to re-arabize the history of Islam, and of Arabs themselves – to see Islam not just as the world faith which it is today, but also as a unifying national ideology, and Muhammad as an Arab national hero.

Something else becomes clear if you go back to the beginning. Philip Hitti, in his big old (and still very useful) *History of the Arabs*, saw the Arabic language as 'the third stage in the series of conquests' by Arabs, after those of arms and of Islam. In reality the Arabic language was the first conquest, and not by but *of* Arabs. Without it, the other conquests would not have happened; there would never have been Arab histories to be written.

One of the best early Arab historians, al-Mas'udi, compared the task of telling the Arab story to that of 'someone who has found a scattered hoard of gemstones of all different kinds and colours, and has then strung them in order and turned them into a precious necklace'.

Eleven hundred years on, the hoard is that much bigger and even more various, but the task is the same. Straightforward chronology fixes the rough order of stringing; the final design depends on how the historian chooses the various shapes and colours and places them together and, to a degree, on the taste of the times. But the success of the necklace also hangs on the strength of the string. Mine is the Arabic language, which I called the 'deepest strand of "being Arab"'; it would be worth briskly reeling through 3,000 years of it over the next few pages, before the events themselves – many of them curious, dazzling and distracting – are strung. Language, the word, is the hidden thread: it is, after all, what Arab unity has itself so often gathered itself upon.

IN THE BEGINNING WAS THE POET

Over the three millennia of recorded Arab history, the gathered word has set off three waves of unity. To use Ibn Khaldun's term again, *'asabiyyah*, 'group solidarity', has always got its momentum from *'arabiyyah*, the high Arabic language par excellence. The scale of these waves, however, has been far greater than the Khaldunian one of tribe or dynasty. The first wave, ancient, slow, but deep, was one of ethnic self-awareness, swelling over a millennium before Islam. The second was a tsunami of physical expansion, the Arab conquests of the seventh and eighth centuries and their aftermath, that dissipated as quickly as it began and ended in a long lull, but left behind a rich and enduring sediment of language. The third wave, powered by dormant forces that were awakened by nationalist movements in nineteenth-century Europe, was one of rediscovery of the ethnic, cultural – and, later, cultic – self. That last wave is still breaking now. The three waves shape the larger sections of the coming book into three groups, unequal in years but roughly equal in pages: 'Emergence' and 'Revolution' (900 BC to AD 630); 'Dominance' and 'Decline' (630 to 1350); 'Eclipse' and 'Re-emergence' (1350 to now).

The beginnings of the first wave, of self-awareness, are obscure and hard to fix in time. It seems that with the increased mobility that came from domesticating camels as pack-animals, and with Arabs working in long-distance transport and trade, a language had to form that could be understood by speakers of different North Arabian dialects (South Arabians spoke another group of languages, distantly related but incomprehensible to the northerners; the distance was something like that between German and Italian). Later, at some time well before the fifth century AD and possibly in the central peninsula, a 'high' form of the unified northern language also took shape. This, the *'arabiyyah*, was not everyday speech but a 'mystical tongue' used for 'oracle giving and recitation of poetry'. Those who could command this special tongue – above all the *sha'ir*, later on a 'poet', but in its oldest sense probably more like a seer or a shaman – could attract followers. In time of raids, the *sha'ir* also played the role of Whitman's poet, 'the most deadly force of the war . . . he can make every word he speaks draw blood'.

The dust raised by Islam's impetuous entry on the field of history blots out a lot of what was there before. And yet a few features are clear in the murk that extends from that earliest mention of Arabs in 853 BC to their sudden appearance in the international spotlight. Human existence across much of early Arabia was mobile, fissile, fractious; lineage groups roving a harsh environment will, by their nature, divide and compete for survival. Time was measured in the names of ancestors rather than recorded in monuments or annals. Towards the end of the first millennium BC, however, the outer margins of this heterogeneous society (if it could even be called that) had already begun to gain shape through contact with the imperial neighbours – Rome, Persia, and South Arabia, that fertile land of mountains in the heel and instep of the peninsula, where Saba (the biblical Sheba) and its successor empires ruled over largely settled folk.

Empires, hierarchical and pyramidal by nature, prefer to deal with clearer chains of command than the horizontal structures of tribes and clans can offer. Arab hierarchies thus began to emerge through recognition by the great powers, including phylarchs (tribal leaders) and, later, 'kings of the Arabs'. The old nomadic, fluid life began to settle, to set at the edges: the kings ruled from centres between the desert tracts and the sown lands that were half camp, half capital. It was as if society, in the Arab lands of north and central Arabia, was solidifying from the outside in, like wax in a mould.

And if kings need recognition from their neighbours, they also need it from their own people: they live off praise and propaganda, the stuff of poets in their later guise. Here the high language came into its own, and took the shape it still has today. The language held the potential, too, of a deeper-felt unity. Herder, one of the founding theorists of modern European nationalism, knew the power of poetry. 'A poet,' he wrote in 1772, 'is the creator of the nation [*Volk*] around him; he gives them a world to see and has their souls in his hand to lead them to that world.'

In Herder's Europe, that world was still new: in some areas of France at the time, for example, 'To walk in any direction for a day was to become incomprehensible', and the ideal of a unified national language was far from being realized. Not so in the Arabic world. Reynold Nicholson, who understood it better than most, was right to say that poetry made Arabs 'morally and spiritually a nation long before Muhammad'.

No one, of course, spoke the language of the poets in real life. 'Nationhood' was a poetic ideal, a reality only in rhetoric. It always has been.

THE WORD SPREADS

In the sixth century AD, as this process of ethnic construction, physical settlement and spiritual nation-building was gathering momentum, the powers around Arabia went to war: Romans (now Byzantines) against Persians, and the Ethiopian empire of Axum against Himyarite South Arabia. As the imperial mould around them cracked, the half-formed society of Arabs itself imploded. With the loss of their imperial backers, the kings of the Arabs lost their *raison d'être*, the Arabs lost their definite article, and Arabia re-bedouinized, a mobile mêlée of competing rhetorics, each tribe with its poets, and now – for the profession of words had multiplied and specialized – its *khatib*s, orators, and *kahin*s, diviners or seers.

Out of the ferment of words and prophecies came Muhammad. But he took the rhetoric immeasurably further than his predecessors. What became Islam was empowered by language; not only by the new and thrilling audio-spiritual universe of the Qur'an, whose language arose from the old oracular high Arabic, but also by the use of slogans – above all the one that proclaimed the power of the old high god of Mecca: *Allahu akbar*, Allah is greatest. Muhammad was both the messenger of Allah, and His messager.

As Ibn Khaldun puts it, Muhammad 'gathered the Arabs together upon the word of Islam'. It was the paramount example of a paramount shaykh's function – gathering the word; and it was the prime example of the way words can be used for the instant dissemination of ideas, and for the insertion of these ideas into minds. Perhaps, in fact, it is the supreme example in human history of how language, rather than simple Darwinian self-interest and physical strength, can win dominance. For within less than a hundred years of Abu Sufyan's amazement at the discipline instilled by Muhammad, the Arab forces of Islam had conquered, or perhaps more accurately raided and patchily occupied, an area far larger than that of the Roman empire at its height. A few decades later, Arabs went global with their new capital, Baghdad, its four main gates leading to the four corners of the known world. The language went global too, founding and then binding – faster, in both senses, than could religious dogma – the great and enduring cultural empire called Islam.

At the same time, Arabs were to be the victims of their own success. The language that had given them cultural unity before Islam, and political unity under it, now destroyed that unity. In a few more short generations, the old, oracular, poetic *'arabiyyah* – high Arabic, the ethnic 'marker' above all others – had become the medium of culture, worship and administration across the empire; the word, once gathered, was now scattered across a vast spectrum of arabicized peoples from the Pamirs to the Pyrenees. Genetically, Arabs were everywhere. Linguistically, their speech laced this far-flung culture with its distinctive savour. But they themselves became invisible, dissolved by their own empire like salt in seawater.

A literal if late illustration of this absence can be seen in Eugene Rogan's *The Arabs: A History*, which covers the period 1500 to 2000: the first two plates are not of Arabs, but are Florentine portraits of ethnic Turks. As we shall see, the centuries of 'invisibility' in fact conceal an Arab expansion almost as remarkable for its extent as the first eruption of Islam – maybe more remarkable, as it was so low-key; but it was an expansion only through the Arab world's back door, into the Indian Ocean. Elsewhere, Arabs stayed at home and looked on as others took over the job of empire-building.

Perhaps histories have 'grammars' that can be parsed; if so, then most Arabs, who had been so active and so present in the world, had now lapsed into a long passivity lived in their own past. In actual Arabic grammar, the passive is called the 'unknown' or 'anonymous' voice – and to an extent, Arabs lost their name and disappeared into the greater totality of Muslims.

THE REAWAKENED WORD

The long anonymity was ended, too, by words. Just as Germans and Italians had rediscovered their national identities in literature before they tried to hammer them out in politics, it was the poets who sounded the Arab call – for example, Ibrahim al-Yaziji's summons of 1868:

> Awake, O Arabs, and arise!
> Misfortune's flood is lapping at your knees.

And yet, for Arabs, the way to 'nationhood', from anonymity to a new unanimity, would be a hard one. The nineteenth-century *Nahdah*, the 'arising' or 'awakening' (often called in Western accounts, with confusing connotations, the 'renaissance'), emerged from earlier European ideas of linguistic-ethnic-territorial nationalism. But it was largely an awakening of intellectuals; most Arabs slept on. Besides, that third element of the European nationalist model – the territorial – proved to be the problem. Al-Yaziji and his fellow intellectuals and poets were addressing an audience whom they defined as Arabs, above all, because they spoke Arabic. These early nationalist writers saw themselves as demiurges: they belonged to the recent European tradition of theorists like Herder, but also to that of the distant Arabian age before Islam, the age of ethnic construction. But what had been possible in the ancient peninsula, and was happening now in the new Europe of nation-states, would be much harder in the vast arabophone zone that had grown with Islam: it stretched nearly a quarter of the way around the globe. The Arabosphere was just too big and too disparate, not least economically, to form a stable whole; the Ottoman empire, which had tried to rule much of that vast area, was now exhausted by the centuries-long effort. After the First World War, hopes of territorial unity were hardly helped by the way in which the Ottoman imperial carcase was hacked about by the victorious powers. Add the small but excruciating wedge driven into the heart of the Arabic world by the Zionist project, plus the simultaneous discovery that some of the blankest bits of the map contain some of the richest oil fields – and borders, and daggers, were drawn.

Nationalism failed to gather the Arab word, or to unite the Arabic world. In more recent decades, some Arabs have pursued the mirage of unity by an older path – the one that led to Islam. Today, however, language, identity and the ideal of unity are still as interwoven as they were in the ages of pre-Islamic praise-poetry and of Qur'anic revelation. *'Arabiyyah*, the high language, 'is regarded by most Arabs as the most significant unifying factor of the Arab world'.

The trouble is, even if people write in it (or try to, and fall far short), nobody actually *speaks* it; nobody ever *has* spoken it as their mother tongue, not since the mists of time when it began to be constructed. High Arabic is an imagined bond, but also a bind – an unattainable ideal that constricts free expression. The reality is dialect, and disunity. Arabs have never been united in speech, or in any other way, only in speeches; never in real words in the real world, only on paper.

High Arabic is shared by more than 400 million people as the idealized literary form of their spoken language (not to mention another 1.4 billion Muslims as their liturgical language). On the ground the situation is different. Even in quite a small country like Tunisia, with eleven million inhabitants, there are four different dialect words for 'I' (in high Arabic, *'anā*): *anī*, *'anī*, *nā* and *nāy*. Another more extreme case is that of the small island state of Bahrain (with an area of 660 square kilometres), where the ruled Shi'i majority – the 'Baharnah', or (native) Bahrainis – speak a 'settled' dialect, and the ruling Sunni majority – the 'Arabs', as they are still called, who took over in a raid in 1783 – a 'bedouin' one. Sectarianism apart, what hope is there for unity, even in a kingdom smaller than the Isle of Mull, when its inhabitants speak two different tongues?

THE BOOK OF THE STICK

The ninth-century expert on arabness, al-Jahiz, believed language to be the chief 'national characteristic' of the people who were his subject. He also knew the importance of gathering the word, and devoted a short but important monograph to it, *The Book of the Stick*. The strangely titled work was a rebuff to a growing movement of protest, mainly among Muslims of Persian origin, that claimed the message of equality and harmony preached by the Prophet Muhammad had been subverted by Arab supremacists, characterized as rough tribesmen with loud voices who had a habit of ranting and waving sticks about.

Al-Jahiz defended traditional arabness by celebrating the very rod that was used to beat Arab backs. The stick, he says, has been a tool of power ever since the staff of Moses had miraculously become a serpent. The stick is the sorcerer's wand, the sceptre of rule, and the symbol and support of the orator – a baton to conduct the masses, a literal rhetorical prop to lean on, a firestick to ignite revolutions, a cudgel to suppress them. Others have extended al-Jahiz's images further – the stick, in the form of the scribe's reed pen, dispenses both balm and venom:

> Fear the reed, and yet desire it, for it is that which
> is known to spit poison and theriac.

The stick is the consummate metaphor for the potency of speech, for power over people, for the whole concept of the gathered word. And once the word is gathered and unity imposed, to fight against that unity is 'to split the stick'.

Those Persian dissidents were not alone. Across the Arab empire, Muslims of Coptic, Berber, Iberian and other origins railed against inequality, and were accused of splitting the stick. In time, however, most of these would-be splinter groups were accommodated, even assimilated; racial memories are not as long as one might think. The Persians, though, reasserted their own history, and reclaimed their own language and culture; relations with their Arab neighbours are still fraught with discontents.

In Arab lands, however, a basic, systemic problem remained and still does: success in gathering the word does not necessarily depend on the objective truth of that word. The mass manipulation of truth is, of course, not an Arabic monopoly. But Arabic is particularly good at it. As Ibn Khaldun observed, 'Both poetry and prose work with words, and not with ideas. The ideas are secondary to the words'. In short, if the rhetoric persuades enough people and creates group solidarity, that is proof enough of its truth. The prime example in Arabic is the miracle of the Qur'an: it is a miracle, and true, because so many people believe in it.

Mass acts of faith, however, are not confined to belief in sacred rhetoric alone. Adonis, the Syrian-born poet and essayist, has noted that because of the 'organic relationship' between religion and politics, 'politics becomes a sort of submission (*islām*) and an act of faith in the existing regime; anything else is tantamount to rebellion and blasphemy'.

Elsewhere, he goes further and explains that *tawhid* (the doctrine of divine unity) is both theological and political: 'To understand how this *tawhid* works at both levels is the first basis for understanding the nature of authority in Islam, and for understanding Arab history.' In other words, saying 'Yes' to everything authority says or does is the equivalent of saying 'Amen' to God's commands. The extraordinary discipline Abu Sufyan witnessed in the scene at the beginning of this Introduction has imposed itself on secular life as much as sacred; opposition is heresy. That, at least, is what secular leaders seem to think.

Those leaders are supported by etymology, if nothing else; the whole semantic foundation of 'politics' is radically different in Arabic. The Arabic word for 'politics', *siyasah*, has nothing at root to do with living together in the *polis*, the city. *Siyasah* is, in its first meaning, 'the management and training of horses, camels etc.'.

Because of all this, the whole idea of the individual voice runs dead against the grain of *'asabiyyah*, against the gathered word. There are, of course, still a few other parts of the globe where diversity of expression is silenced. But the power of rhetoric and the fear of splitting the stick are still so great in the Arabic world that the silencing is much easier there.

The uprisings of 2011 were a stage in which, for a brief season, individual voices could be heard: 'Everybody, everybody here has become an orator,' wrote Ahdaf Soueif of the protestors in Cairo's Liberation Square. 'We have found our voice.' Now, once more, nearly all those voices have been silenced, drowned out by the gathered word.

ATAURIQUE

There is another kind of unity, larger than the temporary solidarities and polities that rhetoric creates. An anecdote from early ninth-century al-Kufah, Iraq, illustrates its breadth. Ibn al-A'rabi, 'the Son of the Bedouin' (the name is a singular of *a'rab*, those nomads of the Qur'anic verses quoted above), was holding his usual literary salon. A renowned expert on the pure Arabic speech of his bedouin namesakes, he had also written on the history and genealogy of Arab tribes, Arabic poetry, the pedigrees of Arab horses, the cultivation of date palms and many other subjects of Arabian interest. One disciple of his who attended the salon for ten years said that during that time he had never seen a book in Ibn al-A'rabi's hand, even though he had dictated from memory 'camel-loads of volumes'.

Following his main lecture on this particular day, Ibn al-A'rabi noticed two strangers deep in discussion on the subject of the talk. He asked where they were from: one turned out to be from a district of Turkestan near the borders of Tang dynasty China; the other was from al-Andalus, in the far west of Europe. Ibn al-A'rabi rose to the occasion and quoted an appropriate pre-Islamic verse on a meeting between two companions from distant origins:

> We are two friends from far apart whom Time has joined,
> for sometimes from afar two come together and unite.

The ancient poet had been describing a meeting between two men from the opposite ends of Arabia. The two fans of Arabic culture in Ibn al-A'rabi's salon came from the opposite ends of Eurasia, nearly 7,000 kilometres apart. But something about the anecdote is more surprising still, and that is the origin of 'the Son of the Bedouin' himself. Far from being the offspring of a nomad, or even of an ethnic Arab, he was the son of a slave from Sind – part of modern-day Pakistan. His knowledge of all things Arab had earned him his name.

The greatest achievement of Arabs has been not the brief gathering of their own word, but its dispersal. The diaspora has been global and millennial. That metaphorical stick of the orators is also the root-stock of a culture that is planted in ancient Arabia, but which has spread horizontally through space and vertically through time. The growth is both vegetal and formal, a three-dimensional ataurique or 'arabesque', continually throwing out new shoots, but also sending down new tap-roots into other cultures, hybridizing all the way to Andalusia, Turkestan, Sind and far beyond.

As a language of international culture, Arabic has been as important as Latin and English. In terms of geographical spread, its script is second only to that of Latin. Maybe it was always destined to go far. The primary meanings of the Arabic word for script, *khatt*, are a line, a line of travel, a path: Arabic writing is as much to do with wending ways as weaving texts, and that is appropriate for its Arab originators, whose identity, like the marriage of Odysseus and Penelope, joins the wanderer to the weaver, the mobile to the settled. And as the Arabic word spread via scribes and travellers, so the socioreligious ideology it empowered spread too. It also hybridized, and finally, far from its Arabian roots, bore the fruit of the Arabian spirit that had first inspired Muhammad: that fruit – harmony – that seems to have eluded so many of his own Arab people. It is an irony that, apart from those two short centuries or so of solidarity and dominance, Arabs seem to have benefited least from his message; that the unity which so impressed Abu Sufyan in Medina has proved a mirage only briefly grasped.

The continuing pursuit of the mirage has sometimes taken Arabs to wild and lonely places, far from the luxuriant growth that they seeded. The usual Arabic word for 'unity' is *wahdah*, which shares a root with *wahid*, 'one'. But its oldest sense is that of 'isolation, exclusion, apartness': *wahdah* is oneness, but also lone-ness. It is not the isolation of a heroic lone individual, but of a heroically lone society. On a crowded planet, the sort of places where a whole society can be culturally self-sufficient are hard to reach; Utopia was built over long ago. And yet the quest, for some, goes on. A country like the Kingdom of Saudi Arabia (to give an admittedly extreme example) rejects many of the norms of the rest of the world, not least most forms of democracy and all freedom of expression. In 2018 the lifting of bans on cinemas, and on women driving and going to football matches, has been touted as a major step forward for the Kingdom, and in a way it is, for a society that insists on being so self-consciously *different*. But many, many more bans remain.

Perhaps it all comes from being in origin an island race, as Arabs are in their own cultural imagination. But the reality is less simple and much more interesting: the origins are many, the race is not a race, and the island is not even an island.

EMERGENCE

900 BC–AD 600

CHAPTER ONE

VOICES FROM THE WILDERNESS

EARLIEST ARABS

THE ISLAND OF THE ARABS

To begin with the land is to put the etymological cart before the horse: there were probably Arabs before there was a place called Arabia, and certainly long before their name applied to the whole Arabian Peninsula. Besides, with such a mobile future ahead of them, the Arab story is more about people than places; more about chaps than maps, to borrow E.C. Bentley's rhyme. That said, since Arab origins are hard to tie down, a subcontinent – the peninsula and its neighbouring regions – is a suitably large area from which to start. More important, its landscapes have shaped the destinies of Arabs who are now spread across a far wider sweep of earth. We cannot begin to understand those people and where they have got to without knowing where they came from.

The most prominent feature of this Arabian subcontinent, the peninsula itself, resembles a stumpy club-foot that is aiming a kick at the underside of Iran – except that hard on its heel comes the rhinocerine Horn of Africa, cramping Arabia's back-swing with a well-aimed butt. Other comparisons are perhaps more useful, and especially with the two other subcontinents attached to the rest of Eurasia: India (including Pakistan, Nepal, Bangladesh and Sri Lanka) and Europe (not including the European parts of the old

Soviet Union). Arabia is, after all, a true subcontinent by one possible definition of the term, in that the peninsula, together with the Fertile Crescent of Iraq and the Levant, sits on a single tectonic plate (or perhaps, given its relatively small size, a tectonic saucer) called the Arabian Plate.

All three subcontinents are much the same size – rather more than 4 million square kilometres in area. And there the similarity ends. Within the Himalayas, India presents few physical barriers to human movement and interaction; it is a land that lends itself to unities, to longish-lived kingdoms and empires, albeit punctuated by wars in which the players reposition themselves in games of musical thrones. Europe, roughly bisected by a mountain range that raises a jagged welt all the way from Cape Finisterre in Spanish Galicia to the Balkans, frayed ragged at the edges into ever-diminishing sub-peninsulas, calving offshore islands like Britain, is an arena of more fitful empires, a patchwork of truculent tribes that have grudgingly coalesced, late in the historical day, into nation-states. Most of Arabia is, like India, clear of obvious barriers; but there is one obstacle greater than Europe's gulfs and mountains, and that is the lack of fresh water. India and Europe are refreshingly blue on the rainfall maps, Arabia a parched brown fenced off by the 250-millimetre maximum annual rainfall line. Only at the furthest corners is there much relief (in either sense): down in the far south-western peaks of Yemen; at a few spots in Oman, notably al-Jabal al-Akhdar, 'the Green Mountain', in the furthest east; and up in the north-western mountains of Lebanon. The Tigris and Euphrates in the north-eastern extreme are the exception, with their copious and accessible waters; but the Fertile Crescent that they irrigate only serves to highlight, by contrast, the vast infertile peninsula to the south.

It is not surprising, therefore, that Arabia differs from the other two subcontinents in another way. India, with a a population of around 1.7 billion, has always been a migratory end in itself, a crowded cul-de-sac. So too Europe, with its population of 540 million, although half a millennium of colonial emigration has taken off some of the pressure. Even including with it those richer lands of the Fertile Crescent, Arabia's population is less than a tenth of India's – around 160 million. Only a single lifetime ago, before the influx of oil wealth and the various species of expat – labourers from Bangladesh, office-wallahs from Kerala, Texan oilbillies, 'Jumeirah Janes' and other denizens of downtown Dubai – it was perhaps a fifth of that, and the population of the peninsula alone less than ten million.

The drier peninsula has always been drip-fed with inhabitants from the Fertile Crescent. But it has never been absorptive of people; rather it seems mostly to have been a place en route. Geography helps this. The peninsula is separated from its neighbours at three points by strategic straits. At its heel and toe are two water-straits: Bab al-Mandab, at 26 kilometres wide only little more than the crossing from Dover to Calais, and the Strait of Hormuz, at 54 kilometres roughly the distance from Cape Cod to Nantucket. The third point of separation, the dry 200-kilometre 'strait' of Sinai, is broader, but easily navigable. And that is the point: all three straits separate, but also join. They invite crossings.

Crossing them seems to be what early hominids and humans did, on their journey out of Africa – both *Homo erectus*, nearly two million years ago, and *Homo sapiens* at various possible times between 45,000 and 125,000 years ago; perhaps even earlier (much research remains to be done). One route of exodus led them through Sinai and across the top of the Arabian Peninsula; the other route took them over Bab al-Mandab, when sea-levels were much lower and the strait even narrower, then through the south of the peninsula and on across the equally diminished Strait of Hormuz.

In contrast to these three straits, the seaward prospect from the instep of the peninsular foot, the south coast, does not invite crossings: there isn't a whole lot of land ahead of you until you reach Antarctica. But that same south coast lies in the realm of seasonal winds that would eventually take Arabian sailors and settlers round the Indian Ocean rim, in a great and growing mercantile crescent that would stretch from Mozambique to the Malacca Strait and beyond. Their camels of the sea would be as sleek and hardy as their ships of the desert, and the winds they would domesticate and make their own: 'monsoon' is from Arabic *mawsim*, 'season for sailing'.

Turning to the north, where the peninsula articulates with the main body of Eurasia, there is no barrier, no Himalaya to stop you crossing from Peninsula to Crescent and into further lands. That is what Arabians have often done, from way before Islam, leaving their peninsular transit-camp for a more central position in Eurasia and in geo-history. A 'wave theory' has pictured surges of nomads periodically pouring out of the peninsula and making for the valleys of the Tigris, the Euphrates and the Nile. While there is clear evidence for this – and none clearer than the last and greatest wave, the tsunami of Arabians set off by Islam – nothing suggests that there was any regularity to the currents of emigration. And, vital to remember, movement by this northern route has been both ways: linguistic evidence shows that, at least in historic times, the Arabian Peninsula has largely been peopled with incomers *from* the Fertile Crescent. The Levant, the land to the east of the Mediterranean, is almost without doubt the region in which the 'Semitic' family of tongues originated, and Arabic has preserved, pristine, many of the earliest features of those tongues. This is another reason to look at both areas together, as a subcontinent in terms of both plate tectonics and linguistics. The wave might thus be better pictured as an alternation of tides – most recently, that incoming tide from all over Eurasia and beyond, drawn by the gravitational oil field of petrodollars.

All this goes to show that the Island of the Arabs, as Arab geographers were to call their ancestral peninsula as far as the Tigris–Euphrates valley – older Arabic doesn't distinguish between *insula*, 'island', and peninsula, 'almost-island' – is noticeably *un*insular, and in fact rather well connected with its neighbouring land-masses. Any insularity is more in the mind than on the map.

It also goes to show why humans in Arabia have often been in motion – and, internally, in commotion – and why Arabia has been a place of comings and goings, slow influxes and sudden diasporas. In some respects, the Island of the Arabs resembles another well-connected island – one that was also to found an empire and export people and language: Great Britain. Like Britons too, it might be true to say that Arabs have often taken a little of their psychological insularity abroad with them. But there is a major difference: other than as a place of pilgrimage, Arabia itself was swiftly sidelined after that greatest exodus, the Islamic one. It was as if, as the British empire grew, Britain itself had become a backwater.

ARABIAN LANDSCAPES

Part of the reason for this net export of people is the brown on the rainfall map: the Fertile Crescent may be irrigable, but the rest of the subcontinent is not at first sight a land of milk and honey, let alone of petroleum and gas. And yet there is much more variety than first appears.

The three classical divisions of Arabia are still a useful shorthand. Arabia Petraea, 'Rocky Arabia', comprised the north-western parts, principally the Nabataean region whose capital was Petra – itself meaning 'Rock' (the local name is not known). Arabia Felix, 'Fortunate Arabia', covered a large area –

the southern two-thirds or so of the peninsula, subject more or less to the rule of indigenous South Arabian kingdoms. Parts of this area were certainly more climatically fortunate than the rest, but the felicity was due as much to the vast amounts of foreign cash that went in there as to the frankincense and other gums that came out to fuel temple rites and perfume the living and, especially, the dead of Mediterranean lands. The perfumes of Arabia Felix come, in fact, from spiky and stunted trees that thrive in spiky and dry environments. Parts of the region, principally in present-day Yemen, are indeed green and pleasant for humans; but, as we shall see, they need human intervention to become productive in food as well as exportable gums. The third division, Arabia Deserta, 'Desert Arabia', signified the sparsely inhabited regions of eastern Syria and Mesopotamia.

The classical divisions were as much to do with politics as with topography. And yet they do also give an idea of landscape. What Mediterranean geographers did not realize was that the actual rocky and otherwise desert parts of Arabia are the majority: climatically, most of the Arabian subcontinent is decidedly *in*felix. What modern scholars have realized is that the desertification has been relatively recent. Arabia as a whole was much wetter than it is now: people lived and hunted in the dried-out heart of the peninsula that is now called the Empty Quarter; you can still pick up their flint arrowheads by hollows in the dunes that were once water-holes, where hippopotami wallowed in the then Watery Quarter. This, the most recent 'major wet period', has been dated to around 8000–4000 BC or a little later, and was caused by fluctuations in that vast and fateful weather system, the monsoon. The big dry took place quickly. Climate change can happen fast, even without human help.

And yet even in the driest desert there is variety: 'empty' quarters are not empty to those who know them intimately. The early tenth-century geographer al-Hamdani, for example, lists terms for desert features in his *Description of the Island of the Arabs*, categorizing dunes, plains and steppeland with wonderful precision. To take just one class of terms, nouns containing repeating pairs of consonants, *nafanif* are 'lands that lengthen journeys by their ups and downs', *sabasib* or *basabis* are level, 'flowing' plains devoid of herbage, water and human company, *dakadik* are sandy plateaux between mountains, especially those on which the *rimth* or salt-bush grows; and the list goes on, with *fadafid*, *'atha'ith*, *salasil*, *sahasih* . . . There is a rhythm, even a poetry, to the most minimal of landscapes.

SOWERS AND MILKERS

This relative dryness, so recent in the geological timescale, took hold not long before the beginning of written human history in the Arabian subcontinent. And yet it has had far-reaching effects on that history. In fact, environment, and particularly the way in which people in drier and wetter regions relate to each other, has been a – maybe *the* – fateful factor in that history.

Arabia may not be an island as such, but it is insular in that other sense, far deeper than the sea-bed, sitting on its own tectonic plate. Moreover the fault line to the west, running along and beneath the Red Sea, is a continuation of one of the biggest and busiest faults on earth – the same one that has created East Africa's Rift Valley and, to the north, the deepest valley on earth, that of the Jordan. Tectonic movement is pushing up the heel of the peninsula, raising and ruckling its south-west corner. Over millions of years, the lifting has formed a long line of mountains. This sticklebacked chain, called by Arab geographers al-Sarah, 'the Ridge', is well within the Tropic of Cancer, too far south – and, with its highest peak standing at 3,700 metres, also not high enough – for snows and meltwaters. But the cool summits do suck up precipitation from the humid coastal plain beneath and, more important, they catch the edge of the monsoon.

So in the south and west of the peninsula, as in the Fertile Crescent, there is water – but no Tigris or Euphrates: people need to harness rainfall and run-off with manpower-intensive, often large-scale works. A verse attributed to a pre-Islamic Yemeni ruler describes the scene in Yahsub, a montane plain in the Sarah chain:

> In the green garden of Yahsub's land
> Water ever flows, springing from eighty dams.

The number may not be exaggerated: the locations of over sixty pre-Islamic dams are still known in the area. Not far away at Baynun, pre-Islamic hydraulic engineers cut a 150-metre-long tunnel, big enough to drive a car through, in the base of a small mountain, in order to channel irrigation water from one valley to another. The most famous of all irrigation works lies further to the north-east at Marib, where there is a massive dam-controlled run-off from a catchment area of 10,000 square kilometres. All this harnessing of nature necessitates, and in turn reinforces, social organization and stability; disorganization and instability lead inevitably to decay. In time the inevitable happened, and the bursting of the Marib Dam inspired a parable for societal collapse in the earliest and still the most authoritative Arabic book – the Qur'an. The moral of the story is also one of the morals of history (if such things can be said to exist): if you want to build and maintain dams and sluices, tunnels and terraces, you also have to build and maintain a working settled society. Civil engineering, in other words, is as much to do with law and order as bricks and mortar.

In contrast to the south and west of the peninsula, rainfall is scant in the desert and semi-desert areas, and never wholly predictable. There can be sudden, surprising verdure: 'The wormwood has put forth leaves,' reported a ninth-century *ra'id*, a pasture-scout of the nomadic camel herds,

> the salt-bush is sprouting, the thorn-tree is in leaf. Herbage covers the ground, the water-courses are green, the valley-bottoms are verdant; the hillocks are clothed in grass and the tussocks in new shoots; purslain, trefoil and mallow have sprung forth.

But finding such ephemeral, pastoral paradises means being on the move with your flocks and tents, and when everyone else is doing the same, there will be competition for resources, and social instability.

All this gives rise to a duality: *hadarah*, the settled life of the wetter south and west and of the watered Fertile Crescent, which imposes stability (and has a flipside – stasis, at times stagnation); and *badawah*, the wandering life of the *badiyah*, the open steppe and desert, which impels mobility (and also has a downside, that of political and social fragmentation). A plural adjective deriving from *badawah*, *badawiyyin*, gives other languages the word 'bedouin'. It is an essential human pairing, as old as the biblical Cain and Abel, the settled agriculturalist and the mobile pastoralist. There is a plausible theory that the names of the two sons of Adam are cognate with Arabic *qayn*, 'metalsmith' – the defining occupation of settled existence from the Bronze Age on – and *abil*, 'camel herd'. Arabic, which loves doublets, preferably rhyming ones (Cain and Abel are themselves Qabil wa-Habil) characterizes the duality by *madar wa-wabar*, '[people who live in houses] of clay and of camel hair', or *zar' wa-dar'* 'seed-sowing and udder[-milking]'.

Another doublet appears in the Qur'an: *sha'b*, 'a people, a folk', and *qabilah*, 'a tribe'. The Qur'anic verse alluded to in the title of this book suggests that it is a duality, an antithesis as basic as that of gender:

> O mankind, We have created you from male and female, and made you into peoples and tribes . . .

Most commentators have interpreted the verse as referring to settled *Persian* peoples and nomadic Arab tribes; some scholars argue, more convincingly, that this interpretation is anachronistic, and that the pairing in fact refers to the fundamental and age-old social duality within the Arabian sphere itself.

We shall return to these two groups: the way in which they interact explains many of the strengths and the tensions that run through Arab history as a whole. For the moment, it is enough to point out that a *sha'b*, a people, is defined by place, not by kinship, and – apparently from early on – united in large and relatively stable blocs by allegiance to a single chief deity. In contrast, a *qabilah*, a tribe, defines itself not by shared residence in a particular area, but by an idea of kinship. Often that idea proves flimsy on investigation: one example is that of the tribes of Asir, who were all of Qahtani lineage until, at some time before the tenth century, they switched completely and claimed Nizari descent. There is no exact European equivalent, but it would be something like an old Anglo-Saxon family suddenly denying their roots and asserting that, in fact, they had come to England with the Normans. Similar graftings from one 'family' tree to another still take place: only a generation or two ago, two major sections of the Yemeni super-tribe of Bakil fell out with their comrades and joined the other super-tribe, Hashid; the process was called *mu'akhah*, 'brothering'. Ibn Khaldun put it bluntly:

> A pedigree is something imaginary and devoid of reality. Its usefulness consists only in the resulting connection.

Also in contrast to the settled *sha'b*, the *qabilah*, or tribe, may share in the worship of one divinity or another, but their main loyalty is to earthly leaders.

These interwoven dualities (never dichotomies) of *hadar/badw*, 'settled/nomadic', *sha'b/qabilah*, 'people/tribe', only become clear with time. What is clear in the murkier beginnings, long before Islam and before even the

Christian year dot, is that the more mobile sort of people who defined themselves by ancestry include the first people known as *'arab*.

DESERT AND SOWN IN DIALOGUE

More mobile doesn't necessarily mean fully nomadic. But an inherent footlooseness, a sense that location and loyalty are moveable, is part of what has given Arab history its peculiar flavour: the history is epic, but it is epic in motion, *Odyssey* rather than *Iliad*. Like the *Odyssey*, a lot of it is about encounters, some productive, others destructive. In its most recent chapters it is about the protagonists searching for a way back home, back to their defining identity and then, as did Odysseus, finding home changed by time (or is it they who have been changed by the journey?). Even when the motion appears to stop, the potential energy is there – which may be part of the reason why the Arab experiment with the territorially based state, from the twentieth century on, has been so fraught. For what is a state if not static? Borders and wanderlust don't go together.

At the same time, those unsettled *'arab* were also to share their name with a succession of settled peoples. *'Arab*, the term for a peripheral, mobile minority, would eventually become a blanket term, covering people of the desert and the sown and everything in between. Today, proportions of nomadic to settled Arabs are probably less than 1:100; but the nomad's-eye view of history still skews the way both Arabs themselves and others view the Arab past. Nomadism and mobility are only part of the story. Without the settled element in their make-up, Arabs would have been a minor tributary of world history, along with the Tuareg and the Roma, or at most a flash flood that devastated then dissipated, like the Mongols. Importantly also, while a duality is easy to grasp, reality is more complex. *Badw* almost certainly originate in settled *hadar* populations; they are often reabsorbed into them; settled people may not generally up sticks en masse, but they can be culturally 'bedouinized'. *Badawah* itself has as many shades and textures as the landscape, from part-time pastoralism through transhumance to the rarity of rootless, full-blown tumbleweed nomadism.

So the *badw–hadar* duality has never been Manichaean, desert and sown and the twain never meeting. On the contrary, the two meet, and overlap, and interact, and never more fruitfully than when the stationary and the mobile intersect at halts on highways: oases and suqs, caravanserais and pilgrim shrines, of which the *locus classicus* – but by no means the prototype – is Mecca. The word *suq* is in itself a semantic intersection: it is the place where you stop to sell your animals, but the root sense of the word is the act of driving them there.

Hadar and *badw* can also counteract as well as interact. The Qur'anic verse quoted above expresses, with beautiful economy, the ambiguous relations between settled *sha'b* and mobile *qabilah*. God has created them, 'that [they] may know one another . . .' However, the phrase (a single word in Arabic, *li-ta'ārafū*) contains a double sense: the 'foreground' meaning is that of 'get to know one another, i.e. by mutual contact'; but there is also a background shade of 'distinguish between each other/tell one other apart'. The hope of unity and the lurking possibility of disunity coexist.

Ernest Gellner examined the sociology of Islam in the light of a binary system, 'urban' versus 'tribal', and has been criticized for it. Islam, as the world religion it has become, is far too big, too various to be seen from a binary perspective (let alone as a monolith). And yet, in Arabian history, it is clear that there has been a 'dialogue' between *badw* and *hadar*. I believe the dialogue goes further – that it is one of the keys to understanding Arab history as a whole, not just in but also beyond Arabia, and from the earliest times right up to the present.

A PEOPLE APART

The very earliest times of all are hard to make out. So far we know little about the palaeolithic people who left scatterings of tools across the uplands of the Arabian Peninsula. It is clear that they were widely if thinly distributed; the peninsula was no void. Neither is their history a blank. Recent studies of palaeolithic sites in Saudi Arabia have shown that, over time, these earliest Arabians were undergoing and adapting to early changes in climate. Of those neolithic hunters of the once watery Empty Quarter before the big dry set in, we know almost as little. We are, however, beginning to get a picture of other aspects of neolithic life. People were herding cattle by the sixth millennium BC; around 2,000 years on, they were starting to grow crops and – importantly, as it suggests evolving social structures based on ever closer cooperation – to develop irrigation systems in the regions where the highlands sloped down into the increasingly dry interior. Also by the fourth millennium BC, people on the long Arabian coastline, and particularly that of the Gulf, were exploiting its mangrove-fringed, shellfish-rich shores for building materials and food. By the early Bronze Age, the people of the coast were also exporting that precious by-product of their shellfish, the pearl, which became one of the earliest and most valuable items of Indian Ocean trade. Over time, the peoples of the seaboard would remain politically as well as geographically marginal; but their 'fertile fringe' would remain economically vital, and thus the target of raiders from the interior. It would also be the springboard for Arab expansion around the Indian Ocean.

The oldest Arabic histories would have hazy, landlocked and almost entirely fabulous ideas about prehistoric Arabians, whom they rationalized into tribes that fitted into later notions of Arab identity. Foremost among these were Ad and Thamud, about whom not much seems to have been known except for the fact that they were wiped out in large numbers at some unknown time in the distant past. The sixth-century poet Imru' al-Qays speaks, for example, of the site of a massacre 'as if it were of Thamud and Iram' – Iram being the legendary capital of Ad and a sort of Arabian Atlantis or Shangri-La. The two tribes make many appearances in the Qur'an, in parables about divine retribution for human sin: 'Have you not seen how your Lord dealt with Ad?' one verse asks. What He did was to wipe them out with a thunderbolt or a 'barren' wind for rejecting the monotheistic message. It is tempting to see this heavenly blitzkrieg as a dramatic compression of a lengthy process of desiccation and desertification, and the people of Ad as a memory of those neolithic hunters whose way of life ended, around 4000 BC, with the last major wet period. Elaborations of the Qur'anic story make the idea even more tempting. For example, what may be the earliest surviving Arabic history, a supposedly mid-seventh-century collection attributed to Abid ibn Sharyah, says that Ad suffered three years of drought before their destruction. But the account slips into ever more dubious territory: when at last the destructive wind strikes, it spares a woman called Hazilah and wafts her to Mecca – an Adite version of Dorothy in *The Wizard of Oz* – so she can impart the news. Later historians are understandably sceptical: 'Those who discuss [Ad],' wrote the reliable Abu 'l-Fida' in fourteenth-century Syria, 'differ greatly among themselves, and everything they say is confused and far from the truth, so we have refrained from reporting it.'

With the extinct tribe of Thamud, we are on firmer, and datable, ground. The name is known as that of a real tribe in the west of the peninsula who, among their other relations, maintained links with the Romans in the second century AD, supplying them with levies. Like Ad, they appear in the Qur'an rejecting monotheism and paying the price; like Ad, they were mythicized by later Arab memory: for example, knowing their own nemesis to be approaching, they plastered themselves with myrrh, wrapped themselves in leather shrouds and lay down to die in ready-carved tombs – a nice folk-aetiology for the leather-bound mummies which presumably once occupied rock-cut sepulchres in the Hijaz, as they still do in a few less accessible spots further south.

Ad, Thamud and similar mythical or mythicized tribes are remembered by Islamic-era historians as *al-'arab al-'aribah*, 'the true/arabophone *'arab*'. All others who were to come after them were classed as *'arab muta'arribah*, 'arab(ic)ized *'arab*', and *'arab musta'ribah*, 'arab(ic)izing *'arab*'. The accumulating affixes – arabo*phone*-arab*(ic)ized*-arab*(ic)izing* – probably reflect a sort of reality: the people who became known as Arabs gained whatever unity they had by a gradual process of acculturation, principally by being absorbed into the language. More important still is the other reality the traditional historians implicitly accepted: that, in origin, Arabs were not a neatly unified people, but a thoroughly mixed bunch.

Turning from later Arab historical memory to the earliest surviving written evidence, one thing is immediately clear, and that is who Arabs were *not*: none of the peoples of the settled Fertile Crescent, the coastal fertile fringe or southern Arabia originally called themselves Arabs. To the settled populations of the Crescent, the Fringe and the south, Arabs were clearly a people apart.

LOOKING IN FROM THE OUTSIDE

To the Assyrians, who left the earliest certain mentions of them, 'Aribi' were indeed a people apart, both geographically and socially, 'who live far away in the desert and who know neither overseers nor officials'. While one or two biblical references may be even earlier, later editing muddies the chronology. Thus the oldest incontrovertibly datable reference to Arabs known so far comes in the inscription left by the Assyrian King Shalmaneser III: the king records that in 853 he fought and defeated a Syrian-Palestinian coalition reinforced by that first known Arab, Gindibu, and his camels – a thousand of them, no less. Mentions of Arabs (and their camels) multiply after this date, and are eventually joined by others in Greek as well as Hebrew sources.

Robert Hoyland, the historian of early Arabia, argues that because both Assyrian and biblical texts begin to refer to Arabs – apparently independently – at about the same time, then 'Arabs' is what the people concerned must have called themselves. If so, then they were remarkably coy about owning up to their name in writing: they only came out of the epigraphic closet as Arabs some twelve hundred years after that first Assyrian mention. Nevertheless, to judge by their names they are unmistakably Arab in those early texts. That first personal name, 'Gindibu', or in standard Arabic transliteration 'Jundub', is borne by Arabs regularly, if infrequently, over the coming millennia. It means 'Cricket' or 'Locust' and presages a long history of calling people after animals. At the tribal level, tribal names like 'Kalb' (Dog) and 'Asad' (Lion) may be totemic; at the personal level, animal names are apotropaic. As the historian of ancient Arabia, Ibn al-Kalbi, said, Arabs 'named their sons with their enemies in mind'.

Not untypical was a tribesman called Waki' (Strong Horse), whose ancestors included 'Dog son of Lion' (or perhaps of Wolf or Cock or several other possibilities) and 'Desert Rat son of Colcynth' – the name of bitter or spiky plants performing a similarly off-putting function to those of non-cuddly animals. Sadly, such names are now out of fashion. Others that appear in the Assyrian texts are still used, however – for example 'Hamdanu' (my first house in Yemen belonged to a Mr al-Hamdani).

The Aribi of the Assyrian inscriptions are unmistakably Arab in other ways, too – most obviously in their use of camels, which they seem to have monopolized, but also in the mobility that the camels give them: they form a mobile auxiliary force fighting, as in that earliest Assyrian inscription, for one side or another. Their hardy mounts gave them a sly advantage, enabling them to move through, and make tactical use of, terrain that was in itself hostile to large, unwieldy and hungry armies. Then, as the inscriptional mentions multiply, they appear more and more as carriers in the overland aromatics trade, transporting northward the fragrant gums of South Arabia and later emerging as players in that trade, trying to gain control of the commercial routes.

The references proliferate, and so do the camels. The Assyrians were in expansive mood, seemingly keen to control the trade of Arabia and ever boastful about their subjugation of uncivilized nomads. In a relief commemorating the victory, in the third quarter of the eighth century BC, of Assyrian King Tiglath-Pileser III over Shamsi, 'queen of the Arabs', a stocky but handsome Aribi woman is seen leading a flock of camels, just a few of the

30,000 the king claims to have seized in the accompanying inscription. In the following century, King Assurbanipal captured so many herds from *mat Aribi*, the Arab land, that, 'Within my land one bought a camel at the market gate for a few pence'.

The Assyrian came down on the Arab not like Byron's mere 'wolf on the fold', but as a camel-rustling collective of multinational dimensions. Of course, it made perfect sense to deprive Arabs of the main vehicle for their mobility and independence.

That latter case of punitive mass rustling (and, naturally, enslavement of humans) was incurred by Arabs supporting, as had Gindibu two centuries earlier, an enemy of the Assyrians – in this case their main superpower rival, the Babylonians. At the same time, however, Arabs had themselves been coalescing, gathering their own word and their own power. Several themes emerge from all this that would be recapitulated over time.

First, the kernel around which this earliest known, tentative unity formed was a centre of cultic pilgrimage and worship – Dumah, in the north of the peninsula, sacred to a number of tribes. The most powerful of these was a polity, perhaps a tribal confederation, called Qedar. Qedar, which existed between about 750 and 400 BC, is only scantily understood, but may in fact be the first known exercise in Arab – as opposed to South Arabian – history in forging a unity larger than the kinship-based tribe. And it is perhaps not irrelevant to Arab history as a whole that this first known statement of the theme of unity was sounded out at a centre of pilgrimage. It was a theme that would eventually emerge in full thirteen hundred years later and 1,100 kilometres to the south, in another place of tribal pilgrimage, Mecca.

Another theme that would be heard again and again is that of neighbouring powers giving royal status to Arab tribal leaders. Thus the Assyrians call the defeated Shamsi and the Qedari leaders Zabibah (730s BC; her name means 'Raisin') and Hazael (early seventh century BC) respectively 'queens of the Arabs' and 'king of the Arabs'. At one point in the seventh century BC, the Assyrians imposed their own puppet 'queen', a Qedari woman named Tabua, on the polity. King-naming – and at times king-making – by outside powers would be a recurring theme through three millennia of Arab history, with its own consequences for Arab identity and solidarity.

A third theme that would reappear regularly across time was the way in which, when they weren't punishing them for siding with other powers, the Assyrians would use Arabs as a buffer against these rivals: this was particularly the case with respect to Egypt. A reference in Herodotus also suggests that the Persians were to employ Arabs to insulate their territory from the Egyptians in the fifth century BC. Such symbioses would recur again and again down the coming millennia.

All in all, to their northern neighbours, Assyrian, Babylonian and, later, Persian, Arabs were marginal, but often extremely useful when they weren't being annoying. The expectation was that, even if they could never be docile, they would at least be tractable, and duly grateful. Assurbanipal records, for example, that following his campaign against *mat Aribi*, 'The people in Arabia asked each other: "Why has such a disaster befallen Arabia? It is because we did not abide by the great oaths of Assur, we sinned against the kindness of Assurbanipal."' Many Arabs reading that now would hear it as an early statement of yet another theme that recurs right down to today, a theme that is repeated in their relations with superpowers even in the post-Cold War era: toe the line, or pay the price.

To the north, then, lay a fissile crescent of empires, with whose interests those of Arabs overlapped or clashed as the case might be. To the south, also, in the rain-fed mountains, plateaux and desert 'estuaries' where great wadis flowed into the wilderness, lay a clutch of settled kingdoms that, at various times over the millennium and a half before Islam, came together as an empire, small in extent but powerful in its cultural reach. Most prominent of these South Arabian kingdoms over time was Saba, or Sheba.

To begin with, Arabs hardly get a mention in the inscriptions of the southern kingdoms. It is only from the last few decades BC onward that the rovers from the north begin to feature prominently in the southern record, almost entirely as mercenary fighters. The clear inference is that Arabs spread southward from the desert borders of the Fertile Crescent in the latter part of that last millennium BC. Even when they do begin to appear regularly in the southern inscriptions, 'it is clear,' according to the late great scholar of the texts, A.F.L. Beeston, 'that they are intrusive elements not fully incorporated into the typical [South Arabian] culture'. As in the north, Arabs were a people apart.

In time, incorporation would take place, but in an unexpected direction: South Arabians would be culturally and linguistically arabized. It was the first statement of yet another recurring theme, one that would be so prominent in the headlong expansion of Arabdom associated with Islam – but in which linguistic and cultural 'conversion' was always more thorough, and probably also more rapid, than religious conversion. Indeed, Sabaeans and other South Arabians would be adopted so fully into Arabdom that by the ninth century AD, in al-Jahiz's view, '(peninsular) Arabian' had come to equal 'Arab': 'All Arabs are one and the same, because their habitation and their Island are one, their ethical values and innate dispositions are one, and their language is one.' (Their politics, of course, were almost never one.)

What is more, the South Arabians arabized themselves, as we shall see, to the extent that they completely rebranded themselves as *the* original Arabs. More sophisticated historians would always remember the distinction between Arabs proper and South Arabians. Ibn Khaldun, for example, lists three main groups of 'Semites': 'From Sam [Shem] are descended the Arabs, the Hebrews and the Sabaeans' – meaning by 'the Sabaeans' the South Arabians in general. The Arab–Hebrew rift haunts history. North–South Arabian distinctions are, however, now dead and all but forgotten; but their ghosts may be raised from time to time – for example by propagandists in the conflict outside my window, which in some interpretations is between southern and northern Arabs. As one commentator has said of the ancient North–South divide, 'It may be useful for political scientists to have this additional insight into why Arab unity is so hard to achieve'.

That realization is the tip of an iceberg of insights. Looking north, for example, the originally non-tribal settled agriculturalists of the northern Fertile Crescent would take far longer, as we shall see, to be accepted into Arabdom in early Islamic times than had their southern counterparts. Moreover, the acceptance was grudging, and incomplete. The lurking disunity tends to be expressed – as in present-day Iraq – in sectarian, Sunnah–Shi'ah terms.

So much for what early Arabs were not. For insights into who or what these marginal and elusive people actually were, we must look to the terse but eloquent records left by themselves. For persons of no fixed abode and no obvious pretensions to a written culture, they left a surprisingly large amount of writing.

'S¹LM WAS HERE'

Littered across the stony deserts of modern Syria, Jordan and northern Saudi Arabia, where the peninsula is mortised into the Fertile Crescent – that is, in precisely the area where those earliest Arabs roamed with their herds – are scores of thousands of graffiti, pecked into the boulders that dot the landscape. The main script used is Nabataean, the precursor of Arabic script. The date is quite a lot later than those early Assyrian and biblical references to Arabs – probably from the end of the last millennium BC on; but before the appearance of Nabataean in the final third of that millennium, the writers probably had no letters in which to express themselves. The language is not quite Arabic as we know it, but it is close – closer, perhaps, than Anglo-Saxon is to English. Bending the linguistic taxonomy a little, it wouldn't be far out to say that these are our first authentic Arabic documents. And, even if the word 'Arab' doesn't appear in them, there is little doubt that they are our first home-grown Arab documents.

One might well be surprised: surely ancient nomadic Arabs, whose very arabness subsisted in living 'far away in the desert and who know neither overseers nor officials', as the Assyrians had put it, are the last people who would have a use for writing? Yet it seems they did, and the most plausible explanation is that it was all a game, a pastime. If you are sitting in the lee of a rock watching camels graze all day long, the temptation to pick up a pebble and peck away at the rock will be irresistible. To depict on the rock what you can see in this minimalist landscape – camels – may be artistically satisfying, and pictures of camels are indeed frequent. But the pleasure of portraying camels eventually palls, and to write your name, and almost invariably your lineage, is even more pleasing: it is both a proclamation of individuality and a declaration of membership, of family, of tribe. If this means importing letters from your Nabataean neighbours, it is no different from importing other products of settled society like spearheads and knife blades. (It is not entirely different from importing Sudokus along with Sony.) M.C.A. Macdonald makes a useful analogy with modern-day Tuareg nomads, who 'have their own writing system, the Tifinagh, which they use purely for amusement'. But writing of any sort is rarely pure amusement, and in proclaiming, 'I was here,' Kilroys over the ages are making the archetypal statement of history.

The language of the graffiti is termed 'North Arabian', and it comes in several varieties. The most common variety in what the Assyrians called 'the land of the Aribi' is known as 'Safaitic', after 'al-Safa', the Arabic name of the lava-strewn steppe where most of them are found. About 18,000 Safaitic graffiti are known. Most of them are names, and most of the names have lineages – 'A son of B son of C . . .' Sometimes the lineages extend back an extraordinary fifteen generations and more (how many generations of your ancestors can you remember?); extraordinary and, in the cases where with luck and scholarly patience they can be cross-checked with other graffiti, consistent. The present-day equivalent would be to remember one's pedigree back to the time of Shakespeare or the Pilgrim Fathers.

But the graffiti-writers were not just walking family trees. There are everyday glimpses such as that of a herdsman who 'spent the [early spring] on this [plain] and fed on truffles', and more poignant records like that of one S^{1}lm (there are no vowels, so he might be Sālim, Sallām, Salīm, Aslam etc.) son of Mn son of S^{1}lm son of Bdr son of Ḏn of the ʾl ʿbs^{2}t clan or tribe, who 'helped the goats bring forth [their young] and so O Lt [the goddess Lat] [grant] security. And he mourned for Mn'l, his son, who had died, distressed, overshadowed'. The grief is audible even now. But there is fun too: another informal epigrapher wrote that 'he was very love-sick . . . for a maiden, and had joyous sex with her'. And there is ribaldry, as when graffiti writers add 'something rude' to the inscriptions of their rivals. There are also plenty of scratched heads among the present-day interpreters of these ancestral voices: does the verb *ʾtm*, for instance, mean to mourn, to finish, or to fuck? Graffiti being what they are, the context is often as minimal as the landscape.

What is perhaps most remarkable, however, is the social context and its continuity. Patterns of pastoral migration that can be teased out of the graffiti repeat themselves not just in the past, 'this is his camping place year after year', but also down to the present. So too, do figures of speech: in one graffito, the writer records that 'a torrent made him flee in [the season of] Suhayl', that is, in late August, when the star Suhayl or Canopus rises. In the same area 2,000 years later, in the twentieth century, the Rwala bedouin proverb warns, 'When Suhayl's overhead, trust not the torrent-bed'. And there is another theme, mentioned in words and prayers and shown in pictures, one that will repeat itself with catastrophic regularity and which 'clearly played a part in both the culture and economy': raiding other people's herds.

Herding and raiding took these people to the steppelands, kept them on the move, and ensured they remained politically disunited. And the pattern all began long before these earliest authentic voices, before the Assyrians and Genesis.

BORN OF THE *RIMTH* BUSH

There is a very old myth that claims the camel was created from the *rimth* bush. Al-Jahiz, who mentions the story, is suitably sceptical but says the unappetizing *rimth*, a highly saline plant, features in it because only the camel can eat it. Then again if, as the saying goes, we are what we eat, there is a grain of truth among the many grains of salt: after all, the camel is par excellence the domesticated animal that can survive where, and eat what, no others can.

The history of the camel has been much written about. The consensus seems to be that it was domesticated for milking at some time in the third millennium BC, probably in the south-east of the Arabian Peninsula; the use of camels for transport developed over the following millennium. What is in no doubt is that by the early part of the first millennium BC, when camel-borne nomads begin to appear in the written records of their neighbours, the employment of camels as pack and riding animals had developed to a high degree and had spread to the north of the peninsula. By the time of that first datable mention of Arabs – 853 BC – camels were big business, given that Gindibu the Arab could hire out as many as a thousand beasts (he presumably didn't lend them for love). Soon after this the Assyrians, as we have seen, were lifting camels in their tens of thousands, although one should perhaps beware of zeros.

The centrality of the camel to ancient Arab life is clear from its significance in the rites that followed ancient Arab death; such rituals can be glimpsed in mentions by poets of the sixth century. If the deceased was a warrior, a riding camel would be immobilized by his grave and left to die there, or sometimes slaughtered and buried with its owner. Like dead Mongols and their horses, and dead Vikings and their ships, dead Arab warriors presumably needed vehicles to make them posthumously mobile. Of the innumerable uses of living camels, the ancient female orator Hind bint al-Khuss – said to belong to a remnant of that archaic tribe of Ad – neatly summed up the most important three as, 'bearers of men, stanchers of blood, buyers of women'. Camels were carriers, but they were also currency to pay the price of blood and thus stanch feuds, and to pay the bride price. However, it was as a vehicle of transport that the camel would play its most important part. It would eventually be a hemiglobal role: when the second caliph of Islam, Umar, warned conquering Arab generals not to go anywhere he couldn't reach by camel, that meant in practice no less than most of the Afro-Eurasian landmass.

The beginnings of this history of mobility were more modest, of course. Yet it was the camel that enabled the people who would be called Arabs to uproot themselves from the Fertile Crescent, to head beyond the fringe of civilization and make for the savage south, the Wild West of the settled Semites: it was the camel, in a sense, that made people Arabs in the first place. The attractions of the wilderness may have seemed limited to most of those settled peoples, but they were explained by an Arab to the sixth-century AD Persian ruler Khusraw Anushiruwan:

> [Arabs] own the land without it owning them. They are secure from the need to fortify themselves with walls: their whetted blades and pointed spears suffice for armour and citadels. To own a spot of earth there is tantamount to owning all of it.

And there were other attractions, that might be called psychosomatic:

> [Arabs] weighed up the matter of cities and buildings, and found them not only wanting but also harmful . . . for places suffer illness as do bodies . . . So they dwelt in the far-spreading lands . . . which are free from pollution, full of fresh air, and insulated from plagues.

And, of course, healthy minds belong to healthy bodies, for 'where fresh air is generated, so too are reason and perception'. The call of the desert is no mere Western Orientalist topos.

As for the identity of the people who answered that summons of the wild, we can only surmise that their origins, like those of North American cowboys and frontiersmen, were from among the farmers and traders of the settled populations. Being Arab might well have been, to begin with, a question of choice, or of necessity, not of birth: one *became* Arab. And the people drawn to a home on the Arabian range were probably, like their American counterparts, a rag-tag bunch.

ARABS OR *'ARAB*?

There is a possibility, implicitly accepted by the earliest Arab historians, that 'rag-tag' is what *'arab* may imply in its earliest, etymological sense. Arabic lexicographers, too, give one of the meanings of *'arab* as '[disparate people] joined or mixed together'. If this is indeed so, then inherent disunity, *and* an attempt to unite, are implicit from the start. Certainly, many other long-enduring names of Arabian groups originate in words that contain a sense of 'to join, to unite, to ally'. These groups include the great southern confederations of Hashid (*hashada*, 'to collect people together') and Bakil (*bakala*, 'to mix'), and the Prophet Muhammad's tribe, Quraysh (*taqarrasha*, 'to come together, gather'), and perhaps even the important South Arabian people, Himyar (Sabaic *hmr*, a 'type of pact, alliance between communities'). Admittedly, Semitic etymology is perilous territory: it is a wilderness of meaning haunted by fascinating mirages, and it is easy to make things mean what one wants them to mean. But such a coincidence of sense in these names goes beyond chance or fancy.

Another long-accepted view is that *'arab* originally meant 'desert people, nomads'. In other words, *badw*, bedouins, and *'arab* are the same thing. This was certainly the case in the early inscriptions, both Assyrian and South Arabian. It was also certainly the meaning later on, and until recent times: well into the twentieth century, most of the sort of people who are proud to be called 'Arabs' nowadays would have been less than pleased at being classed as *'arab*, bedouin bumpkins. Whether it was the 'original' sense, however, is debatable, and much debated. Yet another meaning of *'arab* – 'speakers of Arabic' – is without doubt not early. Some scholars would put its date well into the Islamic period; but, as will become clear, Arab self-consciousness as an ethnic group, part of whose ethnicity depended on shared language, began much earlier.

There are further possibilities. Looking at cognate words, *'arab* could conceivably mean 'from the west' – presumably of the peninsula. And possibilities congregate: one fervent Arabologist, Jan Retsö, has surveyed at length all the available early material and concluded that *'arab* were marginal communities, led by heroic leaders, dwelling in tents, protecting cultic centres, and famous as soothsayers and border guards, and that in particular they are 'those who entered into the service of a divinity and remain his slaves or his property'. This is all doubtless ungainsayable. But as a definition, it seems simultaneously too wide and too narrow: too wide in that the terms are too many, too narrow in that many people regarded anciently as *'arab* would not have ticked all those boxes.

I incline – for linguistic reasons set out in the following section – towards the first possible sense of *'arab* above: that of mixture or union. But in the end, to be honest, we don't and perhaps can't really know the original significance of the word. The Egyptian intellectual Taha Husayn put it more strongly: we are 'in utter confusion' over the meaning. It seems that when you try to draw meaning from the very bottom of the semantic well, it comes up muddy.

Altogether, there hardly seems a good basis for writing a history of Arabs if we don't even know what their name means. So perhaps it is better not to stare down semantic wells, but instead to look over the horizon and say not what exactly or who precisely Arabs had been, but whom they resembled and how they fitted into the wider human environment. A useful comparison comes from further east in Asia: 'It is doubtful whether the term *arya* was ever used in an ethnic sense', says the Indian historian Romila Thapar of the Aryans – and she might have said the same about 'the Arabs', or rather, about *'arab*, in italics and lower case. And there are further resemblances. Both infiltrated subcontinents; both are mobile, migrating, plundering pastoralists (of cows/camels); both, early on, have classes of seers and supernatural experts (*risi*s/*kahin*s); importantly, both develop a strong linguistic self-definition, in distinction to those who do not speak their languages (*mleccha*/*'ajam*), and both develop early on a remarkable oral literature that was put in writing many centuries later (Vedas/pre-Islamic poetry); both develop a prestigious and often cryptic sacral speech that becomes widespread as the language of written culture (Sanskrit/high Arabic) but eventually fossilizes.

These are all no more than rough parallel lines drawn between *'arab* and *arya*; similar parallels could probably be made between *'arab* and many other mobile groups, Nordic, Mongolian, Celtic and so on. But such lines may delineate something of the position of Arabs in broader human history. And, importantly, they also demonstrate the importance of language in turning what looks in origin like a common noun (*arya*/*'arab*) into a proper name (Aryans/Arabs). For – to return to that idea of *'arab* as the 'mixed' people – if they weren't united by genetics, they seem to have been linked, increasingly over time, by linguistics.

SONS OF SAM

At least from as far back as their written records go, nearly all the diverse people of Arabia and the Fertile Crescent, settled and wandering, have used related languages, all belonging to what eighteenth-century German philologists termed the Semitic family. It takes its name from Shem son of Noah, in Arabic 'Sam', whom the traditional genealogists claim as ancestor of Arabs, Hebrews and other collaterally 'related' groups. Later philologists, by playing what could be called 'the "proto-" game', have constructed a family tree for Semitic languages, tracing each back to a hypothetical root version – proto-Arabic, proto-Hebrew and so on – and then to an original rootstock, proto-Semitic. In addition, by estimating rates at which language changes happen and then measuring backwards in time, one can guess, very approximately, the age of the languages concerned; in other words one can, so to speak, count the rings of the linguistic tree. Various dates have been given for the origin – almost certainly in the Levant – of proto-Semitic; what is more certain is that Arabic has preserved features that are older than those of any other Semitic language, and that some of these features may have branched off the Semitic root very early on – perhaps as early as 4000–5000 BC. Then again, perhaps that Semitic root is not in fact the rootstock, but itself belongs to a wider, 'Afroasiatic' family . . . Only connect.

This is all cerebral stuff, to do with cracking codes, crunching numbers and Bayesian analysis. But as we are dealing with ancient nomadic people who, because of the way they lived, left almost no archaeological remains, the great spoil-heap of language is the Arab equivalent of Troy or Knossos. The evidence can be pleasing, and particularly that which proves ancientness and continuity. Jonathan Owens, for example, gives two verb paradigms, remarkably similar, which he labels 'Iraqi' and 'Nigerian Arabic' – only revealing afterwards that the 'Iraqi' is in fact Akkadian from 2500 BC, while the Nigerian example was recorded in AD 2005: continuity, geographical, over 4,500 kilometres, and chronological, over 4,500 years. And then there are those interesting bits and pieces of evidence that complicate the continuity, where the tree has undergone cross-pollination. In Arabic these include very early loan words like the names of the two weapons that always vie in might, those primal tools of civilization and its opposite number, Greek *kalam*^{os} → Arabic *qalam*, 'reed, (reed-)pen', and (probably) Greek *xiph*^{os} → Arabic *sayf*, 'sword'. And what about Latin *taur*^{us} → Arabic *thawr*, 'bull', and Greek *oin*^{os}, 'wine' → Arabic *wayn*, 'black grapes' and South Arabian *wyn*, 'vineyard'? Or should the arrows in some cases go the other way? Or both ways? Question marks are valid, as we seldom know. What is clear is that there was not only loaning very early on, but perhaps too what has been called a pre-Semitic 'Mediterranean substratum', shared linguistic ground that antedates and underlies the borders between 'Semitic' and 'Indo-European'.

Turning to Arabic itself, its origins are in a 'dialect bundle' of the branch of Semitic called North Arabian. Those languages of the graffiti – Safaitic, Thamudic and various other '-ics' – form another bundle of now-dead twigs springing from that same North Arabian branch. All these North Arabian tongues would have been mutually intelligible, probably with ease. South Arabian, on the other hand (or, on the other branch) included the languages of the settled peoples of the southern and western peninsula – Saba/Sheba, Himyar and so on – and would not have been intelligible to North Arabian speakers. Most of the South Arabian branch withered and died with the creeping arabization and arabicization that took place well before Islam. But a few new South Arabian languages appeared in far-off corners – the Gaelics of Arabia, spoken today by several tens of thousands of people in Yemen and Oman. Listening to their speakers, for example to mountain-men in the Island of Socotra off the Horn of Africa, as an Arabic-speaker I wiggle my ears in perplexity, feeling I *ought* to understand but picking up only the odd gist of a cognate word.

When it comes to classifying the different '-ics' within the same branch, things are not so clear. The distinguishing feature of Arabic is usually said to be its '*al-*' definite article; Safaitic and its sisters, in contrast, have '*h-*' or '*hn-*' as the definite article. One of the earliest appearances of '*al-*' is in the fifth century BC in Herodotus, who says that 'Alilat' – al-Ilat, otherwise written as al-Lat or simply Lat (who appears in the graffito of the grieving S^{1}lm above) – is the deity of the Arabs; compare her masculine counterpart, Alilah, al-Ilah or Allah, *the* God. But in reality, classifying languages by their definite articles is rather like grouping screwdrivers not by the shape of their heads, but by the shape of their handles. In present-day Yemen, for example, many Arabic speakers use '*am-*' as the definite article; even the Prophet Muhammad, the Arabic-speaker par excellence, was known to switch to '*am-*' when conversing with those who used it.

An illustration of how thorny are the problems of classification, even within the wider Semitic family, is one of the earliest supposedly *echt*-Arabic texts, a tomb inscription of AD 267 from Hegra/Mada'in Salih that heaps curses on anyone desecrating or trying to re-use the sepulchre. Formerly said to be Nabataean, it is now classed as Arabic with Nabataean touches. And as an illustration of just how hybrid linguistic practices could be, what is now thought to be the oldest known Arabic inscription – a three-line prayer of thanks for delivery from a suppurating wound, found at En Avdat in the Negev and dated to the first century AD – is embedded in an otherwise Aramaic text.

To sum up, one has to admit there was no such thing as Arabic, singular; rather there were – and still are – many Arabic*s*. 'Arabic' was never a neatly espaliered sub-branch of Semitic or a homogenous collection of shoots, but a gnarled and multiply engrafted outgrowth bearing some very old and very odd features. The very diversity of the 'dialect bundle' that became Arabic reflects the sense of *'arab* as a mixed bunch, a genetic and linguistic omnium gatherum, and one that had been absorbing new members regularly from very early times. This is all crucial evidence about the earliest era of Arab history. That old 'wave' theory of emigration from the peninsula tells only part of the story: not only is it clear that ripples of people kept flooding *in* – a perennial human undertow from the Fertile Crescent; also, that admittedly rough date suggested above – 4000–5000 BC – for when the oldest traits of their language separated from the proto-Semitic rootstock, may give a clue to when the ripples began, and to the true age of our earliest *'arab*.

Solid home-grown evidence to support this is hard to find. But the Arab mythic memory may confirm this linguistic and genetic diversity, as well as a settled origin in the Fertile Crescent for Arabs and their tongues. One story, for example, tells how, after the debacle at Babel and the proliferation of tongues, ten original Arabic speakers fanned out from Mesopotamia: each headed for a different part of the peninsula with his family and followers, each uttering a poem about himself as he went. 'All of them . . . were *badw*, and they spread out across the land.' This and other similar accounts have the unreality of dream; but like dreams they may emerge from long-stored memories of waking fact.

ARABS HAVE A WORD FOR IT (AND OFTEN VERY MANY WORDS)

All the early and subsequent diversity and accretiveness of Arabic mean that the lexicon is embarrassingly rich. Multiple synonyms include 80 for 'honey', 200 for 'beard', 500 for 'lion', 800 for 'sword', and 1,000 for 'camel'. The last figure seems if anything rather low: an old saw among Arabists that says every Arabic word means three things – itself, its opposite, and a camel – is not entirely untrue. There are precise terms for such things that one would never imagine needed a precise term, like the droppings of bustards as opposed to ostriches, and different types of farts, categorized by loudness, and the sound of locusts eating, and the spaces between the fingers, each space having its own term.

Ancient diversity is one of the reasons why no fewer than fifty Arabic dialects, not to mention eight foreign languages, have been listed as contributing to Qur'anic vocabulary. It is also a reason why *qamus* – an arabicization of Greek *okeanos*, 'ocean' – has become a synonym for 'dictionary'. 'The Arab tongue,' wrote the great eighth- and ninth-century scholar al-Shafi'i, 'is the widest-ranging of tongues, and the most copious in vocabulary. We are aware of no person who can encompass a complete knowledge of it, unless that person be a prophet'. Al-Shafi'i's contemporary, al-Jahiz, went further: no one can know all the possibilities of Arabic, he said, 'but He who knows the number of droplets in the rainclouds and of the particles of dust, and that is Allah who knows what was and what shall be'.

If Charles de Gaulle could question the governability of a people – the French – who make 246 varieties of cheese, then the same question might be posed about people who have 1,000 names for the camel. Less flippantly, that apparent diversity in the very beginnings of their language – the dense dialect bundle growing from the North Arabian branch – begs an important question: did the earliest *'arab* have any sense of their own unity?

SEARCHING FOR A UNIFIED VOICE

Their neighbours in the early first millennium BC certainly gave *'arab* a sort of unity by giving them that name, whether or not *'arab* was what the people concerned called themselves. And, from around 750 BC to 400 BC there is evidence for the existence of that multi-tribal grouping called Qedar – a polity of some sort, if not exactly a unity. Seeming unity, of course, can often be in the beholder's, the outsider's eye. But for *'arab*, a shared and mobile lifestyle – camel husbandry, the pursuit of pasture, the camel-borne carrying trade – meant that their paths criss-crossed and must have woven at least a tentative sense of shared identity, of cultural if not political oneness.

Language was probably as important in this respect as lifestyle: the very fact that all those '-ics' are so hard to classify shows how close they were. Robert Hoyland sees language as linking and distinguishing *'arab* even in that first millennium BC, and as the most important condition of *'arab* identity.

This is long before the emergence of the unified 'high' language, the *'arabiyyah*, that would become, and still remains, the supreme totem of Arab unity.

At the same time, the voices of the desert stones – all that Safaitic vox pop – suggest diversity, plurality: they are the voices of people, not *a* people; of individuals in a loose and segmenting society, following the forking paths of their own ever-lengthening patrilines. Words were mutually comprehensible for users of the various '-ics'; but their word, in its wider, political sense, was still far from gathered. We can only guess at the dialectics at work between dialects, can only imagine what shibboleths may have divided them.

As for the broader currents of history, *'arab* had only dipped their toes in them as mercenaries for and carriers between settled peoples. Life as it appears from the graffiti was pastoral and parochial. But as the first millennium BC drew to a close, new perspectives were opening up. An improved type of camel saddle was developed, enabling riders to travel much longer distances. And outside involvement in the region increased: *Rum*, 'Romans', begin to appear in the graffiti. *'Arab* begin to appear regularly in the formal inscriptions of the South Arabian kingdoms. And the graffiti themselves begin to appear in unforeseen places – in what is now Lebanon and even on a corridor wall in a theatre in Roman Pompeii. The camel herds of the Arabian fringe were moving on to new pastures.

CHAPTER TWO

PEOPLES AND TRIBES
SABAEANS, NABATAEANS AND NOMADS

'WHEN IN ZAFAR . . .'

In Yaqut's geographical dictionary, the entry on Zafar includes the following anecdote about the ancient south-west Arabian city:

> It was the seat of the kings of Himyar, and the origin of the saying, 'When in Zafar, speak as the Himyaris speak'. According to al-Asma'i, an Arab man arrived for an audience with one of the Himyari kings. The king, who happened to be up on a high roof terrace of his palace, said to the man, '*Thib!*' [Arabic for 'Jump!'] So the man jumped off and was dashed to pieces. At this, the king said, 'We have none of that Arabickt here. When in Zafar, one must speak as the Himyaris speak'. In the Himyari tongue, '*thib*' means 'be seated'.

The source of the story, al-Asma'i, was a respected and generally reliable eighth-century antiquarian; *thib* is from a genuine ancient South Arabian verb meaning 'to sit'; the king's pronunciation of *'arabiyyat* for *'arabiyyah* (imitated above in 'Arabickt') is authentically archaic too. But the tale has a strong whiff of later, Islamic urban legend.

Whether or not the death-leap really took place, the setting is right. The hilltop city of Zafar, royalty, a multi-storey palace, would have been alien to an Arab visitor who only knew stony steppelands, homespun chieftains and hair tents; out of his social and linguistic context, he would indeed be dizzied and disorientated. The royal reaction feels right, too: one can picture the ruler looking down from his parapet and uttering the punchline with a shake of the head. Even if the Arab hadn't taken him at his word, the comment is still *de haut en bas*, urbane host to barbarian guest.

This hauteur of a civilized south towards a nomadic north rears its head again in the Islamic age: 'If a Tamimi [Arab] comes and boasts that he is better than you,' said the poet Abu Nuwas, al-Asma'i's contemporary, addressing an audience of South Arabian origin,

> then say to him, 'Enough, you lizard-muncher!
> *You* dare to boast before the scions of kings, you fool,
> you filthy piss-a-leg?
> Let noble people vie in noble deeds; and as for you – take up your stick
> and shoo your goats, you whose mother got the runs and shat herself!
> *We* ruled the world both east and west
> while your old chieftain was a droplet in his father's loins.

As we shall see, the theme of civilized versus nomadic, of a North–South divide, was exacerbated by the politics of Islamic times. But it does arise from ancient realities. As the story of Zafar shows, the people of Arabia were joined by a landmass but separated by language; Semitic roots united them, but semantic ramifications divided. At the sociological level, the differences went even deeper. The groups called *'arab* would give their name to the ethnic compound who would be known to history as 'Arabs'; but they were only one part of this compound, alongside the Sabaeans, the Himyaris and other settled peoples of the Arabian subcontinent who are the main subject of this chapter. It is important to see at this early stage how settled and nomadic Arabians differed from each other, and how they began to come together. Then it will become clear in later times – the brief time of unity brought about by Islam, and during the multiple disunities that arose after it – how the old differences have given Arabs their extraordinary strengths and their fatal weaknesses.

To recap what we know about the nomadic groups early on: *'arab* were numerically few, probably of mixed origins, and were characterized – at least by outsiders, from the early first millennium BC – by the way they eked out a life from the less promising parts of the landscape. We don't know how they defined themselves to begin with, or even if they saw themselves as a group at all. But by the time we begin to hear the earliest authentic *'arab* voices, scratched on desert stones towards the end of that first millennium BC, there are plenty of forces in place that could create a nucleus of ethnicity: shared lifestyle and constantly crossing paths; an interest, sometimes an obsession, in lineage; closely related languages.

The nomad tribes seemed entirely different from the settled peoples; as different as the meanings of 'jump' and 'sit'. But over the early AD centuries, things would begin to change. That special, 'high' language of prophecy and poetry developed among the tribal *'arab*. Together, the new poetic tongue and the old mobile lifestyle would become the two main ethnic markers – essential items of *'arab* 'national dress'. The metaphor is doubly apt: like clothes, ethnicity has changing styles; like clothes, too, fashions can spread and become trends far from their origin. Along with this apparel, *'arab* would begin to sport the label by which others had been calling them for so long: in a sense, they would become Arabs with a capital A. And the strangest part of it is that other Arabian societies, avowed non-Arabs, radically different in lifestyle and language, would, from the third century AD or so, not only take on these pieces of Arab dress, slipping into Arab costume and custom, but would also eventually, in the seventh century with Islam, adopt the label 'Arab' – and even end up claiming that the label and the language were their very own to start with. As an ethnic fashion statement it was surprising, coming from the settled, civilized peoples of the south – the Sabaeans and their neighbours, including the Himyaris. Even in Zafar of the high palace and haughty Himyari king, they would exchange their ancestral tongues for the 'Arabickt' of the hair-tent-dwelling herdsmen. They would join the growing sociopolitical mix that was Arabdom, and wear the Arab national dress with pride.

A later but literal example of this ethnic cross-dressing is that of the islamized Himyari king Dhu 'l-Kala', who visited the first Islamic Caliph Abu Bakr, 'accompanied by a thousand slaves . . . [He was] wearing a crown and the sort of striped garments and other robes that we have described', that is, of brocade heavy with gold; in contrast, the ascetic Abu Bakr was clothed in the simplest Arab style: 'and when the king saw what he was wearing, he took off his finery and dressed in the caliph's manner. He was even seen one day in one of the suqs of Medina with a sheepskin on his shoulders.' There is something in this of the twentieth-century bourgeois revolutionary donning a Mao suit. Naturally, the story is given a high moral gloss: one can only show obedience to Allah if one shows humility in this world, the shabby-chic but pious king concludes. Then again, obedience to Allah was, by this time, another part of becoming Arab.

All this, however, was in the future; the details of how Arab style dressed a whole peninsula will unfold in the coming chapters. To start with, as the story from Zafar shows, for the southerners and especially for their paramount polity of Saba, *'arab* were anything but chic. Gnawing roasted lizards and sharing vermin with their scabby flocks, they were beyond the pale – almost beyond the lofty palace-purview – of the settled, civilized southern kingdoms.

THE ORIGINAL ARABS (BUT NOT JUST YET)

Like *'arab*, the Sabaeans, whom we have already glimpsed as the best-known South Arabians, may owe at least some of their origins to the Fertile Crescent; so too may other South Arabian groups like the Himyaris. Unlike *'arab*, the Sabaeans may have been a reasonably cohesive group. Looking at the Sabaic language for clues about their beginnings and comparing it with other branches of Semitic, it has been suggested that 'the proto-Sabaeans should have left the fringes of Syria-Palestine well after 2000 BC'. Linguistic evidence is supported by alphabetic: the South Arabian script 'is the survivor of a Proto-Canaanite alphabet which had died out in Palestine around 1200 BC'. (In turn, a descendant of the South Arabian script survives in Ethiopia, where it is used to write Amharic and related languages.) Other analyses, however, place Sabaean origins further east in the Fertile Crescent. But in either case, the subsequent course and chronology of the supposed migration of early Sabaeans to South Arabia is unknown.

Then again, archaeology has thrown a spanner (or rather, a trowel) in the linguistic and epigraphic works. As we have seen, organized irrigation was in place in the region as early as the fourth millennium BC; the great Marib Dam, already mentioned, was the culmination of a long period of evolution in the harnessing both of water and of human resources. Exactly how the Sabaeans and other groups related to and interacted with extant local people is still not fully understood, and some scholars give much more weight to the indigenous beginnings of South Arabian civilization. What is clear from the evidence on the ground, however, is that the Sabaeans developed a flourishing settled civilization in the south, as did other settled peoples of similar language, the Minaeans, Qatabanians, Hadramis and later Himyaris. Together, over time, these peoples formed their own 'Fertile Crescent' in South Arabia.

The two Fertile Crescents bracketed that huge peninsular parenthesis; but from early in the first millennium BC, thanks to *'arab* and their pack camels, the South Arabian peoples began to trade across it. The southerners were themselves middle-men, forwarding north the luxury goods of the Indian Ocean region that came in through the fertile fringe of the coast. They were also exporters in their own right, mainly of aromatics. But the mainstay of their existence was always agriculture.

The virtuous circle in which the need to harness rainfall necessitates the building of a settled society, which in turn accelerates agricultural development, has already been touched on. The rich corpus of inscriptions left by the Sabaeans and their neighbours constantly underlines the importance of water: the earliest Sabaic inscriptions, probably dating from the eighth century BC, thank the divinity Athtar for rain. Some of the last Sabaic inscriptions, from the sixth century AD, record in the name of the Trinity repairs to the ailing Marib Dam, which were carried out by the Christian Axumites from Ethiopia then occupying the south. A typical dedication from some time in between, for a statue at the temple of Awam – the main Sabaean place of worship, not far from the Marib Dam – states that the dedicators

> give as an offering to the god Ilmaqah . . . the Lord of Awam, this gilded statue, in praise for his blessings on them of plenteous crops from both irrigated and rain-fed land . . . and of the harvest from their terraces and fields and farms watered by irrigation channels and dykes, and from all the farmland of their villages . . .

Again and again such inscriptions occur, down the centuries of Sabaean harvests.

As for that greatest of all irrigation works, the Marib Dam itself, it probably reached its final shape and size in the sixth century BC; it continued to function from that time for over a thousand years. Designed to divert and distribute seasonal run-off from the mountains (rather than to store water), it may be one of the most successful works of civil engineering in human history. The silt deposits of its 'two gardens' mentioned in the Qur'an are still clearly visible, as are the two ancient surviving sluices that irrigated them (the barrage wall itself does not survive). The depth of the deposits suggests that the Sabaeans were farming here from a thousand years before their first surviving inscriptions, or that pre- (perhaps proto-) Sabaean inhabitants began the work of irrigation; the extent of the silt shows that the two gardens covered 9,600 hectares at their greatest expanse. All this was the fruit of cooperation. (In contrast, modern irrigation, nearly all from artesian wells, tends to promote competition, with neighbouring farmers raiding a fast-retreating water table.) In time, however, that cooperation would cease, disaster would strike, and the Marib Dam would play a new part in Arabian history – or rather, in a sort of roving folk-epic, an Arab *Odyssey* in which the paths of fact and fantasy cross and recross.

PEOPLE AND PILGRIMAGE

Also at Marib was another great structure which, every year in due season, brought together streams from a similarly large catchment area. This structure was a temple, the Awam temple of the inscription quoted above, a great elliptical temenos containing shrines, and the streams were human. They came in the month of Abhay; appropriately for a hydraulic civilization like that of the Sabaeans, it coincided with the summer rains. The conditions imposed on the pilgrims, including special dress and abstinence from sexual activity and fighting, were echoed in other pilgrimages across Arabia. They still are, today, at the pilgrimage of another great deity – arguably the same one – in Mecca.

Although the Marib pilgrimage was by no means unique, it was vast: 'the House of Ilmaqah', as the Awam temple was often called, was home to one of the great Arabian gods, the patron deity of Saba. After so long in retirement, he has become an obscure figure: he may have been in origin a god of war or of vegetation; one scholar has seen him as a male hypostasis of the (usually female) sun deity. According to the Qur'an, the Sabaeans did indeed 'worship the sun', but the reference could be to one or another of its female versions. The god's name doesn't help particularly in delineating him. However it should be vowelled – perhaps 'Almaqah' – his name seems to be composed of 'Il', the general name of the paramount Semitic deity (as in 'al-*Il*ah' → 'Allah'), plus another element that is possibly from the Sabaic verb *wqh*, 'to command': thus Ilmaqah might be 'God the Commander', or 'the Ordainer'.

Whatever his name means, it is clear that Ilmaqah was central to the whole identity and unity of the major *sha'b*, or people, called Saba – itself a confederation of lesser *sha'b*s. In theological terms, he probably 'represents functionally the collective will of the *sha'b*'. The Sabaeans were seen as the 'children' of Ilmaqah; new members of the confederation had to make the pilgrimage to Marib, and would thus become in a sense adoptive children of the god. A key inscription found in the highlands 130 kilometres west of Marib imposes this duty on the *sha'b* called Sam'ay, which seems to have been newly adopted into the Sabaean confederation. Sam'ay's own patron deity, Ta'lab, decrees to his people that they must not fail to go on pilgrimage to Marib (in the chain of divine command, deities knew their place). Ta'lab also reminds his people that on the Marib pilgrimage they must abstain from sex and from certain types of hunting, and that they should slaughter 700 sheep on each of two days. Again, the dos and don'ts and hecatombs are all strongly reminiscent of Mecca today. Ta'lab even tells his people that if they are to slaughter a camel at Marib, they should ride it there gently – a piece of advice that was repeated in the Meccan context by the Prophet Muhammad, several centuries later. There were also features that would be unfamiliar at present-day Mecca, and one that would be shocking: the fact that Ilmaqah was not alone. Not only does Ta'lab defer to him, but dedications at Marib were made, usually jointly, to a whole pantheon of lesser deities – or perhaps a constellation, since many of them were celestial.

Despite this major exception, it should be clear by now how wrong it is to think of 'Arab history' as beginning with Islam, or even necessarily with 'Arabs'. South Arabians, who in their heyday never considered themselves Arabs in any sense, underlie this history; both Islam and Arabs were part of a very long continuum, one which cannot be pressed into a few prolegomena to a Muslim year zero. Many Muslim Arab historians were well aware of this: in the tenth century, as we shall see, al-Mas'udi's compendious histories would give full justice to the pre-Islamic past; his Yemeni contemporary, al-Hamdani, largely ignored Islamic dynastic history, and viewed current events as a continuation of pre-Islamic struggles. Other long-surviving features emerge from looking at this fuller picture of the past. For example, given the ancient, Sabaean association of the body politic with the will of the deity, an idea inherited by the Islamic community, the recent coinage 'political Islam' looks – at least in its home constituency of the Arabian subcontinent – to be a rank tautology.

Another feature of the ancient south that would elide into the wider civilization of Islam is the way in which it was rooted in places, not pedigrees. A South Arabian *sha'b*, unlike a tribe, defined itself by its territory – to which it was bound by the need to harness water – and by its sanctuaries and urban centres. Its members were the children of a god who had a house in a particular spot; they were not the offspring of some putative wandering ancestor. Compared with the peninsula as a whole, the south was highly urbanized: though some of them must have been pretty small, over a hundred places described as *hjr*, 'town', are mentioned in the pre-Islamic South Arabian inscriptions. Admittedly, a northern tribal grouping like Qedar could coalesce around an 'urban' sanctuary like Dumah; but in the case of the settled southern peoples, sanctuaries would actually be established in order to express and define group unities. The tribal self-definition, by lineage, would form another strand of Arab-Islamic ethnicity; by itself, however, it would not have taken Islam beyond Arabs. Without the legacy of the south and its civic centres, Islam might still have become a world religion – but one that like Judaism remained attached, however tenuously, to the idea of bloodlines. For Islam there are no Twelve Tribes, no Gentiles, and at least part of the reason is its South Arabian heritage.

South Arabia also presented a model of political unity that later ages would aspire to but rarely achieve; in this, too, it may have left a vital legacy for Islam. Early Sabaean inscriptions often feature the title *mkrb*, possibly to be read as '*mukarrib*'. (The root sense may be that of the Arabic *muqarrib*, 'one who brings near, who takes someone as an associate'; a similar Arabic term, *mujammi'*, is used in a political sense as 'unifier'.) The *mkrb* was the king of the dominant *sha'b* in a confederation of *sha'b*s – but only when he was wearing, so to speak, his other crown, as head of the confederation; the role has been nicely compared to that of the British queen as head of the Commonwealth. One important type of inscription, which scholars have called a 'federation formula', clarifies the *mkrb*'s role as unifier: 'he established every community of god or of patron, of treaty (*hbl*) or alliance.' These unions were thus founded in the names of the high god Ilmaqah and the lesser patron deities.

And out of the formula jumps a word, the term for the divinely sanctioned 'treaty': the Sabaic *hbl* will resurface in the Qur'an as *habl* –

> and hold fast, all of you together, to the *habl* of Allah and do not be divided among yourselves.

In Arabic, *habl* can be a 'rope', but it is also a 'binding covenant'. I am not suggesting that seventh-century AD Meccans had studied seventh-century BC Sabaean constitutional terminology, but there is no doubt that the term is the same one, and that the two communities shared ideas about political union in the name of a god or gods – or in the later case, of God. And therein lies the difference: the unity proposed by Islam was ultimate, both political and theological. One polity, one deity.

Philip Hitti, in his detailed *History of the Arabs*, first published in 1937, said that the Muslim community of Medina, 'was the first attempt in the history of Arabia at a social organization with religion, rather than blood, as its basis'. He was well over a thousand years too late in his dating. Of course, much of what we know about South Arabia (and for that matter the little we know about Dumah, the northern religious centre of the Qedar federation) was not known when Hitti was first compiling his work. But subsequent historians have been equally and less excusably islamocentric. An academic disconnect between Islamic and pre-Islamic studies has meant that most scholars do not see the dots that make the bigger picture, let alone try to join them up. When we do take that longer, wider view, we find that Islam was not something that shot up suddenly in Mecca; it is a vast, slow growth whose roots lie deep in time and all over the peninsula – particularly in its south, where they were cultivated by a people who did not even call themselves Arabs.

Today, that Qur'anic verse about holding fast to God's covenant is quoted regularly by seekers after those ever-elusive goals of Arab and Islamic unity. They do not realize how old that call is, or how, again, it comes from before Islam and beyond Arabs.

THE CLINCH OF CIVILIZATIONS

From the ancient Mediterranean perspective, the politics and theology of the South Arabian Fertile Crescent were as much a closed book as they were, until recently, to modern historians. What fascinated Greeks and

Romans was the South Arabians' production and export of aromatics, especially frankincense and myrrh. Pliny the Elder, for example, worked out that a camel carrying frankincense from its source in Arabia Felix to the shores of the Mediterranean would have to travel 2,437,500 (human) paces, and would thus add 688 *denarii* to the incense merchant's expenses. Almost as long, and a thousand years earlier, was the tenth-century BC Queen of Sheba's biblical trek bearing aromatics and other goods to Solomon. While the queen's exact identity has puzzled generations of scholars, most of them have agreed that she came from South Arabian Saba. To date, nothing has been found in her homeland to confirm or deny her existence; but finds of Sabaean products in modern Jordan prove that her countrymen were making the journey at least as early as 800 BC.

In the later centuries BC, the Sabaeans' neighbours, the Minaeans, were the most active and far-ranging merchants. One, for example, left an altar to the god Wadd ('Love'; later anathematized in the Qur'an) on the Greek island of Delos, probably in the second century BC; another left himself, mummified, in the Egyptian town of Memphis. His mummy case records that he imported myrrh for use in Egyptian temples, and in return exported cloth to his home country. Later, during the Himyari ascendancy in the first century AD, the compiler of the Greek *Periplus*, a merchant mariners' guide, wrote of the vast traffic of Muza, not far inside the entrance to the Red Sea. All this busy trade is eloquent evidence of how an Arabian 'nation far off', as the Book of Joel calls the Sabaeans, were tied multiply into distant economies. Then it was perfumes and gums, now it is petroleum and gas.

Another people connected by trade with wider economies were the Nabataeans, whose domain straddled the trade routes where they were funnelled out of the north-west of the peninsula. Unlike the Sabaeans and their South Arabian neighbours, the Nabataeans almost certainly spoke a form of Arabic; like the Sabaeans, however, they almost certainly did not consider themselves *'arab*. Not only were they a settled people, but living as they did in the Levant, in the lap of the Mediterranean rather than out on some Arabian limb, their cultural contacts had made them true cosmopolites. Vulture-like, they picked over what they fancied in the dominant neighbouring cultures, Aramaean, Hellenic and Roman, and returned to their rocky redoubts to digest and regurgitate their pickings. The results were splendid: the most enduring one, the classical architecture of their capital, Petra, is of course all facade; but it is no sham, no Hollywood set. And the fact that it is not built but carved in solid rock gives it all a Titanic magnificence – soaring colonnaded cliffs with pedimented peaks that sprout gigantic urns.

To the north-east, but occupying a similar borderland between cultures, and between fertile zone and wilderness, was the mercantile city-state of Palmyra. The Palmyrenes were also Arabic-speaking non-*'arab*, and deeply cosmopolitan. Their own Graeco-Roman-inspired architecture was in the round; it was the people themselves who had classical facades. Thus, the prince Wahballat ('the Gift of al-Lat', the female supreme deity) appeared on coinage as 'Caesar Wahballat Augustus', while his mother Zenobia (a Latinization of the still current Arabic name 'Zaynab') gave herself even more eclectic foundations by not only adopting the name 'Augusta' but also claiming descent from Cleopatra. It was out of this multicultural mélange, and at the same period, that a Janus-like figure such as Philip the Arab – a native of Damascus – could rise through the ranks of provincial administration to become praetorian prefect and eventually, in AD 244, Roman emperor. For the influences went both ways: even a century and a half before, Juvenal had observed that:

> *Iam pridem Syrus in Tiberim defluxit Orontes*
> *Et linguam et mores.*
>
> Long since has the Syrian Orontes flowed into the Tiber,
> Bearing modes of speech and ways of life.

It is all as far as possible from the Clash of Civilizations; rather, it is a Clinch of Civilizations.

Of course, the embrace of the powerful can end up smothering weaker partners, and Rome, in time, snuffed out both Nabataean and Palmyrene independence. (Empires raid as readily as tribes: that is how they come about.) The Nabataean realm was annexed by Rome in AD 106. Palmyra had been plundered very early on by that ravisher of the Orient, Mark Antony; the Roman state eventually took it over in AD 272. Much more recently, the culture-vultures of Palmyra have been posthumous prey to other dangerous raptors: the so-called 'Islamic State' waged a planned and publicized campaign of vandalism against the city's ancient monuments, defacing and demolishing. They should have pondered the fate of an earlier (and much milder) vandal: the Umayyad Caliph Marwan II is said to have unearthed at

Palmyra a statue of a queen bearing an inscription that cursed anyone who disturbed it. Soon after, the Umayyad dynasty fell, and the caliph was hunted down and killed. Now, the 'Islamic State' has fallen too.

The Nabataeans and Palmyrenes may have been arabophones, but with their settled, sometimes sybaritic ways and imported tastes, they lacked that foremost marker of being *'arab* – the stripped-down, nomadic lifestyle of the steppe. In time *nabat*, the Arabic name for the Nabataeans, would come to be seen as an antonym to *'arab*. Opposites can, however, attract. Indeed, all these Arabian elements were connected, both with each other and with a wider world, and were becoming more so over time.

CARAVAN TOWNS

Like the Sabaeans and Nabataeans, Arab camel nomads were benefiting from links with world economies. If Arabians as a whole were the mercantile mediators between the Indian Ocean and Mediterranean orbits of trade, then Arabs were becoming the mobile middlemen between those poles of Arabian settled life, the southern and northern fertile crescents. Far from living some hermetic, eremitic life in the desert, they too were connected with outside worlds. Not only were the *rm*, the Rum or Romans, beginning to appear in their graffiti; clashes between *rm* and *frs*, the Persians, were reported in the Safaitic samizdat, together with names of international personalities – *grmnqs* (Germanicus), *qsr* (Caesar), *flfs* (Philippus).

Interest was reciprocal. As the Arab gaze reached beyond the peninsula, outsiders cast acquisitive looks into its interior. The Romans sent an expedition in 26 BC under the prefect of Egypt, Aelius Gallus, that got as far as Marib before giving it all up as a bad job: reports that Arabia Felix was a veritable Eldorado turned to dust as the troops slogged deeper into the parched steppe near the Sabaean capital. The expeditionary force included Nabataeans, who themselves had made independent inroads into the peninsula and established a foothold at Hegra (now Mada'in Salih in Saudi Arabia), which became a sort of Little Petra. Earlier, South Arabians too had maintained trading colonies far to the north of their domain, such as the Minaean one at Dedan, a little to the south of Hegra. Such caravan towns were theatres for the growing dialogue between *hadar* and *badw*, settled and nomadic peoples.

Perhaps most significant of all for a developing Arab identity were the links that would develop from the third century AD between a tribe of camel-nomads, Kindah, and the South Arabian states. Unlike rose-red Petra, Kindah's caravan town of Qaryat Dhat Kahl (present-day Qaryat al-Faw in Saudi Arabia) remained unsung by Victorian poets, not because its name would be hard to fit into English verse, but as its importance only emerged in the 1970s. The evidence, if less immediately impressive than the monuments of Petra and Palmyra, shows that just as the latter were hellenized and romanized, Arabs in Qaryat were South Arabianized. For example, a man of Qaryat with an undoubtedly Arab name, Ijl ibn Sa'd al-Lat ('Calf son of the-Luck-of-al-Lat'), whose patronymic invokes the supreme female deity of the nomadic north, was commemorated by a grave-stele with a Sabaic inscription invoking a southern deity, Athtar Shariqan. The two scenes carved on the stele are also expressive of the meeting of Arab and South Arabian: below are two camels, one with the deceased on board, holding a stick and a lance, those tools of herding and raiding; above, the dead Ijl is shown feasting – and making use of those prime accoutrements of settled life, a table and chair. The *'arab* trackers and truckers of the wilderness were making their debut in society, wining and dining with the best. Soon they would be transformed from marginal extras into major players.

THE RECORD OF THE ARABS

Although the death of Ijl was recorded in lapidary Sabaic prose, he would also almost certainly have been mourned in the more mercurial medium of oral Arabic, probably in poetry. Kindah, the tribal masters of Qaryat, were to produce some of the earliest named poets in the language. We have no elegy datable to the age in which Ijl lived; but, significantly, that oldest known Arabic inscription – the first-century AD prayer mentioned in Chapter 1 – seems to have a repeating rhythm. It is likely, then, that prayers, and probably dirges too, took poetic forms in early times. So too did paeans: an early foreign reference to Arabic poetry just after the heyday of Qaryat comes in a Greek history, which mentions fourth-century Arabs celebrating victories in *odai*, 'popular songs'. In the final couple of pre-Islamic centuries, poetry would come to encompass for Arabs every aspect of life and death. It would be 'the archive of their history, their wisdom, and their nobility'. Again, according to an old saying, four attributes are peculiar to Arabs: 'Turbans are their diadems, girdles are their curtain-walls, sword-blades are their fences, verses are their archives.'

Poetry – the *diwan*, the archive – is a record purely oral in origin, in a speech that is rhymed, rhythmic and, importantly, inflected; the inflections of high Arabic affect not only the endings of words but also their beginnings and even their insides, and they are fiendishly difficult. Poems began, however, almost certainly as a statement not of deeds past, but of future or unseen events, as the medium of tribal seers and shamans. One theory, already mentioned, has it that the language of fully developed Arabic poetry started off as a mystical, oracular tongue: the original meaning of *shai'r*, eventually 'poet', is almost certainly 'soothsayer', and in its most basic meaning, a *sha'ir* is 'one who perceives that which others cannot'.

Although there is nothing obviously like poetry in all those thousands of Safaitic inscriptions on rocks in the wilderness, many of poetry's later themes – love, lust, loss, raiding, longing – appear in them. And while the oldest complete odes that we have are by Kindah poets of the sixth century, it seems impossible that they could have hatched, *ab ovo*, not only fully fledged but flying high. Poetry must have been developing in those early centuries AD, going on its oral travels up and down the trade routes, picking up its material and forming its character along the way. Indeed, much of the oldest verse is about departures, journeys, mounts. 'Go!' urged al-Shanfara, early in the sixth century,

> You have all you need: the moon is out,
> The mounts are girthed to go, the saddles too.
> . . .
> Yes, by your life! The world has room for one
> Who seeks or flees by night . . .

Epic it is not; but, like Homeric Greek, its special form of Arabic, elevated above everyday speech, brings together diverse elements from many dialects. It all builds up into a glittering linguistic collage that is formal, often severely stylized, but made from found objects. To listen to Arabic poetry is, still, to enter an elaborate grotto of words and sounds, familiar yet unfamiliar, and, at its best, still possessed by something of that ancient divinatory magic. All around Arabia, not just in caravan capitals like Qaryat but also by campfires in the great dark voids in between, Arabs began to fall under the spell of poetry. To understand its power, you must forget the rarefied and marginal place of poetry in the English-speaking world. For Arabs poetry was (and to some extent still is) a mass medium, as ubiquitous as satellite TV and as beguiling as Hollywood; it played a huge part in laying the foundations of a monoculture for a mixed and mobile people.

It was above all that last feature, mobility, that gave the impetus to an Arab virtuous circle. Diverse but mobile *'arab*, working as carriers across Arabia, mixed with each other and had to be able to communicate; mutual borrowing between dialects led to a levelling of language – especially, it seems, in Najd, the area in which Qaryat was situated. Poetry created a further version, a language that was not only levelled, but also elevated – a high plateau to which the poets, orators and leaders of all tribes aspired, and their people with them. In other words, the mobility of *'arab* was the mother of Arabic, and Arabic was the mother of Arabs – neither a nation in the modern sense, nor a *sha'b*, a 'people', in the South Arabian sense, but a collection of tribes that was something more than the sum of its parts – an ethnic gestalt. To use the terms of German nationalism, if a *Staatsnation* was as yet unimaginable, a *Kulturnation* was forming. The Arab virtuous cycle was gaining momentum, and for a period from the third century into the fourth the caravan town of Qaryat was probably its major hub. In time the momentum would move into higher gears, and the hub would shift – eventually to Mecca, another emporium of wares and words, whose people prided themselves in using what was best of all in Arab speech, and where, in the Qur'an, that speech would reach its highest plateau, level with heaven.

Also in the early centuries AD, that other, surprising change was beginning to take place. As dialect differences between Arabs began to iron themselves out, the nomad tongue also wormed itself into settled populations. Nomad Arabs were playing an ever-increasing role, not just as mercenaries in the pay of local rulers but also as power brokers, actually influencing the outcome of disputes among the settled southerners. The written record begins to mention two elements in the southern societies. From the second century AD, for example, the inscriptions of the increasingly influential South Arabian Hamdan federation speak of 'the *a'rab* of Hamdan and its *hjr*-people' [townspeople]. From the following century, the rulers of the largest southern polity would style themselves 'kings of Saba and Himyar . . . and of their *a'rab* of highland and lowland'. *'Arab* had arrived, both physically and socially, in the south. The haughty kings in their towering palaces were coming more and more to rely on their grubby guests.

In the last century or two before Islam, *'arab* would become the most important people, politically, in southern society. But their speech seems to have begun drowning out other languages long before. As early as the third century AD the Himyaris, for example, although they still wrote their inscriptions in Sabaic, the 'Latin' of South Arabia, may well have seen it as a purely epigraphic language and have spoken something else – probably including ever-increasing amounts of Arabic. (By the early tenth century AD, what the learned Yemeni antiquary al-Hamdani regards as the 'Himyari' language, still surviving in isolated pockets, is essentially Arabic with a few Sabaic features.) If it is also true that most South Arabians were forbidden by some clerical taboo from using the Sabaic script, this too would hardly have helped the ancient language to survive. Not only were nomad Arabs developing a single standard language; Arabians as whole were on their way to being arabophones, and thus in a new, united and much wider sense, Arabs. It is a sense that still holds today, and a unity that still joins people together when religion and politics do their very best to separate them.

But even in those first centuries AD, if language was gathering the word of Arabia, other forces were pulling it apart.

JUST THIEVES

With their poetry, Arabs were serenading each other. Increasingly, too, they were raiding each other. Looking back to the grave-stele of Ijl, the lance-bearing, camel-borne warrior, one wonders if he has rustled the second, riderless camel.

Raiding was a way of nomad life as early as Genesis, which depicts Ishmael as the consummate raider and outsider:

> he shall be a wild ass of a man; his hand shall be against every man, and every man's hand against him.

The Assyrians, too, noted the fondness of Arabs for raiding (a case, perhaps, of a very big pot and a small kettle). Later, Arab Banksys depicted raids in their graffiti art, and offered up written prayers for booty. As a way of life, raiding was not haphazard: in time, it became a formal economic institution, with a fixed etiquette and shares – usually a quarter or a fifth for the leader of the raid, plus a few extra perks such as the pick of any particularly desirable items. Raiding was not just endemic but systemic.

For modern Western people, a mental gear-shift is needed to understand how raiding was – indeed still is – seen as something other than roving robbery, dry-land piracy. To an extent it resembles the old maritime practice of privateering, or for that matter the culture of prize-taking in the regular state navies: until as recently as 1918, Britain's Royal Navy allotted that significant quarter of the prize to the captain, and lesser shares to the rest of the ship's company. The prize had to be an enemy ship in wartime, of course; then again, what is a state of war but a legal gloss on raiding? Equally, it might be said that reciprocally raiding tribes are in a chronic state of war.

In a herding-raiding economy, animal rustling was seen as a way of enlarging one's holdings when other methods of husbandry fell short. The nature of the herding-raiding nexus is revealed by words: *ghanam*, 'sheep and goats', may originally have meant any sort of herded animals; its close cognate *ghanimah* means 'plunder, booty, loot'. Revisiting the parallels between *'arab* and *arya*, the Sanskrit word for 'cow' (the *arya* equivalent of the camel) is *go* and provides the first element in that for 'war', *gavisti*, literally 'cow-wish'. War and raiding were, in both those mobile, herding societies, a matter of adding not to one's immovable territory, but to the mobile animals that grazed it. In a society in which the concept of landed 'real estate' is absent, perhaps notions of ownership in general are looser: as with the ownerless high seas and naval prizes, so too with the desert and its 'ships'.

In time, raiding came to be seen, with Darwinian detachment, as the survival of the fittest: 'Fertility,' wrote al-Jahiz, quoting an anonymous speaker, 'invites one to engage in enmity, to raid one's neighbours; it invites the strong to eat up anyone weaker'. The ranks of raiders generated their own nobility, whose credentials were the opposite of those of a landed gentry founded on old money: 'You may criticize me,' said the poet and aristocrat of the raid, Durayd ibn al-Simmah, whose long life began in about 530 and ended in opposition to Muhammad,

> but I tell you that new wealth
> is dearer far to me than old.

At the same time, raiding could provide social security for the weakest in society. Urwah ibn al-Ward, a sixth-century 'vagabond' leader, would gather the sick, the old and the feeble, would feed them up, and then take them off raiding to support themselves. Raiding and redistribution of wealth go together, and the redistribution takes place first between raided and raider and then within the raiders' own tribe.

A neat characterization of an eleventh-century Arab ruler of Mosul named Qirwash calls him *wahhab nahhab,* lavishing-ravishing – that is, lavishing gifts and ravishing other people's property, 'according to the established customs of the *'arab*'. Although established practice was to avoid bloodshed, Qirwash had to admit, 'I have the blood of five or six bedouins on my hands. As for that of the townsfolk, Allah takes no notice of them.' Something like Qirwash's epithet is still used of a latter-day lavisher-ravisher, the man who for a third of a century ruled my adoptive country and siphoned off the chiefly portion from its economy. His supporters say '*Ya'kul wa-yu'akkil*', 'He eats, but he feeds others'. These others – again, his supporters – also call him *sariq 'adil,* 'a just thief'. His unfed detractors say he is just a thief.

Raiding, whether of flocks or states, fuels the sempiternal cycle of unity and disunity. Eating and feeding, ravishing and lavishing, seizing and distributing plunder provide the quickest way to forge a unity. 'His hands filled with booty,' it was said of al-Barraq, leader of the great tribe of Rabi'ah in the late fifth century, 'and the tribes of the Arabs fell under his sway'. But in most cases the resulting unity will be of the flimsiest. It goes without saying that a 'system' of plunder and redistribution was, and is, inimical not just to the formation of a centralized tax-collecting state, a commonwealth of citizens who share in rights and duties, but also to any sort of long-term stability. Transfers of power will be inevitably disruptive, often bloody. Raiding perpetuates an ancient, internecine clash of cultures: between *qabilah*-tribe and *sha'b*-people, between competition and cooperation, segmentation and symbiosis, personalities and institutions, unison and polyphony; between a society subsisting on reciprocal raid and one built on mutual aid.

How, then, of all mobile peoples, did Arabs become raiders par excellence?

BORN OF THE GATHERED WIND

Folklore had it that the camel was created from the *rimth* bush. To a higher authority, supposedly the Prophet Muhammad himself, was due a legendary account of the creation of the horse:

> Allah, when He wished to create the horse, sent word to the south wind, saying, 'I shall create from you a creature, so gather yourself together,' and the wind gathered itself together. Then Allah gave a command to Gabriel, who took a handful of the gathered wind. Then Allah said, 'This is my handful.' Then Allah created from it a horse, a dark bay. And Allah said, 'I have created you as a horse, and made you Arab, and favoured you above all the other beasts that I have created, by granting you breadth of livelihood, for booty will be borne home on your back . . .'

There is metaphorical truth in all this. The horse blew into the Arabian subcontinent on the wind of change from outside (albeit from the north), and it did indeed become not only a vital part of Arab life, but, *tout court*, 'Arab'; even in English, the word, when it doesn't refer to a person, usually means a horse. As for their more concrete history, precisely when horses entered the Arabian scene is unknown. Recently discovered evidence may indicate some sort of domestication of equids (if not horses as such) back in the mists of the major wet period, 6,000 years ago or more. Undoubted horses drawing chariots are depicted in petroglyphs from the north of the peninsula that date back perhaps to 2000 BC. Horses for riding seem to have appeared in the second half of the last millennium BC, a period some would narrow down to the fourth to second centuries BC.

What is clear is that horses rapidly gained enormous importance in Arab life – and death, for like camels they were sometimes sacrificed and buried with deceased warriors. If a passing mention by al-Baladhuri is to be believed, horses were even worshipped in Bahrain. They are sworn upon in the Qur'an, at the beginning of a chapter named after them, 'The Runners':

> By the running horses, panting,
> Striking sparks,
> Rushing to the dawn raid . . .

And they are celebrated endlessly in the oldest surviving poetry – perhaps earliest and most famously in the sixth-century Kindah poet Imru' al-Qays's brilliant *crescendo e accelerando*,

> charging, fleet-fleeing, head-foremost, headlong, all together
> the match of a rugged boulder hurled from on high by the torrent ...

By the time of those lines, some tribes could field up to a thousand cavalry, and the tribal leader was at times known as the *faris* – the Horseman or Cavalier. A thousand cavalrymen is a surprisingly high figure to be able to mobilize, even for the biggest tribes of the time, given the demands of horses and the difficulties of feeding and watering them in unforgiving terrain. Indeed, by itself the horse might have remained merely prestigious, costly and about as useful in battle as a Lamborghini. But add the camel to the horse, and you have the perfect double-act . . . you plod to battle on your camel, which also carries your horse's fodder and water, and then rush headlong into the fray on your steed. The combination is mentioned in the later Safaitic graffiti, probably dating to the second to fourth centuries AD, and in the formal inscriptions of the declining South Arabian states, whose *a'rab* mercenaries relied on it while their regular armies fielded only footsoldiers. By early Islamic times any warrior worth the name would be inseparable from his two mounts: 'On clouded nights when thunder rolled but no rain fell,' said a contemporary of the Prophet Muhammad, remembering a famous raiding chief,

> he would set out on a slow-paced camel, with a restive horse at his side,
> a heavy lance in his hand, and the cloak all but slipping from his back,
> seated between the waterskins; and thus he would ride till dawn,
> smiling all the way.

It is hard to overstate the importance of that pairing of camel and horse, unique to Arabs: the camel is the spearshaft that gives you reach, but the horse is the spear*head*. It is what gives you *shawkah* – point, power, sting, the thorn in the side of others. Thus armed, Arabs also had a military edge over those others. The edge was further honed by the invention, probably in the second or third century AD, of the saddlebow, which helps you fight from camel-back. Yet another technological development that aided fighting and raiding, the stirrup (and to begin with it may indeed have been singular, and made of wood), seems to have reached Arabs a little later, possibly in the fifth century AD. Arabs immediately found the stirrup 'one of the best aids for anyone thrusting with a lance or striking with a sword'.

Stirrups were imported innovations. But the camel+horse combination was exclusively Arab, and may have been decisive in the transformation of *'arab* from plodding hauliers into dashing warriors. It may have been the crucial factor that brought them into closer contact with the neighbouring powers, north and south, first as mercenaries, then as power brokers, finally as power-breakers – and brought them ultimately, as conquerors and imperialists, on to the international stage. It may too have been a *hamartia*, a tragic flaw that sealed their destiny, their disunity: as a military innovation that spread rapidly and became common to all Arabs, it ensured that none of them ever gained the upper hand over the others for long. It perpetuated a seething stalemate, and sparked an explosion in raiding.

'ALL THE ARABS'

Among Arabs a virtuous cycle was in motion, a gradual standardization of language that was beginning to create a cultural 'nation'. But running counter to it were many smaller tribal cycles of raid and counter-raid, whose effect was chronically divisive. They were fuelled by an increasing amount of horsepower, and by a gradual drop in overland traffic that left camels and cameleers out of work and pocket. In particular, the fall of Petra and Palmyra in the second and third centuries AD, and instability in the southern Fertile Crescent, had disturbed peninsular trade. But at least since the time of the first named Arab, Gindibu, whose thousand camels saw service against the Assyrians, Arabs had freelanced for their powerful neighbours in logistics and then in border control as well as in commercial haulage. Now, as trade gave way to raid, came renewed opportunities for a change of career, from mercantile to mercenary.

The Roman takeover of Palmyra in 272 had brought the two great imperial spheres, Rome and Persia, into closer contact than ever before. For Arabs this proximity brought risks, but also advantages. As Eugene Rogan has said, 'The Arabs were always most empowered when there was more than one dominant [neighbouring] power to the Age'. Rogan was thinking of more recent powers – Britain and France, NATO and the Warsaw Pact – but his insight applies equally to the age of Rome and Persia (and for that matter to the age of Assyria and Babylon). One piece of evidence for such empowerment in the fourth century is a tomb inscription discovered in 1901 near the fortress of al-Namarah, 120 kilometres south-east of Damascus. Written in 'a developed form of the Nabataean alphabet, well on its way to becoming Arabic', it is no easy read. But despite the possible variants and cruces, it is a foundational text of Arab history as important as that first Assyrian mention of Arabs. The Namarah epitaph is not only one of the earliest in what was becoming the standard, unified Arabic; it is also the first known mention of Arabs as such, by themselves, in their own language. 'This', it begins, 'is the monument of Imru' al-Qays son of Amr, king of all the Arabs . . .' It goes on to record that he subjugated four major Arabian tribes of the day, and raided Najran, 1,700 kilometres south of al-Namarah, 'in the irrigated land' of the Himyari ruler. It concludes, 'no king had matched his achievements up to the time when he died . . . in the year 223, the seventh day of Kislul'. The year, given according to a local calendar, coincides with AD 328.

There is general agreement over that much of the text. But in addition to the linguistic puzzles in the rest of it, there is a historical enigma. Later Arab historians list Imru' al-Qays as the second ruler of al-Hirah, in Persian-dominated Iraq, and a Persian inscription confirms that his father was a vassal of the Sasanian empire. But his tomb at al-Namarah is 750 kilometres from al-Hirah, and well within the Roman sphere. There may be other explanations, but the likeliest reason is defection – that he and at least part of his tribe, Lakhm, had 'gone over' to Rome; one Arab historian claims that he had gone over in the religious sense, and become a Christian. Furthermore, a possible reading of a contested phrase in the inscription has it that he appointed as viceroys the nobles of the *sha'b*s, the peoples, 'and they became leaders for the Romans'.

Whatever the truth of the matter, it is clear that superpower politics were part of the picture, and more than possible that Imru' al-Qays took advantage of them to give himself a trans-Arabian presence, all the way from the northern Fertile Crescent to the 'irrigated land' of its southern counterpart. It is also clear that in the fourth-century round of the Great Game – the seemingly perennial confrontation of empires north of the Arabian subcontinent – Arab pawns were starting to cross the board and become kings, major players in their own right. (Queens seem to have gone out of fashion with Palmyra's flamboyant but vanquished Zenobia, who must have been a hard act to follow.)

The Game was as old as that oldest mention of Arabs, a thousand years before the fall of Petra and Palmyra, and it is far from over now. But the particular part played in it by Imru' al-Qays, 'king of all the Arabs', begs a question: was the royal title assumed by himself, or bestowed by one or other of his imperial neighbours? There are later examples where the superpowers handed out royal titles. Procopius, for example, mentions the Romans dubbing their early sixth-century Ghassanid client-ruler 'king of the Arabs', as a riposte to Persian support for Imru' al-Qays's dynasty, the Lakhmids (long back in the Persian bosom). On the other side, later Arab sources confirm that the Persians were the ones who bestowed the title 'king of the Arabs' on Lakhmid leaders in this period. It seems more than possible that Imru' al-Qays was an early beneficiary in this titular tit-for-tat, in other words, that he saw himself as 'king of all the Arabs' because someone else, either Rome or Persia, told him he was that.

If the supposition is right, then it begs a further question: did a first sense of all-embracing Arab unity come not from within Arabs themselves, but from outside – from their non-Arab neighbours? There could be nothing like being told that you're a king, officially, by one or other (perhaps even both) of the two great powers of your age, to make you feel and act like a king; to make you look on your potential subjects, however divided they might be in reality, as a unity – 'all the Arabs'. Perhaps, after more than a millennium of being told by their neighbours that they were Arabs, a discrete group with an identity, the message had finally got through. Admittedly, I am reading between the lines of Imru' al-Qays's epitaph. But it is undeniable that from the time of his rule in the fourth century, as we shall see, the power of a unified Arab culture would surge – importantly, under the patronage of the imperial client-kings who succeeded him on both the Roman and Persian sides.

Certainly, empires and their shennanigans have nurtured national identity and spurred the pursuit of political unity in more recent times. A century ago, the British promoted their own self-proclaimed 'king of the Arabs', Sharif Husayn of Mecca. Subsequent imperial double dealings and dashings of hope would fuel resentment and nourish nationalism. So too, almost certainly, in the days of Rome/Byzantium and Persia. The imperial masters held out crowns to their Arab protégés; but they were just as ready at times to snatch back the crowns and to undermine the unity they symbolized by setting Arabs against each other. In the end it could all only strengthen an Arab sense of identity. The seed of selfhood, even if planted by the imperial Others, would grow in contradistinction to those Others: it would grow into a search for self-determination.

In King Imru' al-Qays's time it was, however, still a seed. No doubt the vast majority of 'all the Arabs' would have been bemused, at best, by the idea of belonging to a single body of people with a single king. Both royal pretensions and imperial policies, whether of the unite-and-rule or divide-and-rule sort, were trumped by the reality on the ground – by the fact that Arabs remained divided and unrulable. And yet the king's successors would sit on their borrowed thrones, and the superpowers would loom over them and over Arabia, crowning and dethroning, for three more centuries to come. As a commentator of the early Islamic age would put it, Arabs of these times were 'stuck on top of a rock between two lions, Persia and Rome' – which sounds, if anything, even more uncomfortable than being caught between the proverbial rock and hard place.

CHAPTER THREE

SCATTERED FAR AND WIDE

THE CHANGING GRAMMAR OF HISTORY

Up on their rock between the two imperial lions of Persia and Rome, Arabs often had a third lion to contend with: the Himyari empire of the south.

If the boast of Imru' al-Qays, 'king of all the Arabs', is true, his people had already twisted the southern lion's tail by invading the Himyari King Shammar's irrigated lands around Najran. But such lion-baiting was exceptional and short-lived, and probably instigated by one or other of the northern powers: there is a mention by the early Islamic historian al-Tabari of the Sasanian shah of Persia ordering a mighty expedition against the tribes of the peninsula at about this time; this might well be the campaign mentioned in Imru' al-Qays's epitaph. If so, then to raid King Shammar's fertile southern lands would have been a tempting side-track to the main campaign against these tribes – and especially useful in Persian eyes as Shammar himself had been in expansionist mood in the early fourth century, campaigning far north and east into Arabia. Well into Islamic times, writers of fabulous accounts of the ancient south would claim that the Himyari king's campaigns had taken him as far as Samarqand in Central Asia (to which, in legend, he gave his name – *Shammar-kand*, 'Shammar destroyed it') and even that he had led Himyaris to Tibet. For the Persians, who were expanding their own influence in the east of the peninsula, that Shammar had got as far as central Arabia was threatening enough.

It seems likely, then, that before his probable defection to the Romans, Imru' al-Qays acted as cat's paw for the Persian lion, subduing truculent tribes. But the expedition would have more fateful consequences for the South Arabians than a one-off raid on Najran. Along the way, Imru' al-Qays says he 'chastised' a major tribal conglomeration called Madhhij. At about this time, and probably because of Persian pressure, Madhhij and their tribal overlords, Kindah, upped sticks from central Arabia and moved south *en masse*. As we have seen, some of Kindah led a semi-urbanized existence in their caravan-capital, Qaryat; but at heart they and the tribes associated with them remained *badw*, and their policy when the odds were against them was not to strike back, but to strike camp and move out of harm's way.

The arrival of tens of thousands of nomads and semi-nomads in the settled south – Madhhij in the foothills to the east of the lush Himyari highlands, Kindah in the heart of the fertile Himyari-ruled complex of valleys called Hadramawt – would bring irreversible change. Arabs and their language had already made inroads in the old Sabaic-speaking south; now, the influx of tribal nomads increased, and as the Himyari lion grew older and weaker, they would gnaw away at the foundations of his settled civilization. The skyscraper palaces of Zafar would soon be tottering.

THE RAT WITH IRON TEETH

In the south, with its patchwork of kingdoms, claims to unity were expressed by the rhetoric of royal titles. Saba had remained the senior kingdom from the earliest days. In its shadow, lesser kingdoms had risen and decayed around the 'shores' of the inland desert – the short-lived states of Ma'in, Qataban and Awsan. Early in the first millennium AD, the Himyari people living in the mountains between the desert and the Red Sea had become prominent; the next few centuries saw struggles for control, and at times coalitions, between Himyaris and Sabaeans. Further to the east beyond a gulf of the sands, the great oasis of branching canyons, Hadramawt, had long maintained its independence and its irrigation systems, but fell to the Himyari-dominated Sabaean state towards the end of the third century. By the time of Hadramawt's conqueror, the expansionist King Shammar who reigned from the late third to the early fourth century, South Arabia was as unified as it ever would be – certainly more unified than it is as I write. Shammar's title proclaimed this: he was, 'King of Saba, Dhu Raydan [the

Himyari palace, symbolizing the Himyari realm], Hadramawt and Yamanat'. That last term, Yamanat, 'the Southlands', probably means the former kingdoms of Awsan and Qataban. To this list, later Himyari kings would add, 'and of their Arabs of the Highlands and Lowlands', in a nominal attempt to contain a growing problem.

It was that last and most recent element, the Arab one, which would unravel the rest of the royal title and end the short-lived unity of the realm. *A'rab* mercenaries in the king's service were joined by ever more hangers-on – tribesmen who had been pushed south and west by Persian pressure. Under a strong king like Shammar, the mercenaries could be a useful force. Later, weaker rulers used the *a'rab* 'to pursue vendettas ... The only result for the land was destruction' and, two centuries after Shammar, successive occupations by Ethiopia and Persia. The pattern of the mercenary undermining his master would repeat itself through Arab history. So too would that of the nomad destroying his settled neighbour's way of life. It is worth noting again that Ibn Khaldun observed, with the hindsight of a thousand years from the time of King Shammar, 'how civilization always collapsed in places where the [Arab] Bedouins took over'. He goes on to cite the example of South Arabia and then the later ones of Iraq, Syria and his own North Africa. (The pattern repeats itself now outside my window, where gun-slinging tribesmen from the northern highlands have been unleashed on the capital of Saba's successor by an ex-ruler pursuing a vendetta. So too, *mutatis mutandis*, in Iraq, Syria and Libya, two-thirds of a millennium on from Ibn Khaldun.)

The long and bitty narrative of the decline and fall of settled civilization in South Arabia would be simplified by later Arab memory, boiled down into the story of the literal fall of the Marib Dam, a tale told and retold in verse, prose and sacred text. The tenth-century version by al-Mas'udi begins by describing Saba in its heyday:

> The Sabaeans enjoyed the finest and most luxurious standards of living ... in the most fertile land imaginable ... They wielded military might, and their word was gathered ...

That is, they were a united people who spoke with one voice. Their wealth, and the fertility of their land, were due to the mighty wadi-spanning dam of Marib. One of the greatest works of hydro-engineering in the ancient world, it was 680 metres long, 18 metres high and, as we have seen, channeled the run-off from a catchment area of 10,000 square kilometres to irrigate an area of as many hectares – the size of Rhode Island, or five times all the Royal Parks of London put together. According to the folk version, the trouble began when the king's *kahinah*, or seeress, began to have nightmare visions of destruction, and then daytime glimpses of the natural order overturned: three gerbils standing on their hind legs, covering their eyes with their front paws; a tortoise stuck on its back, urinating; trees swaying when there was no breeze. Solving the algebra of these portents, she told the king that he would find a rat undermining the dam. 'And there was the rat, using its paws to roll a stone [out of the dam] which fifty men could not have rolled . . .'

Al-Mas'udi, perhaps fearing for his credibility, prefaces the tale with a more sober account in which general neglect results in the dam's destruction. In the much sparer Qur'anic account, the dam and its blessings are portent enough. They are a favour from Allah, and to ignore Him invites destruction:

> There was for Saba a sign in their dwelling-place: two gardens, one on the right hand and one on the left . . . a fair land and a forgiving Lord.
>
> But they turned away [from divine favour,] so We sent against them the flood of the Dam; and We gave them, instead of their two gardens, gardens of bitter fruit, and tamarisks, and a few lote-trees.
>
> . . .
>
> . . . And so We made them as tales once told, and We scattered them far and wide . . .

That last phrase also means, 'and We tore them apart in every manner of tearing'. As both ancient Sabaeans and modern-day Arab refugees know to their cost, it is a warning of what happens when the foundations of a settled and united society are allowed to crumble.

The Marib Dam probably suffered its final, irreparable breach in the Prophet Muhammad's own lifetime, early in the seventh century. But inscriptions at its site suggest that the problems had been going on for almost three hundred years before that: instead of the regular maintenance needed to clear build-ups of silt, long periods of neglect were interspersed with frantic bouts of emergency repair. It all bears witness to the gradual breakdown of central authority, which had formerly organized regular maintenance of the structure. The breakdown was accelerated by the Ethiopian and Persian occupations of the sixth century, but it was due, ultimately, to the infiltration and growing power of *a'rab* tribes over the two preceding centuries. It was 'these human rats,' says a modern-day Yemeni historian of ancient South Arabia, still palpably angry about the disaster, 'the *badw* and *a'rab* mercenaries . . . that played the major part in finishing off its last [independent] state'. Their growing numbers and military strength had turned them from mercenaries into power-brokers, then into power-breakers and power-grabbers; once in charge, their tribal methods of rule, relying chiefly on arbitration, were – in the flipside sense – arbitrary. The rodent effect on centuries-old civic structures ate into the foundations of settled society.

Like all the best parables, the story of the Marib Dam's decline and fall works at different levels. For the farmer and folk historian, it is a warning about what happens when the portents of nature are ignored; for the prophet and his people, it is an example of what goes wrong when divinely given order is not maintained; and for the social historian, it is a parable of the increasing permeability of another legendary 'dam' – the ever-porous barrier between nomad and sedentary – and of the resulting human floods.

If there was indeed a great diaspora of settled peoples as a result of the breakdown of irrigation and society in the South, as the stories claim, the dispersal would have happened long before that last, late pre-Islamic damburst. The folk histories, as we shall see, go on to speak of the migration from Marib of the great tribe of Azd and its important sub-tribe, Ghassan, which must have taken place a few centuries earlier. Whether there was in fact a single mass migration is not known; a gradual ebbing away of settled populations is much more likely. But in either case it would have far-reaching effects: it may not have been a cataclysm, but the setting in motion of settled people in large numbers would be a catalyst for change across the Arabian subcontinent. With nomads percolating into the old settled lands and, now, previously settled people leaving those lands, the old unitary states were dissolving and the boundaries between *badw* and *hadar* breaking down: 'The kings have left their homelands,' says a poem attributed to a pre-Islamic southern ruler, 'and gone to other lands where both *badw* and *hadar* dwell'.

Arabia was on the move, and entering an age of dynamic disunity – a shake-up that would eventually set off the epochal migrations and conquests of Islam. And if the grand old southern civilizations were destroyed in the process then, as the saying goes, you can't make an omelette without breaking eggs.

THE ACTIVE VOICE OF HISTORY

The most memorable character in the Marib story is Tarifah, the *kahinah* or seeress who foresaw the dam's collapse and then led the migration of her people, Ghassan. The male ruler of Ghassan defers to her: it is Tarifah who chooses the route of the migration and, when it is blocked by enemies, incites her people to do battle with them. All her pronouncements are made in the form of high Arabic called *saj'*, prose with rhyme and rhythm but without the metre of poetry, that would reappear later in the Qur'an. Her special, eloquent speech, *bayan* ('exposition', or 'the unveiling of meaning'), is used for making statements based on supernatural insight. What she says is necessarily true *because* she utters it in this special speech. The argument is impenetrably circular; the historically more recent kind of truth, the sort based on empiricism and quantifiable 'facts' that arose in Europe some five centuries ago, does not come into it. The ultimate proof is whether enough people believe her – and they do, when she swears an oath:

> By the truth of my knowledge of the eloquent speech that has alighted on me,
> and of my tongue and what is recited by me . . .

Telling the truth is thus like telling a joke: it's the *way* you tell it that matters.

As someone who can see what others do not see, and who can speak as others cannot speak – and thus can inspire and lead – Tarifah foreshadows a later figure endowed with prophecy, eloquence and command. That later figure, Muhammad, is solidly historical; Tarifah may be inspired by a genuine person, dimly remembered, but the often Grimm-like details of her character almost certainly belong to the realm of the fairy tale. We must not kill her off because of that. The telling of the tale of the Dam and of Tarifah by the earliest known Islamic folk historians (at least as early as Wahb ibn Munabbih, who lived in the first Islamic century) suggests that they understood how the 'new' religion had emerged from an old and thoroughly

Arabian background – and, moreover, one that covered the old, settled south as well as Muhammad's immediate Meccan environment.

Wahb was himself a southerner and, without doubt, pride in the past of the South spurred him and other fellow southerners to stress the region's importance to the broader, later history of Arabdom. They were right to do so. Ghassan, and the other settled folks who had been set in motion, were no longer South Arabians: they had become Arabs. They had ceased to be 'Sabaeans' or 'Himyaris', self-centred and self-sufficient in their far-off fertile lands, and were seen instead from a pan-Arabian perspective as Yemenis – Arabians from al-Yaman, 'the South' of the peninsula. In a sense, the story of the Marib Dam diaspora – of the stirring up of populations, the mixing of people into a new collective identity – is the Arab 'national' epic. It can be told in a page or two, so it is hardly epic in size. But subsequent events make it seem much bigger than it is, a maquette for a great monument: it is the prototype for the seventh-century diaspora of Arabs into three continents, and for the global epic of Islam.

If the Marib story isn't strict history, it also shows how important a dash of myth is in compounding a new identity, a whole new ethnicity for the diverse peoples and tribes who would be united by Islam. As parahistory, it is as significant as the *Mahabharata* or the *Aeneid*; nations, Renan said, come out of getting history wrong. But perhaps 'wrong' is the wrong word. A fiction can be truthful, even if it isn't true; national identity, like religion, turns on questions of faith rather than matters of fact. A historian, of course, must try to distinguish between the two, but it is often hard. There is no doubting the factuality of the cyclopean remains of the Marib sluice gates, for example, or of the three millennia of alluvial deposits in the 'two gardens' which they irrigated and which are mentioned in the Qur'an. Equally factual is the new Marib Dam, bankrolled in the 1980s by the late Shaykh Zayid of the United Arab Emirates. But were Shaykh Zayid's distant but direct ancestors really of the tribe of Azd who migrated, so it is said, from Marib along with Ghassan and Tarifah? That is a matter of faith, for there is nothing to prove it except poems and tales told long after the alleged fact.

What is certain in all this is that for the last few pre-Islamic centuries there were large-scale tribal movements across Arabia, and that they belong to an even longer history of migrations. For these there is some independent external evidence: tribes recognizable as Tanukh, Abd al-Qays and Banu Ulays, for example, are located by the second-century geographer Ptolemy in the north-east of the peninsula, where they seem to have arrived since the first-century works of Strabo and Pliny.

All these diasporas, factual or fictionalized, highlight a feature of the 'grammar' of Arab history: the sense that Arabs are active on the move, passive when settled. Arabs would only remain great, said the early Islamic orator and sage al-Ahnaf, 'if they strap on their swords, tie on their turbans, and ride off on their horses'. To stay inactive at home is to remain *majhul* – 'unknown', that Arabic term for the passive voice of a verb. As in Jack Kerouac's *On the Road*, which inverts the usual metaphor of life as a journey, 'the road *is* life'.

Mobility is a theme that has always been present in Arab history – from the first appearance of Gindibu and his expeditionary force of camels, and before that from the unrecorded day the first voortrekkers left settled lands for the steppe and *'arab*hood, through the Prophet Muhammad's *hijrah*, or 'migration', to Medina, and the hundreds of thousands of *hijrah*s out of Arabia during the two succeeding centuries, and continuing to latter-day journeys like the poet Jubran Khalil Jubran's to *bilad al-mahjar*, '*hijrah* land', in his case Boston's Chinatown and New York's Lower West Side, and those of present-day refugees to Europe and beyond. Fouad Ajami quotes Nietzsche, 'You shall be fugitives . . . You shall love your children's land . . .', as a reflection of the restless Zeitgeist of the 1950s and 1960s. But the words apply equally to the tricontinental super-raids of early Islam, and to the earliest known migrations that preceded them, as well as to the floods of refugees of the twenty-first century.

NO FIXED ABODE

Mythicized though many of the early migration accounts are, there are places where they lead into a tangible past. In one sequel to the story of the seeress Tarifah and her people, Ghassan, they pitch up in Byzantine-ruled Syria, settle down – and are promptly presented with that certificate of civilized life, a tax bill. In their years of wandering, Ghassan, like the Assyrians' Aribi, had known 'neither overseers nor officials'; *pace* Benjamin Franklin, in the *badw* world-view taxes, unlike death, have never been inevitable. Most of Ghassan refused to pay up, and turned back to the peninsula, freedom and poverty.

This sequel shows not only how mobile populations were, but also how fluid *hadar*/*badw* identities could be at this time. Ghassan, who claimed to have begun life as a settled people in the south, spent a long period as migrants – if not necessarily nomads – and then divided into two groups, one resettling, the other resuming a wandering life. The settled group had also now migrated from the shifting lands of legend to solid historical ground: around AD 490, the Jafnah branch of Ghassan did indeed put down roots in Syria as Byzantine clients, ousting a previous Arab group as Constantinople's buffer against Persians and nomads. Their leaders were given the title *patricius* (Arab *bitriq*; in time the word came also to mean 'haughty' and, much later, 'penguin' – because of an imagined similarity in appearance?) and were granted the crown of client-rulers. Later, in the mid-sixth century, beginning with the Ghassanid al-Harith ibn Jabalah, they were given the exalted title *basileus*, 'king'. Most of them also became fervent Christians, though of the Monophysite persuasion that differed from imperial orthodoxy.

The roots, though, were shallow. The Ghassanids kept a foot in both camps, nomadic and settled – or rather, a foot in camp and a foot in court; for all their trappings of kingship (including the -id attached to their surname that for Western historians marks a dynasty), they led a semi-mobile life and never had a fixed capital. The nearest they got to one was in their royal camp of al-Jabiyah in the hills of the Golan, a tented palace for kings on the edge of civilization, interspersed with fixed buildings that included a monastery. Linguistically too, they were of no fixed abode: they maintained their Arabic but also used Aramaic for writing, which had long been the default spoken language of the settled peoples in the Levant. They wrote in Nabataean characters, the common script of the region, and they enjoyed Greek pop music, judging by the later Ghassanid who had five singing slave-girls who performed in '*rumiyyah*'.

Ghassanid roots in Syria may have been tenuous, but they proved tenacious. Under Islam, some of their people would join the new religion, but others would hold to their Christian faith; some present-day Syrian Christians and Lebanese Maronites claim descent from them. For the moment, however, these Byzantine border guards-turned-buffer states, marcher lords-turned-mercenary monarchs, enjoyed power and a high degree of autonomy.

Of course, they were not alone. Eugene Rogan's insight about superpower rivalry empowering Arabs also applied to the east, in the Persian sphere. As rivals in empowerment, the Ghassanids had those long-established successors of Imru' al-Qays ibn Amr, 'king of all the Arabs', the Lakhmid dynasty of al-Hirah in Iraq, client-kings of the Sasanian empire. Once more, that image of Arabs stuck on a rock between two imperial lions looks rather too simple: for as well as the third lion down in the south, Arabs were in fact on two adjoining rocks, and instead of fighting off the lions they were, increasingly, fighting each other.

RIVALS IN THE GREAT GAME

The Lakhmids, whose ancestors had also moved north from the peninsula, had been acting as a semi-nomadic neighbourhood watch for Persia almost since the establishment of the Sasanian dynasty in the third century. Like the Ghassanids, they maintained a mobile court, but had a fixed centre at al-Hirah, south of the later Baghdad.

'Al-Hirah' is from the Syriac *hirta* meaning, appropriately for semi-nomads, 'encampment'. Like Ghassanid al-Jabiyah, it was a borderline place where cultures met and blurred, and the Lakhmids, while remaining Arab, inevitably picked up Persian influences: the prime symbol of their kingship, for example, the crown, was a Persian import, as is the loan word for it in Arabic, *taj*. But they were also open to Byzantine influence, especially in the form of the Nestorian Christianity adopted by many of their people. And, like the *qariyah*s down in the peninsula – settlements in nomad areas, of which Kindah's Qaryat Dhat Kahl was the prime early example and Mecca, 'the Mother of *Qariyah*s', the foremost later example – the Lakhmids Camptown was also a fusion of nomadic and settled lifestyles. An anecdote from after the fall of al-Hirah to the Muslims illustrates this. Nomadic Arabs referred to the settled agricultural peoples of southern Iraq as *nabat*, 'Nabateans', and when an aged sage of al-Hirah was asked whether its people were Arabs or Nabataeans, he pondered for a while then said, 'We are nabataeanized Arabs . . . and arabized Nabataeans'. The informant's alleged age, 350 years, should be taken as a guarantee of his wisdom.

By the start of the sixth century the Lakhmids were already seasoned players of the Great Game. We have seen the Lakhmid king Imru' al-Qays (probably) leading a large Persian-backed expedition into the peninsula in the early fourth century, and then (probably) defecting to the Romans. Two hundred years on, with Constantinople promoting the Ghassanids as its own major satellite in the area, the Persians increased their support for the Arab rulers of al-Hirah. When the two great empires clashed, as they did increasingly in this period, it was usually in the persons of their Arab proxies. Some of these vicarious encounters were extremely nasty. In about 544, the

Lakhmid King al-Mundhir III captured a son of the Byzantines' *basileus*, al-Harith ibn Jabalah, and sacrificed him to the Arab goddess al-Uzza; about a decade later, al-Harith's champions, personally perfumed by his daughter and wearing both the chain-mail of warriors and the shrouds of potential martyrs, were able to capture the Lakhmid ruler in a death-or-glory operation and to put him to death in revenge.

This devolution of violence was matched by the Persians' delegation of policy towards tribes in the north-east of the peninsula. The area of what is now southern Iraq known as al-Sawad, 'the Blackness', or perhaps 'the Dark-Greenness', because of its dense, dark palm groves, was a common target of raiding, and the Lakhmid rulers would 'sub-let' fiefs to nomad chieftains in an attempt to stop the incursions. The Lakhmids also tried to tax the tribes: the taxmen, predictably, often came to sticky ends (stoned to death at the bottom of a well, in one case). Hostage-keeping was an effective way of dealing with tribal unruliness, and al-Hirah in the sixth century was home to 500 sons of tribal chiefs – a sort of forcible boarding school, with terms of six months at the end of which the youths would be changed for others. And if nothing else worked, the Lakhmids would send caravans into rebellious territory that – true to their intermediating position between *hadar* and *badw*, empire and tribe – combined raiding with trading.

Like the Ghassanids, the Lakhmids bestrode the linguistic divide between settled and nomadic tongues, speaking Arabic but writing in Syriac; also like the Ghassanids, they used the Nabataean script. But this was changing.

LK NW VWLZ

Because Arabic script is – like the language it records – so important to the Arab story, we need to look briefly at its sinuous, problematic workings.

Islamic-period sources claim that the script was used by Adam to write on clay tablets; infinitely further back in time, it existed in heaven on the 'Preserved Tablet', the original of the Qur'an, which was as old as God Himself. The more down-to-earth origins of the script are attributed, quite plausibly, to the Lakhmid capital al-Hirah and another town called al-Anbar, further south in present-day Iraq. Looking at the shapes of Arabic letters themselves, it is obvious that they grew organically out of Nabataean script, perhaps with influences from other Arabian writing systems. From al-Hirah the new letters spread slowly. There are very few graffiti in recognizably Arabic script earlier than the fifth century, and the idea that it reached Mecca 'a little before Islam' – at the end of the sixth century – is backed by a claim that, early in Muhammad's prophethood, fewer than a score of Meccans could write. Unpromising beginnings; but over the next few generations, the need to preserve a scripture, propagate an empire and promote a culture meant that the Arabic script went viral. It inscribed itself across space and through time to become, after the Latin alphabet, the most widespread writing system in the world.

An experiment by the eighth-century caliph, Hisham, gives an idea of how the script works. The caliph noticed a milestone by the road, and without looking at it asked an illiterate *a'rabi* in his company to 'read' it to him. For, even if illiterate, *a'rabi*s could read, famously: they could read the landscape, the sparse green growth that revealed hidden water, the tracks of beasts from camels to beetles and of their own and others' wanderings; they could decipher a whole moving history from the palimpsests of abandoned campsites. In the old desert poetry, signs on the ground are sometimes compared overtly to writing. The late pre-Islamic poet Labid, for example, could read the traces of the camp where his beloved had been,

> marked by relics dim
> Like weather-beaten script engraved on ancient stone.

Nomadic Arabs lived in a legible world. Looking at the script engraved on the milestone,

'Theres a shepherd's crook'

حـ

the bedouin said, 'and a ring

ـمـ

'and three things like a bitch's dugs

ـسـ

'and a thing like a sand-grouse's head.'

ـة

Hisham put the characters together in his mind,

حمسة

or, with the dots,

خمسة

which transcribes as *khamsah*, 'five [miles]'.

It is all beautifully logical. At the same time, there are inbuilt problems. Unlike Latin script (which, ultimately, comes from the same fount – or font – of inspiration,* the ancient Phoenician writing system), it doesn't usually show the short vowels; for instance, that word for 'five' above actually reads as *kh-m-s-h*. Thus, in other languages, you read to know what the text is saying, but in Arabic it helps to know what it is saying in order to read it. The section heading above, 'Look: no vowels!', written in Arabic-like notation, may therefore have been puzzling. And to make things trickier, in Arabic there are no capital letters. (I remember trying to read the phrase *strtfwrd 'bwnyfwn* when I was first learning Arabic. *Strtfwrd* . . . obviously, 'straightforward' was the last thing it was. Attempting to insert vowels, the only sense I could make was *satarat fa-warada abū nīfūn* – 'She covered [who was she? what did she cover?], then the father of Nīfūn [who the hell was he?] arrived.' And then a blessed bit of context turned up – *shyksbyr*, obviously the Bard – and the mysterious words became, with the *b* and the *f* standing for un-Arabic *p* and *v*, 'Stratford-upon-Avon'.)

A means of showing the vowels was developed in time, but even today it is only sporadically used; capitals still don't exist. With practice, reading Arabic does get easier. But it involves different mental processes to those of decoding Latin letters: reading Latin script is like playing chequers; Arabic is chess. And Arabic was even less user-friendly in the beginning, before dots were added to distinguish different consonants with the same written shape: both unvowelled and undotted, a simple two-letter group,

ٮٮ

could in theory be read in 300 ways. Now, all texts are dotted; but none except the Qur'an are regularly vowelled. This superadds a layer of difficulty to what is already an extremely difficult language – and remember, written Arabic is no one's mother-tongue: speakers of Arabic have to read and write in a 'foreign' language. The result is that readers are always approximating the meaning of what they are reading, and sometimes guessing wildly.

The other great problem, which only became apparent when printing presses were developed, is that Arabic is cursive: beautiful to look at, a joy to write, but a confounded nuisance for typographers and typesetters, and the very devil for users of old-fashioned typewriters. We shall revisit the problem later. For the moment, it is enough to say that both the Greek invention of separate characters for vowels, and the fact that their script retained its non-cursive form, might have given them, and those who derive their alphabets from Greek characters, a small but significant developmental edge. Arabic script is the glory and the main ingredient of Islamic art, the prime emblem of Arab and Islamic culture, a calligraphic culture that – unlike its vast but ultimately parochial equivalent in China – became intercontinental. But if histories can be said to have *hamartias*, tragic flaws, then for Arabs their script may be another one, alongside the beautiful and lethal combination of the camel and the horse.

THE KING'S BURIED POEMS

Kings, like scripts, can have a remarkable unifying effect on culture; the Lakhmid dynasty, who ruled from the likely birthplace of Arabic writing, al-Hirah, certainly did. Having a powerful and wealthy Arab person to eulogize meant that poets flocked to al-Hirah, and met with each other, and vied in verses. This may have been going on since as early as the first known Persian client-ruler, Amr ibn Adi, the father of Imru' al-Qays the probable defector. There was also a knock-on unifying effect on the evolving 'high' language, which as we have seen seems to have developed first in central Arabia, and particularly in the area including the Kindah capital of Qaryat. Now, to the north-east, high Arabic gained even greater prestige as a sort of 'King's Arabic'.

By the sixth century, with important kings in two places, there was healthy competition between the Lakhmids and Ghassanids in 'collecting' poets; this rivalry resembled that between, say, the Medici and Sforza dynasties in their sponsorship of the arts of the European Renaissance. All this was wonderful for the poetry market: traditionally minded lovers of Arabic poetry still maintain that the later part of that sixth century was its high point. It is hard to single anything out, and harder still to suggest in translation the power of the Arabic sounds; but a classic example of eulogy is al-Nabighah's description of the last Lakhmid king, al-Nu'man III, which concludes:

> Crowned with every honour high your glory's brow
> and in the battle-fray a ramping lion – and beauteous as the moon!

On hearing this fanfare of syllables, 'a look of pure joy lit al-Nu'man's face. He ordered the poet's mouth to be stuffed with gems, then said, "If kings are to be praised, then let it be thus".'

Panegyric may ring hollow in some modern ears. But its force and its truth lay – as ever, with the high speech – more in its sound than in its sense. And its importance went way beyond rhymes for royalty. In the sixth century, the courtly poetry spread like wordfire: kings and courts are there to be emulated, and it is not surprising that the main meme in the mimetic process was poetry. Beyond the few semi-urban settlements, society was short on both artisans and material artworks; any cultural products had to be portable and made of the most readily available material – words. Furthermore, society was still mostly illiterate, so the verbal artworks needed to be not just portable but also memorable. Poetry is made doubly memorable by metre and rhyme: quite a lot of it survives from before the days of writing, as does a fair amount of *saj'* – the speech of the seers that is rhymed and rhythmic, but not metrical; no plain prose survives, except what was indelibly inscribed on unportable stone. Lakhmid and Ghassanid patronage of poetry thus helped to unify further the high Arabic language, by setting a single prestigious standard, and not just in the royal courts but also in suqs and guest-tents and camp-fires – anywhere people met and spoke and recited together. Thereby, they also did more than anyone else to unify Arabs.

Even when poetry had become, for its Lakhmid and Ghassanid patrons, a cultural product, an artwork, it still had more than a touch of the ancient supernatural: it is shot through with the magic that would soon resurface with such power in the Qur'an. It is said that one of the kings of al-Hirah was so entranced by an ode of al-Harith ibn Hillizah that he would only allow the poet to recite it when in *wudu'* – the state of ritual purity later deemed necessary for Islamic prayer. Another story from the Lakhmid court is less credible, but it still sums up the way in which the history of poetry at al-Hirah intersects with that of script. Al-Nu'man III 'gave orders that the poetry of the Arabs be written down for him in volumes. He then had them buried in his White Palace'. A century or so later, an early Muslim governor of the area

> was told that there was a treasure buried beneath the palace, so he had the place dug up and brought out the poems. This is why the people of al-Kufah are more knowledgeable in poetry than those of al-Basrah.

Admittedly, the Kufan source of the story had been caught out more than once committing Chatterton-like forgeries, designed to discredit the Kufans' great rivals, the Basrans. But if nothing else, the telling of the tale shows how poetry was seen by later Arabs as the greatest treasure of their pre-Islamic ancestors. It is the gold in the spoil-heap of language.

THE IDENTITY WITHIN

High Arabic – 'the King's Arabic' – is sometimes known after the Greek model as a poetic koine, a literary language common to a wide area. Developing apace alongside it was what could be called an ethnic koine. If, as already suggested, the elusive original sense of the word *'arab* is that of 'a mixed people' from different origins, then a language both shared by and named after them – *'arabiyyah* – could only reinforce *'asabiyyah*, the feeling of group solidarity. Put another way, the gathering of words – a unified language – fed into the gathering of the word – a united political voice.

In the poetry of the century before Islam, this voice would be raised against the voices of others. Arabs were already constructing an identity for themselves; the next stage was to strengthen that identity by building a boundary. The complementary pairing *'arabiyyah-'asabiyyah* was thus ring-fenced by a pair of opposing terms, *'arab/'ajam*, Arabs/non-Arabs. The second term is closely connected with *a'jam*, 'unable to speak properly', so the pairing is comparable with *arya/mleccha*, Greek/Barbarian, Slav/Nemtsi and so on. This sort of linguistic 'nationalism' has been differentiated from the fully fledged territorial-linguistic nationalism of the nineteenth century onwards; but it is half way there. And the opposition in *'arab/'ajam* signifies even more: as the late Moroccan critic Muhammad al-Jabiri said, 'Arabs love their language to the point of sanctifying it. They consider the hold it has over them to be an expression not just of its power, but of their own power too.'

Like all humans, al-Jabiri goes on, Arabs are speaking animals, but they are also the only truly 'eloquent animals': all the rest are less eloquent, and so less powerful, and in a way less human. The progression of ideas may not seem 'logical', but it is, if you accept – as did the people of Tarifah, the seeress of Marib – that truth is inherent in the sounds and in the syntactic soundness, not in the sense, of the *logos*, the word. Thinking in Arabic, Ibn Khaldun wrote, is a matter of divine inspiration, not logic; non-native speakers are thus handicapped in the thought processes employed by Arabs. The tenth-century philosopher Abu Hayyan al-Tawhidi put it in a nutshell: 'Syntax,' the way words work together, 'is the logic of the Arabs; logic is the syntax of reason.' Then again, 'I think in Arabic,' declared the twentieth-century Lebanese linguist Abd Allah al-Alayli, 'therefore I am an Arab.'

Finally, if bathetically, 'I'm an Arab, by God!' cried a less philosophical person whose arabness had been called into question. 'I have no socks to darn,' he went on, with a swipe at the bestockinged, trouser-wearing *'ajam* par excellence, the Persians, 'and I don't wear breeches, and I'm no good at foreign gabble!' (Old-school Arabs regarded hosiery as effeminate, and like the wilder Scots went bare-arsed underneath their kilts.) It is not just that other people's tongues are less manly; they are less meaningful. If all of this smacks of the sentiments of a linguistic master-race, the implication is probably true.

The more contact Arabs had with jabbering foreigners – and especially, via the client-court of al-Hirah, with Persians – the more they asserted their own identity through opposition to them. This identity-by-antagonism would strengthen as the sixth century progressed and the Persians themselves became more assertive on multiple military fronts: against the Byzantines in the northern Fertile Crescent, in the north and east of the peninsula and, as we shall see, even in that other Fertile Crescent, the peninsular far south-west. As gabbling, trouser-wearing Persians closed in on their 'island', antagonism would become another major feature of being Arab.

So far, neighbouring empires had been defining arabness – and inevitably shaping Arab identity – by appointing or confirming 'kings of the Arabs'. In turn, those semi-settled satellite kings, the Ghassanids and Lakhmids, pulled nomad tribes into their own orbits. The beginnings of wider political unities were there, with big blocs like the multi-tribal alliances of Rabi'ah and Mudar allied loosely to the Byzantines or Persians. Towards the end of the fifth century that third 'lion', the now ailing Himyari empire of the south, would also summon up enough eleventh-hour energy to undertake a burst of expansion and appoint its own new 'king of the Arabs'.

But if pressure from the three neighbouring powers was forcing Arabs into ever more united blocs, the process was two-way: as well as being shaped from the outside, Arab solidarity was also coming about by reflex, as if in a mould formed of those neighbouring others: like the artist Rachel Whiteread's rooms, in which empty interior space suddenly takes shape and becomes visible, the long-overlooked people of the margins and of the apparent emptiness within them were gaining in identity and visibility. The metaphor of the uniting mould appears in al-Jahiz:

> When the *'arab* became one, they became equal as regards habitation, language, characteristics, ambition, pride, violence, and temperament. They were moulded in one mould, and cast in one instant.

The casting wasn't instantaneous. The solidification of society was a process that took centuries; it began at the edges, where Arabs had contact with non-Arabs, and worked inwards. And for the identity to emerge, at last, in full, the enclosing mould – those surrounding empires – would first have to be smashed. This would happen soon: the unified high language would inspire a new rhetoric which would in turn, and in time, be the motive force for the biggest diaspora ever, and the longest-running cycle of unity and disunity in Arab history – that of Islam. For a glorious couple of centuries at the start of that cycle, Arabs, for so long hedged about by other peoples' empires, would hatch their own empire. The grammar of their history would be unstoppably active, and they would earn not just a capital letter but also a definite article. For a time, they would truly be '*the* Arabs'. But the years before the breaking of the matrix were a time of particular commotion: the matter in the Arabian mould underwent a kind of internal combustion.

CHAPTER FOUR

ON THE EDGE OF GREATNESS

THE DAYS OF THE ARABS

A CURTAIN FALLS – AND RISES

The sixth century AD was the time when Arabia became irrevocably more like it is today – more Arab, less South Arabian. Looking back from now, Saba/Sheba and its South Arabian successors appear as they did to the writer of the Book of Joel, 'a people far off', with the added distance of time. Their monuments with their bull- and ibex-friezes and horned alabaster moons, the strange elegant semaphore of their script – it all seems ancient and alien. In contrast, one can feel distinct vibrations on the threads that run from that arabized sixth century to the present: to track a tribe like Anazah from its present homelands, a swathe that cuts through the borders of Iraq, Syria and northern Saudi Arabia, back to al-Haddar in the east of the peninsula, from where their ancestors set out well before Islam and where their stay-at-home cousins still live, is to follow such a thread. And there are more than just vibrations. There are distinctive voices coming down the line, loud and clear. The late Moroccan scholar Muhammad al-Jabiri listed the sixth-century poet Imru' al-Qays – not his earlier namesake, the (probably) defecting king – as the first in his list of great Arabs, 'who we sense are still here living with us, or standing there before us . . . on the stage of Arab culture, a stage on which the curtain has never once fallen'. We will return to Imru' al-Qays the poet – and failed uniter of tribes.

In the first part of the sixth century the curtain was about to drop on that earlier, South Arabian act. The immediate cause was the Himyari King Yusuf As'ar's official adoption of Judaism and persecution of non-Jews; his reasons were probably less doctrinal than political, for he was an opponent of intervention by the Christian Ethiopians. In particular, he is said to have massacred many Christians in Najran in about the year 518; the event is commemorated as a holocaust in the Qur'an. The Christian Axumite kingdom of Ethiopia, which already had a history of attempted military interventions in South Arabia, had more recently been building up a presence by backing Ethiopian trading enclaves there. Now, with the Najran incident, they had the pretext for a full-scale invasion.

But there were other, older reasons for the South Arabian demise. Over the previous two centuries, raids by *'arab* tribes on settled people had been increasing; at the same time, central state rulers relied more – at their own peril – on *'arab* mercenaries for protection. These *badw* tribes were the fly in the ointment; or perhaps the fly of the supposed prophetic tradition, which has poison in one wing and antidote in the other. But the poison was gaining on the cure, and the South was becoming less 'settled' in both senses – more turbulent, and more 'bedouin'.

The Ethiopians knew that this time, unlike the response from the powerful old Sabaean-Himyari state to previous expeditions, resistance to them would be far from concerted. The South Arabians seem to have tried to pull their act together at the last gasp: a late Himyari inscription, for example, boasts of the continued 'inseparable joining' of the palaces of Silhin and Dhu Raydan, symbols of the old Sabaean state and the newer Himyari one, merged in a united kingdom. But the reality was disunity. Yusuf As'ar had come to power in a coup, never a good idea for stability, and the kingdom of Saba, Dhu Raydan, Hadramawt, Yamanat, and of their Highland and Lowland Arabs, fell apart. In 525, King Yusuf is said to have spurred his horse into the Red Sea from which his conquerors had come, and disappeared into the waves.

The Ethiopians first installed a tractable Christian ruler, a Himyari, but he was soon replaced by the Ethiopian general Abrahah. In time, Abrahah, with the moat of the Red Sea and a rampart of Arabian mountains between him and his Axumite master, assumed the old royal titles of the

Sabaean-Himyari realm and began mounting his own expeditions northward. One of these is recorded in a Sabaic inscription and dated to the year 552. This may be the same as an expedition commemorated not in laconic Sabaic, but in the thrilling Qur'anic 'Chapter of the Elephant', which tells how the Ethiopians and their war-pachyderm were repulsed from an attack on Mecca by flocks of divinely directed dive-bombing birds armed with pebbles; if it is the same campaign, the Sabaic record omits these details. The 'Day of the Elephant' may have happened on another Ethiopian expedition, and indeed it is traditionally placed in 570; but if – as tradition claims – Abrahah himself led it, he must by that time have been a very old man. None of this would matter a jot, except that the Day of the Elephant is said to have occurred in the year in which the Prophet Muhammad was born, and it would be good to know precisely when that was.

The Himyaris in particular had been good at dating things. Later, Islamic-period perceptions of pre-Islamic time go pear-shaped: even the mostly reliable al-Mas'udi can say of King Yusuf As'ar, for example (who, after all, shared a century with the Prophet Muhammad), 'he reigned 260 years or, it is said, rather less than that . . .'

When the curtain fell on the ancient South, it was as if that whole thousand-year act of the Arabian drama had been a dream.

GULFS APART

The lion of the South, the old Himyari-Sabaean empire, now lay dead. Over the sixth century, too, the Byzantine and Persian empires were getting ever more mangy and moribund, and their support for their Arab client-kings in the north was waning. In the south-west, however, an opportunity arose for the Sasanian shah that was too good to miss. At some time soon after the year of the Day of the Elephant, Sayf ibn Dhi Yazan, a Himyari noble, approached the shah through his Lakhmid vassal and complained of Ethiopian tyranny. The shah sent a naval force which, according to legend, was made up of convicts (not entirely implausible: navies would have a long history of pressing convicts into service). The now independent Ethiopian king of the old Himyari lands, Abrahah's son, was duly defeated, and Sayf installed in his place as tributary to the Persians. Sayf, however, was soon assassinated, apparently by Ethiopian hands, and a Persian viceroy appointed in his place – which was no doubt what the Sasanians, busily interfering in the Arabian subcontinent as they had been since the dawn of their dynasty, had intended all along. Perhaps emboldened by their near-effortless takeover of its southern Fertile Crescent (or at least of its towns), they also began looking greedily again at its northern counterpart. That they were to take their eyes off the Peninsula in between would be their undoing.

It is impossible to judge how much the Sasanian takeover of the south enhanced consciousness of an *'arab/'ajam*, and specifically Arab/Persian, split – and thus of a sense of Arab identity, an ethnic whole that spanned the peninsula. But it is certain that such a consciousness had been growing fast in the main Arab–Persian interface in the north-east. There, three centuries of political alliance had done little for race relations: when the Sasanian shah sent a request to his client-king of al-Hirah, al-Nu'man III, to marry his sister, al-Nu'man is alleged to have said, 'Aren't the cattle of al-Sawad enough for him, or does he have to have Arab women as well?' The very idea of a Persian taking an Arab for his wife was 'a vile abomination', he added (naturally, the converse was perfectly acceptable in al-Nu'man's patrilineal view).

Al-Nu'man's riposte belongs to the twilit region between history and myth. What is clear, however, is that the theme of Arabs versus Persians has played throughout history, with variations: tribes versus empires, shaykhs versus shahs, Arab cultural reactionaries versus Persian cultural revivalists, Sunnah versus Shi'ah, Iraq versus Iran, and now, outside my window, what is in part (or at least in the imagination and the rhetoric of both sides) a proxy war between Riyadh and Tehran. Arabia and Persia may be all but joined physically at the Strait of Hormuz, but they are separated by an abyss of antique antagonisms older than Islam and deeper than the Persian Gulf . . . or is it the Arabian Gulf? It matters terribly which side you take. Speaking in later times, when the Abbasid caliphate was dominated by Persian warlords, that most Arab and popular of poets, al-Mutanabbi, said,

> A people's fortunes mirror those of its kings – and never
> Will Arabs be fortunate when their kings are Persians.

There is even an idea, to which we will return, that the original Islamic state in Medina came about as an Arab response to the increasing Persian presence in Arabia.

While it is impossible to measure objectively how far the Persian presence reinforced the growing sense of arabness, there is no doubt that the double destabilization of the south, first by Ethiopians and then, hard on their heels, by Persians, handed more power to the *badw* – the *'arab* – elements in society. As later adventurers in the same south of the peninsula, for example the Ottomans and the British, were to discover (and as the Americans were to discover in Iraq), it is all very well to breeze in and rule the towns, but the outsider's writ doesn't go far into what is often an impenetrable landscape. The rough rural hinterland of the south had long been infiltrated by *'arab*. Now, with repeated foreign intervention, the old institutions of the settled areas were breaking down, and the flimsy tissue of relations between *hadar* and *badw*, town and country – always a matter of faith, not of contract – was ripping apart. It all enhanced the power of the *'arab* and of their leaders, personalities whose legitimacy rested above all on their control not of institutions, but of rhetoric.

WALLS AND WEAPONS OF WORDS

It is hard now to appreciate just how important rhetoric was. But in such a restive century as the sixth, when the balance of power was shifting from settled societies to *'arab* tribes, words were not just the most portable cultural product; they also acted as defensive walls, and as offensive weapons. Politically, tribes were led by their most eloquent elders, men (sometimes women) who 'gathered the word' of the people; militarily, tribal clashes were preceded by battles of poets, skirmishes in verse, and then recorded by the victors in odes.

Three titles recur among the orator-leaders: *sayyid*, 'chief, lord', *khatib*, 'public speaker', and *sha'ir*, 'poet'. The functions were not necessarily distinct, and often blur in the same person. A *sayyid* would usually come from a family who enjoyed particular inherited 'honour'; but lordship depended ultimately on personality and prowess in battle – also, vitally, on eloquence, which might be expressed in prose or verse or both. A *sayyid* was thus swordsman and wordsman, wordlord and warlord – with a touch, inherited from the old shamanistic magic of *bayan*, 'unveiling of meaning', of the warlock. When a tribe had a hereditary line of *khatib*s, they often combined the role with that of tribal genealogists and historians, something like European heralds – or, perhaps more nearly, the *jeli* families of West Africa.

In terms of pure rhetoric, the role of the poet was anciently the most important, but became debased when poets got into the business of selling their praises to kings and their emulators for cash. However, war-poetry has retained something of its magical force throughout history. The force was that of a curse uttered under supernatural inspiration; to silence the curse, captured poets had their tongues tied, literally, with thongs, even while they were being slaughtered (enemy orators, too, might be punished by having their lower front teeth knocked out, thus wrecking their enunciation). The force would survive into the age of prophecy: the Prophet Muhammad himself admitted that the shafts of his poets were 'deadlier to [the unbelievers] than a volley of arrows in the dark of night'. And the force is still with us: 'We have cut off his hand,' incanted the ruler of Dubai recently of the Iranian-supported Huthi leader whose own slogans flutter beneath my window,

> and he has stared defeat in the face:
> His army has shattered in the clash –

and, with an extra shaft shot at his backers in Tehran (personified by the name given to the defeated pre-Islamic Iranian kings, 'Khusraw'),

> the rout has rolled up Khusraw's battle-banners!

So far, the claim looks premature: the banners still flutter.

Also prominent in the aristocracy of rhetoric were *kahin*s like Tarifah, who led the legendary diaspora from Marib. The title – and the function – are cognate with those of the ancient Hebrew *kōhēn*; their ability to divine what others could not perceive came, al-Mas'udi thought, from their tendency to be alone in wild places, to spend a lot of time in reflection, and to view the world with 'the eye of enlightenment'. In addition, al-Mas'udi says, many of them were physically deformed, and made up in spirit for what they lacked in body: the celebrated legendary *kahin* Satih, for example, supposedly had no bones in his body, and could be 'rolled up like a gown'. Their rhymed and elevated supernatural speech resurfaces, as we shall see, in that of the earliest Qur'anic revelations. As Ibn Khaldun points out, however, truth differs from *kahin* to prophet: prophets connect directly with the angelic sphere of truth; *kahin*s are 'inspired by devils' and thus mix truth with falsehood. Of course, most people are not able to appreciate this all-important difference in perception; ultimately, the ability of both seers and prophets to persuade and lead depends not on the inherent truth of what they say, but on their command of rhetoric – on *how* they say it.

The old settled South, as central institutions broke down, probably also saw the rise of orator-leaders. During the period of dissolution and then of opposition to foreign rule in the sixth century, the title *qwl* becomes common for regional strongmen or warlords: it may indicate a 'word-gathering' role – in Arabic the root *qwl* is to do with speaking (for example, *qawl*, 'speech', *qawwal*, 'speaker, orator'). What is certain is that the stronger the *qwl*s were, the weaker central rule was, and that as they proliferated and vied for ever-decreasing amounts of available power, so their own raiding and plundering increased.

The rhetoric of all these word-gatherers united tribes or peoples, and by creating *'asabiyyah*, the spirit of solidarity, powered the revolutions of the wheel of fire.

THE INSTIGATORS

It is not surprising, given all the loudly competing voices, that the long sixth century was an age of many 'days' – the so-called Days of the Arabs. These battle-days were sometimes a case of organized raiding getting out of hand, more often of minor disputes over grazing, alleged insults and the like blowing up into violence. But whether small skirmishes or outright wars, they still usually had a sort of chivalric order to them, their own Queensberry Rules. Eventually a neutral party would intervene, and the combatants would make peace, or at least reparations: the total dead would be worked out, and blood-money paid to the side that had suffered more. Sometimes the 'monetary' cost was enormous, as in the reparations paid after a war between the tribes of Abs and Dhubyan – 3,000 camels for three years of hostilities.

The archetypal clash of this age was the War of al-Basus, which set two 'brother' tribes against each other – Taghlib and Bakr, whose territories were in the north-east of the peninsula and extended into southern Iraq and the Syrian desert, neighbouring those of the Lakhmid kings. Both tribes claimed descent from the same ancestor, Wa'il. The conflict began probably at some time in the 490s, dragged on for forty years and, rather like the War of Jenkins's Ear, was sparked off by an event that in itself was not exactly earth-shattering: what was shattered was a clutch of lark's eggs in a nest in a *hima*, an area of reserved grazing, monopolized by the Taghlib chief Kulayb. The culprit, Kulayb decided, was a clumsy-hoofed she-camel called Sarab, 'Mirage', belonging to an associate of the tribe of Bakr. Kulayb had married a Bakri wife, and it was her brother whom he blamed for allowing the interloping camel to enter his own grazing lands. Taunts followed, but nothing more – until the suspected she-camel, waiting in line one day to be watered after the camels of Kulayb, broke loose and jumped the queue. Kulayb, incensed, took his bow and shot her in the udder. The brother-in-law's aunt, al-Basus, equally incensed by the insult to the camel's owner, who was under her protection, tore her headscarf in indignation and let rip a string of verses. The verses, which came to be known as 'The Instigators', conclude,

> But now such folk I dwell among that when
> The wolf comes, 'tis my sheep he comes to tear!

At this point, the soap-opera events turned nasty: al-Basus's nephew, Jassas, killed Kulayb, leading to all-out war between the brother tribes. It was a war in which words were in the vanguard, but it was no less deadly for that: poet upon proud and posturing poet poured incendiary odes on the fires of conflict, and the days and the death-toll mounted. And should the power of poetry be in doubt, the whole horrible affair is called not after Kulayb, or his killer, or even the camel, but after the old woman whose verses ignited it all. Nor were other women the least of the combatants, tearing off their headscarves, baring their heads to the battle and wielding their words: 'War! *War!* ***War! WAR!*** ' screamed one,

> It has blazed up and scorched us sore.
> The highlands are filled with its roar!

The forty-year roar was only ended by the utter exhaustion of the combatants and the intervention of the Lakhmid king.

The great Egyptian critic, Taha Husayn, thought that much of the account of the war was back-projected from Islamic-era squabbles. Whether he is right or not, the War of al-Basus and other such conflicts (like the War of Dahis, which was sparked off by alleged cheating in a horse race) mirror the chronic social fragility and disunity that haunted the pre-Islamic century.

And as a second epic-in-miniature of pre-Islamic Arabdom, it reveals the destructive downside of the Marib Dam diaspora: settled people set out on their trek to pastures new – and then killed each other over the right to graze those pastures. The father of Jassas, the killer of Kulayb, realized the deep and divisive significance of the murder: 'You have sundered the union of your people . . . By Allah, never will the tribe of Wa'il be one, not after what you've done.'

In a sense, the War of al-Basus still isn't over. It is a cautionary tale whose lessons have yet to sink in. It foreshadows a disunity that has proved all but perennial and, 1,500 years on, lights the present with flashes of déjà vu. Then, al-Basus tore her headscarf in protest; now the women still do the same, or burn them. Kulayb (whose name means 'Little Dog') is the model of the successful and beloved chief, the 'benign dictator', who loses his grip and becomes, as they always do if they last long enough, malign. And the vendetta between our own once-'benign' dictator and those who encroached on his pastures has been called, by more than one friend of mine, always with a sad shake of the head, 'the War of al-Basus, again'.

THE WANDERING KING

Just as the 'father' tribe of Wa'il split into the opposing 'brother' tribes of Taghlib and Bakr, a tendency towards division sundered other groups that had enjoyed at least an imagined unity of origin. Nor does the phenomenon apply only to bedouin tribes: the historian-geographer al-Hamdani gives a list of towns divided into two opposing factions, Arabian Montagues and Capulets. The fissile tendency gives rise to a further scenario that recurs down the centuries: tribes or other factions of a single notional origin fall out; they call in – or have imposed upon them – a leader from outside their own factional milieu; this new leader brings about a new unity; the factions soon tire of living amicably, throw out the new leader and return to their factionalism. The even more unhappy ending is when the eventual successors of the new leader fall to fighting among themselves.

The most notable example of this in the long sixth century is that of Kindah and its relations with the tribes of the centre and north of the peninsula. Kindah's own origins are probably in central Arabia, where from the old trading town of Qaryat Dhat Kahl, as we have seen, they cultivated relations with the settled south. Towards the end of the fifth century, the rulers of Himyar-Saba backed the Kindah leader Hujr as a client-king over the fissile tribes to the north. The unity Hujr brought about ended with his death, but from about 500 his grandson, al-Harith, re-established Kindah's leadership of the tribes, and even ousted the Persians' Lakhmid client-king of al-Hirah for a time. The Lakhmids, however, regained their kingdom, and al-Harith was killed. From then on, things went very wrong for al-Harith's family: before his death, he had appointed his five sons as rulers over the five main constituent tribes. Two of these sons now went to war with each other, supported by their respective tribesmen, while a third of the tribes rose and killed a third brother. The unity of the northern tribes, needless to say, went to pot again.

From this background of collapse emerged a remarkable figure. When news of that third brother's assassination reached his estranged and prodigal son, exiled for chasing women and then publishing his amours in poetry, he happened to be as drunk as a lord could get before the Islamic alcohol ban. 'Today I can't be sober,' he is said to have slurred, 'but tomorrow, drinking's over. Today's for booze; tomorrow's for business.' He would never see the business through, but the attempt to avenge his murdered father has given Arab history its first fully rounded tragic hero – the poet-prince Imru' al-Qays. In one sense the obscurities of his life are so deep that he can never outrun his own legend. In another, as Muhammad al-Jabiri said, he is still here on the stage today, Hamlet soliloquizing in the chaos of the sixth century.

That makes him sound like a very 'modern' man, and in a sense he is. Part of him was an old-fashioned *sha'ir-sayyid*, a tribal poet-lord, with an old-fashioned name ('Imru' al-Qays' is probably 'the Servant of [the sky-god] Qays'). But he is also his own poet, who loved and celebrated women like she of the 'breastbone burnished like a looking-glass' . . .

> And hair cascading black to grace her back, intensely black
> and hanging dense and tangled as the bunches of the palm-tree fruit,
> The tresses at her crown piled high in plaits –
> a maze of straight and twisted ways where hairpins stray . . .

'Imru' al-Qays is the forerunner of the poets,' said Caliph Umar. 'He dug down to the wellspring of poetry, and made it flow.' The caliph was thinking not of the ancient cursing, battling bards, but of poets much more in the sense in which we know them now.

But Imru' al-Qays's fame as a poet also eclipses the fact that he may also have been 'the last ruler of the state that made the last attempt to unify the Arab tribes of the peninsula, before Islam'. This is perhaps to credit him with a grander design than he ever consciously contemplated. What is in no doubt is that he courted Byzantine support in his attempt to regain power. Although the exact dates are unknown, the attempt was made not many years before Sayf ibn Dhi Yazan, the Himyari noble, sought and gained Persian help against the Byzantine-allied Ethiopian occupiers of his land. As Sayf found to his cost – in the form of an Ethiopian assassin's dagger and the subsequent Persian takeover of the South – to play the Great Game was to play with fire. Imru' al-Qays never got his Byzantine backing, and died disappointed – supposedly from the effects of a poisoned robe, his come-uppance for courting not only Byzantine political support but also a Byzantine princess.

It is hard to disentangle fiction from non-fiction (in the absence of concrete evidence, to say 'fact' is to claim too much). Sayf ibn Dhi Yazan, would-be restorer of the fortunes of Himyar, became a hero of fanciful folk-tales; Imru' al-Qays, would-be restorer of the fortunes of Kindah, might-have-been uniter of Arab tribes, is seen today almost exclusively as a literary lion. In their political efforts, both had become embroiled with the super-powers, the prowling imperial lions, and both had fallen foul of them. But where the patriot and the poet had failed, a prophet would soon succeed – founding a new, and thoroughly Arabian, superpower.

As with the War of al-Basus, Taha Husayn thought a lot of Imru' al-Qays's biography was back-projected, particularly from that of an Islamic-period exile and would-be father-avenger and leader of Kindah, Abd al-Rahman ibn Muhammad ibn al-Ash'ath. Again, he may be right. But just as the War of al-Basus distils the internecine violence of the sixth century into one event, so Imru' al-Qays, the poet-prince who ends up an outcast – the so-called 'Wandering King' – embodies in one person the many dislocations of the restless pre-Islamic age. He moves from ode to ode, from woman to woman, and from Hadramawt to Asia Minor to Bahrain. His is a life and a century in motion, in search of the unattainable.

Have I not worn out my mounts in every wind-blown waste,
far of horizon, glittering of mirage?

PUSHERS TO THE FARTHEST BOUNDS

The young Imru' al-Qays, the libertine sent packing by his severe father, had for a time gathered round himself a band of *su'luk*s, 'brigands' or 'vagabonds'. It is worth looking briefly at this exceptional group. Like Imru' al-Qays, many of them were poets; they too are emblematic of a restless, atomistic age; and they are a brilliant last burst of absolute individuality and pluralism that would be extinguished, at least in theory, by the communalism and monism of Islam. It is tempting to romanticize the 'vagabonds', and present-day Arab intellectuals tend to do so. They are doubly free, both as poets – poetry, as Adonis has written, is where the Arabic mind is free from ideology – and as outcasts from their tribes. They are one of 'the most notable Arab examples of antinomianism for the sake of discovering truth' (the other example being that of Sufism, the spiritual current in Islam). But there *is* something Romantic about their individualism, their intense emotion, their closeness to the natural world, even if their Romanticism is of the hard-bitten, hobo sort. At the risk of further anachronism, Hunter S. Thompson might have had the *su'luk*s in mind when he advised his admirers to 'Walk tall, kick ass, learn to speak Arabic, love music and never forget that you come from a long line of truth-seekers, lovers and warriors.'

The Arabic that the *su'luk*s learned to speak was the high language of rhetoric and poetry. Most Arabs who used this elevated register were the word-gatherers, mouthpieces and leaders of their tribes; the *su'luk*s were the refuseniks, regarded as outcasts because of crimes against honour and thus against *'asabiyyah*, the binding solidarity of the tribe. Some were extreme in their rejection of norms. When the early sixth-century brigand-poet Ta'abbata Sharran was killed in a fight, his kinfolk

> rode to the place where his body lay, meaning to take it away for burial. When they reached the spot they found the body surrounded by the corpses of wild animals, birds of prey and vermin that had gnawed at his flesh.

His entire body had become poisonous, it was claimed, from living on a toxic diet of vipers and colocynth. The most famous and eloquent rejection of tribal values is the resounding ode of Ta'abbata Sharran's contemporary al-Shanfara, whom the former described as

a sayer of words
strong and sound, a pusher to the farthest bounds . . .

Al-Shanfara's ode begins:

Sons of my mother, get your camels up!
For I choose other company than you.
. . .
I have some nearer kin than you: swift wolf,
Smooth-coated leopard, jackal with long hair . . .

It continues in the same powerful tone of rejection. As the nineteenth-century Arabist Gifford Palgrave wrote, it is 'the absolute individualism of a mind defying its age and all around it'.

Many *su'luk*s, however, lived and raided in bands or, as we have seen in the case of Urwah ibn al-Ward, would gather disadvantaged individuals from the edges of tribal society and take them off raiding to support themselves. While rejecting their own tribe, they therefore often formed alternative non-tribal groups of their own. Urwah's alternative society was founded, if we are to believe the sentiments of his poetry, on social justice:

All those wealthy chiefs can never rule by wealth
alone: their rule rests only on their deeds.
If my friend has plenty, I do not compete with him
in wealth, nor do I spurn him if his fortunes change.
If I am rich, my gain will be my neighbour's
gain, my fortune his, that is my guarantee.
And if I'm poor, you'll never see me seeking favours from
my brother – for his favour's in my hand before I ask.

The *su'luk*s were the exception that proved the Arab tribal rule – and, at least in some cases and senses, a precursor of the alternative, non-tribal and socially equitable community that the Prophet Muhammad was about to found.

But only in some cases and senses. That absolute individualism of the *su'luk*s, their Quixotic, Whitmanesque assertion of what is usually thought of as a 'modern' type of selfhood, would be negated by the eventual totalitarian nature, both theological and political, of that coming society. It would also be negated by the concept of *sunnah* in its Islamic form – the idea that there is one perfect individual whose practices must be imitated by all. For the sixth-century time being, however, the *su'luk*s provided an alternative to tribal mores and to religious norms, such as they were. They were the seers and celebrants of a man-centred universe. Like Whitman, they saw 'eternity in men and women'.

POLITICS AND POETICS

There often seems to be something Titanic about the century before Islam: great warriors, great poets, archaic heroes stride and ride over the vast stage of the subcontinent, clashing in the violence of battle and of verse, ravishing and lavishing. The impression is partly misleading, for it is Titanism in a teacup: the heroics are almost entirely to do with squabbles over camels, and for the unseen majority beyond the limelight life was a matter of survival: finding that bit of pasture where the first rain had fallen in years; keeping your meagre possessions and your daughters safe from Axumite or Sasanian troops; not being raided or ravished by the tribe next door; not dying in too much agony. All the same, the 'heroic' martial ethos of the times does have a certain reality. Raiding (and thus fighting) was a way of life, a major economic activity, and the poetry that celebrated it was not the luxury and rarity it has become for us: for example, the most famous ode by Amr ibn Kulthum (great-nephew of Kulayb, whose killing began the War of al-Basus) 'was so revered by the tribe of Taghlib that all of them, young and old, could recite it', an impressive feat, given that the poem is over a hundred lines long.

For Arabs to be unified politically was beyond anyone's wildest imagination. But it was in this sixth century that Arabs were unified poetically, and inseparably, in a cultural coalition that has survived all the Days, the numberless wars, ever since. It is now that Imru' al-Qays can speak of the women he woos as 'Arab'; it is in this same sense that the Qur'an will speak of Muhammad as 'Arab' – not as an *a'rabi* defined by his nomadism, which Muhammad was most definitely not – but as a member of a subcontinental culture whose members were all joined by the same high over-arching tongue. Not all could use the tongue themselves, by any means, or even understand it in its complex entirety; but all could appreciate it, aspire to it, and respond to it. It was this shared response that made them Arab.

Today, the shared response still links Arabs everywhere: they inhabit the same united *Kulturnation*; they love its language, even if they hate having to learn its grammar. Political union is still unthinkable: as T.E. Lawrence told Robert Graves, 'Arab unity is a madman's notion – for this [twentieth] century or next probably. English-speaking unity is a fair parallel'. But Arabs remain a single people in the realm of rhetoric, whether nationalist or Islamic, even if an abyss of disappointment gapes between the politics and the poetics.

Of course, our view is skewed towards the importance of poetry: it is almost the only Arab artefact, literary or otherwise, that survives from before Islam (as opposed to all the artefacts of settled South Arabian culture – the dams, idols, ibex-friezes, inscriptions and so on). That does not necessarily put historians at a disadvantage. In many other cultures which have left few written texts, or none, we understand the past via archaeology, by excavating built structures and examining their remaining contents. In *'arab* Arabia, ancient physical buildings are rare; but Arabic poems are metaphorical structures, dwellings made of metrical units called *asbab* ('tent ropes') and *awtad* ('tent pegs'), which in turn make up hemistichs called simply *shutur* ('halves') or *masari'* ('leaves of double doors'), two of which together build a line of poetry, a *bayt* ('tent, room, house'). As a group, the ancient Arabic poems are thus the Knossos, the Pompeii of pre-Islamic Arabia. This was realized early on: the Persians left a permanent record of their past, al-Jahiz wrote, in their buildings; Arabs left their record in poems, which may in the end be more lasting, as succeeding generations often demolish the physical monuments of those who came before them. What is more, poetic structures echo audibly with the voices of their time. 'A line of poetry is like a building,' said the eleventh-century analyst of poetics Ibn Rashiq, extending the structural metaphor, 'its basis is natural talent, its roof is the ability to transmit poetry [from earlier poets], its pillars are knowledge, its door is practice, and its inhabitant is meaning. A "house" that is uninhabited is no good.'

Given the vagaries of memory and the forgeries of later transmitters, it is of course possible that little of the ancient poetry has survived in its original condition. A few critics, like Taha Husayn, dismiss all but a few lines as later fakes: such critics spike, so to speak, the entire canon. This is going too far. Reading pre-Islamic poetry may in fact be rather like looking at English Gothic churches, zealously but artfully 'restored' in a more recent past:

some is undoubtedly original, some a clever Abbasid/Victorian pastiche, and the joins are hard to see. To dismiss it all and demolish those structures built of words or stones is vandalism. Other than that oldest Arabic book, the Qur'an, and a few glimpses from non-Arab observers, the archaeology of poetry provides the best – almost the only – picture of pre-Islamic Arab life, belief and events.

IMAGINE THERE'S NO HEAVEN

In that picture, time is ephemeral, not eternal like Islamic time: we come out of a void and end in nothingness. We pay or receive dues on our deeds – but in the way we are remembered, not in heaven or hell. And without that blur of eternity shadowing its edges, life is often pictured in the sharpest focus:

> the descriptions of nature, of the life of the desert, of night-journeyings and day-journeyings, with their various incidents, of hunting, and stalking, and lurking for game, of the tending of camels, of the gathering of wild honey, and similar occupations, are most admirable.

The poet Imru' al-Qays, for example, recalled heading towards the firelight of a friend,

> one hungry chilly dusk,
> While the old big-humped she-camel padded into the falling night,
> deaf to the soft calls of the milkers in the fold.

It is a totally unremarkable scene; but preserved pristine, like the illuminations of rural life in medieval European Books of Hours.

The world of the pre-Islamic poets comes over as savage, politically parochial, but marvellously mobile in other ways, covering great physical distances and also lurching across the moral gamut, from lust and drunkenness to sternest application of *muru'ah* – *virtus*, honour ('Today's for booze; tomorrow's for business'). Organized religion is absent, but there is a binding ethical code that enjoins generosity, bravery, hospitality, and loyalty to family, tribe and ancestors. People who honoured this code could be memorialized for posterity, as Imru' al-Qays did for those who, like the clan of Banu Thu'al, gave him protection in his wanderings. To infringe against the code could, equally, condemn one to a different sort of posterity: 'Himyari,' said Imru' al-Qays of a man who had failed to protect his murdered uncle,

> was not faithful, and neither was Udas –
> And neither was the arse of a donkey itching from the crupper.

Poets performed the role of the recording angels of Islam, and while there may have been no heaven and no hell, there was still an afterlife in which one's memory, if not one's soul, would be rewarded or punished. Whatever one's *nasab*, one's genealogical ancestry, commemoration of noble or ignoble acts added up to the parallel idea of *hasab*, a sort of genealogy of good and bad deeds that would be passed on to future generations.

All these features of Arab belief were prominent by the sixth century; they would survive, and still do, at least in the realm of the ideal. So too would such concepts as *din*, the obligation to follow the ways of one's ancestors, and *sunnah*, the practices of those ancestors. Islam would move *din* on to a different plane, and make it a set of obligations to Allah – 'religion', in short (similarly, the first sense of Latin *religio* is 'obligation'); *sunnah* would become specifically the practices of the Prophet Muhammad. For the pre-Islamic time being, however, the terms were to do with conduct and duty, not doctrine. When trying to understand what *din* was, one has to forget the associations that spring from the English word 'religion', connected as they are with Judaeo-Christian-Platonic thought – with the 'quaint Alexandrian tutti-frutti', as Norman Douglas called eventual Christianity. *Din*, rather like Buddhist *dharma*, is originally a matter not of theology but of keeping society on track: the track is that of the ancestors. And it would be equally wrong to conflate the later and earlier senses of *din* and to think in terms of pre-Islamic Arab ancestor 'worship'; but when one remembers the writers of those ancient Safaitic graffiti recording the names of their ancestors over fifteen generations or more, and when one finds that Quraysh, Muhammad's tribe, hung portraits of all their ancestors in the pre-Islamic Ka'bah (did it resemble a Chinese ancestral shrine?), one can begin to understand something of the reverence paid to the progenitors.

The older senses of *din* and *sunnah* may underlie the thinking of many (particularly Arab) Muslims even today: the extraordinary rootedness in the past of that thought, the obligation to the ancestors, the equally extraordinary devotion to Muhammad – a man who, despite all his insistence that he was just another human being, was clothed with the mantle of the founding hero-ancestor of the new super-tribe, the *ummah* of Islam. The twentieth-century poet Muhammad Iqbal went as far as to say, 'You can deny God but you cannot deny the Prophet' – and when God is so deliberately non-human as He is in Islam, it is not surprising that the feelings of devotion should be transferred to the slightly more approachable figure. Denying God is a matter of theology; denying the Prophet goes against something much older and deeper. To see 'religion' in that ancient light might explain a lot.

THE COLLECTIVE MEMORY

Poetry too is still largely rooted in the past. The literary traditions laid down in the sixth century have endured: they include the form of the *qasidah*, an ode in a single rhyme which in its fullest form begins with a prelude on love and loss, then takes the listener on a journey, including descriptions of the poet-rider's mounts and of the landscape through which he passes, and finally gets to the 'destination' – panegyric, elegy or whatever. And some of those traditions have much older roots: Imru' al-Qays, at the start of his most famous ode, recalls

> a love and a lodging
> by the rim of the twisted sands between Ed-Dakhool and
> Haumal, Toodih and El-Mikrát, whose trace is not yet effaced
> for all the spinning of the south winds and the northern blasts
> . . .
> what is there left to lean on where the trace is obliterated?

But already, in many of the Safaitic graffiti, half a millennium older than those lines, the writers record their sadness on returning to an abandoned campsite and finding traces there of the passing of loved ones.

Nostalgia is only one of the moods of the sixth-century poets. Above, we have seen Imru' al-Qays celebrating present beauty as well as past love. The late pre-Islamic poet al-A'sha was himself so celebrated for his descriptions of female beauty that he was in demand as a 'marriage bureau', producing airbrushed poetic advertisements for plainer girls. As the sixth century progressed, poets themselves gained in celebrity: when, towards the end of the century, Muhammad's tribe of Quraysh founded the pan-Arabian fair of Ukaz on the main trade-route leading into Meccan territory from the south, poetic competitions were the biggest attraction. Contestants arrived on the most expensive mounts and, wearing their flashiest clothes, duelled in verse. Poets were the pop-stars of the time. And the importance of places like Ukaz was more than literary: they were places of truce, where warring tribes could meet without the ever-present pressure to pursue feuds and extract vengeance. In a chronically divided land, the inter-tribal fairs were enclaves of peace and temporary unity.

Even today, traditional poets still compose *qasidah*s. The idea of poetic duels has never died, and the celebrity version has been revived with the Abu Dhabi TV show *Sha'ir al-Maliyun*, 'Millionaire Poet', which even has its own dedicated channel. Like Ukaz, it is more than some greenery-yallery eisteddfod: in a land where rulers attack their enemies with odes, poetry is still portentous and powerful.

There were other wielders of words, however, preachers who would do the rounds of the great gathering places and would prove even more influential for the Arab future. The most charismatic of these in the period just before Islam was Quss ibn Sa'idah, who would preach on morality and mortality in rhyming prose; he would frequent fairs like Ukaz and other inter-tribal meeting places such as Najran, like Mecca a cultic centre, and his customary pulpit was the back of his camel. 'Where now are Thamud and Ad?' he would ask, as would the Qur'an, of the long-extinct ancient tribes

Where are the fathers and the fathers' fathers?
Where is the good deed that went unpraised?
Where is the evil deed that went uncriticized?
Quss has sworn an oath by Allah,
That Allah has a *din* which is more pleasing to Him than this *din* of yours.

Quss was a 'freelance' *khatib*, an orator or preacher not attached to a particular tribe, and al-Mas'udi highlights his super-tribal importance by calling him *hakim al-'arab*, the Sage of the Arabs. That importance is also clear in Quss's mention of Allah, the supreme deity of Quraysh who was already gaining followers across Arabia. Of Quss's many fans, one was particularly fervent:

> It was the Prophet of Allah, [Muhammad] peace and blessings be upon him, who communicated the speech of Quss, and his preaching from his camel at Ukaz, and his spiritual counsel; it was he who communicated it to Quraysh and to the Arabs, and who inspired their admiration of its beauty and revealed the accuracy of its message . . . Quss was the preacher to all the Arabs without exception.

And it was Muhammad the Prophet who would also preach to all the Arab tribes and peoples without exception, and would deliver his own farewell sermon from the back of a camel.

Some Islamic depictions of Quss paint him as a sort of John the Baptist to Muhammad's Jesus. 'There is,' Quss proclaimed, 'on the face of the earth no religion better than a religion the time of which has come, with its shade to protect you . . .' In the Islamic view, Quss is only a herald, an announcer of the coming revelation, but not a part of it. In literary critical terms there are striking resemblances between Quss's gnomic rhyming prose and that of the oldest parts of the Qur'an. But in doctrinal terms, while Quss's rhetoric is human, Muhammad's is divine and thus can have no precursors. Borges said that 'every author creates his own precursors'. The exception is the Qur'an, which – if we accept the orthodox view of its authorship – destroys its precursors.

Altogether, the preaching and the poetry, the whole magniloquent rhetoric of the century before Islam, 'founded a collective memory'. As the poet Adonis has put it, 'a large part of the Arab group unconsciousness is stored there . . . it is not only our first memory but the first wellspring of our imagination'. Without this collective poetics and rhetorical idiom, the Qur'an (if we suspend belief in its eternity) and Islam, and probably the whole idea of Arabs as a 'people', would have been impossible. The memory and the idiom still unite Arabs where borders, wars and doctrines divide.

There would be a price to pay. With the word so central to identity, those who can control it have always been able to control the people for whom it forms the core of their ethnic and religious selves. Poetry and preaching can be exploited politically, made viscerally effective as propaganda. The exploitation can be grotesque: outside my window, now, preachers and poets are inspiring fourteen-year-old boys to go off and get themselves blown to pieces by fellow Arabs; they explain that those fellow Arabs are in fact Americans and Jews; when they are killed, they explain that it had to happen because it was divine will, and persuade their parents to rejoice at their 'martyrdom', to smile through their tears as they bury their children, as my neighbour has just done to the remaining bits of his son. *If any question why we died, / Tell them, because our fathers lied* . . . But perhaps lies are not enough to account for the tragedy. Words themselves can be guilty, and it is a cruel irony that a single one, *shahadah*, includes in its meanings both 'martyrdom', 'profession of [Islamic] faith' and '[school] certificate'. Context clarifies meaning, of course; but propagandists play with context. They stage '*shahadah* days' at every school, exhorting students to go and die: what you lose in the examination hall you gain in heaven.

It all goes to show that of the three outstanding conquests of Arab history – those of arms, of Islam, and of Arabic – the first and most enduring has been the victory, over themselves, of the tongue that bears their name.

VISIONS OF UNITY

By the end of the sixth century there existed an unshakeable idea of Arabs as an Arabia-wide, 'supra-tribal . . . ethno-cultural group', as Kees Versteegh has called them, adhering to a fairly consistent ethical code. Arabs had come a long way from their beginnings as the boondockers and bushwhackers of the Semitic world, the flotsam and jetsam of the desert shores, the wandering, plundering Ishmaels of Genesis, the hillbillies and haulage contractors who lived in the gap between empires. Whatever their diverse origins, they had by now accumulated enough common values and language – and, simply, enough shared history – to qualify for a unified ethnic identity.

Where they had got to might have been enough. They might have stayed in their semi-detached 'island', an appendage to the main body of Afro-Eurasian history, challenging each other to raids and odes. Their onward journey, from ethnic and ethical solidarity to political unity, from *Kulturnation* to *Staatsnation* – let alone the ultimate stage of the journey, to empire – was by no means inevitable. A thousand years earlier, Greece had achieved cultural nationhood and a shared high language, but never enjoyed any overarching political unity; more than a thousand years later, the nineteenth and twentieth centuries would see a rebirth of Arab cultural unity, and a re-death of the idea of Arab political unity.

Nevertheless, there had been times when peoples and tribes, *hadar* and *badw*, ideals and interests, had found an equilibrium, and when the tribes themselves had been brought tentatively together. Kindah's efforts to promote unity have been mentioned; so too the tribal blocs that coalesced under the Ghassanids and the Lakhmids. But all these experiments were dependent, more or less, on the existence and the will of external powers, South Arabian, Byzantine and Persian. To achieve any further unity, the will would have to come from within. Like Salman Rushdie's post-independence united India, a united Arab subcontinent was 'a mythical land, a country which would never exist except by the efforts of a phenomenal collective will – except in a dream we all agreed to dream'. For Arabs, visions of a possible greater unity were there: that pair of opposites, *'arab/'ajam*, Arabs/non-Arabs, was already firmly in place as the sixth century neared its end, together with the sense of 'ourselves alone', walled off from the others. What was lacking was the collective will to come together within the wall, and without it the visions always turned out to be mirages.

Sometimes, too, the visions turned into nightmare. As it had opened with the War of al-Basus, the long pre-Islamic century closed with yet more turns of the wheel of fire. 'When their descendants became wealthy and numerous,' it was reported of an inter-tribal attempt at forming an agricultural settlement, 'they all forgot their good fortune, and severed the ties of loyalty, and war flew among them until they had exterminated each other'. Even more disastrously, the tribe of Udwan, which had once been so prosperous and numerous as to include '70,000 youths not yet circumcised', also fell to internecine raiding and war and utterly destroyed their own unity. As their poet put it,

Authority and excellence and wisdom were all theirs
until, at last, Time took them in its fateful turn:
The tribe was torn apart, its limbs dismembered,
and its people scattered far and wide in bands.
Barrenness befell their land, and then their women's wombs;
the accidents of fate had ruined them for evermore.

The accidents of oral transmission may also have added a zero or two to the population of Banu Udwan. More personal, and thus perhaps more powerful as a record of an Arabia ripped apart by raiding, is the lament by a man called Harithah for a single loss – that of his young son, Zayd, taken in a raid:

I've wept for Zayd, not knowing what's become of him:
is he alive, and to be hoped for? or has death come to him?
The sun reminds me of him at its every rising;
his memory returns each day at fall of dusk;
His recollection stirs with every breeze that blows –
how long my grieving for him, and how fearful.

(*At the going down of the sun and in the morning / We will remember them.*) Zayd was alive, as it happened, but not to be hoped for: the child had been enslaved beyond redemption. The theme of the verses, unlike laments for glorious dead warriors, is rare: children may be lamented in private, but they have accumulated no *hasab*, no record of noble deeds worthy of public commemoration. The lines probably owe their preservation to the identity of the child's future owner and adoptive father, an obscure citizen of Mecca who was about to come on to the stage of great Arabs – and to steal the show.

ADVENT

As the sixth century closed, there were developments of more than personal or tribal consequence. Both the Byzantines and the Persians dispensed with the services their Ghassanid and Lakhmid buffer kingdoms, and tried to defend their borders with regular armies recruited from their own people. The now jobless Arab kings still attracted eulogy, however, and there is a new note of defiance and 'national' feeling in it. 'Your rule in Syria,' said Hassan ibn Thabit of the Ghassanid king Jabalah ibn al-Ayham, 'to the bounds of Byzantium, is the pride of every Yemeni'.

The Lakhmids fared less well. In 602, the Sasanian shah had the Lakhmid king – the same al-Nu'man III who had rebuffed the shah's attempts at a marital alliance – trampled to death by elephants. No particularly high politics seem to have been involved; only personal animosity, a sordid palace plot and a denunciation. However, by so decisively ending their 300-year association with the Lakhmids, the Persians had made a big mistake. Two years later they and some remaining Arab allies suffered an embarrassing defeat at a place called Dhu Qar by a consortium of Arab tribes led by that of Bakr, one of the opposing parties in that War of the Camel's Udder. In itself, this burst of tribal unity looks like a large-scale raid that ended in the usual squabbles; and, as it happened, the defeat seems to have brought the

Sasanians to their senses – and even to have put them on the offensive. From 610 they managed a late last expansion of their empire, trouncing the Byzantines and moving into Syria and even Egypt. But there was a sense that with the Persian defeat at Dhu Qar a corner had been turned. Muhammad, still the obscure citizen of Mecca, is said to have exclaimed on the day of the distant battle, 'Today the *'arab* have demanded vengeance from the *'ajam*, and have won'. Whether the statement is the result of telepathic insight or historic hindsight is an open question; what is not in doubt is that Arabs were about to win far bigger victories, and not just over the Persians.

Looking back on the century before Islam, it was as if a pressure had been building from all the migrations and raids and battle-days, energies that had to find release if they were not to cause implosion. But that release would come and, moreover, the energies would be channelled. The Arab word, and the Arab will, were about to be gathered; for a while, Arabs would all agree to dream the same dream, and to make it a waking reality. The poet Hassan ibn Thabit would soon be eulogizing a new master – not a king, but that obscure yet insightful Meccan, the unsuspecting founder of an empire that would, within a a generation of his death, embrace those proud expatriate Yemenis of the far Ghassanid north, their much-removed cousins in the Persian-colonized south, their surviving Lakhmid rivals in al-Hirah, and – astonishingly, briefly – all the perennially bickering tribes in between. In Muhammad not only would the rhetoric of the tribal *kahin*, *khatib*, *sha'ir* and *sayyid* – oracle, orator, bard and lord – unite with extraordinary originality and charisma; the rhetorical roles would amount to much more than the sum of their parts: to prophethood.

A prophet is someone who 'speaks for' a deity. In Muhammad's case it would be a deity who, like those of the old South Arabians, would function as, and guide, the collective will of His worshippers. The difference was that this deity would suffer no partners, no rivals: His was an uncompromising theological unitarianism, and for a brief but heady season it would impose another unity – not just of language and culture, but also of doctrine and even of arms – and not just on a settled commonwealth but on the whole population, *hadar* and *badw*, of the peninsula, and send them out, Arabs all, from their 'island'. The 'Days of the Arabs' were far from over; still, now, they come thick and fast. But Arabs were about to have their day in the history of a wider world.

REVOLUTION

600–630

CHAPTER FIVE

REVELATION, REVOLUTION
MUHAMMAD AND THE QUR'AN

THE BLACK STONE

'When Quraysh rebuilt the Ka'bah,' goes the story of the Meccan shrine's reconstruction in 608 after a flash flood had destroyed the earlier building,

> . . . work progressed as far as the place of the [Black] Stone . . . but then the Qurashis quarrelled over who should lay the Stone in position. In the end they agreed to abide by the decision of whoever should happen to enter first from the Gate of Banu Shaybah. The first person to appear before their eyes through that gate was the [soon-to-be] Prophet [Muhammad], peace and blessings be upon him. They already knew him as '*al-Amin*' [the Trusted One], on account of his gravity, his sound judgement and the truth of his speech, as well as his avoidance of uncleanliness and filth. They asked him to decide in their dispute and agreed to follow his adjudication. At this he took off the cloak he was wearing . . . spread it on the ground, took the Stone and placed it in the middle of the cloak. He then told four of the men of Quraysh, all of them chiefs and leaders [of different sub-clans of the tribe] . . . to take hold of the cloak, each grasping a side of it. They lifted it up and took it over to the place of the Stone, and the Prophet laid the Stone in position with all

of Quraysh looking on. This was first of his public acts in which he displayed his merit and his wisdom.

The Black Stone is still a focal point of the focal shrine of what is now Islam: it is the fervent desire of every Mecca pilgrim to kiss it. And yet the precise reasons for this are unknown. Thirty years or so after Muhammad relaid the Stone, Caliph Umar, his second successor, said he knew that 'it did neither good nor harm'. So why, then, did he and other pious people kiss the Stone? Because, the caliph said, that had been the Prophet's custom. For something to have been a *sunnah*, a practice, of Muhammad, is reason enough for Muslims to emulate it. But as the story of its relaying shows, the Stone also had a past that went back, possibly a very long time, before the year zero that marks the beginning of Islamic time and, supposedly, the consummation of all previous history.

At the time of its final pre-Islamic reconstruction, the Ka'bah housed a whole bevy of idols representing the deities of different Arabian tribes. We do not know whether Allah – the supreme deity of Muhammad's tribe, Quraysh – had a physical symbol or not. If he had had no symbol at all, he would have been exceptional; conversely, if he had indeed had a symbol of some sort, it would have been natural for the fact to be covered up in Islamic times: the Ka'bah, as represented by Islam, is the most ancient shrine of a strictly aniconic monotheism, dating back to Abraham or in some accounts to Adam; even perhaps to before the creation of mankind, when the angels would gather to worship at its site.

The assumption that the Stone had some association with Allah would be a reasonable one, even if unprovable. It may be supported by the unusual word used for Muhammad's act of kissing it – *istalama* – which is found in ancient South Arabian inscriptions with the sense of 'gaining security with a deity'. The equally aniconic deity of the Jews, after all, is known to have been associated with sacred stones – unworked stones like the Black Stone, that is, not figurative 'graven images' such as the one at Bethel in Genesis. ('Beth El' is the same as 'Bayt Allah', 'the House of Allah', the official name of the Ka'bah.) It is also known that unworked stones were used by Arabs to represent deities. When halting on their travels, the antiquarian Ibn al-Kalbi says in his *Book of Idols*, they would select four stones, using three of them to support their cooking pot and one as their 'god'. They would make sacrifices to these *dieux trouvés* and circumambulate them, just as they would process around the Ka'bah. The most binding oaths were sworn on sacred stones, and in another rare glimpse of the Black Stone before Islam, an alliance of Qurashi clans was sealed by the washing of the Stone, the drinking of the rinsings, and the making of vows.

There are a couple of less convincing glimpses: of Abraham's son Ishmael/Isma'il receiving the Stone from the Archangel Gabriel during the building of the Ka'bah (a 'heavenly' origin is not impossible – the Stone may be a meteorite, although this has never been proved); and of its having been originally white, and then being blackened by the sins of the pre-Islamic 'Age of Ignorance'. But, whatever its lost pre-Islamic meaning had been, the Black Stone gains enormous symbolic significance for Arab history from that first public act of Muhammad, two years before the beginning of his revelations. It is the foundation stone of something absolutely new, but whose substance comes from an ancient past. Over twenty years later, when Muhammad returned from his new power-base of Medina, his first act on capturing pagan Mecca was to kiss once more the Black Stone; the kiss sealed the reconciliation with his native town and his native Arabian tradition. When he then smashed the idols of the Ka'bah, the Stone was the point of continuity that allowed the mostly pagan past to elide into the monotheistic future; its customary place, in the eastern corner of the shrine, became a turning point. Most important, because of Muhammad's wisdom and leadership on that earlier occasion, the Stone ceased to be a source of disunity, a stumbling-block. Instead, it mediated, literally, between the disputing clans; it brought them together to carry it; and it became the property of none of them and all of them, a point not of contention but of conjunction. Muhammad had gathered the word and the will of the people.

Almost none of the millions of pilgrims who crowd in to kiss the Black Stone today in emulation of Muhammad have any idea why it is so significant; yet its significance grows a little with the touch of every pair of lips.

THE MOTHER OF EMPORIA

As with any other permanent settlement in Arabia, Mecca's location depends on water. In Mecca the water was supplied not by human cooperation, as in the settled South, but by nature – or by God, as the Islamic-period story of Hagar and Isma'il tells. Abraham, the story goes, took the young Isma'il to Mecca and left him there with his concubine mother, Hagar (Hagar's successful delivery of a child had incurred the jealousy of Abraham's free-born wife, Sarah, who had so far failed to become pregnant). In their Meccan place of exile, Isma'il became desperately thirsty. His mother searched for water, in vain – until by divine agency the miraculous spring of Zamzam bubbled up. Later, Isma'il married into the tribe of Jurhum, who controlled Mecca; in another version, Jurhum, originally from South Arabia, were given permission by Hagar to settle by the spring of Zamzam when their southern homeland was ruined by drought. In all the versions of the story, Isma'il, originally a speaker of 'Syriac' or some other Semitic tongue, learned Arabic, either from Jurhum or through divine inspiration. Confused though the story-lines are, they probably do give some hints about the Meccan past – the town's links with South Arabia, migration caused by climate change, acculturation to the Arabic language. As for Zamzam, still regarded as a holy well today, it may have been holy early on: Muhammad's grandfather Abd al-Muttalib is said to have found two gold figures of gazelles in it when digging the well out. They may have been hastily hidden treasure, but they may have been offerings to the well.

Looking at the less murky and less miraculous Meccan past, it is clear that as a *qariyah*, a caravan-emporium, the town was a successor to Petra, Palmyra and Kindah's cognate Qaryat. It stood on an already ancient north–south trade route, at a geographical mid-point between the two Fertile Crescents; it also occupied a cultural mid-point between the more settled west of Arabia and the more nomadic east, between *hadar* and *badw*. Its sacred role may be old, too: in Ptolemy's second-century map of Arabia a toponym, 'Macoraba', corresponds roughly with the site of Mecca. It could represent a Sabaic word, *mkrb*, the vowelling of which is not known, but which seems to mean 'temple'. 'Macoraba', however, might equally represent 'Maghrabah', an Arabian toponym for places like Mecca that lie between hills. All that can be said with certainty is that, whether or not we take Mecca's holy history back as far as Ishmael, Adam, or even the pre-Adamic angels, it is likely to have been a cultic centre for at least several centuries before Muhammad's time.

Like other emporia in the pre-Muhammadan centuries, Mecca seems to have led a mercantile life of its own that survived the various periods of 'protection' (with the Mafioso shade of meaning) by successive tribes. In the traditional histories, Jurhum and other tribes had fought for control and afterwards, possibly no later than the early third century, conflicts over the town broke out between the tribes of Mudar and Iyad. By this time the Black Stone had entered the scene, and – whatever its significance may have been – was already revered enough to be hidden for its own safety; so well hidden that the hiding-place was, apparently, forgotten. Enter another tribe, Khuza'ah, who just happened to have come across the Stone . . . They would be delighted to return the much-missed relic, they said, on condition that they could be its guardians. Presumably the guardianship was as much to do with money as with love. At any rate it was Khuza'ah, in the later monotheist narrative, who diversified the attractions of Mecca by introducing idolatry into what had been the House of the One God. In particular their leader, Amr ibn Luhayy, imported an idol of the deity Hubal ('spirit, vapour' in Aramaic) from Syria. Khuza'ah remained in charge until the fifth century AD, when a new era of Meccan history began. It is an era that has not yet ended.

The new epoch started with the arrival in Mecca of an Arab man called Qusayy. His origins are obscure, but those who claim descent from him have been in the spotlight ever since: they – the tribe known as 'Quraysh', after the supposed name of Qusayy's own ancestor – are the most successful family in Arab history, perhaps in human history as a whole. No one can be sure about that earlier name; genealogies, as we have seen, tend to be 'something imaginary and devoid of reality [whose] usefulness consists only in the resulting connection', and this seems to be true of Qusayy's pedigree. Qusayy is sometimes known as al-Mujammi', 'the Connector, the Uniter'; 'Quraysh', as we have also seen, is often said to derive from the verb *taqarrasha*, 'to gather people together'. All this suggests that Quraysh may have been a group of mixed origins. Others, however, have derived the name from *qarsh*, 'making money', an activity in which Quraysh were to excel. Yet others go for the most literal derivation, from the common noun *quraysh*, 'little shark'. The following verses are attributed to a pre-Islamic Himyari poet called al-Mushamrij ibn Amr:

> A *quraysh* is that which lives in the sea
> and from it Quraysh were called Quraysh.
> It eats both lean and fat and leaves
> not a feather of any two-winged thing.
> Thus, on land, are the tribe of Quraysh:
> they eat lands up and gobble them down.

At the end of time a prophet they'll have –
many he'll kill and slap in the face.
His horsemen and footmen will fill the earth
and drive the mounts with a crackle of fire.

Or, perhaps, ' . . . with a slither of snakes'. Whatever the truth of the etymology, the poem is almost strange enough to be genuine.

Whoever he was, Qusayy was able to gain control of the Meccan shrine. The traditional account of how he did so is, like the verses above, unexpected enough almost to be credible: the rather seedy Khuza'i guardian of the time was down on his uppers, and Qusayy simply persuaded him to part with the keys to the Ka'bah for a camel and a skinful of wine. Whether or not the long and still unbroken link of Quraysh with the Meccan shrine did in fact have such bathetic beginnings, according to the traditional record the position of Quraysh as guardians of the Ka'bah and chiefs of Mecca was later confirmed by agreements drawn up with the three Arabian powers, the Ghassanids, Lakhmids and Himyaris. If true, this would place the ultimate origins of the Islamic state in that ancient mesh of Arab relations with foreign superpowers – the Ghassanids' Byzantine overlords, and the Lakhmids' Persian suzerains.

What is certain is that the fate of the neighbouring powers would have a direct effect on the fortunes of Quraysh, who had quickly added trade to shrine-management in their portfolio of activities: pilgrim-routes are ready-made highways of commerce. Their third guarantors, the Himyaris, had been a superpower in their own right, but in the later fifth century they were already in decline. The decay of their southern-based empire was to Quraysh's advantage, as the newcomers were able to gain more control over the Arabian trade routes in general. Towards the end of the following century, Qurashi trade also benefited from Byzantine–Persian hostilities of the time, which caused a shift of traffic from eastern Arabian routes to western ones, already dominated by Mecca. Throughout, the Qurashis were busy cultivating a network of alliances with the *badw* tribes, who could be paid and otherwise persuaded to protect Meccan caravans and to keep out or raid those of potential interlopers. The network grew until it covered much of the peninsula. As it did so, probably also towards the end of the sixth century, the new – for Meccans – technology of Arabic writing boosted the book-keeping capabilities that were vital for keeping track of large-scale merchant ventures. Also in this century began a practice that would be crucial for mercantile expansion – *mudarabah*, the mass pooling of capital for investment in ever bigger caravans trading ever further away. All these developments made Mecca the hub of commerce for the whole Arabian subcontinent. And, as the Dutch, English and French would discover with their East India companies of a thousand years later and their far-ranging fleets, large-scale commercial cooperation could sow the seeds of imperial domination.

The most famous Meccan caravans were those that went on the 'winter and summer journeys' mentioned in the Qur'an. The winter caravan headed south to the ancient port of Aden, the summer one north to the Levant and its main port of Gaza, thus linking the traffic of the Indian Ocean and Mediterranean spheres. The link revived already ancient mercantile patterns: long before the turn of the millennium, merchants from the South Arabian state of Ma'in had traded north and south, and had enjoyed particularly close relations with Gaza. Increasingly, however, the Meccans enhanced that other dimension of the pattern – their town's own attractions as a pilgrimage venue for the peninsula. Trade and pilgrimage both led each other on and fed off each other; Muhammad's uncle al-Abbas, for example, used to buy perfume in Yemen and sell it in Mecca during the pilgrimage. Equally important, the Meccans' cosmopolitan trade would shape the patterns of their future imperial expansion. It is no coincidence that Amr ibn al-As, the eventual conqueror and governor of Egypt, used to trade in Gaza, the gateway to the rich land of the Nile. Nor is it surprising that the first ruler of the first dynasty in Islam, the Umayyads, relocated the capital from Medina to Damascus, or at least not when we realize that his wealthy father, Abu Sufyan, had already invested in land in the rich Bekaa Valley, not far from Damascus in what is now Lebanon.

With commerce abroad and the Ka'bah, a magnet of pagan pilgrimage, at home, the Meccans traded in both goods and gods. They also traded in words. The old everyday dialect of Quraysh had probably been rather far from high Arabic; as late as the end of the sixth century, it may even have had some points of similarity to the old South Arabian tongues. But with their increasingly cosmopolitan connections, the speech of the Meccans was becoming ever nearer to the Arabic lingua franca of travel and trade, and ever richer. Quraysh are said to have 'selected from the speech and poetry [of visiting delegations of pilgrims and others] the best of the local variants and the purest speech, and these were added to their innate linguistic ability'. This makes the process sound more conscious than it would have been; it is more like the deliberate way in which Arabic would be standardized in later centuries. But there is no doubt that when the high speech was needed for formal public utterances, some Meccans had a way with words: a visiting poet compared their speech to 'rain on parched earth'.

As Meccan merchants and Meccan speech grew richer, so the town's population expanded. If it is true that its inhabitants numbered 15,000–20,000 by the early seventh century, then it would almost certainly have earned its Qur'anic title of *umm al-qura*, the Mother of Emporia, the Metromarket, on the basis of size alone. But by this time Mecca was also wielding her matriarchy as a cultic as well as a commercial emporium. The little city was comfortable, lucrative, smug; but in world terms it was still peninsular, an appendage to events. No one knew that it was poised to turn from a self-centred market town into an epicentre that would send shock waves around the globe.

THE NAVEL OF THE EARTH

At about the time of Muhammad's birth, Mecca's sanctity had been boosted by the apparently miraculous way in which the Ethiopians were repulsed, by squadrons of avian fighter-bombers, on the Day of the Elephant; the town's allure as a pilgrimage centre was increasing. There are hints that the mountain of Arafat, scene of the climax of rites in the Islamic version of the pilgrimage, was the main draw in pre-Islamic times, and that the Ka'bah itself was something of a local side-show. Pilgrims would arrive at Arafat in tribal groups, belting out ritual chants peculiar to each tribe and imitating the cries of the tribe's particular totemic animal. One interpretation of the scant information has it that sites around the Ka'bah were the centre of an 'urban' pilgrimage, mainly for settled *hadar* people, while a separate *badw* pilgrimage focused on the area around Mount Arafat; Islam would unite the *hadar* and *badw* rites into a single pilgrimage.

It is impossible to get into the heads of pre-Islamic Arabian tribespeople. But it is likely that, just as the borderline between the spiritual and the political has always been porous, so too was the line in their minds between the spiritual and the commercial. For a *badw* society in which the main economic institution was raiding, the spiritual draw of Mecca may have been little different from the attractions of shopping and fun at the associated fairs like Ukaz. Peace, too, was another draw: the pilgrimage fell in the middle of an annual three-month truce in which trading replaced raiding, and raid- and feud-weary warriors could breathe easily and listen to duelling poets and camel-borne preachers. The three spheres – political, commercial, spiritual – intersected, and at the very centre of their conjunction was, and is, the Meccan temenos.

The current focus of that temenos, the Ka'bah, the 'Cube', seems sempiternal, archetypal. Muslim geographers called it 'the navel of the earth', the same term used by Greeks for their pilgrimage-centre of Delphi (where the precise 'navel' was symbolized – perhaps not coincidentally – by a sacred stone); some also compared Mecca to a womb that expands to accommodate ever-growing numbers of pilgrims. The Ka'bah seems almost to have arrived rather than been built, like the black alien monoliths that haunt human history in *2001: A Space Odyssey*. But the Ka'bah too has been subject to change, decay and rebuilding no less than any other monument. It has also had a shifting population. The idol Hubal, supposedly introduced from Syria at some time before the fifth century, presided over popular and lucrative divinations: at a cost of 100 *dirham*s or one camel, arrows inscribed with 'Yes', 'No' and other words would be jiggled in a sacred quiver in front of the god's image, and visitants given advice on the basis of the arrows drawn. Qusayy, the Qurashi founding father, added to the inhabitants of the shrine by bringing together there the three most popular female deities of Arabia, al-Lat, Manat and al-Uzza, the trio that later featured in the notorious 'satanic verses'. By the time of Muhammad there was a fair old pantheon, and the attractions of the Ka'bah included a pair of statues called Isaf and Na'ilah, a couple who had allegedly fornicated in the shrine and been turned to stone. By this time the Ka'bah also doubled as a portrait gallery of Quraysh ancestors, while around it were ranged the meeting-houses of the various Qurashi clans, and a house of convocation that brought all the clans together. Not least, from the rebuild of 608 and possibly from earlier, the shrine contained an image of Jesus and Mary, later spared by Muhammad from his mass destruction of pre-Islamic paraphernalia.

The Ka'bah of Mecca, however, was not alone. There was a Ka'bah of Najran, developed under Ethiopian auspices as the martyrion of the Jewish King Yusuf As'ar's Christian victims, and also a Ka'bah of Sindad in southern Iraq, about which little seems to be known. But towards the end of the sixth century the Meccan Ka'bah was becoming the major centre of worship and pilgrimage. In those disunited days it offered something for everyone, a one-stop divine shop with Hubal and his divinations as the main draw. Allah was widely recognized, but seems to have been rather parochial in his active cult. He was regarded as the patron, or paternal, deity of Quraysh: 'We've been the family of Allah since times long past,' Muhammad's grandfather Abd al-Muttalib is said to have declared. But all that was about to change.

MUHAMMAD

Muhammad's life straddles the precise mid-point of recorded Arab history. And just as the first, pre-Islamic half of that history is often obscure, so too is the first part of that life. The date of Muhammad's birth is often given as 570. That is a stab in the dark that has stuck; as we have seen, it depends on the problematic dating of the year of the Day of the Elephant and – like the tale of the blind Sufis and the elephant – we can do no more than feel around the problem. That traditional date of 582 for the boyhood trip to Syria is equally debatable. Only with 610 – usually suggested as the beginning of Muhammad's revelations – does time firm up. Thereafter, likelier dates begin to dawn: some of Muhammad's followers went to Ethiopia, perhaps in 616; his first wife, Khadijah, may have died in 619. Muhammad's relocation from Mecca to Medina in 622 is the first indisputable waymark in his life, and thus the start of the Islamic calendar. From then on the dates are certain: the decisive raid at Badr in 624; the Meccan siege of Medina in 627; the truce with the pagan Meccans in 628; Muhammad's takeover of Mecca in 630; his death in 632.

Later piety has not only fleshed out the half-buried bones of a life, but foreseen it in retrospect long before it began. The 'Comforter' whom Jesus promised would come to console the world is interpreted by Islam not as the Holy Spirit, but as Muhammad. Prophethood, too, was prophesied. As a boy, Muhammad is supposed to have gone on a trading trip with his uncle, and to have met a Christian Arab monk in southern Syria who saw in him the signs of divine grace. Another story has his friend Abu Bakr going to Yemen and meeting a monk who showed him a portrait of 'Muhammad, the prophet'; Abu Bakr was bemused, but returned to Mecca to find that Muhammad had indeed declared his prophethood.

As well as these elisions with the wider Judaeo-Christian past, there are others that bind Muhammad into specifically Arabian tradition. One tradition says that, in the middle of the sixth century Satih, the supposedly boneless seer already mentioned, was consulted about a Persian nobleman's dream of 'stubborn camels leading Arab horses' across the Tigris and spreading through the Sasanian realm. Not surprisingly, Satih predicted the coming fall of the Persian empire to invading Arabs and their unstoppable camel+horse combination; but he also went on to say, 'Arab fortunes will be raised up high: I believe Muhammad's birth is nigh'.

Interpretations of the Gospels and the Qur'an are matters of faith, and thus in a sense beyond scepticism. However, one may well be sceptical about boneless seers and telepathic monkish portraitists. The same goes for biographies of Muhammad. Even when they are not being obviously fanciful, they need to be approached with reserve: nearly all are later than the first Islamic century; they disagree on many points; and, most dubiously, 'the later the sources are, the more they claim to know about the life of the Prophet'. The *hadith* literature, too needs a cautious approach. Collectors of *hadith*s – reports of the speech and deeds of and concerning Muhammad – amassed as many as a million alleged such 'Traditions', which works out at about one for each eight minutes of his waking life as a prophet. Of the million, around 5,000 are supposed to be reliable – four or five for each week of his prophethood. That latter figure sounds more possible. But that looming mass of unsound evidence, 200:1 in proportion to the reliable Traditions, is a warning of how piety (or necessity – the need for prophetic precedent) can manufacture the past.

Muhammad himself was aware of this when it came to his own antecedents. Later grafted on to the family tree of biblical prophets via Isma'il, the infant asylum-seeker in Mecca, Muhammad himself forbade anyone to try and trace his pedigree back that far: beyond Ma'add, the putative ancestor of the northern tribes, he knew that the record was unreliable. 'Genealogists,' he said bluntly, 'tell lies.' Then again, both those statements come in *hadith*s. What can you believe?

Looking at his more recent ancestry, Muhammad was not only an orphan, but also from a poorer clan of Quraysh. In the fissile tribal tradition, the two grandsons of the Quraysh founding father Qusayy had fallen out: one account has these two, Hashim and Abd Shams, born as conjoined twins and cut bloodily apart with a sword. If it is not true, it should be: lashings of gore would mire relations between their descendants, the Hashimis and the Umayyads (named after Umayyah, the son of Abd Shams, whose own name – 'Slave of the Sun Goddess' – would have sat strangely on the future dynasty of Islamic caliphs). The blood still flows today from the open wound separating Sunnah and Shi'ah, which is a follow-through from that first legendary severance. Over the two generations after it, the Meccan economy began to boom, and the Umayyad line did better than the Hashimis in the capitalist free-for-all. Wealth also meant power, and during the youth of Hashim's great-grandson Muhammad, the Umayyads effectively pushed the Hashimis out of the ruling elite of Quraysh.

Muhammad the orphan, posthumous son of Abd Allah ibn Abd al-Muttalib ibn Hashim, did not have a deprived childhood. He was brought up lovingly by his paternal uncle Abu Talib, and cosseted by household slaves and an Ethiopian nurse. By some accounts, he spoke Ethiopic, presumably learned from the nurse. To the 'rain on parched earth' of Meccan speech and this possible bilingualism was added further richness: following Meccan tradition, Muhammad was sent out as a very small child to the *badiyah*, the *badw*-land or steppe hinterland of the town, to live with the nomad tribe of Sa'd ibn Bakr. This bedouin kindergarten served both to toughen up Meccan infants and to improve their language – elocution by immersion. Nomad mobility had been the mother of the Arabia-wide, elevated form of Arabic, and it was seen almost as an innate attribute of the mobile tribes. Cities, in contrast – even relatively eloquent Mecca – were regarded as inimical to pure speech, places where one's glottal *hamzah*s would wither and drop as surely as a Cockney's aitches or a Cajun's final consonants. Strange though the custom of the bedouin education seems, therefore, it is no stranger than sending small boys off to boarding schools. It was also older than Muhammad's time and more widespread than Mecca: in a late Sabaic inscription from the time when the South was being widely arabicized, the writer mentions sending his sons to be wet-nursed by nomadic *a'rab*. Later, after their move to the fleshpots of Syria, the Umayyad caliphs continued the practice: in an exception, Caliph Abd al-Malik admitted that he had spoiled his son al-Walid by not sending him to the *badiyah*. Much later – in fact as late as the 1920s – better-off Meccans were still sending their sons out to the *badiyah* boarding school.

The experience seems to have left Muhammad with a positive view of the neighbouring nomads, and a sense of their symbiosis with Mecca. Much later, when his wife A'ishah referred to the nomads of the Meccan hinterland as *a'rab*, Muhammad retorted, 'They are not *a'rab*. They are the people of our *badiyah*, and we are the people of their *qariyah*'. From this, however, it is also clear that Muhammad was wary, to say the least, of the further-flung, wilder nomads. As we shall see, his relations with the latter would be fraught. He would be willing to make use of their tactics, but ever aware of their dangers.

For the moment, Muhammad's brief and seemingly happy nomad education – it might be called arabicization, even arabization – would have an importance far greater than just personal. Looking at the wider Meccan milieu and the broader currents of Arabian history, Muhammad was from a perfect background to mediate in the long-running dialogue between *hadar* and *badw*, and eventually to try to gather their word into one. He was from an urban, commercial background, but one that was embedded in a nomad environment and had to rely on the nomads for its trafficking. It has been claimed that politically, culturally and religiously, Meccans were much like their nomad neighbours. But they were genteel – or, one might say, using terms derived from words for 'city', polite or urbane – versions of nomads. If the visions of paradise in the Qur'an can be used as a guide, they aspired to the sort of lifestyle enjoyed by their more distant civilized neighbours. The Qur'anic paradise is described as if it were an eternal Hellenistic, or perhaps Palmyrene, symposium, where the elect wear silk, recline on raised thrones and drink from vessels of silver and crystal plied by youthful cupbearers. Its gardens are watered by rivers that invariably flow underground, like the subterranean *qanat*s developed by the Persians. But through their bedouin homestays Meccans were made aware from an early age of the nomad reality – sour milk from goatskins and brackish water scooped from gritty holes. At home they occupied a middle ground, the *qariyah* in the *badiyah*, the market town in the steppeland, watered by the revered – if somewhat bitter-tasting – spring of Zamzam.

The rest of Muhammad's early life is a blank, except for that possible Syrian trip in his boyhood, accompanying his merchant uncle. Later on, as a young man, he made another trip to Syria on behalf of an older woman, a Qurashi widow named Khadijah who was a businesswoman in her own right. This was a success, and among the results of it was their marriage. Six children were born – four girls and two boys. The latter died young, as did Muhammad's later son, Ibrahim. The boys were posthumously islamicized with the names 'al-Qasim' and 'Abd Allah', but according to his main biography he had named one of them Abd Manaf, 'the Slave of [the Goddess] Manaf', the given name of his uncle and guardian Abu Talib.

As this shows, Muhammad was a part of his pagan Meccan environment. He is known to have made offerings to the pagan deities on at least one occasion, when he sacrificed a white sheep to the goddess al-Uzza. But, as we shall see, Mecca was not immune to the divine environmental shift that had affected much of the region over the previous three centuries. Monotheism had spread around the entire rim of the Mediterranean, overwhelming ancient pantheons and seeping up towards the far islands of Britain (Augustine was taking Christianity to Canterbury at about the time Muhammad was taking Khadijah's caravan to Syria). Monotheism had also taken over both Fertile Crescents: in the old Sabaean-Himyari south, for example, its various forms – Christianity, Judaism, and an indigenous and little-understood product of local evolution, Rahmanism – had jostled, sometimes battled, for supremacy. Mecca was still a pocket of theo-diversity, but al-Uzza and her like were an endangered species. We will return to this divine evolution below.

At some time in the first decade of the seventh century, Muhammad began emulating other contemplative Meccans by going into retreat; a favourite destination for this was Jabal Hira', the mountain overlooking Mecca. That is just about all that is known about the practice. The preceding couple of centuries had seen Christian stylites and other hermits proliferating, especially in Syria and other regions to the north of the peninsula. To speculate about some inspiration from them may be justified, but it is no more than speculation. At any rate, it was during one of these retreats that the revelations began. At first Muhammad was afraid – afraid, as he told his wife Khadijah, that he was turning into a *kahin*, a seer; if he already had monotheistic leanings, then the idea that he might have fallen into the clutches of the daemonic spirits of ancient Arabia would indeed have been frightening. That was also the diagnosis of his eventual successor, Umar, and of other impartial observers: later, hearing him mention that he had not experienced any revelations for a while, a Qurashi woman said, 'His *shaytan* ['satan', or inspiring daemon] is keeping him waiting!' But by that time Muhammad had realized his revelations were different from those of the ancient Arab soothsayers. For a start, the supernatural intermediary who brought them was no *shaytan*, but an angel.

Together, the revelations would form the Qur'an. It is not just the only indisputable record of Muhammad's life, but also his chief miracle as a prophet. Its rhetorical power would fuel the greatest of all wheels of fire, a cycle of unity and fragmentation that is still in motion today. It is the masterpiece of the Arabic language and, in a sense, the centrepiece of the Arab story – the hidden thread of history made suddenly, dazzlingly visible. We must step for a while out of the obscurity of Muhammad's earlier life and look into that miraculous book.

RECITE!

According to later Islamic legend, Isma'il had received the Black Stone from Allah via Gabriel. Now, Muhammad received from Allah not an obscurely symbolic lump of rock but a living word: *iqra'!*, '*Recite!*', was the first word of the Qur'an, 'the Recitation', revealed by Gabriel to Muhammad. It is proof, if it were needed, of the primacy not just of the word, but of the sound of the word. 'I am no reciter,' Muhammad replied, confused and terrified. At this, according to Ibn Hisham's biography, Gabriel is said to have stuffed a cloth inscribed with writing into Muhammad's mouth, almost making him choke. After three attempts, Muhammad got the words out, in both senses. In recently monotheized Britain, Muhammad's near contemporary the hymnist Caedmon would also recoil from a divine visitor ('*Sing!*' 'I cannot sing'); and the painful annunciation has been compared to Isaiah's angel touching him with a burning coal.

'Annunciation' suggests a Judaeo-Christian context, which is partly appropriate: following Gabriel's annunciation to Mary, the Word of God was made flesh; with that to Muhammad, the Word was made sound. Both Mary and Muhammad were virgins – Mary literally, in that she had no experience of procreation, Muhammad in the sense that he had no experience of recitation. But the context disguises the underlying subtext: as the Qurashi woman who spoke of Muhammad's *shaytan* realized, Gabriel also performed the function of a sort of super-daemon, such as those that had inspired the ancient *kahin*s.

To Muhammad's original audience, it was the *kahin*-like nature of the early revelations that was most obvious – even to Muhammad himself, worried about becoming a seer. To show why, it is enough to compare the oath of a *kahin* judging in a dispute between those earlier Qurashis, Hashim and Umayyah, with an oath preceding an early Qur'anic chapter. First the *kahin*:

By the moon that shines brightly,
By the star that shows clearly,
By the clouds that give rain,
By all the birds in the air . . .

Then the Qur'an:

By the sun and its forenoon brightness,
By the moon when it follows it,
By the day, revealing it,
By the night, veiling it . . .

Later, however, Muhammad would express his dislike of the *kahin*s' rhyming speech, in order to distance himself from them. He had ended and surpassed their tradition, he declared: 'There can be no *kahin*hood after prophethood.'

As well as being thought of as a *kahin*, Muhammad was accused by his early detractors of being one of those other adepts of the high Arabic tongue, the poets. Both accusations were denied in the Qur'an:

This is indeed the word of a noble messenger.
It is not the word of a poet: how little is your belief!
And it is not the word of a *kahin*: how little you reflect!

Linguistically, the revelations were undeniably uttered in the same high Arabic language that the rhymed speech of the seers shared with poetry: for its hearers, a circle of Meccans that rippled outwards from Muhammad's close family and for whom the special speech was a guarantee of the message's supernatural origin, this was all part of the proof of its truth. But the subject-matter of the Qur'an was clearly different from that of the already classic poetry of boasting, panegyric and love. 'Do you not see,' the Qur'an asks of the poets' fanfaronade,

that they wander in every wadi,
And that they say things that they would never do?

But was the subject-matter always so different? In western Arabia about the time of Muhammad a new, if rare, strain of what could be called 'devotional' poetry was appearing. Its best-known exponent was Umayyah ibn Abi 'l-Salt who hailed from al-Ta'if, a town 60 kilometres from Mecca. He was an ardent *hanif*, the term used in the Qur'an for one practising the 'original' but somewhat misty pre-Muhammadan monotheism that went back to Abraham and had remained free of subsequent accretions, Jewish and Christian. This Umayyah is said to have read the older scriptures, worn hair shirts, eschewed alcohol and had a penchant for destroying idols. Lines attributed to him include the sort of material that also appears in the Qur'an – on divine unity, creation, heaven and hell, the ancient prophets, the 'extinct' tribes of Ad and Thamud, and matters of more local interest like the Day of the Elephant. One of his verses goes,

> On the Day of Resurrection, Allah will consider every *din* –
> other than the *din* of the *hanif*s – false.

Compare with this Qur'anic verses such as,

> So set your face towards religion as a *hanif* . . . that is the straight religion, but most people do not know.

Other than his being a contemporary of Muhammad, Umayyah's dates are unknown. What is clear is that he was, and remained, an opponent of Muhammad: after the setting up of the state of Medina, he would compose elegies on those killed in Muhammad's raids.

For believers, the Qur'an is the eternal word of Allah and can have no precursors. If we willingly suspend belief, however, there is the obvious question of who influenced whom. Orientalists like Clément Huart tried to show that Umayyah influenced Muhammad; Muslim free-thinkers (and you have to be a free-thinker to engage in the debate at all) like Taha Husayn tried to show the opposite. Neither is convincing, and no one *can* be convincing as long as we cannot answer crucial questions about the dating and authenticity of Umayyah's poems. Regarding the latter, it is generally agreed, 'that there might well be some authentic material' among the verses ascribed to him. That is all. And all that can be said with certainty is that, in western Arabia in late pagan times, there was a kind of oral circulating library – of parables from ancient times, snippets of knowledge about the Jewish and Christian scriptures, and ideas about creation and the nature of the monotheistic God. All the *hanif*s drew from these, and to try to decide which way influences went between them is probably a pointless exercise. What is clear is that Muhammad was not alone in his beliefs. Even the verb *aslama* and its noun *islam*, as a term for 'submission' to the One God, was shared. Compare the beginning of the last Qur'anic verse quoted above with some lines by Zayd ibn Amr ibn Nufayl, a Meccan *hanif* who predated Muhammad but may have overlapped with him:

> I have submitted [*aslamtu*] my face to Him to whom
> the Earth submitted, bearing heavy rocks.
> He spread it out, and when He saw it lying evenly
> on the waters, He set mountains firm upon it.

Like Muhammad, Zayd would go regularly into retreat on Mount Hira'; also like the later adherents of *islam*, he would submit his face in prayer and prostration to the One God, Allah, literally 'facing' His house, the Ka'bah. 'Islam', 'Submission', only gained its capital letter as the system of the cognate 'Muslims', the 'Submitters', after the move to Medina and the shift in focus from spiritual to political. Until then, Muhammad and his followers and predecessors were all *hanif*s together.

If the Qur'an is not unique in content and thought, it is, however, unique in form. It went much further than any poetry, devotional or other, and than the old magic speech. The latter seems to have been uttered in snatches. The Qur'an 'descended' in this way too. But it builds up into something much more sustained, and something that beside even the longest pre-Islamic odes (rarely more than a hundred lines) looks truly epic: it builds into nothing less than the first ever, and for a long time to come the only, Arabic book.

THE WORD MADE BOOK

It has been said that, 'With an alphabet, a people . . . sets out upon a journey'. And with a book – and especially such an omnibus volume as the Qur'an, that takes in heaven, earth and all of time from the moment of Creation on – there is a vehicle for the journey. The Qur'an is therefore not only the scripture of Islam; it is also the founding text of Arabdom as we know it, with all the historical weight of a Pentateuch, a Magna Carta and a Declaration of Independence.

Anyone who looks into Arab history must dwell on the Qur'an. Like that other gift of Gabriel, the Black Stone, it is a turning point on which a lot of history hinges: while at first glance 'the influences which stamp the world's history are wars, uprisings or downfalls of dynasties,' to quote Whitman again (he does tend to put his finger on things),

> yet, it may be, a single new thought, imagination, abstract principle, even literary style, put in shape by some great literatus, and projected among mankind, may duly cause changes, growths, removals, greater than the longest and bloodiest war . . .

The long and bloody wars would come as well, and soon enough. But it was the book and the supposedly 'illiterate' literatus, Muhammad, that wrought the change.

As that first word revealed – '*Recite!*' – shows, *qur'an* really means an oral text, read aloud and listened to. Even today, printed and electronic versions reproduce a standard edition done in Egypt in the 1920s which itself relied not on manuscripts, but on oral tradition. Individual copyists have always been regarded as more fallible than the mass memory of Qur'an reciters. But as the story of Gabriel stuffing the inscribed cloth into Muhammad's mouth recognizes, reciting and writing are intimately bound up from the beginning. Furthermore, that first revelation continues thus:

> *Recite!* In the name of your Lord who has created . . . Who has taught by the pen.

Reciting and writing go together from the start of the revelations, and writing as much as reciting is a divinely inspired act; it is not impossible that there are influences at play, yet again, from the earlier civilization of South Arabia, where writing may have been an activity restricted to priestly scribes. Another early revelation, the Chapter of the Pen, begins with an ancient sacred oath sworn on that instrument of modernity –

> By the pen and what they write . . .

The old oral, magical world of the *kahin*s had come together with the new era of recording technology.

If the phrase 'recording technology' suggests associations with hi-fi, they are not out of place. In Arabic, 'the written symbol is considered to be identical with the sound indicated by it'. Letters are not just phonetic; they are phonic, acoustic, '. . . script that fills the ears of him that sees it', as the poet al-Mutanabbi was to call them. Robert Byron, writing on Kufic, the earliest Arabic script, is spot-on when he says that it 'seems in itself a form of oratory, a transposition of speech from the audible to the visible'. What this means in practice is that a written version of an oral text is not a separate entity, a next stage in composition; it is seen (or heard) rather as a direct audio-recording, not so much a dictation as a notation, like that of music. Thus an old saying, 'The pen is a second tongue'.

From early on, the Qur'an had a material, written presence. The revelations were jotted down on anything that came to hand – leaves, bones, bits of hide, pieces of wood, potsherds, stones, recycled scraps of imported papyrus. And at some stage, probably quite early in the second decade of the seventh century, written portions of it started circulating. Umar, who had imagined Muhammad to be just another *kahin*, is said in some accounts to have converted to the Prophet's cause on reading a single leaf that he happened to find in his sister's house. Such leaves probably began as a form of aide-mémoire to recitation for Muhammad's followers among his family and acquaintances. Later, in Medina, recording became systematic, and Muhammad would dictate Qur'anic verses – often hot off the heavenly airwaves – to 'the scribes of the revelation'. Once, when a verse that had already been revealed had slipped Muhammad's memory, a scribe had to prompt him, a case of the recorded version collaborating with the live performance. In another case, one of the scribes would maliciously substitute wrong words in his copy; he was found out, fled back to pagan Mecca – and a Qur'anic verse duly descended to criticize him. The revelations themselves take account of this shift from oral to written: earlier ones tend to speak of a *qur'an*, 'recitation', later ones of a *kitab*, 'writing, book'.

That the Qur'an became the first Arabic book is not just a fact of literary history. The Qur'an is more than those disparate jottings bound together; much more than the sum of its parts. A major part of Muhammad's argument against the pagan Meccans was that they had no scripture to prove the truth of their eclectic spiritual beliefs. For example, the Qur'an challenges the pagans for asserting that supernatural beings like angels are the daughters of Allah:

Or do you have clear authority?
Then bring forth your Book if you are telling the truth!

Of course, the pagans had no book to bring forth. Muhammad trounced them by producing not only the old sacred language but also by producing a new sacred scripture.

Furthermore, part of the miracle of the Qur'an is that its recipient, Muhammad, was *ummi*, a word often glossed as 'illiterate'. But a better gloss may be 'gentile': in other words, Muhammad was from a community – Arabic *ummah*, Latin *gens* (hence 'gentile') – who, unlike the Jews and the Christians, did not have a scripture. There are some indications that he could write. In the story mentioned above about the monk displaying Muhammad's portrait and predicting his prophethood, Abu Bakr's first reaction was to say, 'But Muhammad cannot write well,' not that he was unable to write at all. Stories from the Medina period may confirm that he had some ability to write.

What is certain is that Muhammad knew the *power* of writing, and would use it widely in the later community- and state-building years at Medina. As Benedict Anderson argues in his *Imagined Communities*, there is no more powerful fundamental unifying force for a community than language. For the language to come from a deity, and to be written in a book for the first time, could only increase that force exponentially. Part of Muhammad's genius, whether he himself could write or not, was therefore to grasp the potential of writing – the earthly power that pens can wield alongside swords. In this respect if no other, he may have resembled the chief of the Nambikwara tribe with whom Claude Lévi-Strauss stayed in Brazil: 'I could not help admiring [his] genius in instantly recognizing that writing could increase his authority, thus grasping the basis of the institution without knowing how to use it.' Perhaps, too, he resembled the legendary king Cadmus, said to have disseminated the Greek alphabet – and also to have grown himself an army sown from dragon's teeth. (The king, like both Greek and Arabic letters, is also said to have been Phoenician in origin.)

So who did know how to use writing in early seventh-century Mecca? As we have seen, it was probably a newish technology there, one that had filtered down the trade routes from the Lakhmid-ruled north-east of Arabia by the later sixth century. It had revolutionized Meccan book-keeping, and raised commerce to new levels. A poet is said to have congratulated the Meccans in verse on the benefits of their newly acquired Arabic script,

> by which you now can keep account
> of wealth that had been scattered and disordered.
> . . .
> You ply your pens back and forth along the lines
> as nimbly as the scribes of Khusraw and of Caesar;
> You have no need for the ancient script of Himyar . . .

The verses make a historical point of great importance. It was not just that Meccans were discovering the joys of accountancy; Arabs were at last joining, as independent members, the regional club of literate civilizations – Khusraw's Persians, Caesar's Roman-Byzantines, and the now superannuated Himyaris of South Arabia. Henceforward, Arabs would compete with these imperial neighbours on equal terms. Soon, with the added benefit of their God-given (or at least Allah-based) solidarity, they would outstrip them.

Altogether, seventeen Qurashis are said to have been literate at the beginning of Muhammad's prophethood, but the number soon increased and started to include women. Significantly, among those seventeen were some of Muhammad's closest companions: five of them acted as his secretaries, and it was those five who would eventually succeed him in turn as heads of the new state that he founded. By the time of the fifth successor, the state had become an empire. Only an administration based on writing could have kept that empire up, running and expanding; faith and arms alone would never have been enough.

The spread of writing, until now confined to the courts of the client-kings in Lakhmid al-Hirah and Ghassanid Syria, transformed Arabs. By learning to form their own Arabic characters in ledgers and scriptures, they were also forming their character as a people, and inscribing it on the pages of a bigger history.

RHYME IS REASON

During Muhammad's life, 'scripture' meant a loose-leaf, unbound mass of texts. Putting them together as a single book would take a long time, and would not be completed until nearly thirty years after his death. Part of the problem was the editing: the editors had to splice, but, given the divinity of the material, they couldn't cut. The volume that eventually appeared is, not surprisingly, full of repetitions and internal echoes. One must expect not to read a sequentially constructed narrative in the Qur'an, but to hear a set of themes and variations. To think in visual terms, it is not an exercise in linear perspective, but a synoptic view of a cosmic subject by a compound eye and from multiple angles; it is not just cubist but endlessly polyhedral. It is aware of its own potential infinitude:

> If all the trees on the Earth were pens and the seas were replenished after it with seven seas [of ink], the words of Allah would not be exhausted.

It is not that the Qur'an is physically long: even in translation, which is inevitably much wordier than the original, it is the length of a moderate paperback. But it has generated hundreds of commentaries, each many times the length of its subject, and the story of the commentator who spent thirty-six years delivering an oral exposition and still never got to the end bemuses, but doesn't surprise.

Part of the reason for this excess of exegesis is its multiple inbuilt ambiguities. Edward Said thought the inexplicability of the Qur'an to be an Orientalist cliché. But the inexplicability is there in the Qur'an:

> In it are verses that are entirely clear . . . and others not entirely clear . . . None knows its hidden meanings save Allah. And those who are firmly grounded in knowledge say, 'We believe in it: the whole of it [both clear and unclear] is from our Lord.'

In the end, what matters more in the Qur'an is not what it says, but how it says it. It is not the logic that counts, but the magic – 'magic' in its first and now forgotten sense: for the earliest Greeks, *magoi* were the keepers of oral tradition in Media. Muhammad compared the experience of receiving revelations to the shrill clang of a bell. The simile of striking, 'abstract' sound is appropriate: the ideas, as Ibn Khaldun said, are secondary to the words. It is a strange claim: surely truth is inherent in what you say, not how you say it . . . Yes; but not when what you say comes straight from God. For those of us who live in a post-supernatural environment, there may be an analogy with the visual arts: one can look at a portrait by, say, Francis Bacon, and sense that even if it is far from photo-realist, it reveals another sort of reality – that it contains a deeper truth about the subject, that it is inimitable and even in some way 'inspired'. For seventh-century hearers of the Qur'an, for whom supernatural beings were real and words the only art, there was no doubt about the inspiration and inimitability of Muhammad's revelations. The irony of it, as Geert Jan van Gelder has said, is that the dogma of the Qur'an's divine origin 'has denied Muhammad a place among the world's most gifted and original authors'.

The Qur'an inherited the ancient magic of the *kahin*'s speech. This magic, now promoted to divinity, is proof of the book's own truth. In the end, truth would out in the events of history.

The linguist Joshua Fishman pointed out that language, 'is not merely a carrier of content . . . Language itself is content . . .' The Qur'an is a particularly egregious case of language-as-content. This is not to say that the content it carries is unimportant; far from it. Many Muslims over the ages have pondered the content deeply, and digested its messages sincerely and faithfully. But it is possible to get away with much less. The ninth-century founder of the Hanbali school of Sunni Islam said,

> I saw the Almighty in a dream and asked, 'O Lord, what is the best way to manage to be near You?' He replied, 'My Word [i.e. the Qur'an], Ahmad.' I inquired, 'With understanding or without understanding?' He said, 'With or without understanding.'

AND THE WORD DWELT AMONG US, AND WE IN IT

In time, the Qur'an's inbuilt obscurities would invite conflicting interpretations and inspire bitter clashes; many of Muhammad's most sublime spiritual messages would be buried under the business of running a state, then ruling an empire. But to start with, the obscurities didn't matter. What counted – and still counts above all – was not logic, but the direct appeal to the ear, the heart, the soul, bypassing the brain. Ibn Qutaybah, a ninth-century polymath, said that the time of Moses was 'the age of magic' (transforming staff into serpent, dividing the Red Sea); that of Jesus 'the age of healing' (curing the sick, raising the dead); and that of Muhammad 'the age of *bayan*', of the clear, eloquent speech of the Qur'an. Earlier miracles were supernatural; Muhammad's was superlinguistic.

The Qur'an was Muhammad's main miracle. But for Arabs, it was enough. The proof of the miracle was and is the great number of people brought together by belief in it:

> If you [Muhammad] had spent all that is in the earth, you could not have united their hearts. But Allah has united them.

As al-Mas'udi put it, with the Qur'an Muhammad 'challenged the most eloquent of all peoples [Arabs] . . . and he stunned their hearing and disabled their minds'.

No clearer proof is needed: the Arabic language is not only the third of a series of conquests by Arabs of others, after the victories of arms and Islam. It was the first conquest, of themselves by themselves, and without it the others would never have happened: Arabs would have been a footnote to world history, not a continuing and important chapter. The language that bears their name both ensorcelled them ('enchanted' is not strong enough), and empowered them and their coming empire. The point needs to be restated, because the many books that the Arab chapter of history has inspired have never made it clearly enough. It is the reason we can speak of 'the Arab world' – really, the Arabic world, the Arabosphere – and the reason why that world is still alive, while the Roman world is as dead as its language. Arabic, as its early twentieth-century celebrant Mustafa Sadiq al-Rafi'i wrote, 'was built on a magical foundation which gives it eternal youth, never growing old or dying'. Some would disagree about its eternal youth; none can deny that it is still alive.

Jan Retsö has gone as far as saying that Muhammad and the Qur'an revived the whole idea of arabness, which had been on the verge of disappearing. Retsö is speaking of his own complex definition of *'arab*, as traditional soothsayers and guardians of local cults. It would be truer to say that whatever *'arab* had been or had become, Muhammad redefined them through the book he gave them, not just as guardians of marginal local cults but as the vanguard of a global culture. The culture would include non-Muslims and embrace non-Arabians. To quote al-Rafi'i again, 'The Qur'an is a linguistic nationality that unites disparate lineages to the Arabic language'.

Returning to my own earlier metaphor, the high formal language of pre-Qur'anic poetry had given Arabs their most prominent item of 'national dress'. Now, in the Qur'an, it also served to clothe a transcendent deity and thus make Him visible, if veiled. (It has been rightly said that the Qur'an is the equivalent not of the Gospels, but of Christ, the Logos: the Christian godhead veiled Himself in flesh and became man; the old high god of Mecca veiled Himself in a text, a textile of words.) But the consequences of the Qur'an went way beyond theology. Arabic, the national dress, had been loose. As the Islamic centuries progressed, exegetes and lexicographers would turn it into something much more uniform – a uniform that could be adopted to make Arabs of people far beyond Arabia. It was, and still is, formal wear: people feel uncomfortable in it, and speak day to day in the motley of dialects. And yet that difficult and formulaic tongue, stiff with the starch of millennia, is still the medium of reading and writing. It still unites Arabs 'from the Ocean to the Gulf'. Whatever 'Arab' has meant in the past – marginal camel herds, cultic guardians, tribal raiders – it now means, primarily, users of the Arabic language. As Munsif al-Marzuqi, the Tunisian intellectual and recent head of state, has written, 'Our [Arab] community, unlike all others, does not live in a land; it lives in a language'. He meant the old language that goes back via the Qur'an, and ultimately to the poetry and magical speech of pre-Islamic Arabia. Arabic is something to put on, a habit in its oldest meaning, but also something to *in*habit.

LA ILLAHA ILLA 'LLAH

If the stuff of the Qur'an is secondary to the style, the content to the form, certain messages stand out, and one above all others. It is the first phrase of the Islamic creed:

> There is no god but Allah

– lumpy in English, but in Arabic mellifluous, mantra-like and mesmeric:

> *La illaha illa 'llah.*

For the idol-rich Meccans, however, whose current economic boom was at least partly due to trading on the Ka'bah's popularity as a divine hypermarket, it would hardly be a popular mission-statement. In Mecca, there were lots of gods beside Allah: the place was crowded with images of deities from all over Arabia and beyond. But, looked at in a wider context, Muhammad was only following the regional zeitgeist. The Hijaz was the last great island of paganism in the Mediterranean-Arabian world, and Muhammad was going with the monotheistic swim. But which way would he go?

The One God in His various guises had been moving in on western Arabia in a long slow pincer movement. It began with the dissemination of Judaism to the north during the first millennium BC, and perhaps a tentative early monotheism in South Arabia with the worship of Dhu 'l-Sama', the God of Heaven, half way through that millennium. By the the fourth century AD, Christianity had a firm hold over the regions to the north, while a new indigenous monotheism spread in the south with the worship of al-Rahman, 'the Merciful' (about whom little is known except that He begins to supplant the old pantheon in inscriptions). Judaism was also to gain a foothold in the south, as we have seen with the early sixth-century ruler Yusuf As'ar; the Christian presence there increased with the Ethiopian takeover that ended Yusuf's rule. In the same century, Christianity also spread in the Ghassanid and Lakhmid Arab client-kingdoms in the north. There were major pockets of Judaism in the Hijaz itself, notably in Yathrib, Muhammad's future Medina. Even in pagan Mecca, Christianity made inroads: several Meccan Christians are known by name, and among the sacred furnishings of the holy of holies was that icon, the Virgin of the Ka'bah.

Most notably, the Hijaz was home to the *hanif*s whose monotheistic devotional poetry, as we have seen, shares features with Muhammad's message, including the term *islam*. The sharing may even go further than themes and isolated words. The *hanif* Khalid ibn Sinan al-Absi, who lived just before Muhammad's time and was accepted by him as the penultimate prophet, was said by some to have pre-empted him by reciting a whole chapter of the Qur'an, that known as the Chapter of Purity, or of Unity: 'Say,' it begins,

> He is Allah, One . . .

It is one of the shortest chapters, but it is the one most often recited after the opening chapter, and the purest distillation of Qur'anic theology.

Under this combined monotheistic pressure from without and within, paganism was looking more and more parochial; the old divinities were losing their powers. They were liable to rough treatment if they didn't do their job. In the mid-sixth century the poet Imru' al-Qays, for example, is said to have sought the sanction of the god Dhu 'l-Khalasah for avenging his father's blood, but when the god's divinatory arrows repeatedly said, 'Don't Do It', the poet lost his temper and snapped them. Similarly, the tribe of Banu Hanifah had an idol moulded from a mixture of dates, flour and ghee: when the deity refused to answer their prayers in a famine, they ate him. The growing impotence of the old idols meant that some strange consortiums appeared. Ibn al-Kalbi, for instance, mentions an oath to which the witnesses were that divinatory deity Dhu 'l-Khalasah, Allah and, to make assurance triply sure, the Christian God. Flexibility and eclecticism were the order of the dying pagan day.

For Meccans, however, Allah was the default deity. Their oaths were sworn,

> By al-Lat and al-Uzza and those who in them Believe,
> And by Allah, verily He is greater than both.

Assuming the lines are genuine, this and other similar oaths show how the Meccans, even if goddesses like al-Lat and al-Uzza and other deities were a fall-back, looked to Allah as their high god. As the Qur'an says of the pagan Meccans,

> And if you ask them who created them they will surely say, 'Allah'.

Also,

> And if you were to ask them who sends down water from the sky and gives life therewith to the earth after its death, they would surely answer, 'Allah'.

Allah's primacy in Mecca was even confirmed by the offer – if not the actual execution, in a famous recorded case – of human sacrifice. Muhammad's grandfather, Abd al-Muttalib, had vowed to Allah that if he fathered ten sons who lived to maturity, he would sacrifice one of them. The prayer was answered, lots were drawn, and Muhammad's father Abd Allah was chosen as victim – but, in the nick of time, ransomed by the substitute sacrifice of a hundred camels. The Abrahamic echoes are loud, even if inflation had raised the ransom from the ancient single ram.

Already in the centuries before Islam, Allah's supreme status in Mecca, and the town's sanctity, meant that He enjoyed a wide reputation among Arabs as a whole. It is impossible to assess rankings among the shifting pantheon of ancient Arabia, but He may have occupied a place similar to Zeus/Jupiter and Brahma among their own pantheons – the acknowledged but rather distant chairman of the board, whom most people felt happier approaching via intermediaries. Muhammad's achievement was to get so many Arabs to see Allah not just as the super-god, but the only God. And with theological unitarianism came both the idea of political unity, and the means of achieving it. But maybe, in this also, the revelation wasn't as revolutionary as it seemed.

MOST BEAUTIFUL NAMES

The old South Arabians, as we have seen, had for many centuries held notions of political unity deriving from worship of a shared deity. Saba, for example, was the core *sha'b* or 'people' of a wider commonwealth: other peoples who wanted to join this larger unity had to pay homage to the Sabaean 'national' deity, Ilmaqah, in an annual pilgrimage. It is likely that the Islamic idea of unity is an heir to these old notions, and perhaps even a descendant of them, at least collateral if not direct. That the Qur'anic concept of *habl Allah*, Allah's uniting and binding covenant, is the same as the Sabaean term for a divine covenant, *hbl*, is more than circumstantial evidence. So too is the shared concept of the ancient *sha'b*s being the children of their patron deities, and of the Meccans being *āl Allah*, the folk or family of Allah, as both the pre-Islamic Abd al-Muttalib and his grandson Muhammad put it.

There is no proof positive for the link; but the similarities between the South Arabian and Islamic systems are certainly more than coincidental, if probably less than conscious. A possibly conscious import from the South, however, is the most important alternative name for Allah, 'al-Rahman' ('the Merciful, the Most Gracious'), which had already been in use by southern monotheists for at least three centuries. Muhammad began to receive verses including this name about two years into the revelations. At first the Meccans were unhappy, but a verse descended to give the usage Allah's imprimatur:

> Say: 'Invoke "Allah" or invoke "al-Rahman". By whatever name you invoke Him [it is the same], for to Him belong the Most Beautiful Names.'

'Al-Rahman', together with its cognate 'al-Rahim', were given pole position as part of what would be the opening verse of the whole Qur'an:

> In the name of Allah, al-Rahman, al-Rahim.

The formula is still used at the head of all texts written by Muslims that have any pretence to being formal or official, and before all sorts of acts from getting married to having breakfast. That the divine name 'al-Rahman' was used first in South Arabia is undeniable. So too, perhaps, were some of the other 'Most Beautiful Names' mentioned in the Qur'anic verse, which highlight aspects of Allah's nature: 'Al-Bari' ' ('the Creator'), 'al-Mughith' ('the Reliever'), 'al-Khaliq' (also 'the Creator') and others appear in pre-Islamic South Arabian inscriptions as attributes of the One God. Was the adoption by the old Meccan high god of the names and attributes of His South Arabian self part of a conscious policy – to draw the southerners into Muhammad's unifying mission? It is a reasonable hypothesis, but again unprovable.

Even more debatable would be the idea of any conscious inspiration for Muhammad's project from the neighbouring empires of the north, those of the Byzantines and Sasanians. But it should be remembered that they, too, were increasingly promoting political union through religious orthodoxy, Christian and Zoroastrian. It is unlikely that Muhammad was aware of these trends in any detail. But within a few years of his death, his followers would absorb vast areas of those empires, and with them vast numbers of people who were used to being told that obedience to God and to Caesar, or to Ahura Mazda and the Shah, were same thing. For them, Islamic ideas about toeing a single sacred-secular line would not have seemed strange; equally, the still highly malleable Islam may itself have been shaped further by Byzantine and Persian ideas about orthodoxy, political and theological.

This was yet to come. For the moment, all the ingredients of what would be Islam were sourced locally. The genius of Muhammad (or, if you like, Allah) put them together in a heady cocktail, in which the political theology of South Arabia was mixed with the metaphysical theology of imported Christianity and Judaism, and poured out together in the supernatural, spellbinding language of the old *'arab* poets and seers. The mixture coursed around Arabia along the arteries of trade and raid, and reached the parts no other ideas could have reached. No wonder people had their hearing stunned and their minds disabled, as al-Mas'udi put it. And it all went even further –

to an ultimate unity both in heaven and on earth. To understand that this unitarianism works at both levels, as Adonis realized, is to grasp the key to Arab history: Muhammad gathered the word not only of Arabs, but of angels and of Allah Himself.

People being what they are, the earthly unity was doomed. 'And if your Lord had so willed,' the Qur'an admits,

> He could surely have made mankind one community. But they will not cease to disagree.

And yet the tension between heavenly ideal and earthly reality is one of the great forces driving human history.

FIRST FANS, FIRST FOES

The power of the Qur'an is evident in the way it magnetized from very early on a small but fervent, and growing, body of believers. Long before organized worship began, they would spend much of the night awake in prayer vigils. The Quraysh *ancien régime* was at first amused by this excess of zeal, then – as the implications of Muhammad's message sank in – horrified. It was precisely the pluralism of worship at Mecca that had made it so attractive to so many Arabians – that one-stop shop for idolators, marketing itself with all the acumen of the traders who had developed it. Here was someone preaching directly against that pluralism, as had Zayd ibn Amr, the campaigning *hanif*; they had run him out of town. And Muhammad's mission was going even further: many of the 'economic' messages in the Qur'an are truly revolutionary. For example,

> Woe to every slanderer and backbiter
> Who has gathered wealth and counted it:
> He thinks his wealth will make him last for ever.
> Far from it: he will be cast into the crushing Fire!

Muhammad's biographer Ibn Hisham narrates how the Qurashi Establishment warned their fellow townspeople that Muhammad's revelations were *sihr*, '[black] magic', that would force apart fathers and sons and thus destroy the community. On the latter point they were quite right.

Muhammad, the orphan since before his birth, had no father to be estranged; but a whole chapter of the Qur'an descended to curse his paternal uncle Abu Lahab and his wife and consign them to the eternal estrangement of hellfire. And when a son of Abu Bakr, one of Muhammad's first followers, fought against his own father in the coming Raid of Badr, it was far from the only case of its kind. The Qurashi old guard had foreseen, accurately, how their *'asabiyyah* would be dismantled, their comfortable and prosperous community destroyed.

But another community would be born. The wheel of fire was turning again, and it would be its biggest revolution ever. The spin-offs – lesser cycles of unity, meltdown and re-formation – still turn today and, in various degrees, affect us all.

CHAPTER SIX

GOD AND CAESAR

THE STATE OF MEDINA

SEVERANCE

Abu Sufyan, the pagan merchant-prince of Mecca, was astonished by the sight of the praying ranks at Medina. Never had he seen such discipline, he said, 'not among the noble Persians, nor the Byzantines with their braided locks!' Another onlooker, Urwah ibn Mas'ud, was equally amazed. He had visited the rulers of Ethiopia, Persia and Byzantium, he said,

> But I have never seen people more obedient . . . They stand around [Muhammad, as motionless] as if birds were perched upon their heads. At the mere gesture of a command from him they hasten to act. When he performs the ritual ablution they divide the [used] water among themselves [considering it blessed]. When he expectorates they rub their faces, their beards, and their skins with his sputum.

Muhammad was no longer just a harmless *hanif* – a monotheist devotee – or even, as he had more recently become in Meccan eyes, a subversive dissident preaching not just against Mecca's pagan traditions but also against its merchant plutocracy. Having realized that he was a prophet, prompted to speak by a force beyond his self and his control, he had also discovered, like all prophets, that he was without honour in his own country. He had found the logical, if extreme, solution: *hijrah*, a move to another country. And in that other country he had found not just honour, but obedience and adulation: he had created a super-*'asabiyyah*, a sense of solidarity and unity like none before.

The strength and potential of this new unity were obvious to Abu Sufyan and Urwah a few years after the *hijrah*, the move to distant Medina. But at first Muhammad's kinsmen, seeing how he was destroying their old *'asabiyyah* – dismantling the social structure of pagan Mecca – had been far from impressed. 'O Allah,' the Meccan Abu Jahl would soon cry out as he fought against Muhammad's raiders at Badr, 'bring woe upon him who more than any of us has severed the ties of blood!' The word *hijrah* was later to gain more meanings; but 'severance' is what it meant to the Meccans, and in a tribal setting where kinship ties real or imagined were the main defence against societal dissolution and anarchy, Muhammad's schism was shocking. Moving to a far land was what you did if you had committed murder within the tribe.

It was also the first step on a journey that would give Arabs a definitively active voice in the 'grammar' of world history. Although *hijrah* meant severance, it also came to mean mobility, exertion, salvation – not unlike the ethos of the old dissident refuseniks of tribalism, the *su'luk*s or 'vagabonds', but translated into a mass movement. *Hijrah* was immediately equated so closely with Islam that some early activists believed 'you cannot be a Muslim if you do not undertake *hijrah*'. Muhammad himself dismissed the idea, and said you could be a Muslim wherever you lived. But as we shall see, soon after his death when the far expeditions of conquest began, *hijrah* was again billed – this time officially – as a virtual prerequisite to Islam. Conversely, to return to one's old home and old ways – *ta'arrub*, literally '(re-)arabization' – was seen almost as apostasy. A whole redefinition of being Arab would come about: Arab mobility would be blown wide open; Arabs would be severed from their tribes, their roots, their ancestral pathways and pastures, even from their 'island' of Arabia, from everything that had always made them Arab.

That, at least, was the theory.

YATHRIB

With their *hijrah* of 622, however, Muhammad and his few score followers were following ancient practice by taking themselves off and forming an alliance with another tribal grouping. As it became clear that the Meccan old guard were planning to silence him – by exile, perhaps, or worse – Muhammad had first opened negotiations with the people of al-Ta'if with a view to moving there, but these had fallen through. With the inhabitants of Yathrib, a town 350 kilometres north of Mecca, he was successful. He already had a useful connection with the place: his father's father, Abd al-Muttalib, had been brought up there in his own Yathribi mother's house. That connection may have been significant to the people of Yathrib, many of whom (including Muhammad's great-grandmother's family) were of South Arabian origin and perhaps less fervently patrilineal than the Meccans; there is evidence that women played a much more independent role in ancient South Arabia than they did in northern, tribal societies. The Yathribis may also have been less fervently polytheist. Certainly that was the case with the other main ingredient of Yathrib's population – several tribes of judaized Arabs, or perhaps arabized Jews.

Several months after an advance party of his fellow *hanif*s made it to Yathrib, Muhammad arrived there in September 622. It is the first definite date in his life, and literally epochal (although the official epoch was actually made to start on 16 July 622, the beginning of the lunar year). The migrants found themselves in a place that was very different from their home town: whereas Mecca was hemmed in by hills, hidebound by ritual and crowded with gods and pilgrims, Yathrib was a much more open place, a sort of loose garden city whose diverse inhabitants lived in hamlets among the fields and date groves on which their livelihood depended. In place of natural defences or city walls, the landscape was punctuated by many small towers in which the people could take shelter from attack. Yathrib was open to incomers, too: its two main tribes, Aws and Khazraj, were themselves originally migrants from South Arabia; the Jews were also immigrants, possibly of varied origins, although legend sees them as refugees from the Babylonian king Nebuchadnezzar's campaigns early in the sixth century BC.

Pious tradition asserts that Muhammad was given a hero's welcome in Yathrib. 'The full moon has risen over us!' the Yathribis chanted, as people still do to bridegrooms when they arrive at their wedding parties. The citizens vied with one another to host him, and immediately put him in charge of their town. Why they should have treated the leader of a small band of refugees in this way – let alone rubbed themselves with his sputum – is not immediately obvious. It is reason enough for pious tradition, of course, that

Muhammad was who he was; no further explanation is needed. But Muhammad himself offered an explanation, saying, 'Medina was conquered by the Qur'an.' The claim makes sense: Yathrib – or Medina, as it was about to become – was one of the most literate places in Arabia beyond the old Lakhmid and Ghassanid spheres, and it is more than likely that the vanguard of Muhammad's followers had been busy not only broadcasting the mesmeric messages of the Qur'an's Meccan chapters to the Yathribis, but also delivering them in their written form – the unprecedented form of Arabic holy scripture – in preparation for Muhammad's arrival. But it may not be wholly cynical to imagine that Mammon influenced the Yathribis as well as God. Muhammad was, after all, a Meccan, from the boomtown of Arabian commerce. One of his first acts would be to declare the market of Yathrib a tax-free zone; the traditional market-day there was Friday, the day he now earmarked for congregational prayers. It did not become a 'sabbath' of shuttered shops: instead, the influx of worshippers would fuel a brisk Friday trade in the suq. The simple mosque Muhammad established, with its palm-tree columns and palm-frond awnings, also became Yathrib's new political headquarters. As they always had in pagan Mecca, political, commercial and spiritual spheres intersected.

In Yathrib, that third sphere began to take on distinctive form and colour. At first, the impressionistic content of Muhammad's monotheism began to take firmer doctrinal shape; much of its shape is comparable to that of material in Christian and, particularly, Jewish scripture. The Qur'an itself declares that it confirms the book of Moses in the Arabic tongue. The people of Moses evidently agreed: even later in the seventh century in a Jewish document, widely circulated, 'Muhammad's message was described as an act of God's mercy – *i.e.*, a true religion'.

As time went on, however, and Yathrib became known as Madinat al-Nabi, 'the City of the Prophet' (or simply as al-Madinah/Medina, the City), the Qur'an grew away from other monotheistic beliefs. The need to build a community, and to give it 'brand recognition', was most easily fulfilled by saying what that community was *not* – certainly not like the polytheists; but also not quite like the Jews or the Christians. Islamic identity solidified, as had Arab identity, through contact with others: through attraction, then repulsion. It was around this time that 'Muslim' started to be used as the official name for adherents of Muhammad's monotheism, rather than the broad-church old term, *hanif*. The realities of worldly rule were pulling against the universalist ideals of monotheism: the One God joins mankind together; men, in their quest for earthly powers, inevitably pull themselves – and their God – asunder.

A question hangs over this intensely formative period for Islam, and for the whole of Arab history: what part did the originally South Arabian element of Yathrib/Medina's people play in it all? The two tribes, Aws and Khazraj, are always seen by traditional history in an ancillary role, as the Ansar, the 'Helpers', of Allah and Muhammad. There are hints, however, that they too may have influenced the development of Islamic practice. Ritual ablutions, for example, had been part of ancient South Arabian worship, with channels and cisterns incorporated into temples at Marib and elsewhere; it seems the southerners had brought the practice with them to Yathrib. This may be another case – as with the divine name 'al-Rahman' and the whole idea of unifying 'political theology', the *habl* or binding covenant with a god – where old South Arabian practice accords with what was, or became, Islamic custom. The most successful of all attempts to unite Arabs – the Islamic state of Medina – may have its deepest roots in the non-Arab past of the old South, roots buried beneath the ground zero of the new era, the year AH 0.

The usual 'Orientalist' take is that there was an arabianization of Islam at Medina 'in direct response to the Jews' rejection' of Muhammad. But the arabianization was more accurately a de-judaization. Islam was already firmly planted in its Arabian setting, and was shaped by it all along.

THE SUPER-SOCIETY

The political shape of Medina was also moulded by traditional Arabian models. The new polity resembled the sort of tribal alliances that had been formed in the pre-Islamic past, and gave Muhammad paramountcy in resolving disagreements and taking decisions. Before, most such alliances had been sealed by oaths and rituals performed around fire; Muhammad, who knew so well the power of writing, had his alliance between the old groups of Yathrib society and the new incomers from Mecca set down in documents known today as the Constitution of Medina. Even in this, however, he was following tradition: his grandfather, Abd al-Muttalib, is said to have drawn up a written document of alliance with the tribe of Khuza'ah and to have hung it up in the Ka'bah.

But the new *ummah*, or community, that Muhammad founded went beyond the old model of tribal alliance. It was a super-tribe, owing its unity not to an ancestor real or imagined, but to the super-deity, Allah. The pagan Meccans had seen themselves as 'the family of Allah'; the old South Arabian peoples had been the 'children' of their respective patron deities. Allah in His Islamic guise is Creator but – heaven forfend! – not Procreator. Instead, the new community is fathered symbolically upon Abraham, the first monotheist; Muhammad's own wives are the 'mothers' of the community, and the individuality of its members is displaced by the person of Muhammad, who is

> closer to the believers than their own selves.

There were, however, a few unfraternal disunities. Not all the tribesmen of Aws and Khazraj were in favour of the incomers, and these dissidents built their own rival mosque-headquarters. Their leader, Abu Amir, was swiftly ousted; he escaped to pagan Mecca and from there to Syria, where he is said to have adopted Christianity. But to begin with, the community was generally pragmatic and inclusive: Muhammad's original Constitution took in not only the Jews of Medina and but even its polytheists.

Seen in isolation it might look revolutionary, a new start from that Year Zero. Looked at in context, against the *longue durée*, the state of Medina can be seen emerging from its Arabian background. True, everything about Muhammad and his community was superlative: he was a super-soothsayer with a super-daemon – the Archangel Gabriel, no less – to inspire him; Allah was the super-deity, and the *ummah* was Muhammad's super-tribe, Allah's super-*sha'b*; they had a super-*'asabiyyah*, and very soon it would take them on super-raids, to rustle not camels but empires. And yet it was all a superlative version of something that had been there in the Arabian past. This is something Arab historians themselves recognize: while non-Arab histories of Arabs tend to start with their subjects suddenly bursting in full cry on to the stage of world history with the new-born phenomenon of Islam, Arab historians tend to take a longer view that takes in the pre-Muhammadan millennia and sees 'the Island of the Arabs' as part of an archipelago of cultures and empires. In fact they usually take the longest *durée* possible and start with the Creation.

There was one major point of departure from the Arabian past, however. We do not know how much authority was wielded by the heads of the old

South Arabian *sha'b*-commonwealths, the *mkrb*s, but it seems unlikely that their rule was absolute. In the tribal tradition of the north, to which the new community was a more direct heir, the rule of chiefs was rarely autocratic – they governed by consent, and made decisions on the basis of consultation with fellow elders. To assume dictatorial powers – as did Kulayb, who shot the fateful arrow that set off the War of the Camel's Udder – was to invite nemesis. Muhammad, in contrast, speaking on behalf of Allah, could exercise not just a super- but a hyper-authority, and it soon become clear that there could be no opposition to it. When the question of who could use the traditional tribal grazing grounds came up, for example, he declared that from now on they belonged to Allah and His prophet; that is to say, they were for the use of the whole community, the *ummah*. In the cognate modern-day term, he had *ammama*, or 'nationalized', them.

As totality of control was established, everything that rejected it became an opponent, an Other that shaped the new community by reflex. The original pluralism of the *ummah* withered, and a culture of opposition, even antagonism, grew in its place. The opposition was literal: for Muhammad and his *hanif*s in the early days at Yathrib, the direction of prayer had been towards Jerusalem. Now, in the second year after the *hijrah*, there was a volte face of almost 180 degrees and the newly designated Muslims, 'Submitters', turned their backs on Zion and submitted their faces instead to Allah, the Lord of the Meccan Ka'bah. It was a 'conversion' in the most basic sense: a turning around. But it was also a turning back: the Arabianness of the new ideology was reasserting itself.

Antagonism increased towards other versions of monotheism. In contrast to early conciliatory pronouncements, new, more strident Qur'anic verses descended:

> O you who believe, take not the Jews and Christians as friends. They are but friends of each other, and if any among you take them [as friends], then surely he is one of them.

On the ground in Medina, the antagonism came to a head with the expulsion in 626 of one of the two Jewish tribes, Banu al-Nadir, and the seizure of their property. In the following year, 600 of the other Jewish tribe, Banu Qurayzah, were killed for allegedly acting as a fifth column for the pagan Meccans who, having realized how dangerous a rival Medina was becoming, had sent an army to besiege the city; the survivors were expelled. Qur'anic verses descended in justification.

Regarding this last point, it is clear that while the form of revelation remained as elevated as ever, the content moved distinctly down to earth in the Medina period. The need to decide who should belong in the new community, and then to build that community, called for constant divine intervention. Some editions of the Qur'an implicitly admit this change in the nature of revelation by labelling chapters 'Meccan' or 'Medinan'. A rare recent revisionist and visionary, the Sudanese Mahmud Muhammad Taha, went as far as claiming that 'The latter are clearly historical in nature and content and have no relevance to modern conditions'. He was hanged for apostasy in Khartum in 1985, in his mid-seventies. He still provokes strong reactions: the anniversary of his execution, 18 January, is commemorated (by some) as Arab Human Rights Day; conversely, I have been in a room that emptied at the mere whiff of some of his ideas.

With the shift from Mecca to Medina, Muhammad had come face to face with the challenges of founding a community and building it into a state headed by himself. Where previous religious figures, famously Jesus during his time in the wilderness, had rejected tempting offers of earthly power, Muhammad embraced it and made it part of his mission. Jesus was king of the Jews only in the sardonic inscription on the Cross; when Muhammad died, he was *de facto* lord of the Arabians – their *sayyid*, a courtesy title his descendants still accord themselves. The inevitable questions about power-building and power-holding in Medina had been answered by divine revelation: thus, while the Qur'an's core messages are worthy of the Prince of Peace, it can also touch on matters for *The Prince* of Machiavelli. This, and not the rejection of beliefs about the Crucifixion or the Trinity, is the biggest point of difference with Christianity. It has also left an enduring legacy. For most Islamic moralists, the business of gaining and keeping power has never in itself been tainted with suspicions of sin; they let rulers get on with it, and acquiesce in what often looks like moral ambiguity. Figures like Thomas Becket and Thomas More are rare enough in Christendom; they are all but unknown in Islam.

COMING WITH A SWORD

As the new state expanded, however, Muhammad was happy for Jews elsewhere to stay where they were – especially when they could work the land as sharecroppers, as they did at Khaybar, 150 kilometres north of Medina. And there were other continuities from before. One of these was on the military-economic front. At first, when Muhammad was militarily weak, Allah told him to

> overlook their [i.e. the unbelievers'] faults with gracious forgiveness.

With his gathering strength in Medina, this soon changed. 'Anthropology', Daniel Varisco points out, 'has . . . played a role in showing where Islam definitely does *not* come from', namely, not from 'the desert', with its 'never-ending cycle of feuds and raids that define the newer monotheism as violent and uncivil'. History confirms this: Islam comes from the urban setting of Mecca, and – as I hope I have shown – owes something to the ancient and eminently civilized, if not always non-violent, South Arabian past. Islam comes from all this, and within it from a deep fount of spirituality, from a sense of almost inexpressible wonder at the majesty of creation, the mystery of eternity, and the perfect oneness of the divine originator of it all. The most vehement atheist would be hard put to deny the presence of something supernatural in the earliest revelations; the most violent cynic is disarmed by the beauty of holiness, 'never – nowhere – aught so solemn, so impressive as this', declared the arch-cynic Richard Burton on first contemplating the Ka'bah. Islam comes from this, and it will return to that perfect oneness of its origin: 'Whatsoever is on it [i.e. earth] will perish,' the Qur'an says of the end of time,

> And the face of your Lord will remain.

So far on this great return journey, however, it has passed through periods in which, being a sociopolitical ideology as well as a faith, it has made use of the military option. One of these periods began a couple of years after the *hijrah*.

Along with the power of the Qur'an, the personal magnetism of Muhammad, and the shuttling of envoys, the successful use of raiding tactics was a reason behind the rise of Medina as a power. It was in that light that the earliest Arabic sources view that rise: the earliest biographies of Muhammad are called *kutub al-maghazi*, 'books of raids', and they are serial accounts of his armed expeditions. There were almost thirty major operations, and

Muhammad took an active part in about a third of them. There is more to the 'books of raids' than derring do, but in essence they belong to the tradition of the 'Days of the Arabs', the accounts of pre-Islamic battle days that constitute the oldest Arab historiography.

The first major encounter was in many ways the most fateful, and it was Muhammad's success in it against superior numbers that convinced him and his people that Allah was on their side, militarily as well as morally. A rich Meccan caravan was returning from Syria in AH 2 under the leadership of Abu Sufyan (the pagan grandee who would be so amazed at Muslim discipline). Muhammad, with about 300 men, decided to hit the Meccans where it hurt – in the main artery of their most lucrative trade. He set out to intercept the caravan at a watering-place called Badr, on the trade route from Mecca to Syria, south-west of Medina; but Abu Sufyan got wind of the planned attack and sent ahead to Mecca for reinforcements. By the time the Meccan force of more than 900 arrived at Badr, Abu Sufyan had taken the caravan by a different route; the Meccan reinforcements decided, however, that they should teach the dissidents of Medina a lesson. It all went horribly wrong for them. Seventy were killed and about the same number captured, to Muhammad's losses of fifteen dead. The sense of righteous triumph on the Medinan side may be imagined. AH 0 was the start of the epoch; AH 2, the year of Badr, the turning-point of Muhammad's fortunes, was the true beginning of the epic.

Popular memory views such battles in black and white, goodies versus baddies. But, as ever, the reality was more complex. As already mentioned, a son of Abu Bakr, Muhammad's right-hand man, fought on the pagan Meccan side. So did al-Abbas, Muhammad's uncle and eponymous ancestor of the future five-hundred-year dynasty of caliphs. And there were other elisions between the pagan past and the Islamic future. Just as in the pre-Islamic Days of the Arabs, battle poetry played a part on both sides at Badr and in later confrontations. In the encounter at Uhud in AH 3 or 4, a rare setback for the Muslims, part of the pagan Meccans' success was due to Abu Sufyan's wife Hind, mother of the first caliph of the future Umayyad dynasty. 'We are the Tariq girls,' she chanted (the meaning of 'Tariq' here is uncertain), egging the Meccans on,

> We walk on carpets fair
> Our necks are hung with pearls
> And musk is in our hair

If you advance we'll hug you
Or if you flee we'll shun you
And we'll no longer love you.

Lest she come over as a bobby-soxed cheer-leader, it must be added that Islamic tradition presents her in a more ghoulish light: another uncle of Muhammad, Hamzah, was killed at Uhud fighting for his nephew, and Hind is said to have mutilated his corpse and gnawed his liver. On Muhammad's side, the most famous poet was Hassan ibn Thabit, already celebrated for his odes in praise of the Ghassanid kings. As the prophet and his revelation, so the poet and his rhymes: the angel Gabriel, who acted as medium for the transmission of the Qur'an, is said to have doubled as Hassan's poetic daemon or muse in the battle poems instead of an outmoded *jinni*. We do not know what Muhammad made of other continuities, like Hassan eulogizing him with a traditional image of fine wine and kisses, although the Prophet is supposed to have said, 'Throw dust in the faces of the panegyrists.' Another would-be panegyrist, A'sha Qays – encountered earlier, improving girls' marriage prospects with airbrushed poetic descriptions – was dissuaded from working for Muhammad by the pagan Meccans, who bought him off with camels and frightened him off with warnings about the teetotalitarian life of Medina.

There was yet another continuity with the Arabian past. The raids were not unproductive of booty; Muhammad, as a traditional raiding-redistributing chief, controlled a fifth of the proceeds and handed shares of it to his kin, the descendants of Hashim. He is said to have made a point of declaring that he was the only prophet for whom booty had been made licit. But it was all sanctioned in any case by Arabian tradition, and further sanctified by the Qur'an, for example by its chapter called 'The Spoils of War'. The business of shares and distribution was all carefully controlled: warnings of hellfire descended to ensure that no one cheated. Sensibly, Muhammad also earmarked substantial sums from his chief's fifth to distribute to opponents, in order to bring them round to his cause –

those whose hearts are reconciled,

as the Qur'an describes them.

'Do prophets come with a sword?' asked a ninth-century Christian Iraqi commentator, thinking of the generally quietist beginnings of his own faith and comparing them with those of the two other great monotheisms. That writer's answer was a clear 'No'. A fairer answer in Muhammad's case, however, is that he didn't come with a sword at first, but that the precedents of the Arabian past, the pressures of the present, and the promises of the future, all conspired to place a sword in his hand; and that perhaps other more apparently pacific prophets would have taken up swords if they had left their countries, lands where they were without honour, and had gone on their own *hijrah*s – in other words, if they had seen their revolutions through. For the *hijrah* was a severance, but also a transition from spiritual and moral activism to political action. At the time, political action meant, as it still usually means in the region, forming a new *'asabiyyah*, a new solidarity group, taking up arms, taking over as much as you could and holding it for as long as you could. Indeed, very soon the word *hijrah* would come to mean the resettlement of tribesmen in garrison towns. One authority bluntly glosses *hijrah* itself as 'military service'. In one sense, a religion is a cult with an army; but while most cults take a while to get hold of one, Islam got its army almost straight away.

That Muhammad was so successful in his political and military roles at Medina should never cause anyone, whether Muslim or not, to forget the spiritual and moral underpinnings of his mission, the Meccan years. They are the heart of the faith of Islam; they are what will last. Those few eventful years at Medina brought about the development of Islam as a sociopolitical phenomenon. But they also form the second of the three instalments of the Arab national roman-fleuve, along with the legendary migrations from the ancient South, and with the coming conquests across three continents. It is a drama in, and on, three stages – Marib, Medina and the world – and it is part of what now inspires some young European Muslims to migrate from the lands of the heathen and make, via the 'Islamic State' and dreams of world conquest, for the fourth, final and eternal stage: heaven.

I have mentioned an aim of 'de-islamizing' Arab history. To do so would, in Samir Kassir's opinion, free Arabs of a 'millstone' and reclaim their history from its current malaise. Looking at Muhammad in Medina, I realize it is not possible fully to do so. As one commentator has written, 'Islam is a religion, but it is also a form of religious nationalism . . . Some have gone so far as to call Arabism and Islam "unseparated Siamese twins"'. Separation can be bloody, as with the severance of those ancestral Meccan twins Hashim and Abd Shams, as with Muhammad's *hijrah*. And sometimes it seems that

Arab and Islamic history are conjoined not just at the hip, but at the heart. That said, what we can and should still do is to see Islam not as the start of it all, but as a part of it all. Not only is the 'millstone' no monolith; it was also carved from much more ancient and variegated rock than might at first appear.

THE SMILING GUARDIANS

Mecca capitulated in January 630. Medina had gained the military upper hand, but had not scored the decisive victory; there had been parleys and truces; there had been that reconciling of hearts and minds with the proceeds of raiding, and very little fighting for the previous two years. In the end, the Qurashi old guard knew that even if they might be able to beat Muhammad eventually, it would probably be more profitable on balance to join him. It would not be the last time in Arab history that an *ancien régime*, in order to prolong its life, threw itself into the arms of a young ideology. In more recent times the example of Al Sa'ud and the Wahhabis comes to mind.

By joining Muhammad's revolution, the Meccan Establishment had not exactly hijacked it; but they had hacked into it, and were probably happy for it to serve their own ends. Allah alone knows the true intentions of Abu Sufyan, his son the future caliph Mu'awiyah, and all the others who came over to Muhammad's side. But it is hardly unlikely that the main chance played a part in their decision, as well as the spiritual message (and that ready money to reconcile hearts). After all, two great figures of the Meccan past had made the city a successful pilgrimage centre – Amr ibn Luhayy and Qusayy, who between them had brought the gods of the Levant and Arabia together in one place; Muhammad, in a sense, was taking their idea one stage further, by bringing those gods together in one God. The old Meccan chiefs may have sensed that, in an age when monotheism was eclipsing the ancient pantheons, Muhammad's plan would draw ever more pilgrims – and cash – to their city. What is clear is that the pagan Meccans had made a wise decision: their recognition of Muhammad, and Muhammad's confirmation of the Ka'bah's centrality, have ensured the prosperity of their city ever since, and for the foreseeable part of eternity.

With Mecca as the shrine of the ultimate monotheism, the pilgrimage destination was streamlined and rebranded, but the management remained the same. In one department it has remained the same ever since. The

Qurashi clan of Banu Shaybah, who started out as the sacristans of the goddess al-Uzza and then were granted the keys to the Ka'bah, still hold the keys to the Ka'bah today. An old Meccan saying went, 'The Shaybah clan are wreathed in smiles: this must be a day for opening the Ka'bah', because, of course, they charged entrance fees. After so long, the smiles must be part of their genetic make-up, a *risus sardonicus*. In other senses, too, Muhammad's revolution turned out to be more in the nature of evolution. Mecca's ruling clans had undergone a shake-up, and the city's wealth would be redistributed, to some extent, across the branches of the Quraysh family tree. But life went on, pilgrims circumambulated the Ka'bah as ever, and trade circulated along Mecca's mercantile arteries. For the city's people, the Annus Hegirae, the Year Zero, was far from being a Khmer Rouge-style reset of history.

But in yet another sense, the revolution had only just begun. Muhammad, who united in himself the old voices of *kahin*, *khatib*, *sha'ir* and *sayyid* but also transcended them, now went on to unite perennially dissonant Arab voices like no one else before or since.

MEDINA MEDIA

Even before Mecca's capitulation, a truce with the pagan city in 628 had enabled Muhammad to focus his burgeoning forces on more distant Arabian horizons. At times, the force was military. Traditional raiding tactics only went so far; in the case of al-Taif, the fortified urban centre of a fertile area south-east of Mecca and power base of the tribe of Thaqif, heavier weaponry was needed. A siege catapult and a cow-hide *dabbabah* – a *testudo* or shelter for sappers – were used to invest the town in 631. They show how much the state of Medina had grown in confidence, and how it had opened to military innovation (*dabbabah*, literally 'crawler', is now the word for 'tank' in the military sense). But other campaigns were also afoot, using other tactics and technologies. At least for the moment, Islam would conquer most of Arabia without the use of arms.

Over the preceding century, Muhammad's Qurashi ancestors had spun a web of commerce across much of the peninsula. In this web, a warp of trade routes combined with a weft of tribal alliances; the balance of complementary interests – those of nomad carriers and guards on the one hand, and of the merchant masterminds of Quraysh on the other – gave the system tensile strength and durability. It was this web that Muhammad used to spread his message, ultimately realigning the network towards himself, in a way comparable, perhaps, to that in which the early twentieth-century Bolsheviks used their close contacts with workers on the imperial rail network to spread their ideology across the Tsar's domains.

Muhammad achieved this realignment by diplomacy, and also with the help of technology. As he was also doing with the Qur'an, the supposedly 'illiterate' prophet was harnessing the media, and especially the barely exploited development of Arabic writing, to communicate with distant tribes and peoples. 'The only phenomenon with which writing has always been concomitant', wrote Claude Lévi-Strauss, 'is the creation of cities and empires, that is the integration of large numbers of individuals into a political system'. Muhammad already understood the possibilities of writing as a tool of control: in his Meccan days, written public announcements (like that of his grandfather's tribal alliance) had sometimes been fixed to the wall of the Ka'bah – presumably not in the expectation that anyone other than the score or so of literate Meccans could actually read them, but rather as a form of official proclamation, like publication in a gazette. But for most Arabs, especially tribal Arabs, writing in any form was a new and even more powerful phenomenon, invested with magic and mana. Its political potential was enormous, and Muhammad made full use of it.

Medina also had a recent tradition of literacy, and Muhammad set about enhancing it. In addition to his own Muslim Meccan scribes, already at work recording Allah's words in the scriptorium of Qur'anic revelation, he gave orders that each literate pagan captive from the Raid of Badr should have his ransom commuted into teaching ten Medinan boys how to write. Alleged originals of documents issued by Muhammad and supposed to have survived into later centuries give an idea of the ends to which he used writing. Apart from divine revelation, there was an example of his own wisdom preserved on the spot – a *hadith* about the nature of faith, dictated to his cousin and son-in-law Ali. But other documents were more prosaic, such as a land-grant written on the stem of a palm-branch, demands for tribute from a Jewish community and from the Kindi ruler of Dumah, and a letter to the Hadramis, telling them to pray to Allah and pay their dues to Medina. Many texts of letters like this last one survive, and if some are pious fabrications, they probably do reflect the output of the Medina secretariat. Such missives, written in a script that was regarded with supernatural awe, recited by eloquent missionaries, must have had an impressive effect on their recipients. To the Yemenis, who had used the archaic South Arabian script but are supposed to have abandoned it by the time of Islam, Muhammad sent not only letters, but a teacher of Arabic letters: 'I have sent you a scribe,' he said to them of his envoy Mu'adh ibn Jabal.

Less clear is the part played in this campaign of integration by the supreme example of the scripted supernatural, the Qur'an. Muhammad has already been quoted saying that Medina was 'conquered' by it. Clearly, the Qur'an was also being broadcast further afield in some form. Its language was accessible to most Arabs, whatever their everyday dialect, as it is the same as the high language of poetry that had been infiltrating every corner of the peninsula for centuries: as al-Mas'udi said, it 'stunned their hearing and disabled their minds'. But to begin with, it probably stunned them in bits and pieces, orally transmitted, particularly the shortest, earliest, most powerful chapters. The text as a whole is too diffuse, and often too difficult, to work as propaganda, besides which, there was no text-as-a-whole, no collected edition, until well after Muhammad's death. But Muhammad had yet more words to deploy in his media campaign.

Observing events outside my window, and wondering about the extreme rapidity with which people have been converted to a new cause, it is clear that what has stunned them into belief in it is not long and subtle holy texts – and certainly not logical argument – but a blunter instrument: the slogan. Here we have the Iranian-origin *sarkhah*, the 'yell':

> Allah is great!
> Death to America!
> Death to Israel!
> The curse of Allah upon the Jews!
> Victory to Islam!

Belted out *en masse* at public occasions – Friday prayers, rallies, funerals – it is 'gathering the word' by brute force. (The Arabic for 'missile', *sarukh*, 'yeller, screamer', is cognate with *sarkhah*.)

It may not always be sound practice to extrapolate backwards, but I suspect that if Medina was conquered by the Qur'an, most Arabs were conquered by slogans and sound-bites that were more eloquent and meaningful than the ones I hear today. First of all there was

Allahu akbar
Allah is great/the greatest

(i.e., your old tribal deities are puny). Then there was the mellifluous, memorable,

La illaha illa 'llah
There is no god but Allah

(so in fact your tribal deities don't exist at all). And then,

Muhammadun rasulu 'llah
Muhammad is Allah's messenger

(so everything he says is unquestionable). The devil may have all the best tunes, but Allah has even better lyrics.

The lyrics have had an amazingly long run. Those same slogans still work perfectly today, and the community is still 'on message': the first words a newborn Muslim hears are the second and third phrases above, whispered into the right ear; they are also whispered into the ear of a dying Muslim. Christians are summoned to worship by bells, joyful but meaningless; Muslims are summoned to their more frequent prayers by words – including those of the three phrases above, now amplified (4,000 loudspeakers in the new system recently installed at the Meccan mosque, and audible 9 kilometres away). They are uttered constantly as interjections. They appear on the flag of Saudi Arabia and on the piratical-looking black and white banner of the so-called Islamic State. Over his life, a Muslim will hear and pronounce them countless times: if he had just one mosque within earshot and lived to seventy, he would be told that God is great three-quarters of a million times. It is almost as hard to stop believing as it is to stop breathing.

Muhammad was thus the messenger of Allah, and also His messager. He and his followers disseminated the word of Allah in writing, and also distilled it into oral/aural slogans. These were innovative ways of creating an unprecedented *esprit de corps* among Arabs, a super-*'asabiyyah*. And the slogans have played their part not just in maintaining *'asabiyyah* but also in preserving *'arabiyyah*, the Arabic language. As the eleventh-century observer of non-Arabs, al-Biruni (himself Iranian in origin), noted,

> How often have tribes of subjects congregated together, in order to impart a non-Arabic character to the state. But they could not succeed in

> their aim, and as long as the call to worship sounds in their ears five times a day . . . they have got to submit.

Muhammad's media, spoken, written and sound-bitten, poured out of his Medina. Qur'anic chapters and sacred slogans did the rounds of the Arabian network. So too did written invitations, or summonses, delivered by literate envoys to tribal chiefs. The chiefs were intrigued, responded to the call and went to Medina. There, like Abu Sufyan and Urwah, they were magnetized by Muhammad's power and personality – and, in a hierarchical society, if you magnetize the chief you attract the whole tribe. It was all perhaps less a matter of Muhammad 'gathering the word' than of his occupying the silence with his own words, his messages. Nothing quite like them had been heard before. To use Martin Nowak's expression again, language enables dominance through the insertion of ideas, and how much more powerful the ideas will be if, as in early seventh-century Arabia, there are no preconceptions to counter them.

Delegations flocked to Muhammad from ever further afield, especially in 630–1. Some, notably Christian Arabs from Najran and from north-eastern Arabia, came not to 'convert' but to express their allegiance to the rising power: *islam*, 'submission' in more than one sense, was (in some ways still is) as much a matter of politics as of dogma. Diplomatic contacts were established with Christian Ethiopia and Constantinople: the Byzantine emperor sent Muhammad a fur coat, which the Prophet tried on before passing it on to the Negus, who probably had more need of it in his chilly Abyssinian highlands. Tribes and peoples from afar became allied with Muhammad, including by numerous marriages. Something of the tension between the rising and falling powers of Arabia comes out in an anecdote about Muhammad's wedding night with Asma', a daughter of the old ruling family of Kindah. When invited to the nuptial bed, she replied at first, 'Does royalty give itself to trade?' But the prophetic charisma worked on her too.

It seemed to work on everyone. More and more Arabians entered the contract to pray and pay – to pray to Allah, to pay allegiance on earth to His prophet, and to pay the dues of membership. It is unclear how much the latter amounted to at the beginning; rules concerning the amount of *zakah*, 'alms tax', were only formulated later. But sums were probably not great. Still, the very idea of any payment at all was anathema to many Arabians – certainly to *badw* – and the fact that they agreed to it shows just how forceful

Muhammad's character was. And if that force was not enough by itself, he could always fall back on using one group to put pressure on another: in particular, he employed nomad tribes like Hawazin, who had long roamed the western and central peninsula, as persuaders.

Little persuasion was needed. Success bred success, and then the fear of being left behind by the bandwagon – although in the generally wheelless world of the peninsula, the bandwagon was a caravan. Chief after chief, tribe after tribe, they tagged on to the ever-lengthening line that snaked around Arabia, knowing that the short term offered safety in numbers, and the longer term a chance of profit, whether earthly or heavenly. The caravan effect worked brilliantly, and peninsular Arabia was united for the first time in its history. It would also be the last time.

A PERSIAN FACTOR?

There is an alluring possibility about the ultimate reason behind this unprecedented unity: that the state of Medina was a response to Persian encroachment on the Arabian subcontinent. This has been mooted by at least one recent historian, and at first sight it is a perfectly plausible idea. The Persians had a powerful presence – a viceroy, no less – in the south-west, in Yemen; they had long been active and influential in the east, in the region of Bahrain; recently they had been scoring notable successes against the Byzantines in the north, in the Levant and even Egypt. It does all look like a triple-pronged attack – not unlike how Shi'i Iran's influence in Lebanon, Iraq, Bahrain and now Yemen feels to the rulers of Saudi Arabia and the states of the Gulf littoral. Further odd pieces of evidence may support the idea of widespread Persian penetration, like the claim that Khalid ibn Sinan al-Absi (acknowledged by Muhammad as the last prophet before himself) saved Arabia from wholesale conversion to the Persian state religion, Zoroastrianism: he had gone the rounds of the peninsula's growing number of Zoroastrian fire-temples, snuffing out the sacred flames which were the focuses of their worship.

The idea that Muhammad's unitary state was a closing of Arab ranks in the face of Persia's forward policy may, therefore, not be unfounded. The evidence, however, is circumstantial. Like crop circles, the grand designs of geo-politics often only become apparent from the heightened perspective of future historians; at the time, on the ground, they can be invisible. Also like crop circles, the grand designs may never have been what they are claimed to be. In Muhammad's mind, standing up to the Persians may well have been a factor in his design of a new state. He had a clear aim to unite the tribes, as Kindah had tried to do, and also to forge a greater unity that took in the peoples of the old southern civilizations. Part of the new, all-embracing Arab identity had been expressed in the apposition of *'arab* to *'ajam*, of Arabs to non-Arabs, and especially to Persians. And there is a hint in the main piece of evidence, the Qur'an, to support the idea of the anti-Persian beginnings of Medina – a statement that Muslims will rejoice at a coming victory of the Byzantines, presumably over their main, Sasanian Persian foes. In the end, however, it is only a hint. Moreover, Muhammad's successor Abu Bakr would actively court the Persian interlopers in Yemen, and use them against his Arab opponent, al-Aswad. On the ground, in real time, realpolitik is what counts, not grand designs.

THE WORST IN UNBELIEF

Within the unprecedented unity Muhammad was creating there were inbuilt dangers. The new community inherited the strengths of the Meccans' trans-Arabian network, that compact between urban traders and nomad traffickers; it also inherited its tensions. The *a'rab*, the *badw* proper, had always been distinguished by their love of autonomy: it has been called the basic premise of their life. But that clearly would not fit happily into the new, all-encompassing *ummah* with its total obedience to Allah's will as expressed by Muhammad.

Muhammad was wary of the *a'rab*. It is claimed that he said, 'I have never heard tell of an *a'rabi* whom I wished to set eyes on, unless it be Antarah', a famous poet and hero, son of a black slave mother. Muhammad and his *ummah* needed the raiding capabilities of the *a'rab* in order to expand; at the same time, these capabilities had to be carefully controlled so as not to threaten the *ummah* itself. To put the dilemma another way, the bedouin *a'rab* were dynamic, but also potentially disruptive and destructive; the settled members of the *ummah* contributed security and stability, but also the likelihood of stasis. The two forces pulled in different directions, and the danger was that the *ummah* would be pulled apart. Muhammad's close companion and second successor, Umar, would describe the bedouins as, 'the origin of the Arabs and the material of Islam'. But much of that material was raw and very volatile. Allah Himself had described them in the Qur'an as

> the worst in unbelief and hypocrisy.

In contrast, Muhammad said that, 'faith is Yamani, wisdom is Yamani', and by 'Yamani' he was almost certainly referring to the traditional antithesis of the *a'rab*, the settled, civilized peoples of al-Yaman, the South.

BELONGING AND BELIEVING

The *a'rab* exasperated Muhammad because they added another tension to his unifying project – between *islam* and *iman*, 'submission' and 'belief':

> The *a'rab* say, 'We are believers.' Say [to them, Muhammad], 'You are not "believers." Say instead, "We have submitted [*aslamna*]," for belief has not yet entered your hearts.'

The idea of belief-less or faith-less *a'rab* recurs throughout the Islamic half of Arab history. Sometimes it takes a comic turn. For example, a group of bedouin were overheard early in the eighth century praying, in verse, for rain:

> Between us, Lord, things really should better –
> Like old times, when You made our weather wetter.
> So send us rain, O You with no begetter!

In the last verse, the rude bedouins are casting aspersions on God's parentage: 'You with no begetter!' means, bluntly, 'you bastard!' (They are also, of course, hitting the theological nail on the head: God is uncreated, unbegotten.) In recent years, too, far from the idea that life in the wilderness inspires contemplation of the eternal, there was a general assumption among many urban Muslims that the wilder nomad Arabs may have been nominally Muslim but had as much sense of the divine as the wilder beasts.

To return to the Qur'anic verse, while it is revealing about attitudes to the bedouins, it also has a further and very surprising import: that one could apparently be a *muslim*, a 'submitter', without being a *mu'min*, a 'believer'. *Islam*, it implies, is outward, public, impersonal, to do with society and politics; *iman*, dwelling in the heart, is inward and private, to do with one's personal relationship with Allah. Muhammad, building a community and a state, was well aware of the two-track nature of religion. It has even been said, perhaps justly, that 'It is very doubtful that Muhammad ever thought of the socioreligious community he founded in Medina as a universal religion'. Plenty of Qur'anic verses show that Jews and Christians were believed to share in *iman*, in that heartfelt belief, by virtue of their monotheism; they could also become tribute-paying associates of the Islamic state. The faith-less bedouin, conversely, could be full, 'card-carrying' members of that state as *muslim*s, submitters, without believing inwardly in its spiritual truths. But perhaps even to describe the community of Medina as 'socioreligious' could be misleading, given the resonances of the English word 'religion': scholars who have studied the reaction to Muhammad's revolution by contemporary poets – the nearest thing to objective observers – see the majority of them as considering Islam to be 'a social and political movement rather than a profound spiritual experience'.

Islam began as a profound spiritual experience with Muhammad's Meccan revelations. Given time and space, it was to regain that spirit. But during the first state-forming decade at Medina in particular, material considerations could at times outweigh spiritual ones: the important thing was to get everyone, including the Meccan aristocracy and the *a'rab*, on your side – whether by subduing them, subsidizing them, or suborning them with the lure of booty – whatever they believed in their heart of hearts. It didn't matter that the spirit was weak as long as the flesh was willing. Provided public conduct was correct, joining the praying ranks, saying 'Yes' to the earthly leader as well as saying 'Amen' to God, conscience could remain a private matter. It is the converse of the state of affairs in the individualist 'West' today, where institutional religion has nose-dived, but where many individuals keep up a deep spirituality. The sociologist Grace Davie has described their condition as that of 'believing without belonging'. In Muhammad's Arabia, the *a'rab* of that Qur'anic verse belonged without believing.

There is an even greater difference, however, between seventh-century Arabia – perhaps between the past of the world as a whole – and the 'West' now. In the former, belonging and believing were contrapuntal but complementary terms, two poles of the same globe; between the poles lay a sliding scale, from politics to piety. Arabic *din*, Sanskrit *dharma*, Latin *religio*, might all be rendered by the English 'religion', but that last word, with its post-Protestant focus on personal piety, skews the English reader to one of the two poles, to seeing religion as primarily a matter of belief. Believing is only part of it. Belonging is the other part, and humans have been saying 'Amen' to God and 'Yes' to Caesar in the same breath as long as gods and caesars have existed. Islam, with its doctrine of total political and theological *tawhid*, unitarianism, is only a heightened example of the phenomenon.

THE DEATH OF MUHAMMAD

A doctrine of unitarianism, however, is not the same as a durable unity. Muhammad was to leave a degree of social and political cohesion unparalleled in all the already long history of Arabs. But he also left a question hanging – that of a successor. Answered unequivocally, it might have guaranteed the unity for at least some of the equally long Arab history after him. The question remains unanswered still.

Towards the end of February 632, Muhammad led his followers from Medina to his Meccan birthplace in what came to be known as the Farewell Pilgrimage. The sermon he preached at its culmination – from camel-back, in the style of his old inspiration, the itinerant preacher Quss ibn Sa'idah – began with a premonition of his own death: 'I do not know if shall meet you in this place again, after this year.' His sermon went on speak of the sacrosanctity of blood and property, and of matters such as marital relations and legacies. But perhaps its most striking passage is this:

> By Allah I bear witness, O my people, that your Lord is one, and that your father is one: for you are all the children of Adam, and Adam is of dust. The most noble of you in the sight of Allah is he who is most pious. Allah is the Most Knowing, the Omniscient. Nor is any Arab superior to any non-Arab, except in piety.

Some versions add, 'nor is black superior to white'. If Muhammad had not always thought of the community he founded as universal, then perhaps this was another premonition – that his message would one day reach around the globe. Then again, the community of Medina was already heterogeneous, and included Persian and black slaves and freedmen. Whatever else it means, it is a clear statement of inclusiveness.

Despite that first intimation, of mortality, the matter Muhammad did not touch on in his sermon was that of succession. It arose all too soon and too suddenly: two months after his return to Medina, he fell ill with the fever that would kill him. During his last ten days he was unable to lead prayers, but said that his companion Abu Bakr should do so in his place. This, and the fact that this same, closest companion had also led the pilgrimage the previous year, were taken by most as evidence that Muhammad wished Abu Bakr to succeed him at the head of the community. Not everyone was to agree immediately, however, and although the lines of contention within the community were at first no more than hairline cracks, and soon concealed by the need for consensus, in less than thirty years the craquelure would widen into chasms.

Muhammad died in the arms of his youngest wife, Abu Bakr's daughter A'ishah. In view of all the pious memories that would spiral out of his life – those potential million traditions – it would be hard to write a thoroughly objective obituary of Muhammad the prophet. It is almost harder to obituarize Muhammad the man, except in fragments: he was a fan of horse-racing, but didn't mind losing; he would eat sitting on the ground, and would lick his fingers; he never beat a slave; he was never seen to laugh with fully open mouth. Regarding the last point, he did not lack a sense of humour, and rather dry humour. Once an old woman asked him if Allah let old women into paradise, and when he told her that He didn't, she wept – at which Muhammad said, 'He changes them first into nubile virgins!' Muhammad also had a sense of fun, and was once spotted on all fours with his little grandsons al-Hasan and al-Husayn on his back, calling out to them, 'O what a fine camel you've got!' These glimpses have the feel of anecdotes that one couldn't, and wouldn't, make up. But many of the less impressionistic elements of the picture are missing – even how old he was. Suggestions as to his age at death varied between sixty and sixty-five lunar years, but doubts about the dating of the Day of the Elephant could mean that he was older.

It is said that, like some of the famous pre-Islamic warriors, Muhammad rarely appeared in public unveiled. With time he has become ever more invisible, veiled in ever denser layers of piety. For most Muslims the very idea of physically portraying him is sacrilege. Even in the looser tradition of Shi'i Iran, other prophets may be depicted, but Muhammad's face is always shown as a blank.

LEGACY

One scholar who has studied the subject at length has claimed that 'the concept of *'arab* [had been] on the verge of disappearing altogether' before

Muhammad. And yet the concept hadn't disappeared: it was aired regularly if infrequently in pre-Islamic poetry; it was a rarely articulated concept, but by no means a dying one. *'Arab*, tribal nomads, and Arabians in general, had already become Arabs, an ethnic group with a language and an identity; contact with *'ajam*, those who could not speak Arabic, had given them solidarity by reflex; and now prophecy had – at least for the time being – given them unity, a collective will guided, as in the old South Arabian non-tribal peoples, by a shared deity.

What Muhammad did was to give that Arab identity, whose deepest foundation was language, a new and durable prominence. His greatest legacy, the Qur'an, reminds its hearers time and again that Allah's final word to mankind is in the Arabic tongue. Muhammad had 'gathered the Arabs together upon the word of Islam', and had gathered the political word of Arabs like no one before or since. In turn, this unified word and united will gave Arabs the potential, at last, to rule others. As yet, however, the potential was unrealized; perhaps even unrecognized. Muhammad is said to have prayed for the fall of Ghassan and Kindah, but not for the fall of Persia and Byzantium. However broad his spiritual horizons were, his political purview seems to have been limited to the arabophone world.

The question now was what would happen next. As was the case with the bedouin *a'rab*, by no means all of those who had answered Muhammad's call had embraced the spiritual 'faith' – *iman* – that gave rise to this call. But they had all signed up to a social contract. It was not a secular contract as described by Europeans of the Enlightenment, in which citizens surrender liberties in return for protection by state institutions, but rather a contract with Allah: He would protect and direct His people, acting as their collective will, in return for their surrender – *islam* – to Him of their individual will, and for their payment of dues in the form of prayers, pilgrimages and property taxes.

The idea of *habl Allah*, that sacred social contract, or covenant, with a supreme deity, had worked reasonably well for centuries in the old Sabaean south. There, allied peoples signing up to it were allowed to hold on to their own identity and independence in the form of their old gods: it was a theocratic state, but theologically loose and decentralized. The covenant of the Jews with Jehovah, too, had worked tolerably efficiently: the deity was unassailably One, but as long as the Jews had an independent political state He inspired a series of spokesmen and spokeswomen – prophets – to reveal His will to His people through changing times and circumstances. What

Muhammad had founded was different: it was a theocratic state, and not only rigorously monotheistic but also monoprophetic. Muhammad was the Seal of the Prophets, and if revelation had started with Adam, it had stopped with him. In the relay of revelation, he was the last recipient of the baton. There was no concept of a Holy Spirit to inspire the community world without end and to reinterpret revelation through successive and changing ages. Muhammad's state was thus extraordinarily centralized, not geographically but temporally. History, in a sense, had ended, or entered an eternal present that would become an ever-present past. As with Francis Fukuyama's more recent pronouncements, however, rumours of the end of history are usually exaggerated. With the end of revelation, a major theme of history – God's relationship with His creation – had indeed ended. But earthly events continued. The clock had stopped, but time went on.

Ibn Khaldun was to write with 750 years of hindsight that 'Arabs can only attain kingship through prophecy'. So far, that kingship extended no further than the central western Arabian region of the Hijaz, albeit with a web of treaty relationships extending over much of the rest of the Arabs' 'island'. And since Muhammad was the prophet to end all prophecy, would even that kingship die with him? It nearly did. For the immediate moment, however, things didn't fall apart. Neither did history end. But it might be said to have held its breath: for it was clear that a change had come over Arabdom, even if the change might not have seemed as radical then as it did to the later developers and definers of Islam.

Something of the nature of the change could and can still be seen one hundred metres from where I'm writing this.

OUT OF THE RUINS

The Great Mosque of San'a was built in 627, by Muhammad's express command, in the Persian viceroy's garden. The viceregal residence loomed over it – the multi-storey Sabaean palace of Ghumdan, itself already 400 years old, with its alabaster windows and hollow bronze birds and beasts on its parapets that shrieked and roared when the wind blew through them. The Great Mosque incorporated material from the dismantled Great Church of San'a, built by the Christian Ethiopian occupiers a century before (mosaics and columns from the church would also be reused in the Meccan Ka'bah). Much of that architectural salvage material was itself inspired by Byzantine models, with acanthus capitals and other classical motifs; one capital still bears a discreet Christian cross. Muhammad fixed the limit of the San'a mosque at a stone called al-Mulamlamah, now buried beneath the floor by later accumulations and extensions but still indicated by a marker. Presumably the stone had some ancient significance to have been given a name that was known as far away as Mecca. The mosque also incorporated the tomb of a revered local monotheist, Hanzalah ibn Safwan, supposedly a prophet sent to the Sabaeans. The building and its orientation to Mecca were new. But it was constructed among, and from, the remains of empires – those of the Byzantine-aligned Ethiopians and the Sasanian Persians. Moreover, it was also founded on, and both delimited and overshadowed by, an old and indigenous Arabian past. The San'a mosque is a scale model of the change wrought by Muhammad: it is a structure to accommodate a whole new society, but built from ancient materials and in a familiar setting.

To return to Medina, to the prototype of that new-old mosque, and to the bowing ranks that had amazed Abu Sufyan and Urwah: what had struck them so forcibly was neither the strangeness of some alien rite, nor the materials of its setting, but the new zeal activating and uniting their own Arab people – people who had been divided ever since they had existed. Perhaps those two observers had also both sensed how these newly united and energized Arabs might even build their own imperium out of the ruins of their neighbours' actual, territorial empires, those of 'the noble Persians and the Byzantines with their braided locks'. If so, they had sensed a basic motive force of history – how a shared ideology makes a society much more effective at conquering others. What they could never have guessed was just how quickly it would all happen, or how their local cult of Allah would become a culture, and then a global cultural hegemony that would long outlive any empire.

DOMINANCE

630–900

CHAPTER SEVEN

CRESCADERS
OPENINGS-UP

THE HARLOTS OF HADRAMAWT

It does not need saying that Muhammad is the dominant figure of the mid-point of Arab history, and a towering figure in human history as a whole. What must be said is that he is not a typical Arab: he was the product of his background, but he went beyond it; he has been carried so much further still, by the collective devotion over time of billions of followers, that he stands with one foot in history and the other in make-believe. Given their diversity from the start, and the fluidity of what their name actually means, 'typical Arabs' are hard to pin down. But the current of events that surged around and past Muhammad's life swept many of his Arabian contemporaries along with it and set them on similar courses into new lives, often far in every way from their origins. Such journeys scattered them physically, but gave them a unity of experience: in a comparable way, the sons of poor Scots crofts and of rich English manors would share in the same British imperial experience. It is hard to capture the process but, occasionally, one Arab seems to summarize in a single life the journeys of many.

One such figure was al-Ash'ath, 'the Tousled'. He was born in the southern Arabian region of Hadramawt, probably towards the end of the sixth century. Like the great poet of that earlier century, Imru' al Qays, al-Ash'ath (or

Ma'dikarib ibn Qays, to give him his proper but rarely used name) belonged to the ruling line of the tribe of Kindah. After its wanderings about the peninsula, its long semi-settled period in and around the mid-Arabian caravan town of Qaryat, its own pre-Islamic attempts to weld and to lead a union of Arabian tribes, and the final failure of these efforts, most of Kindah had migrated south and settled in Hadramawt. Here, in a complex of canyons sunk deep into a plateau of lunar barrenness, they began to lead a life cut off from Arabian events – until Muhammad's envoys arrived. Inspired by the Prophet's summons to join the growing tribal union, al-Ash'ath accompanied the envoys back to Medina in 631, that 'Year of Delegations', at the head of a group from Kindah and, like so many others, fell for the prophetic charisma. Also like many others, he agreed to marry his sister to Muhammad. The Prophet died, however, before the bridal caravan had even left Hadramawt.

We do not know the sister's reaction to the news of her premature widowhood. But al-Ash'ath's reaction to Muhammad's death was the same as that of most Arabs: he broke off all allegiance to Medina. Many in his native Hadramawt were delighted: Islamic historians particularly mention 'the Harlots of Hadramawt', a group of women who sang and danced in celebration of the break. Apparently of noble families, one of the women is said to have been Jewish; the others were perhaps priestesses of the ancient cults, 'married' to their deities (hence the accusation of harlotry). They and the other Kindis may have thought themselves safe in their secluded wadi, 1,500 kilometres from Medina – until, with remarkable swiftness, an army from the distant city descended on them and exacted revenge from the disobedient Hadramis. The 'harlots' had their hands severed and, in an old form of punishment for subversive orators, their front teeth knocked out. Al-Ash'ath himself was besieged, but surrendered under guarantee of safe conduct. It was nearly his last deed: he forgot to put his own name in the document of surrender. Saved at the last moment, he was taken to Medina, where Muhammad's successor Abu Bakr pardoned him and married him, as one did in polite circles, to his sister.

Following this slalom-like series of twists in fate and allegiance, al-Ash'ath entered the long straight out of Arabia. Momentum took him far. In 636 he fought (and lost an eye) at al-Yarmuk, the gloriously decisive Arab battle against the Byzantines. Soon after, he fought at al-Qadisiyyah, the gloriously decisive Arab battle against the Persians. He settled at al-Kufah, the new garrison town in southern Iraq, and from there went on a successful expedition to Azerbaijan in 646–7, where he may have acted for a time as governor. Following the great schism that would split Arab ranks, he took the part of Muhammad's first cousin and son-in-law Ali against Mu'awiyah, leader of the Meccan *ancien régime*, and in 657 fought for Ali in the ingloriously indecisive inter-Arab battle of Siffin. In the wake of the slaughter, he was one of those who persuaded Ali to submit to the farrago of fudge that posed as arbitration between the foes. Al-Ash'ath died in al-Kufah in 661, and because of his disastrous advice has been reviled by the pro-Ali faction – the so-called Shi'ah, or Party, of Ali – ever since.

'Typical' is thus perhaps not the word for Ma'dikarib the Tousled; rather, he is a microcosm of Arabdom at its most active moment in history. Few other Arabs packed quite as much into a single lifetime, but within a couple of generations the lives of many were changed beyond recognition. At the end of the eventful first Islamic century, an Arab of the old school was still able to define happiness as 'a pretty spouse, a spacious house, a fine horse tethered in the yard'. His son, however, had a new definition. Happiness was 'flags that fly, thrones on high, people to cry, "Hail to our lord!"' Arabs had always failed – al-Ash'ath's would-be master-tribe of Kindah is a case in point – in their attempts to rule each other; in other words, to impose unity on themselves. It seemed to be easier to rule non-Arabs, and they quickly acquired a taste for it; not that the pretty women and horses were forgotten. But life became more complicated in other ways. Tribal Arabs had always sat on the democratic, or at least levelling, ground. Sitting on thrones may have been the new fashion, but thrones have to be competed for, and the more elevated the seat, the greater the danger of falls. It may not be coincidental that the usual word for a throne in Arabic, *'arsh*, can also mean a bier for a corpse.

OVERWHELMED WITH VULTURES

The one great exception to the perennial failure of Arab attempts to unify themselves had been that of Muhammad. Now, on his death, his companions had to try to see his project through.

The first question was about the choice and nature of a leader to succeed the Prophet. His tribe, Quraysh, put their heads together and chose one of themselves: admittedly their choice, Abu Bakr, was not one of the Qurashi Establishment, but he was Muhammad's closest companion, and the Prophet's own choice to lead the community's prayers in his final illness. (The very idea of a candidate from among the non-Qurashi native population of Medina seems to have been dismissed out of hand.) Abu Bakr's 'election' was, like so much else, a continuation of pre-Islamic tribal practice; so too was his role as arbiter, not autocrat. But his title was new – *khalifah*, 'successor', hence the English 'caliph', to the Messenger of Allah – and in practice he would wield more authority than the old tribal *sayyid*s. Also in practice, Abu Bakr took over and was then agreed upon: it was an election after the fact, a rubber-stamp, and a smudged one at that. For by no means all of Muhammad's prominent companions accepted the result: Ali and other members of Muhammad's Hashimi branch of Quraysh withheld their approval of the non-Hashimi Abu Bakr for six months. It was not the first contested change of rule in Arab history, and it would not be the last.

The second question came on the heels of the first, and was even more pressing: would there be anyone left to be led? For within a week or two of Muhammad's death, as news of it began to do the rounds of the Arabian network, that unprecedented unity, the great socio-politico-religious caravan of ideas that he had set in motion and to which tribes across the peninsula had tagged on with apparent enthusiasm, began to fall apart. Like al-Ash'ath and his tribe of Kindah in Hadramawt, most of them thoroughly rejected the whole idea of any sort of central rule now that Muhammad was gone.

It was not that they particularly missed their old gods. Muhammad had realized that the chances of Arabs backsliding into a pagan past were real, but remote: 'This world shall not pass away,' he is claimed to have said, 'until the buttocks of the women of Daws wiggle [again] around [the idol] Dhu 'l-Khalasah and they worship it as they were wont to do.' In the mean time, the stone that represented Dhu 'l-Khalasah had been turned into the threshold of a mosque, to be trodden underfoot. Other pagan pockets had been summarily dealt with. In an *Exorcist*-like end, the goddess al-Uzza is supposed to have appeared to the Muslim hero Khalid ibn al-Walid, materializing as a ranting and dishevelled Abyssinian woman. Khalid cut her head in two, and she crumbled to dust and ashes before his eyes. Islamic legend not only deals her a death-blow, but de-arabizes her and makes her an Abyssinian. She is blackened literally as well as metaphorically.

Many Arabs had enjoyed a pragmatic and at times cavalier relationship with their old deities. If the gods didn't come up with the goods, you snapped their divinatory arrows as the poet Imru' al-Qays had done, or you called them bastards, like the sacrilegious bedouin in their rain hymn quoted in the previous chapter. On the move, you picked up cooking-pot-stones and a god-stone, and when you struck camp you left them behind. There was little love lost between the idols and their worshippers. So the problem following Muhammad's death was not doctrinal. Rather, it was that most Arabs who had signed up to his project simply hadn't grasped the political implications of the deal. The most important function of the old gods had been their political role: they had served as 'totems' for tribes or, on a much wider and more formal scale, for the *sha'b*s or peoples of the South. Now, Allah was the totem of a super-tribe, a total tribe, one that demanded totalitarian discipline – and taxes. It was precisely at the time when all these implications were sinking in that the news of Muhammad's death spread. With few exceptions, the old tribes and peoples of Arabia quietly reasserted their autonomy of centuries that Muhammad had persuaded them to renounce for the past year or two. Often they continued to pray in the Muslim way; it was obviously a good idea to keep in with the supreme deity. As for paying taxes to His representatives on earth, they let the matter quietly drop.

This clearly wouldn't do for the captains of Quraysh who had inherited Muhammad's project. To give an idea of what was happening, it is worth quoting in full an exchange that is said to have taken place in AH 11 between the heroic exorcist of pre-Islamic goddesses, Khalid ibn al-Walid, and a prominent alleged 'apostate', Malik ibn Nuwayrah, a leader of the tribe of Yarbu' (and the smiling chieftain described in Chapter 2). Different versions of the story exist, but the most usual one says that Malik had been one of the delegates visiting the Prophet, who appointed him to collect the alms-tax of his tribe. After the Prophet's death, tribal leaders, including Malik, withheld taxes and thus 'went back [on their agreement]' (in its later sense, the verb *irtadda* would mean 'apostasized'). Khalid ibn al-Walid was sent to threaten the defaulters, and confronted Malik.

> 'I still perform the [Islamic] prayers,' Malik said, 'even if I do not pay the taxes.'
>
> Khalid said, 'Do you not know that prayers and taxes go together? Neither is acceptable without the other.' To which Malik said,
>
> 'That is what your companion [Muhammad] used to say.'
>
> And Khalid replied, 'Do you not then consider him your companion too? By Allah, you make me want to cut your head off!' They wrangled at length in this way, until at last Khalid said,

> 'I am indeed going to kill you.' At which Malik said, 'I suppose your companion ordered to do that as well.'
>
> Khalid said, 'You add insult to injury! Now I really am going to kill you.'

Before one of Khalid's men struck his head off, Malik

> turned to his wife, Umm Mutammim, and said to Khalid, 'It is she who is the death of me,' for she was an exceedingly beautiful woman.

Khalid's 'sentence' was carried out; he used Malik's head as the support for a cooking-pot until it was burned beyond recognition (another posthumous blackening); and, as Malik had foreseen, he took Umm Mutammim as his wife. Admittedly, the affair caused scandal in Medina: Malik had performed his devotions, even if he had not paid his dues, and had asserted to the last that he was still a Muslim. But the caliph, Abu Bakr, refused to punish Khalid. He was simply too valuable a commander to be alienated, and he was about to prove his worth in the greatest struggle for the life of the nascent state.

Other tribes went on praying but not paying. They were used to wearing religion lightly; but paying allegiance, let alone cash – or, rather, for most of Arabia, camels and other animals – was a much heavier and more distasteful burden. (At least if you lost camels in a tribal raid, you had a chance of getting them back; with a centralized, camel-taking state, the odds were stacked against you.) In their rebellion they often had forceful and inspiring leaders. These were not only old-fashioned tribal chiefs like Malik ibn Nuwayrah, but also a newly empowered kind of leader. For one aspect of Muhammad's mission had been almost too successful, and the main danger to his project was not from old false idols, but from new false prophets. In one sense they were the sincerest form of flattery; in another, since the new 'prophets' were invariably old-style *kahin*s, one can only imagine how piqued they had been by a man they saw as one of their own kind – Muhammad – doing so well. The great, bright wheel of fire that he had set in motion now began to give birth to numerous incendiary spin-offs.

The most prominent of the imitators was Musaylimah, known to Islamic historians as 'the Liar' – the false prophet par excellence. He gained a huge following in the east of the peninsula; like Muhammad, he had a muezzin to call his followers to prayer, and a 'Qur'an' for them to recite. This aped the inimitable rhythmic and rhyming prose of the original, but supposedly with very different content. The few alleged surviving passages from the book have the look, again, of black propaganda. For example,

> Frog, daughter of two frogs! / Croak! What are you croaking? / Your top half in the water soaking, / your lower half in the mud poking! / The drinker you rile not, / the water you soil not. / We have half the earth and Quraysh the other half, but Quraysh are a hostile lot.

That last verse, however, was for a time not so far from the truth, at least in the confined world of the peninsula. It began as wishful thinking by Musaylimah, who suggested to Muhammad early in 632 that they should split Arabia 50:50; alternatively, Musaylimah would give his allegiance on condition that he should eventually take over from Muhammad. Given the totalitarian nature of Muhammad's ideology, this cut no ice. The True Prophet's death, however, was a fillip to the False Prophet's cause, and at one point Musaylimah looked as if he would be a serious and ineradicable rival to the state of Medina. Abu Bakr despatched his tireless troubleshooter, Khalid ibn al-Walid. In the final clash, Musaylimah was killed, but so too were many Muslims – 700 or 1,700, according to different accounts.

Musaylimah's cause had also been boosted when he joined forces – not just in warfare but also in worship and even in wedlock, by some accounts – with Sajah, a false prophetess in her own right. It is difficult to disentangle the broadsheet truth from the tabloid details with which historians of the winning side recorded this union, but Sajah may have been Christian, or at least influenced by the Christianity of her tribe. Whatever the case, she became a good Muslim on Musaylimah's defeat. So too did Tulayhah, yet another *soi-disant* prophet with yet another 'Qur'an', when he too met defeat. Tulayhah, however, differed from his co-'prophets' in that he had started out as a nomadic tribal leader as well as a *kahin*; Musaylimah and Sajah were from settled *hadar* backgrounds that had long been infused with monotheistic ideas. Musaylimah, if his pseudo-Qur'an is to be believed, disdained nomads: 'You are better,' he told his followers, 'than the dwellers in tents of hair . . . Your cultivated fields, defend them!' Conversely, Tulayhah's prophetic pretences were disdained by his own bedouins, who simply wanted to escape having to pay camels to Medina. In the light of these failures, it is clear once again how much the success of Muhammad's project was due to the way in which it brought together both *hadar* and *badw*, settled people and nomads, however shaky the equilibrium between them.

The south of the peninsula also had its own would-be prophet, the *kahin* al-Aswad al-'Ansi. His given name is disputed, so he is generally known by his black nickname ('al-Aswad' means 'the Black One'). He was also known as Dhu 'l-Khimar, the One With The Veil – that sartorial feature of old-style hero-leaders. Islamic polemic would remove a letter-dot from this and make him Dhu 'l-Himar, the One With The Donkey, and would explain the name by making his most prominent follower a donkey that prostrated itself to him; it further characterized him as a conjuror, 'who captivated hearts by his discourse'. Al-Aswad, like Musaylimah, scored some notable successes: he expelled the Muslim representative, and persecuted the Persian occupiers of the south who had so readily accepted Islam. (It is for this reason that the Marxist ideologues of the short-lived People's Democratic Republic of Yemen would, in the 1970s, rehabilitate al-Aswad as an Arab nationalist. One man's false prophet is another man's freedom fighter; one man's captivated heart is another man's disabled mind.) In the end, Medina collaborated with the Persians of the south, and al-Aswad was defeated and subsequently killed by his own Persian wife, *à la* Mata Hari.

The *Riddah*, the 'Backsliding' on the deal with Medina (the 'Apostasy' in theocratic parlance), had spread around Arabia like wildfire. Just as swiftly, the forces from Medina went about stamping it out. We should not think in terms of generalized armed conflict: in the war in which I find myself today, thousands of tribesmen in thousands of square kilometres of difficult country have held out against the latest airborne, laser- and GPS-guided weaponry for over three years, so far; for the Medina regime to have subdued, militarily, not thousands but millions of square kilometres in under two years with the weaponry, transport and communications then available was utterly out of the question. Rather, there were a few high-profile military defeats, like that of Musaylimah; a few cases of exemplary punishment, like that of the 'Harlots of Hadramawt'; a few of assassination, like that of al-Aswad; and the odd case of stormtrooper tactics, as in Bahrain, publicized in bloody verses to terrify others who might wish to resist:

We left Shurayh dead, striped in gore
like the dyed streaks of the border of a robe from Yemen.
We made the mother of Ghadban weep for her son,
and broke our lance in Habtar's eye-socket.
We left Musma' thrown down upon the ground,
hostage to hyenas, overwhelmed with vultures.

Otherwise, deals were done, chiefs were cowed or coaxed, and that time-honoured but often forgotten factor of history – the apathy and inertia of the vast majority – did the rest. Allah was clearly on the side of His people.

Those spin-offs of Islamic unity had never got far off the ground. Muhammad's caravan was back on track. Moreover, its Qurashi leaders were now both battle-hardened generals and experienced negotiators who could set their sights beyond their immediate 'island', into the further, northern part of the subcontinent, and into the future. Abu Bakr, no doubt sensing that the newly subdued Arabs needed a swift joint action to cement their renewed unity, activated the new communications technology once more and sent letters across Arabia summoning people to fight the Byzantines. His summons would have unimaginable success, but he himself did not live to see it. He died of natural causes in August 634.

If the Farewell Sermon of his friend Muhammad had shadowed forth the way in which Islam would grow into a universal, fraternal faith, then Abu Bakr's last address intimated how it might develop into a secular empire, but one that would be haunted by the spectres of his own people's disunity:

> Today you live in an age succeeding that of prophecy, at a fork in the path of pilgrimage. After me you will see despotic rule, deviant rule, a bold community, blood shed . . . So cling to the places of prayer and take the Qur'an as your counsel. Hold fast to obedience and do not abandon unity . . . And then, just as the nearer lands have been opened up to you, so too will the further lands.

PRUNING THE UNCIRCUMCISED

Abu Bakr and his commanders and envoys had wielded the stick to beat, goad and guide the rebels back into line. Under his successor, Umar, whom Abu Bakr probably designated before his death, came the carrot – conquest

– that would tempt the caravan on . . . and on, into ever further lands. It would get to the ends of the earth, and gather fellow travellers wherever it went. The new adherents would soon come to outnumber by far the original, Arab members. And yet the latter would never entirely discard their less useful baggage – the tribal and racial impedimenta that they brought out of Arabia. For some, that load has kept them weighed down in earthly matters and stopped them looking up to heaven.

Early in Umar's caliphate, however, Islam may in any case have been seen as a purely Arab project, its main aim the political one of unifying Arabic speakers – perhaps in the face of the Persian Threat, according to that alluring but unprovable theory. Certainly, the first campaigns beyond the peninsula proper would seek to unify arabophones. In the northern regions of the subcontinent, the marginal world of Arabia slotted into the main body of Eurasia with its Greek, Achaemenid, Hellenistic, Roman, Sasanian and Byzantine heritage. The junction itself, the northern Fertile Crescent, had its own even longer and richer heritage; in more recent centuries, however, under Ghassanid and Lakhmid rule, speakers of Arabic had infiltrated (or, looking at the longer history of migrations, returned to) these lands, and were interspersed among speakers of the cousin-language, Aramaic. More recently still, Meccans had come to know the area well through trade; the father of that wealthy pillar of the Meccan Establishment, Abu Sufyan, had even bought estates in Byzantine territory. Arabs may have had an 'island' as their principal residence; but it was, to use the estate agents' term, link-detached and most of the folks next door were at least linguistic family.

In the western part of the Crescent and in its Egyptian extension, Byzantium had suffered recent and embarrassing defeats by a briefly resurgent Persia. In the 620s, however, while Muhammad was fighting the pagan Meccans, the emperor Heraclius was pushing the Persians back; by the end of the decade, he had restored lost Byzantine territory. But whereas the old imperial Goliaths had come out of their struggle battered, exhausted and scowling at each other, the young Arabian movement had emerged from its own conflict stronger than ever. Now, in 633, with the whole of their peninsula at last united (at least in theory) by ideology, led by sophisticated caravan-chiefs-turned-tacticians, and above all raring to raid, Arabs were no longer the puny herdboys who had annoyed the Assyrians and their successor empires.

These developments had not yet sunk into the Byzantine consciousness, and when a force of 24,000 appeared in their territory – not from across the usual eastern front with the Persians but from the south, Arabia, the place next door to nowhere – they were caught napping. Moreover, if the Arab forces were lightly armed, their camel+horse combination gave them the invincible weapons of speed and manoeuvrability. Most of the scattered Byzantine garrisons melted away; the tribal Arab population went quietly over to the Muslim side. The 'natives', the Aramaic-speaking peasantry, were conspicuous only by their silence.

Did the Arabic- and Aramaic-speaking Christians of the region see the Muslim invaders as slightly weird co-religionists? It is quite possible. At the time, Islam may still have been much more doctrinally malleable than its own later, fossilizing historians would lead us to think. Besides, the outward forms of prayer were not dissimilar; for example, Muslims shared with Christians in the region the practice of prostration (still part of ritual in the Syrian Orthodox Church). In major cities including Damascus and Hims, as well as in rural regions like the Negev, they also shared churches – something that would have been uncomfortable if each side had viewed the other as hell-bound heretics. In Damascus, soon to be the new caliphal capital, that cohabitation lasted no less than seventy years: at its mosque-basilica, Muslims and Christians 'entered by the same doorway . . . Then the Christians turned to the west towards their church, and the Muslims to the right to reach their mosque'. Cohabitation also spread beyond the realm of religious real estate: the future St John of Damascus, for example, would not only work as a tax official for the Muslims but also become a courtier and drinking partner of the caliphal family. Meanwhile, a long history of intellectual transfer began when a prince of the family hired a Greek monk named Marianus to teach him medicine and alchemy.

What is in little doubt is that the local Monophysite Christian majority of the region, looked down on as heretics by Constantinople, actively preferred Muslim to Byzantine rule. As for the Jews, it is claimed that in Hims they swore on the Torah that they would never have another Byzantine governor. What mattered to all of them, as to most people in most ages, is that they could get on with their lives without being messed about too much. It was what would matter also to the Christian and other inhabitants of Persian-run lands and to the Copts of Egypt, all soon to fall to the state of Medina. Though perhaps 'fall' is not the word: defending armies fought and fell, to be sure; the non-combatant majority bowed to the new rule, grumbled at the new taxes, realized that they weren't that bad, and carried on.

That does not mean it was all a walkover for the Arab forces. There were sieges: the Arabs had to invest the city of Caesarea on the coast of Palestine for a reported seven years before it capitulated in 640 (it was well defended, but no doubt a zero or two have crept into the '100,000' troops guarding its walls; also, the 'seven years' may have been closer to seven months). There was heroism and carnage: an Arab woman, just married and then just widowed in the battle of Marj al-Suffar, went beserk with a tent-pole and killed seven Byzantine soldiers. And there was al-Yarmuk. Named after a river that descends westward to the Jordan Valley near the sea of Galilee, the Battle of al-Yarmuk saw the entire Arab army of 24,000 massing and facing a Byzantine force of at least that number. For a month in the summer of 636, heavy but sporadic fighting flared and died about the foothills of the Golan Heights, before a final mass encounter in which Khalid ibn al-Walid – that successful but not altogether scrupulous captain of the Wars of Apostasy – broke the Byzantine ranks and oversaw their slaughter in the Yarmuk gorges.

Again, Arab women did their bit – including the cheerleading, fire-breathing, liver-gnawing poetess, Hind the wife of Abu Sufyan, now on message for the Muslims. This time she encouraged the troops with the cry, 'Go on! Prune the Foreskinned Ones with your swords!' But if in Hind's mind the battle was one between the 'Roundheads' and 'Cavaliers' of British schoolboy parlance – the circumcised and the uncircumcised – in reality things were not so clear-cut. Al-Yarmuk was not a battle between Arabs and non-Arabs. Far from it: the Byzantine side relied on contingents of Arab troops from Ghassan, Lakhm, Judham, Tanukh, Iyad and other tribes. The commander of the Byzantine vanguard was the Arab Ghassanid king, Jabalah ibn al-Ayham, whose ancestral palace-camp of al-Jabiyah overlooked the battlegrounds. To confuse matters further, Jabalah is said to have switched sides in the middle of the conflict on the grounds that his opponents from the Medinan tribes of Aws and Khazraj were in fact his 'brothers' (they were all of distant South Arabian origin). He is also said to have professed Islam and then, threatened with punishment by Caliph Umar for slapping a man, to have returned to the fold of Constantinople and Christianity: 'I will not remain in a land where others rule me,' he declared, still regal. Like so many others, he had not taken in the political implications of Islam. For Jabalah, blood-ties had trumped older political loyalties; but, in the end, personal honour and independence had trumped all the rest, Islam included.

THE WEST OF THE EAST

In their early encounters with the Byzantines, Arabs as often as not found themselves up against their pre-Islamic selves, men like Jabalah the Ghassanid. In their great simultaneous clash with Persia, Arabs were fighting the Other that had so long defined them.

The otherness is clear in stories like that of the Arab chieftain al-Mughirah parleying with the enthroned Sasanian general and virtual regent, Rustam, and idly poking holes with his spear in the latter's vast and precious Persian carpet – and then trying to cosy up beside the shocked paladin on his throne. Arabs may have been oiks, their historians wish to say, but they would get their turn on the throne; the protocol-ridden Persians were as decadent as their empire. In this attitude Arabs shared, unconsciously, the old Greek and Roman view of Persians as effete and dissolute; like their predecessors, they saw themselves as epic heroes versus epicene Orientals. Even this early on, they were the West of the East, as Lévi-Strauss has described Islam.

Given negotiators like al-Mughirah, it is not surprising that the Arab advance into Persian territory led to another great battle, ultimately even more fateful to the Sasanians than the rout of al-Yarmuk had been to Byzantium. The latter survived another eight centuries, at times fighting back, at others behaving as a truculent satellite of the Arabs. In contrast, the last of the Sasanian shahs, Yazdgard III, resisted for a while, but within little more than a decade ended up stabbed and thrown into a Central Asian river. The old Persian empire died with him. Simple geography helped: the Persian capital, Ctesiphon, lay at the Arabian end of the empire, right in the path of the Arab advance; Constantinople, on the other hand, was insulated from the Arabian subcontinent by nearly 1,000 kilometres of Asia Minor.

The date of the decisive battle has never been agreed upon, but it fell at some time between 636 and 638. What is certain is that for Medina to take on the two superpowers at almost the same time was either mad or inspired. Nor is the site of the battle in dispute – a spot called al-Qadisiyyah, a day or so from the Lakhmid capital of al-Hirah, and lying where Fertile Crescent became infertile steppeland. Arab forces arriving from Medina may have numbered 12,000. Behind them they had their harsh bright 'island'; before them the legendary Sawad of Iraq, that 'Blackness' of dark green palmeries, moist earth and meandering canals that had drawn Arab raiders since time out of mind. They also had before them a Persian army under Rustam that was a lot bigger than their own – 120,000 by some accounts, although one suspects that the David-and-Goliath syndrome is at work again among Islamic historians, as it had been at Caesarea. As usual, speed and manoeuvrability were important early on, but the thick of the battle was waged mostly on foot, and in the end it was archery that proved decisive. '*Spindles! Spindles!*' the Persian troops would yell as yet another swarm of angry Arab arrows headed for them. But they were spindles 'that would rip through the heavy breastplates and double layers of chain-mail that we wore.' Al-Qadisiyyah was the Arab Agincourt.

Arab archery, perfected since ancient times by sharpshooters hunting game in the bare tracts of the peninsula, might have been deadly at a distance, but most Arabs' horizons were still limited to raiding the neighbours. There was a single palm-tree at al-Qadisiyyah, and wounded Arab warriors would catch sight of it and ask, 'Are we nearly at the Sawad yet?' They were, and that palmy land was now theirs. But the greater empire, extending to the Persian heartland of Fars, the far plains rising to the highlands of Armenia and rolling across Asia to the Oxus and the borders of Sind – a territory as big as the entire Arabian subcontinent – all that was for now beyond the imagination of most Arabs. It makes the contrast between the two sides the wider, the bathos of the fall of an ancient power the greater. So too do vignettes of the aftermath of the battle: the captured Persian imperial baker, mounted on a mule, wearing silk brocade and a cap of cloth of gold, surrounded by ceremonial caskets filled with cream cakes and honeycombs; the last of the thirty Persian war elephants, bought by an entrepreneur to be taken on tour and shown, disgruntled, to goggling Arabs.

The fall of the house of Sasan also brought down the remains of its old Arab outhouse, the Lakhmid dynasty. With them fell their capital, al-Hirah, the ancient home of Arabic poetry and writing and, arguably, the birthplace of a united Arab identity. Huraqah, the daughter of al-Nu'man III, patron of poets, who used to ride to her estates along roads spread with silk, now came in sackcloth to beg alms from the Arab victor of al-Qadisiyyah. Al-Hirah itself was soon a ruin haunted by monks; another princess, Hind, now a blind nun, enjoyed a twilight reputation there as an expert on ancient Arabia. But at last even these ghosts of the Arab past faded and the ancient metropolis was home only to owls and to *sada*, spirit-birds that emerge from the skulls of the dead. Al-Hirah, abandoned, rotted away like Babylon or Chernobyl.

The expanding state of Medina would create other ruins and other ghosts. In the far south-west of Arabia, where the old civilization of Saba and Himyar had fallen first to Ethiopians, then to Persians, the ancient Sabaean palace of Ghumdan with its alabaster windows and bronze beasts had survived. It was demolished partially in the time of Muhammad, and almost completely in that of his third successor Uthman. Sometimes the destruction was personal, and wanton. A young and zealous recruit to Islam came across the aged warrior-hero, Durayd ibn al-Simmah, who had clung to his pagan ways. The youth tried to kill him, dealing him several inexpert blows. 'Do it with my sword,' Durayd said. The hero's blade killed its owner instantly. Dead and exposed, Durayd's buttocks and thighs were seen to be like papyrus from years of bareback riding. 'The man you killed,' the zealot's mother told him later, 'set free from captivity three generations of your ancestresses.' The ghosts of tribal heroes, of al-Hirah and Himyar, were family ghosts; but the new Islamic generation left their haunted ancestral home without regrets. They turned their backs on a past that Islam had branded *al-Jahiliyyah*, the Ignorance. *Jahl* is the ignorance of childhood, and Arabs had grown up.

Later, although in fact not much later, when the youthful zeal of Islam began to pass to others – resurgent Persians, insurgent Turks – Arabs would look back and see the Ignorance as blissful, a Golden Age, a pre-dawn glow that was their very own before the universal enlightenment of Islam. It was the memory of that glow that kept a flicker of arabness alive through the long millennium in which the torch of Islam was in the hands of others. It was the same flicker that in the nineteenth century would reignite a sense of Arab greatness and unity, an 'Awakening'. But in the first flush of that youth, Arabs went out of Arabia without a backward glance, as if obedient to the pre-Islamic belief that a traveller who looked behind him as he set out would never complete his journey. The forwardness – the frowardness – worked: the headlong fall of Persian and Byzantine lands was due to lacklustre opposition and to that ever-underestimated military quantity, luck (or in Islamic terms, Allah). It was not due to conventionally wise strategy, unless taking on two empires at once is wisdom. But it was also due to sheer momentum. Qurashi generals had gained plenty of practical experience in the *Riddah* wars, but they also possessed large amounts of chutzpah. Khalid ibn al-Walid is said for example to have led his men across the Syrian desert, slaughtering their camels to drink the juices in their stomachs.

In the end, however, the relentless forward policy simply *had* to work. The *futuhat*, the Arab conquests of the first Islamic century – in their most basic sense the 'openings-up' – were the super-raids of inveterate predators who, now united, could no longer raid each other or their settled fellow Arabians. If you pray with each other, you shouldn't prey on each other; that, at least, is the theory. One might well ask if tribal Arabs could have found another economic basis to existence than raiding. It seems not; or not yet. Besides, the Meccan generals were only too happy to make use of the predatory propensity. As Hugh Kennedy puts it, 'The leaders of the new state were fully aware that it had to expand or collapse'. Empires are usually thought to grow, like Marvell's 'vegetable love', vast and slow. The empire of the Arabs arose like a soufflé.

THE SONS OF AL-ABBAS

The rise of Arab power did not follow the rules governing the growth of empires; it was, as Ibn Khaldun said, exceptional and miraculous. Certainly, the conjunction of circumstances that enabled the expansion – the war-weariness of the neighbouring empires, the battle-hardness of Arabs, disaffection and disunity among the Byzantine- and Persian-ruled populace, Arabs united by an Islamic ideology with an irresistible rhetoric – was all more than anyone could have dared to pray for. But there would be a price: it seems to be a rule of empires, miraculous or otherwise, that the quicker they are won the shorter they last (the Macedonian, the Mongol, the Napoleonic); again on the soufflé principle, they soon collapse, if they are not first wolfed down by others hungry for power. Conversely, slow-grown empires (the Roman, the Chinese, the Russian) live longer. Arabs would control their own united empire for about two hundred years. (The cultural empire that it inspired is, of course, still up and running.)

For the first hundred years or so Arabs were on a roll that mixed raiding tactics with more formal warfare. Having won a pitched battle, they would send out *saraya*, bedouin-style raiding parties, to pursue fleeing opponents and generally show the non-combatant peasantry who was in charge. It was a winning formula, combining doggedness and *élan*, like the old pairing of camel and horse. It is also another case where features of settled *hadar* and mobile *badw* society – in this case, their respective military tactics – are employed together and to great effect. In general, however, the emphasis was on lightness and mobility, unencumbered by lumbering baggage trains. A camel-borne column is its own baggage train; and in any case, an Arab warrior's kit was basic: a shield, a coat of mail, a helmet, one large needle and five small ones, linen thread, broadsword, scissors, nosebag, and a palm-leaf basket, as well as his other weapons – usually lance and bow – and his horse. As treasure from the newly plundered and taxed provinces began to flood into the central treasury at Medina, Caliph Umar endeavoured to pay warriors 4,000 *dirham*s (over ten kilogrammes of silver) up front – a thousand each for his travel, weapons and mount, and a thousand to leave with his family.

This last point highlights the fact that the one piece of kit Arab soldiers usually didn't take at first was their womenfolk. A *badawi*, asked by his wife if she could take to the road with him, replied in verse,

> If you travel, saddle-soreness will make you lose your wits.
> The miles will tenderize you thighs and make you do the splits,
> And you'll feel a cock was crowing down among your nether bits.

Commanders sometimes took their wives along, especially, as we have seen in the case of Hind the wife of Abu Sufyan, if they could turn a good verse or two to egg on the warriors in battle. But in general the conquerors left their women at home. They didn't need to take them: there were plenty to be had out there.

Arab armies travelled light, and it is clear that they were also light in numbers. As with the alleged disproportion of ten to one or even twenty to one at al-Qadisiyyah, the giant-killer syndrome has led Islamic historians to exaggerate the size of enemy forces. In fact, Arab strategists had to cope with the reciprocal and very real problem of a continual and general shortfall on their own side. After the collapse of the main Persian army at al-Qadisiyyah, Arab forces drew breath for a few years. They secured the Sawad and the rest of the lowlands of Iraq for themselves; up on the Iranian plateau, however, Yazdgard the resolute shah was trying to muster support to safeguard the remainder of his empire. The second decisive showdown would take place at Nihawand, a key position that would unlock the Iranian plateau and lands far to the east; in the end, the battle there in 642 proved indeed to be the vital victory that opened further Asia to Arab forces. But for a time Caliph Umar was at a loss as to how he could take on another big Persian army. He considered mobilizing men from Syria and Yemen but realized that this could leave those two lands open to reconquest by, respectively, the Byzantines and the Ethiopians. In the end, he scraped together enough warriors from the garrison towns of newly conquered Iraq. It was a perennial problem of these years of expansion, in which the men of the thinly peopled peninsula set themselves against the armies of more populous lands: there were never enough Arab boots on the ground, or sandals in the sand. Garrisons were established in the main centres of new territory, but the Arab presence elsewhere was usually patchy at best. The answer, as we shall see, was to manufacture more Arabs by various means. But even then, there weren't enough to go round. It was why what are billed as blockbusting conquests were often little more than raids that never got consolidated, and at least partly why the temporal Arab empire would also be a temporary one.

A single generation of Arabs was scattered 'fanwise', as Philip Hitti nicely put it, across 6,000 kilometres of the Old World; but the material of the fan was painfully thin. According to one 'very tentative' estimate, perhaps half a million people emigrated from the peninsula in the first dozen or so years of the conquests. That sounds high. Ibn Khaldun gives a figure of 150,000 as the total number of northern and southern Arabian tribesmen in the time of Muhammad. That may be more accurate for the adult male population, but perhaps does not take into account all the settled southerners. Then again, by no means all of that number emigrated. If it is true that Umar managed to field 30,000 men at the battle of Nihawand, and that he was throwing into it as many men from the Iraqi garrisons as he could spare, then it is clear that he was not troop-rich. It is almost certain that those early conquests involved the movement from the peninsula of a six-figure total of people, nearly all of them men. More than that it is hard to say.

It was the size of the fan itself and the suddenness of its opening that were remarkable. By no means unique were five of Muhammad's first cousins, all sons of his uncle al-Abbas by the same mother, Umm al-Fadl: they died variously in Medina, al-Ta'if, Syria, Tunisia and Samarqand. 'How far between his birth and his death,' said a less-travelled sibling of that last brother, Qutham. (Qutham was to have a far-reaching posthumous existence, too: known locally as Shah-i-Zinda, 'the Living King', his tomb-complex is still the major destination in the city at the end of the golden road.) The sons of al-Abbas not only went forth, from western Arabia to North Africa and Central Asia, but also multiplied: in AH 200 al-Abbas's descendants were found to number 33,000 – a creditable but credible figure. In those first Islamic centuries, Arabs made up for their lack of numbers. But they did so almost exclusively by concubinage and marriage with women of the conquered lands – Berbers, Copts, Aramaeans, Iranians, Kurds, Turks and many others. The label of 'Arab' was passed down the patriline but, generation by generation, the material of the 'fan' became even thinner.

The five Abbasid brothers were especially memorable: their patronymic was that of a future 500-year dynasty. But even of the others who were scattered over huge areas, we can still follow 'footprints' of one sort or another. Most often the traces are bloodlines, religiously remembered, that link present generations in Borneo or Brooklyn with seventh-century Mecca. Sometimes there are fainter tracks to follow, linguistic ley lines: the same very unusual dialect feature, for example, found isolated in the present-day Arabic of Uzbekistan and in a region by Lake Chad, originates from a small area of eastern Arabia, and almost certainly from the time of the seventh-century migrations.

The migrations took place almost entirely on dry land: Caliph Umar had warned his generals to go nowhere that could not be reached by camel. But there were occasional sea expeditions, including in the late 630s a short-cut from Oman across the Arabian Sea to Sind, the lowland regions of present-day Pakistan. Umar was not pleased by the news, and said that men on ships are nothing but '*dud 'ala 'ud*', 'ticks on sticks'. That first attempt on Sind was repulsed, but it would be taken and held early in the eighth century. Elsewhere the diaphanous Arab fan would continue to unfold until, by the middle of the eighth century, its tips reached the Central Asian borders of China and penetrated, briefly, those of France.

Arabs may have been miraculously motivated, but they were not invulnerable. An Arab army of 10,000 was wiped out in the 660s in the gorges of Tabaristan, south of the Caspian. Sixty years later, an Arab expedition had a notable success against Turkish forces in Central Asia, but failed to follow it up and was repulsed. The reason, according to a satire of the Arab commander, was that he and his men were too busy with the female captives:

> You fought the foe, then fun and games allured you double-quick:
> Your sword stayed in its scabbard while, instead, you drew your prick.

The ultimate reason for Arab failures in Central Asia would be disunity, swords drawn against each other. But despite the breaks for rest and recreation, in that first heady burst of expansion the only serious barriers there, and at the far western end of the known world, would be physical. 'O Lord,' the Qurashi general Uqbah ibn Nafi' is said to have exclaimed as he rode his horse into the Atlantic surf in Morocco in the 680s, 'if the sea did not stop me, I would go through the lands like Dhu 'l-Qarnayn, defending your faith and fighting the unbelievers!' Dhu 'l-Qarnayn, 'the Two-Horned One', is an obscure figure who appears in the Qur'an, sometimes taken to be an ancient South Arabian king who achieved legendary far conquests, sometimes associated with Alexander the Great. Whatever his real identity, the seventh-century Qurashi commander was drawing his inspiration from a potent past – the South Arabian past that underlies Islam, and perhaps also the Hellenistic past to which Arabs were becoming heirs, geographically and culturally.

At its greatest, the Arab empire was as big as Alexander's ephemeral imperium; as big as or bigger than the Roman. It had also become something more complex in form and more organic in nature than Hitti's unfolding fan: it had grown into that vigorous, vegetal ataurique or 'arabesque', throwing out new growths but also sending down new roots into other cultures, hybridizing across the Old World.

READING AL-BALADHURI

The fertile complexity and hybridity would come later. For the moment, despite the rhetoric of Uqbah at his Atlantic Ne Plus Ultra, the earlier accounts of the Arab eruption have little to do with faith, and more to do with taxing unbelievers than fighting them.

Writing had played an important part in the initial phases of Muhammad's project. But the great secular writing revolution would take place only from the second Islamic century onwards, so there is little contemporary documentation of the conquests in Arabic. Third-century historians, however, claim to have preserved oral records. One of the most thorough writers was al-Baladhuri, who died in Baghdad in AD 892 (and got his surname from an addiction to *baladhur*, a tropical nut supposed to increase powers of memory). His contents page begins with Muhammad's move from Mecca to Medina, follows the Prophet's own campaigns and then the post-Muhammadan battles of the War of Apostasy in their vortex-like flourish around the peninsula, before that fanwise unfolding across two continents and the corner of a third: the Levant, Mesopotamia, Armenia, Egypt, North Africa, Spain, then the eastward unfurling through the Persian empire into Azerbaijan and Khurasan, to Sind.

When Uqbah said he was 'defending the faith', he was actually bending the truth back on itself: he was, after all, speaking at the westward limit of the longest concerted *of*fensive campaign since those of Alexander, a thousand years before. 'Propagating the faith' might have been nearer the mark; but when one gets into al-Baladhuri's text, it is remarkable how little the fight against the unbelievers aimed to unite them in one true universal religion, and how much it was to do with raiding them and imposing taxes. The conquests were less a matter of hearts and minds than of pockets and purses. Four centuries and more on, the ethical system symbolized by the Cross would have little enough, in all conscience, to do with the so-called 'Crusades' of the European states. (Bedouin Arabs have no monopoly on raiding and booty. Of the Fourth Crusade in 1204, which the civilized Venetian merchants turned into a sack of their fellow Christians at Constantinople, Geoffrey of Villehardouin wrote: 'Never since the world was created had so much booty been won in any city' – and that may be no exaggeration.) It is the same with the Crescent and what might be called – if a little anachronistically, as the crescent moon only became closely associated with Islam later on – the 'Crescades'.

The alleged text of the protection agreement imposed by Iyad ibn Ghanm on the Christians of al-Raqqah in northern Syria in 639 or 640 gives an idea of the conquerors' priorities:

> In the Name of Allah, the Compassionate, the Merciful. This is what Iyad ibn Ghanm has granted to the people of al-Raqqah on the day he entered the city: He has granted them security for their persons, and their properties and churches shall likewise neither be destroyed nor occupied, provided they pay the poll-tax imposed on them, and provided they do not behave treacherously, and provided they do not build any new church or monastery and do not openly use prayer-clappers, or celebrate Easter, or display crosses. Allah is witness to this. 'And Allah is sufficient as a witness.'

Al-Baladhuri adds that the annual poll-tax was four gold *dinar*s per adult male. (Exactly the same tax – four *dinar*s' weight or 17 grammes of gold, worth about $650 – was reimposed on Christians in the area by the so-called 'Islamic State' in 2014. They too have read their Baladhuri, even if they have not been so scrupulous about granting security.) To withhold tax after agreeing to pay it is often termed *kafara*. The verb has a more general sense, 'to be a non-Muslim' (and is the origin of the South African derogatory term 'Kaffir'). But the fact that, in early accounts, it is usually to do with non-tax-paying rather than non-conversion shows where the conquerors' interests lay.

The pragmatism of the system is clear from occasional tax exemptions. For example, the Mardaite Christians of northern Syria, who agreed to raid alongside the Muslims, were excused the poll-tax. So too were the Christian Arab tribe of Taghlib, who successfully argued that, as Arabs, they should not have to pay the tribute imposed on conquered barbarians. Islam in its expansive period had as much to do with economics and ethnicity as with ethics. And Arabs were more often than not 'religious' – in the other, older sense of 'scrupulous' – in the application of their rules: the value of masonry taken from Christian al-Hirah to be reused in the nearby new town of al-Kufah was regarded as tax-deductible. Equally, physical violence to civilians (as opposed to economic violence, including enslavement, because of resistance or non-payment of taxes) was exceptional. One of the rare exceptions was Istakhr, the capital of the Persian heartland of Fars, which surrendered, then revolted and resisted long and hard. Supposedly, 40,000 of its inhabitants were massacred. But in general, Arabs knew perfectly well about geese and golden eggs.

It would be unfair to call the conquests a mob protection racket on a massive scale. But that, in large part, is the nature of conquest and empire. To be cynical, it is also the nature of the social contract in its Enlightenment sense: you pay taxes, the state protects you; you do not pay taxes, the state punishes you (but probably does not kill or enslave you). Moreover, the Arabic terminology invites the comparison as, technically speaking, poll-tax-paying non-Muslims are *ahl al-dhimmah*, 'protected people'. For that matter, the whole business of religion in its developed, 'political' form is underpinned by the notion of dues and payments: *din*, 'religion', is a cognate of *dayn*, 'debt'.

But there were more sophisticated ways of making money from the conquests than imposing poll-tax. There was also *kharaj*, a tax on agricultural land. A large-scale example of such taxation was that imposed on the rich date-producing Sawad of Iraq, with its ancient and carefully maintained irrigation system and its half a million non-Arab, 'Nabataean' peasant farmers

– a number perhaps not far off that of the entire Arab population. Magnet of raiders from the days of Babylon to the battle of al-Qadisiyyah, the Sawad was given special treatment as public *kharaj* land. Caliph Umar, who knew the propensities of tribal Arabs all too well, said, 'I fear that if I divided the Sawad up, you would squabble over the water'. Ali ibn Abi Talib put it to them even more bluntly: 'I would have divided the Sawad between you, if you weren't going to smash each other's faces in.' As it was, the annual revenue of the region plunged from a hundred million *dirham*s at the time of the conquest to forty million at the end of the seventh century.

The conquerors also employed other more sustainable means of generating income and maximizing profits. The very first priority on 'opening', that is, conquering, a town was often that of opening a market in concert with the townsfolk. For example, the people of al-Ruha, now Urfa in south-eastern Turkey, 'opened the gates of the city, and set up a market for the Muslims at the [main] gate'. This, as we shall see later in the founding of the new Arab towns, was an important stage in the long and still ongoing process of social engineering by which pastoral nomads turn into settled traders, bedouins become businessmen. It was a process that had been in train at least since the time of that third-century bedouin emporium, Qaryat Dhat Kahl. Now it had been given new impetus, and was the other 'conversion', less obvious but no less important than the religious one, brought about by Islam. Muhammad, after all, came from mercantile Mecca – the Qur'anic *umm al-qura*, the Mother of All Emporia – and was himself a merchant, a prophet who knew about profits. Markets and mosques sat side by side from Medina onwards.

Booty remained hugely important too. Caliph Umar managed to mobilize extra tribal forces for the Iraq campaign by tempting them with percentages: he offered the chief of the tribe of Bajilah, Jarir, a third of the loot (of course, after the customary caliphal fifth had been deducted). This same Jarir and another Arab chief would squabble violently over who had dealt the mortal blow to a Persian commander in the battle of al-Nakhilah – the killer had the right to despoil the corpse. Very occasionally, loftier motives are put forward: al-Mughirah, who vandalized Rustam's precious carpet, is said to have told the Persian general that he didn't want his money – only that Rustam and his people should embrace Islam; but if they refused, he went on, they would be fought, 'until they pay the poll-tax with willing submission and are humbled'. Often the booty came in human form, as many as '40,000 head' of slaves, for example, taken in a thirty-month period in the Iranian region of Sistan. And just how far the business of raiding had gone beyond its parochial, peninsular origins can be seen in the figures from the second, successful Sind expedition, masterminded in the early eighth century by al-Hajjaj, the governor of Iraq. He admitted that the campaign had cost sixty million *dirham*s, but it netted twice as much: 'We have cooled our rage', he said, 'and taken our revenge, and profited by sixty million *dirhams* and Dahir's head', Dahir being the defeated ruler of Sind. Raiding had become a multinational industry; revenge was less important than revenue.

Arab schoolchildren today learn that the *futuhat*, the conquests or 'openings-up', were about 'spreading Islam'. That is the rhetoric, and it was indeed one end result of that extraordinary era. The reality on the ground, at the time, was that there wasn't much incentive to spread Islam, at least in the sense of getting other people to convert; instead, Islam acted as a unifying ideology empowering Arab conquest and colonialism. Al-Hajjaj, ever keen to store up treasure on earth if not in heaven, actively dissuaded Sawad peasants from converting. On one occasion he even expelled converts from the Arab new towns, and made them pay the poll-tax of the unbeliever. Admittedly, the particularly horrible al-Hajjaj is not typical of administrators in the first Islamic century. Neither, however, was the saintly Umayyad Caliph Umar ibn Abd al-Aziz, whose humility, piety and choice of good governors inspired major conversions both in post-conquest Sind and among the Berbers of North Africa. They are the extremes, the exceptions; the rule that lies between them is that trade follows raid in swift succession, while faith lags far behind. According to one figure, by AD 750 only about 10 per cent of the inhabitants of the conquered lands had embraced Islam. That figure is admittedly conjectural. What is not in doubt is that one will search al-Baladhuri's 450-page history of the conquests largely in vain for claims to moral or spiritual motivation. Perhaps that motivation is meant to be taken as read; perhaps it simply wasn't there.

THE BRIDES OF MEDINA

The openings-up would work both ways. As one commentator has put it, playing with the Arabic double meaning, they were not just a *fath*, a conquest, of lands; they were also a *fath*, an opening, of Arab minds to the intellectual heritage of those lands. But the reverse or complementary conquest was not only cerebral. Medina, the new bastion of Islamic arabness, was 'invaded' by

Persian brides – first and most notably, three daughters of the last Sasanian ruler, who were married into the first generation of the new nobility: their husbands were the sons of Abu Bakr, Umar and Ali, the first, second and fourth caliphs. The consequences would be far-reaching. For example, of Muhammad's two lines of descendants via his grandsons al-Hasan and al-Husayn (the sons of Ali), the entire Husayni line, now millions strong, goes back to that Persian mother. The new blood seemed to revive flagging Qurashi lineages, for the children of those first unions turned out to be 'the most upright and learned' people in Medina. Moreover, the marriages set an immediate trend for fathering children on captured Persian women; before, such offspring had been regarded as socially inferior. The flipside was that, in almost no time, the chaste Arabic of Medina and even of Mecca began to be invaded by Persianisms from the interloping mother-tongue. And not only Persian morphemes and Persian mothers began to take over the holies of Arab holies, but also Persian manners – the supposed love of luxury, the unmanning languor of those arch-'Orientals':

> When Umar saw that the Emigrants [from Mecca] and the Ansar [the native Medinese] were living luxuriously, and that many of them were aping the Persian way of life, he told them, 'You must be proper Ma'add Arabs and keep yourselves rough.'

(Ma'add is one of the blanket names for the 'northern', principally bedouin, tribes.) Umar's plea would be in vain. What he saw as cultural miscegenation at Medina was all a foreshadowing of the Arab–Persian cultural mass marriage that would take place a century later.

Even at this time, however, another reverse invasion had begun – an infiltration of the Arab tribes, and not just by captured women but by converted men. Almost universally in the early period of Islam, a non-Arab could only become a Muslim by first becoming a *mawla*, often translated as 'client' but more precisely an affiliate, of an Arab tribe. Freed slaves generally became the *mawla*s of their former owners' tribes, but the relationship could be entered into by anyone, by mutual agreement. Given the small numbers of tribal Arabs relative to the populations of the lands they had occupied, the *mawla*s soon came to outnumber the original Arabs. By the end of the seventh century, Arabs in the new Iraqi city of al-Kufah would go about on formal occasions each accompanied by between ten and twenty *mawla* followers. *Mawla*s were, in theory, totally assimilated to the tribe as a political structure, sharing in its *'asabiyyah* or solidarity. But distinctions of blood were rigorously maintained. Indeed, the distinctions were said to maintain themselves: when a group of Shaybani tribesmen and their *mawla*s were captured and beheaded by rivals, a witness swore that the pools of tribal and *mawla* blood had refused to mix. In time, however, the inevitable happened, and even the blood blurred; *mawla*s and tribesmen, after all, bore the same sort of names – 'A son of B son of C . . . al-Shaybani', for example. Within a couple of centuries of its moment of highest definition and greatest visibility, Arab identity – as a group not only with its own distinctive language, but also with a scripture, a mission and unbounded energy – was in flux once more. As Ibn Khaldun was to put it, the South Arabian *sha'b* peoples had been mixed from the start. As for the supposedly pure-blooded northern Arabs, those tenders of tribal trees and pruners of patrilines, with the growth of Islam and their minglings with Persians and others, 'the tribes disappeared'.

Sometimes the process of grafting non-Arabs onto the Arab family tree would be obvious, as with the arrant faking of a pure Arab pedigree by the probably ethnic Persian Yahya ibn Hubayrah, in an attempt to gentrify himself when he landed the job of *wazir* or chief minister to the later Abbasid Caliph al-Muktafi. In the vast majority of cases, however, the process is invisible – except in flashes of satire such as that of the poet Abu Nuwas, poking fun at an 'Arab manufactured in the marketplace', who was a humble *mawla* in town, but played his role as a 'genuine' bedouin to perfection when he was in the country. Occasionally an 'Arab's' non-Arab origin came to light unexpectedly: when the grammarian al-Farra' discovered 'something appalling' in the ancestry of his colleague al-Sikkit – that the poor man's forebears hailed from the infra-dig Persian province of Khuzistan – he shut himself away for forty days in order to avoid seeing him (it was another case of pots and kettles: al-Farra' himself was of non-Arab, Daylamite origin). But, in general, being Arab was to become more like being a *cives romanus* or a citizen of the United States; and in time, when the Others – Daylamites, Turks, Mongols – took over the empire that Arabs had won, being genuinely Arab mattered less and less. Genealogy, one of the great passions of Arabs at least since the days of the Safaitic desert graffiti, would become more an art than a science, and a pretty abstract art at that.

That said, the Arab–Persian marriage in particular, and the whole relationship of Arabs with others in general, has never been easy or equal. It was largely non-Arabs who would 'open up' Islam, incubating it, nurturing it and making it the world faith it has become. In a sense, Arabs have always struggled against this reflexive opening-up, struggled to maintain not some imagined racial 'purity', which in reality they have never had, but at least to preserve their primacy and patriarchy – to maintain their missionary position in both of its senses. As with the Persian shah wanting to marry the sister of the Arab king of al-Hirah, it would never do for the non-Arab to be the one on top. The technical term for marriage of an Arab man to a non-Arab woman is *hujnah*, which suggests mere 'hybridization'. The term for the opposite union is *iqraf*, which also means 'loathsome infection'. At the battle of al-Yarmuk, Hind had egged on the Arab troops by telling them to 'prune' the uncircumcised Byzantines with their swords. Another Arab war-poetess, Azdah, went one further in a battle against the Persians: 'If you lose,' she cried, 'the uncircumcised ones will penetrate us!' She was playing on an old and terrible fear, one that has never quite been laid to rest.

SKY OF DATES, EARTH OF GOLD

It was not only the close encounter with others that was changing Arabs. Further changes came from within, and were planned. After the great Arabian 'Apostasy' was put down in 633, a conscious policy of social engineering came into play. The Islamic community was an Arab (to begin with) super-tribe unified, like the old South Arabian *sha'b*s or peoples, by allegiance to a shared deity. Now, *hijrah* became a form of super-migration, a severance not just from one's birthplace, but altogether from one's Arabian roots. The severance enabled far conquest, or super-raids. It was Muhammad's move to Medina, writ large.

In fact, very large. The idea of *hijrah* has some similarities with the modern Zionist idea of mass-migration to a physical Promised Land. But it is that idea blown wide open: all lands are promised. The Wandering Zionist eventually settles in what he looks on as the land of his ancestors; the Wandering Arab forsakes the land of his ancestors and is potentially always on the move. As the Qur'an puts it in one of many passages encouraging travel,

> And Allah has made the earth for you as a carpet spread out,
> That you may go about therein on broad roads.

In one sense this new and vastly expanded *hijrah* was a continuation of pre-Islamic tribal migrations; it was all part of an old, ever-extending figure in the unrolling carpet. And it was not haphazard: it was carefully, centrally designed and controlled. Control depended on the increasing use of writing, and on a growing network of posts. Above all, central policy aimed to create tractable masses of people who could be shifted and settled in garrison towns. As we have seen, *hijrah* was keenly promoted, and its reverse – *ta'arrub*, 're-arabization' – equated with apostasy. It was even claimed that Muhammad had cursed anyone who 'turned bedouin' (*bada*) after *hijrah*. One upshot of all this was that an ancient aspect of being Arab began to wither. You moved from your old *dar a'rabiyyah*, 'bedouin home', to your new *dar hijrah*, 'migratory home': in so doing, you abandoned your *'arab* lifestyle, and ceased being of the *'arab* in the oldest, herding-raiding sense of the word. In the linguistic sense you were still *'arabi*, Arabic-speaking. But, as we shall see, even that was in jeopardy.

The planned mass resettlements began as soon as Syria was conquered in 636. Arabs already there from pre-Islamic times were relocated within the country, and new nomads were shifted from the peninsula to settled areas. But the movement really took off with the foundation of the new cities called *amsar*, whose basic sense is that of 'frontier outposts'. The obvious purpose of the *amsar* was to serve as bases for extending those frontiers. But an additional aim was to balance further the *hadar–badw* equation. This was done in two main ways. First, by being sent to the new towns along with other emigrants from the peninsula, the bedouins were 'collectivized' and their *shawkah* – their 'sting' or warlike potential – was pointed away from Medina. After the near-collapse of their project in the War of Apostasy, Umar and the other leaders in the Arabian capital must have sighed with relief to see the more troublesome tribesmen disappearing to new conquests beyond the horizon, far from the centre of power. (The policy, of course, spread the seeds of destruction for the future empire; one cannot plan for all contingencies.)

Second, settlement in the new towns converted bedouin tribes not just from raiding to regular soldiering (or at least to raiding others rather than each other), but also to trading (or at least to getting others to do the trading and then taxing them). In addition to their other senses, the *futuhat*, as we have seen, were the 'openings-up' of new markets. For tribal Arabs, there were now ways of making a living that were more lucrative and more leisurely than rustling camels. The oral promotional literature played on this:

according to one enthusiastic report on the new cities of al-Basrah, founded in 638, and its twin or slightly younger sister, al-Kufah, the streets of the *amsar* were paved with gold: 'Our thickets are sugar-cane, our rivers are a marvel, the sky above us is fresh dates, the earth beneath us is gold.' It could not have sounded more different from the parsimonious peninsula. Not, of course, that one could sink into opulent inactivity; not yet. The *amsar* may have been golden, but they were gilded garrisons. It was *de rigueur* to teach your sons swimming and horsemanship, and at any time you and they might be sent from relatively balmy al-Kufah to die in sweaty Sind, or from palmy al-Basrah to pine in distant Central Asia. Occasionally, such relocations were on a military-industrial scale: in the biggest, in 671, 50,000 men were moved from overcrowded, under-resourced al-Basrah to Marw, nearly 2,000 kilometres away.

Relocation, collectivization and mass mobilization smack of Stalin. But the ethos in the new towns – that of militarism combined with market freedom, all in the employ of a young empire – has other parallels. Bernard Lewis felicitously saw al-Kufah, al-Basrah and the other major garrison cities, al-Fustat in Egypt and al-Qayrawan in Tunisia, as the 'Gibraltars and Singapores' of Arabs who relied on 'desert-power' as the British were to depend on sea-power: Britannia ruled the waves; Arabia ruled the wilds. But, once again, perhaps the Honourable East India Company provides an even closer parallel: the *amsar* are also inland Bombays and Madrases, functioning like the European factories-cum-fortresses that would spring up round the Indian Ocean rim. A century before the great Arab conquests, Qurashi merchants had come up with the idea of *mudarabah*, the pooling of capital and the basis, too, of those future European merchant ventures. Now, with the *amsar* and the addition of military might, expansion was entering a new, imperial phase, as it would do for the Honourable Company.

For seventh-century Arab leaders, it was all a triumphal outcome of the long-running dialogue between *badw* and *hadar*, nomad and settled. And who better than men from Mecca the Mercantile, the Mother of Emporia, to understand that the slash-and-burn approach of *a'rab* raiders might produce fruitful booty in the short term, but that for sustainable gain you had to cultivate urban markets? It has even been suggested that the developed Islamic usage of the word *hijrah* – migration to new towns – might have come about under South Arabian influence: the Sabaic root *hjr* means not 'severance', but 'town'. This is tempting but debatable: every word we use is haunted by semantic ghosts, but some of them are very wispy. It is more likely that influences – economic, not linguistic – came from the other old imperial neighbours. The Meccan merchant elite, now rebranded as the leaders of the Islamic state of Medina, were directing the tremendous energies released by Muhammad's revolution, and the unprecedented unity it had generated, to remould tribal Arabdom into something that was economically, militarily and even socially more like the former superpowers, Rome/Byzantium and Persia, in their heyday. Now Persia was defunct, Byzantium decimated, and Arabs would succeed them both.

Looking far ahead to other imperial ventures, we have that parallel to the Arab path in the British empire, and particularly in its joint-stock, mercantile beginnings. Looking even further – and there are, admittedly, a lot of *mutatis mutandis* – perhaps the Islamic Arab path was also not entirely different from that of Communist China, redirecting its ideological revolution to accommodate the market, repositioning itself to succeed more recent superpowers.

HOUSES DIVIDED

At first it all worked. The *amsar* sprang up at strategic locations. In Iraq, al-Basrah was built not far from the head of the Gulf, al-Kufah in the long fought-over borderland between desert and sown, near the ruins of both ancient Babylon and more recent al-Hirah. In Syria, which had a long-established Arab population and pre-Islamic links with the Meccan aristocracy, the old cities such as Damascus were kept as administrative centres and the land divided into military districts. In Egypt, only retaken from the Persians in 631, the Byzantines were dazed and demoralized by the fate of their comrades in Syria and put up limited resistance when Arab incursions began in 639. The maritime cosmopolis of Alexandria was to hold out longer, but the inland fortress of Babylon (Old Cairo) fell to an Arab force in 641. Nearby, beside the Nile where Upper and Lower Egypt met and the wedge of the Delta penetrated deepest inland, another *misr* (the singular of *amsar*) was founded – al-Fustat, 'the Tent' in Arabic, or possibly from the Greek *fossaton*, 'ditch'. (The word *misr* is also the Arabic name for Egypt, although chickens and eggs are involved: *misr* is an ancient Semitic word which means at root 'border', and Egypt had been the Semitic *misr* 'border(-land)' long before Arabs founded their *misr* 'border(-town)' there.) Almost immediately, Arab raids penetrated west from Egypt as far as Roman Africa (today's Tunisia) but a fourth great frontier city would not be founded there until 670. Its name, al-Qayrawan (from Persian *karwan*), is usually glossed in Arabic as 'garrison camp'; the mercantile bells rung by the English cognate, 'caravan', are however thoroughly appropriate.

None of the *amsar* is typical; they all developed differently in their different environments. But to look briefly at the first of them will give some idea of what the others were like. Al-Basrah began as a giant camp, a city that could be 'struck': even its public buildings were constructed from enormous reed bundles (like the houses of the nearby 'Marsh Arabs') that were easily dismantlable when the garrison went on extended raids. But the city soon became more permanent, and its population swelled and diversified: in the early years, it included not only Persians but many pre-Islamic immigrants of Indian origin, especially 'Zutt' or Jhats, who allied themselves with Arab tribes. For a time this much-needed addition to the fighting force was given equal rights and army pay to those of Arabs; later in the seventh century, as the Arab population grew, chauvinism hardened and state coffers emptied, they were expelled. By this time al-Basrah had a population of 80,000 warriors and 120,000 dependants – vast by world standards of the time. And despite the growing 'Little Arabia' mindset of its governors and their intolerance of non-Arabs, the city was becoming visually cosmopolitan: captives from Afghanistan built a mosque 'in the Kabul style' which, at the time, may have meant that it had influences from Buddhist buildings. Not least, al-Basrah's position on the conjoined Tigris–Euphrates waterway that leads to the nearby head of the Gulf also made it commercially cosmopolitan. A later Basran boasted of 'our teak and ivory, our brocade and land-taxes, and our rolling river'. It is a neat summary of the hemiglobal sources of the city's wealth – Indian forests, African elephants, Chinese silk, its own vast palm-groves of the Sawad – and all these products borne by its great watery artery.

Al-Basrah was blessed by geography. But it shared features with the other *amsar* – temporary-looking beginnings, tensions between Arab and other inhabitants, inevitable diversification, mushrooming growth. It also shared a design flaw that would hold back the cities' organic urban development and, much worse, doom the cohesion of their Arab inhabitants. To begin with, Arabs of nomad origin only became superficial 'townies': when famine struck in al-Kufah, for example, most people upped sticks and dispersed to forage in the steppelands. For the old survival mechanism to kick in thus was hardly surprising. But they were also, and far more fatefully, only a superficial community: collectivization was never radical enough to erase differences. As early as Abu Bakr's projected Syrian campaign, troops fought under tribal colours: he 'ordered the commanders to assign a banner to each tribe, which would stay in their midst'. The banners stayed in their midst in the eventual conquests: each tribe marched under its own colours, while the smallest tribes grouped together under a joint flag – a sort of 'Minor Counties' team, or a Black Watch tartan. This comparison is by no means flippant; but it is flawed. The super-tribe of Islam was, and remained, an ideal; the conversion of tribal banners into regimental colours, the sublimation of tribalism into sport – changes like these would take place with the rise of the European territorial nation-state. Arabs never fully achieved them. (Indeed, with the apparent failure of the more recent ideal – that imported nation-state – *re*tribalization is a current trend, at least outside my window.) And tribal banners fluttered not only on the march. The *amsar* themselves were physically divided: in al-Kufah, for example, Yemenis ('southerners', as they were still seen, despite the centuries of blurring) were settled in the east of the city and Nizaris ('northerners') in the west; these big divisions were themselves subdivided into tribal cantonments, each tribe having its own mosque. Thus, even on the core ground of the Islamic ideal – congregational prayer – disunity was perpetuated. The house of God had many rooms, and they did not intercommunicate.

Taha Husayn neatly lists some of the splits that would divide Arabdom all too soon after that first brief unanimity of expansion was spent:

> Adnanis [another term for 'northerners'] ganged up against Yemenis, Mudar against the rest of the Adnanis, and Rabi'ah against Mudar. Mudar itself split, with Qays, Tamim and Quraysh each having its own *'asabiyyah*. Rabi'ah split too, with Taghlib and Bakr forming their own *'asabiyyah*s. And the same can be said for the Yemenis – Azd, Himyar and Quda'ah each had their own *'asabiyyah*.

The result was that, 'in all the *amsar* of Islam, the Arabs went back to a state of rivalry and competitiveness even more bitter than that of the [pre-Islamic age of] "Ignorance"'. Arab unity was more like a suspension than a solution: as in a salad dressing, the constituents intermingled happily as long as the mixture was kept in motion, by raiding and conquest. But when the motion stopped and the mixture settled, the constituents began to separate out.

Part of the problem was that the whole moral ethos remained tribal and pre-Islamic. An Islamic moral infrastructure would develop in the new towns and new lands, but only in the following centuries. For the moment, Arabs were so busy trying to chew the territories they were biting off that they had no time to ingest, let alone digest, the ethical implications of Islam – not least the essential equality of Arab and non-Arab, expressed so forcibly in Muhammad's Farewell Sermon. To put it in terms of Christian history, it was as if the Crusades had taken off in the lifetime of the first Apostles. These factors – continued tribalism, the time-lag between building cities and building civil societies – would mean that old-style, peninsular Arabs would be scattered and lost in the empire they had founded, marginalized in every sense.

Even then, the Arab story would be far from over. New sorts of Arabs would arise from the imperial multiplicity, as much a mixture as Arabs had always been – and united, both with each other and with the past, by the old catalyst of language. For, among their other roles, the new cities of the conquests were linguistic hotspots from which Arabic radiated outward to become the medium of trade, culture and everyday life. Many conquerors – Goths, Vandals, Mongols, for example – are themselves conquered by the cultures they occupy. With Arabs it would be the other way round: they themselves 'disappeared', but their language and culture remained triumphant. Thus the poet Ahmad Shawqi could look back from the early twentieth century and wonder that:

> We know no other races, other tongues like this:
> The people passed away, and yet their language lives!
> The line of Hashim's frayed, Nizar's is faded; but
> Their tongue speaks on in never-ending eloquence.

HOW TO SIT ON THRONES

Those new, acculturated Arabs were yet to come. For the moment, the exodus of old Arabs from Arabia was not just a severance of people from a land and from their more distant past. It also marked the start of Islam's own travels away from its Arabian matrix. Arabs and Islam were to travel, as we have seen, at very different rates. At first, Islam lagged behind; but it would catch up, and ultimately go much the further of the two.

Back home, the effect of the exodus was immediate. The peninsula became a place to be left, a holy land whose sanctity increased with distance. It seems that most of the migration out of Arabia itself was over as early as the time of Caliph Umar's death in 644; later migrations were secondary, with the *amsar* in Iraq and Egypt acting as stepping-stones. What is not in doubt is that Arabia had lost a lot of its 'talent' in not much more than a decade, and that it suffered cultural desertification. This would accelerate when in the 650s the caliphal capital moved to Damascus in the far north of the Arabian subcontinent. Looking through an overview of Arab(ic) culture such as Ibn Khallikan's great thirteenth-century biographical dictionary, *Wafayat al-a'yan*, *Notable Deaths*, it is striking that the peninsula hardly features in the lives of those who died after the first Islamic century or so, except as a place of pilgrimage. The *amsar*, and especially al-Basrah and al-Kufah, became the new intellectual as well as military centres: 'The Arabs have no scholarly tradition except in these two cities', complained a critic in the tenth century. Even by the early ninth century, the antiquarian and literary critic al-Asma'i could say of Medina, 'I spent a long time there and found not a single correct ancient ode. All of them were full of errors, or were forgeries.' Earlier still, and most damning, was the eighth-century Kufan scholar Ibn Shubrumah's response to the boast of a scholar in Medina:

> 'Scholarship came out of our city!'
> 'Yes,' Ibn Shubrumah said, 'and it never came back to you.'

It is clear that Arabia suffered severe cultural depletion. The effect of the exodus on the Arabian gene-pool can only be imagined, not quantified. 'The souls of the ambitious,' said an anonymous poet,

> strive to attain high stations,
> while the hapless strive to stay at home.

Another poet went further: the stay-at-homes, he said, are like, 'the inhabitants of tombs'. Persian brides may have brought new blood in the first flush of conquest, but from the end of the seventh century most of the Arabs' island became ever more isolated. There would be genetic minglings at Mecca, with the pilgrimage, and in the outward-looking parts of the Arabian seaboard, the ancient fertile fringe. But the mountains and valleys of the south and east and the steppe of the interior became steadily more inbred and introverted. Peninsular Arabia slipped out of the mainstream histories for the next thousand years and more.

As for the ambitious souls, a spur to their ambition was almost immediately taken away when Caliph Umar set up a welfare system, with pay and pensions from the copious proceeds of conquest. These were doled out to all Muslims who had played any part in the setting up of the state of Medina, in the wars of the 'Apostasy' and, now, in the conquests of further expansion. The amounts mostly ranged between 500 and 1,000 *dirham*s annually, and were heritable. It is hard to give a modern-day equivalent of their worth, but one could live on them. Not surprisingly, Umar was warned that people would come to depend on hand-outs, to which he replied, with disarming honesty, 'That is inevitable'. His vision of a welfare state was far-reaching, and included child-support payments; his economic innovations went as far as contemplating the issue of 'banknotes' in the form of camel-hide *dirham*s. If the text of his advice to his successors is genuine, Umar's intentions were of the best: they show how he intended to carry the revolutionary social and economic aspects of Muhammad's project forward, by investing in the new cities, and by taxing the rich and redistributing to the poor. He concluded with a Qur'anic quotation:

> 'Do not let wealth become something to be passed around among the rich.' And do not shut your door in the people's faces, lest the strong eat up the weak.

Umar's advice was, of course, ignored. The weak may not have been completely eaten up – someone had to be there to do the donkey-work for the strong; but the rich began their inevitable game of pass-the-parcel with the wealth that flooded into the imperial capital, Medina, from conquered lands. (That Qur'anic word for 'something to be passed around', *dulah*, is almost identical with the word soon to be used for 'dynasty, state', *dawlah*.) With so much booty and power involved, the division of the spoils would also cause divisions of loyalties, and corrode the old culture of generosity. Arabs would only remain great, as the sage al-Ahnaf said at about this time, 'if they strap on their swords, tie on their turbans, and ride off on their horses. And,' he went on, 'if . . . they never regard mutual generosity as a vice.' But the sheer amount of lucre would make victims of the old virtues.

Treasure in conquered lands was 'de-thesaurized' – taken out of vaults and turned into coinage – and not a little of the cash made its way back to Arabia, and to the capacious pockets of the few. 'On the day Uthman was killed,' al-Mas'udi records of Umar's successor as caliph,

> 150,000 [gold] *dinar*s and 1,000,000 [silver] *dirham*s were in the hands of his treasurer. The value of his estates . . . was 200,000 *dinar*s. The eighth part of the estate of al-Zubayr after his death amounted to 50,000 *dinar*s. He also left 1,000 horses and 1,000 female servants. Talhah's income from Iraq was 1,000 *dinar*s a day, and his income from the region of al-Sharah was more than that . . .

And so the list goes on. Uthman, admittedly, had been a well-to-do merchant early in life. But still, these were the revolutionaries who had been in on Muhammad's project from the start; about them hangs a whiff of what in different circumstances would be called 'champagne socialism'. (In contrast, Umar, it must be said, shared the Prophet's disdain of wealth. On one occasion, as caliph, he spent sixteen *dinar*s going on pilgrimage and thought himself extravagant.)

The parameters of wealth expanded with the horizons of empire. In a different class from the *nomenklatura* of early Islam, and of a later date, was a ninth-century judge who received a gift of gold and silver from a caliph's wife. His attitude to it illustrates the change that had come over Arabs. A friend of the judge told him the Prophet said that gifts are to be shared with one's close friends. 'Ah,' said the judge, keeping a tight hold of his present, 'that was in the days when gifts were sour milk and dates.' Such tight-fistedness, however, was particularly unwise when your friend was a poet and could record it for posterity:

> 'Hail, great *amir*!' are words I'll never say
> To you, Zayd. No; you'd sooner find me dead.
> You scoff rich puddings in your private rooms,
> And feed your guests on poor men's barley bread.
> A sheepskin coat and rawhide sandals once
> Were all the finery you hoped to own.
> All glory be to Him who gave you power
> And taught you how to sit upon a throne!

MANY BOOKS INTO ONE

If the equitable ideals of ancient Arabia and recent Islam were victims of the new fashions, their greatest victim would be the unity Muhammad had brought about. The wheel of fire would roll on, and it would be given a good hard shove by that first plutocrat of the Islamic half of recorded Arab history, Uthman.

Umar was killed in murky circumstances by a slave. With more foresight than his predecessors, the murdered caliph had appointed a committee to nominate a successor. Their choice, Uthman, was a descendant of Umayyah, the sixth-century ancestor of the clan that had run Mecca in the last decades of the 'Ignorance'. He was thus the first Umayyad caliph, but at least in Sunni circles has escaped the opprobrium that haunts the imminent Umayyad dynasty. He has his own claims to notoriety, as we shall see; but his main claim to fame, and an inestimable contribution to the cause of Arab cultural unity, was to put the Qur'an into the form in which we have it today.

The first caliph, Abu Bakr, had 'gathered the Qur'an between boards' – gathered, but not organized. Uthman and a core editorial team, all of them people who had known Muhammad, now set about arranging, editing, canonizing and broadcasting a unified text of the scriptures. At first the people who for a generation had acted as Qur'an reciters were unhappy. Relying on their memories (supplemented, no doubt, by uncollected, uncanonical written texts), they had exercised control over the Word of God. 'The Qur'an was many books,' they said. Now, they complained, 'you [Uthman] have abandoned all but one'. Their complaints were ignored. Master-copies, probably of large size and certainly written on parchment in the monumental, angular script later called 'Kufic', were sent out across the empire; secondary copies were made from these and distributed to mosques, where individuals would bring leaves to be copied piecemeal by in-house scribes. The Arabic publishing industry had so far produced only one book. But the boost to literacy can only be imagined. Just as important, that single authorized text would play the central part in unifying Arabic, if not Arabs: however much they might disagree with one another, the *ummah*, the super-tribe, now had a standardized written version of their super-dialect in which to do verbal battle.

All this was necessary because, as we have seen, Arabic was beginning to lose its 'purity' – or, to be honest, was continuing to change – even in those bastions of eloquence, Mecca and Medina. The threat of change was greater still for Arabs in the diaspora. Language had given them identity and then, via Muhammad and the Qur'an, unity. But the very success of that unity had spread them far and wide – and thin: they were in danger of being dissolved by their own mobility. Those 33,000 descendants of al-Abbas mentioned above were Arab in the male line, but in their female lines they were bewilderingly multiracial; mother-tongues multiplied down the generations – Aramaic, Persian, Turkish, Coptic, Greek, Berber and more. (We will return to this matter of forking mother-tongues and of hybridity in general.) Uthman's authorized edition of the Qur'an at least ensured that a unified form of written Arabic, and thus of Arabic culture, would not only survive but also thrive. As Ibn Khaldun would put it, 'Qur'an and Sunnah . . . preserved the Arabic language'. But preserving the political unity of diaspora Arabs would be a more daunting challenge by far. And, for the moment, the biggest challenge of all would be maintaining unity back home, in Medina.

CRACKING UP

As Arab armies cracked on across the continents, the consensus of their leaders in Medina began to crack up. It is neat to see things in dichotomies like Sunnah versus Shi'ah, and to trace reasons back to single ultimate causes like the legendary bloody separation of the conjoined ancestors, Abd Shams and Hashim. In truth, of course, there are countless tributary factors that feed into the approaching disunity; equally, neat dichotomies branch into deltas of dispute. Looking at the early years after Muhammad, however, the main problem was not one of policy or piety, doctrine or dogma; all that was controlled by the beneficent will of Allah. The problem was one about power and authority, about who should be king of the castle.

There is a story about Muhammad's first successor, the mature and pious Abu Bakr, that hints at the nature of the coming competition for power. Early in his caliphate, he had reason to remonstrate with Abu Sufyan. Abu Bakr's father was alive at the time, an old man in his nineties. Hearing his son's raised voice, he asked,

> 'Who is my son shouting at?' He was told, 'At Abu Sufyan.' At this the old man went up to Abu Bakr and said, 'So, Atiq Allah [the name by which his father had always called him], you raise your voice at Abu Sufyan, who only yesterday in the "Ignorance" was the lord of Quraysh?

> You have overstepped the mark of good behaviour and exceeded your station!' At these words, Abu Bakr and the Meccans and Medinans who were with him smiled, and Abu Bakr said, 'Father, with the coming of Islam, Allah has raised some people and humbled others.'

As it turned out, the temporarily humbled Umayyads would soon be raised back to their former station. But for the moment, it looked as if Islam had levelled the field, even if all the players were drawn from Muhammad's tribe of Quraysh.

In his two-year caliphate Abu Bakr, who belonged to the rather distantly related Quraysh clan of Taym, had shown neither particular enmity to the Umayyads nor special partiality to the Hashimis; in fact he had alienated some of the latter by excluding Muhammad's next of kin from a share in the caliphal fifth share of booty. Umar, who belonged to another collateral line of Quraysh, had also been an impartial ruler. With the wealthy Uthman, first of the Umayyad clan of Quraysh to rise again, things began to change.

Uthman, although one of the 'Rightly Guided' caliphs (as Muhammad's first four successors are known), seems to have mislaid his sense of direction about half-way through his twelve-year caliphate: his loss at this time of Muhammad's seal, used for authenticating state documents, which he dropped down a well, has been seen by some as a symbol of that loss of bearings. Portents apart, he allowed corruption to spread, and exiled whistleblowers. Worse, he favoured his own Umayyad kin with plum jobs. The governorship of Syria was already in Umayyad hands, those of Abu Sufyan's son Mu'awiyah; Uthman also gave the rule of the Iraqi power-bases of al-Basrah and al-Kufah, and of Egypt, to his relatives. In Medina, he surrounded himself with Umayyad advisers. One might try to defend him on the grounds that he could exercise better control via his own close kin, but neither of his two predecessors as caliphs had felt it necessary to do so, and to many it was blatant nepotism. The wry comment of Amr ibn al-As, mastermind of the conquest of Egypt, sums up the general attitude. Dismissed as governor of Egypt by Umar for extravagant living, Amr was now offered the job of military commander on the Nile, while Uthman's Umayyad placement would have control of the purse strings. 'Then,' Amr said, 'I'd be like someone holding the cow's horns while your governor milked her.' The great Arab conquests were beginning to look like a mega-fief for a small pre-Islamic ruling clan of a single Arab tribe. When one of

Uthman's governors in Iraq described the vast and long-coveted palm groves of the Sawad as 'the garden of Quraysh', it hardly corrected the view.

In 656 numbers of Arab troops in the provinces mutinied, complaining of corruption and inequality, and many marched to Medina: they hoped to make their case to the caliph, who after all had been one of Muhammad's earliest adherents, and was known, despite what later apologists would call his 'excusable errors', for his piety. Prominent among the marchers were those from the milch-cow of Egypt. Uthman acceded to their demands and sent them home. Here the story turns nasty: he had given the Egyptian Arabs' leaders a letter, and on opening this they are said to have found orders that they, the bearers, were to be seized and put to death on their return to the land of the Nile. Instead, they did an about-turn, marched on Medina, rather than just to it, besieged Uthman in his house and eventually, in June 656, killed him.

Such a sequence of events – creeping corruption and nepotism, the inertia and silence of the majority, the noisy disaffection of the few, confrontation, placation, double-dealing, the violent end that will beget more violence . . . it is hardly restricted to Arab history. But the extraordinarily monist nature of Islam had now given it an extra dimension: Allah is One, Allah is Truth, therefore Truth is One. This was the blunt syllogism with which disputants had begun to belabour each other, each convinced that he was utterly, unshakeably right. The pattern runs through history and is multiply visible around the Arab world today; I can see it here, in my adoptive land.

'The killing of Caliph Uthman,' Adonis has written,

> was the signal for the life of Islam to enter a struggle in which each side [of an argument] rejected the other. Politics and culture were characterized less by debate . . . than by denial, with each side believing that it acted according to absolute Truth, while its opponent was utterly in the wrong.

But if the claims to Truth were new, the events leading up to the killing of Uthman also follow the classic cycle of the wheel of fire: a fall-out over spoils, a split in the hub of the wheel, the split radiating out, an end to unity. In this case the split was magnified in direct proportion to Muhammad's success in forging that first great unity. The split has run through time right up to the present, and in looking at neat dichotomies of dogma like Sunnah/

Shi'ah we are only examining symptoms. The root problem is who gets the power – and the cash, the kudos and everything else that goes with it.

That question dominated the next four years of Arab history. Part of the problem was that the new caliph – Muhammad's first cousin and son-in-law, Ali – was apparently not interested in cash or power. Like Umar, he set about the fair redistribution of wealth, but unlike Umar, he emptied the coffers doing so; he also reversed land-grants made by Uthman to his cronies. Again like Umar, he had a firm grasp on the sacred implications of Islam; but, better than any of his contemporaries, he could express these implications in words. 'How far is it from earth to heaven?' he was asked. '*An answered prayer.*' 'And from East to West?' '*A day's journey for the sun.*' Islam, Ali meant, had brought heaven close and revealed the smallness of the world in its cosmic context. But Islam had also sparked off a vast and growing worldly empire, awash with wealth, in which heavenly matters were not at the top of the agenda. Ali was the perfect candidate to rule what Ibn Khaldun was to call that 'rare and remote . . . hypothesis', the ideal city of the philosophers. Others, however, aspired to run what was looking more like Quraysh plc.

Two of those others, Talhah and al-Zubayr, were prominent in al-Mas'udi's Rich List of Muhammad's companions who amassed fortunes. The third was Muhammad's favourite wife, A'ishah the daughter of Abu Bakr. They too had been unhappy with Uthman's rule, but had kept aloof from the violence against him. Now they could wield accusations of complicity in the old leader's murder against Ali, who had unwisely let himself be elected to the caliphate by a group including some of his predecessor's killers. A'ishah, Talhah and al-Zubayr now called for *islah*, 'reform' – that woolly but potent watchword of solidarity-creators down the ages – gathered a band of followers, and set out for Iraq, there to set up a power-base. Ali pursued them, and it all ended in more violence, for which the adjective 'internecine' might have been coined.

The climax of that violence, the so-called Day of the Camel in December 656, set Muhammad's favourite cousin, the widower of his favourite daughter, against his favourite wife, the daughter of his best friend. The Day takes its name from A'ishah's presence in the thick of the fighting, in the tradition of pre-Islamic seeresses, 'on a camel in a litter made of wooden boards covered with thick hair cloth and cattle-hides, under which was a layer of felt, the whole covered with chain-mail'. By the end of the battle, 'seventy men's hands had been severed as they tried to grab the camel's halter

. . . and the litter was so stuck about with darts and arrows that it looked like a porcupine'. News of the battle flew back to Medina – literally, it is said, in the form of one of those severed hands, wearing the signet-ring of its owner and carried by a vulture. But the people of the capital were kept in suspense over the outcome. On the battlefield, however, it was clear: among the 7,000 dead – a 'conservative' estimate – were Talhah and al-Zubayr. The feisty A'ishah lived on, but not to fight another day. (She did however attempt soon after the battle to intervene in another dispute, riding into the thick of it on a mule. But one of the Medinans gently took her aside and said, 'By Allah, we haven't yet washed the dust of the Day of the Camel from our heads, and they'll soon be talking about the Day of the Mule.' And A'ishah laughed and rode away.)

For the time being, it was a victory for Ali; perhaps for the more egalitarian aspects of Islam over older vested interests. Was it also the defeat of a possible resurgence of female authority? Certainly, women had wielded greater public power in pre-Islamic times; even in the 'Apostasy', the prophetess Sajah had gathered an impressive following. In the case of A'ishah, the question is the merest speculation. But that speculation seems to have been current at the time: one report has a fighter on A'ishah's side saying, as he died, that he had been 'duped by the woman who wanted to be Commander of the Faithful.'

A female caliph . . . now there's a what-if if ever there was.

QUR'ANS ON LANCES

In the end, it would not be the spirit of pre-Islamic matriarchy that won the leadership title, but the favourite son of the pre-Islamic Meccan oligarchy. Mu'awiyah – the son of Abu Sufyan, 'who only yesterday', as the older generation had been at pains to remind the younger, ' . . . was the lord of Quraysh' – was already firmly ensconced as governor of Syria. Now he demanded vengeance for his Umayyad kinsman Uthman's killing, to which he considered Ali a party. Forget, for the moment, later dogmas and doctrines, Sunnah and Shi'ah: it was an old-fashioned clan blood-feud, magnified – super-clans have super-feuds. It was also a downside to Muhammad's miracle: the greater the coming together, the worse the falling apart. For the caliphal title fight would make the hardest-fought ancient 'Days of the Arabs' seem like gentlemanly tiffs in comparison, and the crucial battles and raids that founded the Islamic state sandpit scuffles. Beside it, the Day of the Camel would look like a preliminary scrimmage. Even the decisive, empire-busting routs of al-Yarmuk and al-Qadisiyyah were less bloody.

The battle of Siffin was fought over nearly four months in 657, on the right bank of the Euphrates across from al-Raqqah. It began like one of those ancient tiffs, with skirmishes and poetic wind-ups. Ali, for example, taunted Mu'awiyah (and his notorious liver-gnawing mother, Hind):

> Where's that Mu'awiyah? I fight and mean
> To beat him; but he's nowhere to be seen.
> Where is the slit-eyed fat-gut? None can tell:
> His mother hurled him, and herself, to Hell!

It soon got desperate: it was a fight over what was already a vast empire. 'There was such fighting,' al-Mas'udi says,

> . . . as had never taken place before. I found in a certain written account of the events at Siffin that Hashim al-Mirqal, having been thrown to the ground . . . saw Ubayd Allah ibn Umar prostrate and wounded near him. Hashim crawled over to him and, deprived of weapons and of strength, began to gnaw at his nipples until he sank his teeth into one of them. He was found thus, dead, on top of Ubayd Allah.

That is the sort of detail that would be hard to invent. Other details – that Ali, for example, personally killed 523 of the enemy in a day and a night – sound more questionable. But as the battle raged on towards its climax all detail was lost in a descending darkness:

> Dawn broke and they were still fighting. Then the sun was eclipsed, and the dust rose, and the banners and standards were cut down, and they no longer knew the times of prayer.

With the 'colours' and the light gone, so too was tribal and even personal identity. The enlightenment of faith, the passage of time itself, were annulled. The darkness clings there still: it is a millennial theatre of war, from the clashes between Babylonians and Assyrians down to only yesterday, when distant, mutant offspring of Ali and Mu'awiyah – a Shi'ah-dominated Iraqi state and a hyper-Sunni 'Islamic State' – were slogging it out on the endless dusty plains and missiles were slamming into al-Raqqah, the 'Islamic State's' capital in Syria.

> Places, when you reflect on them, resemble men:
> Some are inclined to happiness, others to grief.

It is hard to see through the murk, but Mu'awiyah was probably losing. And then he remembered a weapon in his armoury that was as yet unused: the Book of Allah. Every man on Mu'awiyah's side who had a copy of the Qur'an – 500 of them – tied it to his lance and raised it high. (The idea recurs to Arab leaders, however lightly worn their faith. You can still find pictures, peeled and faded, of our former president here in Yemen, flourishing a copy.) In Mu'awiyah's case, given the large size of surviving early Qur'ans, it seems unlikely that 'pocket editions' existed and that the warriors could have tied whole copies of the book to their weapons. The more probable sense is that individual leaves or sections, kept as amulets, were suspended from the lances. In any case, Ali was unimpressed: 'They are not people of religion and the Qur'an,' he pointed out. But his men were set on submitting to arbitration by the Book of Allah, and Ali deferred to them. As ever, the conquering Arabic word had won: it trumped the force of arms on Ali's side, and the force of argument. And the scene on the battlefield of Siffin foreshadows the conflicting claims to truth that would in time be wielded by Sunnah and Shi'ah: on one side rhetorical truth, the sacred word, as much amulet or talisman as meaning; on the other, apostolic truth, authority vested in a live person, a living imam.

When the dust of Siffin finally settled, 70,000 – the most commonly given number – were found to have been killed over 110 days of fighting, 45,000 on Mu'awiyah's side, 25,000 on Ali's. Some authorities, however, put the total slaughter at over half as much again. As ever, all the figures are questionable; but there is no doubt that Siffin was astonishingly bloody, and that it was the climax of a long series of encounters between the opponents. It is claimed that Mu'awiyah's deployment of the Word of Allah ended the fighting; just as likely, it was that tireless promoter of peace – exhaustion.

Ali, under pressure of many on his own side, all of whom were convinced of the truth of his claim, acquiesced in the idea of arbitration: using the Qur'an as their guide, two judges would decide who should be caliph. The whole business was inconclusive: 'The arbiters,' as the most succinct verdict puts it, 'agreed on nothing.' The Syrian Arabs acknowledged Mu'awiyah as caliph; the Iraqis fumed, and some now went against Ali for his alleged sell-out. With the ranks of the opposition split, recognition of Mu'awiyah's caliphate became more general.

At least the slaughter had ended, for the moment. But that miraculous first and last Arab unity, empowered by Islam, had now been permanently wrecked. The splits would follow tribal and sectarian lines – not that the two are always distinguishable: a sect is often a metaphor for a tribe. Muhammad is said to have prophesied that his community would divide into seventy-three sects. It is a conservative figure: what may have been the longest poem in Arabic, a lost ninth-century ode of 4,000 lines ending in the numbing monorhyme *-nā*, was a catalogue of sects and sectarians. Sad to say, this may be another candidate for the role of national epic.

That tactical deployment of the Word had won Mu'awiyah a reprieve in the battle of Siffin; his eventual victory in the battle for the caliphate had little to do with faith, truth, right or even perhaps with might. It was a victory of the old over the new, of the *ancien régime* of Quraysh over a slightly less *ancien* branch of the regime; of – as the Arabic equivalent of an English saying puts it – the *jinni* you know over the human you don't. Mu'awiyah knew the simple fact behind this crucial swing in Arab history: 'Quraysh,' he said, 'liked me more than Ali.'

Less than thirty years before, Mu'awiyah's father had witnessed that extraordinary unity in Medina. Now the body of Islam had undergone its first great cell-division, the start of a process of decay and regeneration. There have been mutations over time, but the general outlines remain the same, and have given their own unity to Arab-Islamic history, if not to Arabs themselves. Looking at an early account like al-Mas'udi's, you sometimes wonder if you are reading history or current events. Sunnis fight Shi'is over the same ground, literal and metaphorical, as they do today. Opposing sides, beneath banners black or white, green or striped, claim the same monopolies on authenticity, on truth. Ordinary people suffer and die.

George Santayana's famous maxim has it that 'Those who cannot remember the past are condemned to repeat it.' Sometimes, however, the problem is *not* forgetting history; or fixating on its least edifying chapters. It is a problem not just in Mesopotamia but also in Ulster and Kosovo; the banners can be orange or can bear white eagles as well as black script. Then again, the other option – sweeping the dirt of the past under the carpet – can be unhealthy too. Arab schoolchildren know about al-Yarmuk and al-Qadisiyyah, but the Day of the Camel and Siffin may well be met with blank looks. The bright faith is propagated, the darker truth is buried.

In many places, heritage is a tourist attraction; in the Arab world, 'heritage . . . is a socio-political problem'. It is rarely examined with detachment, with irony; how can you do a post-mortem when the subject is alive? In countries like the United States and Britain, where history is alleged to have ended, enthusiasts can for the moment safely revive it: 're-enactment' groups, neo-Cavaliers and neo-Confederates, neo-Unionists and neo-Roundheads, equipped with period arms and Kensington Gore, fight the battles of past civil wars. So do the enthusiasts of Siffin – but the blood is real, and the weapons are bang up to date.

CHAPTER EIGHT

THE KINGDOM OF DAMASCUS

UMAYYAD RULE

A GATHERING OF HEADS

Towards the end of 691 Abd al-Malik, Mu'awiyyah's fourth successor as Umayyad caliph, travelled from his capital, Damascus, to the Iraqi city of al-Kufah. Mus'ab, brother and general of the Umayyads' longstanding rival, the Meccan anti-caliph Abd Allah ibn al-Zubayr, had been killed in battle nearby. Now, in the audience hall of the governor's palace, Abd al-Malik stood contemplating Mus'ab's severed head. One of the Kufans accompanying him later recalled,

> Abd al-Malik noticed that I was perturbed, and asked me the reason. 'O Commander of the Faithful,' I said, 'I came to this palace and saw the head of al-Husayn placed before Ibn Ziyad on this very spot. Then I came here again and saw the head of Ibn Ziyad placed before al-Mukhtar on this same spot. Then I came again and saw the head of al-Mukhtar placed before Mus'ab ibn al-Zubayr. And now here is the head of Mus'ab placed before you – may Allah protect you from evil, O Commander of the Faithful!' At this, the caliph sprang up and ordered that the vault over the hall be destroyed.

The anecdote crams a lot of eventful Umayyad history into a nutshell; or four nutshells. The owner of the first head, al-Husayn, was the son of Caliph Ali; his death in 680 during an ill-planned bid to rally support against the Umayyad dynasty provided the 'party' of his late father, *shi'at 'Ali* – the Shi'ah, in short – with their greatest martyr. Al-Husayn was avenged when his nemesis, the Umayyad governor Ubayd Allah ibn Ziyad, met his own death in 686 in a rising led by the early Shi'i extremist, al-Mukhtar. Al-Mukhtar was killed in the following year when large parts of Iraq fell under the rule of Abd Allah ibn al-Zubayr, who had set up a rival caliphate, based in Mecca, to that of the Umayyads. Now, in October 691, Abd Allah's brother and governor in Iraq, Mus'ab, had gone down fighting despite offers of reconciliation with Damascus. It was all a far cry from the year three decades before when the first caliph of the Umayyad dynasty, Mu'awiyah, had finally emerged from the troubled and bloody struggle for succession as the most widely acknowledged leader of Arabdom. That year, 661, was remembered – ironically, it now looked – as *'Am al-Jama'ah*, the Year of Unity.

THE NOSE OF THE ARABS

'The Year of Unity' was wishful thinking from the start. What it meant was that the pre-Muhammadan Meccan Establishment had revived and reasserted itself in Mu'awiyah, son of the most prominent leader in pagan Mecca, albeit relocated to Damascus, and that most people simply acquiesced in the return to the *status quo ante*. A generation earlier, the tables had been turned by Muhammad. Now they were turned back again; the revolution of Islam had gone through a full 360 degrees, and Arabs were going forward in time into their own past.

Mu'awiyah reasserted his family's hereditary dominance by appointing his son as his successor. The idea of a crown prince clashed with Islamic precedent, such as it was (so far, various forms of election or appointment, but never of a member of the previous incumbent's immediate family). However, opposition to the appointment came in appeals not to as-yet-hazy Islamic ideals, but to the solid old-fashioned notion of nobility. 'So,' the eventual anti-caliph Abd Allah ibn al-Zubayr complained to Mu'awiyah,

> 'you would promote your son over those who are better than him?'
>
> 'Meaning yourself, I suppose,' Mu'awiyah said.

'Well, among the lineages of Mecca, my son's line is superior to yours.'

'But,' Ibn al-Zubayr replied, 'with the coming of Islam, Allah exalted certain lines. *My* line is one of those which He exalted.'

'True,' said Mu'awiyah. 'Along with the line of Hatib ibn Abi Balta'ah.'

Mu'awiyah's final retort is triple-barbed: not only was this Hatib of South Arabian origin, and thus in Qurashi terms socially challenged to begin with, but he had acknowledged his inferiority by making himself a client and thus a dependant of Abd Allah ibn al-Zubayr's father. Most pointed of all, however, is his name, which sounds even sillier in Arabic than it does translated into English: 'Firewood-gatherer, son of the father of Scold'.

In theory – at least in later theory – Muhammad's revolution had shifted the whole foundation and focus of Arab society from tribal to theocratic. *Din* had shifted in meaning from honouring ancestors and tribal deities to worshipping the One God, and *sunnah* from emulating tribal heroes to emulating God's prophet. The revolution had set off mass migrations and great victories. It had brought the peoples of South Arabia under its aegis, and made Persians and Egyptians members of the family of Islam. It had made these peoples equal with Arabs, and Arabs with each other. Superiority, nobility could only come from piety, not parentage. And yet here were two members of the same small tribe arguing about whose immediate family was posher. It was the same argument that the Qurashi ancestors Hashim and Umayyah had had, back in the pre-Islamic 'Ignorance', the same dispute that down the centuries had fuelled posturing poems and blood feuds between cousins. The revolution of Islam might have turned things upside-down around the periphery; the motion at the hub of Quraysh had been far less. It is not unlike V.S. Naipaul's Durkheimian notion of a 'constant inner world' – in his case, of India, where a whole existence remains the same while Mughals and British, Buddhism and imperialism, come and go. There are inner worlds within inner worlds, too, and the inmost one can be quite small, and can turn on questions of who's a nob and who's a pleb.

Muhammad had foreseen what would happen to his revolution. 'After me,' he is supposed to have said, 'there will be a caliphate for thirty years, and then there will be a king or kings'. Such alleged statements may of course be influenced by the anti-Umayyad sentiments of later writers. (Written Arabic history would only take off under the Abbasids, who pilloried and demonized their Umayyad cousins and predecessors.) But it cannot be denied that Mu'awiyah took the *'asabiyyah* created by Muhammad and recentred it on himself, as the head not of the inclusive and egalitarian theocratic commonwealth that was the Islamic ideal, but as an old-fashioned Arab king. Indeed, the Umayyads, the first of the Islamic dynasties, might be thought of equally as the last of the pre-Islamic Arab dynasties. The elision shows in a legend about Mu'awiyah's mother Hind, the liver-eating harridan: accused of adultery by her first husband, she was declared innocent by a *kahin*, who then went on to predict that she would give birth to a king. The annunciation would prove true; it only overlooks the circumstances of that kingship, the intervening matter of Islam.

King Mu'awiyah picked up where the pre-Islamic Ghassanid royal dynasty had left off. (Meanwhile the last Ghassanid king, Jabalah, whom we have seen embracing and then forsaking Islam, elided into Byzantium: he fathered a line which would produce the emperor Nicephorus I.) Mu'awiyah's subjects in Syria were the same, largely Aramaic-speaking, largely Christian populace whom the Ghassanids had ruled under their Byzantine suzerains; further east, the people were equally un-islamized and un-arabized. Mu'awiyah and his successors toed the line of Muhammad's ideology, of course: it was, after all, what had empowered the whole imperial venture and what gave the Umayyads legitimacy at the head of it all. But the ideological line could be very elastic, and many of the Umayyads enjoyed un-Islamic pleasures such as 'the daughter of the grape' – Caliph al-Walid ibn Yazid, for example, is supposed on one occasion to have been so overcome by alcohol and emotion at hearing a song that he insisted on kissing every member of the singer's body, including his penis. Al-Walid, however, crossed the line of propriety when he allegedly shot darts at a copy of the Qur'an and called Muhammad a charlatan. Not for nothing was he called the *khali'* of Banu Umayyah, the black sheep of an already dark dynasty. When judging the Umayyads, one must always factor in the way they were retrospectively demonized. But there is no doubt that, on balance, the temporal side of their rule outweighed the spiritual. Religion had a place in that rule, but it was a duty rather than a pleasure. Among the caliph's chores, for example, was the preaching of a sermon at Friday prayers, and when Abd al-Malik – seen above contemplating Mus'ab's severed head – complained that 'exposing his intellect' thus once a week to the populace had made his own head go prematurely grey, one feels he was being honest. (If there was one area in which religion did become a pleasure – even a passion – it was, as we shall see, in the built monuments of Umayyad Islamic legitimacy.)

Compared with his successors, Mu'awiyah was happier in his public role; but it was the role of traditional Arab leader, not head of a spiritual state. Historians who look askance at the Umayyads cannot deny that the first of their dynasty was a capable, hands-on ruler. He slept little, and constantly listened to edifying tales from ancient Arab history; even while eating, he heard the complaints of his subjects; and he possessed a quality found in only the most successful chiefs – *hilm*, a cocktail of forbearance, justice, wisdom, sedateness and moderation, akin to the Romans' *gravitas*. And Mu'awiyah's rule elided not only with the pre-Islamic Arab past: to a Christian monk from Mesopotamia, it brought back memories of Byzantine rule in its good old days:

> Justice flourished in his time, and there was great peace . . . The peace throughout the world was such that we have never heard, either from our fathers or from our grandfathers.

The Umayyads are chiefly remembered, as Patricia Crone puts it, for their 'impious deviation from an established tradition', the tradition of Islam. And yet that 'established tradition' was less than three decades old when Mu'awiyah came to power; it was still feeling its way. The tradition of Arab kingship, from which he and his house did not deviate, went back well over three centuries, to the beginning of the Lakhmid dynasty of al-Hirah. And he is also part of an even longer continuum. Mu'awiyah might have been the first Muslim dynast and the fifth caliph or successor of Muhammad; but he was also *anf al-'arab*, 'the nose of the Arabs' – their most prominent feature, their chief – and Arab history under him followed through from long before, as naturally as one follows one's nose.

BY THE FIGS AND THE OLIVES

Like the Ghassanids, the Umayyads had a foot in each world, that of the *badw* and that of the *hadar*. Al-Jabiyah, the Ghassanid tented capital in the Golan, became an Umayyad power-base too; the same nomad Arab tribes of the Syrian desert who, before Islam, had fought for the Ghassanids – and against the Muslims at the battle of al-Yarmuk – provided the Umayyads with their military backbone. Umayyad recreations included the bedouin pursuits of the racetrack and the chase. Among their built monuments are a number of voluptuous 'hunting-boxes', miniature pleasure palaces with bath houses and frescos (including the occasional naked lady), plonked, as if by wish-fulfilling *jinn*, at points across the Greater Syrian steppe. In these, too, they had been anticipated by the Ghassanids. But an Umayyad desert palace like Qusayr Amrah shows how much wider horizons had now become. Built in the first part of the eighth century by al-Walid, the son and successor of Abd al-Malik, its mural paintings are labelled in both Arabic and Greek; they show not only the allegorical figures of History, Poetry, Philosophy and Victory, but also the emperors of Byzantium and Abyssinia, the long-defunct shah of Persia, and the very recently defeated Roderick, king of the Visigoths in Spain. The dome of the bath house *calidarium* displays even wider horizons, for it depicts the vault of heaven. Qusayr Amrah is a man-made oasis in which to banquet and to bathe while hunting. But it also acts as a kind of camera obscura, for it projects a panorama of the Arab empire in the process of headlong expansion, and shows how Arabs were now members, under heaven, of the international club of kings and cultures past and present.

The Umayyads' weight, however, was on the other, urban foot – in Damascus, the ancient metropolis set in its immense oasis, the Ghutah. Muhammad is said to have reached the outskirts of the city on a trading trip, but to have recoiled from setting foot in its fleshpots. Now his *khalifah*s, his successors, had rushed in where prophets feared to tread. Compared with Muhammad's Medina, Damascus was Cockaigne or Las Vegas, an earthly parody of paradise. One of Mu'awiyah's commanders against Ali at the battle of Siffin, al-Nu'man ibn Jabalah, expressed this in a wry allusion to the Qur'an: 'By the figs and the olives . . .', one of its early Meccan chapters swears,

> We created man in the finest stature,
> Then we reduced him to the lowest of the low;
> Save those who believe and do righteous deeds. They shall have reward without end.

Sensing that he might miss out on that endless reward in heaven by siding with the worldlier of the two rivals, al-Nu'man said to Mu'awiyah, 'We'll fight for the figs and the olives of al-Ghutah, since we've deprived ourselves of the fruits and rivers of Paradise.' Another of those with his eye on the earthly temptations offered by the Umayyads was Amr ibn al-As, conqueror of the milch-cow of Egypt but subsequently sacked from its governorship.

> 'I will never give up any of my heavenly reward for you,' he said to Mu'awiyah, who was bargaining for his support, 'unless I get a share of your worldly wealth.'
>
> Mu'awiyah asked him to be more specific. Amr replied, 'Bait your hook with Egypt.'

He was reinstated as its governor.

Imperial governors knew they had to keep the funds flowing to Damascus. Ziyad, Mu'awiyah's governor in Iraq, told the caliph, 'I have subdued Iraq for you, and harvested the taxes of its land and sea, and brought you its inmost substance and hidden treasure.' The treasure had to pay for a court lifestyle that was far from the modest lives led by Muhammad and his first successors. An expert on pre-Islamic poetry, Hammad al-Rawiyah, recalled being summoned all the way from Iraq to Damascus by Caliph Hisham:

> I found him in a spacious palace paved with marble, each slab bordered by a strip of gold. Hisham was sitting on a red carpet, robed in red silk and dripping with musk and ambergris. I greeted him, and he returned my greeting and told me to draw near. I did so, and kissed his foot. He had two slave girls the like of whom I had never seen, wearing two earrings in each ear, each earring blazing with a pearl . . . The caliph said, 'Do you know why I sent for you?' I said, 'No.' He said, 'I sent for you because a line of poetry occurred to me, and I do not know who the poet is.' I said, 'What is the line?' And he recited,
>
> > 'They called one day for the morning-draught, and there came
> > a singing-slave who held in her right hand a pitcher.'

Fortunately, given that the caliphal whim had brought him on a two-week journey, Hammad knew not only the poet but also the rest of the poem. (And if he hadn't, knowing Hammad he would have made it up on the spot.)

In ancient Arab royal tradition, the Umayyads were also patrons of contemporary poets; some of these became virtual laureates, like the hard-drinking,

Christian bedouin al-Akhtal, court poet to Abd al-Malik. Vigorous, traditional verse flourished; but the Umayyad age was also one of transition. Emblematic of the change was the chronically love-lorn Jamil. He could compose a verse of which the first half was described as 'an *a'rabi* in a ragged loin-cloth, out in the sticks' –

> Come on, you sleeping camel-riders, up and off!

– and the second half,

> that I may haply ask you: Might a man be killed – by *love*?

as 'dizzy and effeminate'. Not all poets could slip so effortlessly from campsite to 'camp'; but Arab culture as a whole had begun its migration from the harsh *badiyah* to a softer, urban setting.

As well as that major Arab cultural heritage of poetry, the Umayyads were now heirs by adoption to other traditions. Prominent among these, as we have seen, were the architectural and figurative traditions taken over by the caliphs in their desert palaces. But artistic adaptation reached its climax in the religious monuments of the Umayyads, of which the greatest is the Umayyad Mosque of Damascus. The site – previously that of the temple of Damascene Jupiter, and before that of his local counterpart, Hadad – had more recently become that of the city's main church. Following the defeat of the Byzantines, Muslim and Christian worshippers shared the sacred precinct for no less than seventy years. In 708, however, the Christians moved to a new church nearby, and Caliph al-Walid ibn Abd al-Malik began seven years of building. The culmination was the decoration of the walls around the mosque's now immense courtyard with mosaics, for which thousands of Byzantine artists and craftsmen were employed. The millions of scintillating tesserae – pixels of gold, green, purple and many other colours – turned the walls into a gleaming dreamscape of villas and villages, streams and meads. Given Islamic strictures on images, at least in a place of worship, it is empty of people and animals, but planted profusely with trees. Among the mosaic figs and olives in this simulacrum of heaven on earth, al-Walid made a place where the here and the hereafter intersected.

It was the worldly aspect that impressed a Byzantine delegation to Damascus only a few years after the mosque had been completed. On his accession in 717, the new caliph, the ascetic and pious Umar ibn Abd al-Aziz (whom we have seen inspiring conversion to Islam in South Asia and North Africa), was said to have resolved on removing the mosaics and using the copious amounts of gold in them for charity. Just in time, the Byzantine envoys arrived and were shown around the mosque. Their reaction made Umar change his mind: 'Their leader looked about and turned pale. "We Byzantines imagined that you Arabs would not endure long. Now I have seen otherwise."' The newcomers were here to stay. Moreover, their aniconic Islamic take on Byzantine style may have fed back into the tastes of their neighbours. It is not known whether the Byzantine period of iconoclasm owes anything directly to the Islamic dislike of portraying living things, but when in the mid-eighth century the iconoclast emperor Constantine V removed from the Blachernae church mosaics that show human figures, he replaced them with trees and landscapes that might have been transplanted direct from Damascus.

The mosaics of Damascus are glorious, and also symptomatic of the Umayyad relationship with Islam: it was to be celebrated publicly and fulsomely, for it had got them where they were; but, ultimately, its glory was superficial, a glittering veneer. A recent commentator put it more exactly when he described the Umayyad state as consisting of 'an Islamic layer with a pre-Islamic essence, all given a Byzantine imperial gloss'. If that saintly exception, Umar ibn Abd al-Aziz, had seen through to the true worth of the faith, the gold that gave the glitter to that specious surface, he too realized that surfaces were what mattered to most people.

Umar's sainted caliphate did not endure. He sent a return deputation to Constantinople, where his pious reputation was well known. As it happened, while the Arab envoys were in the Byzantine capital, news reached the emperor that the caliph had died. The Arab ambassadors were as yet unaware; the emperor summoned them, received them – 'he had descended from his throne and removed the crown from his head; his features had changed . . . as if he had suffered a calamity' – and told them the news. On hearing it, the envoys wept. 'Do not weep for Umar,' the emperor said,

> Weep for yourselves and for what has befallen you. For he has gone to a better place than that which he has left . . . What amazes me is this: that the world should have lain beneath his feet, and yet that he remained aloof from it, and became like a monk. Good men can sojourn only a little while among evil men.

Umar's monastic caliphate had lasted a little over two years, and had done little to change the temporal tenor of Umayyad rule. Whether the encomium is a true verbatim report is questionable, although it does seem there was a particular mutual respect between the imperial neighbours during his brief tenure. And Umar's monk-like mien is attested by other accounts. Observing him deliver a Friday sermon, one of those present took note of the quality of his clothes – kaftan, turban, shirt, drawers, shoulder-cloth, soft boots, cap – and estimated that together they were worth no more than a bargain-basement twelve *dirhams*. There could have been no greater contrast to Hisham's red silk; or to Caliph Sulayman ibn Abd al-Malik, who would spend the morning pondering which turban to preach in, and even dressed his cooks in richly coloured livery. Nearly two centuries later, the Abbasid Caliph Harun al-Rashid owned a collection of Umayyad caliphal robes: the sleeves of those that had belonged to Sulayman were still stained with grease, from his habit of delving in roasted rams to get at their kidneys.

As ever, we must beware of retrospective blackening, or smearing. And it is equally dangerous to see the sainted Umar as the white sheep, the exception who shows up the other Umayyads as deviants from Islamic tradition. Once again: that tradition had not yet taken shape. The Qur'an existed as the canonical text; but a whole theological, legal and moral superstructure had yet to be built on it. Islam's basic 'pillars' – profession of faith, prayer, pilgrimage, fasting and alms-giving – were religiously upheld; its extant lore and legend were carefully orally preserved, and sometimes written down; but the sayings and doings of Muhammad and his companions had not yet been put into any order, let alone synthesized into an ethical system. The earliest of the synthesizers, the great Islamic doctors of the law, Malik ibn Anas, was born while the Umayyad Mosque was being built, and only came to prominence after the fall of the dynasty. Like their high-profile buildings which helped to establish Arabs as an international presence, the Umayyads were more concerned with what might be called ethnic architecture – building Arab identity to fit its new role and environment – than with promoting ethical structures in which that identity would be lost.

As we have seen in the preceding chapter, Arabs had now become the masters of a huge tranche of the civilized world, from Portugal to the Pamirs and from Aden to Azerbaijan; they needed not just the recent unifying ideology of Islam, nor even that far older unifying factor, the high Arabic language, but also firm and ancient foundation myths with which they could stake out their claims among the longer-established civilizations. This was the age when stories from the distant pre-Islamic past were fully articulated: Mu'awiyah would listen not only to accounts of the *ayyam al-'arab*, the ancient 'battle days' of the bedouins, but also to oral historians from the old settled south like Abid ibn Sharyah. Abid's narratives of the Marib damburst and the subsequent migrations co-opted southerners into a wider Arabian – now Arab – history. As part of this process of co-optation, myths were elaborated according to which the South Arabian conquests were taken far beyond their actual limits (central and eastern Arabia) and extended to Samarqand and the borders of China. The imaginary ancient empire thus mirrored the actual empire of Alexander, and fore-mirrored that of Islam. Listening to a richly embroidered account from Abid of how the Himyaris got to Kabul and beyond, Mu'awiyah said, 'Allah has made us heirs of all that empire of theirs. Today it is ours'.

THE LEGEND OF ISMA'IL

Arabs became heirs not just of other peoples' empires, but also of other peoples' ancestors. One of these was destined – if one can be destined in retrospect – to unite Arabs and make them a 'race'. As we have seen, the earliest sense of *'arab* may well be that of 'a mixed people'. This seems to reflect reality: genealogically, Arabs are not a family tree growing from a single stem, but its water-mirrored reflection; or rather the river itself, fed by multiple tributaries. Under the Umayyads, the search was on for the ultimate source of the river. They found it in Isma'il, the wandering exile.

The Romans of the new imperial age had also needed a source, a founding father. They discovered him in Aeneas, the immigrant from Troy, the exile who both connects to and differentiates from another older culture, who inaugurates a new line and a new unity in a foreign land. Similarly, Arabs needed stories of migration, of founding fathers, acculturation and unification, to rationalize their own historic diversity. And just as Augustus claimed descent from Aeneas, so too was Muhammad's origin traced back to Isma'il.

It was in the Umayyad age that all the elements of the legend finally came together. It tells how the northern Arabs were descended from Isma'il/Ishmael the son of Ibrahim/Abraham by his slave-concubine Hagar; Hagar herself came, according to tradition, from a village in Sinai called Umm al-'Arab, 'the Mother of the Arabs'. We have already seen how Hagar and

Isma'il were exiled in Islamic legend to Mecca, where they almost died of thirst but were saved by the miraculous spring of Zamzam. We have also seen how Isma'il, not originally an Arabic speaker, was taught the language by South Arabians living in Mecca, and how he married into the community of southerners. The story so far, inspired by impressionistic appearances of Isma'il in the Qur'an, back-projects a provenance for several features in the sacred landscape of Mecca. In Umayyad times, however, the account was developed in full, and provided in addition a provenance for Arabs themselves and for their major prophet who, as we have also seen, had discouraged speculation about his more distant ancestry. It was now – probably at some time around or during the short caliphate of Umar ibn Abd al-Aziz – that full pedigrees were elaborated, directly linking a more recent ancestor of Muhammad and the northern tribes, Adnan, with the biblical/Qur'anic Isma'il.

That there are at least three different versions of the line of descent from Isma'il to Adnan hardly inspires confidence. And yet the Isma'il legend works for many reasons: it grafts Muhammad on to the monotheistic family tree; it grafts the South Arabians on to the linguistic tree (thus avoiding the problem that they didn't actually speak Arabic); it backdates by millennia the alliance between the peoples of northern and southern Arabia; it offers in Isma'il a paradigm for the wanderer who settles (useful in an age when bedouins were being turned into colonists); and, most important, it acculturates not just peoples, but a whole past – Judaic and monotheistic – and makes it Arab. If Arabs wanted to assert their place in that wider community of kings and cultures depicted graphically in al-Walid's desert palace, then Isma'il's was a perfect ancestral persona to adopt.

Other ancestors were conjured out of even thinner air. The South Arabians were given a spectral forebear called Ya'rub, which means 'He-Speaks-Arabic'. His original tongue was supposedly, like that of Isma'il, 'Syriac', but he was miraculously converted to the language of heaven by a great wind that blew from Babel: the whole family of actual South Arabian languages, Sabaic and its siblings, was thus blown to oblivion. Furthermore, Ya'rub was deemed to be the grandson of the Qur'anic figure Hud, an ancient Arabian prophet who had been sent to warn the impious tribe of Ad of their coming extinction; the southerners, too, got their own share of inherited prophetic honour. Finally, to tie the knot neatly, the descent lines of both Isma'il and Ya'rub were taken back to join at the son of Noah, Sam/Shem.

All of this is hardly history; it is inspired and inventive autobiography. But it has become part of deep-level Arab collective memory. Nowadays, Isma'il only features in the general Arab conscious as a minor Qur'anic prophet; Ya'rub, if at all, as a dubious invention of the early genealogists. But between them they embody the forces that have created and held together an expanding Arab world. Thus, legendary or even imaginary as they are, they are as important to the story of Arab unity as solidly historical figures like Muhammad or, more recently, Egypt's President Nasser. A recent commentator, stressing the importance of the Isma'il legend, has said that it created 'a unifying "ethnic" identity for the Arabs, which had not existed before'. To be more exact, it gave an alleged biological basis to an ethnic identity that had begun to form long before, in the first millennium BC. What took place was something like the age-old assimilation of outsiders into a supposedly descent-based tribe, but on a massive scale: just as, say, an ex-slave of Persian origin could become affiliated to an Arab tribe, first adopting its language and customs and then its ancestral name, so too could entire non-Arab peoples – in this case, the settled Himyaris, Sabaeans and others of the South. In a process that began centuries before Islam, they had already become Arabs by language and culture; now they had the ultimate imprimatur, a place in the tribal Debrett's or Burke's. But as part of the process, the historic languages and diversity of these peoples were denied; they were 'tribalized', fitted into a system in which political unity derived from shared human ancestors, not just from a shared deity. In a sense, it was the triumph of the *qabilah* over the *sha'b*, of the tribe over the people.

It was also a denial of that basic idea of Muhammad's revolution, that of unity in plurality, or at least in duality:

> O mankind, We have created you from male and female, and made you into peoples and tribes, that you may know one another . . .

The need for Arab national unity to control the earthly Arab empire ran counter to Muhammad's vision of the super-tribal, supra-national unity of Islam. But in either case, unity was doomed. The branches of a family tree inevitably grow apart, competing for the light. Similarly, all roads might lead to Mecca and oneness in Allah, but when the pilgrimage is over the pilgrims take their ever-forking paths, and earthly realities reverse the heavenly ideal.

At least all Arabians were now, in the later Umayyad age, automatic Arabs. They needed to be: despite that supposed equality under Islam, Arabs were in practice the master-race of a ballooning empire, and without the southerners there would not be enough masters to go round; as we have seen, the first Caliph Umar had been painfully aware of the shortfall. One poet said of the southerners,

> Were it not for the swords and lances of Ya'rub,
> ears would never have heard the cry, *Allahu akbar!*

He may not have been exaggerating very much. The sons of Ya'rub, the old South Arabians, were the vital reinforcements without whom the whole imperial project would have failed.

DASHING PENS

By the careful elaboration of legend, Arabians were themselves arabized and arabicized under the Umayyads. But so was something else that would have equally far-reaching consequences.

The Umayyads had picked up where the pre-Islamic Ghassanid dynasty left off. But there was a major difference: unlike the Ghassanids, or the Lakhmids in the old Persian orbit, the Umayyads weren't mere client-kings – they were in charge. At first they adopted imperial know-how from the Byzantine and Persian systems. Their administration was conducted in Greek and, in ex-Sasanian areas, the old Persian language, Pahlavi; Byzantine and Persian coinage provided their currency. But they were not content to camp out for ever in the bureaucratic ruins of their predecessors. They had a vision, a mission, and if it wasn't an islamicizing mission, it was an arabicizing one.

In the year 700, Caliph Abd al-Malik – his own head, despite the curse of all those decapitations at al-Kufah, still firmly on his shoulders and running the empire with aplomb – took a decision with far-reaching results: he had a new coinage struck that bore Arabic legends and, more important still, he decreed that the empire be administered not in the local languages but in Arabic. From now on, across a swathe of two continents, if you wanted to get on in life you had to knuckle down and learn that infuriatingly difficult but infinitely rewarding tongue.

One of those dubious-sounding but hard-to-invent stories explains the change in the language of administration:

> The reason was that one of the Byzantine scribes needed to write something and, finding no water [to thin the ink], he urinated in the inkwell. Abd al-Malik heard of this, punished the scribe and gave orders . . . to change the records [to Arabic].

Whether writers of Arabic are less likely to urinate in inkwells than writers of Greek is a moot point; besides, it must be hard to urinate in an inkwell. But the story should not be dismissed because of its illogicality or triviality: chaos theory can apply to history as much to other disciplines. (Perhaps Borges was right to suggest that 'there is no event, however humble, that does not imply the history of the world and its infinite concatenation of causes and effects'.) What is not in doubt is the repercussions of Abd al-Malik's decree. It was at this point, Ibn Khaldun writes – with some truth, even if he simplifies, compresses and generalizes a much longer process – that 'People turned from the low standard of desert life to the splendour of sedentary culture and from the simplicity of illiteracy to the sophistication of literacy'. As a more recent commentator put it, the caliphal decree 'both reined in and enriched a language of poetry, oratory and proverbs, and changed it into a language of civilization and science'.

Not everyone benefited, however. When Abd al-Malik told his chief scribe, Sergius, of the decision,

> it troubled him, and he left the caliph's presence in a state of depression. Some of the Byzantine scribes found him thus, and he said to them, 'Go and look for some other means of livelihood, for God has deprived you of this profession.'

Others were more adaptable, and could slip into the new system: there were already people in the northern Fertile Crescent – that junction of languages and cultures – with a multilingual, multiliteral background, like the young Hassan al-Tanukhi, a Christian Arab fluent in speaking and writing Persian, Syriac and Arabic who would serve the state as a scribe and translator. One simply had to change or lose out.

The changes came fast. The older, more angular Arabic script, later known generically as 'Kufic', had resembled its Nabataean parent. Now, the sudden need to write much more, and much more quickly, gave birth to a new and rounded form of cursive script, essentially the same as most of the hands and typefaces used today. 'It can be written with a swiftness that is impossible in other scripts', noted the philosopher al-Kindi of the new and dashing style. To make reading easier and quicker, diacritical marks also began to be used more; inherited from Syriac, they had already appeared in Arabic at least as early as a dated papyrus of AH 22/AD 643.

As we shall see, arabicizing the administration was also to have other repercussions. The need for a mass of people suddenly to learn the intricacies of a very tricky language kick-started the formal analysis of that language. Grammar, syntax and philology were the first formal Arab sciences, and they shaped the entire Arab 'scientific method' – a whole way of looking at and understanding complex systems. Contrast this with the beginnings of the classical scientific method, in the observation of and speculation about 'the nature of things' from Anaximander on, and the scene is set for divergence: two angles from which to regard the universe, one rhetorical, relying on the authority of words, of texts; the other empirical, relying *Nullius In Verba*, as the motto of the Royal Society would put it, 'on no one's word'.

As for the coinage, Abd al-Malik issued a new Arabic, aniconic currency bearing pious phrases in place of the Byzantine coins used before. His decision, Ibn Khaldun says, was 'because eloquent words alone were obviously more congenial to the Arabs' than images – as if, for Arabs, the saying about the relative worth of words and pictures is inverted. Congenial images, of course, covered the walls of Umayyad palaces and mosques; but it has been suggested that a 695 Byzantine issue of gold coins bearing the face of Jesus must have clashed too obviously with Islamic strictures on the depiction of prophets. Al-Baladhuri, however, explains the new issue with another dubious but not incredible story. The 'lead-ins', or visible outer ends, of papyrus scrolls exported as writing material to Constantinople from Egypt had, before the Arab invasion, always borne crosses and other Christian symbols and words. The new Arab rulers of Egypt had these changed to Islamic messages, such as the anti-trinitarian Qur'anic verse,

> Say, 'He is Allah, One . . .'

In retaliation, the Byzantines threatened to include anti-Muhammad legends on the *dinar*s they supplied to Damascus – hence Abd al-Malik's decision to mint his own.

LINGUA SACRA, LINGUA FRANCA

Abd al-Malik's arabicization of bureaucracy and coinage was as important to the founding of a durable Arabic culture as the Qur'an had been: it was the second chapter of a written revolution. The Qur'an had been the first chapter: it was the first book and almost certainly still, at the beginning of the eighth century, the only physical one. Now, however, writing – based on the only written Arabic in general circulation, the high Arabic of the Qur'an – would proliferate as the red tape spooled out. (The third chapter would be the paper revolution that began later in the eighth century, when expensive parchment and papyrus were replaced with the much cheaper new writing material originating in China.) Without Abd al-Malik's decree, the Qur'an would have remained a revered holy text, but one that would gradually have detached itself from the mainstream life of the community it had helped to found. The high Qur'anic and poetic version of the language would, like Latin, have suffered a long, inevitable decline – ultimately to become, if not exactly a dead language, then a beautiful zombie, dedicated like Sanskrit to the service of a priestly caste. Indeed, without that sudden and intensive arabicization, today's Arab world – really the Arab*ic* world, a world defined by words – might never have come about. Empires that insist on administration in the language of the imperial masters can be immensely long-lived, like that of the Chinese, or can have a healthy afterlife, like that of the British; empires that make do with the languages of their subject-peoples have a tendency, like that of the Mongols, to break up and melt away.

The longevity of the Arabic world – of the Arabic word – is astonishing. No other comparable diasporic groups – Scythians, Turks, Mongols – have had such a strong and long-lasting sociolinguistic 'glue'. The Greek of the Hellenic world and the Latin of the Roman (and the Roman Catholic) dissolved in time. The standard English of the British empire is dissolving now. A present-day inhabitant of Kingston, Jamaica, would probably have little in common, linguistically or otherwise, with a seventh-century tribesman from Anglo-Saxon Northumbria; in contrast, despite the similarity of distance in time and space, a literate member of the black Moroccan Gnaoua in Tangier could hold a conversation with a seventh-century Meccan. Linguistic links are more powerful than genetic ones; ink is thicker than blood. For this we have to thank Islam, which never had a Pentecost, a revelation in many tongues. We have to thank too the *amsar*, the colonial new towns that were linguistic hotspots. Perhaps we also have to thank that nameless Byzantine scribe, short of ink, caught short and caught out.

The Arabic *lingua sacra* became also the *lingua franca*, and over an ever-widening region. Long-lived, far-flung cultures, however, can also exact a price: as we shall see in more detail later, the conquered tend to appropriate the language of the conquerors, infiltrate their ranks, and ultimately overwhelm them. An early and outstanding example of such an infiltrator is Hammad al-Rawiyah (Hammad 'the Copious Reciter'), a native of Daylam south of the Caspian, already seen helping Caliph Hisham by identifying the author of a pre-Islamic verse. A human search-engine when it came to ancient Arabic poetry and the battle-days of old Arabia, Hammad is said to have been able to recite 2,900 pre-Islamic odes – a hundred for each letter of the alphabet (that is, a hundred in which the rhyme-letter is *alif*, a hundred for *ba'* and so on). Whether or not this many genuine ancient poems had survived is questionable. What matters more is that, whereas traditional Arab transmitters of poetry only preserved the poems of their own tribes, Hammad and other non-Arabs preserved those of all the tribes together. In doing so, ironically, non-Arabs further developed the idea of Arabs as a cultural whole. As in the formative pre-Islamic years, when non-Arab imperial neighbours had shaped Arabs' definitions of themselves, the Other was moulding the Self. (But perhaps it is not ironical, for it can be argued that it is precisely the existence of others that gives us – as people or as peoples – the sense of who we are.)

The acculturated were defining the culture they had joined. But they were also beginning to add to it. Non-Arabs began to represent not just transmitters of poetry, but also poets in their own right. Even a slave from Sind, Abu Ata, could learn the ancient magic and become a poet patronized by the later Umayyad caliphs. Caught off his guard, his pronunciation could be appalling. But Arabic language, even mispronounced, made up for lack of Arab lineage. As the black slave and poet Nusayb ibn Rabah said,

> Some are raised up by their lineage;
> The lines of my poems are my lineage.

Now it was not only the old South Arabian peoples who were being acculturated by the Arabic language. The *futuhat* – the 'openings-up' or conquests – were going into reverse; the whole cultural empire of Arabs was being occupied by outsiders. Nor, as we shall see, did it help Arabs that their ranks were never truly closed: for despite the unifying rhetoric of Islam, and the efforts to synthesize Arabians in all their diversity and make them into Arabs, the old fissile tendency was back at work.

THE 'NORTH–SOUTH' SPLIT

It is always easy to picture things in contrasting pairs, and that of 'Northern Arabs' and 'South Arabians' has been useful so far. It is, however, shorthand for something much more complex. In genealogical terms, there is little basis to it. As we saw above, a theory of two major groupings had developed – that of the descendants of Isma'il (often called Adnanis or Nizaris, after ancestors higher up the family tree who may personify actual tribes) and those of Ya'rub (often called Qahtanis, for the same reason). But this was a rationalization of a much more involved reality, and by Islamic times trying to classify Arabs as 'northern' Adnanis or 'southern' Qahtanis was about as profitless as trying to sort the twenty-first-century population of the United Kingdom into Celts and Anglo-Saxons. There had of course been a linguistic division, but that had all but disappeared with the slow and steady victory of Arabic over the South Arabian languages. In purely geographical terms there was not much basis to the split: there were South Arabian groups like Ghassan in the far north of the Arabian subcontinent, and Northern Arabs had long infiltrated and settled the south. All of them, in any case, seem to have originated in the northern Fertile Crescent not long before the start of recorded Arabian history – that is, by the end of the second millennium BC.

Where the North–South split had greatest reality was in the way topography and climate had affected society from early on, producing the duality of *badw* and *hadar*, of *qaba'il*, tribes, and *shu'ub*, peoples. This sociological split resurfaced in Islamic times. 'What are you Yemenis?' asked a northerner of a southerner in a dispute in eighth-century Baghdad.

> I'll tell you. You're nothing but tanners of hides, weavers of striped shirting, trainers of monkeys and riders of nags. You were drowned by a rat and ruled by a woman, and people had never even heard of Yemen until a hoopoe told them about it.

The rat is the one supposed to have gnawed away at the Marib Dam. The woman is the Queen of Saba/Sheba, brought to Solomon's notice in the

Qur'anic account by a talking hoopoe. The monkeys are the baboons that frequent the southern highlands; the 'nags' are the sturdy horses, more suited to mountain travel than the thoroughbreds of the Arabian steppe. As for tanning and weaving, the two famous luxury industries of the south may have been the butt of rawhide- and haircloth-clad raiders, but were the mark of a settled society of consumers and exporters. For their part, the southerners saw the northern, tribal Arabs as bellowing *gimal* – the 'Himyari' pronunciation (still current south of where I live) of *jimal* – 'gamels', 'camels', who were always trying to order them around: 'We can't abide these loud-mouthed gamels: they think they should talk the talk while we walk the walk.' 'Trade' looked down on 'Raid', and vice-versa.

It seemed the ancient *hadar–badw* dialogue still hadn't got beyond the trading of insults. Most recently and strikingly, Muhammad had brought together North and South: theologically, he had shown the Qurashis' Allah and al-Rahman, the merciful deity of the southerners, to be one God; politically and socially, he had united the two groups by the 'brothering' of the Qurashi migrants and the originally southern Ansar, the native population of Medina. On his death, however, the Ansar had been excluded from any claims to leadership of the new community. That exclusion rankled. The old divisions had already been reinforced during the earliest conquests, when Syrian provinces and Iraqi cantonment cities were parcelled out along pre-Islamic tribal lines. Now, under the Umayyads, all Arabians were Arabs – *hadar* and *badw*, southerners and northerners; but some were more Arab than others, and a snobbish northern tribal poet like al-Farazdaq could dismiss Hadramis from the south of the peninsula as mere clients of Quraysh, as second-class tribesmen, like the unfortunate 'Firewood-gatherer' of Mu'awiyah's put-down. In the face of this kind of northern *'asabiyyah*, the southerners had maintained something of their own ancient solidarities and social structures: the clan of Dhu 'l-Kala', for example, descended from a line of late pre-Islamic *qwl*s or warlords, were a focus of southern unity in Umayyad Syria. But the northern tribal model of society was the dominant one, and such survivals from the old South soon faded away.

If the North–South split of Islamic times opened up ancient – sometimes legendary – fault lines, the movements in these faults were caused by forces in the present. It is not entirely unlike the twenty-first-century present in which the border of Scotland still happens to run, roughly, along the line of Hadrian's Wall, but in which Scottish Nationalism has more to do with oil revenues, taxation and the European Union than with whether one's ancestors were Picts, Celts, Romans, Sassenachs, Gaelic-speakers, Jacobites or whatever. The North–South split was a super-clan dispute, the latest and greatest example of that old tendency of units to divide in two – the Hashim versus Umayyah tendency. As we shall see, it exacerbated and was exacerbated by the power-struggles of Umayyad times. And it sparked off wars, far away in place and time – imminently in Khurasan, later in ninth-century India, in eighteenth-century Lebanon, in twentieth-century Oman.

But there were other, more immediately fatal fault lines.

HEARTS AND SWORDS

One rift was fatal at first only to a few of the family and followers – the *shi'ah*, or party – of Ali. (Seventy years on, however, it would open up and swallow the Umayyad dynasty; another 1,270 years on, it is still undermining Arab and Islamic unity, as fatally as ever.)

After the fudged arbitration that had ended his war with Ali, Mu'awiyah had gained the critical mass of support needed to call himself caliph in fact, not just in theory. The mass went on growing, swollen by the ever-silent majority – all those zeros that in themselves mean nothing, but can turn the '1' at their head into a million. In contrast, Ali's rival caliphate had shrunk until, by 660, it was limited territorially to little more than the region of al-Kufah. In the following year he was assassinated by a Khariji wielding a poisoned sword: a comrade spurned can be more furious than a woman scorned, and the Kharijis, 'the Quitters', loathed Ali for not fighting on against Mu'awiyah. Twenty years later, however, al-Kufah was still the hard core of Ali's *shi'ah*. On the death of Mu'awiyah and the accession of his son Yazid to the caliphate, clearly now the hereditary throne, the *shi'ah* decided to try and nip the dynasty in the bud and start their own. To this end they invited al-Husayn, one of Ali's two sons by Muhammad's daughter, Fatimah, to come from Medina and lead a rising.

Al-Husayn's friends in Medina advised him to send agents and prepare the ground in Iraq before venturing there himself. But he felt sure of his support, and marched off in September 680 with little preparation and only a small force of followers. In the event, the moral support would be there; the martial support would vaporize. As the poet al-Farazdaq is supposed to have said to al-Husayn when the latter asked him about the state of public opinion, 'Hearts are with you, but swords are against you. Victory is in heaven'. It was, as ever, the swords that would matter.

Al-Husayn and his small band of supporters were wiped out by a force sent by the Umayyads' governor of Iraq; the head of the Prophet's grandson became the first of those four grim trophies seen in the governor's palace at the start of this chapter. Soon after, the head took to the road, as grisly proof that the rising had been crushed, and as a warning to any other would-be rebels. When it arrived in Damascus, Caliph Yazid ibn Mu'awiyah is supposed to have addressed it in verse:

> We cleave the heads of men who were beloved
> of us – and then tyranically rebelled!

As he did so, he poked his sceptre in the mummified mouth. But one of those present, an older man who had known Muhammad – and this, his grandson al-Husayn, as a child – reproved the caliph: 'Take your sceptre away from it! By Allah, often did I see the Messenger of Allah, peace and blessings upon him, place his mouth against that mouth to kiss it.'

Hearts had not been enough. Having provoked his rising, the Shi'ah of al-Kufah had left al-Husayn in the lurch.

> They saw that they had committed a great sin: al-Husayn had summoned them to his aid, and they had not responded; he had been killed right next to them, and they had not gone to help him.

The *shi'ah* of Ali still mourn their murdered founder and first imam; his son al-Husayn, however, dying gloriously in battle, gave them their protomartyr, their greatest and most enduring piece of propaganda. When boys I know are blown to bits in our present war – *Martyrs Unite The Homeland!*, says the slogan, a drugged cocktail of the nationalism and political Islam poured out on TV screens and in text messages – it is all a re-enactment of that sacrifice in 680. The continuing Shi'i sense of tragedy is due not only to loss, but also to a burden comparable to Peter's betrayal of Jesus before the last cock-crow. It is a collective burden, and a heritable one. To witness, for example, Iranian pilgrims in the Umayyad Mosque of Damascus, kissing and weeping over a spot where al-Husayn's head is said to have rested on its long Via Dolorosa (perhaps to Cairo, perhaps back to Iraq; no one knows for sure), is to watch an enduring play of passions and emotions, among which is ineradicable guilt.

CALIPH–ANTI-CALIPH

Collective guilt drove collective revenge, and eventually the head of the Umayyads' governor was displayed in his own palace. But another challenge to Umayyad rule was rising far to the south-west in Mecca. Less fateful in the long term than the threat from Ali's supporters, in the immediate present it posed a much greater danger. Fifty years after the death of Muhammad – the man whose revolution had offered liberty from the 'Ignorance' of the past, equality under Allah, and fraternity with all mankind – Arabs were back in their old cycle, the wheel of fire. Worse, the wheel was now powered by competing claims to a single, ultimate truth, a divine right – claims that had begun to clash with the killing of Uthman in 656, and had collided so bloodily at the battle of Siffin in the following year; moreover, Arabic makes 'truth' and 'right' one word, *haqq*. Al-Husayn had only made an ill-judged bid for leadership; Abd Allah ibn al-Zubayr, butt of Mu'awiyah's put-down about 'Firewood-gatherer, son of the father of Scold', actually managed to set himself up as rival caliph with Mecca as his capital. He also managed to take control of a swathe of the empire, including much of the land that had emerged as its crux, Iraq – the pivot between Arabia and Persia, between the subcontinent and Eurasia; his caliphate was even acknowledged in parts of the Umayyad heartland, Syria. He was able to achieve this, in large part, by taking artful advantage of that fault line between 'North' and 'South': Mu'awiyah had been brought to power largely by the southerners in Syria; Abd Allah ibn al-Zubayr courted the northerners and won their backing.

Mu'awiyah, on his deathbed, admitted that Ibn al-Zubayr would need more than jibes to neutralize him. The crown prince, Yazid, was not present, but Mu'awiyah said,

> Tell Yazid from me . . . Ibn al-Zubayr is *khabb wa-dabb*: he'll delude you like a wizard and elude you like a lizard . . . If you get hold of him, chop him up limb from limb.

These were the dying caliph-king's last words.

Ibn al-Zubayr's reptilian counterpart, the *dabb*, is a lizard eaten by old-fashioned Arabs but notoriously hard to catch: it retreats head-first into its hole and can only be pulled by its spiny and flail-like tail, which it uses as a painful weapon. The anti-caliph would prove similarly hard to prise out of his stronghold of Mecca. Mu'awiyah had already sent an army against the holy city under the anti-caliph's own brother, Amr ibn al-Zubayr. This had been defeated, and Amr stripped and whipped to death at the gate of the Ka'bah precinct. The new caliph in Damascus, Yazid, despatched a much bigger force. Mecca was besieged again; this time the Ka'bah itself was the victim, bombarded to bits by mangonels and burned by incendiaries. While this was happening, Yazid and then his own son and successor Mu'awiyah II died in rapid succession, both of natural causes. Undeterred by these ominous events, the Umayyad family conclave chose a rather distant but powerful cousin, Marwan ibn al-Hakam, as the new head of the dynasty, while the anti-caliph rebuilt the focal shrine of Islam. Marwan's caliphate, however, lasted only a matter of months: it was rumoured that he died of poison administered by his wife Fakhitah ('Turtle-dove') – she had previously been married to Yazid, and her son by him had been excluded from the succession. If so, the murder was to no avail: all the Umayyad caliphs to come were descendants of Marwan, and are thus often known as Marwanids.

For a time, disorder was the order of the day. Once again, the extraordinary unity achieved by Muhammad's revolution had been reduced, like its symbol, the Ka'bah, to rubble. And even if the anti-caliph was rebuilding that 'navel of the earth', it seemed the symbol would never again reflect reality: for example, in one year, 688, there were four separate Mecca pilgrimages by supporters of, respectively, the caliph, the anti-caliph, a proto-Shi'i group that revered the memory of Ali, and a Khariji group that reviled it. A final stake was driven into the heart of unity when Marwan's son, the new Damascene Caliph Abd al-Malik, actually forbade pilgrimage to Mecca: the anti-caliph had allegedly begun to force Mecca pilgrims to pledge allegiance to himself. Abd al-Malik declared Jerusalem the substitute destination and, as the focus of the redirected pilgrimage, built the Dome of the Rock, completed in 691. That golden architectural icon of Islam, founded on the vacant temple mount of the Jews and decorated by Christian Byzantine craftsmen, arose from Arab disunity.

The Dome of the Rock, however, was destined almost immediately to become a gorgeous folly. For it was now, in 692, that Abd al-Malik mounted another huge offensive against the lizard in his Meccan lair. The Ka'bah was bombarded again, but this time the city fell too, and the head of Abd Allah ibn al-Zubayr duly made its way to Damascus. The united Mecca pilgrimage was back on track. And, ironically, given that it was now once more the single focus of pilgrims' piety, the peninsula was sidelined politically and in every other way until the discovery there of oil 1,300 years later.

The year of the anti-caliph's defeat is remembered as the second Umayyad 'Year of Unity' . . . Like the first one, three decades earlier, the wish was father to the name. For the Meccan anti-caliphate had bred disunities that continued long after it was suppressed. In particular, it exacerbated the 'North–South' split, which would soon resurface far away, but with disastrous consequences, in the eastern province of Khurasan.

Already, however, problems were bubbling away nearer home, in that crucial land, the crucible of Iraq.

THE TYRANT WITH THE SILVER TONGUE

Not only were the main losers in the first great schism, the *shi'ah* of Ali, gathering their strength again in Iraq. So too were their even bolshier arch-enemies, the Kharijis – the 'Quitters' who had backed Ali, then turned against him. The presence of both groups not only made the idea of unity a phantasm, but also posed a direct threat to the stability of the Umayyad caliphate. So Abd al-Malik unleashed on them his imperial rottweiler, al-Hajjaj, a viceroy whose bite was quite as bad as his bark.

Al-Hajjaj ibn Yusuf had begun life as a schoolmaster of the flogging sort; later, however, he found his true vocation as a soldier and a gauleiter. Already notorious for his harshness, it was he who had masterminded the defeat of the anti-caliph. Over the following couple of years, he acted as a roving troubleshooter, putting down opposition to the Umayyads in various parts of the peninsula. Now, at the end of 694, Abd al-Malik sent him to sort out that most troublesome land of all, Iraq.

The new viceroy was also notorious for his rhetoric. Al-Hajjaj in the pulpit – the mosque, as ever, being the political hub – can make Hitler at the Nuremberg Rallies seem mealy-mouthed. His keynote speech was delivered on his arrival, incognito, in al-Kufah, which at the time was a focus of Khariji dissidence. He ascended the steps of the pulpit veiled in a red Khariji-style turban, surveyed all the other red turbans before him, and began with a line of poetry:

> I am the son of brightness, climber of the folded mountain passes:
> when I unveil myself – *you will know me!*

Thus revealed as Lucifer, dark bringer of light, he continued:

> I come bearing evil for evil, weight for weight. I measure the sandals of evil by their footprints. I reward evil with evil. And I see heads ripe for the picking, heads that are mine to pluck. I see blood oozing between turbans and beards . . .

Armed men guarded the exits, waiting to shed that blood.

Often he would begin a speech softly, almost inaudibly, and then rise in a crescendo until he terrified those in the furthest corners of the mosque. It was not all blood and thunder, however. He could be so suavely persuasive, one of his listeners said, that you would end up thinking that it was he who had been personally mistreated by the Iraqis, and that his harvest of heads was quite justified. In other words, he possessed the ultimate qualification of the rhetorician: he could make you believe a rhetorical truth that was the diametric opposite of observable fact. 'That enemy of Allah,' another contemporary noted after his fall,

> would put on the gaudy garb of a whore, and mount the pulpit and speak the fine words of fine men – and then, when he descended, would act the pharaoh. He lied in his speech worse than the Antichrist.

Acting the pharaoh in Iraq involved putting to death, by some estimates, 120,000 Kharijis and other opponents of the Umayyads in cold blood. Then there were the victims – 50,000 men and 30,000 women – who died in his gaols, and the numberless ones killed in fighting. Are the figures exaggerated? Even reduced by a factor of ten, they would still be terrifying.

Like some other schoolmasters and dictators, al-Hajjaj enjoyed his reputation as a bogeyman: 'I am iron-hearted and malevolent, cruel and jealous', he once admitted. As an orator-despot, he was a darker version of the old tribal *sayyid*s and *khatib*s who ruled with words, and his heady mix of eloquence and violence has exercised a dark fascination: in Ibn Khallikan's great thirteenth-century biographical dictionary of the Arabic world, the thirteen-page entry on al-Hajjaj, the man you love to hate, is one of the longest. The fascination lives on. He was a role-model for the recent ruler of

Iraq, Saddam Husayn, and, like that twentieth-century disciple, has plenty of admirers today. 'No one but al-Hajjaj and Saddam could keep those dreadful Iraqis under control!' is a sentiment I have heard more than once.

Al-Hajjaj, for all his cruelty, was one of the greatest Arab orators in history. Only one person is on record as having silenced him – the wife of Caliph al-Walid ibn Abd al-Malik who, while al-Hajjaj was ensconced with her husband, sent a maidservant to the latter with the message, 'How can you sit with this *a'rabi* bristling with weapons, when you are wearing nothing but a light tunic?' When the caliph sent a message back to say that the *a'rabi* was in fact al-Hajjaj, his governor of Iraq, 'she was horrified, and told him, "By Allah, I don't like you being alone with a mass-murderer!"' Overhearing the exchanges with the maid, al-Hajjaj gave the caliph a lecture on the importance of not listening to women's prattle. This was passed back to al-Walid's wife, and the following day she summoned al-Hajjaj to pay his respects. He was kept waiting; finally admitted to her veiled presence, he was kept standing – and given a lecture in return that began,

> If Allah had not made you the most miserable of His creation, he would not have chosen you to be the one to bombard the Ka'bah!

On it went, concluding with aspersions on his manhood. Al-Hajjaj fled to the caliph and admitted,

> 'She did not stop until I wished the earth would swallow me up.' And al-Walid laughed so much that he pawed at the ground with his feet.

The man who had caused so many deaths was himself destined to die in bed. But there is a chilling twist to his end. Feeling that it was approaching, al-Hajjaj is said to have summoned an astrologer and asked if he divined the imminent death of a ruler.

> 'I do,' said the astrologer, 'but it is not you . . . because the one who is to die is called "Kulayb".' And al-Hajjaj replied, 'No; it is I. For that is what my mother used to call me.'

If another anecdote can be believed, it was the infancy of Kulayb, 'Puppy', that influenced his future career. Having refused to suck his mother's milk or that of wet-nurses, he was made to lick on successive days the blood of two black lambs, a black kid and a black snake. The remedy worked, 'but thereafter he could never resist the shedding of blood, because of what had befallen him at the beginning of his life'.

Al-Hajjaj left Iraq a legacy of blood, added to that which the war between Mu'awiyah and Ali had bequeathed. He also left a legacy of division. As we have seen, the originally cosmopolitan new cities of Iraq, the *amsar*, were turned at his orders into apartheid reserves, forbidden to non-arabophones. When al-Hajjaj founded his own new town, Wasit, 'Midway' – because it was half-way between al-Basrah and al-Kufah – a simpleton is said to have spoken the truth no one else dared to utter:

> Al-Hajjaj is a fool. He built the city of Wasit in the country of the [native] Nabat, then told them not to enter it!

It was all part of the doomed attempt at social engineering, at keeping Arabs as the ruling caste. But al-Hajjaj and his Umayyad overlords were trying to stem an irresistible tide.

MONGREL SPEECH

The flood-tide was nowhere more visible – or, rather, audible – than in the way spoken Arabic was changing. Non-Arabs were learning the secrets of the old high language; at the same time, Arabs themselves were losing the voice that had given them the nearest thing to unity for the longest part of their history. At first, keeping Arabs together in the *amsar* had ensured that they kept their language: having new and thriving cities that were concentrated cores of arabness in Iraq, Egypt and Tunisia meant that, in time, the people outside were arabicized, rather than the Arabs being persianized, copticized or berberized. The locals adopted the language of the powerful group. The opposite happened in regions where there were no *amsar*: in the vast eastern province of Khurasan, for example, by the mid-eighth century most ethnic Arabs spoke Persian.

But in the hearts of the *amsar*, in their inmost chambers, Arabic was changing. Apart from the high Arabic of poetry and the Qur'an, everyday Arabic had always existed in different varieties, but these had been easily mutually intelligible across Arabia. What was happening now was that the language was becoming *muwallad*, mongrel – because even if you could keep the native men out of the *amsar*, you couldn't keep the native women out. Arabhood came from the patriline, but what went for Arabic came as often as not from the other side of the family tree; the term 'mother-tongue' speaks for itself. Further add to the mangled language of concubine-mothers the kitchen-Arabic of wet-nurses and household slaves, and the tongue of angels will fall to earth.

Al-Jahiz collected a chapterful of choice malapropisms. These include the Persian mother of the poet Jarir's sons trying to tell one of them that rats (*jirdhān*) had got at her dough (*'ajīn*) – except that it came out as 'two troops of horsemen (*jurdān*) have got at my backside (*'ijān*)'. The boys asked her to remain silent if they had guests. Another famous blunder was that of a Persian client of Mu'awiyah's governor of Iraq, Ziyad, who needed a donkey (*ḥimār*) but, falling into the perennial *ḥ/h* trap, asked him for a meaningless '*himār*'.

> 'What the hell are you saying?' Ziyad asked.
> 'I asked you to give me an *ayr*,' the man said,

pleased at having come up with a synonym; except that instead of *'ayr*, 'an ass', with a twanging letter *'ayn*, he had asked for a twangless *ayr*, 'a penis':

> 'The second is worse than the first,' said Ziyad.

Indeed, Arabic was going from bad to worse. The very genders were bending: Jarir's concubine might have held her tongue when guests came to dinner, but, he sighed,

> The first I hear from her, when with the sun I rise,
> is feminines made masculine and masculines that feminize.

It was as if the British in India, originally speaking their own regional varieties of English – Scots, Irish, Cockney and so on – but all understanding each other and all writing a standard King's English, had not only never sent their sons home to school in Blighty, but had also failed to keep themselves aloof from the native women. Succeeding generations of Kims would have grown ever darker-skinned and wallowed ever deeper in a Hobson-Jobson in which not only the vocabulary but the most basic grammar was pidginized.

Even the King's Arabic was slipping. Al-Walid ibn Abd al-Malik was prone to making slips because, as mentioned, he never had his elocution lessons in the customary bedouin 'finishing school'. His lapses, a listener complained, undermined his dignity. This is probably no exaggeration in the case of one of his most famous *faux-pas*, when he meant to ask someone,

'*Man khatanuka?*' 'Who is your father-in-law?'

but asked instead,

'*Man khatanaka?*' 'Who circumcised you?'

MORE LOST THAN ORPHANS

If Arabs themselves were losing their grip on their own silver but slippery tongue, non-Arabs were sharpening their pens and taking to the high and increasingly written language with alacrity. Arabic was joining the exclusive club of great world languages. In terms of geographical spread it was to leave its jaded fellow members, Greek and Latin, far behind. It was also leaving Arabs behind; not only that, but the whole business of being Arab was beginning to run away with itself.

Arabicization didn't always mean islamization: there were, and still are, plenty of Arabic-speakers who were not Muslims. To begin with, however, becoming a Muslim did usually entail becoming an 'Arab', in the sense of having to be attached to an Arab tribe as a *mawla*. But becoming a tribal affiliate didn't suddenly turn you into an Arabian tribal person: *mawla*s had their own 'constant inner worlds', to use V.S. Naipaul's phrase again, and *mawla*s were the majority. What was happening was that Arabic and Islam were bringing about a new cultural unity, but of the sort aspired to in the old motto of the United States (and of the *Gentleman's Magazine*) – *E Pluribus Unum*, 'unity out of diversity'. Arabs had long defined themselves in contrast to others, especially in terms of language – *'arab* versus *'ajam* – but now the others were including themselves in the definition, bewildering it with added meanings. An early example of bewilderment is that of Ziyad, the Umayyad governor of Iraq already mentioned. He is usually known to historians as Ziyad 'ibn Abihi' – 'the son of His Father [implying, *whoever his father might have been*]'. His nominal father was a Persian slave; it was alleged that his real begetter was the old pagan chief of Mecca, Mu'awiyah's father Abu Sufyan, and indeed Mu'awiyah did later acknowledge Ziyad as his half-brother. Whatever the truth of the allegation, in Ziyad's case it was his gift of speech that gave him the power he would wield:

> By Allah, if this lad were of Quraysh, he would drive the Arabs before him with his stick,

said a Qurashi who heard him speak as a youth. In the end, Ziyad not only wangled his way into the Prophet's tribe, but finished up as the caliph's brother and viceroy – and above all because of 'his noble character and eloquence'.

Arabic had unified Arabs ethnically even before Muhammad gathered their word politically; after him, it soon began to dissolve them. In the words of a supposedly ancient prediction, *sayyid al-kalam* – Arabic, 'the master of speech' – was making masters of its people; but it was also empowering others. The traditional solution was to adopt these others into the tribal system, if not as actual brothers, then as affiliated *mawla*s. That worked on the old Arabian level, until the time of Ziyad and his brothers. It didn't work when the newly empowered of the conquered lands began to outnumber the conquerors. With the master-race divided among themselves, and its ruling dynasty set on maintaining traditional notions of arabness and kingship, how could they cope with the plurality of an empire?

Many could not cope, and took refuge in that redoubt of embattled empires, chauvinism. Despite Muhammad's famous declaration in his Farewell Sermon, that no Arab is superior to any non-Arab except in piety, some peoples who were not notably impious came in for especial opprobrium:

> Berbers and Slavs [*barabirah wa-saqalibah*], Jarmaqis and Jarjumis [*jaramiqah wa-jarajimah*: Persian desert-dwellers and Antiochian marsh-men], Copts and Nabataeans [*aqbat wa-anbat*], and the dregs of humanity . . .

as one Arab warrior dismissed them in a fit of jingling jingoism. This is hauteur speaking, but also fear.

The fear was well founded. The empire was growing ever bigger and more plural: the super-raid had developed its own momentum, a chain reaction of conquest, and increasingly the raiders were non-Arabs. The conqueror of Spain, to give a particularly egregious example, was Tariq ibn Ziyad, and he was the *mawla* of a *mawla*. His story began, indirectly, when in the 630s the Qurashi commander Khalid ibn al-Walid raided a church in Iraq and gathered a remarkable flock of captives: they included the grandfather of Muhammad's most famous biographer, the future founder of the art of Islamic dream-interpretation, and an Arab Christian called Nusayr. The latter became a slave and then a freed *mawla* of the Umayyad clan; his son, Musa ibn Nusayr, was thus a *mawla* by heritage. Musa was to lead the forces that raided across the top of Africa, getting as far as Tangier in the first decade of the eighth century. His Arab warriors seemed to be on an unstoppable roll – except that, by now, they had both reached the end of the known world, and had gathered so many Berbers along the way that the force could hardly be called 'Arab' any more. And there was another problem: all the extra raiders had to be paid, or at least be given bed, board and booty (and bedfellows). Inevitably Musa's gaze turned north, across the strait to Spain, and it was his Berber lieutenant and *mawla*, Tariq ibn Ziyad, whom he sent over the water in 711 to wrest the Iberian Peninsula from the Visigoths. (En route, Tariq gave his name to the shark-fin mountain in the sea, 'Jabal Tariq', garbled by Spanish tongues into 'Gibraltar'.) The long and glorious history of Arab-Muslim al-Andalus thus began with a Berber ex-slave of the son of a Christian ex-slave. Rather as the Arab minorities of the present-day Gulf states leave the hands-on business of running their countries and expanding their economies to non-Arab masses, mostly from South Asia, Arabs of the Umayyad age were subcontracting the business of imperial expansion.

It seems unlikely, although not impossible, that Tariq the Berber could have delivered the high Arabic speech that is put in his mouth before the decisive battle with the Visigoth king, Roderick (one of those rulers depicted in the Umayyads' desert palace of Qusayr Amrah). But it is worth quoting, for it shows how historians retrospectively arabized the conquest of Spain:

> Men, where can you fly when the sea is behind you and the enemy before you? All you can do is be true and steadfast. For you must know that in this island [i.e. the Iberian Peninsula] you are more lost than orphans at the feasts of evil men . . .

It soon slips into that most anciently Arabian form of high speech, rhythmic, rhyming prose:

> . . . You have heard of the lovely houris whom this isle has brought forth, / daughters of the Greeks [sic] by birth, / maidens trailing pearls and gems / and cloth-of-gold from heads to hems, / secluded in their palaces where kings wear diadems. / [The caliph] al-Walid ibn Abd al-Malik has chosen each of you as an Arab knight / from among his champions for the fight, / is pleased that you and the royal ladies of this island will unite, / and trusts the penetration will delight . . .

That last phrase refers both to the penetration with steel in battle of Roderick's men, and of the secluded 'daughters of the Greeks' in bed afterwards. The pun, if made in reality, would have passed over the Berber troops' heads; so too would the entire speech. But the speech is not a matter of reality: it is an imaginary arabization not only, probably, of Tariq, now an old-style Arabian leader-orator, but certainly also of his Berber troops, converted into 'Arab knights'. In order to conquer and control the empire, South Arabians had already been turned into Arabs; historians, in retrospect, manufactured even more Arabs, and from ever more distantly sourced materials.

It was all very well for Arabs to outsource their further conquests and pass on the imperial impetus to others: spread along so many fronts, there were simply not enough Arabs to keep the impetus up themselves. It was a shortage that had been felt in the first years of the conquests, when that second, Persian front had been added to the original Syrian one. But it meant that Arabs themselves were becoming ever more isolated in their own expanding empire. In the coming centuries, as the distinction between *ersatz*- and *echt*-Arabs blurred, and as blatant non-Arabs – Daylamites and Turks – took over not just the impetus but the imperium itself, those original Arabs would be more than just isolated in the new world they had created: they would be lost, more lost than orphans.

THE FALL OF THE HOUSE OF UMAYYAH

In first part of the eighth century, with the conquest of Spain, the Arabic world had finished realigning itself on a completely new axis. It was no longer orientated north–south, from one Fertile Crescent to another. Instead, it ran east–west, Mashriq to Maghrib, from the land of the rising sun to that of its going down. It was the orientation of a bigger, older stage of history, the vast Afro-Eurasian theatre of events, and the cast of players was similarly intercontintental. Its rulers, the house of Umayyah, were thus at the pinnacle of their power – and they were soon to plunge from it, headlong. For the threats were multiplying: the anti-caliphate in Mecca may have been dealt with, but in the simmering lowlands of Iraq, pro- and anti-Ali factions posed a double danger to the rule of Damascus that even the bloody al-Hajjaj had not been able to contain. And way to the east, beyond the central Iranian desert and hard by Afghanistan, the temperature was rising in another hotbed of revolt, the province of Khurasan.

As early as the caliphate of Mu'awiyah, Arabs in Khurasan had been unwilling to hand over the spoils that piled up from its conquest. Khurasan seemed a world in itself, hemmed in by river, desert and mountain, and an independent-minded leader there could rule the land virtually as his own mega-fief. It helped in building up a core of loyal support when, like one governor of the late seventh century, al-Muhallab, you fathered 300 children; they formed a whole Arab sub-tribe, the Mahalibah. A subsequent governor, Qutaybah ibn Muslim, found it less exhausting to import his support than to father it. Like al-Muhallab but unlike the more malleable contemporary commanders of the west of the empire, Qutaybah was a peninsular Arab by origin, and many of the men under him were raw newcomers from the Gulf region – '*A'rab*,' Qutaybah called them, haranguing them and banging them into shape as a fighting force:

> and what are the *a'rab*? The curse of Allah upon the *a'rab*! I gathered you up as the chaff of the harvest-time is gathered, from the places where wormwood and southernwood grow, from the places where the shower-tree grows, from the island of Abarkawan. You rode on cattle and lived on animal-fodder. And I have mounted you on horses and girded you with weapons, that by your efforts Allah might make this land inviolable and pile up its booty!

The team-building rhetoric worked, and in the first part of the eighth century Qutaybah led his forces across the River Oxus and into the rich lands of Transoxania. Eventually, success went to his head: he wrote to the newly installed Caliph Sulayman ibn Abd al-Malik, threatening to 'cast off allegiance like a pair of sandals', and to send an army against him. But none of his men would back him, and Qutaybah was killed in 715.

The next governor of Khurasan, Yazid ibn al-Muhallab, was one of that earlier governor's 300 offspring. Immensely capable, he had already succeeded once to the governorship but had fallen from grace, been gaoled, and subsequently escaped. Now restored to the post, he set about redeeming his reputation by further enlarging the realm, particularly in the regions bordering the Caspian. As so often, the problem was the division of the spoils: he was accused by Damascus of holding on to booty, was jailed again, escaped again – and this time hit back, like Qutaybah, by casting off allegiance to the Umayyads. Defeated in 720, according to some accounts Yazid had intended making a bid for the caliphate itself. Whether the allegation was true or not, it would not be the last time that Khurasan was a springboard to revolt. Next time, however, the revolt would succeed spectacularly, and would found a new ruling dynasty.

The beginnings of that new dynasty, the Abbasids, and the end of the Umayyads, are bound up with the third of those severed heads in the audience hall at al-Kufah, that of the proto-Shi'i al-Mukhtar. In his brief but bloody uprising in Iraq, al-Mukhtar had promoted as imam the martyred al-Husayn ibn Ali's half-brother Muhammad, known after his mother as Ibn al-Hanafiyyah. On Ibn al-Hanafiyyah's death in the first decade of the eighth century, the notional imamate had passed to his son, Abu Hashim. It was in the name of the latter that a revolutionary movement called the Hashimiyyah took root over the east of the empire, and especially in Khurasan, always a fertile land for faction. Abu Hashim died in 716 or 717 without leaving any sons; however, he magnanimously bequeathed the imamate to the living head of another branch of the family – the one that descended from al-Abbas, paternal uncle of both his grandfather Ali and of the Prophet Muhammad . . . or that, at least, was what the rulers of the Abbasid branch later asserted. The claim about the 'bequest' may be an attempt to cover the usual naked bid for power with a fig-leaf of legitimacy.

Whatever the truth, it was in the name of the Hashimiyyah that the Abbasid campaign began in Khurasan in 747. It was a revolution that brought together a whole stew of discontents – hardline Hashimis, Persian peasants and nobles (mostly still un-islamized), second- and third-generation persianized Arabs, more recent Arab arrivals from that other hotbed, Iraq, all of them fed up with their absentee landlords in distant Damascus – and it was masterminded by a *mawla*, Abu Muslim. It is unclear whether Abu Muslim was of Persian, Arab or perhaps Kurdish origin, but he was bilingual in Arabic and Persian and, most likely, began as a Persian slave. In any case, he was another of those complex products of imperial blurring, one of the hybrid actors who were beginning to inherit the Arab impetus, and the old Arab eloquence. When Abu 'l-Abbas, the eventual first Abbasid caliph, praised his role in the revolution, Abu Muslim would invariably reply in impeccable Arabic verse:

> I have achieved by resolution and discretion that
> which all the gathered kings of Marwan's line have failed to do.
> All along, I strove for their destruction by my efforts,
> while they, that heedless lot in Syria, were slumbering.
> Until at last I struck them with my sword – and they awoke
> from sleep the like of which no one has ever slept.
> Let a shepherd graze his sheep in lion-ridden lands
> and then nod off: he'll find the lion does the shepherding.

At the time, the Umayyads' governor in Khurasan tried to awaken his master to the danger – also in that most pointed medium, verse, also using the metaphor of sleep, but mixed with that of fire:

> Among the ashes I see embers glowing
> that, likely, will be coaxed to flame.
> Fire's kindled with two firesticks,
> war with words –
> And if no men of sense extinguish it,
> its fuel will be of corpses and of heads.
> I say, amazed at the Umayyads: would that I knew
> if they're awake or slumbering.
> For if they're yet asleep, then tell them
> that the time is come to wake and rise!

The wake-up call went unheard. Far from slumbering, however, Caliph Marwan II ibn Muhammad was busy trying to douse a Khariji uprising in northern Iraq, and to cope with several other outbreaks in that incendiary land. Meanwhile, from Khurasan, the fire of greater revolution spread until it was too late to stamp it out.

In little over two years, the rebel armies wiped out Umayyad rule in Persia and Iraq. In a last attempt to save his realm, Marwan II confronted them in January 750 on the Greater Zab, a tributary of the Tigris. Mu'awiyah, first of the Umayyad caliphs of Damascus, had emerged from the apocalyptic darkness of the fight with Ali at Siffin on the Euphrates. Now, with grim symmetry, darkness descended on the last of Mu'awiyah's heirs in a battle by a river on the other side of the Mesopotamian plain. The revolutionaries had chosen black as their colour, and

> in their vanguard black banners flew, borne by men mounted on Bactrian camels . . . Marwan said to those near him, 'Do you see how their lances are as thick as palm-trunks? Do you see the standards on their camels, black as pieces of stormcloud?' As he was speaking, a number of black birds flew from some nearby gardens and alighted together on the first of the banners of Abd Allah ibn Ali [the Abbasid general] . . . Marwan took this as an ill omen and said, 'Do you not see how black is joined to black, and how those birds are as black as thunderclouds?' He then turned to his fighters, and they too had sensed the grief and the dread and the doom. 'You are a fine force indeed,' he said. 'But what use is a force, when time has run its course?'

Everything was being subverted: darkness had dawned from the east, and the fact that it had done so on the backs of those outlandish two-humped camels underlines how alien were the forces ranged against Marwan. Arabs themselves had been divided, at times by reality, at others by propaganda, into those northern and southern Arabian blocs. Their empire, however, now ran on that different, Afro-Eurasian axis: conflicts tended to oppose east to west – Ali in Iraq to Mu'awiyah in Syria, Abbasids in Khurasan to Umayyads in the Levant; later, Abbasids in Baghdad versus new anti-caliphates in both Egypt and al-Andalus. It would be from both west and east that eventual nemesis would descend on the Arab empire – the lesser nemesis of the Crusades, then the darker fate, looming from the east, of the Mongols. Even today conflict, real or imaginary, tends to run along an east–west axis. The Umayyads had never realigned themselves to face the new threats, the frightening plurality.

There were of course multiple reasons for their fall. One of the few survivors of the family listed some of them with great frankness: love of luxury, oppression of the people and the people's consequent unwillingness to pay taxes, emptying of the treasury, unpaid troops enticed to the revolutionary side . . . altogether, a template for dynastic decline and fall. But above all, the unnamed survivor admitted, the Umayyads' collapse was due to their detachment from reality: 'For one of the most potent causes of our downfall was the fact that no one told us what was happening.' Or rather, they did tell them, with those warnings of fire and heads and corpses; but only when it was too late.

Reality had caught up with Marwan II in the form of defeat on the Zab. It now pursued him to Egypt, where he tried unsuccessfully to bury the regalia of the caliphate – robe, sceptre and staff; they were found, and so was he. His head was sent to Abu 'l-Abbas, who had proclaimed his caliphate in al-Kufah. Another head; another symmetry. Abu 'l-Abbas, meanwhile, had made the first of many breaks with the past by adopting a caliphal title, 'al-Saffah'. It is a strangely appropriate title, as it foreshadows all the asymmetries, the self-contradictions that would characterize his dynasty, for it means both 'the Giver of Gifts' and 'the Shedder of Blood'. (Arabic being what it is, it can also mean 'the Wielder of Words'.)

What is in some ways the most 'Arab' period of Arab history – the Umayyad – had also been the briefest, little more than a human lifetime long. But it was a period in which, by the legerdemain of pedigree, the South Arabians were attached to the tribal tree and all Arabians were defined, finally and irrevocably, as Arabs; a period in which their now vast empire was still grounded in the varied landscape of their subcontinental home. As for the Umayyads themselves,

> They were the mother-lode of monarchy, and only
> under them could Arabs live as proper Arabs.

Al-Jahiz, the great 'arabologist' who quotes this verse, should have the last word on the Umayyads. The Abbasid dynasty, under whom he lived, was

> *'ajamiyyah khurasaniyyah*, non-Arab and Khurasani. The [Umayyad] dynasty . . . was *'arabiyyah a'rabiyyah*, Arab and bedouin-Arab.

You can't get more Arab than that.

HISHAM'S PALACE

The Umayyads had also been a deeply divisive dynasty, as the four heads at the beginning of this chapter bear witness – not to mention the tens, if not hundreds of thousands of other heads that fell over their ninety years in power. The divisions would extend deep into the future.

North of the Palestinian town of Jericho is another of those hunting boxes or rural palaces, like Qusayr Amrah with its heavenly vault and frescoed emperors. The Jericho monument is called Khirbat al-Mafjar but is popularly known as 'Hisham's Palace'. No inscriptions or documents actually link the place with Hisham, but its rich decorations would have suited that poetry- and luxury-loving caliph, seen above draped in red silk, dripping with musk and surrounded by marble and gold. Today, the ruins of the palace face those of a more recent structure – a Palestinian refugee camp, al-Nuway'imah. It might be the perfect illustration of the bathos of history. That is how one observer, Sharif S. Elmusa, sees it: 'A more poignant image of the contrast between the state of the Arabs then and now could not have been dreamed up by the wildest poet.' Elmusa should know: he himself is a poet, and he grew up in al-Nuway'imah camp. But the spores of the decline – the family, clan, tribal, sectarian rivalries – were present even before the palace was built. The camp may be a contrast architecturally, but it belongs historically to a continuum of disunity of which the palace is also part. The Umayyads built palaces; but they also built up political camps, including those 'Northern' and 'Southern' blocs, whose rivalries they were happy to use and abuse. Playing one side against the other had helped to set their dynasty up. It had saved it from the anti-caliph in Mecca. But it had also ultimately contributed to the unrest in Khurasan and to their undoing. 'North–South' disunity proved longer-lived than any dynasty, and as damaging in its way as those other rivalries, sometimes connected with it, which ran along the east–west axis. 'In Lebanon and Palestine,' Hitti has pointed out,

> the ['North–South'] issue seems to have remained a living one until modern times, for we know of pitched battles fought between the two parties as late as the early part of the eighteenth century.

Nor has the issue gone away. It lives on under other names, and the deepest underlying issue – the dialogue of *badw* and *hadar* – is far from over. Hisham's Palace and al-Nuway'imah Camp are an image of contrast, but also of continuity, two points on the sliding scale from luxury to misery.

CHAPTER NINE

THE EMPIRE OF BAGHDAD
ABBASID SOVEREIGNTY

AT THE MID-POINT OF THE WORLD

In the year 871, 'seized by a sudden desire', an adventurous citizen of al-Basrah called Ibn Wahb sailed to China. On arrival he was seized by another desire, and made his way to the imperial capital, Chang'an, to call on the Tang emperor. After a long wait, the writing of many petitions and, eventually, the making of inquiries by the imperial court, Ibn Wahb's persistence paid off, and he was admitted to the emperor's presence. Royalty being obsessed with its own precedence, one of the first questions the emperor asked his visitor was,

> 'How are all the kings ranked according to you Arabs?' Ibn Wahb tactfully feigned ignorance, and replied,
>
> 'I know nothing about them.'
>
> Then the king said to his interpreter, 'Tell him we count five kings as great. The one with the most extensive realm is he who rules Iraq, for he is at the centre of the world, and the other kings are ranged around him; we know him by the name "the King of Kings." Next comes this king of ours . . .'

meaning himself. Then came the kings of the Turks, of India and of Byzantium.

The emperor's answer is astonishing. Was not China the Middle Kingdom, and Chang'an the mid-point of the civilized world? Would the Tang emperor really have regarded the Abbasid caliph in barbarian 'Bangda' – Baghdad – as more important than himself? It all seems highly unlikely. Moreover, the wise infidel king who makes pointed comments about one's own society is a recurring literary character: al-Mas'udi, for example, who himself repeats this Chinese anecdote, also has the Christian king of the Nubians pronouncing a blistering critique of the Abbasids' predecessors, the Umayyads, and their irreligiosity. But whether the audience in Chang'an actually took place or not, the point it makes is no less valid. Baghdad controlled the biggest empire in the world; and it does indeed lie exactly half-way along a line drawn from the far west of Africa to the far east of China – the extremes of the busiest band of habitation and trade on the Afro-Eurasian megacontinent, a clime that includes Egypt, the Levant, Persia, northern India and China itself. Baghdad's seaport, Ibn Wahb's native al-Basrah, lies down the Tigris and just inland from the head of the Gulf, which sits half-way round the Indian Ocean rim and is also the spot where the rich littoral of the Old World's greatest trading 'pond' penetrates deepest into its landmass.

A small but tangible piece of evidence that the Arab empire was now at the centre of the Old World, and more than just geographically, comes from that world's far north-western corner. There, in England in 774, King Offa issued a gold coinage in imitation of the *dinar*s of the first great Abbasid caliph, al-Mansur: in addition to the rest of the Arabic inscription, the centre of the coin bears the words 'OFFA REX' sandwiched in Roman characters upside-down between the Arabic,

محمد رسول الله

'Muhammad is the messenger of Allah'. The Islamic creed jingled in English purses; even the Latinate name of the coin, *mancus*, is possibly from the Arabic *manqush*, 'inscribed, minted'. It was not that the Anglo-Saxons of Mercia had suddenly converted to Islam; but it was graphic acknowledgement that the Abbasid *dinar* was the US dollar of its day – that there was now a new superpower, a new superculture, and that the old Classical age had finally ended. Admittedly, it is probably the Arabic that is notionally upside-down: a mint master in the English Midlands was hardly likely to have known which way up the script went, let alone what it meant. But if that reflects a more general incomprehension of the new cultural power, then the reflection is accurate.

ROUND WORLD, ROUND CITY

In the 740s the Abbasids had begun, as did all power-seekers, by forging a new *'asabiyyah*, a new wheel of fire. As the Umayyad governor of their power-base in Khurasan had warned,

> Fire's kindled with two firesticks,
> war with words –
> And if no men of sense extinguish it,
> its fuel will be of corpses and of heads.

The fire had fanned out from the east and consumed everything in its path. Soon, however, it would begin to consume itself: ever since the primeval Titan, Cronus, castrated his father, then went on to swallow his own offspring, revolutions have tended to devour their children. Sure enough, the Abbasids would exclude from power their fellow revolutionaries – the Hashimiyyah, and the pro-Ali faction in general – and then go on to turn violently against them. Once more, a small sub-clan of the Meccan tribe of Quraysh had taken the mould-breaking message of Islam and remoulded it to monopolize power to its own ends. Once more, the ideal, universal unity of Islam was subverted by a particular unity, loyalty to an earthly power.

There was, however, a difference. The Umayyads had been the Establishment before Muhammad, and for almost a century of the new Islamic era they had ruled largely in the manner of ancient Arab kings; their rigidity, their resistance to plurality, had been a large part of their undoing. The Abbasids were made of more flexible stuff. Their ancestor and eponym, Muhammad's paternal uncle al-Abbas, had been one of the Prophet's opponents and had fought against him at the battle of Badr. When it was clear that victory was Muhammad's, however, al-Abbas's sons had entered wholeheartedly into his ever-expanding venture: they ended up, as we have seen, scattered from North Africa to Central Asia. As for the stay-at-home son Abd Allah, great-grandfather of the first two Abbasid caliphs, he is remembered as the first interpreter of Islamic scripture. The Abbasids did not merely toe the line of Islam: they followed it wherever it led them, into the paths of scholarship or conquest. Their flexibility endured, and would guarantee the survival of their own line – even if, paradoxically, it meant the end of the line for Arab power. It also meant that, as a dynasty, they would be multiply self-contradictory. Although they would cling on to the caliphate for three-quarters of a millennium, they would rule for only a century; they would reign for four more, and live out the rest of their time in a gilded cage in Cairo. The greatest Arab dynasty, they would also be the last great Arab dynasty, and in many ways the least Arab.

Abbasid adaptability was visible almost from the start of their rule. The Umayyads had secured their place in the Afro-Eurasian-Mediterranean world but had never detached themselves from Arabia and the long Arab past. Their chosen capital was a prolongation of that past: Damascus was the oasis of Arab dreams, a temperate earthly paradise set in a land of figs and olives. It was also a second-hand city, one of the many seats of government in a millennial game of musical chairs. The Abbasids made a new start. They began by systematically erasing their predecessors in the nastiest way, disinterring and desecrating their remains. The poetry-loving Hisham was subjected to particularly harsh post-mortem punishment in revenge for his crucifixion and burning of an Alid revolutionary, Zayd ibn Ali: Hisham's own corpse, still reasonably whole, was given eighty lashes before itself being burnt. Fortunately for future lovers of Islamic art, this *damnatio memoriae* spared both the Umayyads' great religious monuments and their more out-of-the-way rural palaces.

The Abbasids turned their backs on Syria, and to begin with al-Saffah, figurehead of the Abbasid movement and first caliph of their dynasty, ruled from al-Kufah. But the city had remained the centre of Shi'ah activism, and if the Party of Ali were still fellow revolutionaries they would not remain so for long: they had been used, and soon they too would be erased. Al-Saffah therefore founded a new capital, at a comfortable distance – near al-Anbar, 200 kilometres up the Euphrates. The caliph had hardly moved there, however, when in 754 he died of smallpox. So it was that the real new Abbasid beginning took place under al-Saffah's brother and successor, Abu Ja'far, who took the title al-Mansur, 'the Victorious'.

Al-Mansur is remembered above all for his foundation of Madinat al-Salam, 'the City of Peace' – and of dreams and nightmares – usually known by the name of a small earlier settlement on the site, Baghdad. It was yet another new town in the pivotal land between Arabia and Persia; but its site destined it to be different. Like the old Persian capital, nearby Ctesiphon, it was built on the Tigris, the easternmost of the two great rivers of Mesopotamia; unlike Ctesiphon, it straddled the river, with its eastern, left-bank suburb lying at the start of the road that led to Khurasan. Up to now, the major Arab cities – ancient al-Hirah, and recent al-Kufah and, far to the south, al-Basrah – had been built on the Arabian side of the western river, the Euphrates. Al-Mansur's new capital re-orientated the empire geographically, politically and psychologically to the east as well as to the west. With their initial burst of conquest, Arabs had moved into the Eurasian mainstream; with the Umayyad move to Damascus, they had set their sights north and west, on the old Classical world, while keeping a southward eye on ancient Arabia. From Baghdad, however, Arabs looked east as well, and into the future.

Baghdad was cosmopolitan, imperial and idiosyncratic: its global orientation was reflected in its design, which centred on the great Round City. Planned in concentric cirles like a target with the caliphal palace at the bull's eye, 50,000 workmen laboured simultaneously to build it. In good Meccan mercantile tradition, al-Mansur soon commanded the merchants to come and set up shop; they formed a commercial suburb, called Karkh. Damascus had been an ancient Incense Road town; Baghdad rapidly became the new hub of multiple Silk and Spice Roads that crossed land and sea. The Round City was the caliphal capital, but it was no introverted Forbidden City: its gates at the cardinal points led to the four quarters of the empire, and over each one al-Mansur built an airy pavilion from which he could survey comings and goings. He was aware too of the wider world, and of the position in it of his own vast realm. Anglo-Saxon Mercia may not have featured except as part of a general 'Frankish' blur, but the other extreme did: 'Here is the Tigris,' he said one day, surveying the traffic on Baghdad's river, 'and nothing bars the way between it and China.'

Baghdad, however, was not founded until 762, when al-Mansur had already been caliph for eight years. During that time, he had been busy levelling the political ground, removing all obstacles to autocracy. The first of these was the military commander of the Abbasid revolution, victor of the battle of the Greater Zab with his Bactrian camels and black banners, al-Mansur's own paternal uncle Abd Allah ibn Ali. He made a bid for the caliphate, was besieged, captured and put under house arrest – and then, by the sort of coincidence that happens when potentates are in charge, was killed when the house collapsed on top of him (reliable people were summoned to bear witness that it was accidental). Having dealt with his uncle, al-Mansur then turned to the faithful lieutenant who had captured him, the revolutionary mastermind Abu Muslim. There were indications that the old story would repeat itself and that Abu Muslim would make a bid for independence in his native Khurasan, that rich, distant and troublesome province. Al-Mansur had him killed – then had to deal bloodily with a revolutionary splinter group that arose in this Abbasid Trotsky's name. Next, just as al-Mansur was at last beginning work on his new capital, an Alid element of the Abbasid former revolutionary coalition itself rose in revolt. The leaders, two great-great-grandsons of Ali, were soon eliminated, one in Medina, the other near al-Kufah; in that place of falling heads, the latter was of course decapitated. By flogging dead Umayyads in revenge for their treatment of the descendants of Ali, the Abbasids had literally beaten the lessons of history into their predecessors. For all the lessons they themselves learned, they might as well have flogged dead horses.

Built though it was on hypocrisy, wilful amnesia, treachery and avunculicide, Baghdad and the wider Abbasid empire would be stable for a time. The *futuhat*, the armed Arab 'openings-up', had reached their furthest limits in the two decades before the Abbasid coup. Now the borders of empire were consolidated, and a network of control and communication was built up. Those five far-flung Abbasid brothers of the first Islamic generation had ended up in locations as various as North Africa and Samarqand. Similarly, in early Abbasid times two brothers, Yazid ibn Hatim and Rawh ibn Hatim, could find themselves as governors respectively in North Africa and Sind; the difference was that when the first one died, the second was appointed to his post – a transfer from one end of empire to the other, and across half the width of the known world. The Round City was the hub of control and communication for a massive but mobile empire: al-Mansur's grandson al-Rashid was overheard addressing a cloud, 'Go and rain wherever you will, for your crop tax will come to me.' There was nothing whimsical in the command. Revenues, reports and officials would come with increasing speed from increasing distances. It was possible, for example, to travel express, posting from the far end of Khurasan to Baghdad in as little as twelve days – a distance of more than 1,500 kilometres. Even the crops themselves could be sent by the equivalent of FedEx: myrobalans, a plumlike fruit, could be sent 2,500 kilometres from Kabul to Baghdad and arrive fresh.

Given this carefully cultivated interconnectedness, and the fact that the Department of Posts also operated as the caliph's most effective intelligence department, one had to go a long way to hide from the Abbasids. Surviving dissident descendants of Ali thus ended up scattered across a vast arc from the borders of India to the shores of the Atlantic. Many would remain in secluded obscurity: I once visited the ancestral Mauritanian stronghold of an Alid family, a mud fortress on the furthest edge of the Sahara from Baghdad, where members of the clan still held out against their persecutors of 3,500 kilometres away and 1,250 years ago. Some, however, were able to set up independent states, such as that of the Idrisids in Morocco, founded in 788. Most remarkably, an adventurous young survivor of the ousted Umayyads made it hot-foot to Spain and founded a western offshoot of the old dynasty even before the first brick was laid in Baghdad's Round City.

The 'King of Kings' in Baghdad may have ruled the biggest realm in the world, but he soon found out that the bigger the realm, the flakier the edges.

MEASURING THE WORLD

If it hadn't been clear to their Umayyad predecessors, it was obvious to the Abbasids almost from the start that such an empire could not be held together by military force alone. It needed something more central, much more powerful – gravity, not pressure.

Umayyad rule of their ever-broadening empire had been exclusive and aloof. As the base of the imperial pyramid had become ever more plural, so the apex had risen until it had lost touch with the ground. A new imperial architecture was needed – a structure in the round that would encompass plurality, which would centre on the caliph and celebrate him, but which would be built on the level; a structure not unlike the Round City. It was not – of course – that the Abbasid empire was in any political sense level; rather, the caliph was seen to share the same cultural ground with his subjects, whether they were descended from Persian noblemen, black slaves, migrant Indian peasants or bedouin Arabs. Under the Umayyads, the dominant culture had been Arabic, Arabian and elitist. Now it was Arabic, Islamic and increasingly accessible. Being a 'true' tribal Arab or a *mawla*, a tribal affiliate, was to matter less and less; as in the ancient, non-tribal South Arabian societies, it was submission to the unifying deity that made one a member.

Long before, Arabic had given its speakers a sense of unity. With Muhammad, its rhetoric had given Arabs a sense of purpose and inspired the empire-building super-raids under his successors. Now, at long last, began the third conquest after those of language and arms – that of Islam. Up to the time of al-Saffah and al-Mansur, the rate of conversion remained very low: most Persians, for example, were still Zoroastrian. This changed under their successors: Islam would complete its transformation from cult to cultural hegemony. The part that subsequent caliphs played in it all was central, but usually closer to that of British monarchs as ex-officio heads of the Church of England than of medieval popes as *de facto* secular princes, or of more recent popes as infallible interpreters of divine will: caliphs were defenders of the faith, but not necessarily paragons of its practice. To take the case of alcohol, as with the Umayyads few of them would have passed a breathalyser test. The attitude was neatly expressed by al-Ma'mun, their greatest thinker:

> Drink, but always know that it's a sin,
> and seek forgiveness from a kindly Lord.

It was enough for their subjects that they were there, at the heart of things, and that they derived their name and their descent from Muhammad's uncle.

The subjects, meanwhile, covered the imperial gamut. Something of their diversity comes across in the list of people mimicked and satirized by the late ninth-century Baghdad comedian Ibn al-Maghazili: *a'rabi* bedouins, Turks, Meccans, Najdis from central Arabia, indigenous Nabati peasants from Mesopotamia, black Zanjis, Sindis from the valley of the Indus, Jat Indians, and 'types' such as camp homosexuals, judges, caliphal eunuchs and grammarians. Arabs accounted for only a few of these personas, and if they enjoyed any primacy it was mainly in their own eyes. To be an Arab in ninth-century Baghdad was not unlike being a WASP in twenty-first-century New York: important to oneself, perhaps, but increasingly irrelevant to the demography of 'Baghdad on the Subway' (as O. Henry aptly called his city).

This diversity under the early Abbasids fuelled an intellectual ferment that bubbled with questions – not least questions about that belatedly cohesive force, Islam. Baghdad itself was not the major centre of learning: its inhabitants were dismissed by one scholar as 'the camp-followers of the caliph's army'. Rather, it was al-Kufah and al-Basrah that acted as the twin, often rival, intellectual capitals, a sort of Abbasid Oxbridge or Harvard and Yale. Debate was lively, thought free. According to a recent writer,

> The most important stage of Arab intellectual growth was in the Abbasid period. It was then that most of the questions were posed that are still posed today. Debate was marked by such extraordinary fearlessness that even heretics were able put forward their views. Today, we dare not pose the smallest fraction of the questions some of our forebears asked, and in this sense, we have regressed from those times.

Among the questions were ones about the nature of God, about predestination and free will, sin and repentance. Foremost in debate in the earlier Abbasid period were the scholars known as the Mu'tazilah, who tended to stress the role of the individual, and in particular one's ethical responsibilities and ability to make one's own sense of scripture. They emphasized the importance of *ijtihad* – a cognate of *jihad*, 'struggle', with its various implications – but, for the Mu'tazilah, meaning the individual struggle to understand what Allah communicated to mankind through His messenger Muhammad. Their ideas were given a huge fillip when they were espoused by Caliph al-Ma'mun; at the same time they were fatally jeopardized for, in 833, only four months before his death, al-Ma'mun was to take a 'papal' turn and make them official dogma, thus turning what had been points of view into rights and wrongs. In particular, al-Ma'mun backed the view of the Mu'tazilah that the Qur'an was created by Allah, and not eternally co-existent with Him. At first glance, the point may look like a theological nicety. But when one considers the battles, theological and political, fought over the equivalent Christian questions in the early Byzantine period – about the exact relationship of God and His Logos, Jesus, and the nature of the Trinity – one will realize that the stage was set for bitter dispute, accusations and counter-accusations of heresy, even for inquisitions.

It had taken two centuries for Islam to produce its first orthodoxy. In that time, however, Allah had come a long way from His beginnings as the tribal deity of Quraysh; but then, so too had Quraysh. The caliphs of its Umayyad clan, by depicting the great rulers of the world on the walls of their palaces, had signalled that they had staked their claim to territory on the world map of kings. For those of the Abbasid clan, that claim was now secure: they wanted a stake in learning as well as land, to found an empire of the mind as well as on the map. Rather as imperial Romans had looked across and back to Greece, and imperial Russians to France, so the rulers of the Arab empire looked to their neighbours present and past to build up their intellectual property portfolio. The theological debates of the time were thus part of a general intellectual opening-up, an opening that reached its widest during the earlier part of al-Ma'mun's caliphate. An anecdote attempts to explain why this was. Under the heading, 'The reason why books of philosophy and of the other ancient sciences have proliferated in this land', the bookseller and bibliographer of Baghdad Ibn al-Nadim wrote,

> One night al-Ma'mun dreamed that a man . . . was sitting on his caliphal throne. 'It was as if I were standing before him,' he said, 'and filled with awe by him. I asked him who he was, and he said, "I am Aristotle." I was overjoyed, and said, "Great sage, may I ask you a question?" "Yes," he said. So I asked him, "What is goodness?" He replied, "That which reason deems to be good." And I said, "And then what?" He replied, "That which the law deems to be good." And I said, "And then what?" He replied, "That which the mass of the people deem to be good." And I said, "And then what?" And he replied, "And then there is no more 'then'."'

At least in al-Ma'mun's dreams, it seemed Baghdad might become that hypothetical city of the philosophers. In pursuit of the ideal, al-Ma'mun 'wrote to the Byzantine emperor [Leo the Armenian] asking him to consent to sending a selection of such works on the ancient sciences as had been preserved and passed down in Byzantine lands. To this the emperor agreed, after some initial reluctance'.

The dream may itself have been dreamed up to rationalize al-Ma'mun's interests; but the interests were real, and there is nothing hypothetical in the way he put some of them into practice. 'Al-Mamun was fascinated by the sciences of the ancients and wished to prove their theories', says a biography of the three sons of Musa ibn Shakir, joint authors of a famous book on mechanical contrivances. In the course of his perusal of those 'ancient' sciences – that is, Greek and Hellenistic studies of the physical world – the caliph had read, for example, that the circumference of the terrestrial globe was 24,000 miles, and commisioned the Banu Musa brothers to put the figure to the test. They scouted around for the flattest and largest area possible and decided on the desert around Sinjar. There, they measured the elevation of the Pole Star, then travelled due north until they reached a point where the elevation had increased by one degree. Measuring with pegs and rope the distance travelled, they found it to be sixty-six and two-thirds of a mile. They then repeated the experiment by travelling due south until the elevation of the Pole had decreased by one degree, and found the distance to be the same. They then double-checked their figure in the desert around al-Kufah. Multiplied by 360 degrees, it gave a product of 24,000 miles – QED.

The point is not in the originality of the experiment, 'the ancient metrologists had themselves performed it', but in the fact that the Banu Musa brothers, under al-Ma'mun's patronage, 'were the sole ones in the community of Islam to have applied themselves to it, and to have taken it out of the realm of theory and into that of practice'. The experiment had never been repeated in Islamic lands as far as the writer knew, and he was writing 450 years later. After his time, Mongol and Mughal Islamic rulers would become enthusiastic backers of the applied sciences, but among Arab rulers al-Ma'mun's caliphate marks an apogee for practical research.

Alongside the sciences of the non-Arabs (often called *al-'ulum al-'aqliyyah*, 'the rational sciences'), the Arab sciences (*al-'ulum al-naqliyyah*, or 'traditional sciences') were also flourishing. The latter were really the Arab*ic* sciences, as they revolved around texts – the written text of the Qur'an, and the vast body of sayings and doings of Muhammad and his companions, which existed as oral texts or jottings. In early Abbasid times, this second corpus began to be codified and committed to papyrus and increasingly, as we shall see, to paper. From it – at last – formal ethical and legal structures began to emerge for Islam. Of the four founders of the main 'schools' of Sunni jurisprudence – based, that is, on the *sunnah* or practice of Muhammad and his followers – three were 'genetic' Arabs; the fourth, Abu Hanifah, was a *mawla* and the grandson of a slave from Kabul. The next generation, however, those who elaborated and disseminated the founders' ideas, tended to be as cosmopolitan as the empire. Not untypical is al-Qasim ibn Sallam: born in Herat, Afghanistan, to a Byzantine slave father, he eventually became a judge in Tarsus on the Mediterranean, and died in Mecca shortly after the time of al-Ma'mun. Similarly, Shi'ah ethics and jurisprudence were laid down by imams of the house of Ali, but built upon by their non-Arab followers. It was these 'foreigners' who took the kernel of the Qur'an and the amorphous raw material surrounding it, and pressed it into shape as a fully rounded religion.

Al-Ma'mun was also the beneficiary of the traditional Arab sciences, for he had been schooled in the nascent study of Hanafi jurisprudence as a youth. With this background, his Aristotelian dreams and his measurement of the globe, he was clearly equipped to be a broad-minded thinker, even if he would come late in life to pontifical conclusions. Nothing, however, prepared the empire for another experiment of his – one which seems not to have been repeated anywhere, in any form, until the twentieth century. It was a political experiment, and it sought to bridge the great rift in Arab and Islamic unity: that between the Shi'ah, the Party of Ali, and the rest. It was a rift that had begun as a simple if perilous crack in the Arab power-base, but one that had already swallowed so many lives and loyalties from the battle of Siffin onward. It had also been gaining new dimensions – as a division in the very nature of authority, between caliphate and imamate; between an authority subsisting in texts and their interpretation by scholarly consensus, and another more esoteric, apostolic kind of authority inherited with the blood of the martyred Ali and al-Husayn.

Al-Ma'mun's recent forebears, the first Abbasid caliphs, had hardly promoted love between the two blocs by coming to power on a Shi'i ticket and then proceeding to rip that ticket to pieces by arrogating power to themselves. But in 816 al-Ma'mun apparently decided to renounce the Abbasid monopoly on rule: he designated Ali al-Rida, the eighth imam of the Shi'is, as heir to the caliphate, and gave him his daughter in marriage. Dazed by the decision but dutiful, those closest to the caliph went along with it; some Shi'is scented success, at last, for their cause, while others smelt a rat; Abbasid dynastic hardliners were appalled. As it happened, Ali al-Rida died two years later, and the business was quietly forgotten – except by the Shi'is, who put his death down to a plot and a poisoned pomegranate. They may be right. Whatever the truth of the matter, the caliph buried Ali al-Rida beside his father, the late caliph al-Rashid, where the latter had died on an expedition to Khurasan. The place became known to Iranian Shi'ism as al-Mashhad, the Sanctuary, and is still the holiest site in Iran.

Conspiracy theories abounded and still do. There was even a niggling rumour that al-Ma'mun secretly exhumed and swapped the two bodies. If it is true, when Shi'i pilgrims stand by the tomb of their eighth imam and pray for his soul, then cross over and curse, triply, al-Rashid's grave, their prayers and curses are at cross-purposes. God is the one who knows.

The next official attempt at Sunni–Shi'i reconciliation would not take place until the 1940s, with the foundation of an ecumenical body, the Jama'at al-Taqrib; within two decades, that too would fizzle out and die. But for a brief season in the early ninth century, it seemed that the great hemiglobal organism that had gestated in Arabia and been born in the time of Muhammad might, at last, have grown to maturity and left the squabbles of its Arab infancy behind. But once more, the community of Islam stood, as it had done in years immediately after the Prophet,

> at a fork in the path of pilgrimage.

Now, two centuries on, the choice was between intellectual routes: on the one hand that of tradition with its textual, rhetorical truths, on the other that of reason, with its empirical truths; and between political paths – the authority of the Sunni Abbasid caliphate, or of the Shi'i Alid imamate . . . Or, as the mercurial al-Ma'mun had shown by making the imam heir to the caliphate, there might have been middle ways to pioneer, ways of compromise but also ways to unity. But, as always, it was easier to agree to differ than to compromise, and to let the future suffer the consequences.

FOUND IN TRANSLATION

Despite divergences intellectual and political, one bond above all still gave the vast and complex organism unity and identity: it still wrote, even if it rarely spoke, in the old high Arabic language. Spoken Arabic might have been splitting up into new dialects, but as Islam expanded to become a world religion and a world culture, Arabic provided the words for that world. In the Qur'anic version of a biblical story, Allah taught Adam the Arabic names of all things in creation; now, with Islam recreating the world in its own image, Arabic was again supplying the vocabulary. It could provide much of it by spontaneous generation: Arabic had always been supple, subtle and versatile, its root-system spontaneously producing offshoots. But just as marriage with the women of the conquered lands had given birth to new hybrid Arabs and new hybrid Arabics, so the language was also enriched from other tongues. Arabic's own word-world expanded.

In this expansion, formal translation played as important a part as day-to-day communication. The translation movement had begun slowly in

Umayyad times, with Arabic versions of texts on chemistry done in Alexandria from Greek and Coptic for an enthusiastic Umayyad prince. Now the programme accelerated, and with the new Abbasid eastward orientation it took in new source-languages: to the first three languages to be mined – Greek, Coptic, and the Syriac of Fertile Crescent scholarship – were added the Persian language, Pahlavi, and Sanskrit. The range of sciences expanded too, with works translated on medicine, botany, pharmacology, astronomy, astrology, geography, geometry, engineering, music, mathematics and more. And the enrichment was not just of the Arabic language and Arabic-thinking minds, but of world knowledge as a whole. If nothing else, the Arab adoption of *sifr*, the 'cipher' – the figure zero, hitherto confined to India – and their communication of it to the rest of the Old World via 'Arabic' numerals, would have done much to take that world into the modern age.

Arabic civilization, however, was no cipher itself, no mere hyphen between east and west, ancient and modern. Arabic-speaking scientists were to add much of their own to ancient knowledge, particularly in the spheres of medicine, trigonometry, mathematics and astronomy – as witness the giveaway *al-* words like 'alcohol', 'algebra', 'algorithm', and star names like 'Altair' (*al-tayr*, 'the bird'). Others are less obvious: when Hollywood borrowed the name of a star, Betelgeuse, for that of a movie, *Beetlejuice*, did the movie men realize it was the Arabic *ibt al-jawza'*, 'Orion's armpit'?

As al-Ma'mun's dream shows, philosophy was eagerly consumed, particularly Aristotle's, but also that of Plato and the Neoplatonists. Al-Ma'mun was the greatest sponsor of translation and scientific endeavour, and gave the lie to the jibe about Baghdad being nothing but an overblown garrison town by founding a sort of Royal Institution in the city, the Bayt al-Hikmah or House of Wisdom. The Abbasid institute focused on translation but also on the heavens, with astronomical observatories in Baghdad itself and in Damascus. Sponsorship also went on at less exalted levels, even if few could match the sum paid by the three Banu Musa brothers to their own in-house translators – 500 gold *dinar*s a month, at a time when the pay of a foot soldier was twenty *dirham*s a month, or about two *dinar*s. Eventually, as Dimitri Gutas has written, 'the majority of pagan Greek books on science and philosophy . . . that were available in Late Antiquity throughout the eastern Byzantine empire and the Near East had been translated into Arabic'. The translation movement had not run out of energy; it had run out of texts.

Even then, however, the literary drive did not end. It changed gear, for the translations had begun to inspire a broad range of original thinking in Arabic, and the thinking was now being set down in what for Arabic was a completely novel way – plain prose, with neither rhythm nor rhyme, composed directly in writing: prose like that which I am writing now. A whole new medium of expression unfurled. At last, users of Arabic could think in ink as well as in sound: the language could serve intellectuals as well as poets, orators and imperial book-keepers. Admittedly, few of the intellectuals were Arabs 'proper'; they covered the genetic spectrum of the empire. But in philosophy, the first and one of the greatest was the ninth-century 'Philosopher of the Arabs', al-Kindi, a prolific author in and defender of science in all its forms. He belonged to that immensely talented clan of princes, poets and pioneers, the ancient ruling house of the tribe of Kindah who had produced the fourth-century king Imru' al-Qays, author of one of the earliest known Arabic texts, his namesake the sixth-century wanderer and greatest of the pre-Islamic poets, and that seventh-century rebel reconciled to Islam, the far-travelled warrior al-Ash'ath.

It has often been said that if had not been for Arabs, Europeans would have had no Renaissance. It might be better said that the Abbasids, and especially al-Ma'mun – an unstinting patron greater than Maecenas or the Medici, and mid-way between them in time – were themselves princes of the Renaissance, of which the later European episode was a continuation after a long hiatus.

A REVOLUTION ON PAPER

The Abbasid Renaissance, and the birth of written scholarship in Arabic that came with it, were both powered by paper. This was the third stage in a writing revolution that had begun with the recording of the Qur'an, and had then spread with the need to run the empire in the language of its rulers.

The change from writing little, and slowly, on expensive parchment and papyrus to writing a lot, quickly, on much cheaper paper was a leap in information technology no less important than the leap from paper to screens in our own age: it, too, generated words, not all of them worth generating, but all adding volume to the literary buzz of the times. The traditional account tells how paper came west with Chinese papermakers captured by Arabs at the battle of Talas or Taraz, east of the Syr Darya River, in 751 – the clash which marked the furthest penetration of Arab forces into Asia. The story is almost certainly a simplification of a longer and woollier process; the bibliographer Ibn al-Nadim, for example, says that 'Khurasani paper' made from flax was known in the west in Umayyad times. What is not in doubt is the sudden spread of paper under the Abbasids. Al-Ma'mun's father, al-Rashid, is said to have ordered the use of the material in government offices to prevent the 'cooking of the books': writing on paper is difficult to erase, unlike that on parchment and papyrus, which can be scraped off comparatively easily. From al-Rashid's time comes the oldest known surviving paper from the Arab empire, a Greek manuscript written in Damascus in about 800. It is not known where the leaves for it were made, but by that date a papermaking industry had begun in Iraq and was about to spread westward.

The smoothness of paper compared to other writing surfaces further helped the growth of more rounded and cursive Arabic scripts, originally developed by Umayyad imperial scribes to help them speed through their increasing piles of copying. And, just as it had done in its native China, paper also enhanced a whole calligraphic aesthetic, one that would unify the world of Islam and keep it rooted in its Arabic origins: a lot of 'Islamic' art is really Arabic calligraphic art. As sculpture was to ancient Greece and the movie is to the modern United States, so calligraphy has been to Arabs through the second half of their long story. Even when they 'disappear' from that half, when their role changes from active to passive, the script inscribes itself on and on – saying nothing new, perhaps, but providing a line of continuity, a lifeline for Arab identity that would lead Arabs to their nineteenth-century reappearance in world history.

The calligraphic aesthetic is all-embracing: it literally describes and inscribes both the divine, in the revelation of the Qur'an, and the human – the kiss-curl of the beloved is the letter *waw*:

و

and the lovers entwined are a *lam-alif* of the elaborate 'Kufic' sort:

and, to complete the aesthetic circle, letters in their wider sense are described in terms of human beauty:

Perfume the literature you write with only the finest ink,
for literary works are luscious girls, and ink their precious scent.

As yet, in the Abbasid stage of the writing revolution, most writers had no time for such whimsicalities. Written scholarship had a lot to catch up with, and now it began to do so in industrial quantities. A scholar of Nishapur in Iran, for example, would hold open lectures on *hadith* in which 500 inkwells would be set out for those attending to take down his words. There was a seemingly unstoppable flow of ink: by the early tenth century the *wazir* Ibn al-Furat could return to his office from sick-leave to find a thousand letters waiting for him to deal with, and another thousand chits to be signed – the equivalent of the bursting email inbox. Sometimes red tape spooled out of control, as in a story of an official with loose bowels who had to submit a written application to use the only available lavatory. By the time it came back, approved, and the illiterate janitor had sent for a clerk to read it out, it was almost too late: a case of logorrhoea and diarrhoea at odds with each other.

At the other literary extreme of this writing society, libraries abounded and played their own part in ensuring cultural cohesion. The ninth-century poet Abu Tammam, for example, marooned by snow in the Iranian city of Hamadhan, shut himself away in the library of one of the local notables, poring over pre-Islamic verse. The scene is a miniature of the cultural empire: an Arabic poet of ambiguous but probably Greek origin, travelling through Persia, reading the works of his ancient Arab predecessors. Libraries grew apace with the outpouring of words. The great statesman of the tenth century, al-Sahib ibn Abbad, was offered a tempting career change, but declined it partly on the grounds that his library alone would need 400 camels to transport it. This was also the age when weighty individual works were appearing, themselves an attempt to contain and control the never-ending flood of ink – books like the tenth-century histories of al-Tabari and al-Mas'udi, both running to many volumes. Al-Mas'udi's is lost, but its surviving four-volume abridgement – *Muruj al-dhahab*, *The Meadows of Gold* – is compendious in itself. It is one of my main sources: it gives an Abbasid world-view of history, in which the Arab empire is both part of a continuum beginning with Adam, and central (as the Tang emperor observed) to a human geography that includes Copts and Persians, Franks and Chinese.

Al-Mas'udi had himself observed a fair portion of that geography, and was thus eminently qualified to present the Abbasid perspective. An Arab descendant of Muhammad's learned companion Abd Allah ibn Mas'ud, he grew up in Baghdad but would visit many lands – Egypt, Persia, Sind, India, Sarandib (Sri Lanka), and possibly Indo-China, China, the East Indies, and then Madagascar and East Africa on his way back home via the Arabian Peninsula. Later he toured what are now the north and west of Iran, and the lands of the Levant. As the personification of an increasingly bookish and mobile age, he has been compared to Herodotus. But he also embodies a restlessness that had always been endemic in Arabia, had been released after Muhammad when Arabs set out to pioneer a political empire, and was now finding its outlet in travels in search of knowledge. Dual empires of territory and information, such as Edward Said describes in his *Orientalism*, were not confined to later Western conquerors.

Few if any individuals could have rivalled al-Mas'udi's explorations, either on the ground or on paper. But the Arabic language and culture he and others used and exported travelled even further. Well before al-Mas'udi's time, as we have seen, the salon of the poet Ibn al-A'rabi – 'the Son of the Bedouin', who was actually of Sindi origin – brought together visitors from Andalus and Turkestan, the extremes of empire. The encounter was not the only one of its kind. 'I was reciting in the entrance hall of my house one day,' the later Baghdad poet Ibn Nubatah remembered,

> when there was a knock on the door. 'Who is it?' I said.
>
> 'A visitor from the Mashriq [the east of the empire],' came the reply.
>
> 'How can I help you?' I asked.
>
> He said, 'This verse is yours, is it not:
>
> "A man who dies not by the sword, still to him death will come:
> the causes may be many but the malady is one."'
>
> 'Yes,' I said, 'it is mine.'
>
> 'May I then recite it on your authority?' he asked.
>
> 'Certainly,' I replied. He went on his way. At the end of the day there was another knock on the door.
>
> 'Who is it?' I said.
>
> 'A visitor from Tahart, in the Maghrib [in Algeria],' came the reply.
>
> 'How can I help you?' I asked.
>
> He said, 'This verse is yours, is it not:
>
> "A man who dies not by the sword, still to him death will come:
> the causes may be many but the malady is one."'
>
> 'Yes,' I said, 'it is mine.'

'May I then recite it on your authority?' he asked.

'Certainly,' I replied. And I was amazed that this verse should have reached both East and West.

Another poet, al-Buhturi, caught the world-spanning mood of the times:

The caravan of my widely travelling verse will surely always
follow you . . .

The Abbasid age was mobile, physically, artistically, intellectually. Al-Kindi, descendant of that most talented of Arab families since long before Islam, vigorously opposed intellectual stick-in-the-muds, obscurantists who would attack philosophy in the name of religion. 'It is right and proper for us,' he wrote,

never to shy away from admitting the value of truth [*al-haqq*] and acquiring it for ourselves, wherever it may come from – even if it comes from races who are distant from us and societies quite different from our own.

Only in a society and culture sure of its own strength could such an idea have been thought, let alone expressed.

The influence of this new and cosmopolitan superculture spread not just to Chinese emperors and Anglo-Saxon coinage. In the shrinking rump of the classical world too, in Constantinople, they were imitating Baghdadi architecture and dress: the emperor Theophilus, who fought Arabs on the battlefield in the 830s, built a Baghdad-style palace by the Bosporus, while wealthy Byzantines went about *à l'arabe*, in turbans and kaftans. Even on the streets of Tang-era Guangzhou, the Arab-style kaftan or *hufu*, 'foreigner's robe', was in fashion. But, while the world was becoming ever smaller and more Arabic – both in the words it spoke and wrote, and in the modes of its life and dress – it was becoming, at least to the traditionally minded, ever less Arab.

THE LONG ECLIPSE BEGINS

The last Umayyad governor of Khurasan had warned his masters in Damascus of the Abbasid revolution. If they failed to extinguish it now, his poetic fire alarm concluded, then 'to Islam and to the Arabs – farewell!' The Abbasid victory had not brought about the end of Islam; instead, it had enriched it in many ways. But what about arabness? As we have seen, the great arabologist al-Jahiz, writing a century after the Abbasid takeover, branded the Abbasid dynasty as *'ajamiyyah khurasaniyyah*, non-Arab and Khurasani. Certainly, their revolution had begun in Khurasan, and they had always used troops from that region; they were 'Khurasani' in that sense. But *'ajami*? Surely al-Jahiz was overstating a rhetorical point: *'ajami* had always served as the opposite – in language, but also in ancestral origin, lifestyle and every other way imaginable – by which *'arabi* defined itself.

The Abbasids were of course still Arabs in language and in the all-important male lineage. But in lifestyle they had come a long way in a short time. Al-Mughirah, that epitome of rough bedouin arabness, parleying with the shah's viceroy a little over a century before the Abbasid rise, had vandalized the Persian's precious carpet and thrust himself on to the viceregal throne. Now the Abbasids were the ones with carpets and thrones. The Arab 'kings of kings', as the Chinese emperor called them, even if they had not officially adopted that persianesque title, had embraced Persian 'ornamentalism'. In contrast to the accessibility of old Arab and most early Islamic rulers, the first Abbasid caliph, al-Saffah, had adopted the Persian custom of sitting behind a curtain when in public audience. Admittedly some of the Umayyads had done so too. But the later Abbasids went much further. They began to wear the *taj*, a Persian word for 'crown' but perhaps, for the Abbasids, a turban adorned with gems. They employed court astrologers – in al-Mansur's case a Zoroastrian, who gave him a veneer of legitimacy in the land of the 'Magi', where the majority still clung to the old religion. And policy was persianized as well: al-Mansur's assassination of Abu Muslim is said to have been inspired by a similar killing of a trusted lieutenant by one of the Sasanian shahs. It was a deed that would hardly have been imaginable under the Umayyads who, even if they fought their enemies to the death, were generally more loyal to their friends.

A metaphorical curtain was coming down between the rulers and their origins, between the new, cosmopolitan Arab and the old-style *a'rabi*. The disconnect is revealed in a story about the third Abbasid caliph, al-Mahdi, getting lost while hunting in the wilderness and taking refuge with a bedouin. The bedouin plies him with wine and, cup by cup, the caliph gradually reveals who he is: first that he is from the court; then that he is one of the caliph's commanders; then that he is the caliph himself. The bedouin, meanwhile, looks on askance.

> 'Bedouin,' al-Mahdi said, 'pour another cup.'
>
> The man replied, 'No, by Allah, I won't let you drink another drop.'
>
> 'Why?' the caliph asked . . .
>
> 'Because I'm afraid that if you have a fourth, you'll be telling me you're the Prophet of Allah.' When he heard this, al-Mahdi laughed.

At this point the caliph's distraught escort finally find him. The bedouin is at first aghast, then collects himself and says to the caliph,

> 'So you *were* telling the truth. But if you'd made the fourth claim – *and the fifth* – you'd have been going too far.' And al-Mahdi laughed so much at 'the fourth claim – *and the fifth*' that he nearly fell off his horse.

The fifth claim being, presumably, that the caliph was God . . . In conclusion,

> Al-Mahdi commanded that the bedouin be paid a pension, and took him into his circle of close companions.

It reads like a parable about the transformation, begun with Islam and now gathering pace, of old-style Arabs into city-dwellers: the *a'rabi*, the peripheral, the outsider from the wilderness (albeit a wilderness well supplied with wine), is taken into the eye of the circle – admitted behind the caliphal curtain, transported into the heart of the new urban society. It also feels like the end of an era. The future of caliph-hood would be not that of al-Mahdi unknown in the wilds, but that of his son al-Rashid in his fabulous *Thousand and One Nights* persona, incognito in the urban wilds of Baghdad; not disbelieved in the desert but disguised in town.

As to lifestyle, then, al-Jahiz was right: the Abbasids, throughout their long era the first family of arabhood and the prime symbol of Arab solidarity, were far removed from traditional Arab existence. But even in those two spheres where they might still have seemed purely Arab, in language and lineage, their arabness was being undermined; or to be precise, their language and lineage were also being removed from the old environment. Umayyad caliphs may have made mistakes in the case-endings of high Arabic; much worse, al-Mahdi's grandson, al-Mu'tasim, admitted that he was 'illiterate' when he didn't know the meaning of the word *kala'* – it is the most important word in traditional Arab life after *ma'*, water, for it means 'pasture'. And although the patriline was now the one that mattered, descent on the mother's side had been of almost equal importance in old Arab society. In pre-Islamic times, the children of slaves often went unacknowledged by their fathers, unless they were sons who had produced their own offspring. But of the thirty-seven Abbasid caliphs over the 500 years until their effective extinction by the Mongols, only three would have free-born Arab mothers. The other mothers were slave-concubines of hugely varied origin, including Afghan, Khwarizmian, Byzantine, Slav, Berber, Persian, Turkish, Armenian and Abyssinian. 'The world has intermingled,' the eleventh-century poet al-Ma'arri noted, 'the people of the plain with the daughters of the mountain; the mother of the race of Numayr is a Turk; she of 'Uqayl is a slave from Samarkand.' It was all an accurate reflection of the complex diversity of empire, but very far from the home life of the old Arabian subcontinent.

Hadarah, the successful, settled coexistence of diversity, had prevailed for the time being over *badawah*, 'bedouinism'; the *sha'b* or 'people' in its broadest, cosmopolitan-Islamic sense had reduced the *qabilah*, or tribe, to a minor and marginal role. Society – the part of society that mattered – was no longer tribal; genealogy might still have been important for some, but people with widely different genes could still live together within the family of Islam. Importantly, non-Arabs were no longer just clients or clerks or concubines, but were becoming people of importance in their own right.

Under the Abbasids, the *wazir* or 'vizier' would increasingly be in charge of the hands-on running of the empire. Foremost among the *wazir*s of the earlier Abbasids were those of the Persian Barmak family, whose ancestors had been hereditary sacristans of the temple of Nawbahar at Balkh, in what is now northern Afghanistan ('Barmak' is Sanskrit *parmak*, 'superior, chief', 'Nawbahar' the new *vihāra* or Buddhist monastery). Three generations of the family served the Abbasids in various capacities, most famously Ja'far, the companion of Harun al-Rashid in the story collection that became *The Thousand and One Nights*. The relationship of the two was close; so close, according to legend, that al-Rashid had a special 'Siamese-twin' garment that accommodated both of them, their heads poking out of individual collars. (Is this the origin of a proverbial expression for a close friendship, 'Two pairs of buttocks in one pair of drawers'?)

The legends do not end there: the coming together of Persian and Arab was said to be so close that the old taboo – as old as the pre-Islamic Lakhmid kings – was broken, and al-Rashid married Ja'far to his sister, Abbasah. And then, the story goes, things went wrong: the union, meant to be a *mariage blanc*, was consummated, and a son born. Al-Rashid, enraged at the thought of the Persian 'paper groom', bosom pal or not, sullying his sister's Arab purity, had Ja'far executed, imprisoned the rest of the family and confiscated their stupendously valuable properties.

Is the story true? Probably not. Ibn Khaldun, for one, dismisses it as ridiculous – then rather undermines his case by asking of Abbasah, 'How could she . . . stain her Arab nobility with a Persian client?' Ibn Khaldun may be the father of sociology; he is shakier on what happens in the bedroom. More persuasively, he then goes on to suggest that the Barmak family were in fact planning a coup against al-Rashid. There is no clear evidence to support this, and yet the pro-Barmak elegies that have survived may include coded references to it. One, for example, includes the lines,

When you were here, the whole world was a bride;
now it is bereft of husband, and of child.

Ja'far's marriage was not just to the caliph's sister, this implies, but to his realm. Now the Persian wedding to the world was off.

The fall of the house of Barmak has never been explained. Vicious court rivalries were in play, especially between the Barmaks and another close aide of al-Rashid, al-Fadl ibn al-Rabi'. But perhaps in the end it was a resurfacing in al-Rashid of the ancient fear – that of the *'ajami* being the one on top, whether in bed or on the throne. It may not be insignificant that in Arabic the two items of furniture can be expressed by one word, *sarir* (as we have seen, another word for 'throne', *'arsh*, also means 'bier'). It may also not be insignificant that, just before his move against the Barmaks, the caliph had been on the pilgrimage to Mecca, that ritual reconnection with Arabian roots. He was the last Abbasid caliph to renew that ancient link.

The fear of the Other, even if ancient, was justified: Arab supremacy would soon be lost. Persians – Turks, even – were about to assert their dominance not over Arab women's bodies and thus Arab 'honour', but over the whole Arab body-politic. Their climb to power would begin in earnest in the next caliphal generation; within only one more generation after that, those non-Arabs would turn into an incubus of a thousand years.

THE BARRENNESS OF KINGSHIP

Big declines and falls – that of the dinosaurs excepted, perhaps – always have many causes, often so trivial as to evade detection; but sometimes among them are tragic flaws, twists of character or of circumstance from which disaster spirals out. 'When Allah Almighty intends a people's destruction,' wrote Ubayd Allah ibn Sulayman, 'and the end of their happiness, He provides reasons for it'. In other words, He does not play dice. With Arabs, the usual suspect – the perennial, internecine disunity they brought with them out of Arabia – goes a long way to explain their fall from power.

It does not need to be said that ruling-family rivalry is not an exclusively Arab flaw: the Kurdish Ayyubid dynasty 'united and flourished, then disunited and perished', according to the confidant of their founder, Saladin; similarly, their near contemporaries in India, the Turkic Delhi Sultans, 'united to destroy their enemies and disunited to destroy themselves'. Nor is it a flaw peculiar to Muslim ruling families: it would set Pedro of Castile and his illegitimate brother Henry of Trastámara against each other in Spain, and pitch the cousin-houses of York and Lancaster into the Wars of the Roses. Infighting is part of dynastic dynamics. But it is exacerbated by polygamy, concubinage and the resulting multiplicity of stepmothers and half-brothers. And in the Abbasid case, with Arabs as a whole already dispersed and disunited, when the last great symbol of their solidarity and continuity – the caliphal family – was split apart by sibling rivalry, the consequences would be direr than ever before.

Al-Ma'mun, philosopher-caliph, patron of the sciences, had got where he was by the time-honoured means of a fight to the death with his nearest, if not his dearest; neither Abbasids nor Arabs would ever recover from it. Between the 'golden prime' of Harun al-Rashid and the intellectual golden age of his son al-Ma'mun lay a war in which the unity of the whole empire was shaken. Rather as the legend of the bloody separation of the conjoined twins Hashim and Abd Shams foretold the split within their ancestral clan of Quraysh, so too is an anecdote about the young Abd Allah (al-Ma'mun) and his brother Muhammad (al-Amin) an omen of their future falling out. The scholar al-Kisa'i was visiting al-Rashid, and the doting caliph summoned his two young sons to show off their recitation of Qur'anic passages and poetry. The unremarkable couplet Muhammad recited was about wealth, generosity and honour. Abd Allah's piece was different. It was about fate and patience in adversity, and ended with a strange image:

> You will see the shaft of my lance, when gripped
> by the bite of the straightening-vice, slow to break.

Al-Kisa'i was full of praise and prayers for the boys. But, he recalled,

> Al-Rashid drew them together to himself and held them tight. When he loosened his hold I saw that tears were coursing down on to his chest. He sent the boys away, and when they left he came close to me and said, 'It is as if your presence has brought on their fate, called down their destinies from the heavens, and taken what is written to its conclusion. For their word, once gathered, has now diverged, their ways have forked, their enmity is made plain. Thus they will remain, until blood has been shed, until many lie dead, until the veils of the women are torn, until many living wish that they had not been born.'

Whatever the truth of the story – and of the rumoured existence of a book, alluded to by al-Rashid, in which the fate of the entire Abbasid dynasty was predicted – there does indeed seem to be an inevitability about the princes' falling out. Muhammad al-Amin's mother Zubaydah ('Butter-pat'), a patroness of grand charitable works and lover of gemstones (she even wore gem-studded boots), was one of those very few caliphal wives who were both free-born and Arab; she was herself a member of the Abbasid family. Worried for the future of the dynasty when her growing son showed a marked preference for slave-boys to slave-girls, she began dressing the latter in boys' clothes – and sparked off a fashion for *ghulamiyyat*, 'gamines', as well as for diamanté heels. Abd Allah al-Ma'mun, slightly the elder of the two, had been born in the more usual way to a slave-concubine. There was no love lost between the two mothers: the Sarah versus Hagar, Isaac-and-Ishmael syndrome was at play. As so often in Arab history, the existence of rival mothers, and the absence of the blunt but serviceable instrument of primogeniture, would complicate the transfer of power. In this case al-Rashid hit on a disastrous 'solution', worthy of King Lear: he made al-Amin the first heir to the caliphate

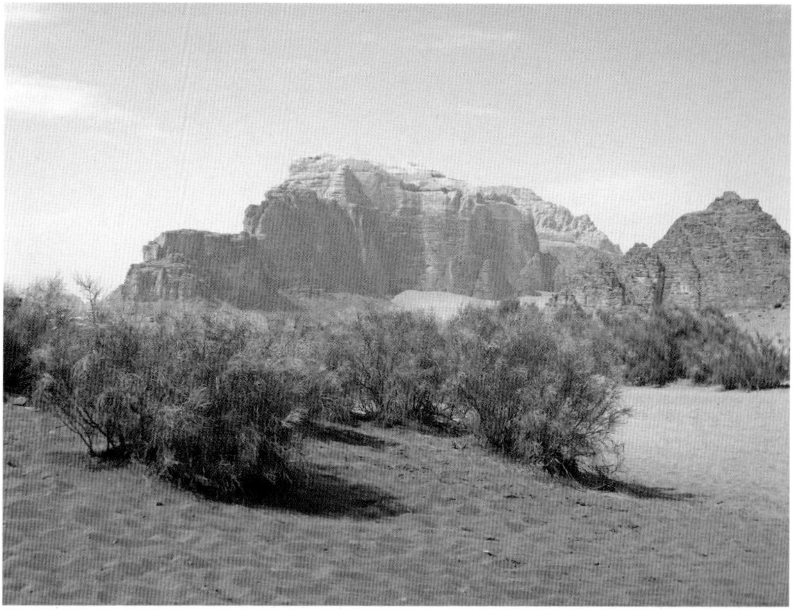

1 Parsimonious beauty, short commons for the herds, but a livelihood of sorts. *Arabias Petraea* and *Deserta* intersect in Jordan's Wadi Rum.

2 *Arabia Felix* . . . and yet felicity only comes with social organization and hard graft. Building and maintaining these terraces is labour-intensive, but they retain the precious topsoil. A village near al-Tawilah, north-western Yemen.

3 *A handbag?* No, a vase. The gesture with the other hand is one of submission or despair: this was one of the times it didn't help Arabs to be neighbours to empires. Gypsum wall panel of 728 BC from Nimrud, Iraq. The woman and camels have been captured in Assyrian campaigns against the Arab 'queen', Shamsi.

4 Alluded to in the Qur'an, this great hydraulic monument has proved to be one of the most durable structures in the history of civil engineering. Part of the southern sluice of the sixth-century BC Sabaean dam at Marib, Yemen. It remained in use for over a thousand years.

5 *A'rab* of nomad origin riding roughshod through settled South Arabian society. A first–third-century AD South Arabian calcite-alabaster stele commemorating a certain Ha'an ibn Dhu Zu'd.

6 Kiss like a butterfly: black power meets the Black Stone. Boxing legend Muhammad Ali at the Ka'bah, Mecca, in 1972.

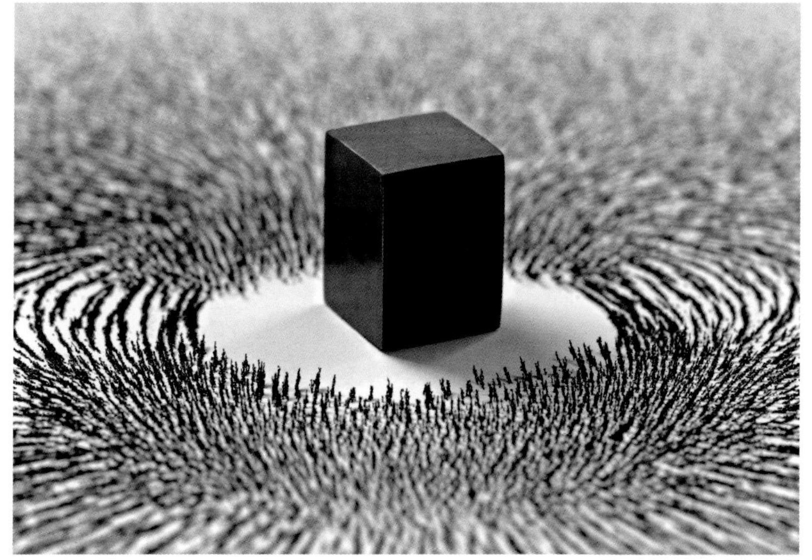

7 Circling the square. The central magnet attracts; beneath the surface, other, unseen magnets exert a centrifugal force. Saudi artist Ahmed Mater has created a simulacrum of the Meccan Ka'bah and its orbiting pilgrims. Perhaps, too, he has captured, in a moment, something of the way opposing forces work across time.

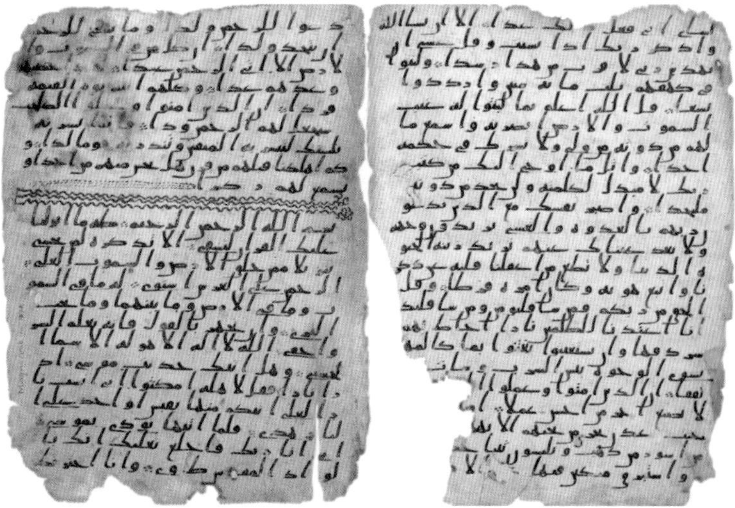

8 Perhaps the earliest surviving Qur'an manuscript, these folio parchment leaves have been carbon-dated to a time before AD 645.

9 A gilded paradise empty of people. Early eighth-century mosaics from the west side of the courtyard, Umayyad Mosque, Damascus.

10 In Baghdad itself, nothing remains above ground of the great Round City of the early Abbasid caliphs. This provincial survival hints at the grandeur of the imperial metropolis. The eighth-century Baghdad Gate, al-Raqqah, Syria.

11 To those with Anglo-Saxon attitudes, it looks upside-down. But, taking a world-view, it was the old Classical order that had been overturned by the newly coined Arab empire. A gold coin of AD 774, minted by King Offa of Mercia, England, in imitation of the contemporary Abbasid *dinar*.

12 Brutalist beauty: Sultan Qabus of Jurjan's mortuary skyscraper, in which his corpse is said to have hung in mid-air in a crystal coffin. The Arabic proclaims, 'This lofty palace . . .' Gunbadh-i Qabus, tower-tomb of AD 1006, in the town to which it gave its name, Iran.

13 A final fanfare for the caliphs before the coming of the Mongol hordes: a poignant image used on countless book jackets. An AD 1237 manuscript miniature from al-Hariri's *Maqamat*, showing the caliph's mounted standard-bearers.

14 'Allah is the Light of the heavens and the earth. The parable of His Light is a niche wherein is a lamp . . .' Marble tombstone, fourteenth or fifteenth century, commemorating one Ali ibn Uthman Al-Mursi. Found in Aden, Yemen, but imported there from a workshop in Cambay, India.

15 The East of the-West-of-the-East: Islam goes native in Arabic chinoiseries. A panel over the entrance of the Great Mosque, Xi'an (formerly Chang'an), China.

16 Liberty, equality, fraternity? Or just the next imperial lion? A nineteenth-century woodcut of tricolours and turbans in the Great Pyramid during Napoleon's 1798 visit.

17 A far-travelling pavilion, empty of content but filled with the symbolism of power and pilgrimage. The procession of the Egyptian *mahmal*, or ceremonial camel-borne pavilion, leaving for the Mecca pilgrimage, *c*. 1917.

18 Taming the latest imperial lion . . . King Ibn Sa'ud of Saudi Arabia charming US President Franklin D. Roosevelt via his interpreter, aboard the USS *Quincy*, Egypt, 1945.

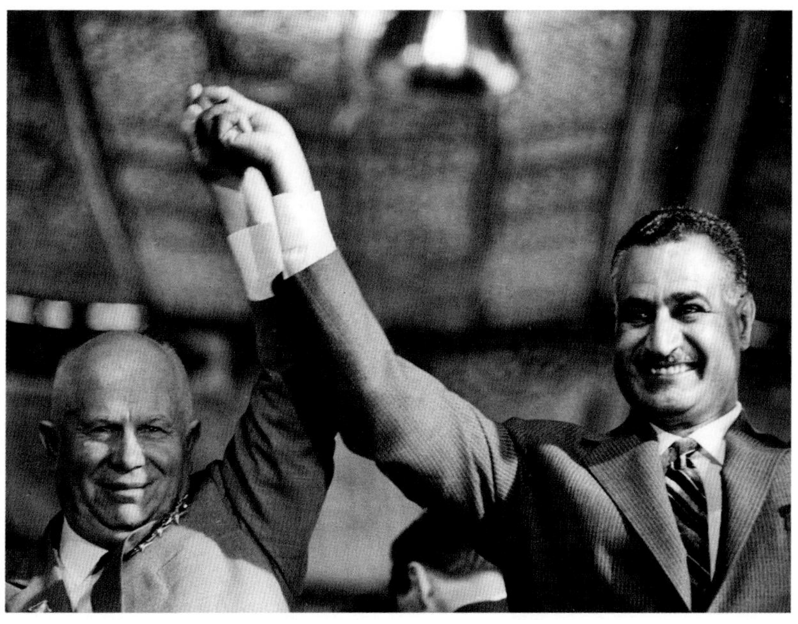

19 . . . and melting another Cold War emperor's heart. Comrades-in-arms-deals: Nasser of Egypt with Nikita Khrushchev of the USSR, 1964.

20 Engineering liquid assets: 2,500 years ago it was the water in the Marib Dam (cf. Plate 4); now it is the oil in the Dhahran refinery. A Blakeian vision of Saudi Aramco's main installation, at Dhahran on the Gulf coast of Saudi Arabia.

21 & 22 Before and after. As a famous line of Arabic poetry goes, ‘O that my youthful self could come back for a day, / That I might tell him what grey hair has done . . .’ Libyan leader Mu’ammar al-Qadhdhafi, near the beginning and near the end of his forty-two-year rule.

23 This and other works have inspired what might be termed the West Banksy school of graffiti art. Graffito by Banksy on the Israeli-built separation wall, Palestine, 2012.

24 Still giving them stick: latter-day *a'rab* ride roughshod over civil society (cf. Plate 5). A camel-borne hireling of the Mubarak regime scatters anti-Mubarak protesters in Cairo, February 2011.

25 The sledgehammer school of history. Are they simply denying the past? Or are they wreaking revenge on that oldest imperial lion nearly 3,000 years too late (cf. Plate 3)? 'Islamic State' iconoclasts 'cleansing' the Nineveh Museum of ancient Assyrian 'idols', Iraq, February 2015.

26 Butcher or bosom pal? Both, when the mass Stockholm syndrome is at work. Teenage fans of Bashshar al-Asad at a rally to support his candidacy in the forthcoming presidential election, Damascus, April 2014.

27 A Bach fugue for the eyes. Detail of the late thirteenth-century *minbar* (pulpit), formerly in the Great Mosque, Aleppo, Syria. At the time of writing, its whereabouts are unknown.

and al-Ma'mun the second, but also divided responsibility for the empire between them and a third brother, al-Mu'tamin. Al-Amin was given Baghdad and overall power; al-Ma'mun was appointed to run the original Abbasid powerhouse, Khurasan; al-Mu'tamin was put in charge of the Byzantine marches. In an act of great symbolism with parallels to the pre-Islamic practice of the Abbasids' tribe of Quraysh, a document promulgating the division was hung up in the Ka'bah at Mecca. And in another ominous scene, it is said that, as the proclamation was being raised up, it fell down.

Al-Rashid's division of the empire needed no omens to fail. On his death, al-Amin succeeded to the caliphate, and then (the gamines having had their effect) appointed his infant son to be his heir, in place of his brother al-Ma'mun and in opposition to their father's wishes. Many were shocked. So alien was the concept of primogeniture and infant crown-princedom that a poet could say,

Most astonishing of all, that we
should swear allegiance to a little child
Who hasn't learned to wipe his nose!

Al-Ma'mun was already ensconced in Khurasan, that breeding-ground of wars, and from there his forces marched on Baghdad where his half-brother was ill-prepared for martial exertions (he was more interested in interior decoration and ornamental fish, his favourite being adorned with gold gill-rings). A long and brutal urban war began. It ground on for more than a year: 'Brother fought brother, and son father, Aminists against Ma'munists. Houses were destroyed, palaces burned, goods looted.' Poets, the war-artists of the time, record stark images of dissolution, of a whole society falling apart: 'Severed,' one ode begins,

are the birth-bonds that joined kin together.

. . .

Baghdad might have never been the finest sight,
the loveliest resort that eyes beheld.
Thus it was; but now its beauty's gone,
its harmony destroyed by fate's decree.
Theirs now the fate that once befell the people of the past:
they too are tales told to others near and far.

Those 'people of the past' are all those who were doomed by disunity – back, the poet hints, to the ancient people of Saba who in the Qur'an became 'as tales once told'. Looking at Baghdad today, and Damascus, and out of my own window, it is clear that the tales are not yet over.

In the end al-Amin was captured while trying to escape by boat. His last hours were recorded by a fellow captive, an old *mawla* of his named Ahmad:

> Al-Amin said, 'Come near me. Hug me. I feel a dreadful loneliness.'
>
> I hugged him and felt the violent beating of his heart . . . Then he said to me,
>
> 'Ahmad, I don't doubt they'll take me to my brother. Do you think my brother will kill me?'
>
> I replied, 'No, for the bond of kinship will make him pity you.'
>
> And he said, 'Forget that. There is no kinship in kingship. It is barren.'

In one sense he was literally right: the word for 'kinship' – translated in the poem above in the plural as 'birth-bonds' – is *rahim*, which also means 'womb': with their different mothers, a womb, a birth-bond, was precisely what the two brothers did not share. Some anti-Aminist historians even 'efface' their shared paternity and call al-Amin, after his mother's name, 'Muhammad ibn Zubaydah'. Al-Amin was not sent to his brother. He was killed there and then; the usual trophy, his head, was sent instead. (The third brother and joint ruler, al-Mu'tamin, had wisely bowed out of the fight and spent the rest of his life in obscurity.)

Al-Ma'mun was victorious, and would go on to be a philosopher; but the ties of family – let alone of clan or tribe or race – had, as the poet and the caliph realized, been fatally severed. Increasingly, from now on, rulers would buy loyalty, relying on non-Arab followers and mercenaries. The trend had begun as early as the second Abbasid caliph, al-Mansur, who had depended on his slaves and freedmen in preference to Arabs. But al-Ma'mun would now greatly accelerate it by importing Transoxanian troops to Baghdad and putting them on the official payroll. Soon, as we shall see, military and then political power would slip from Arab hands. Of all the reverse *futuhat* – reciprocal 'invasions' of Arabs by those whose lands they had conquered – this was the most decisive, for it would end for ever Arab supremacy, and any pretence of political unity.

Add to that the linguistic infiltration of Arabic by non-Arabs, and the genetic invasion at every level of society by the monstrous regiment of concubines, and it all meant that Arab identity was sliding out of control. But not before an official version of the Arab past – of what it had been to be Arab, and might be once more – had been preserved.

SETTLING DOWN, SETTING DOWN

During the century and more of pell-mell imperial expansion from the 630s onward, Arab vision had been blurred by the sheer speed of movement. Arab energy had been absorbed by the need to maintain momentum and, less successfully, cohesion. Now, for a time, Arabs could take stock: like astronauts settling into orbit after the thrills and perils of the launch, they could look at where they had got to, where they had come from and, importantly, at themselves.

In their attempts to keep a grip on the world they knew, Arabs would do what they would do in later times, and what many still do now: they would cling to the past. Not just to the recent, revolutionary past of Muhammad's time, but also to the earlier Arabian past from which Islam had emerged – that old, self-completed past of their ancestral 'island'. Nostalgia is an underrated force in history: time goes forward; but people often flee backwards, from crisis and complexity to imagined simplicity and purity. The past can be another country, but it can also be a homeland.

For Arabs in Abbasid times, that past had first to be retrieved and recorded. The movement has been called *'asr al-tadwin*, 'the age of setting down'. It was a kind of foil to the translation movement – a foil almost in the literal sense of the foil that backs the mirror, for the translation was not from outside, but inward and backward into the Arab self. It was also the beginning of a slippage that still affects the life of Islam – between that introspection on the one side, and on the other a greater openness to the world beyond Arabia. Those who were open to the wider world used the medium of Arabic and the material of Islam to create a global civilization, in which inherited Arabian ritual was enriched by the indigenous pre-conquest wisdoms of other lands. The result has been aptly compared to Hellenistic civilization. But it was, and is, a civilization from which many would yearn to go on pilgrimage back into its Arab past.

CREATION OF A LEGACY

The trouble was that much of the past had been lost. The continuity, the mirror of memory, was broken: in the new settled society, it was not only the caliph who had forgotten the meaning of 'pasture'. To put this right, scholars turned to those whose lives still revolved around pasture – the bedouin.

From the later eighth century onward, philologists, lexicographers and ethnologists from the towns descended on the remaining Arabs whose lives were supposedly uncontaminated by urban ways and speech. Their object was to gather folklore in its widest and most etymological sense – the whole inherited knowledge of a people. The movement is sometimes reminiscent of that in the changing Europe of a century and more ago, when Cecil Sharp and Béla Bartók gathered dances and tunes. But the Arab version was not just inspired by artistic curiosity or folksiness: it was rescue archaeology performed on the living remains of a people's past, and in a mobile society in which words had always been more important than places or artefacts, it focused on language. Like some other, later archaeologies – those, for example, of Zionism and Hindu nationalism – it had a programme, and was happy to present a particular view of the past. In the Arab case it was the bedouin past, or at least that part of it which had survived into the present among the nomads of the north-east of the peninsula, the part nearest to the Iraqi Oxbridge of al-Kufah and al-Basrah. The other major Arabian past, of settled non-tribal societies, of great dams and temples, lay far away and forgotten in the deep South, the dark side of the Arabian moon.

The bedouin subjects of these studies were often bemused by the questions they were asked: whether, for example, one should say 'Isra'il' with a glottal stop, or 'Israyil' with a *y*, and whether 'Filastin', 'Palestine', had a genitive case . . . 'How long,' asked one *a'rabi* informant, 'will you go on asking me about these nonsenses? How long will I make up fine answers for you? Can't you see your beard's going grey?' One lexicographer benefited from being kidnapped for several years by a bedouin tribe. Some researchers paid ready money for their information, while some informants moved to the towns to sell their knowledge. Often, researchers were not over-careful about their informants. As al-Ma'arri said of them,

> how often do grammarians quote any tiny tot, who knows of letters not a jot? Or any person of the female gender, in need of men to defend her?

Of course, the point was to find subjects who *didn't* know their letters; moreover, women are often the best informants, being more conservative in speech than men.

The lore was in essence linguistic. But the study of language often entailed the collection of poetry, and understanding poetry entailed, in turn, the gathering of information on the topography and genealogy of the pre-Islamic past. And it would all have repercussions far beyond the interests of antiquarians and the preservation of a rich and curious heritage: it would, in fact, define and refine for all time the whole Arab 'brand'. The brand is still with us today, stamped on people of great diversity from Mauritania to Muscat. Once again, as with those early wanderers of varied origin whom their neighbours lumped together under the same designation nearly 3,000 years ago, the label of 'Arab' has proved its strength and durability.

THE RETURN OF THE NOMAD

The Abbasid reality was that of a largely urban, agrarian and settled society, increasingly plural and diverse. Bedouin Arabs had served their purpose as spearhead of the conquests; since then, they had been absorbed into the new society or, if they had maintained their old existence, had faded back into the political and geographical margins. When they do appear, it is either as linguistic informants or as a subversive force – taking part in a two-year war between 'Northern' and 'Southern' tribes in Syria in the time of al-Rashid, for example, or raiding the Mecca pilgrim caravans, as did a force of 6,000 Tayyi' nomads in 898. This latter phenomenon would continue on and off for over a thousand years, until the rise of the centralized power of the Al Sa'ud. Arab pirates attacking Muslim pilgrims . . . there could be no better illustration of the continuity with the old herding-raiding past, or of the disconnect between Islam and its peninsular origins.

At the same time, in recording the past for posterity, it was precisely that herding-raiding past that was made prominent and given a heroic gloss. The *badw* ethos was inserted deep into the collective Arab cultural memory. It became the ideal, whatever the reality might be. In other words, it became a kind of national persona. As a recent critic put it, it was now, in the age of setting down, that 'Arab personality began to be conscious of itself'. But if it was the beginning of self-consciousness, it was also the latest stage in a long period of development. That Arab personality had existed in embryo for centuries; it began to take on recognizable features before the Christian era; it was born before Islam, around the time of the Lakhmid kings, and further shaped by its environment – particularly by the presence of powerful non-Arab neighbours; it was weaned on a diet of post-Muhammadan conquest, and further nourished in Umayyad times with the transfusion of South Arabian blood. Now in the diversity of the empire it faced a more complex and threatening world than it had ever known, and in self-defence it had set about establishing, in retrospect, its own identity. The personality had, in effect, matured to adulthood, and if with the self-consciousness there also came a certain self-deception, it is by such shifts that adults confront the world.

The supposedly changeless bedouin world filled a growing library of poetic commentaries, works on philology and history, and the first dictionaries. In the 'non-Arab, Khurasani' reality of Abbasid society, however, urban Arabs who actually tried to return to their *a'rabi* roots were ridiculed. They included the poet Hays-Bays, who affected archaic, bedouin speech: his nickname itself was a long outmoded bedouin expression, often used by him, meaning 'Dire Straits'. He claimed membership of the great tribe of Tamim, and was told,

> you haven't a Tamimi hair on your head!
> But go eat lizards, nibble dried colocynth,
> And, if you really want, drink ostrich piss . . .

But the old-fashioned bedouin persisted as the dormant identity, the default personality. For a thousand years from the ninth century to the nineteenth, from 'the age of setting down' to 'the Arab Renaissance', the meaning of 'Arab' would split in two: on the one hand, all those who used the Arabic language were in a cultural-linguistic sense Arabs; on the other, and in usual parlance, Arabs were uncivilized lizard-munching nomads, even if their ancestors were heroes. Exactly the same split is visible in Yemen today: 'Oh, they're just *qabili*s, tribesmen,' someone might say dismissively of uncivilized, gun-toting rustics. But insinuate that the speaker himself is not of tribal origin, and you will insult him to the quick. The relationship between the two halves of this split personality is all part of the continuing dialogue between *hadar* and *badw*.

The extraordinary valorization of the bedouin past meant that anyone with literary pretensions, or who wanted to find employment in the bureaucracy, had to have a knowledge of 'the Days of the Arabs', the raids and battles of the pre-Islamic tribes. There were a lot of such Days: al-Isfahani's collection described 1,700 of them. The obsession continued across time and distance. Poets in fourteenth-century urban Andalus would celebrate bedouinness, and so would the emigrant Lebanese-Brazilian poet Ilyas Farhat, celebrating tents and camels in twentieth-century São Paulo. Often, the bedouin ethos would, and does, override Islamic ethics; raiding Mecca pilgrims is only the extreme example of a mass of less obvious cases in which customary laws and mores trump Qur'anic ones. Often, too, it would come in for harsh criticism. 'It may not be an exaggeration,' the late Muhammad al-Jabiri suggested,

> to say that the *a'rabi* is in fact the creator of the 'world' of the Arab, the world inhabited by Arabs on the level of words, expressions, visualization and imagination, or indeed of the mind, values and emotions; and that this world is deficient, impoverished, shallow and desiccated, a world of sense and nature, ahistorical, reflecting the 'pre-history' of the Arabs – the age of the Ignorance, before the conquests and the foundation of the state.

Today, this other world underlies the visible one. Even in the Arabian-Gotham urban settings of Doha and Dubai, poet-princes still celebrate heroic bedouinness. To say, as Fouad Ajami did, that desert nostalgia is 'strange to the culture' is astonishing: desert nostalgia has been embedded in the culture since Abbasid times. The 'traditional' Arab self-image is much closer to that in the 1,700 Days than to its urbanized, persianized version in *The Thousand and One Nights*.

The whole of Arab history since the Abbasids has been haunted by a sense of disjuncture with the rest of the world and where it is going, and by a chronic harking back – at times to the supposed uncomplexity of Islam before it left Arabia, at times to that narrow, nostalgic view of the deeper Arab past. This mass nostalgia is not altogether bad: it offers a kind of unity, prolonging the life of the *Kulturnation*, and is another reason why we can write 'Histories of the Arabs' but not of the Anglophone world (which has supposedly abandoned its national myths and come to grips with the global). But, like language, nostalgia is a bond in both senses – of brotherhood, but also of servitude. It is the reason why the poet Nizar Qabbani could say,

> . . . I am exhausted by my arabness.
> Is arabness a curse, a punishment?

GUARDIANS OF THE LEXICON

Under the Abbasids, Islam was looking forwards, to ever broader horizons; the view back into the Arab past continued to narrow. The vigour of expansion was spent, and Arabs began to focus on their own national myth. Thus Arab personality advanced rapidly from adulthood to middle age, to the climacteric, the age when all will begin to decline and decay. As with the 'gigantic bluff' that was the British empire, when the small and rag-tag population of a marginal island (or in the Arab case, peninsula) get to rule a large slice of the world for a couple of hundred years, they need to have tales about heroic pasts; all the more so when their rule is under threat from others.

It should not come as a surprise that the scholars who retrieved this past, philologists and others, were mostly non-Arabs. A recent commentator has put it bluntly: by collecting and organizing knowledge of the past, 'the non-Arab *mawali* [*mawla*s] were the ones who actually constructed Arab identity for the Arab community'. 'Reconstructed' would be more accurate. But in either case it is a statement with which Ibn Khaldun agreed: he devoted a chapter to the monopoly of scholarship by non-Arabs. Yet again, as when the old non-Arab empires created a first sense of Arab selfhood by creating 'kings of the Arabs', Arab identity was being shaped by others.

This shaping was also affecting that constant and major player in Arab history, the Arabic language. Arabic had been greatly enriched by the translation movement; but little of the richness made its way into the dictionaries that were now beginning to be compiled. Urban intellectuals looked outwards to the peoples of the empire and its further neighbours in India, China and Constantinople; linguists looked backwards to the world of the bedouin, who tended not to bandy about Sanskrit-derived mathematical terms or Graecisms such as *sūlūjismus*, 'syllogism', while they were milking their camels. Moreover, the philologists and other guardians of the lexicon further narrowed the language by ironing out the many variants that existed between the speech of different tribes. An example of such variants was given by al-Asma'i, an antiquarian and philologist of tribal Arab descent, famous for his prodigious memory, who died in 828:

> Two [bedouin] men differed over the word for 'falcon'. One said it was *ṣaqr*, with an [emphatic] *ṣ*, the other that it was *saqr*, with a [non-emphatic] *s*.

> They agreed to abide by the decision of the first person who came along. When someone appeared, they put their dispute to him. He said, 'I don't agree with either of you. It's *ẓaqr*.'

In the end, only *ṣaqr* has got into the dictionary. This is because the philologists' policy was to see what the majority usage was, then brand it as the only acceptable one.

In the real world, then, Arabic was expanding and changing: it had always existed in many tribal variants, as well as in the high speech of poets and prophets; with conquest and racial intermingling it had further branched off into new dialects; the written vocabulary of the intellectuals had also been expanded by translation and the growth of new sciences. But now written high Arabic was contracting. The term for it, *fusha*, is from the word *fasih*, meaning pure milk, free from froth. The milk is still rich, but ever since the age of setting down it has been homogenized and pasteurized.

Written Arabic is thus a construct, and by synthesizing this pan-Arab language, linguists further enhanced the idea of the diverse tribes and peoples being a single race – '*the* Arabs'. The race, like the language, is a construct.

A GOD MADE OF LETTERS

For a time, the old national dress of language had been variegated with new colours. But the language scholars were countering the trend and making Arabic a uniform in the limited earth-colours of the bedouins. In time, it would become a straitjacket that would restrict literary movement, and even thought itself.

By arabicizing government, the Umayyads had already inspired a mass of non-Arabs to learn their difficult tongue. This had meant that the language had to be analysed; thus, grammar, syntax and the other linguistic studies became the first formal Arab sciences. Now, when other Arabic-Islamic – as opposed to imported – studies developed under the Abbasids, they grew along the lines of those linguistic sciences, rather than the lines of the physical and speculative sciences of the non-Arab 'ancients' that had inspired al-Ma'mun. The rules of grammar were applied in particular to *fiqh*, Islamic jurisprudence, and would shape its whole thought-world. Al-Ma'mun, al-Kindi and their like had engaged with a whole world of thought;

al-Ma'mun, indeed, had measured the world. After them, however, faced with that fork in the intellectual path, Arabic civilization took the route of textual truth, and remained on it. There would, of course, be many great empirical Arabic minds, unrestrained by the language they thought in, but they operated in isolation or at the margins. In general, thought would remain shackled to the study of texts, and truth rhetorical rather than empirical. Abd al-Samad ibn al-Fadl, for example, whose ancestors had been hereditary orators at the Persian court, could deliver three long and brilliant lectures on the mosquito; but the brilliance was in the eloquence, not in the observation. That would have to wait for Hooke and the microscope.

Anyone who doubts the intense, introverted and navel-gazing centrality of the Arabic language to Arabic thought should reflect on the fact that, 'from the period between 750 and 1500 we know the names of more than 4,000 grammarians'. Even with a language as rich as Arabic, few of them had anything new to say: most merely recycled what had been said before, a wheel of words. Naturalists, physicians, chemists, astronomers, geographers and others might all amount to as many as three figures over the same period; but they are far outstripped by grammarians. Of al-Sahib ibn Abbad's 400-camel-load library mentioned above, no fewer than sixty camel-loads were books on Arabic philology. Why this obsession?

By Abbasid times it was rare for anyone to use high Arabic without an enormous effort – except for the few remaining linguistically 'uncontaminated' and much-researched bedouins, and then only when they were reciting poetry. Even in polite court circles, the effort had been abandoned by about the year 900. In less elevated settings, high Arabic was unknown: a philologist using high-flown words in the suq was thought to be possessed by a *jinni* speaking 'Indian'; a poet declaiming his high Arabic verses by the Nile was pushed in and drowned by a yob, for supposedly casting a spell on the river; a grammarian conjugating aloud in a palm-grove the imperatives of a rare form of verb was attacked by the date-picking peasants for, as they thought, parodying the Qur'an. This last anecdote gives a clue as to why there were so many grammarians. In a culture where even the least educated were inculcated with the idea of truth residing in texts, one text in particular, the Qur'an, was believed to contain the sum of all truth: now, as high and low Arabic diverged, the language-scholars were the only ones who could give access to the high language. Increasingly, therefore, 'grammaratchiks' monopolized truth, became sole mediators with a text-based God, and began to occupy a place not unlike that of the priesthood in a Christian setting. Indeed, like a priesthood, from Abbasid times onwards the scholars were treated as a class apart, distinguished by their dress; it often included a particularly voluminous turban, and a waist-sash in which a pen-box would be stuck at a jaunty angle, like a dagger. They were priests not of the spirit, but of the letter. The development was not inappropriate, considering that the Abbasids themselves were descended from Abd Allah ibn Abbas, the first great exegete of the Qur'an.

Crucial to the growth of this new 'hierarchy' – and to the whole future of Arabic intellectual history – was the about-turn in dogma under al-Ma'mun's third successor, al-Mutawakkil. Probably to curry popular favour via the support enjoyed by traditionalist scholars, under him the Mu'tazilah intellectuals and their debates and discussions were banned, the very idea of the Qur'an as a created book open to interpretation by the individual became anathema, and the principle of *taqlid*, or 'imitation', was imposed; from now on, one could only understand the word of God according to officially recognized interpretations. *Naẓar* and *ra'y* – two words that mean 'looking' but had come to mean 'speculating and forming an opinion' – were now tainted with the suspicion of heresy. It was another case of narrowing: just as lexicographers were acting as verbal bouncers, banishing anything they regarded as *outré* from the dictionary, so 'the gate of *ijtihad*,' the individual struggle to extrapolate meaning from God's revelation, was closing. And, as a recent commentator has put it, 'To shut the gate of meaning is to shut down thought'. As often, alleged sayings of Muhammad turned up in support of the policy change. One of these states, for example, that

> He who interprets the Qur'an on the basis of his own opinion will be wrong, even if his interpretation happens to be right.

Some poets, Sufis and sectarians have always flown beneath, or above, the dogmatic radar and made their own attempts to understand the word of Allah without interpreters, without intermediaries. By and large, however, the community of Islam, which has always prided itself on having no priests, has since the middle of the Abbasid age approached the divine via that hierarchy of linguists, exegetes and other authorities, most of whom died well over a thousand years ago. Meaning was mummified.

Those old authorities were usually diligent and subtle scholars. But often God is in the detail, and the subtlety is lost with time and repetition. An example is that of the Fatihah, the opening chapter of the Qur'an. The equivalent in some ways of the Lord's Prayer for Christians, it is repeated several times by worshippers in each of the five formal daily prayers and on many other occasions, and concludes by asking Allah to

> Guide us to the straight way.
>
> The way of those on whom You have bestowed Your grace, not of those who earned Your anger, nor of those who went astray.

My edition of the Qur'an with a parallel English text and commentary – an edition much relied on by Muslims who do not know Arabic (even if they can recite the sounds of it) – goes,

> Guide us to the Straight Way.
>
> The Way of those on whom You have bestowed Your Grace, not (the way) of those who earned Your anger (such as the Jews), nor of those who went astray (such as the Christians).

A footnote explains the glosses about the Jews and the Christians as deriving from an alleged statement by Muhammad quoted in the works of two ninth-century authorities, al-Tirmidhi and Abu Dawud. All well and good: the authorities are both excellent. But the very fact that the glosses have crept into the body of the English text of holy scripture, even between brackets, gives them near-divine status. And in practice, as I find on quizzing Muslim friends, the brackets are usually forgotten, and so are the words 'such as'. Even with purely arabophone Muslims, so effectively has the gloss covered the underlying substance that the two groups simply *are* the Jews and the Christians. To suggest, for example, that terrorists who kill people in the name of Islam might well be equally worthy of inclusion among those who incur Allah's anger and have gone astray is usually met with bemused surprise.

From the age of setting down, then, but especially that of al-Mutawakkil's dogmatic volte-face, written texts and the guardians of their meanings began to gain an increasingly powerful grip on the mind of Arabic civilization. Of the three great conquests in Arab history, the first – that of the Arabic language – was also proving to be the most relentless, writing roughshod, so to speak, over the empire it had helped to win. As for that first, inimitable text, it was now the official line to regard the Qur'an as uncreated and coeval with Allah, the Logos as literally literal *logoi* – words inscribed since before the beginning of time on the 'Preserved Tablet' mentioned in the Qur'an. One of the most extreme proponents of the idea of Qur'anic apotheosis, an eighth-century Shi'i of hermetic leanings named al-Mughirah ibn Sa'id al-Bajali, had gone so far as to conceive the inconceivable Deity as having 'members of the number and form of the letters of the [Arabic] alphabet'.

The Word was with God, as the Gospel puts it, and the Word *was* God. That was an admittedly extreme and shocking view. But in the new Abbasid orthodoxy of the tenth century, the Letter had prevailed over the Spirit. Those who were moved by the Spirit had to beware how far it took them.

THE DEATH OF AL-HALLAJ

The two-hundred-year flash flood of Arabs had ebbed, or been absorbed into the lands it had covered. But it had left behind it a rich layer of language. It was this, then, that the Abbasid state aimed to control. Theirs was a new version of the old policy of 'gathering the word', and it sought to unify not just voices, but also meanings and thoughts.

Dissident voices and minds were raised against the newly gathered word, one of them that of the early tenth-century nonconformist al-Hallaj, who would be executed in 922. Al-Husayn ibn Mansur al-Hallaj was in several ways a man of his times. Born in Fars in 857 or 858, it seems his first language was Arabic, but his ancestry is ambiguous – he may have been Arab, but no one is sure. Like his contemporary al-Mas'udi, he took advantage of the mobility of the age and travelled, spending time in India; also like al-Mas'udi he was culturally adventurous, observing Buddhist and Hindu societies.

So why did al-Hallaj pay the ultimate penalty? His famous declaration, 'I am al-Haqq!' – taken to be a claim of *hulul*, 'indwelling', by the deity under His appellation of al-Haqq, the Truly-existing – was certainly enough to make dogmatists stretch their eyes. But there is perhaps a more than subliminal, etymological suggestion in al-Hallaj's exclamation that he was asserting his *haqq*, his 'right', to speak 'the truth', *al-haqq*, as he himself experienced it – that he was breaking the rulers' and scholars' monopoly on what was true.

In the 920s, truth was no longer to be revealed in a caliph's dreams about Aristotle, or adopted, as al-Kindi had suggested, 'from races who are distant from us and societies quite different from our own'. That had been possible a hundred years earlier, when Arab identity was less in question; now, as it dissolved, that identity clung to ever-narrowing definitions of its language, its history, its religion, even of truth itself. Truth subsisted alone in al-Haqq, the Truly-existing God, and access to it was strictly controlled. Lone voices and thoughts were dangerous. 'Indwelling' meant anarchy.

There was another reason, however, why al-Hallaj incurred the wrath of the authorities. He advocated the practice of a symbolic, substitute Pilgrimage that anyone unable to go to Mecca could perform in his own home, circumambulating any object he chose (like the old bedouins did with their god-stones), and then feeding and clothing thirty orphans. Pragmatic, indeed laudable though this sounds, in one sense it was the ultimate heresy for, like his notorious declaration of indwelling, it asserted the individual over the corporate: it undermined the physical enactment of unity-in-the-divine that went back via Mecca to the most ancient pre-Islamic pilgrimages such as the South Arabian one to Marib, centuries before Muhammad. As Christians express their unity in breaking bread together, Muslims and pre-Muslims do so most powerfully in the sacrament of travelling together. Al-Hallaj's promotion of the individual – the idea that God could 'visit' a particular person, and that people could visit Him on a personal, spiritual pilgrimage – was seen as subversion of the most dangerous sort.

Al-Hallaj remained a controversial figure long after his killing: views differed over him, Ibn Khallikan wrote 350 years later, as they did over Jesus. At times, he was also a protean figure. During his final imprisonment, the slave who attended him recalled,

> 'One day I took him his plate of food as I did every day, and when I went into his cell I found that he had filled it with himself from ceiling to floor and from wall to wall, leaving no empty space. I was terrified, and threw down the plate and ran.' The terror of what the slave had seen brought on a fever in him which lasted a long time, but he was disbelieved . . .

It does sound incredible, except in terms of the altered physics of *Alice in Wonderland*. Or did al-Hallaj possess powers of mesmerism? 'One day,' al-Ma'arri wrote, 'al-Hallaj moved his hand, whereupon the odor of musk spread to the people. Another time he moved it and *dirham*s were scattered . . .', just as with the 'godmen' of India, whom we might guess he had observed.

Shaykh or charlatan, martyr or mage, al-Hallaj undermined the Abbasid order. As an individual voice raised, he would not have seemed so dangerous in the days of the pre-Islamic *su'luk*s, or 'vagabond' poets. But he would be regarded as equally subversive if he were alive in the Arabic world today, when truth is still what it is instructed to be, and those who speak independently – like the Sudanese visionary Mahmud Muhammad Taha – can still pay with their lives.

Truth has always been seen to disrupt social order, way back via Oedipus solving the riddle of the Sphinx to the original scrumping of the Tree of Knowledge. But there were even more present dangers to Abbasid society than from maverick divines. To return to the beginning of this chapter, Ibn Wahb – the Basran who met the emperor of China – was not travelling entirely on a whim, 'a sudden desire': he was, in fact, a refugee from the heartland of the empire. The Arab King of Kings may have reached the top of the international royal rankings, but his realm was not just flaking away at the edges: it was already rotting from the inside.

DECLINE
900–1350

CHAPTER TEN

COUNTER-CULTURES, COUNTER-CALIPHS

THE EMPIRE BREAKS UP

MEDALLION MAN

In late September 938, a decade and a half after the killing of the visionary al-Hallaj, the tutor of Caliph al-Radi went to pay his respects to his former pupil. It was the day of Mihrajan, a pre-Islamic Persian festival celebrated by the pleasure-loving Baghdadis. 'I went by boat along the Tigris,' the tutor recalled,

> and as I passed the residence of Bajkam the Turk, I saw there such scenes of wanton and frivolous merrymaking as I had never before witnessed. Going on to al-Radi bi 'llah, I found him alone and immersed in gloom. I hesitated to approach him; but he told me to come closer, and when I did so I saw that he was holding a gold *dinar* and a silver *dirham*. Each was several times the usual weight, and each bore an image of Bajkam, bristling with weapons and encircled by the words,
>
> Know ye: all power's a sham,
> Save mine – Amir I am,
> Great lord of men, *Bajkam*.
>
> On the reverse of the coins was another portrait of Bajkam, but showing him seated in his audience hall, looking contemplative and inscrutable.

> Al-Radi said, 'Do you not see what this . . . this *person* is doing? How high his ambition is reaching? How far his pride is taking him?' And I could say nothing in reply.

There was nothing to say. The coins, a Mihrajan present from Bajkam, said it all: beware the Turks bearing gifts. For not only had a Turkish slave-soldier – supposedly there to guard the caliph – pushed himself on to the currency, the preserve of sovereignty. He had also done so in person, in a portrait, in contrast with the chaste calligraphic coinage that for a quarter of a millennium had been a symbol of Arab power and had been imitated even in the English Midlands. He had enlarged the coins and turned them into flashy medallions. And to add aural insult to visual injury, he had replaced the godly legends of Arab coinage with a crass jingle celebrating himself, *Bajkam* . . . The alien name ends the rhyming Arabic with a thump: to Arabic hearing it sounds both comical and faintly sinister – perhaps something like 'Boojum' or 'Bogyman' to English ears. It means in Turkic, 'Horsetail' or 'Yaktail'. The caliph's regnal name 'al-Radi bi 'llah' is, in contrast – and appropriately for someone who had no one else to turn to – 'he who is content with Allah'.

As their shared festival of Mihrajan showed, Arabs and those archetypal non-Arabs, the Persians, had come to an accommodation. Turks, however, still seemed to come from beyond the fringe of the acceptable. Portraits of other early Turkic warriors on surviving medals show them armed, appraising the viewer through narrow and alien eyes; to be *akhzar*, 'slit-eyed', as all Turks were popularly supposed to be, was to be physically as un-Arab as possible. Turks were not just another kind of non-Arab, but a sort of anti-Arab, and the past resounded with warnings about them. The Abbasids' ancestor, Ali ibn Abd Allah ibn al-Abbas, had supposedly predicted that his descendants would inherit Arab rule, but only 'until the time when their slaves shall own *them*, slaves with small eyes and broad faces, faces like hammered shields'.

From earlier still, a saying attributed to Muhammad went '*utruku 'l-turka ma tarakukum*', 'Leave the Turks alone as long as they leave you alone.' It has the proverbial sense of 'Let sleeping dogs lie'. But, far from leaving them alone, the Arab rulers of the empire had stirred them up, taken them on as caliphal guard dogs, taken them into the centre of power, the eye of the Round City – and then watched powerless as they had taken over. From now on, in one form or another, Turks would dominate most of Arabdom for most of the next thousand years.

That day of Mihrajan, the caliph's tutor tried to console him with historical precedents of rulers getting pushed aside by their own followers but then reasserting themselves; this did nothing to lighten al-Radi's depression. He only perked up when the tutor reminded him in verse that, after all, it was a festival, and that if he couldn't beat Bajkam he could at least emulate him by opening a bottle or two of the finest vintage with a few friends. Friends and bottles multiplied until the caliph's party rivalled the Turkish shindig along the Tigris. But for al-Radi, his Abbasid dynasty, and the Arab masters of the empire, the party was a final farewell to real power.

'And so,' said the historian al-Mas'udi, now writing not history but current events, 'the Arabs fell, and passed away. Their power disappeared and their rank was lost.' It was just three centuries since those miraculous few years in which they had set out from their Island and taken on two empires.

A DIMMING RADIANCE

Under the Abbasids, the wheel of fire – the old cycle of unity and disunity that for centuries had repeatedly welded Arabs together, then ignited them against each other – had grown into something much bigger and, for a time, apparently more stable: something more like a solar system, pulling ever more peoples into the gravitational field of Arabic culture and Islam. At the same time, the whole nature of Arab rule had changed. Muhammad's original successors had governed in the manner of pre-Islamic Arab shaykhs and the Umayyads in that of pre-Islamic Arab kings. The Abbasids had made themselves more like the pre-Islamic Persian *shahanshah*s, kings of kings, crowned, enthroned, elevated on a stage and concealed behind a curtain like players in a royal drama, yet ruling over an empire so huge that even the added gravity of Islam could not hold it together for long. The stability was thus short-lived: the radiance of the caliph at the centre of the Round City progressively dimmed, and Arabs themselves were pushed out into ever more distant orbits. As we shall see, some of those Arabs at the edges gained in strength, forming the nuclei of their own new systems.

In the meantime, the power at the original centre, the caliphate, was being hollowed out by the very people who had been brought in to preserve it – Turkic slave-praetorians like Bajkam. They were proving the most successful challengers to Arab power. But earlier threats had already undermined the whole notion of Arab primacy, an idea grounded in Arabs' sense of their own right to rule: from Arabia, they argued, had come both the prophet whose inspiration and revolution had sparked off the empire in the first place, and the language that held it all together. With the complexities of empire under the Abbasids, however, friction between Arabs and others was inevitable. Sometimes it would be expressed in words; at other times the fight would be bloody.

SLAVES AND PEASANTS

The first and in some ways the most shocking blow to Arab notions of supremacy was the so-called Zanj Rebellion of 869–83. It was all very well for Arabs to fight each other; they had done so since the year dot, and it seemed they would do till Doomsday. But the depradations of the Zanj – the usual name for black East Africans – seemed to overturn the natural order. They were slaves, and not even military slaves like the Turks, but plantation slaves; and yet they caused truly frightening destruction to the Iraqi heart of empire. Ibn Wahb, whom we met in the previous chapter in audience with the emperor of China, was in fact a refugee from the ruins of his native city, al-Basrah: the Zanj had devastated it.

At the domestic level, slavery had always been a feature of Arab society. The problems came with the conquests, and the desire to exploit great tracts of land with cheap manpower that was, in theory, easily controlled. Revenues from agriculture in southern Iraq had fallen dramatically under the Umayyads, and slave-labour was seen as the quickest way of upping profits again. The rich merchants of al-Basrah therefore invested in tens of thousands of East African slaves and put them to draining the marshlands near the city. But exploitation of land meant exploitation of men: their conditions were appalling, and in time the slaves rebelled. They were joined by others opposed to the Arab monopoly over power, money, land, life, and were united by an ambiguous figure called Ali ibn Muhammad – perhaps Iranian, perhaps Arab, perhaps even a descendant of the Prophet's cousin and son-in-law, Ali, as he claimed. No one seemed to be sure. There was no doubt, however, that it was he who channelled the seething discontents of the region into violent and successful insurrection.

Statistics about the destruction caused by the rebellion are uncertain. Al-Mas'udi's supposedly conservative estimate of the total number of victims was 500,000, including 300,000 alone in the sack of al-Basrah; but he admitted that no one knew the true figures, and it may be that a stray zero has crept in. What is not in doubt is that the Zanj caused a temporary inversion of the order of things: slaves became slave-masters, buying and selling freeborn Arabs for a few coins, using female descendants of Muhammad as concubines and making them work as maids to their own womenfolk. When one of these Arab *sharifah*s, noblewomen, dared to complain that she had been misused by her own former slave, she was told, '*He*'s your *mawla* now!' – a nice irony, as *mawla* is a 'bipolar' word that means both 'dependant, client' and 'master'. The vocabulary of society, of slaves and masters, remained the same; its polarity was overturned.

The revolt was eventually put down by forces from Baghdad led by commanders from the caliphal family, but at great cost in life and treasure. Discontent, however, seemed now to be endemic in the flatlands of southern Iraq – a region long raided by Arabs before Islam, ruled bloodily and ruined agriculturally by them in the first Islamic century, and most recently racked by revolt. Only a few years after the Zanj were suppressed, the region's long-suffering indigenous 'Nabataean' peasants rose under the leadership of another demagogue, Hamdan Qarmat. Of probable Iranian origin, he too was opposed to Arab supremacy and monopoly over the life and wealth of the empire; he found in the growing Isma'ili branch of Shi'ism, which had split in the later eighth century from the main *shi'at Ali* because of a disagreement over which of Ali's descendants should inherit the leadership, a vehicle for radical revolution. The motive force of revolt he found in the over-taxed and marginalized peasantry, now shaken out of centuries of servility by the example of the slave uprising. His following gathered more groups, including Arabs in eastern Arabia who had long felt themselves sidelined by the imperial project. It was also in eastern Arabia that the Qarmatis founded a republic that claimed, and possibly achieved, a level of egalitarianism unknown elsewhere in the Arab empire: visitors admired its civil institutions, which included the provision of social security for citizens. 'There are mills,' wrote an eleventh-century traveller from Iran, 'that belong to the authorities and grind grain for the people free of charge. The authorities bear the expense of their upkeep and the wages of the millers'. Later ages may not admire the reliance on imported African slave labour that underpinned it all.

The republic was to survive well into the eleventh century. But in its most active early decades, from the end of the ninth century on, Qarmatis managed to cause havoc further afield – in Iraq, the Levant, and over much of the Arabian Peninsula. Their most daring coup (or most dastardly crime) was a raid on Mecca in 930 in which they stole the sacred Black Stone from the Ka'bah, the dark gem at the navel of Creation. It was to remain in their hands for twenty years, until the rising Fatimid counter-caliph persuaded them to return it. (As we shall see, both the Fatimids and the Qarmatis were Isma'ili Shi'is, but the Fatimids claimed descent from Muhammad and, as supposedly born of the line of the Quraysh, were bound to respect the sacred centrality of their ancestral shrine in Mecca. To them the Qarmatis were wayward schismatics, the 'loony left' of the Isma'ilis.) But the point had been made: the looting/liberation of the Stone had shaken the empire to its core, for it suggested – even if symbolically and temporarily – that the Qurashi axis of the whole cultic and cultural system was not inviolable.

Furthermore, the Qarmatis called into question not just the centrality to Islam of Quraysh, but also the essential arabness of its whole cultural edifice, so recently enshrined for all time in the Age of Setting Down. Under their auspices, a group called Ikhwan al-Safa', 'the Brethren of Purity', compiled in the last third of the tenth century an encyclopaedic collection of treatises that attempted to bring together all the sciences then existing in the known world. The treatises, or 'epistles', were intended for higher instruction among the Qarmatis and their Isma'ili co-sectarians. The Brethren's interests resembled those of the open-minded Caliph al-Ma'mun in the previous century, but drew on an even wider range of influences. In philosophy, Greek sources predominate, and include the Pythagoreans, Aristotle, Plato and the Neoplatonists, but in other fields the range of influences is wider: astrological ideas, for example, come from Persia, India and ancient Babylon, while the treatises on divine revelation draw on both the Hebrew Bible and the New Testament; shades of the cult of Mithraism have been detected too. The Brethren's mode of expression was the Arabic language; their range of sources, however, was global. As with their hijacking of the Black Stone, the Qarmatis had shown – this time through their intellectual wing – that the old Arab-centred world could be made to wobble on its axis.

THE LEVELLERS

Throughout the ninth and tenth centuries, there were other challenges to Arab supremacy. In contrast to those of the Zanj and the Qarmatis, they were generally bloodless; but they were still bitter, and in one form or another they would spring up across the empire from Spain to Transoxania, endangering the newly implanted arabness of that tricontinental tranche of the globe.

The discontents arose first with the Persians. They had enjoyed a special, love–hate–love relationship with Arabs since the beginning of Islam: the conquests that followed Muhammad's revolution had joined Arabs and Persians in a kind of marriage – often literal marriage, as when the three captured Persian princesses had been wedded to the three most prominent young men of the new Medinan nobility. But the relationship was unequal, a joining of conqueror and captive, dominant male and supposedly submissive female, and so it would remain. The story of Harun al-Rashid reversing the usual roles by giving his sister in marriage to his Persian bosom friend, Ja'far al-Barmaki, then executing him when the couple dared to consummate the union, may have no basis in fact; but it is a powerful parable about Arab–Persian relations, and Arab fears.

It was thus not only the physically exploited and the economically maltreated, the slaves and the peasants, who kicked against the Arab pricks: so too did educated Iranians, who soon tired of Arabs always being the ones on top. As the Abbasid age progressed, and Arabic and then Islam began to spread more widely through the old Sasanian domains, their discontent increased. Ever more Persians were now joined to Arabs by a script, a scripture and a faith that proclaimed the equality of all believers. Had not the Prophet himself, in the sermon he preached on his Farewell Pilgrimage – perhaps Muhammad's equivalent of Jesus's Sermon on the Mount – declared, 'Nor is any Arab superior to any non-Arab, except in piety'?

The backlash began in early Abbasid times. Bashshar ibn Burd, the first great non-Arab Arabic poet, celebrated his non-arabness by declaring,

> My father never urged
> a scabby camel with a song;
> . . .
> I never dug for, never ate
> a lizard from the rocks,

and after many more such bedouin-bashing verses ended by celebrating Islam – but as a Persian Muslim with his own glorious past:

Our wrath is a most worthy wrath
for God and for Islam.
I, son of double Persian stock,
defend it zealously.
We bear our crowns and own our strong,
disdainful sovereignty.

As the eighth century turned into the ninth, such sentiments spread and inspired a movement with a name: Ahl al-Taswiyyah, the Levellers, because they demanded equality with Arabs. But they soon came to be known by another name, one with more dimensions – the Shu'ubiyyah. The immediate word-association is with that seminal Qur'anic verse that tells how Allah

> created you from male and female, and made you into peoples [*shu'ub*] and tribes [*qaba'il*], that you may know one another.

In the same spirit as Muhammad's final sermon, it continues,

> The most honourable of you in Allah's sight are the most pious.

By evoking the verse through their name, the Shu'ubiyyah were therefore identifying themselves as 'peoples', societies joined by shared geography like the ancient South Arabians, not by alleged ancestry like the tribal northern Arabs. But other associations hover: they are settled peoples, 'civilized' in the most basic sense; but they are also 'civilized' in that they do not serenade scabby camels or nibble lizards.

While Arabs were polishing their own self-image as natural leaders sprung from rough, tough but innately noble stock (compare imperial Rome's pride in its own rustic heroes of earlier times, and Hollywood's in the frontiersmen of the American West), the Shu'ubiyyah were doing their best to smear it. The Arab ancestors, they said, were no noble savages; they were savages, *tout court*, and their roughness still clung to them like the whiff of their animals:

> You were herdsmen living among camels, sheep and goats . . . and because you were so long accustomed to speaking to your camels, your

> speech became harsh and your vocal organs coarse. Now, even when you are speaking to people in the same room, you sound as if you are addressing the deaf.

Very little of the Shu'ubis' own words has survived; but as that quotation (preserved by one of their main foes) suggests, a lot of their invective probably centred on the force that had shaped so much of Arab history, the Arabic language. The Shu'ubis were a literary movement: most of them came from the large and growing class of Arabic-literate non-Arabs, who had made the written language virtually their own. Arabs had formed the *spoken* language and its rhetoric, and had themselves been shaped and united by them. But it was non-Arabs who, as we have seen, took the infant *written* language – a language that was still, so to speak, learning its letters – and pressed it into the service of their imperial masters. An almost entirely oral culture of poetry and incantation had made it into ink with the Qur'an, at first the only regularly written Arabic; then, under the Umayyads, largely non-Arab scribes had begun to use written Arabic for record-keeping. It was only in Abbasid times that Arabic prose began to appear as written literature. Its most important pioneer was a Persian, Ibn al-Muqaffa', and Persians and other non-Arabs would be instrumental in its development. These literate non-Arabs thus felt that, just as they were sharers in Islam, they now had a stake in Arabic equal to that of its original owners. Arabs disagreed. Thus began a struggle in which, even if no blood was spilled, plenty of ink was shed.

Beset by accusations of backwardness, belaboured as loud-mouthed lizard-eating bedouins, Arabs counter-attacked. Or rather, other non-Arabs counter-attacked on their behalf: with few exceptions, 'genetic' Arabs had still not taken to sharpening their pens; just as they were relying more and more on Turkish soldiers to defend them militarily, so they depended on non-Arab clients to defend them in the debate with the Shu'ubiyyah. Thus the greatest ideologue of arabness, the copious author known as al-Jahiz, was no noble scion of some ancient Arabian tribe, but the 'pop-eyed' (*jahiz*) grandson of a black slave in al-Basrah.

Al-Jahiz believed that the Shu'ubiyyah were whipping up palpable hatred of Arabs that would imperil the empire and Islam. His most forceful counterblast, *The Book of the Stick*, has already been mentioned in passing. In it he takes the Shu'ubis' disdain of stuck-up, stick-waving, word-wielding bedouins, and uses it to strike back at them. In the stick, both he and the Shu'ubiyyah had hit on a powerful image. Sticks are an essential feature of traditional Arabian kit: they appear in pre-Islamic reliefs, in the hands of camel-riders of the ninth century BC, and of ritual dancers of the later centuries BC; today they are still carried, like swagger-sticks, by conservative tribesmen; one may find a camel stick on the dashboard of the latest SUV (and perhaps a falcon's hood on the gear knob). But sticks are also a tool of Arab rule and Arabic rhetoric, a rebus of control. In Shu'ubi eyes, Arabs used sticks and loud words to herd their camels, and they thought they could do the same to people.

Al-Jahiz, however, defends the stick – and thus the whole business of being Arab – in his strange, stream-of-consciousness style. Sticks, he suggests, can indeed be used to herd animals, but also to guide people to the true religion, as Arabs guided Persians via the message of Muhammad (in a Christian context, the shepherd's crook is also a bishop's crozier). But above all for al-Jahiz, the stick is the tool of the Arab orator, and the symbol of rhetoric. Like a conductor's baton, it acts as an extension of the orator's hand, emphasizing his gestures. It is the essential adjunct of Arabic public speech, of – most importantly of all – a rhetoric that none but Arabs themselves can aspire to master. 'Orators are to be found among the Persians,' he admitted,

> except that for them all speech, and for non-Arabs in general all meaning, can only ever result from lengthy thought and mental exercise; from periods of solitary contemplation and other periods when ideas are discussed and exchanged with others; from meditation and book-learning . . . Whereas for Arabs it is all a matter of intuition and extemporization: as it were, of inspiration . . .

Has al-Jahiz got into some inmost part of 'the Arab mind'? No, because such a singular object has never existed. He has certainly grasped a lot about the old high language and its origin as a special, supernatural tongue, evidence of 'inspiration' in poets and seers. But his assumption that Arabs have some innate, quasi-genetic disposition to eloquent speech is wishful thinking on behalf of the Arabic culture he had embraced; they arise from his fears for the future of that culture. He and other defenders of arabness were becoming more vehement the more Arabs lost political control. There was no hiding that loss: Turks like Bajkam were taking over in broad daylight, turning themselves from slave-soldiers into praetorian princes. But Arabs would never concede the loss to others of their language; it was the factor above all that had made them Arabs and kept them Arabs over history. There is a saying attributed to Muhammad, supposedly uttered in defence of his Persian companion Salman and much quoted by the Shu'ubis: 'He who speaks Arabic is an Arab.' With most Arabs, it cut no ice. They were happy for non-Arabs to use their language for worship, book-keeping, and immortalizing the heroic Arab past. To make further claims on it, as the Shu'ubis did, was to try to steal what they saw as the very soul of arabness.

Arab attitudes to Arabic can still be possessive. I have found that to speak the language is at first praised and encouraged – until one speaks it well enough to disagree with its owners. Many of them do not see this as debate, but as disloyalty – the 'splitting of the stick', of the gathered word. The feeling is seldom put into words; a rare example is that of the contemporary Moroccan scholar Abdelfattah Kilito, who admits in one of his books that he dislikes foreigners knowing his language, and feels they have 'robbed' him of it. The English title of the book is eloquent: *Thou Shalt Not Speak My Language*. (Professor Kilito himself teaches French, and presumably speaks that language.) As an old Spanish proverb warns, 'Do not speak Arabic in the house of the Moor'.

THE WOBBLING PEDESTAL

Elsewhere, feelings of inequality gave rise to similar conflicts between Arabs and others. In Egypt and North Africa, there were Copt and Berber Shu'ubis. In the Spanish far west, discrimination against local converts to Islam led, at times, to uprisings and bloodshed. Non-Arab Muslims had often retained their old family names, arabicized, such as Banu Bashkuwal (Pascual), Banu Gharsiyah (Garcia) and Banu Quzman (Guzman); some Arab supremacists, however, referred to them by derisory blanket terms like *banu 'l-'abid*, 'sons of the slaves'. When the discrimination persisted into the second century of Arab rule, a few of the native Muslims revolted and managed to found their own short-lived statelets. In time the revolts were contained and the rebels placated. But that Islamic ideal of equality was, again, unrealized; Arab chauvinism always weighted the scales. By the eleventh century a late, literary Shu'ubiyyah arose among Spanish Muslims of Berber and European origin, very much like the earlier movement in the East.

In the furthest southern corner of the empire, too, at the far end of their own 'island', Arabs found even their supposedly long-arabized South Arabian brethren turning against them – or at least against the narrow, bedouinized view of arabness promoted in the Age of Setting Down. We have already heard the poet Abu Nuwas, not himself an ethnic southerner but a *mawla* of southerners, laying into backward bedouins. Sometimes his attacks are outrageous: Abu Nuwas was famous for his homosexual love poems, and his satires of the rough *a'rab* can be filled with queeny spite, as when he declares that if the old macho bedouin poets were alive in the Baghdad of his day, they would be poncing around like perfumed Persians and drooling over pretty boys. Nor did Abu Nuwas's satire spare Quraysh, the tribe of the Prophet and his Abbasid successors. As a result, the poet spent a long spell in prison by command of Caliph Harun al-Rashid. The fictionalized Abu Nuwas of *The Thousand and One Nights*, al-Rashid's amusing companion, has had his sting removed.

Abu Nuwas's attacks were in part a symptom of the 'North–South split', which had been so deepened by the struggles of Umayyad times. Now, as the ninth century progressed and the Persian Shu'ubiyyah intensified their own literary attacks, down in southern Arabia itself there was a resurgence of pride in ancient Saba and its sister-civilizations – the original *shu'ub*. Local rulers began to assert both their political independence from the caliph in distant Baghdad, and their descent from the indigenous pre-Islamic nobility. Local writers like the tenth-century antiquarian and geographer al-Hamdani would try to resurrect the forgotten glory of the South. But their efforts hardly impinged on the bigger cultural picture of Arabdom: they were memorializing ruins in what was now the back of beyond. Just as tribal nomads had infiltrated and arabized the old South in the centuries before Islam, so in the centuries following it, and especially in the Abbasid Age of Setting Down, the narrative of history itself had been effectively bedouinized.

In their attempts to meet Arabs on even ground, the Shu'ubi levellers of all lands had set themselves an impossible goal. They never succeeded in knocking Arabs off the pedestal they had built themselves as the Prophet's folk, the original owners of the language of the Qur'an. Politically too, Arabs were the kings – still, just, nominally – of the castle; they were up on their rock, and the lurking lions had, for the moment, skulked away. Nevertheless, the Arab perch was precarious, both politically and culturally, and the peoples whom Arabs claimed to rule were doing their best to wobble it.

Shu'ubi sentiments would reappear over time. Urban lampoons of lizard-munching tribesmen would persist for centuries. On the Arab side, their nineteenth-century 'Awakening' would revive the language of the debate: Ottoman nationalists and, later, opponents of Arab Nationalism and even Marxists would be accused of Shu'ubism. Saddam Husayn's Iranian adversaries were labelled as Shu'ubis in the war of the 1980s. Now too, in the conflict outside my window, the Iranian-influenced Huthis have been accused of pursuing a Shu'ubi agenda. In terms of timescales it is as anachronistic as calling Great War Germans 'Huns'. But it may not be quite so inaccurate. Like all conflicts, the fight before me now is in part a fight over identity. The Huthis have built themselves an idiosyncratic identity from the fragments of several nonconformist pasts, sectarian, cultural, political. Their opponents, Saudis and others, see themselves as part of the bedouin-Arab narrative of history. They still twirl their sticks with swagger.

(Then again, the Huthis, accused at the end of 2016 of firing a missile in the direction of Mecca, have been further likened to the Qarmatis who plundered its sacred Black Stone, and to that even earlier assailant of the holy city, the sixth-century Abrahah the Ethiopian. History has too many themes and variations ever to recapitulate exactly. It is the rhetoric that repeats itself.)

CUCKOOS IN THE CALIPH'S NEST

Defend their cultural imperium as they might, it seemed there was nothing Arabs could do to stem the haemorrhage of their political power. Bajkam the Turk, whose portrait medallions so dismayed Caliph al-Radi, was a paradigm for the new power-holders: he had risen from being a lowly slave-soldier in the provinces to the post of al-Radi's Prefect of Police, before imposing himself on the caliph as commander-in-chief and *de facto* ruler in 938. He may have been the first interloper actually to portray himself on the seat of power; but others of his kind had been aiming for it for some time. Nearly 200 years before, the second Abbasid caliph, al-Mansur, had set a precedent by relying on guards who were slaves and ex-slaves in preference to free Arabs; in the early ninth century, al-Ma'mun was bringing increasing numbers of non-Arab troops to Baghdad from his original eastern power-base in Khurasan. It was al-Ma'mun's brother, al-Mu'tasim, who took the trend even further. During a reign that began in 833, he imported ever more slave-soldiers, and especially Turks. It would only be a matter of time before that large and growing body of armed men would start to throw their weight about politically.

Slave-soldiers make sense: in the absence of a strong abstract state as the focus of allegiance, the loyalty of free soldiers – and particularly of those from the sort of ready-armed tribal background from which Arab soldiers tend to be recruited – can be bought by the highest bidder or the most persuasive speaker. (I am watching a country fall apart because of this: the apparent Yemeni army devolved overnight into a rag-tag bunch of private militia; perhaps it was never really more than that.) But the loyalty of slaves is not negotiable; that, at least, is the theory.

For al-Mu'tasim, Turks were the cream of slave-soldiery: 'Turks . . . are the bedouins of the non-Arabs', wrote al-Jahiz at the time – from him, high praise indeed. Their skill as riders and archers was legendary, their vigilance almost supernatural: 'The Turk has two pairs of eyes, one at the front and the other at the back of his head.' We do not know whether al-Mu'tasim's preference for Turks was influenced by the fact that his mother was herself a Turkic slave-concubine, but it can hardly not have been a factor. He stockpiled prime-quality Turkic warriors as Saudis stockpile the latest laser-guided missiles; three years into his reign, he had amassed 4,000 of them. But the narrow-eyed centaurs refused to champ at the bit in their barracks; instead, they cantered about Baghdad, causing havoc. Al-Mu'tasim's solution was a combination of lateral thinking and grand design: build them another Baghdad.

Al-Mu'tasim founded his new capital, Samarra', 125 kilometres up the Tigris from Baghdad, in 836, and moved his Turks and other foreign troops to it. Samarra' has been likened to Versailles; but it was also an overblown Aldershot or Fort Hood, a military metropolis of mud-brick and dust inhabited by Central Asian cavalrymen and caliphal camp-followers like al-Mu'tasim's jester, Ali the Cobbler, who would store his farts in his capacious sleeve then waft them over the more po-faced courtiers. As for the troops – not only Turks, but also Khurasanis, Farghanans from hard by the Tien Shan range, North Africans and others – they were divided by origin into cantonments whose relative positions echoed the geographical disposition of the various races' homelands: Samarra' was a scale model of the empire. It also mushroomed into one of the biggest cities in the world, at least in area. But its time as capital would also be small in scale – it lasted less than sixty years before it was abandoned. That there are six variant ways of writing the name in Arabic seems only to reflect its impermanence. And yet the irony is that while almost all traces of Abbasid Baghdad have long been buried under later layers of habitation, the Great Mosque of Samarra' survives, at least in outline, with its curious helical ziggurat-minaret rising still like a helter-skelter from the dust, marking the centre of that now silent Babel.

The overwhelming turkification of the army brought with it other ironies. In 838, for example, al-Mu'tasim raided far into Byzantine territory, destroyed the city of Amorium south-west of Ankara, and took numerous captives. The exploit was celebrated by Abu Tammam ibn Aws in one of the most famous and sonorous of all Arabic poems, a Tchaikovsky-last-movement of an ode. It begins:

> Sword tells more truth than books; its edge is parting wisdom from vanity:
> In gleaming blades, not lines of dusky tomes, are texts to dispel uncertainty and doubt.
> Knowledge is found in the sparkle of lances, glittering between opposing ranks, not in the seven sparkling lights of heaven . . .

It is all a paean to bedouin Arab martial prowess, a declamation of the flashing rhetoric of sword and lance that puts mere written, prosaic truths (penned, of course, by Persians and other Grub Street foreigners) in the shade. And it is a homage to the ancientness of that other, sharper truth. As one recent commentator has said, 'The poet . . . transforms the ethical values of his [al-Mu'tasim's] pagan tribal ancestors into the moral foundation of the Islamic state.' But further investigation reveals the slippages from reality. The poet was himself by birth not the hyper-Arab-sounding 'ibn Aws' but actually ibn *Thad*aws – the son of Thaddeus, a Christian tavern-keeper of Damascus. And what he does not admit is that the ancient Arab heroism was being recapitulated by an army of Turks. Neither does he mention that, back home, al-Mu'tasim's nephew al-Abbas ibn al-Ma'mun was making an unheroic and decidedly underhand bid for the caliphate, thus scuppering his uncle's plan to follow the victory through with a march on Constantinople.

The raid on the neighbours – pre-Islamic tribal war writ large – was splendidly traditional; so in a different way was the enemy in the family. But in the case of the former, Arab tradition had been outsourced to foreigners, and ultimately the foreigners, the Turks, didn't give a damn for tradition. They cared only, of course, for power. They had the weapons, the numbers and, increasingly, the sort of *'asabiyyah* or group solidarity that had empowered Arabs; and whether might is right or not, power makes people cower – even the caliph.

BLINDED TO THE BEAT OF DRUMS

The crisis came with the caliphate of al-Mu'tasim's son and second successor, al-Mutawakkil. By his time the Turkish pawns had crossed the board and become major players; the Abbasid family, fount of honour and arabness, were themselves no more than pawns. From now on a catalogue of caliphs would start their stints on the throne with bewilderingly similar regnal names, and finish them, for the most part, with similarly violent ends.

Al-Mutawakkil favoured his son al-Mu'tazz to succeed him; another son (from another mother), al-Muntasir, plotted with the Turkish praetorians to ensure his own succession. The plotters chose a night in December 861 to act. The caliph was drinking with his closest courtiers. 'He was exceedingly drunk,' recalled the poet al-Buhturi, one of those present.

> About three hours of the night had passed, when suddenly Baghar [one of the Turkish commanders] appeared with ten other Turks, all veiled and clutching swords that glittered in the candlelight. They dashed towards us, making for al-Mutawakkil. Baghar and another Turk leaped on to the caliph's dais. Al-Fath [ibn Khaqan, al-Mutawakkil's secretary and himself an arabicized Turk] shouted, 'Woe to you! This is your lord!' The cup-bearers, courtiers and cup-companions who were present flew headlong when they saw the Turks. Only al-Fath remained in the audience-hall and tried to fight them off. Suddenly I heard al-Mutawakkil cry out: Baghar had struck him on his right side – with a sword that al-Mutawakkil himself had given him – and sliced him open down to the waist; he then dealt him a similar blow on his left side. Al-Fath had rushed up to try and fend the Turks off the caliph, but one of them plunged his sword into al-Fath's stomach till the point came out of his back. And yet al-Fath held his ground and did not flinch. Never did I see a braver soul, a nobler man. He threw himself on al-Mutawwakil to protect him; but they died together. They were rolled up in the carpet on which they were

> killed. Thus they remained for the rest of the night and most of the following day, until al-Muntasir had been confirmed as caliph. He ordered that they be buried together.

There is a sequel. Ghoulishly, al-Muntasir took to sitting on the carpet, his father's first shroud – until it was pointed out to him that it depicted an ancient Persian prince who had killed his own father, the shah; this earlier parricide, an inscription on the carpet said, had lived only six months after his crime. And so it was with al-Muntasir. Apparently he died of a chill caught from sleeping in the lower chamber of a wind-tower after a sweaty game of polo. But rumour had it that his death might have been accelerated by another Turkish plot – unwisely, he had tried to assert his authority over his fellow conspirators – and a poisoned scalpel.

More wisely, al-Muntasir's sidelined brother, al-Mu'tazz, kept out of the fray of succession. Even when his mother thrust his father's bloodstained shirt in his face and urged him to take vengeance on the Turks, he could only say, 'Mother, give up, or you'll have two shirts instead of one' – the second, of course, his own. For the time being a cousin, al-Musta'in, was placed on the caliphal perch. Power was in the hands of the two Turkish commanders, Bugha the Younger, mastermind of al-Mutawakkil's murder, and a fellow general, Wasif. Of these two, a contemporary poet said,

> Bugha and Wasif
> Beggar all belief:
> They're masters of the age;
> The caliph's in a cage!
> He meekly talks their talk,
> A polly-parrot's squawk.

But blood would soon flow again, and Abbasid annals turn into a drawn-out version of the end of *Titus Andronicus*. Al-Mas'udi, who was born in Baghdad in the middle of the drama and witnessed some of its later acts, does not skimp on the sensational details and suq rumours. Particularly valuable, however, are the contemporary verses he quotes: poets were the pamphleteers of the age, reflecting and shaping reaction to events. When the Turks eventually forced al-Musta'in to abdicate – and then for good measure beheaded him – al-Mas'udi quotes another outspoken verse:

How marvellous to see the Turkish horde
fend off cruel fate's advances with the sword –
Then use that sword for their next regicide,
thus spreading fear and terror far and wide!
They've carved a realm up, too, its ruler's fate
to be their guest in his own caliphate.

Violence begat violence. Al-Mu'tazz, the parricide al-Muntasir's brother, was at last persuaded by the Turks to overcome his squeamishness about high office. They installed him in the gilded caliphal cage but soon appeared to contemplate replacing him with another brother, al-Mu'ayyad, who at the time was out of harm's way in prison. Moving quickly, al-Mu'tazz had this brother smothered in a poisoned bedsheet. Now fearing that Bugha the Turk would 'swoop down on him from the sky or rise up at him from the ground', al-Mu'tazz employed a band of North African slave-soldiers to assassinate him. At first the other Turks seemed stunned. But they eventually regrouped and deposed al-Mu'tazz, too; he was killed in gaol a few days later.

The next caliph would also fall to the Turks, but for different reasons. Despite (or because of) being the son of al-Wathiq, the louche anti-hero of William Beckford's Gothic-Saracenic novel *Vathek*, al-Mu'tazz's cousin al-Muhtadi was that rarity among Abbasids – a puritan; he tried to model himself on Umar ibn Abd al-Aziz, the pious exception to that dynasty of black sheep, the Umayyads. Raised to the throne, he soon managed to shock public immorality. It was all very well for him to whitewash over the figurative murals in the palace and to disband the orchestra, to do away with the caliphal fighting cocks and fighting rams, and to slaughter the beasts in the menagerie; if he chose to sleep, as he did, in a hair shirt, that was his own business. But to try to ban alcohol and singing slave-girls throughout his territories was going too far; for one thing, except in name the territories were no more his. According to al-Mas'udi, some of his more sybaritic subjects arranged the now usual solution with the real rulers, the Turkish guard. In fact, there seems to have been a complex power-struggle involving the caliph and different Turkish factions. Whatever the cause, the end was the same: the ascetic caliph was killed by a drunken Turk, who allegedly drank his victim's blood.

Earlier, al-Muhtadi had been asked why he was trying to implement such unpopular reforms.

> He replied, 'I wish to guide the people on the path of the Prophet of Allah – peace and blessings be upon him – and of his family and the four right-guided caliphs.' To which the response was, 'The Prophet of Allah – peace and blessings be upon him – was surrounded by people who had renounced this world out of desire for the world to come . . . Your men are Turks, Khazars, Farghanans, Maghribis and other species of non-Arab . . . whose only aim is to get what they can from this world, and as quickly as possible.

The retort, cynical but truthful, shows once more how far Arabs had come since leaving their 'Island' less than 250 years before, how lost some of them now were in the wider world – and how that older, smaller world was itself a lost ideal. Al-Muhtadi would not be the last Arab to want to recreate the ideal.

For a time there was relative stability. Al-Muhtadi's cousin, al-Mu'tamid, survived an extraordinary twenty-two years as caliph. The latter's nephew, al-Mu'tadid, lasted ten, and actually managed to restore some of the territory and authority that had been lost in the Zanj and Qarmati upheavals, but only within Iraq. Anywhere further afield – Persia, Egypt and elsewhere – had by now, as we shall see, slipped for ever from the rule of Baghdad. After the six-year reign of al-Mu'tadid's son, however, succession problems resumed with a vengeance. Some of the Turkish praetorians, dissatisfied with the official appointee, al-Mu'tadid's grandson, got hold of his uncle, al-Mu'tazz's son Abd Allah, and installed him as their candidate. Ibn al-Mu'tazz (he didn't last long enough to acquire a regnal name) was a connoisseur of rare vintages and fine verses, and himself a first-growth modernist poet. One imagines him dragged complaining at dawn from his ivory tower:

> Another glass!
> A cock crow buries the night.
> Naked horizons rise of a plundered morning.
> Above night roads: Canopus,
> Harem warder of stars.

For Ibn al-Mu'tazz, the caliphate was the usual poisoned chalice, but one he was able at least to down in a single draught: as if to make up for the two long reigns before him, he lasted less than a day before being strangled by the partisans of his nephew.

Ironically, Ibn al-Mu'tazz had himself commented, in his refined poetic voice, on the caliphate's decadence. Other, earthier voices continued also to versify their thoughts about the mayhem at the palace. Ibn Bassam, for one, did not mince words. Having attacked the regent al-Muwaffaq and every important officer of state by name in a swingeing ode, he could only conclude,

> Let's chuck this age in: let the villains reap its benefit –
> Till God consigns them, with His curses, to the fiery pit.

It might be the voice of the man in the suq today: We want justice! But we know it will always be postponed, post mortem.

Turks and other foreign power-holders did not escape the venom of Ibn Bassam's verse. They included

> Our alien *amir*,
> Called Donkey, son of Ass.
> When he took over here,
> Islam took flight, alas!

The donkeys, nevertheless, were firmly in control. By the time of Bajkam, minter of medallions, the fact had been recognized in the title he held: *amir al-umara'*, *amir* of *amir*s or Generalissimo. His nominal master, al-Radi, faded away of dropsy at the age of thirty-one. But with al-Radi's brother and successor al-Muttaqi, relations with the Turks turned nasty again and the Grand Guignol resumed. Deposed after a few years in office, he was blinded while drums were beaten to drown his screams. 'That,' said his uncle al-Qahir, an earlier caliph who had also been deposed and blinded, 'makes two of us. Now we need a third.' Sure enough, al-Muttaqi's cousin and successor al-Mustakfi was dethroned and blinded too – though not by Turks, but by a band of Iranian hillmen. In the repetitive chronicles of the Abbasid decline, it comes almost as a refreshing change.

At last it seemed the Turkish hold on power might have been broken. It would soon become clear, however, that one species of cuckoo in the caliph's nest had merely been replaced by another, equally voracious for power.

IRANIAN INTERMEZZO

The three Buwayhid brothers who took over swathes of western Iran, Iraq and, from 945, the caliphal capital of Baghdad, came from the mountains of Daylam, south of the Caspian. Politically, however, they seemed to come from nowhere. Stories arose to explain their sudden appearance. The most usual account said that they came from humble origins – their father, Buwayh or Buyah, who gave them their dynastic name, was a fisherman – but that their fortunes had changed when one of them found a hoard of buried treasure. Whatever the truth of the legends, the brothers were recent converts who used their Islamic label as a ticket to rule, first serving in the armies of rising local powers in Iran, and then manoeuvring their way to even greater power themselves.

That their Islam was of the Shi'i sort was to be expected. Precipitous Daylam and the damp, squelchy Caspian coast skirting it were fertile ground for Shi'i missionaries, prevented from propagating their beliefs in more congenial parts. In any case, the Shi'i affiliation made little difference. Some of the Buwayhids' bitterest enemies were the Hamdanids, an Arab dynasty in northern Iraq and Syria, who were themselves generally pro-Shi'ah. Besides, the Buwayhids did not try to impose their sectarian beliefs – probably woolly at best – on Baghdad, which was always a second city to them; their main capital was Shiraz in south-western Iran. In fact, as heterodox bosses of the Sunni centre, they were in a perfect position: they could let the caliph enjoy his pretence of holding sway over the world of orthodox Sunni Islam and, as Shi'is, feel no moral onus to respect his authority – an authority that, in any case, was by now purely theoretical. Ultimately, sectarian labels mattered little. Religion, as so often, was a bloated red herring that hid a lean and power-hungry shark.

In their policy towards the last great symbol of Arab rule, the Abbasid caliph, the Buwayhids carried on where the Turks had left off. Their first tame caliph was another brother of al-Radi, aptly entitled al-Muti', 'the Obedient' – nominally to Allah, but in reality to whomever Allah placed in charge over him. In this case it was Fanakhusraw ibn Buwayh, to whom the caliph gave the title Mu'izz al-Dawlah, 'Strengthener of the State'. In fact, the caliph did not have the option *not* to grant the title: the fount of honour issued titles and offices, but others controlled the flow. 'Al-Muti',' wrote al-Mas'udi in a late *post-scriptum* to his history, 'was in Mu'izz al-Dawlah's hand, with no power to command or forbid.'

Like most of the Turkish amirs before him, Mu'izz al-Dawlah the Daylamite spoke no Arabic. But, as their -id suffix shows, the Buwayhids managed to found a dynasty and to become, as one scholar has put it, part of an 'Iranian intermezzo' between the Turkic warlords and the Turkic dynasts to come. They were thus around long enough to be conquered, like so many others, by the Arabic language: Adud al-Dawlah ('Strongarm of the State'), the second-generation Buwayhid ruler of Baghdad, was fluent enough to compose Arabic verses in praise of wine. Interloping power-grabbers had once more been cemented into established society by the glue of language. But the relationship would be short-lived: within a generation of the Buwayhid takeover of Baghdad, a new wave of Turks loomed from the north-east. Far from being slave-soldiers, these were their own men, and they were approaching under their own ever-growing power.

EMPEROR OF THE WORLD

The Saljuqs were a clan of the great Oghuz super-tribe of Turks, who can be traced back to the eighth century and the region of Lake Baykal. By the early tenth century, they were leading a nomadic life between the Volga and the Aral Sea. Then, like the Buwayhids and at about the same time, they adopted Islam and used it as a ticket to military service in the rising Muslim states further south – and as a passport to power for themselves. Unlike the Buwayhids, however, they were in no hurry: they entered caliphal territory around 970, and only reached Baghdad in 1055. Also unlike the Buwayhids, their Islam bore a Sunni label. They could therefore justify their seizure of the caliph's city by airing the increasingly rotten red herring of sectarianism. They were good orthodox believers, they said, saving the caliphate from the Buwayhid Shi'i heretics.

There was another difference from their predecessors as 'protectors' of the caliphate. Like his Buwayhid forerunner Mu'izz al-Dawlah, Tughril, the first Saljuq ruler in Baghdad, could only speak to the caliph via an interpreter. But during their slow but thorough takeover of the old Iranian realm, the Saljuqs had adopted newly renascent Persian as their cultural first language. It seemed now that, except as an archaic liturgical tongue, the days of the ancient high Arabic, last vestige of Arab primacy in the expanding world of Islam, might be numbered. Unexpectedly, as we shall see, it was under the Saljuqs that Arabic and its whole cultural empire would get the biggest boost imaginable.

First, however, Arab prestige had yet more waning to do. Tughril was so powerful that he was able to cross that ancient red line, impenetrable since at least the time of the pre-Islamic Lakhmid kings half a millennium before: he, a narrow-eyed, flat-faced Turk, forced himself into marriage with the caliph's daughter, a pure-blooded Qurashi maiden and first cousin, if rather removed, of Muhammad (in the patriline; on the female side, of course, 400 years of slave-concubines from across the Old World had made her gloriously intercontinental). If any act could symbolize the fall of Arabdom, it was this. Even Alp Arslan, Tughril's nephew and eventual successor, was embarrassed; he sheepishly returned the daughter to her father after his uncle's death. Alp Arslan, however, himself penetrated another barrier, both symbolic and material: he was the first Turk to cross the Euphrates – the border, the psychological maidenhead, of the Arabs' inviolate 'Island'. And if there was any remaining doubt about the power of this all-conquering clan from the far Asian steppe, then Alp Arslan's son and successor dispelled it. Malikshah, a Turk whose name appropriately unites the Arabic and Persian words for 'king', who bore the honorific name Abu 'l-Fath, 'Father of Victory',

> ruled an empire such as none of the kings of Islam had ruled since the days of the former caliphs. It was an empire that encompassed the whole of Transoxania, of the lands of the White Huns of the Oxus, of the Gate of Gates [the eastern Caucasus], of Anatolia and Diyar Bakr, of Mesopotamia and the Levant. Prayers were raised for him as ruler from all the pulpits of Islam, save only those of the Maghrib, for he ruled a realm that stretched in length from Kashghar, a city in the furthest lands of the Turks, to Jerusalem, and in breadth from Constantinople to the lands of the Khazars and shores of the Indian Ocean. Such was the extent of his dominions that he was reckoned emperor of the world.

If there had been any doubt before that Arabs had passed on the baton of imperial rule, there was none now.

As for the caliph, he had 'nothing but his title'. Under the Saljuqs, however, in contrast to the earlier Turkic praetorians, he usually got to keep his life as well (an exception was the killing in 1138 of Caliph al-Mustarshid by Ghiyath al-Din, the Saljuq sultan). But however negligible or disposable its holders were, the actual office of *khalifah* – that whole link with the Arab past through *khilafah*, succession, from Muhammad – was still of great symbolic importance. It was their title that enabled caliphs to crown Saljuq princes and invest them with other symbols of temporal authority, including the ceremonial armlets that would be shared with European monarchy. In not dissimilar circumstances, Otto, warlord from the far German north, had been crowned Holy Roman Emperor in 962 by an impotent pope. But the parallel is not precise: the Saljuqs' own title – the now official one of *sultan*, 'power' – had no tint of holiness. Sultans, particularly alien ones from the steppe, needed the touch of sanctity still conferred by quasi-apostolic succession from the Arab Prophet.

The caliphate, and Arabdom, had lost their temporal power. But that residue of spiritual power remained. Further afield and later on – in the twelfth-century Syria and Egypt of the Turkmen Zangids and Kurdish Saladin, even in the fourteenth-century India of the Turco-Mongol Delhi sultans – Abbasids would remain useful as Arab-Islamic mascots, a living link with ancient Mecca. But they were little more than that. 'The non-Arab rulers,' Ibn Khaldun was to write, '. . . showed obedience to the caliph in order to enjoy the blessings [involved in that], but royal authority belonged to them with all its titles and attributes. The caliph had no share in it.' Furthermore, the caliphs' loss of earthly power was another symptom, and perhaps the decisive one, of nothing less than 'the disappearance of Arab group feeling [*'asabiyyah*] and the annihilation of the race and complete destruction of arabness'. Elsewhere, however, Ibn Khaldun revises that melodramatic diagnosis: what happened with the Saljuq takeover was that 'Arabs turned in on themselves'. As events long after Ibn Khaldun would prove, this was the juster judgement. Moreover, that turning inward was the latest twist of introspection that had begun in the first Abbasid century when Arabs, lost in the empire they had created, first looked back into themselves and into their past. The reverse *futuhat*, the counter-conquests, now seemed complete: conquered peoples, above all Turks, had got their own back. Except that the old Arab conquest, the first one of all, was not yet over.

ARROWS TO THE THRONE OF GOD

From the middle of the eleventh century, persianized Saljuq Turks were the political masters of the old Arab empire's centre and of most of its vast Asian wing. Beyond the edge of Saljuq rule, too, Iranian culture was beginning to rebuild itself. Firdawsi dedicated his late tenth-century *Shahnameh*, *The Book of Kings*, the first great work of the Persian renaissance, to Mahmud of Ghaznah in today's Afghanistan. But Arabic language and culture were about to have their own revival – in a movement that began in the east, too, but would spread over the coming centuries across the former Arab empire and beyond. It would ensure the survival of the old high Arabic as more than just a language of worship. Ultimately, more than four centuries after Ibn Khaldun had looked back on the annihilation of arabness, it was that dormant but still living language and its culture that would spark off the resurrection of Arabs as a 'race'.

Arabs today might therefore feel grateful to the Iranian Nizam al-Mulk, vizier of the two great Saljuq Turks, Alp Arslan and Malikshah (and patron of Umar al-Khayyam, the great mathematician better known in the West for his Persian poetry). Born in Khurasan in 1019 or 1020, he became fascinated early on by the science of *hadith* studies that had grown up around the sayings ascribed to Muhammad. He did not claim to be a specialist, but was admitted nevertheless into the elite circles of oral *hadith*-transmitters: 'I wish,' he said, 'to bind myself to the camel-train of those who have passed down the sayings of the Prophet of Allah – peace and blessings be upon him.' Through ever-extending chains of transmitters – Nizam al-Mulk's 'camel-train' – Muhammad was still gathering the word four centuries after his death. Nizam al-Mulk's importance was that, by founding the first great *madrasah*s, colleges of Arabic and Islamic studies, he ensured that the train would extend into the future. He used a different metaphor, however, more suitable for a warlike Turk, when lobbying for funding for his new institution from his master, Malikshah:

> 'The best marksmen in your army could not shoot a mile . . . But with this money, I could muster for you an army the arrows of whose prayer would reach the throne of Allah . . .' And the sultan wept and said, 'My father, make this army even greater . . . and you may have all the wealth in the world.'

The *madrasah*'s origins go back further than Nizam al-Mulk. But by tradition it was he who took the teaching of Arabic and Islamic studies, put it in a dedicated building, gave it a formalized curriculum and, importantly, endowed it richly with inalienable income. Nizam al-Mulk's first college, the eponymous Nizamiyyah in Baghdad, founded in 1065–7, provided board and lodging for its students and taught the Qur'an and the pagan classics – pre-Islamic poetry – as the basis of all learning. The Nizamiyyah also taught jurisprudence according to the Sunni school of al-Shafi'i, but later *madrasah*s would often provide teaching in all four main Sunni schools and in other subjects, sometimes including Sufism; the *madrasah* complex would always include a place for prayer, and often the tomb of its founder. The funding of colleges soon became the ideal vehicle for conspicuous charity: the Balliols, Yales and Wafic Saïds had their predecessors in the *madrasah* builders of the middle centuries of Islam (it has even been suggested that some aspects of the European university system were consciously imitated from the *madrasah*). For temporal power-holders, building a *madrasah* was also an ideal way to save one's soul, a kind of spiritual money-laundering. Thus a poet in Cairo, addressing the tomb of a member of Saladin's Ayyubid dynasty in the *madrasah* he had built, could say with tongue only half in cheek,

> You've built fine colleges to safeguard erudition;
> Perchance you've saved yourself, come Doomsday, from perdition.

*Madrasah*s, along with mosques, have proved to be the most enduring built monuments of the Arabic-Islamic world. Of Abbasid Baghdad, for example, in its heyday the centre of the Old World, very little remains visible above ground. One of the few exceptions is the Mustansiriyyah *madrasah*, founded by an early thirteenth-century caliph in the tradition of the Nizamiyyah. It is much restored but still extant and, despite eight hundred years of occasionally over-eventful history, still teaching on a new site as the Mustansiriyyah University. Perhaps more important, the *madrasah* curriculum still survives. Traditional jurisprudence is still taught along the lines laid down in the old *madrasah*s; as for the *qawa'id*, the 'foundations' or grammar of the high Arabic that underpin the only real unity of the Arab world, 'The university student of our days is essentially offered the same course in Arabic grammar as the student of a late Abbasid *madrasah*'. And to think that this grand and enduring tradition was founded by an Iranian and funded by a Turk.

Perhaps that is Nizam al-Mulk's greatest legacy – that *madrasah*s would do so much to preserve the cultural unity and continuity of the old Arab empire, flaking so visibly apart in his age but metamorphosing into the expanding community of Islam. But if *madrasah*s provided an anchor, they also exerted a drag: the focus on the pre-Islamic classics projected, through time, the ancient Arabian bedouin heritage that had come to be the Arab persona. And, in another way, they fed into disunity. By design, *madrasah*s were pro-Sunni, anti-Shi'ah, and it was in them, in the halls of learning as much as on the battlefield, that the dichotomy would harden.

AN ARAB INDIAN SUMMER

Their empire had taken Arabs into a west–east, Maghrib–Mashriq theatre of events. But Ibn Khaldun saw Arab rule as just one phase in a longer history. From the seventh century to his own fourteenth century, its time was also measurable on another axis, in great north–south pendulum-swings between Arabs and Turks,

> the former in the southern lands, the latter in the north. Over time they have taken turns in ruling the world, so that for a period the Arabs were in control and displaced the non-Arabs to the furthest north, while at another time the Arabs were themselves displaced to the ends of the south by Turks and other non-Arabs.

Writing while the Ottoman empire was still in its infancy, Ibn Khaldun was not to know how the pendulum would follow through into the Turkish side and stay there. But even in the earliest stages of Turkish dominance nearly five hundred years earlier, the picture was even more complex: not just some giant imperial swing, but also local oscillations of power. In some of these, Arabs retained their old primacy.

One family who did so were the Hamdanids, prominent in northern Iraq and northern Syria for much of the tenth century. They traced their ancestry back to the mobile tribe of Taghlib, one of the belligerents in the forty-year conflict of al-Basus, ancient Arabia's Trojan wars; sections of Taghlib, including the Hamdanids' forebears, had migrated into northern Iraq well before Islam. More recently, the family had taken on a Shi'i shade – not that it seemed to matter very much: Caliph al-Radi's brother and successor al-Muttaqi, for example, figurehead of Sunnism, had offered to hand over power to them, in order to get shot of his Turkish protectors/persecutors. Conversely, it was the Hamdanids who fought the bitterest battles against the Shi'i Buwayhids.

The Hamdanids were famous for those ancient Arabian pursuits of raiding and poetry. Their most famous leader, Sayf al-Dawlah, 'the Sword of the State', was said to have been buried with his cheek resting on a brick made from the dust shaken from his clothes after his many raids into Byzantine territory. And like the old pagan warriors, he had a way with words as well as with swords. They showed a gentler side to him, however, for he could compare a rainbow

> To petticoats trailed by a pretty girl,
> a multicoloured underlapping train.

As that sophisticated image suggests, the Hamdanids were a product of the urban, Abbasid age as much as of their ancient hair-tent heritage; they were readers as well as raiders. Patrons of cosmopolitan scholars, they cosseted men like al-Farabi, an immensely talented Turk from the lap of the distant Tien Shan range who had studied with Christian Aristotelians in Baghdad and who wrote on philosophy and music. Sayf al-Dawlah's court at Aleppo became

> the meeting-place of writers, the arena of poets. It is said that, after the caliphs, no other rulers had so many of the shaykhs of poetry and the other literary stars of the age congregating at their palace gates.

Most notably, Sayf al-Dawlah was the patron of al-Mutanabbi – still, today, probably the most famous Arabic poet since Islam. The prince's generosity was matched by the poet's love of money, preferably in quantities so big that they had to be weighed, not counted. A visitor recalled seeing al-Mutanabbi,

> with an amount of cash, gifts from Sayf al-Dawlah. The coins had been poured on to a palm-fibre mat that he had spread out; they were then weighed and put back in their bag. One coin, however, the smallest of the hoard, had got stuck in a tiny gap in the mat, and the poet applied himself so single-mindedly to the task of trying to prise it out that he completely forgot about his guests.

Perhaps not surprisingly, jealous rivals poisoned the court against him and he fled to another ruler. As we shall see, this new patron was as different in origin from the Arab Hamdanids as possible, and yet typical of the cultural empire that Arabs had founded.

A PERSIAN PURDAH

The hollowing out of authority at the centre was one thing; at the edges, power was sheering away with alarming rapidity. In the furthermost east, the Arab position had always been tentative. As we have seen, descendants of Arab tribesmen settled in Khurasan were soon subsumed into their environment, becoming Persian-speakers. Beyond the Oxus in Bukhara, the Arab invaders had been obliged to leave the local rulers in charge; before Islam took root there, they had even experimented with paying the locals two *dirham*s each to go to Friday prayers, and had allowed a Persian version of the Qur'an to be used. For worship and for writing, Arabic would soon prevail everywhere. But in speech, most people in the old Persian realms that stretched eastward from Iraq continued to use the Iranian languages.

Iranian discontent had found its literary voice early and widely, in the Shu'ubiyyah movement, and in Arabic. Rather later, it began to express itself politically in the form of independent states. Particularly successful was that of the Saffarids of Sistan, an area straddling the modern border between Iran and Afghanistan. Around the time of al-Mutawakkil's killing by the Turkic praetorians in 861 – that fateful turning point for Arab fortunes – Ya'qub ibn al-Layth al-Saffar made himself governor of Sistan. Baghdad was no longer in a position to argue, or to object when the governorship became hereditary in Ya'qub's family; for the next century and a half, while the Saffarids paid lip service to the caliph, they paid him no taxes. Ya'qub, however, did send the caliph al-Mu'tazz a flat-pack mobile mosque, big enough for fifteen worshippers and made of silver. It was perhaps subconsciously symbolic – as if Islam had gone travelling and had come back to its origins with added value. But there was no hidden meaning in another act of Ya'qub's: he took an army deep into the heart of the caliphal territory and claimed the rule of all Persia and Iraq. The claim never came to anything more than a raid; but the fact that Ya'qub's threat loomed just as the Zanj slaves were devastating the south of Iraq showed how the Abbasid Round City of Baghdad had ceased to be a bastion, and was now a target – with the Arab caliph at the bull's eye.

The eventual takeover of Baghdad by the Buwayhids, and its status as second city to their capital in Persian Shiraz, were further symptoms of

Iranian resurgence. With the subsequent persianization of the 'world'-ruling and long-lasting Saljuqs, the whole east wing of the empire would be lost not just to Arab control but, in the long term, to Arabic culture. Divines and other scholars would, of course, continue to be fluent in the ecclesiastical language of Arabic; the new *madrasah*s would ensure that. And the new Persian would be interwoven with Arabic words, a richly figured linguistic carpet. But the warp, the basis, was Iranian. From the Caspian to the Gulf a cultural curtain, a Persian purdah, descended across the gates of the east. Beyond it would flourish Firdawsi, Sa'di, Hafiz, and a whole Persianate future all the way to Safavid Iran, Mughal India and Ayatollah Khomeini.

It was in the west that arabness persisted, even intensified. However, that did not mean Arab political unity; far from it.

THE ALCHEMY OF ARABNESS

It was the interconnectedness of their empire that helped the rot run wild through Arab rule. Even in Egypt, it was those mobile and troublesome Turks from furthest Central Asia who were the first to challenge the sovereignty of Baghdad. In 868, as the Saffarids were consolidating their own rule in the east, and as the anger of the Zanj was about to boil over in southern Iraq, the lieutenant-governor of Egypt declared his own independence from the caliph. Ahmad ibn Tulun's father had been a slave-soldier from Farghana, in the service of Caliph al-Ma'mun; now, yet again, the Arab outsourcing of security would mean their slaves and freedmen gaining mastery over them. Worse, within a couple of decades Tulunid forces overran Syria and clashed with the caliph on Iraqi home ground. What with the Iranian Saffarids from the east, the Turkic Tulunids from the west, the East African Zanj in the south, and the praetorian peril at the centre, it was no longer helping the Abbasids to be – as the Tang emperor had pointed out – in the middle of things.

The Tulunid mini-dynasty did not last, however, and for a time the caliph reasserted himself over Egypt and Syria. But in 935 far-off Farghana provided a second short line of independent rulers in Egypt when another governor defaulted on taxes and fealty: like the Tulunids, the Ikhshidids took over Syria, and even added parts of western Arabia to their domains. As it happened, they proved to be a micro-dynasty – and a microcosm of current history as a whole, for they were displaced by their own cuckoo-in-the-nest, Kafur.

A black eunuch slave, Abu 'l-Misk Kafur ('Father-of-Musk Camphor') was the power behind the Ikhshidid throne of Egypt for over twenty years and sole ruler for two, from 966 to 968. That he looms much larger than he might in the Arab chapter of Egypt's long history is largely because of poetry, and in particular a clutch of odes by al-Mutanabbi, last seen fleeing his old patron in Aleppo. Kafur – illogically, a common name for black slaves because camphor is so white – seemed an unlikely new patron. He had been bought for a paltry eighteen *dinar*s; but he had risen fast in the Ikhshidid household, and on gaining control of Egypt he set about showing his true worth. Appropriately for someone whose name changed his colour from black to white, he was well aware of the power of spin and spared no expense on it. When, for example, an earthquake shook Egypt and a clever versifier declared –

> You think the earth of Egypt quaked because of mere mischance?
> No! Egypt's joy at Kafur's justice made it belly-dance . . .

– Kafur paid him 1,000 *dinar*s. It was supposedly the glint of that gold that made al-Mutanabbi head for the land of the Nile. A string of odes in praise of Kafur ensued. But, ever the poetic prima donna, al-Mutanabbi soon fell out with his new eulogee as he had fallen out with Sayf al-Dawlah. At the last minute he switched from praise to satire, having first planned his getaway in secret, and his final, over-the-shoulder fling at Kafur ends,

> A well-hung, well-heeled white man's sense of gratitude soon palls;
> what thanks can be expected from a black man with no balls?

Imperial fragmentation may have been death to unified Arab rule, but it gave new life to Arabic culture: it meant more patrons, more travelling poets like al-Mutanabbi, and more peripatetic scholars like al-Farabi. It is precisely because of the force and flexibility of that culture – illustrated in the muscular language of al-Mutanabbi, and in his own mobility as he flitted from court to court and from praise to satire – that we remember Kafur and many others in Arabic terms. It might be argued that it was also Islam that united these disparate people, all the poets and princes, the scholars and sultans of diverse origins. In theory, it was. On the ground, however, Islam has tended to be a divider as much as a uniter; that said, one of its most important functions has been as a vessel to preserve and transmit Arabic language and culture.

That is the triumph of Arabs: they lost their empire, but in the end their culture won.

Egypt has been a brilliant example of this victory, a crucible of arabization that has unified extraordinary diversity. The Tulunids and Ikhshidids, from what is now the junction of Uzbekistan, Tajikistan and Kyrgyzstan, and Kafur from sub-Saharan Africa, were not the only alien rulers of Egypt who would be absorbed into Arab history. The alchemy would continue working on successive incomers: Fatimids (dubiously Arab, as we shall see), Kurdish Ayyubids, Qipchaq and other Turkic Mamluks, Ottomans from the Balkans. Well into the nineteenth century, the son of the Albanian viceroy Muhammad Ali Pasha declared, 'The sun of Egypt changed my blood and made it all Arab'. By the time Arabs themselves got to rule Egypt again, in the revolution of 1952, being Arab would be more complicated than it had ever been, a many-layered *tell* or Troy-town of identity. Undeterred by the complexity, Nasser, the great showman, would promote Egypt as the heartland of *'urubah*, arabness. In a sense he was right: Egypt was the millennial melting-pot, a Pharaonic-Ptolemaic-Hellenistic-Roman-Byzantine-Coptic cauldron with ingredients sourced from around the Mediterranean, the northern Fertile Crescent and Black Africa. But for the thousand years up to Nasser the dominant flavour had been intensely Arab.

So when Kafur's rule ended and a new power took Egypt by storm – this time, for a change, from the west – the ambiguous arabness of the newcomers didn't seem to matter too much.

BLOODLINES AND TIDELINES

Kafur had not lacked metaphorical balls: among the many threats to Egypt that he successfully fended off were the Fatimids, an Isma'ili dynasty who had been established for some decades in Tunisia. His immovability prompted their agents in Egypt to give him a wry nickname, 'the Black Stone'. Their extremist fellow Isma'ilis, the Qarmatis, had recently removed the actual Meccan Black Stone; the Fatimids had to wait until 968 for death to remove Kafur. The news was the signal for the Fatimids' commander-in-chief to advance on Egypt. A freedman of probable Eastern European, possibly Sicilian, origin called Jawhar, 'Gem', he was one of a long line of foreigners to whom the Fatimids, like the Abbasids, would delegate defence and governance. That their new city of Cairo, founded in 969 by Jawhar and ruled by other foreigners – Kurds, Turks and Albanians – for the latter 800 of the next thousand years of its history, would succeed Baghdad as the metropolis of Arabdom, is yet more evidence of the alchemy of Arabic culture: it absorbs, and transmutes.

As for the Fatimids, even their ancestral arabness is in doubt. Their dynastic name declared that they were not just Arabs, but Qurashis and descendants of Muhammad through the marriage of his daughter Fatimah to his first cousin Ali. Few outside their domains believed in the pedigree, however. These critics were well aware that arabness, and especially membership of Quraysh, was another useful red herring: like sectarian affiliation, it could be a lure to get a hook on power. Existing power-holders naturally did their best to unhook rivals by subverting their supposed lineages, and this is what may have happened with the Fatimids. The story was circulated that their ancestor was not only a Persian but, to boot, from al-Ahwaz – the nearest part of *'ajam*dom to Arabia, for whose inhabitants long familiarity had bred particular Arab contempt. Another version claimed that the Fatimid dynastic founder, Ubayd Allah, was in fact the stepson of his alleged father, and that his actual father was a Jew. There is also an anecdote which, if true, insinuates that the Fatimids themselves were touchy about the subject. On his arrival in newly founded Cairo – al-Qahirah, 'the Victorious' – the Fatimid ruler al-Mu'izz soon became aware of the whisperings about his family tree:

> When he was securely installed in the citadel, he summoned the people to a general assembly . . . He half-drew his sword and said, 'This is my pedigree.' Then he scattered large amounts of gold among them and said, 'And this is the record of my noble deeds.' And they all cried out, 'We hear and obey!'

Admittedly, the story might itself be a piece of black propaganda. In the end, the only conceivable way to clear the Fatimid name – or perhaps to cloud it for ever – would be the miraculous discovery of some lost Fatimid tomb (none is known to survive) containing genetic material, and then the comparison of the genes with those of (supposedly) undoubted living Alid–Fatimid descendants. But who would dare to open that can of DNA?

Once established in Cairo, the sword and the gold, the control and the cash mattered for the Fatimids more than their name. With power, an obedient populace and, importantly, the wealth and commerce of Egypt in their hands, they could set themselves up as rivals to the unfortunate, Turk-ridden Abbasids. They affected the full caliphal look, complete with jewelled turban. The title of caliph they had used since Ubayd Allah's Tunisian days. Given that yet another claimant to the office – a tit-for-tat title in response to Ubayd Allah's assumption of it – was, as we shall see, at large in the far west wing of the empire, there were now three simultaneous caliphs. For a time it seemed as if the Fatimids were easily the most active of them; having secured comfortable, enervating Egypt, however, Fatimid forward policy flagged. They degenerated into a dynasty of dilettantes, variously into books, gemstones, alcohol, racing pigeons, weird alternative medicine, unorthodox sex and downright sadism. The business of everyday rule they left to a succession of viziers of varied ethnic origin. In sectarian matters, although themselves Isma'ili Shi'is, they were rarely rigorous, letting the Sunni majority get on with their lives. The laid-back attitude extended to those of other faiths: one of their viziers, for example, was an Armenian who doubled as Commander-in-Chief and as a result sported the title, though he was Christian, of Sayf al-Islam, 'the Sword of Islam'.

Despite the questions about their antecedents, the Fatimids contributed enduringly to the future of Arabic civilization. Not only did they create Cairo, still, today, called Umm al-Dunya, the Arabic 'Mother of the World', if now a somewhat frowzy dame; they also founded its great teaching mosque, al-Azhar, nowadays the nearest thing to a Vatican in priestless Sunni Islam. But their most important contribution to the future of the Arabic world was unplanned. Among their less obedient subjects was a huge, semi-nomadic and rowdy Arab tribe, the Banu Hilal. Long before, they had roamed Najd in central Arabia, but had moved to Egypt at some time in the eighth century. Later they proved disruptive, abetting those mobile and troublesome schismatics, the Qarmatis. As a result, the Banu Hilal were sent up the river to Upper Egypt. For the Fatimids, this was not far enough, and in the eleventh century they banished them further still, inflicting them on points further west. With this forced migration and that of another unruly tribe, the Banu Sulaym, came a belated but far-reaching arabization of North Africa, until then still almost entirely Berber in speech and culture outside the Arab-founded towns. As Ibn Khaldun put it, 'The Arabs outnumbered and overpowered the Berbers [and] stripped them of most of their lands.'

'Outnumbered' is an exaggeration: even if the Arab mass migrations numbered a (highly unlikely) million – including the sparser ones of early

Islamic times – as contemporary sources claimed, there were still a lot more Berbers. But overpower the region they did, both militarily and linguistically, in a slow but unstoppable flood that took a couple of centuries to roll to the far west of Algeria; the Berber languages survived, but only in highland areas above the reach of Arabs and Arabic. It was all a contrast to the flash flood of the seventh-century conquests, and much more like the creeping arab(ic)ization of the Arabian peninsular south that had taken place in the centuries before Islam. But in all three cases the Arabic tongue proved as complete a conqueror as Arab arms. If the principle of survival of the fittest can be applied to languages, then Arabic is among the fittest of them all: it had added to its conquests the whole blunt end of a continent.

With the advent of the Banu Hilal, the Banu Sulaym and other groups, the old settled life of North Africa was permanently disrupted. Ibn Khaldun remarks that,

> Formerly, the whole region between the Land of the Blacks and the Mediterranean was settled. This is attested by the relics of civilization there, such as monuments, architectural sculpture, and the visible remains of villages and hamlets.

With the coming of Arab nomads, however, the region was, 'depopulated and laid in ruin'. The Khaldunian verdict is harsh. Other factors such as climate change had also affected the region. Even so, there is no doubt that along with their language the incomers brought with them the ancient bane of raiding. It would stalk the region for centuries to come. The late thirteenth-century Moroccan pilgrim al-Abdari, for example, complained that 'the traveller, from the time he leaves the territory of Morocco until his arrival in Alexandria, never ceases to face death at the hands of malefactors'. Those malefactors were tribal Arab raiders. Given that the Mediterranean was equally malefic – when it was created, it supposedly threatened to drown God-fearing travellers and was thus cursed by Allah – those travelling between the far west and the central Arab lands faced a Hobson's choice, between the *badw* and the deep blue sea. Ibn Khaldun himself entrusted his family to the latter when they travelled from the west, intending to join him in Cairo: the ship sank, and his wife and five daughters were drowned.

The long westward swell of migration would roll on. Another big nomad conglomeration, that of al-Ma'qil, also passed through Egypt early on and went the way of the Hilal and Sulaym tribes. But they went further: from the fifteenth century, they began infiltrating Mauritania and soon came to dominate there. Arab migrations were thus reaching their high tideline at the far end of the Old World as European migrations were taking to the water and making for the New: another imperial baton passed on. And this last pushing of the boundaries of the Arab world completes a historical arc as well as a geographical trajectory. Al-Ma'qil, whose descendants are known in Mauritania as Hassanis, trace their ancestry back ultimately to the great Arabian grouping called Madhhij – that ancient and peripatetic tribe, well known from both the South Arabian inscriptions and the seminal Arabic epigraph of al-Namarah. And, for me, their spoken Arabic completes a linguistic circle: I strain to catch the urban patois of Morocco; in the Hassani speech of Mauritania, spiced though it is with Berber and Wolof speech, I hear the rhythms and timbres of Arabia, and realize I am understanding.

But by the time of the *hijrah* of al-Ma'qil to the far west, the days of the great tribal migrations were past. A different sort of mobility had taken over – one which, during centuries of Arab introversion would, as we shall see, help keep the *Kulturnation* alive, and expand it in new and surprising directions: the mobility of merchants and missionaries. But there was still one other land in the west, another 'island' in which Arab culture flourished.

THE FALCON AND THE PEACOCK

If the Fatimids' Qurashi Arab origins were in doubt, there was no question about those of their rivals in the farthest west. In the latter part of the tenth century, the third of the three caliphs, the ruler of Cordova and of most of the Iberian peninsula, received a letter from his Fatimid rival in Cairo. It was a most undiplomatic letter, venomous and scornful. The caliph of Cordova did not waste words in his reply: 'Sir: You know who we are, and have satirized us. If we knew who you were, we would have replied in kind. Greetings.' Arabic being so snappy, the original is only half the length of the English. Perhaps a better translation would be that down-the-nose put-down of English snobbery, 'Do we *know* you?'

Admittedly, if anyone in the western Arab world could have been justified in looking down his nose, it was the Umayyad caliph of Cordova. Some 250 years earlier, his ancestors had been almost entirely liquidated by the Abbasids. But one young survivor – Abd al-Rahman, grandson of the Syrian silk- and musk-loving Umayyad Caliph Hisham – escaped with his life and made it to the fringe of empire in Spain. His pluck and his far flight earned the admiration even of his enemies: al-Mansur, the second Abbasid caliph, called the young prince 'the Falcon of Quraysh'. For nearly two centuries, the Falcon's descendants were busy enlarging and feathering their western nest. In the 920s, however, the Fatimid state, still based in Tunisia, began to threaten Spain: it was in response to this, and in high dudgeon at the Fatimids' presumptuous use of the title of 'caliph', that in 929 Abd al-Rahman III of the Umayyad line of Cordova staked his own claim to the hallowed office. This meant there were now three concurrent caliphates – and by a semantic quirk the Arabic plural, *khilafat*, 'caliphates', also means 'controversies'.

Seen from Baghdad, which still regarded itself as the eye of empire, al-Andalus was the back of beyond. Moreover, there was an old notion that the map of the inhabited world was 'in the shape of a bird, with the eastern lands forming its head, the south and the north its wings and the lands between them its body, while the west is its tail'. Western Arabs travelling to the east, and particularly those from al-Andalus, were not allowed to forget that they came from the bird's backside. But one victim of this low teasing had a response: 'Shame on you! Do you not know what kind of bird it is to which the world has been compared? It is a peacock, and its finest part is its tail.'

He had a point: the descendants of the Falcon of Quraysh flaunted their Arabic culture with a peacock's pride. Rather as British Columbia and other tail-ends of the British empire preserve the concentrated essence of the old home country, al-Andalus became more Arab in some respects than Arabia. The arabness was genuine: in contrast to most of North Africa, fertile Spain drew Arabs in the mobile early centuries of Islam, and Tariq ibn Ziyad's largely Berber incursion had soon been followed by a wave of Arab settlers. The indexes of Arabic works on al-Andalus are thus rich in the names of tribes and peoples from the peninsula, and especially from its south, who had colonized Spain – Azd, al-Aws, al-Harith, Himyar, al-Khazraj, Khawlan, to look only at the first few Arabic letters of one such list. Just as Canada attracted Scots settlers, so the Arab New World drew colonists from the Arabian 'Celtic' fringe of the south.

Unlike the mass movements of Banu Hilal, Arab migration to Spain usually took place in fits and starts. Ibn Khaldun's own family history illustrates the sort of patterns of motion that emerged. His distant ancestor Wa'il ibn Hujr was from Hadramawt in South Arabia, and thus a descendant of the legendary southern progenitor Qahtan. With the first migrations of Islam, this Wa'il ended up in the southern Iraqi new town of al-Kufah; a seventh-generation descendant moved from there to Spain, where his own descendants joined communities with shared if distant Hadrami origins, first in Carmona, then in nearby Seville. They also negotiated the maze of politics, surviving several regime changes as public servants. Later, with the Christian takeover of Seville in 1248, Ibn Khaldun's more recent ancestors shifted to North Africa. It is all a microcosm of Arab mobility over six centuries and three continents.

The arabicized came too, drawn by the increasing prosperity of al-Andalus. They included those who transplanted to the west the seeds of the new Abbasid Perso-Arab urban culture, like Ziryab, 'Goldwater', a famously hip ninth-century Persian lutenist and musical innovator, the Mozart or Prince of the age, who moved from the court of Baghdad to that of Cordova. (Cordova's music-loving monarch, Abd al-Rahman II, also sent the female director of his orchestra, Qalam, 'Reed-pen', a slave from Navarre, to study at the conservatoire in Medina.) And with the increased glamour of the newly proclaimed caliphate in the tenth century, other cosmopolitan figures flocked to Spain. One such was the famous philologist al-Qali, born in Armenia, educated in Baghdad, and imbued with an encyclopaedic knowledge of high Arabic as spoken by all the tribes of the old Arabian homeland. His knowledge was in demand: the interest of Spanish Arabs in their ancestral lands and language was insatiable and led to some remarkable feats of long-distance publishing and book-buying. One such was when the caliph of Cordova commissioned works on ancient Arab history and genealogy from the Baghdad scholar al-Isfahani, and books and payments travelled back and forth across the 4,500 kilometres that separated the two capitals. But tastes in scholarship were cosmopolitan too: like the earlier al-Ma'mun in Baghdad, the second Spanish caliph, al-Hakam, ordered books from Byzantium – including, for example, a fine copy of Dioscorides's famous *De materia medica*. Also,

> he had agents in Cairo, Baghdad, Damascus and Alexandria whose task it was to commission copies of all worthwhile books, whether old or recent. His palace was so full of books and bookmen that it seemed to be a factory in which none but copyists, binders and illuminators were to be seen.

Al-Hakam's library was said eventually to have contained 400,000 volumes which, if true, was an astonishing number: the British Library, for example, did not reach that figure until the second half of the nineteenth century. Nor was bookishness the preserve of the caliph. Cordova, a city with 113,000 households, is said to have been served by innumerable bookshops and no fewer than seventy libraries.

This intellectual high summer continued even after the fall of the Cordova caliphate and its replacement, from about 1030, with a jigsaw of Muslim statelets ruled by an eclectic lot known as the Party Kings. In fact, just as earlier in the east, competition between rival rulers probably increased levels of literary patronage. But in contrast to the east, where free-thinking was discouraged after its brief season under al-Ma'mun and his immediate successors, scholarly openness prevailed in Spain. Rationalism and individualism flourished, for example, in the thinking and writing of the eleventh-century Ibn Hazm, who believed that 'every individual has the power of forming his own judgement, according to his particular abilities', and that even the untutored 'common folk' were not obliged to follow accepted authority. In the following century, too, the revolutionary thinker Ibn Rushd investigated the old duality of truth – the truth of faith and the truth of reason – and accepted their amicable coexistence. Latinized as 'Averroes', he was to gain a following in Christian Europe, where his thinking would reverberate down the centuries and into the European Renaissance.

The history of Arabs in Spain would last almost 800 years, from the *mawla*-general Tariq ibn Ziyad's footfall on his eponymous rock, Gibraltar, until the loss of the last foot-hold in Granada. Throughout this time ran a deep vein of nostalgia for the old country, the Arabian subcontinent. The Falcon of Quraysh himself is said to have confided in a fellow 'exile' – a lone date-palm in his Spanish garden. 'O Palm,' Nicholson's version goes,

> thou art a stranger in the West,
> Far from thy Orient home, like me unblest.
> Weep! But thou canst not. Dumb, dejected tree,
> Thou art not made to sympathize with me.
> Ah, thou wouldst weep, if thou hadst tears to pour,
> For thy companions on Euphrates' shore;
> But yonder tall groves thou rememberest not,
> As I, in hating foes, have my old friends forgot.

Andalusian nostalgia was to express itself in countless verses memorializing the Arabian past, and in the curious genre of letters addressed to Muhammad in his tomb at Medina, a virtual crossing of time and space; the actual Arabian pilgrimages of Spanish Muslims would give rise to a rich travel literature. But relatively few were able to undertake the journey, and Iberian Arabs suffered from a chronic longing for that other peninsula, for its sanctity and its lore. Their tail-end of the world may have been gorgeous, but beyond it there was nothing but the Lands of the Franks in one direction, and in the other the Circumambient Ocean. Bounded by the dangerous and the unknown, they looked back fondly to what was old and familiar.

Nostalgia combined with an outpost mentality made al-Andalus a bastion of arabness. Despite the racial and denominational mix on the ground, an alchemy of arabization was at work that was even more potent than its Egyptian equivalent. In a strange inversion of King Offa's Arabic coinage, the earliest gold pieces minted by Muslims in Spain had borne a Latin legend: *In Nomine Domini: Non Deus Nisi Deus Solus*, 'In the Name of the Lord [God]' – that is, the Arabic invocation, *Bismi 'llah*, plus that greatest of all slogans, lumpish in Latin and English but hypnotic in Arabic,

La illaha illa 'llah,
There is no god but Allah.

By the middle of the ninth century, however, the tables had turned completely: the Christians were totally arabicized – 'intoxicated', as one of them wrote, 'with Arab eloquence' – and studying alongside Muslims in the splendid new mosque of Cordova. Soon, they could no longer read their Latin scripture, and an Arabic Bible had to be produced for the Christian 'Mozarab' population. That term, a Hispanic garbling of *musta'rib*, 'arab(ic)ized', is the same one that was used for the anciently arabicized peoples of that other peninsula, Arabia. Arabic was continuing to conquer, to absorb.

The Arabic conquest of Spain has proved lasting. Islam was extirpated, but its holy language still haunts the land and its speech. Along with about 4,000 undoubted Arabic loan words in Spanish, the name of the ancient tribal god of Quraysh may even persist in the most stereotypically Spanish of settings. As the matador (itself from Spanish *matar*, 'to kill', perhaps in turn from Arabic *mata*, 'to die') dances with his victim and the crowd exclaims, '*Ole!*', I for one hear the echo of another word: the syllables are nearly the same, the intonation and the awe precisely the same, as those of an Arab football crowd transfixed by some expert striker and exclaiming, '*Allah!*' But He is the most-knowing, in etymology as in all else.

A SHIFT IN THE NATURE OF TIME

Arab identity remained strong in Spain and Egypt; but it was a new sort of identity, urban, linguistic, composite. Old-style Arabs, the raiding, herding *badw*, had been the leaven of an empire. That empire had risen and, now, had been divided. A flavour of the old arabness lingered in every part, but the substance of it all was much more complex, and much greater. The millions of members of the cosmopolitan Arabic world no longer called themselves 'Arabs': the term had reverted to its old sense, that of a marginal, tribal minority, often living more or less nomadic lives. It was losing its capital letter, becoming *'arab* again.

The relationship between these marginal *'arab* and the civilized centre had also reverted to something more like it had been in the days of the former empires, Assyrian, Babylonian, Roman, Persian. *'Arab* were once again a diverse group defined by their apartness from settled life. If, like the Abbasid caliph al-Qa'im, you found yourself shut out of your own capital while the Turkish slave-soldiers were doing deals with your Fatimid rival, whom did you turn to for asylum in the wilderness? To the local *amir* of the *'arab*, al-Muharish ibn al-Mujalli ibn Alith ibn Qabban. Even his name, which might mean something like 'Quarrelsome (or Dogfighter) son of Leadinghorse (or Hawkeye) son of Barleybread son of Steelyard', marks him as alien to the cosmopolitan Islamic persianized civilization from which the caliph came. A void now lay between the vast majority, the 'linguistic' Arabs, and the marginal minority of 'lifestyle' *'arab*. Moreover, while Arabs in the first sense still formed a puissant cultural empire, they were now sidelined from political power almost everywhere: they were culturally central, but politically marginal. In other words, the Arab *Staatsnation* had reverted to being a *Kulturnation* – and culture, to paraphrase Emile Enriot, is what people cling to when they have lost all else.

Moreover, Arabs had entered a new kind of time – a sort of passive eternal present quite different from the distant, ephemeral present of pre-Islamic tribal life, a brutish and short one; but different also from the active, dynamic present of early Islam, a present that had been rife with possibilities for the future. The energy and velocity of that seventh-century expansion had been impossible to keep up: Arabs had slowed to stalling speed and had, as al-Mas'udi put it, fallen. It was not a fall into oblivion, but rather a fall down to earth, to being unexceptional. As Salman Rushdie has said, 'nations and fictional characters . . . can simply run out of steam', and in a sense, a nation is itself a fiction.

But a fiction can, of course, have more than one episode. And in the interim, if the wheels of fire had burned themselves out for the time being, the cultural empire kept on growing outward from the ashes.

THE LOFTY PALACE OF QABUS

That growth can be tracked by following Arabic script as it spread across continents in its relentless arabesque. It spread not just on paper, but also on ceramics, textiles, plaster, wood, brick, stone, metalwork, coins, gems, arms, armour, amulets, bindings, buildings. It retained its old rhythms and rhymes too: poems were engraved and embroidered on everything from inkwells to saddles to the sleeves of robes. It made Arabic culture visible, and legible. Script linked non-Arabs to early Arabia in a concatenation of words: just as Nizam al-Mulk tagged on to the 'camel-train' of *hadith* transmitters, so calligraphers would inscribe themselves into 'genealogies' of pupils and writing-masters that joined their script to that of Muhammad's Meccan secretaries and companions, and of the pre-Islamic scribes of al-Hirah. Such lines of descent, not bloodlines but inklines, can still be traced back from the present, back 1,500 years.

The craft of writing Arabic had some unexpected practitioners. One was Qabus ibn Wushmagir, an Iranian ruler of the region of Jurjan south-east of the Caspian in the late tenth century, who excelled in the arts of tyranny, poetry, astrology and calligraphy. He was as adept at turning Arabic verses as he was at twisting necks; but he shone brightest in Arabic penmanship. On seeing an example of it, al-Sahib ibn Abbad – who as the owner of the famous 400-camel-load library of manuscripts was well qualified to judge – exclaimed, 'Is this the hand of Qabus, or the wing of a *tawus* [a peacock]?' No known examples of his calligraphy on paper remain, but he has one splendid memorial in brick – the Gunbadh-i Qabus, a soaring tower-tomb in which his body was said to have 'floated' in mid-air, in a glass coffin hung from the ceiling. The levitating corpse has gone, but the tower remains.

Robert Byron, stern and brilliant critic of buildings, wrote of its 'extraordinary momentum . . . unlike anything else in architecture . . . [It] ranks with the great buildings of the world'.

A fifty-metre funerary rocket caught in eternal take-off from the Caspian steppe, it was all very far from Arabia, and from the more recent urban Arab world of Damascus or Baghdad or Cairo or Cordova. But it is joined to that world by a band of Kufic script above the door and another far, far up beneath the cornice, both almost certainly designed by Qabus himself. The lower inscription says that the tower is the 'the lofty palace' of Qabus and that it was built in AH 397, or the year 375 by the Iranian solar calendar. The AD equivalent is 1006.

Like his earlier contemporary the philosopher al-Farabi (and like so many others), Qabus was a brilliant example of acculturation into the Arabic world. But the journey was in a different direction: al-Farabi came from the edge and was absorbed into the centre of the culture; people like Qabus were bringing the culture out *to* the edge. The calligraphic bands that bound his resting place are a part of a vast and widening cultural circumference.

The circumference would continue to expand, growing ever further from its point of origin in the magical poetical oral culture of ancient Arabia. In one sense, the powerless Caliph al-Radi who began this chapter is the final direct link with that starting point: Arab historians call him 'the last real caliph', meaning that he was the last one to deliver the sermon at congregational prayers in the capital of empire. With his death, the orator-leader – *khalifah*, successor, to the *khatib*s and *kahin*s, the preachers and seers of pre-Islamic times, as well as to the Prophet Muhammad – had, for the long time being, fallen silent. It is a symptom, minor yet eloquent, of the Arab fall itself.

The old rhetoric would reverberate on – but now resounding from grandiloquent towers of brick and stone, from the 'lofty palace' of Qabus, from the Minaret of Jam in the mountains of Afghanistan, from Delhi's Qutb Minar, exclamation marks that punctuate the march of Arabic across a continent.

CHAPTER ELEVEN

THE GENIUS IN THE BOTTLE
THE HORDES CLOSE IN

SHADOW-FANTASY

Cairo has always been the screen capital of the Arabic world. High Arabic costume dramas set in early Islamic times have made it into a Muslim Hollywood, or Mollywood. Egyptian soap-operas have long been the staple tele-fodder of the region. And, surprisingly, the history of the Egyptian screen goes back to the early period of Mamluk rule in the thirteenth and fourteenth centuries. This was the time when *The Thousand and One Nights* and other story-cycles, performed to live audiences, took the shapes we know today. It was also the period when the popular street entertainment called *khayal al-ẓill*, 'shadow-fantasy', took off. In this, hinged two-dimensional puppets similar to those already known in South-East Asia (perhaps their original home) were worked behind a brightly lit screen on which their shadows were cast. Surviving scripts are in high Arabic, but they revel in low humour, sharp satire and touches of smut. It is on such a screen that we should view the caliph of the age.

If the tenth-century Abbasid Caliph al-Radi was 'the last real caliph', God's shadow on earth, then his fourteenth-century successor al-Mustakfi Sulayman was hardly a shadow of the shadow. He was a genuine Abbasid; but the coming of the Mongols to Baghdad in 1258 had, as we shall see, made his family exiles in Egypt. Now the Abbasids were mere shadow-puppets worked by yet more Turks, the military dynasty of the Mamluks. Worse, Sulayman had fallen out with the Mamluk sultan in Cairo and been sent into a second exile in Qus, far up the Nile near Luxor. He had no illusions about his position, and in a rhyming complaint that might have been spoken by one of those Cairene Mr Punches, he said,

> Such as I / live when we die. / The world's a joke / until we croak. / Those Mamluks won't disburse / my privy purse. / They pray, 'God save His Majesty the Caliph!' / I say, 'God save My Travesty from the bailiff.' / The sultan sits enthroned in opulence; / the only wind Sulayman gets of thrones is flatulence.

Al-Radi and the other later caliphs in Baghdad were impotent, but at least they were on home ground. Sulayman was doubly in exile, and he and his family were so strapped for cash that they had to sell their clothes.

Islam was on the up; it had gone travelling long since and was crossing new frontiers, especially in a tropical clime that stretched from sub-Saharan West Africa to the East Indian Spice Islands. Arabic was the language of its holy book, and Mecca the Arabian navel of the world for Muslim pilgrims. At the same time, Islam had cut the umbilical cord that had tied it to its Arab parent: it had grown up into a world faith. Arabic culture had a new and hybrid foster-parent – Cairo, that fertile 'Mother of the World'. The two earlier counter-caliphates were long extinct; but Sulayman the Abbasid was still seen by a few as titular head of the first family of the faith and of Arabdom – of the 600-year dynasty descended from Muhammad's Meccan uncle. And yet so irrelevant had he become that he could be packed off, penniless, to a Nilotic Siberia. How did this come about?

A MULTIPLICITY OF THREATS

Over the two centuries before Abbasids became asylum-seekers, the remains of the Arab empire – fragmented as it was, but much of it still paying at least nominal allegiance to descendants, real or alleged, of its Arab founders – had been under increasing pressure from new forces. There were threats from Christendom at both ends of the Arabic world: the Crusades in the Levant, the Reconquista in Spain. In addition, Arabs in Spain were under a double pressure – Christian Latins from the north, Muslim Berbers from the south. Crusades would also encroach on Egypt which, since the re-persianization of the east and the rise of the Fatimids, had become a new centre of the Arabic world. Unlike the Reconquistadors, the Crusaders would be repulsed; but the upheavals they caused would bring another non-Arab people to the fore, Saladin's Kurdish dynasty. The Kurds were a tiny ruling minority, and they did not seem out of place: the Levant and, especially, Egypt had long been used to Muslim rulers of all complexions. But after only a century of rule, and in yet another example of the Cuckoo Syndrome, they would be displaced by a further sub-species of Turkic slave-rulers – the shadow-caliph Sulayman's Mamluk minders. For two and a half centuries from 1250, this self-perpetuating military caste would be the dominant force in the region. Their influence would endure even when their very distant Ottoman Turkish cousins had become the great imperial power (indeed, it would take Napoleon and Muhammad Ali Pasha to remove the Mamluks from the scene once and for all). But even with the Mamluks the list of new forces was not complete: just as they took over, the Mongols loomed out of the east.

By the time the shadow-caliph Sulayman's grandfather had fled Baghdad and the Mongols, therefore, the political value of Arabs had already been reduced almost to zero. Sulayman, stuck in his Mamluk gulag 600 kilometres up the Nile from Cairo and civilization, was thus an ironically appropriate figurehead for Arabs in general. Their history had been great when it was mobile, history on the hoof. Now, though, they had been hemmed in by other peoples on the move, all of whom seemed to be converging on the millennially important junctions where Africa and Europe, Africa and Asia, Asia and the Arabian subcontinent meet. With their genius bottled up and stoppered, it seemed that the active Arab days were finally over, and that they would now be the passive spectators of history, and its victims.

FRANKISH FOES AND FRIENDS

Looking briefly at those other peoples on the move, the most surprising were the European invaders who would be called Crusaders, generally known in Arabic as Firanj, Franks. In contrast to the waves of nomadic, mostly Turkic, incomers who had headed westward for the northern Fertile Crescent from the wide expanses of inner Asia, the Franks came from a cramped, dead-end continent, fractured by gulfs and mountain chains into statelets whose people tended to be tied, by geography and necessity, to the land. Looking back to the end of the eleventh century, when numbers of them first mobilized and headed east in the name of religion, it is tempting to see the movement as a belated response to the earlier Arab expansion, Crusades as a reflex of Crescades. The reason the Europeans themselves gave – to liberate the Holy Land of Christianity from Muslim rule – seems to confirm the view. It is as if Arabs, even if they were no longer the major motive force of history, were still propelling it at a remove, by setting off an equal and opposite reaction.

In the event, the Crusades themselves would be far from equal to the Arab expansion. The small and short-lived states that arose from them in the Levant were no re-run of the Arab empire; rather, perhaps, they were a pre-run of later European imperialism. None the less, there are parallels between Arab history in the seventh and eighth centuries and European history in the twelfth and thirteenth, when Europe forged its own wheels of fire. Crusaders shared with Crescaders the use of 'oppositionalism' to unite themselves and end baronial wars, the European equivalent (*mutatis*, as usual, *mutandis*) of the pre-Islamic tribal wars in Arabia. As godfather of the Crusades Pope Urban II said in 1095, it would be better to redirect 'against the pagans the fighting which up to now customarily went on among the Christians'. For Urban, Jerusalem was, like Mecca, 'the navel of the world', and the riches of that world were to be reaped by Crusaders as they had been won before by Crescaders: 'The possessions of the enemy, too, will be yours, since you will make spoil of their treasures.' Religion, again, was serving not only to create a large if temporary unity, but also to provide a fig leaf for naked ambition – for land, plunder and power. The despoiling of treasures, however, was often much more violent than in the time of the Crescaders. European chroniclers themselves admitted, for example, that the taking of al-Ma'arrah in northern Syria at the end of 1098 had involved not only massacre but even cannibalism. The slaughter of Muslims and Jews in Jerusalem in the following year was a shocking contrast to its peaceful occupation by Arab forces, 360 years earlier.

Resistance was stymied by disunity among the Muslims. When, for example, the people of Damascus sent a delegation to Baghdad in the year of Jerusalem's fall, the Saljuq sultan was off fighting his own brother in Iran: 'The sultans were at loggerheads with each other, and this enabled the Franks to occupy the country.' The caliph made sympathetic noises but was powerless. The conflict, however, was by no means always as simple as

Christians versus Muslims. A decade or so later, in 1111, another plea arrived in Baghdad, this time from the Crusaders' co-religionist, the Byzantine emperor Alexius: the Franks had occupied his territory, too, and Alexius wanted Muslim help to expel them. On this occasion the Saljuq sultan mobilized, but his campaign was derailed when another brother, the ruler of Aleppo, refused to join it. Another century on, the Doge Enrico Dandolo notoriously redirected the Fourth Crusade against his fellow Christians in Constantinople and filled the treasuries of Venice with Byzantine gold. The fig leaf had fallen away: lust stood exposed.

Apart from harvesting heads, lands and gold, however, the Crusades did also manage to sow the seed of new markets. The presence of the Europeans and of their colonies, and the penetration of Levantine trade by foreign merchants, caused an upsurge in traffic across the Mediterranean. While fighters fought and died, merchants bought and sold and – those horrific early massacres apart – the conflicts did not necessarily disrupt civilian life: 'The men of war were busy with their war, the rest of the people were perfectly happy, and earthly rule went to the winner', noted Ibn Jubayr, a late twelfth-century observer from Spain who undertook the Mecca pilgrimage (supposedly in expiation for having been forced by his sultan to drink alcohol). Ibn Jubayr also remarked on the generally friendly relations between Christians and Muslims on the ground, including even reciprocal alms-giving. His contemporary, al-Harawi, happily picked the brains of Crusading knights to compile his Islamic pilgrim-guide.

The frankest Arab observer of the Franks was Usamah ibn Munqidh, foe and friend of the invaders, who belonged to a family of local power-holders in Syria. He was impressed by the Crusaders' military prowess, but not by their other qualities: 'They have the qualities of bravery and excellence in fighting, but that is all – just as beasts of burden have the qualities of strength and excellence in carrying loads.' He admitted, however, that a few of the older Frankish hands who had mixed with Muslims had taken on some of their polish. Usamah became close to one or two of these knights, although at times the friendship was too close for comfort. One of his Frankish companions

> would address me as 'my brother', and we enjoyed each other's company. When he eventually decided to set sail for home, he said to me, 'My brother, I am going to my homeland, and my wish is that you will send

with me your son' – my son being with me at the time, and fourteen years of age – 'to come to my country to see our knights, and to learn reason and chivalry. He would then come back as a man of reason.' These words of his that rang in my ears were *not*, however, such as would come from the head of a man of reason. For even if my son were to be taken captive in battle, no worse fate could befall him as a captive than precisely that – to be taken away to the land of the Franks. So I replied, 'By your life, this is *exactly* what I was hoping myself, except that something prevented me from mentioning it. You see, the boy's grandmother loves him so much that she won't even let him go out with me unless she has extracted a solemn promise from me that I'll bring him safely back to her.' The knight said, 'And is your mother alive?' I said, 'Yes.' And he said, 'Then do not disobey her.'

Most Franks, however, remained a people apart, physically present but beyond the cultural pale. Usamah brought some of them into the Arabic fold, nominally: Benedict became 'Ibn al-Daqiq', 'Son of the Slender One', and Bohemond 'Abu 'l-Maymun', 'Father of the Fortunate One' (or perhaps 'of the Ape'). Occasionally they arabicized themselves: the Frankish lord of al-Shaqif, near the Syrian coast, for example, became fluent in the language, studying Arabic histories and even *hadith*s of Muhammad. And a few Franks would stay on, to become permanently arabicized and to found lines whose names preserve the memory of their foreignness, like the Lebanese families of Dikiz (de Guise), Shanbur (Chambord), Franjieh (Firanjiyyah, 'the Frankish Woman'), Salibi ('Crusader', from *salib*, 'cross') and Bardawil (Baldwin). But by the end of the thirteenth century most of them had gone.

Arabic and its culture had conquered, absorbed and forcefully embraced one people after another. In the incomers from Latin Christendom, however, it had met, if not its match, then its own like pole. The Franks went back to their cold halls in the north, taking, as we shall see, keepsakes, linguistic and cultural, of the doomed relationship. Perhaps it is the spurning of the embrace, as much as memories of the enmity, that has marked relations since.

RECONQUISTA

Meanwhile, at the far end of the Mediterranean, other Latin Christians were piling the pressure on to a fragmenting Muslim Spain. The Umayyad caliphs of Cordova, descendants of the Falcon of Quraysh, had been crowded out of power by their own cuckoos-in-the-nest – in their case, successive influxes of Berber mercenaries. The last Umayyad's reign had ended in 1031 in a welter of popular revolts, and that motley band of strongmen known as the Party Kings had cut up the caliphal cake of al-Andalus. Some of these rulers were of Arab lineage: the Abbadid mini-dynasty of Seville, for example, were descendants of the pre-Islamic Lakhmid kings of al-Hirah. Others were of Berber origin, or Saqalibah – 'Slavs', a term which in Spain meant slaves of European origin. But, perhaps predictably, the party turned into a brawl as the Party Kings started to squabble. Meanwhile the Reconquista pushed down into Iberia. After the fall of Toledo in 1085, when it looked as if Cordova itself would be next, an emergency meeting of Spanish Muslim scholars issued their statement of the obvious: 'The Franks have conquered the cities of Islam, while our kings are busy fighting each other.' It was the same *cri de coeur* that would soon be heard in the Levant. Here in Spain, however, there was no longer a caliph, even an impotent one, to cry out to. So the appeal for help was directed to the only united Muslim power in the region, a conglomeration of Sanhajah Berber tribes across the strait in North Africa. They called themselves al-Murabitun, 'Defenders of the Frontier Forts', and, not unlike that of the slightly later Crusading order of the Templars, the name has both holy and warlike resonances.

Known in English by their Hispanicized name, the Almoravids were the lesser of two evils for Spanish Islam. With their strange tongue and their fashion for male veiling, they seemed as alien to Arab ears and eyes as the Franks. But as the Arab ruler of Seville, al-Mu'tamid ibn Abbad, put it, 'It is better for our children to herd the camels of the Veiled Ones than the swine of the Franks'. The second option was real: later on in the Reconquista, according to a German visitor, Spanish Christians used the threat of compulsory swine-herding to keep their Muslim subjects in line. In the event, a different fate awaited al-Mu'tamid's heirs when the Almoravids took over and dethroned the Party Kings. His young grandson, who had borne the honorific title Fakhr al-Dawlah, 'Glory of the State', became a refugee in Morocco, working the bellows of a goldsmith to keep the family alive. With that boy, one more branch of the 800-year, 4,000-kilometre tree sprung from the ancient Lakhmid ruler Imru' al-Qays ibn Amr, first 'king of all the Arabs', withered into oblivion.

Spain had been the last major dominion of the Arab empire that had remained under indisputably Arab rulers. Ibn Khaldun was to write of the

Almoravid takeover that, with it, 'Arab rule dwindled to nothing, and the Arab tribes faded away'. It seemed to be the mirror-image of that Arab fall in the east. But in fact the fade-out would end in a small but grand finale: at the tail-end of the world, the successors to the Falcon of Quraysh would have their swan song.

For the moment, however, not only were Latin Christians and Muslim Berbers between them squeezing Arabs out of Spain. In the last third of the eleventh century, pressure was also increasing on Arabs in Sicily, another outstation of the Arab empire and 'the daughter of al-Andalus'. Sicily's recent history had indeed been a microcosm of Spain's, with an Arab dynasty, the Kalbids, running to seed and being supplanted by a tangled growth of warlords. This time the pressure on them came from that exceptionally mobile race of raiders – perhaps the sea-borne European equivalent to Arabs – the Normans, the former Norsemen (simultaneously, they were taking over a more marginal European island – Britain). The result was that reverse migration accelerated, taking asylum seekers from Spain and Sicily across the water to the urban centres of North Africa where their fellow Arabs were concentrated. The migrants would take with them an almost unbearable load of nostalgia, especially for their lost Andalusian paradise,

> The meadow-land of all the world, for all the rest's a wilderness . . .

But if Arabs themselves were in retreat, their culture and language continued to advance across the western part of their old empire.

TRANSFORMATIONS AND EXHUMATIONS

The Berber Almoravids did not just occupy Arab territory: they also took over Arab history by genealogically arabianizing themselves. Arab political might had ebbed away, but Arabs still retained a powerful aura, as founders of a great faith and culture: by tapping this numinous force, Berbers – B-team players in history – saw themselves as increasing their own prestige and legitimacy. Picking up loose ends of legends in which pre-Islamic Himyari expeditions had become entangled with Alexander the Great's conquests and with the even more ancient Phoenician colonization in North Africa, Berbers would weave a web of myth in which they claimed a South Arabian origin. The Almoravid conqueror of Spain, Yusuf ibn Tashfin, is thus always called 'al-Himyari' in the traditional histories. Sober historians like Ibn Khaldun would dismiss the claims; the myth of the Arabian-Berber link, however, is still alive in our less sober present.

In the following century, the Almoravids were followed into Spain and supplanted there by another great Berber conglomeration, also usually known by the Hispanic version of their name, the Almohads. As the Arabic name – al-Muwahhidun, 'the Unifiers' or 'Unitarians' – reveals, they too used religion to create a strong political bloc: as in early Islam, the main message of the Qur'an, that of *tawhid* or the unity of the divine, provided them with a totalitarian template for earthly life. By imposing a oneness that was both theological and political, the Almohad founder Muhammad ibn Tumart forged a super-tribal unity among Berbers that attempted to rerun Arab history from the time of Muhammad ibn Abd Allah, the Prophet. (The template, and even the name, 'al-Muwahhidun', would be reused again another 600 years on by the Arabian reformer Muhammad ibn Abd al-Wahhab: his own Unitarians are still active, even if they are usually known today, after their founder, as 'Wahhabis'.)

Within a generation, the Almohad movement became a dynasty, and the dynasty a new counter-caliphate: for the first time in its 500-year history, the title of 'caliph' was assumed by overt non-Arabs and non-Qurashis. But from their rough origins in tribal Berber North Africa, the Almohads swiftly translated themselves into natural denizens of the urban Arab culture of al-Andalus. In particular Yusuf ibn Abd al-Mu'min, the second Almohad caliph, who ruled 1163–84, was a scholar of *hadith* and philosophy who mixed with some of the greatest and freest minds of the day. Thus the Almohads were a repeat not just of early Islam, but of 300 years of Arab history, from the tribal fastness of Arabia to the cultivated, cosmopolitan court of al-Ma'mun in Baghdad – but replayed *prestissimo*. The speed and strangeness of the transformation seemed wondrous to the Berbers themselves. One day, the Berber poet al-Jarawi, who composed in Arabic, and the Berber physician al-Ghumari, went to call on Yusuf. Hearing that they were at his palace gate, the caliph exclaimed,

> 'Ah, the wonders of the world: a poet from [the Berber tribe of] Jarawah, and a physician from [the Berber tribe of] Ghumarah.' The comment reached al-Jarawi, and he said [quoting from the Qur'an], '"And he puts forth for Us a parable, and forgets his own creation –" for more

> wonderful still than either of us, by Allah, is a caliph from [the Berber tribe of] Kumyah.'

Arabs may have become the passive onlookers of history, but their own great past would be plagiarized again and again among the ruins of their empire.

During Yusuf the Almohad's reign, in 1169, but at the far end of the Mediterranean, his powerful Kurdish namesake Yusuf ibn Ayyub entered that other great centre of Arab urban culture, Cairo. First his uncle Shirkuh, then, on the latter's sudden death, Yusuf himself – better known as Salah al-Din or Saladin – became nominal viziers to the Fatimid caliph. That, however, was as far as niceties went. As others had done before them, the Kurds played the sectarian card: they were orthodox Sunnis, their suit matched that of the Sunni majority population, and they soon trumped the heterodox Isma'ili Fatimids. In 1171, Saladin abolished the Fatimid caliphate and re-established the nominal sovereignty of the Abbasid caliph in Baghdad.

The Fatimids' dubious arabness had always been the skeleton in the dynastic cupboard. Saladin, however, made no bones about his own antecedents: as with the Almoravids, there were attempts to arabize the Ayyubid pedigree, but Saladin himself dismissed them. The great commander had a good working knowledge of Arabic, and could quote poetry; his younger brother composed proficient Arabic verses. But, for these Kurdish dynasts of the new, post-Arab age, as for most of the peoples of the former Arab empire, arabness of blood no longer mattered. What counted was arabness of mind, instilled by constant draughts of language from the holy chalice of the Qur'an and from the ever-expanding literature of Islam; often too from the more ancient vessel of pre-Islamic poetry. Earlier, rougher arrivistes like the Berber Almoravids might have claimed an imaginary transfusion of ennobling Arab blood, but now ancestry was no longer so important. This is clear in *Notable Deaths*, the great cumulative biographical dictionary of the Arabic world compiled by the thirteenth-century Ibn Khallikan (himself of Iranian origin), many of whose notable dead have been exhumed in this chapter: occasionally the book gives long pedigrees going back to Arabia for older entries, but they dwindle as the centuries progress. Arab origins were becoming as irrelevant as Arab caliphs.

All the same, Arabia itself remained the holy land. Saladin exhumed his uncle Shirkuh and his own father, Ayyub, from their tombs in Cairo and sent them for reburial in Medina. The two dead Kurds were not alone in making the journey. There were even instances of corpses being taken to circumambulate the Ka'bah and perform the other Meccan rites before burial. Such posthumous pilgrimages were a reflection of what had happened to Arabdom and to Islam. Before, the Egyptians had fought to keep the body of Nafisah, a fifth-generation descendant of Muhammad, when her husband had wanted to return it to her home town, Medina: they meant to make a corner of their foreign field for ever Arabia, for ever holy. Now, in contrast, Egyptian corpses of Kurdish origin were heading for Muhammad's city, and the dust of Arabia itself was being internationalized. It was another aspect of the reverse conquest, of the opening up to others not just of Arab minds and Arab genes, but even of the sacred earth of their 'Island'.

Live Kurds, however, found no rest in the peninsula. The Ayyubids managed to set up a branch of their dynasty in Yemen; its ruler, Saladin's brother Turanshah, soon became homesick for Cairo, and complained of the impossibility of getting ice in his punishing posting. Another Ayyubid ruler in Yemen lost his mind. Except as a destination for pilgrimage, the Arabs' 'Island' had regressed into a state of isolation from which parts of it have only emerged in very recent times. (I have heard echoes of Turanshah's complaints from Cairenes who served time as soldiers and teachers in Yemen in the 1960s and 1970s.) The regression had begun long before, with the shift of Arab power to Damascus, then Baghdad. But it had accelerated as Arabs lost power entirely and 'turned in on themselves', as Ibn Khaldun had put it. Now, however, introversion was affecting Arabs everywhere. It is symptom enough that the Frankish historians of the Crusades rarely mention Arabs: they almost always call their opponents 'Saracens' – a word of disputed origin, bristling with contrary etymologies, but already in use for many centuries.

For the Franks, the most celebrated Saracen was no genetic Arab, but that borderless product of the post-Arab Arabic empire, Saladin. A century and a half after his death, he would be remembered in Europe as the model of Saracen knighthood: England's Black Prince had Saladin's exploits embroidered on his bed-curtains, and Boccaccio embroidered his life, in words, in the *Decameron*. At home, he towers over the middle history of the old Arab imperial heartland – a member of an Iranian race, albeit born in Iraq, raised in the service of Turkic rulers in Syria, himself ruling in Egypt and Syria, fighting across the Levant and dying in Damascus. He has the longest entry in *Notable Deaths*, longer than any prince or poet, caliph or commander of actual Arab origin. Like Kafur, the black eunuch slave who ruled Egypt two centuries before him, we remember Saladin in Arabic terms. He needed no imaginary transfusion of Arab blood; instead, he was the perfect product of the fusion catalysed by Muhammad's revolution, and by the even older catalyst of language.

TALLY-HO

All these incomers, Frankish, Kurdish, Berber, may have finished off the remains of the Arab *Staatsnation*. But the Arabic *Kulturnation* was still in good shape, and growing. Its influence would not only spread to Muslims like Saladin, but would cross over into Christendom. Spain, Sicily and the south of mainland Italy had long been interfaces for the transfer of Arabic culture. This is clear from the number and nature of Arabic words that infiltrated their languages. We have already noted that Spanish uses around 4,000 Arabic loan words. These are not just the vocabulary of exotica: even something as basic as the respectful pronoun for 'you', *usted*, is from the Arabic *ustadh*, 'master, professor', itself from the Persian *ustad*. In traditional Sicilian dialect, there are other down-to-earth loan words in the many terms of Arabic origin used by farmers; among the stranger Sicilian arabica is the name of Piazza Ballarò in Palermo, once the Arabic Suq Balhara, a market for foreign luxuries that took the Arabic name of a famous Indian monarch, Balhara.

The Crusades accelerated the process of transfer, spreading Arabic words and Levantine ideas much further afield in Europe. Not surprisingly, many military and associated innovations were imported from the east, such as crossbows, carrier-pigeons and maybe even heraldic charges. But the inspiration went further. The first organized European hospitals were probably influenced by Levantine models, and life in general was enriched by physical imports – for example of crops like rice, lemons and sugar cane, and of many new types of textiles and dyestuffs. And the fact that even the more peripheral Europeans took part in the general Crusading mobilization meant that technology and vocabulary were flung far across the continent. Thus, even English has well over 2,000 Arabic-origin words. If you write a cheque (*sakk*, written agreement) for a carafe (*ghiraf*, measure for scooping grain) of alcohol (*al-kuhl*), or for a coffee (*qahwah*, admittedly long post-Crusades, but the word is an old Arabic one for wine), a sherbet, a sorbet with syrup, or a glass of old-fashioned shrub (all four from the root *shariba*, to drink); if you wear chiffon (*shiff*, diaphanous cloth), mohair (*mukhayyar*, 'select' cloth), muslin (*mawsili*, cloth from Mosul), satin (*zaytuni*, from Citong, an old name for Quanzhou in China) or even a jacket (*shakkah*, chain-mail upper garment) or a jumper (*jubbah*, gown); if you sit on a sofa (*suffah*, bench) or a mattress (*matrah*, mat, sleeping-mat) stroking your tabby cat (*'attabi*, striped cloth, named from a quarter of Baghdad), then you are using Arabic. Much of that Arabic came to Europe during the love–hate, clinch-and-grapple period of encounters via Crusaders and Reconquistadors, merchants, pilgrims and scholars. Perhaps, too, if you go hunting and cry, 'Tally-ho!', you are using Syrian dialect, *ta'ali hun*, 'come here!' . . . Perhaps: for as with so much in etymology there is nothing to prove it.

Looking beyond the dictionary to the atlas, Arabic is even further flung. It is not only confined to Spain and its many Arabic placenames (like the Guadalquivir – al-Wadi al-Kabir, the Big Valley). Via the Iberian Peninsula, Arabic makes it to London's Trafalgar Square (al-Taraf al-Agharr, the Gleaming Point), and to the New World and San Francisco Bay, where Alcatraz is the island of *al-ghattas*, the diving bird, the pelican (the word wandered even further and metamorphosed into 'albatross'). On the Brazilian coast, Recife is the Arabic *rasif*, quay, while up the Amazon one can encounter people of mixed Portuguese and native blood called, disparagingly, *mamalucos* (*mamluk*s, slaves). Beyond the Andes and out to sea again, even Chile's Robinson Crusoe Island has a local administrator called an *alcalde* (*al-qadi*, the judge) and a guest-house called an *aldea* (*al-day'ah*, the country estate).

KINGS WEAR KUFIC

This sort of linguistic permeation was organic, and slow. But there were also swift and highly organized transfers of Arabic culture and knowledge to Europe. When Alfonso VI of León and Castile took Toledo in 1085, he ensured that the old Arabic learning continued, and even called himself 'King of the Two Faiths'; the present heir to the British throne, Prince Charles, would approve (he has announced his intention to be 'Defender of the Faiths'). Similarly, when the king of Aragón captured Murcia nearly two centuries later, he was impressed by a scholar of the city, Muhammad ibn Ahmad al-Raquti,

> a scholar of high lineage, well acquainted with the ancient arts of logic, geometry, computation, music and medicine, who was also a philoso-

> pher, an accomplished physician and God's gift to languages [literally 'a sign of Allah' – an *ayat Allah* or 'Ayatollah' – in languages] . . . The tyrant of the Romans [i.e. the king of Aragón] recognized his worth when he captured Murcia, and built him a school where he could teach Muslims, Christians and Jews, and this king continued to regard him with great favour.

The Christian reconquerors had realized that by winning territory they were losing the knowledge that had always filtered through to them. They therefore founded programmes of translation from Arabic, and maintained the old Arabic academic traditions, which continued to permeate through to further Europe. Thus, medical students at the University of Paris would study Arabic texts on physic in Latin translation, and would sometimes benefit from human teachers – 'Moors' who went north in the brain-drain of the age; their students were known as *arabizantes*. Such a monopoly did Arabic learning gain over the medical faculties of Europe that Petrarch took to mocking Italian arabophiles:

> We [Italians] may often equal, and occasionally surpass, the Greeks, and therefore all nations – except for the Arabs, as you say! O madness! O vertigo! O benumbed or extinguished genius of Italy!

Petrarch's arabophobe attitude is said to have become so extreme that he would refuse to take medications with Arabic names.

As Petrarch's lamentations suggest, Italy as well as Spain was a major channel for the transfer of Arabic science into further Europe. This was especially true of Sicily and southern Italy under the rule of the protean Norman and Hohenstaufen kings. In particular, the significance of Norman Sicily was far wider in space and time than its own limited confines: it was not a mere afterthought to the Italian mainland, but the centre of an interconnecting zone that was truly *mediterranean* – mediating between territories and their cultures. A material illustration of this is the old Graeco-Italian wind rose used by navigators. Its centre 'seems to be somewhere off Sicily, the heart of the Mediterranean', for it mixes Latinate-origin terms like 'Levante' ('rising [of the sun]') for the east wind with Arabic-origin ones – Souróko for the south-east wind (*shuruq*, also 'sunrise'; cf. *scirocco*). Another tangible illustration is the magnificent mantle made for the Norman king of

Sicily Roger II (r. 1130–54), embroidered with lions, camels and a palm tree and bordered by an Arabic inscription in monumental Kufic script recording its origin in the royal workshops and its date, AH 528 or AD 1133–4. The mantle is now in Vienna, as it was used for no less than five centuries by Roger's successors, the Holy Roman Emperors, as a coronation robe. At the most sacred moment in their lives, they would clothe themselves in Arabic.

For a few decades, Sicily seemed to be the centre of a world with few boundaries. Its centrality was celebrated in a huge planisphere – a flattened hemisphere – weighing 400 pounds and teeming with toponyms, made for Roger by a North African scholar, al-Idrisi. The planisphere itself, the consummation of geographical knowledge to date, has not survived, but al-Idrisi's accompanying book is extant, a map in words. The Island of Anqiltarrah (England), for example, resembles an ostrich's head (of which Cornwall is the 'beak'). And there is human geography too, for 'its people are steadfast, firm and resolute. It always rains there'. (Even then, stiff upper lips and wet weather were prominent features of England.) To render them in Arabic script, al-Idrisi necessarily tweaks placenames, such as Hastinkash (Hastings), and my own local metropolis when in England, Aghrimas (Grimsby). More notably, he also arabizes his Norman patron with stately rhyming prose and regnal names borrowed from the Abbasids and their sultanic sidekicks, extolling '*Rujar al-Mu'tazz bi 'llah wa 'l-Muqtadir bi-qudratih . . . Mu'izz Imam Rumiyah*', Roger, the Glorier in the strength of Allah, Empowered by the might of Allah . . . the Strengthener of the Imam [the Pope] of Rome.

Another Arab in Norman Sicily was Ibn Jubayr, already quoted above on the Crusades. He is a sort of Usamah Ibn Munqidh through the looking-glass: Usamah fought, observed and befriended the inhabitants of Christendom on his own territory and terms; Ibn Jubayr travelled through their parallel world. He was in Sicily in the time of Roger II's grandson, William II (r. 1166–89), who both read and wrote Arabic well and had a whole palaceful of Muslim functionaries, including his head chef. Sicily for Ibn Jubayr was a land of 'lofty palaces and elegant gardens, particularly in the royal seat, Palermo'. And just as the king's grandfather, Roger, had attracted scholars like al-Idrisi, William too was a patron of the Arabic learned:

> Whenever he is informed that a physician or astrologer is passing through his country, he orders that the man be detained – and then bestows on him such a copious salary that he gives up thought of

> his homeland! May Allah by His grace protect the Muslims from such temptation . . .

Perhaps the last sentence is a sideways sneer at people like al-Idrisi, inveigled into the Nazarene's service; perhaps there is also a hint of envy, given the decline so depressingly evident in much of Ibn Jubayr's Arabic home territory. For, in contrast to his guarded enthusiasm for Palermo, the traveller had summed up Baghdad thus:

> Of this ancient city, even if it remains the seat of the Abbasid caliphate, and the base of the mission of the imams descended from the Hashimi clan of Quraysh, most of the traces are gone, and nothing of it remains but its famous name.

The mid-point of an earlier boundless world in the ninth century, Baghdad had later lost its old centrality to newer hubs in Cairo and Cordova. Now, however, the centre of hemiglobal gravity was shifting again, towards a pre-renascent Europe; it hovered for a time mid-Mediterranean, in Sicily, and the open sea-roads drew men with open minds – geographers like al-Idrisi, travellers like Ibn Jubayr, polymaths like the Syrian Ibn Wasil, even accomplished eulogizing poets like the Egyptian Ibn al-Qalaqis – from the Arabic world to the courts of Palermo and its offshoot in Calabria. The Baghdadis, meanwhile, whom Ibn Jubayr had found alternately ingratiating, grasping and arrogant, had not yet caught up with the reality of their marginalization, for 'it is as if they do not believe that anywhere or anyone else exists on God's earth'. He had been kinder to the caliph of the day, al-Nasir, whom he spotted crossing the Tigris:

> a young man with a full fair beard clipped short, handsome and good-looking, of pale complexion and medium height, with a bright and pleasant face, about twenty-five years old, wearing a white robe like a gown with gold stripes and, on his head, a gold-embroidered cap with a band of black fur of some valuable kind such as marten or a higher quality. This Turkish style he adopts in an attempt to go about incognito.

That sort of word-portrait is rare in Arabic prose, and it makes the bright young caliph stand out even more prominently against the gloomy background of Baghdad. But it is, none the less, a portrait of doomed youth in a dying city, where to go unnoticed one had to adopt the dress of the Turkic interloper. And, within the span of a human lifetime, far worse was to befall Baghdad and its Arab caliphs.

A TALE TO DEVOUR ALL TALES

If Ibn Jubayr the Frank-watcher was a kind of reflected Usamah, then the slightly later Yaqut al-Rumi ('the Roman', i.e. the Byzantine) was a sort of inverse Idrisi, for he was a descriptive geographer – among his other skills – but one who crossed from Christendom to the world of Islam. Unlike al-Idrisi, however, Yaqut had no choice in his transition, as he was brought to Baghdad as a five- or six-year-old slave from Byzantine territory. An illiterate merchant bought him, soon realized that Yaqut was exceptionally smart, and gave him an education. The young slave went on business trips on his master's behalf, especially around the Gulf; later, they fell out and Yaqut was given his freedom. Thereafter he set out on his own career of travel and writing. Long after the end of Arab political power, Arab language and culture were still assimilating outsiders like him and launching them into the mobile world which they had created.

Yaqut was the epitome of the scholar-gypsy, a man who could quote from the heart the old sayings about the blessings of mobility: *Fi 'l-harakah barakah wa 'l-ightirab da'iyat al-iktisab*, 'God gives grace to those who move from place to place; exile's pain can lead to gain.' In the well-stocked libraries of Marw, in modern-day Turkmenistan, he found books 'that made me forget home and homeland, nearest and dearest . . . I fell upon them like the greediest glutton . . .' He travelled throughout his life and, appropriately, spent the last part of it in a caravanserai outside Aleppo. The journey he never made, however, was the one that would have taken him away from his roots: he longed to translate himself from Yaqut, 'Ruby' – a name only given to slaves – into Ya'qub, 'Jacob', but the new name never took root. In the end, the literary name he earned was far greater. His dictionaries of Arabic poets and prose writers are still indispensable nearly 800 years after his death. And it is fitting that such a footloose scholar is best remembered for his great Arabic geographical dictionary, *Mu'jam al-buldan*, *The Lexicon of Lands*. And yet Yaqut's sort of mobility, so much a feature of and a reason for the continuing spread of Arabic culture, suddenly found itself under deadly threat.

In 1219 there was a double disaster, with the Crusaders taking the important Egyptian port of Damietta and – 'the greatest calamity of all' – the coming of the Mongols to the lands of Islam. There are different explanations for the appearance of Chingiz Khan and his Mongol horsemen in Khurasan, at this time part of the territory of Khwarizm, whose capital was south of the Aral Sea. One is that the expanionist Turkic Khwarizm Shah destroyed his buffer states in eastern Central Asia and thus let the Mongols in. Another says that the bright young Abbasid Caliph al-Nasir, his brightness now dulled, encouraged the Mongols to invade Khwarizm in order to deflect a Khwarizmian invasion of Iraq. Yet another explanation has it that the Khwarizmian generals beat off the advancing Mongols, but then fell out over booty and let them in. Whatever the reason, they would probably have come anyway.

Their advent seemed apocalyptic. 'The news of the Tatars,' as Arabic writers called them (after a Turkic people they had subjugated and who then joined their campaigns), 'is a tale to devour all tales, an account that rolls into oblivion all accounts, a history to make one forget all histories.' So it seemed to Abd al-Latif, a physician of Baghdad. In contrast Ibn al-Athir, the great contemporary chronicler, saw the Mongols in the light of a dark future: 'Probably not until the end of time will a catastrophe of such magnitude be seen again.' One of those caught up in the catastrophe was Yaqut. As he wrote in 1220 from Mosul to a patron in Aleppo, his bookish Central Asian sojourn east of the Caspian had been ended by the Mongol advance, a calamity

> that whitens the hair of youth and rips out the guts of the brave, that blackens the heart and confounds to the core . . . I reached – but only just – the safety of Mosul after suffering many perils and trials, sorely tested, my sins atoned for. Often I beheld death and destruction, for my path took me between drawn swords, through the ranks of routed armies . . . wading through blood outpoured that cried for vengeance . . . In short, had not my appointed span still had time to run, I would have joined the thousand thousand thousand thousand thousand or more victims of the godless Tatars.

However many zeros the number of the dead actually included, even apologists for the Mongols never denied that dreadful urban massacres took place. At the same time, a major depopulation of the countryside and the resulting neglect of sensitive irrigation systems caused rural devastation; from this, arguably, parts of Central Asia have never recovered. As for the old tide of Arabdom, which had rolled on and on and absorbed almost all those whom it reached, it seemed that it had finally turned; or, rather, had been rolled back by a force greater than itself.

THE FALL OF THE FIGUREHEAD

Following their invasion of the east, there was a long lull in the Mongol advance. But in 1258, under Chingiz Khan's grandson Hulagu, it would sweep on to the old capital of the Arab empire and roll its last living symbol into oblivion.

Iraq was already in trouble. There was not only the general decline from greatness noted by Ibn Jubayr in Baghdad; society itself was in decay. The same traveller passed through al-Kufah and found it more than half-ruined in raids by the Khafajah tribe. In the following, thirteenth century, Baghdadi townsfolk often took to violent rioting, with the various quarters of the city battling each other. But all this was only a minor prelude to the destruction wrought by the Mongols. In the most usual account, it was the vizier of the last caliph in Baghdad, al-Musta'sim – a great-grandson of the fair-bearded al-Nasir – who incited them to take Baghdad: as a Shi'i, the story goes, the vizier was incensed by a punitive caliphal raid on a Shi'i town. If true, the account would be the starkest example of disunity leading to destruction: divided we fall. But it may well be an example of anti-Shi'i propaganda. Whatever the case, the Mongol momentum now seemed unstoppable. They were less a factor in history than a force of nature.

The fate of al-Musta'sim is uncertain. He was either strangled, drowned in the Tigris, or tied in a sack and kicked to death. It sounds harsh to say that the Abbasid caliphate was thus put out of its misery; but it had been living on borrowed time. Exactly 500 years before, the first of its thirty-six caliphs in Baghdad and the founder of the city, al-Mansur, had begun the borrowing by relying on slave-troops; less than 200 years after that, the alien praetorians had smothered Arab power; since then, the caliphate had been in a vegetative state, on life-support provided by its own Turkic or Iranian minders. But even at its height, the intimations of mortality were there. In the time of al-Rashid and al-Ma'mun, the Arab philosopher and astrologer al-Kindi

> is said to have made complete forecasts concerning the Abbasid dynasty. He indicated that its destruction and the fall of Baghdad would take place in the middle of the seventh [thirteenth] century. We have not found any information concerning al-Kindi's book, and we have not seen anyone who has seen it. Perhaps it was lost with those books which Hulagu, the ruler of the Tatars, threw into the Tigris.

'Only in war,' as Mandelstam knew,

> our fate has consummation,
> And divination too will perish then.

The Abbasids would have that shadowy afterlife in Egypt. But the destruction of al-Musta'sim and Baghdad was a massive psychological blow to Arabdom: both the human focus and the geographical locus of arabness had been wiped off the map. Not only that: although Arab political power had disappeared long before, Arabic culture had gone from strength to strength. Now, the coming of the hordes seemed to put into reverse 600 years of forward motion. The Mongols drove Yaqut and other standard-bearers of Arabic culture before them, pushing them back to the west; they overwhelmed the urban centres of that culture, and razed the libraries where Yaqut had lost himself – and his slave origins – in the study of a glorious Arab past. They wiped out history itself.

It seemed, too, that the Mongol hordes had wiped out 600 years in which *hadarah*, settled civilization, had been in the ascendancy over *badawah*, tribal nomadism. From now on, for example, tribal Arabs would continually raid into the settled heartland of Iraq, preying on farms and villages. Such changes were part of a much wider trend. Ibn Khaldun, in a moment of ballistic overview, saw the Umayyads and the Abbasids not only as a single Qurashi dynasty, but also as the culmination of a series of polities that began with those of prehistoric, settled South Arabia and elided into those of Islam – the movement that had brought together the settled and the nomadic, peoples and tribes:

> [There were] Ad and Thamud, the Amalekites, Himyar, and the Tubba's [the later Himyari kings] . . . and then, there was the Mudar [North Arabian] dynasty in Islam, the Umayyads and the Abbasids.

But with the fall of the latter, 'when the Arabs forgot their religion, they no longer had any connection with political leadership, and they returned to their desert origins'. It is striking that Ibn Khaldun saw Arabs as losing their 'religion' . . . He does not mean that all Arabs suddenly stopped calling themselves Muslims or gave up praying (although bedouins, at least in townsmen's eyes, have always been virtual infidels). Rather, the equilibrium Islam had created between Arabian peoples and Arab tribes was now being upset. Moreover, Arabs as a whole, for whom Islam had always been a sociopolitical phenomenon as well as a faith, had lost something else – not just the equililbrium, but the fulcrum on which it had been balanced. Al-Radi, who had died more than 300 years earlier, had been 'the last real caliph', that is, the last to preach at Friday prayers. But the office of imam, prayer leader, had persisted in potential as long as there was a caliphal line in Baghdad. For the vast Sunni majority the Abbasids had always been 'the imams descended from the Hashimi clan of Quraysh', as Ibn Jubayr had described them. An imam is first and foremost – in every sense – the leader of congregational prayer. Now, with the killing of al-Musta'sim, the line of imams was severed. For the first time since Abu Sufyan had watched his Hashimi cousin Muhammad leading the bowing ranks in Medina, and had marvelled at the vision of discipline never seen among Arabs, there was no leader of the unity, however symbolic. It didn't matter that, for centuries, caliphs had been no more than figureheads. Now they were gone, people realized that however broad the ranks of worshippers, however deep the rows, however various the people who made them up, it had been precisely the figurehead, the frontman, the imam, who had held them all together.

LOST BOYS

After the fall of Baghdad and the Abbasids, it seemed that the Mongols would follow through and wipe Islam off the map, even without the help of Crusaders and Reconquistadors. Where was the saviour, the Saladin of these latter, terrifying times?

Saladin's descendants had done what almost every dynasty before them had done: they had subcontracted security to Turkic military slaves, then fallen out fatally among themselves. And when the Cuckoo Syndrome operated yet again and the Turks took over, it was they who in 1260 would save Islam, stopping the Mongol advance almost at the gates of Africa, at Ayn

Jalut in Palestine. Moreover, they went on to do what no purely military Turkic power-holders had done before, and made themselves into a dynasty, or rather an establishment – that of the Mamluks, or Slave-soldiers. The establishment was self-perpetuating, and in a manner that ensured longevity much more successfully than the chancy business of begetting sons: Mamluk *amir*s constantly brought in selected new young recruits, mostly from the Qipchaq Turkic tribes settled to the north and east of the Black Sea, and later on from the Circassian peoples of the Caucasus. These recruits would rise through the ranks and recruit their own replacements, and so on *in saecula saeculorum*; or at least for the next 500 years and more, until the last Mamluks were defeated by the Napoleonic horde in 1798 and then finished off by Muhammad Ali Pasha in 1812.

As in all successful ruling cliques, the establishment was based on an elite education and the chance of glittering prizes. The recruits were placed in barrack-schools, divided into 'houses' with eunuch 'matrons', and taught Arabic and the basics of Islam. There was a particular focus on shooting, team games like polo, and, of course, on OTC drill. The idea was that the Mamluks would emerge from this as naturalized rulers and gentlemen,

> masters in the administration of kingdoms, leaders fighting the good fight on the path of Allah, men who knew how to rule, doing their utmost to display good manners and fending off the tyrannous and aggressive.

It might be the British self-image in its muscular imperial heyday. Qipchaq fathers queued up to send their sons to the Mamluk Rugbys and Wellingtons of Cairo. And there were no school fees! Instead, it was the fathers who got the fees (there was a downside: they would never see their sons again). Succession did become genetically dynastic from time to time. The prime example was that of the long-ruling Mamluk sultan al-Nasir (r. 1293–1340, with a couple of gaps), whose eight sons, two grandsons and a great-grandson reigned after him. The average reign of these younger generations, however, was about three years, and most of them were under the heavy hands of Mamluk *amir*s from outside the family.

It was a singular system. But it worked, for under the Mamluks Egypt and Syria were reasonably stable, and Cairo boomed, 'boundless in multitude of buildings,' as Ibn Battutah's *Travels* describes it under Sultan al-Nasir in the 1320s, 'peerless in beauty and splendour . . . she surges as the waves of the sea with her throngs of folk and can scarce contain them'. In fact Cairo was probably the biggest city in the world at the time outside China. Much of its prosperity was due to its being a double metropolis – of both the Mamluk *Staatsnation* and the Arabic *Kulturnation*. The Turkic soldiers and their Circassian successors were politically dominant, but the overwhelming cultural power was always that of high Arabic, that first and still unbeaten conqueror. For the Arabic alchemy of Egypt worked on Mamluks too: Turks and others were arabicized, never the other way round. The arabicized, however, mixing with the subject-people, lost their lofty detachment and ceased to belong to the ruling class. But the elite was always topped up with new young recruits – lost boys from beyond the Crimea and the Caucasus, whose own offspring would eventually find their place in a new world, ever-diversifying but always united by Arabic.

At the same time, 'true' Arabs were not completely out of the picture, and some had maintained a measure of political independence. But they were back exactly where they had started, 'on a rock between two lions'. For a time after the Mamluks had stopped the Mongols in their tracks, the two military superpowers glared at each other across the northern Fertile Crescent, the Mamluks in Egypt and Syria, the Mongols in Iraq. Tribal Arabs in the region and its adjoining wildernesses had reverted, meanwhile, to their position in ancient (and also coming colonial) times, when rival empires chose 'kings of the Arabs'. One example was Muhanna ibn Isa, the Mamluk-appointed *amir* of the *'arab* in the bedouin-lands of Syria. Muhanna was the leader of the tribe of Tayyi', a force in the area since well before Islam. Now, like the ancient Lakhmids of al-Hirah and other, even more ancient, mercenary tribes in the fringes of the Fertile Crescent, he went about playing the great powers against each other and switching sides as it suited him: he fought the Mongols on behalf of the Mamluks; then fell out with the Mamluks and went over to the Mongols, and on their behalf attacked Aleppo with 25,000 tribesmen. Later, after a period independent of both sides, when he survived by the old Tayyi' métier of raiding pilgrims in the desert, he returned to the Mamluk fold. His son and successor Fayyad got into trouble with the Mamluks by plundering merchants and did a flit back to the Mongols. 'He was badly behaved', his biography concludes curtly. The hordes may have bottled most Arabs up; some, however, remained mobile, at least in their loyalties.

MONGOLS AND MICROBES

The Mongol columns, advancing in their scaly armour, had resembled a crocodile devouring Eurasia. In religion, however, they were chameleons: at least nominally Buddhist early on, they also clung to even more ancient shamanistic practices; in the period after Chingiz Khan, they passed through a spectrum of beliefs, including various shades of Christianity. But towards the end of the thirteenth century, while their far eastern wing morphed into the Buddhist-Confucian Yuan dynasty of China, their three western divisions began to take on an Islamic colouring. Like that first conqueror from Arabia, the Arabic language, Islam itself seemed indefatigable, even when the people who had first professed it were reeling from defeat. But the Mongols resembled the last great wave of nomads from the east, the Saljuq Turks, in that they adopted Persian rather than Arabic as their cultural first language. Thus the hordes of Chingiz and Hulagu added a further barrier between the Arabic and Persian parts of the Islamic world: the Saljuqs had drawn a linguistic curtain across the south-western entrance to Asia; the Mongols turned it into a shutter, and Arabic was further diminished as the paramount language of the Islamic world. Yet, at the same time, they opened a door. Having digested their victories, they settled down to the business of ruling in relative peace, and presided over the so-called Pax Mongolica. For the first time since the brief height of the Arab empire in the Abbasid ninth century, truly trans-hemispheric trade and travel were up and running once more . . . and then, just when you thought it was safe to take to the Silk Road again, the Black Death struck.

The first onslaught of plague in the 1340s and 1350s killed perhaps a third of humanity in a swathe across Eurasia and North Africa, and it did so at least partly because of the mobility which the newly unrolling land- and sea-roads offered microbes as well as mankind. The Black Death seemed like another horde from the East:

> Ah, woe to him on whom it calls! / It found the chinks in China's walls – / they had no chance against its advance. / It sashayed into Cathay, made hay in Hind / and sundered souls in Sind. / It put the Golden Horde to the sword, transfixed Transoxiana and pierced Persia. / Crimea cringed and crumpled . . .

Thus wrote the Syrian scholar Ibn al-Wardi; and there is a touch of levity in the original too, black humour in the face of black horror. The history from which it comes ends with a crowd of obituaries, and then stops mid-chapter: the Death had killed the author too. The Silk Roads may have unrolled again, but along them, as Ibn Khaldun put it, had rolled 'the all-consuming plague, rolling up Earth's carpet and everything upon it'. It all seemed as final as the fate of caliphs.

But there was more to come, late in the fourteenth century, in the form of the delayed Mongol aftershock of Timur Lang or Tamerlane, who shared an ancestor with Chingiz Khan. His invasions reaped another harvest of death, particularly grim among the sedentary Arabic-speaking populations of the Levant. In Aleppo, for example, he had the heads of the dead arranged in pretty pyramids, all 20,000 faces looking outwards. (Alas for Aleppo: Hulagu in 1260, Muhanna in 1311, Timur in 1400; more recently, in 2016, Bashshar al-Asad.) Next came Damascus. Ibn Khaldun was in the city as the Mongols bore down on it, left there in the lurch by the fleeing Mamluk sultan in whose suite he had come; Timur, however, had a soft spot for scholars, and spared the historian's life. But there was a *quid pro quo*: Ibn Khaldun found himself having to write Timur a guidebook to North Africa, which was then translated into Mongolian. For a man who sought to out-conquer Chingiz Khan, this was inviting a Baedecker raid on the entire west wing of the Islamic world. Ibn Khaldun did, however, salve his conscience by subsequently writing to the Berber sultan of Morocco and telling him what to expect, in the form of a useful description of Timur and his hordes.

The master of historical hindsight was too close to events to get the bigger picture. But he does give two glimpses of what Arabs had come to at this latest horrible juncture. At one end of the social scale, an Abbasid chancer was hanging around Timur, trying to get recognition from the warlord as a rival to the Mamluks' puppet caliph. At the other end, after his own close shave with the Mongols, Ibn Khaldun himself was plundered by bedouin Arabs on his way back to Egypt, and left naked in the wilderness.

AN AGE OF SURFACES

If Timur was planning incursions into the Maghrib, Ibn Khaldun's guidebook in hand, he never got to carry them out. Had he done so, he would have found that in the far west, beyond Mamluks and Berbers, Arabs were singing their swan-song and basking in the last rays of their long imperial day, down on the Costa del Sol and in the lap of the Sierra Nevada. Spain's

Berber Almoravid rulers had given way to their fellow Berbers, the Almohads. But the advancing Reconquista had driven them out, leaving a tenuous pocket of Arab culture in Granada.

Perhaps because it was the last Arab state in the great diaspora beyond the Arabian subcontinent, a wizened rump of empire at the Andalusian peacock's tail, a parson's nose plucked bare of its dependencies and often paying tribute to its Castilian neighbours, Granada clung fast to its arabness. Its Nasrid rulers flaunted their descent from Khazraj, one of the two main tribes of Yathrib before it became Muhammad's Medina, and the arabness of the population was stressed by local historians. Granada had in fact been founded by Berbers; even so, and even if your family had been thoroughly arabized for nine generations, you could still be classed by unforgiving biographers as 'a [Berber] Masmudi client of [the Arabian Qurashi clan] Banu Makhzum'. This sort of genealogical apartheid had been largely abandoned elsewhere: it no longer reflected hybrid reality, nor did it do so in Granada, which was a racial paella compounded from Berbers, Goths, ex-slave 'Slavs' from across Europe, and Jews and Muslims of all sorts who had fled the Reconquista. In fourteenth-century Granada, Ibn Battutah even met immigrants from West Africa and India. 'True' Arabs (that is, Arabs in the patriline, however exotic their maternal ancestry), though, provided the garnish and the dominant flavour, and in this sense Granada was a boiled-down microcosm of the Arab empire as well as its last bastion. Its eventual end, too, was bathetically typical, as Castilian forces advanced on a state in which an uncle and a nephew were battling it out for possession of the sultanate. Granada was the victim of its own disunity as much as of Christian Spanish unity.

Granada's fall in 1492 came not many decades after the fall to the Muslim Ottomans of its mirror-image at the eastern end of the Mediterranean, Constantinople. There, in the eastern Roman empire, also shrunken to a rump of a city-state, the Palaeologue emperors had presided over a final flurry of artistic endeavour. The same happened under the Nasrids in Granada, and their most famous monument could not be more fitting. The sprawling palace of the Alhambra is important as it is the only such place that has survived; but it is also the perfect memorial to the stage-set Arab state that Granada had become. It is an architecture of facades, a pop-up palace adorned with beautiful, bombastic Arabic. If we look for solid architectural vigour at this time, we find it instead in the brutal-beautiful buildings of

Mamluk Cairo, like the mid-fourteenth-century mosque-*madrasah* of Sultan Hasan. In contrast, the Alhambra belongs to an age of surfaces, and it is as much text and textile as building. As the Granadan poet and vizier Ibn Zamrak wrote in an ode carved self-referentially in the palace's Hall of the Two Sisters,

> Fortune desires
> That I outshine all other monuments.
> What pleasure I provide for eyes to see!
> . . .
> Clothed in a woven raiment fine as this
> You can forget the busy looms of Yemen.

Building has become clothing, and the verse, its voice, is finely woven too; except that the reference to Yemen's looms has itself by now worn thin – 800 years earlier, the poet Imru' al-Qays had wrapped up his 'Suspended Ode' with an image of Yemeni cloth, and his successors had been churning out the same old simile ever since. Of course, thematic originality is the last thing one looks for in high Arabic poetry; it is about form, not content. But even the kindest critic would have to admit that the Arabic language, the ever-fresh first conqueror, was beginning to look a bit jaded. It had crossed continents; now it was doing crochet.

INSCRIPTIONS ON RUINS

The loss of literary vigour had begun centuries earlier, with the loss of rule; swords and pens had become blunt together. Of the great Arab art-form, poetry, it is often said by non-Arab commentators that there was little or nothing that was sharp or shining after the death of al-Ma'arri in 1058. A well-read critic from within the Arabic world can also admit, 'If I were asked to name a poet from [the twelfth century onward] I would be at a loss to answer'. There was always a lot of verse about; but less and less of it was poetry in its old sense of inspired, 'magical' utterance. As one observer has put it, poetry 'could not outrun its own shadow'. In fact the shadow was winning.

In Arabic literature as a whole, too, the old fires were burning out. The period is often called *'asr al-inhitat*, the Age of Decline; others have called it *'asr al-taraju'*, the Age of Retrogression. But whether downward or backward, it was also an age of going round and round, and the sum result was a descending spiral, a wheel not of fire but of waffle: 'It was an age of condensations and exegeses, of condensations of the condensations and exegeses of the exegeses, and of commentaries on all these.' The spiral accelerated with the centuries. Now it seemed that with the shock of the Mongols and the fall of the caliphate, Arabs had lost not only their great symbol of unity, but also their tutelary, literary spirit, their *genius linguae*; the introversion – Ibn Khaldun's 'turning in' – had reached the empty heart of the helix, culturally as well as politically. A century after Ibn Khaldun, the decline was even more painfully obvious. Recalling al-Sahib ibn Abbad's great tenth-century library with its sixty camel-loads of books on Arabic philology alone, the fifteenth-century literary historian al-Suyuti wrote, 'Most books disappeared in the upheavals caused by the Tatars and others, so that the works on philology surviving nowadays . . . would not make a load for a single camel'.

The spiral would continue to descend; some observers think it still does. In the diagnosis of Adonis, the Arabic world has been in retreat from modernity since the fall of Baghdad; in that of al-Jabiri, it has been ruled for all these centuries by what he calls 'the resigned mind'. And the poet Nizar Qabbani might be speaking of this same continuum, from the ruin of Baghdad through the fall of Granada to the latter-day ruins of Beirut, Baghdad again, Mosul, Palmyra, Aleppo . . . when he says,

> Half our verses are inscriptions . . . and what
> Use is an inscription when the building's falling down?

Or, indeed, being demolished by its own inhabitants?

FAREWELL THE CLARIONS

But not everything was falling down. If al-Ma'arri, born in 973, was the last great Arabic poet, his life also coincided with the birth of a whole new genre. *Maqamat*, tales of picaresque heroes told in rhyming prose, are the offspring of the magic speech of ancient seers and of the Qur'an, but twisted to a quite different end – storytelling – and packed with such verbal acrobatics that they sometimes read like *Finnegans Wake*. The stories and their cunning, cavorting characters quickly reached the furthest corners of the Arabic world; the influence of their devilishly clever prose can be heard in much of subsequent Arabic writing – as in that jingling account of the plague's progress quoted above – and is hard to escape from entirely, even for more minimalist modern-day authors.

The *maqamat* sparked off imitations in Persian and even Hebrew. Their magic realism also gave rise to something else: graphic illustration, all but unknown in earlier Arabic books (except scientific texts). The most celebrated example is a manuscript of al-Hariri's *Maqamat*, probably illustrated in Baghdad and dated 1237, a couple of decades before the city's fall to the Mongols. All the images are brilliant, jewel-like; but the most powerful and memorable of all is a tight group of horsemen, the mounted standard-bearers of the caliph. The uprights of their banners are bordered by diagonals of clarions and gonfalons; their eyes peer outwards beyond the margin of the page, as if they are ready for the off; horses champ, hoofs paw. All the old energy of empire seems captured in that frame.

The image is gorgeous, but doomed. The caliph, court and capital that it celebrates are doomed by the approaching hordes; but so too is a wider Arab world that still, just, looks to the caliph's standards as its rallying-point. And the image itself is fated to be the captive of its own success. Time and again, it has been reproduced on the covers and jackets of books on Arab history and culture (one of mine included). That, of course, shows just how brilliant it is; but it is a brilliance that highlights the long eclipse to come. It is as if every Arabic book on Western history and culture (not that there are many) had, say, the *Mona Lisa* on its cover. There would, of course, be plenty of brilliant 'Islamic' miniature painting to come; but it is Persian, Ottoman, Mughal. Painting in Arab lands never again quite attains the power and the splendour – indeed, the standard – of those standard-bearers; quite soon it fades to nothing. The horsemen are fated to march on, flying the flag, getting nowhere.

In the spheres of political power, prose, poetry and, now, painting, Arabs seemed stuck in a recurring present, following the path of pilgrimage, never leaving the frame. Admittedly, it didn't help to have Mongols and Mamluks, Berbers and Franks forming that inescapable border, blocking their access to the broad Eurasian stage of events; not to mention Timur and the Ottomans looming, just as that same Eurasia was convalescing after the first onslaught of the Black Death. But there would be an escape route, a back door via the fertile fringe of Arabia's coastline. For if continental prospects were blocked, there was still an ocean opening out from the far south of the Arabs' island: a whole monsoon world, from Mozambique to the Malacca Strait and beyond.

The hero of al-Hariri's *Maqamat*, Abu Zayd, was to venture through the back door. An illustration in the famous manuscript shows him as one of a row of queasy faces aboard a leaky-looking dhow. Another shows the dhow beside an island inhabited by apes and parrots, but also by fantastic creatures with human faces. That island belongs to fiction, but there were plenty of solid islands and coastlands explored by real-life adventurers, traders, scholars, Sufis, chancers, beachcombers: individuals who were following through, belatedly, from the great Arab diaspora of the seventh and eighth centuries. Together they would propel a second, slow, eirenic wave of conquests, a trans-oceanic swell of Arab culture. These conquests have few heroes, because the adventurers tended to go off and never come back; one of the rare ones who did, and wrote about it, was Ibn Battutah. Most of the rest are lost, but now and again other, extraordinary journeys can be pieced together.

ECLIPSE

1350–1800

CHAPTER TWELVE

MASTERS OF THE MONSOON

ARABS AROUND THE INDIAN OCEAN

THE LAMP IN THE NICHE

Ibn Battutah, born in Morocco at the beginning of the fourteenth century, who made his way to Mecca but went on to criss-cross the Old World from the Niger to the Grand Canal of China and from the Volga to the south of Tanzania, may well be the most widely travelled human before the age of steam. His real-life Odyssey, with himself as its accident-prone but ever optimistic hero, is the epic of Arabic travel literature. It does not matter that he was a 'genetic' Berber; culturally, he was Arab through and through, steeped in the Arabic of the Qur'an and of Islamic jurisprudence, looking to Cairo and Mecca as the intellectual and spiritual poles of his world.

Ibn Battutah, however, was no hero to his children. Married at least ten times and owner of countless concubines, he fathered and abandoned offspring from Damascus to the Maldives. Leaving Delhi in 1341, for example, he entrusted a son named Ahmad to a friend, and later admitted, 'I do not know what God has done with either of them'. The lax father was a tireless social climber, and of all the expatriate Arabs in India this friend, Ghiyath al-Din, was the grandest possible 'godparent': he was the great-great-grandson of the penultimate Abbasid caliph of Baghdad, and thus a distant – in both senses – cousin of the Mamluks' shadow-puppet caliph in Egypt. Like Ibn Battutah himself, Ghiyath al-Din had been attracted to Delhi by its sultan's campaign to draw Arabs and thereby, as we shall see, to bolster his legitimacy. The far-flung Abbasid's credentials as a guardian are less obvious: Ibn Battutah devoted two pages of his book to anecdotes about the man's avarice.

We still don't know what God did with Ghiyath al-Din or the abandoned young Ahmad. But, because of a chance survival, we do know what happened to Ghiyath al-Din's own son, Abd Allah: his tombstone was found in an old royal cemetery in northern Sumatra, near the sea on the bank of the Pasai River. Here was the capital of Samudra-Pasai, the first Islamic state in what is now the country with the biggest Muslim population in the world, Indonesia, and here the rootless Abd Allah died. The Arabic inscription on his stone gives the date as 809/1406–7, and five generations of ancestry back to Caliph al-Mustansir and Baghdad. It is a monument that joins the pomp of pedigree with the pathos of exile; Abd Allah was a prototype of those wandering White Russian princes of the twentieth century, exiled from their homeland but still trading on their noble origins. In Abd Allah's case, the trade seems to have paid: the neighbouring grave, probably that of his wife, is that of the sultan's daughter.

If Abd Allah ibn Ghiyath al-Din ended up marrying a princess, the fate of a half-brother back home in Baghdad was very different. On his way back from the East, Ibn Battutah was moved by the scene of a mosque imam in the city, now a ghost-metropolis, having to plead for arrears of his pay – a paltry *dirham* a day. It turned out that the young man was an elder son of the traveller's Abbasid friend from Delhi. 'By God,' Ibn Battutah wrote,

> if [his father] had sent him a single pearl of all those pearls which adorned the robes of honour that he received from the Sultan [in Delhi], the boy would have been well-off. May God protect us from such a state of things!

Given Ibn Battutah's own shortcomings as a father, motes and beams come to mind.

The contrast between the two half-brothers illustrates what was happening to Arabs in these post-Mongol centuries: stagnation in the old homeland, but opportunities for those who moved abroad. And the Indies were only part of a bigger picture. Abd Allah the footloose Abbasid in Sumatra may seem like a one-off. But he was part of a 12,000-kilometre arc of oceanic wanderers, and one of the things that joins them all together is his monument – that Arabic gravestone. The memorial came, as he almost certainly did, from India, and in particular from the port of Cambay up in the nook at the north of India's west coast. Here were the workshops of the most successful monumental masons in history. Working with a fine local marble (sometimes robbed from ancient buildings, as the undersides of some monuments reveal), the craftsmen of Cambay produced Arabic-inscribed headstones, table-tombs and other memorials that were exported around the Indian Ocean rim from East Africa to South-East Asia. Cambay memorials have been found in Kilwa Kisiwani off the southern Tanzanian coast, Mogadishu, Aden, Dhofar in southern Oman, Lar in Iran, Cambay itself, Goa, Kollam in Kerala, Trincomalee in Sri Lanka, Kinolhas Island in the Maldives (where I discovered one, half buried in a patch of jungly scrub), Sumatra, Gresik in Java.

It is not immediately obvious why a family in, say, Tanzania should order their late relative's Arabic tombstone from India, 5,000 kilometres across the ocean, at enormous cost in money and time; or not until we realize that all those who were thus commemorated could well afford it (the family on Kilwa controlled the export of gold from southern Africa), and that the annual alternation of the monsoon meant that ocean communications were in fact as regular as clockwork – albeit a slow-running clock, timed to the solar year. You sent the text of the epitaph off on the south-west monsoon; back came the stone on the north-east monsoon. And there was your dear departed, commemorated indelibly in Arabic script, that vigorous growth that had already spread across Central Asia and over the passes into northern India, and was now putting down roots all around the Indian Ocean's tropical shoreline. Ordering such a monument was a way of declaring membership of a wealthy and cosmopolitan culture. Today, Chinese plutocrats order Aston Martins; then, oceanic sultans and merchant princes ordered Cambay tombstones. And it was all less bothersome than being sent to Arabia for reburial, as Saladin had done with his father and uncle: with a Cambay stone, Arabia came to you in Qur'anic verses of your choice, executed by the most painstaking Indian craftsmen.

The Cambay stones bear more than Arabic words. Most noticeably, the ogival tops of the headstones often contain the image of a bulbous, vase-like glass lamp hanging in a niche. This is almost certainly meant to recall a striking image from the Qur'an:

Allah is the Light of the heavens and the earth.
The parable of His Light is a niche wherein is a lamp –
the lamp is in a glass, the glass as it were a glittering star –
lit from a blessed tree, an olive,
neither eastern nor western.
. . .
Allah guides to His Light whomever He wishes.

The script on the stones also sometimes transmits unexpected messages, such as a quotation from a Persian poem by Sa'di; other decorative elements include motifs borrowed from the wider artistic environment of Cambay, particularly from Jain temples. Together, the stones commemorate a diversity of dead: Arabs like Abd Allah ibn Ghiyath Din, but also the newly islamized – Swahili, Somali, North Indian, Tamil, Indonesian.

Arab wheels of fire might have long burnt out. But from the late thirteenth to the fifteenth century the oceanic arc was itself a niche, with Arabia at its centre, radiating the light of Islam, dispersing Arabs and their words east and west. The Arab eclipse was edged with brightness.

IDOLS, ELEPHANTS AND ARABIC

Arabs in the heartlands of their former empire may have been hemmed in by the hordes from further Asia and Europe. But at the edges, as Ibn Battutah's *Travels* shows, there was still motion, expansion: in the aftermath of the first great Mongol conquests of the thirteenth century, Arabs and the arabized were pushing out ever further, not this time as military conquerors but as merchants, missionaries and adventurers. They were driven by acquisitiveness. As Muhammad said, 'Two hungers are never satisfied: the hunger for knowledge, and the hunger for worldly things'. Together, the new frontiersmen founded an informal mercantile and cultural empire around the oceanic arc, in which the dominant culture was Arabic and Islamic. The oldest and longest-lasting Arab polity, the Abbasid caliphate in Baghdad, had fallen in 1258, and with it the last pretence of Arab unity. But, in its own unobtrusive way, the Arab-Islamic diaspora of the following 250 years or so, until the coming of the Europeans into the Indian Ocean, was as important and as far-reaching as the military explosion of the seventh and eighth centuries: it shaped the map of today's Islamic world.

It was the old story of dynamic disunity, breaking the egg to make the omelette.

The new expansion also shaped the ways in which a good fraction of the world population would speak, write and think, for the conquering Arabic language spread too, and not only on tombstones for Muslims. Even Ibn Battutah, the great explorer of the diaspora, could be surprised by how far Arabic had reached. A strange instance came when, probably in 1346, after leaving Samudra-Pasai on his way to visit the Arab and Persian expatriate communities in southern China, he landed at a place he calls Kaylukari. The people there worshipped idols, kept elephants and were governed by a princess named Urduja who had a guard of female warriors. She herself was a warrior, and had sworn only to marry a man who could defeat her in single combat; so far she had remained undefeated (no one had dared to challenge her) and resolutely virgin. Urduja has defeated all commentators too. Some have concluded that Kaylukari existed only in Ibn Battutah's heated fantasies; others that it mixes fact and fiction, like that island in al-Hariri's tales where parrots and apes cohabit with a harpy and a sphinx. Clearly, yarning sailors are partly to blame: the most sensational information about the princess was provided by the captain of Ibn Battutah's ship. Ibn Battutah, however, provides another couple of details that stand out because they are unsensational, but still unexpected: '*Dawah wa-batak katur*,' the princess said to an attendant, wishing to impress the traveller, meaning, 'Bring an inkwell and paper'. They were brought, and she wrote: *Bismi 'llah al-rahman al-rahim*, 'In the name of Allah, the Merciful, the Compassionate'. The first unexpected detail – that she spoke with Ibn Battutah in a kind of Turkish – is hard to explain. The second, that 'she wrote Arabic well', is less inexplicable.

If the meeting *is* real, we don't yet know where it took place. The Philippines have claimed Urduja as theirs; other locations, in southern Vietnam or Borneo, may be nearer the mark. But wherever it was, Kaylukari is most likely to have been a colony of the widespread seaboard empire of Majapahit, whose capital was in eastern Java. And if that is the case, for the princess to have known a bit of Arabic script is not beyond the bounds of possibility. Arabic had begun to be used as the script of Old Malay, the language of some of Majapahit's possessions. Suggestively, too, there exist Majapahit coins – perhaps, rather, tokens or amulets – that show on one face the Javanese tutelary spirit Semar together with Krishna and an elephant, all depicted in shadow-puppet style; on the other, in Arabic script, is the Islamic declaration of faith,

> There is no god but Allah: Muhammad is the messenger of Allah.

It is gloriously syncretic. And it proves, if nothing else, that solid archaeological evidence can be as surprising as sailors' yarns and travellers' tales.

THE BLESSED SEA

The travels of Arabs and Arabic were helped by those regular monsoons, and encouraged by the wealth of the ocean and its surrounding lands. In contrast to the spiteful Mediterranean, cursed by God, the Indian Ocean was blessed with precious products. It is, according to the oldest Arabic travel book,

> the Sea of India and China, in whose depths are pearls and ambergris, in whose rocky isles are gems and mines of gold, in the mouths of whose beasts is ivory, in whose forests grow ebony, sapan wood, rattans, and trees that bear aloeswood, camphor, nutmeg, cloves, sandalwood, and all manner of fragrant and aromatic spices, whose birds are *fafagha* (parrots, that is) and peacocks, and the creeping things of whose earth are civet cats and musk gazelles, and all the rest that no one could enumerate, so many are its blessings.

Moreover, the ocean meshed with a wider network, as the thirteenth-century Persian poet Sa'di realized. His own verses would travel the network and appear in unexpected places: not only on a Cambay tombstone found in Sumatra, but also in a song heard by Ibn Battutah on a boat in the Chinese city of Hangzhou. And Sa'di himself wrote of meeting, on the Gulf island of Kish, a merchant who day-dreamed about the ultimate trading journey:

> I shall take Persian sulphur to China . . . China-ware to Greece, and Grecian brocade to India, and Indian steel to Aleppo, and mirrors of Aleppo to Yaman, and striped cloth of Yaman to Persia, and after that I shall give up trading.

The merchant, in fact, was no longer in the best position in Kish: the Mongol depradations had shifted the western terminus of trade from the

Gulf, Persia and Iraq to the Red Sea and Egypt. Otherwise, however, the later thirteenth century was a propitious time for international commerce. First, the Mongol ravages on land had 'energized' ocean trade. Then, when the heirs of Chingiz Khan chilled out and settled down, the resulting peace gave a burst of energy to land trade too. Under the Mongols that whole broad swathe of Asia was loosely united, from the northern Fertile Crescent to the Yellow Sea. Individuals took advantage of the new hemiglobal currents; so did trading corporations, most lucratively that of the Karim, based in Egypt and the Levant. The meaning of their name is unclear: they were Muslim, but their origins may have been eclectic; they are often glossed as 'spice merchants', but their interests were much wider. They had already existed for several centuries; now they too were revived by the Pax Mongolica, and they set about realizing Sa'di's merchant's dream and more, operating a hemispheric trade network that stretched from the Atlantic to the Pacific the long way round.

Sometimes, as in the early history of the Arab empire and in the coming history of European empires, the flag followed trade. In one far corner of the arc, the family who commissioned the south-westernmost Cambay monument were rulers of a tiny island sultanate – Kilwa Kisiwani. Ensconced there since the last quarter of the thirteenth century, they were expatriate Arabs from Yemen, and perhaps originally from Muhammad's Hashimi clan. In Kilwa, however, they joined the borderless culture of the ocean rim: their gravestones came from India, their tableware – the finest *qingbai* porcelain, as well as the standard celadon – came from China, and the source of their wealth, gold, came from the southern African interior. By cornering its export, they were forerunners of Cecil Rhodes. But their sultanate was no Rhodesia: far from being racially or culturally segregated, it rapidly creolized, adding to the already diverse Afro-Arab mix of the *sawahil*, the 'coasts'. Kilwa was only a few kilometres long, but it belonged to both the 'Swahili' sphere of East Africa and to the whole great oceanic arc, just as it belonged to a future that would give birth to Zanzibar, Singapore and Hong Kong.

Kilwa's near-monopoly of gold was, however, untypical; ocean trade was open and organic. But the riches that flowed into the island meant that its sultans could build to last, including what was for many centuries the biggest stone mosque in sub-Saharan Africa, and a sprawling warehouse-cum-palace. The palace incorporates the perfect rich man's touch, still intact: an infinity pool, overlooking the blessed sea.

THE PHANTOM EMPIRE

As with the actual empire of the seventh and eighth centuries, not only Arabs but also Persians, Berbers, Turks and others contributed to the virtual, cultural empire of post-Mongol times. And as with the earlier, military expansion, the cultural empire gained its own momentum. Muslim merchants and others spread knowledge of the sophisticated civilization of the Islamic zone; in ever more distant lands, rulers – particularly newly established ones with no credentials other than brute force – adopted Islam; they then encouraged Arabs and others, especially Muslim scholars, to attach themselves to their courts, legitimizing themselves with the glamour of learning and the whiff of holy places. Mercantile and missionary traffic increased, and Islam spread horizontally across the hemisphere and, more slowly, downwards through society.

The example of the lands around the Strait of Malacca illustrates how the cultural empire spread during the fourteenth and fifteenth centuries. As we have seen, the rulers of Samudra-Pasai in northern Sumatra (to which Samudra gave its name) had adopted Islam early on – at least by the end of the thirteenth century. A century later, it seems that the sultanic family were pleased to have a blue-blooded Abbasid as a son-in-law. Later still, it is claimed that merchants from Sumatra advised the chief of Melaka (Malacca) to become a Muslim too, in order to attract trade. How the islamization of the East Indies had begun in the first place is not clear. Local histories claim that missionaries were sent direct from Mecca to Sumatra; Islam and Arabs, however, tended to arrive in South-East Asia not in one leap, but via the oceanic stepping-stone of India.

India also acted as a portal from continental Asia into the ocean arc. Delhi had been captured by Muslim Turkic adventurers in the later twelfth century. Soon after, the Mongol catastrophe had propelled a stream of mainly Central Asian Muslims into the subcontinent. The flow increased throughout the thirteenth century; news of Indian opportunities spread through the mercantile web, and via the sounding-board of the Mecca pilgrimage. By the second third of the fourteenth century, under Muhammad Shah ibn Tughluq, sultan of Delhi and host of Ibn Battutah and Ghiyath al-Din, the flow had become a flood.

Muhammad Shah came from a mixed Turco-Mongol background, and like the later rulers of India of Mongol origin – the 'Mughals' – he set his sights on the conquest of the entire subcontinent. Campaigns in the south made Delhi the richest Muslim state on earth, awash with gold and slaves, and there took place a migration of which the recent surge of Indians to the Gulf is a mirror image. On occasion, Muhammad Shah sent fleets of ships to the Gulf to recruit Arabs. They gathered round Muhammad Shah, a contemporary wrote, 'like moths around a candle'. Arab courtiers adorning the royal audience chamber, the Hall of a Thousand Columns, could amass stupendous wealth: in his Delhi palazzo, Ghiyath al-Din had the ultimate plutocrat's bauble, a gold bath; the buttons of his coat – just one of which would have got his son in Baghdad out of hock – were pearls as big as hazelnuts. Ghiyath al-Din, scion of caliphs, was specially favoured; but Muhammad Shah was besotted with Arabs of whatever background, addressed them all as 'my lord', and showered them with gifts.

One was always there, however, at his majesty's pleasure. Among the prominent Arabs who turned up in Delhi in the 1330s was a youth named Ghada, a grandson of Muhanna ibn Isa, the *amir* of the Arabs in Syria whose loyalty had oscillated between the Mamluk and Mongol superpowers. Muhammad Shah assigned the young man the income of vast provinces – the equivalent of the modern state of Gujerat, and more – and married him to his sister in the society wedding of the season.

> The sultan showed him immense honour, but [Ghada] was a raw bedouin, who did not measure up to this standard; the rudeness of the desert folk was his dominant trait, and it brought him to disaster only twenty days after his wedding.

The bedouin princeling started knocking high-born officials about and ended up in the sultan's gaol. Eventually, however, he was given a reprieve and 'learned good manners and refinement'.

The already refined Ghiyath al-Din the Abbasid, however, could do no wrong. The sultan would share his betel with him, which he did with no one else; the part of Delhi where Ghiyath al-Din lived was renamed 'the Abode of the Caliphate'; and on one occasion, having unintentionally slighted him, Muhammad Shah lay on the ground and forced Ghiyath al-Din to place his caliphal foot on the sultanic neck. But the sultan's almost manic obsession with Arabs, and above all with the Abbasid family, went even further. Before Ghiyath al-Din had arrived in Delhi, Muhammad Shah, the richest Muslim monarch on earth, had given his empire away – to that impoverished exile in Egypt, the man who was forced to sell his clothes to live, the Mamluks' puppet caliph al-Mustakfi Sulayman.

No doubt, Sulayman was bemused. But he duly sent Muhammad Shah a document declaring the sultan of Delhi his vassal, and a set of robes in black, the Abbasid dynastic colour. Little good did it do the new nominal overlord of India: by the time Muhammad Shah finally received the diploma in 1343 and substituted Sulayman's name for his own on the coinage, the caliph was dead. Undeterred, Muhammad Shah sent for a new diploma from his son and successor. In practical terms, it all meant rather less than Queen Elizabeth II being head of state of Australia. To Muhammad Shah, however, it meant more; perhaps everything. He was the man who *had* everything, materially. But as the second in a dynasty of Turco-Mongol marauders, recent converts to Islam, he had no legitimacy other than his own worldly power. While this has not bothered most rulers, it troubled Muhammad Shah, one of the most fascinating, frightening and complex monarchs in world history. As a fragment of autobiography reveals, he had fallen into a deep spiritual malaise, almost an existential crisis:

> My father prevented my search for the rightful imam . . . My condition became such that no designs of mine could be actually realized . . . [and I] would have preferred (in despite of Islam) to become an idolator.

Muhammad Shah saved himself from idolatry by finding his rightful imam – in those tenuous, shadowy caliphs in Egypt. In them, in the black robes, in the Abbasid foot on the sultanic neck, the old Arab empire kept a phantom hold on the wealthiest ruler in the world.

A CENTRIFUGAL CENTURY

If the enigmatic and arabophile Muhammad Shah was a special case, his Delhi was only one destination in a hemisphere of mobile Arabs. And by no means all the globetrotters and fortune-hunters were the offspring of Abbasids or great tribal *amir*s. The Berber-blooded Ibn Battutah was from a respectable but modest family of Tangier; in Delhi and then again in China he bumped into a fellow Moroccan called al-Bushri, a traveller of similarly middling background from Sabtah (now the Spanish-run Ceuta), up the road from his own birthplace. Later, he stayed with al-Bushri's brother on the north-western edge of the Sahara. 'How far apart they were!' he exclaimed (about 12,500 kilometres, as the crow flew). Just as the diaspora of the seventh and eighth centuries had flung Arab families apart, like the five sons of al-Abbas scattered from Tunisia to Samarqand and the brother governors in Tunisia and Sind, so too did the centrifugal century after the Mongol calamity. Now, too, new regions were opening up to the adventurous, and not only around the Indian Ocean. South of the Sahara in the Sahel – the *sahil* or 'coast' of the desert – Ibn Battutah found that the great West African empire of Mali (far more extensive than the modern state of Mali) was home to many expatriate Arabs. Most were from North Africa; some, like the distinguished Granadan scholar and architect al-Sahili and the merchant al-Kuwayk of Iraqi origin, whose tombs Ibn Battutah noted in Timbuktu, were from further afield.

Most Arabs, of course, stayed at home; unlike the mass migrations of the first Islamic centuries, this was a diaspora of the edges, of an adventurous minority. It is impossible to estimate numbers; but judging by names on the surviving Islamic gravestones from one destination in the far east – Quanzhou, the Hong Kong of its day, in China's Fujian province – Arabs, and especially Yemenis, were a prominent component among Muslims of other origins, mostly Persians and Turks. Here, in what the Chinese called 'the richest city under the heavens', no fewer than twelve of the twenty-two governors under the Mongol Yuan dynasty were Muslims. Nor were the Arab and arabized wanderers all Muslim. North of the Caucasus, for example, in what is now southern Russia, Ibn Battutah met a Jew from al-Andalus who had travelled overland via Constantinople in four months; local informants regarded such a journey as unremarkable. Travellers and traders to distant parts also turn up regularly in documents from the Cairo Geniza, a repository for discarded documents attached to a synagogue. This giant waste-paper basket has turned out to be a mine of information on Egyptian and further Jewish communities from the eleventh century on. Patient paper-chasing has enabled researchers to trace the lives of people ignored by standard histories: Abraham ibn Yiju, for instance, a Tunisian Jewish businessman in the India trade, and Abu Zikri ha-Kohen, originally from Sijilmasah in southern Morocco, who dealt from Cairo in Indian Ocean goods and had a brother-in-law acting as his agent in Sudanese Sawakin.

These far travellers may not all have shared a faith or a genetic origin; but they did share a global, or at least a hemiglobal frame of mind, and they were fluent in its major language. It was because of the spread of Islam, but also of Arabic, that people like Ibn Battutah could feel at home in places as far apart as West African Mali, Maldivian Male, and even on the margins of the known world, with Urduja the pugnacious princess.

VIRILE VOCABULARY

Like today's travellers for whom English plus a bit of French or Spanish will cover most eventualities, fourteenth-century globetrotters could get by in Arabic, with a smattering of Persian and perhaps Turkish; speaking Arabic then, like speaking English now, made travel easier. The irony was that, back home, the old high language was decaying. In 1327, listening to the sermon at Friday prayers in al-Basrah, the Iraqi Ivy League town where the laws of the language had been laid down, Ibn Battutah was shocked to find that 'when the preacher rose and recited his discourse he committed in it many gross errors of grammar'. Complaining to a local scholar, he was told bluntly, 'In this town there is not a man left who knows anything of the science of grammar.' The political and social breakdown that had afflicted the old heartlands for centuries, followed by the Mongol onslaught, seemed to have undermined even the oldest and firmest base of Arab unity, the Arabic language. The *qawa'id* – both the 'foundations' and the 'grammar' – were decaying alarmingly.

As if in compensation, Arabic was enlarging its overseas empire. It had already colonized Persian and Turkic; more recently, Arabic loan words had made inroads into European languages. Now it was going on to conquer new lands and tongues in sub-Saharan Africa, India and South-East Asia. Arabic script, too, spread with trade and Islam, and with the material culture that they carried: it was the literal expression of that culture. Not much later than the earliest Cambay stones in Sumatra, inscribed in Arabic, comes the first extant Old Malay text written in Arabic script: found across the strait in the Malay Peninsula, it may be as early as 1326. The list of languages written in Arabic script was to lengthen and cover much of the Old World: to Arabic itself, Persian, the Turkic languages and now Malay, would be added Kurdish, Pashtu, Sindi, Kashmiri and Urdu, Uyghur in Chinese Turkestan, Swahili in East Africa, Fulani and Hausa in West Africa; even, for a time, Croat in the Balkans, 'Cape Malay' – really a form of Afrikaans used by nineteenth-century South African Muslims and written in Arabic script – and certain 'secret' languages among the clans of southern Madagascar. Often, additional letters were needed; sometimes a whole new style of script was designed, like Persian *nasta'liq* – supposedly inspired by a dream in which Ali ibn Abi Talib, Muhammad's son-in-law and one of his scribes, told the calligrapher to look for inspiration in the anatomy of *ducks*. In the far east, meanwhile, the ancient transition from the chisel of angular, epigraphic Nabataean and Kufic to the cursive reed-pen of the caliphal chancery was taken even further in the Chinese Arabic scripts, written with the ink-brush and looking as if they had descended from cloud-scrolls.

How far Arabic penetrated the languages themselves can be judged from numbers of loan words. In post-Ottoman Turkish in 1931, 51 per cent of newspaper vocabulary was Arabic; even after a generation of de-arabicization, the proportion in 1965 was still 26 per cent. In Farsi, there were attempts to persianize the lexicon in the nineteenth century, but at least 30 per cent of the vocabulary remains Arabic. Arabic travelled via Persian to the Indian subcontinent, where not only Hindi and particularly Urdu but also many of the related languages are rich in Arabic words; thus, for example, a concept as indigenous as Sikh *khalsa* can turn out to have an Arabic name – *khalisah* is 'pure'. India's recent colonial history also meant that a minor secondary wave of Arabic words made it the long way round to Europe, and particularly with the nabobs (the *nawab*, Arabic 'deputies') to 'Blighty' – itself from Arabic *wilayah*, 'dominion, realm', via Persian into Indian *bilayati* 'of the foreign land, especially Europe/Britain'. Arabicization is continuing in at least one part of the Indian subcontinent, as Bangladeshi Bengali replaces Sanskrit loan words with new ones of Arabic origin.

Further south and east around the ocean arc, Arabic has bequeathed modern Indonesian as many as 3,000 loan words. From the East Indies, it still had further to go – not just to Ibn Battutah's hazy Kaylukari but also to Elcho Island, off Australia's Arnhem Land: there, the Aboriginal name for God, '*Walitha'walitha*', apparently came via early contacts with Makassar Muslims from the Arabic phrase *Allahu ta'ala*, 'Allah, exalted is He'. In the opposite direction, in Africa, the belated Arab tribal migrations of the Banu Hilal and others from the eleventh century onwards arabicized the lowlands, but Arabic would also steal into the Berber languages, a quarter to a third of whose vocabulary is now Arabic. From the Maghrib, traders, missionaries and tribesmen also took Arabic itself as far south as Bornu in northern Nigeria, where a form of the language is still spoken by inhabitants of Arab origin. No less importantly, from the *sawahil*, the coasts of the western arm of the oceanic arc, Swahili spread inland through trade to become the national language of Kenya and Tanzania. Swahili is a Bantu language, but Arabic has loaned it perhaps as much as half of its vocabulary. Like Turkish and many other languages that were long written in Arabic script, Swahili has romanized itself. But, as in Bangladesh, the lexical penetration continues: Greek-origin *saikolojia*, for example, is giving way to Arabic-origin *elimunafsi* (*'ilmu 'n-nafsi*, 'the science of the soul').

Given that language is already gendered in other ways – notably 'masculine' and 'feminine' – it may not be wrong, or even impertinent, to see the whole process as one of virile Arabic vocabulary (and it is always vocabulary, never grammar) penetrating a succession of grammatical matrixes, Indo-European, Turkic, Hamito-Semitic, Austronesian, Bantu. Just as seventh- and eighth-century Arab men scattered abroad and begot generations of talented *muwallad*s, so in later times their language continued to father a rich and expanding creole world. If only in retrospect, it makes up for the political impotence.

A DISTANT VIEW OF MECCA

As Islam spread, it too penetrated and enriched one culture after another. It had long outgrown its Arabian origins. But over the centuries a web of attachments grew that kept the wider Islamic world joined to Arabia and the world-navel of Mecca. The most powerful link was the inviolable Arabic of the Qur'an and of worship. And there was another binding and physical link in pilgrimage, one of the five 'pillars' of Islam and therefore a duty, but only for those who were physically and financially able to undertake it. Very few were; even fewer did.

But there were other kinds of attachment. Sometimes these were corporeal and personal, like the tombs of expatriate Arab matriarchs and patriarchs: Nafisah's in Cairo has been mentioned, as has that of Qutham, one of those five sons of al-Abbas, in Samarqand (where, for a time, the superintendent of the shrine was that real live Abbasid – Ghiyath al-Din, en route to Delhi). Sometimes the wish was father to the corpse. Thus, 'Abu Waqqas', supposedly Sa'd ibn Abi Waqqas, the Companion of Muhammad, is buried and venerated in both Tamil Nadu and Guangzhou, leading a posthumous double life like the Christian St Thomas – or indeed triple, as the real Sa'd was buried in Medina.

Non-human remains could also bring Arabia close. One example is the sacred house in Kangaba, Mali. Known as the Kababolon, 'the Vestibule of the Ka'bah', it is said to contain relics of an unspecified and mysterious nature brought from Mecca by a mid-fourteenth-century ruler of the Mali empire.

If you could not reach Arabia by the usual means, you could always take yourself there supernaturally, compressing time and distance. Nizam al-Din, the great Sufi saint of Delhi, is an extreme case: he is said to have visited the Ka'bah every night on a flying camel. Sometimes, though, lesser mortals can share in something of the same experience. At a site called Daftar Jaylani, deep in the Sri Lankan jungle, there is a cave that for ten years in the twelfth century was supposedly home to the Baghdad-based saint Abd al-Qadir al-Jaylani; he, too, would go on supernatural pilgrimages. Even today, by crawling into the narrowest part of the cave and looking through a peep-hole, a sort of psychic telescope, thousands of visitants are convinced that they have seen Mecca, 5,000 kilometres away.

TRANSLATING ISLAM

Despite all these various points of attachment to Arabia, Islam 'creolized', rather as those Arabic-enriched languages had done. In the ninth-century Baghdad of al-Ma'mun, it had begun to develop from an Arabian *religio*, a set of inherited obligations, into a cosmopolitan faith that added philosophy and ethics to cult. Now, in the post-Mongol centuries, it spread around an even wider world, acclimatizing and gaining accretions as it went. Islam was going global; also, inevitably, it was going native.

At home in the old Arab empire, Islam tended to remain a unitary ideology that had long ceased to unify. Its living word, the Qur'an, was embalmed in sanctity and shrouded in layers of exegesis; so too was *hadith*. Except among Sufis and esoterics, public rituality tended to be more important than private spirituality; debate, such as it was, centred on textual minutiae – on individual words, syllables, letters, dots – and generated ever more texts. Writing of his own fourteenth century, Ibn Khaldun entitled a chapter, '*The great number of scholarly works available is an obstacle on the path to attaining scholarship*'. He went on to brand academic overkill 'an evil that cannot be cured, because it has become firmly ingrained through custom'. Many scholars could no longer see the wood for the trees – or hear the Word for the sounds. But for non-Arab Muslims the sacred sounds were not enough: they had to look for the larger meaning, the sense, as one inevitably does when one translates. The curious upshot of this is that some non-Arab Muslims may in fact understand the message of the Arabic Qur'an as well as, if not better than, many of their Arab co-religionists. As a recent researcher in sociolinguistics was told, the latter 'are Arabs and already speak Arabic, [so] there is no need for translations'. But Arabs do not 'speak Arabic' – that is, they do not speak the high Arabic of the Qur'an; they never have done, or not as a 'native' language of daily life. That is the point of the Qur'an: it is elevated beyond human expression. And it does not help that the numerous exegeses try to attain the same high language as that of the text they are trying to explain. Arabophones may well respond to the mystical medium of the Qur'an like no other hearers; sometimes, however, the message may elude them.

At the same time, while the essential texts, rituals and doctrines of Islam crossed oceans and deserts intact, and were explained through translation, they were nearly always relocated on foundations of previous local beliefs. These might be hidden, but they were rarely eradicated; upon them new superstructures arose – cultural, ethical, philosophical, mystical – that belonged less to seventh-century Arabia or ninth-century Baghdad than to Islam's new settings. Just as, say, the spiky mud mosques of Dienné in Mali, the Hindu temple-style mosques of Kerala, the elaborately carved wooden mosques in the Maldives that are built on the foundations of Buddhist temples, and the moon gates and curly eaves of Chinese mosques are all in harmony with their local history, so while the words and the worship are the same as those of Arabs, the local 'architecture' of surrounding practice and underlying belief can be different. Different superstructures are easy to spot, like the cave eremism that Indian Muslim ascetics adopted from their Buddhist peers, or the *pranayama* breath control that they learned from yogis. In the fourteenth century, Ibn Battutah observed many Muslim penitents studying ascetic techniques with Shaivite saddhus at Khajuraho; he also saw Haydari dervishes who had taken over the practice of penis-piercing from Naga *sanyasi*s. The infrastructure of earlier beliefs is harder to see, but the case of Jalal al-Din Tabrizi, the early thirteenth-century Muslim proselytizer of Bengal, is probably far from unique: he converted a Hindu temple into his main centre of worship, gave it an Indo-Arabic name, 'Deva Mahall', and simply took over the resident Hindu devotees, who 'presumably' converted along with the building. Over the next two centuries, Isma'ili missionaries in India would identify Islamic figures with members of the

Hindu pantheon: Adam was the equivalent of Shiva, Muhammad of Brahma and Ali of Vishnu. Inevitably with such 'translations', something would be lost, and something gained.

It helped that Sufism was surfing a wave in these expansive Islamic centuries. Most memorably, the great early thirteenth-century Andalusian divine, Ibn al-Arabi – ironically, perhaps, in view of his name – was freeing Islam from its Arabian matrix. For him, Mecca was still the beloved mother-city, the Ka'bah the navel of the world, but that did not necessitate navel-gazing or preclude other loves:

Receptive now my heart is for each form:
For gazelles pasture, for monks a monastery,
Temple for idols, Ka'bah to be rounded,
Tables of Torah and script of Qur'an.
My religion is love's religion: where'er turn
Her camels, that religion my religion is, my faith.

At times the creolization of Islam went so far that it gave birth to beliefs that would be disowned by mainstream Muslims, or were classified as new religions, like those of the Sikhs and the Baha'is. Sometimes the Islamic symbol and the sanctity lingered, but the ritual context changed entirely, as with the metamorphic masks worn by Poro society members in Guinea. One example has a human face and a hornbill's beak, and is lined with paper inscribed with Arabic letters and allusions to the Qur'anic chapter in which Muhammad's uncle is cursed. There are other surprising cohabitations. Around the corner from the Kababolon, that West African repository for Islamic relics, and resembling it on a smaller scale, is a traditional pre-Islamic fetish house, supposedly founded by a servant of the Mecca-visiting emperor of Mali. Outsiders, I was told, 'came here and brought Islam, and our kings went to Mecca and brought back Islam, but the people kept their own beliefs as well'. Promiscuous, but pragmatic.

OTHER PEOPLE'S EMPIRES

Even though Ibn Battutah and many other travellers and traders had made it almost as far south as Mozambique, the further reaches of Africa were extremely hazy. The consensus, illustrated by al-Idrisi's map, was that the continent bent eastward and nearly met the far end of Eurasia, all but enclosing the Indian Ocean and making it an enlarged mirror-image of the Mediterranean. It was the early sixteenth-century Arab navigator Sulayman al-Mahri who put his fellow mariners right. Reporting a recent discovery by the Franks, he revealed that Africa extended much further south than had been thought – to where the elevation of Ursa Major was seven 'fingers' below the horizon – and, far from stretching to the east, the shoreline turned sharply north and west at what the foreigners had named the Cape of Bunasfarans: Bõa Esperança, or Good Hope. Africa had unbent; the Indian Ocean was not a near-lake. And all of a sudden the kindly sea of Arabia and the Indies had been thrown open to interlopers.

The Ming revolution that ended Mongol rule in China in 1368 had already closed Chinese ports to foreign traffic: direct ocean trade between the west and the far east had therefore ceased more than a century earlier. Now, in 1488, the Portuguese had appeared via that unexpected south-western route, and they wanted to turn what had been a *mare liberum* into another *mare nostrum*. The ocean would prove too big for them to do so; but they still did their best to stymie Arabs as middle-men, building a ring of forts around the oceanic arc and patrolling with their strange new ships, square-rigged, square-pooped, and held together with *nails* (in all the western part of the Indian Ocean, ships were still 'sewn' together with coir cord).

The Europeans also stymied some other, nearer neighbours. In 1453, the Ottoman Turks had joined up the most significant dots of their Eurasian empire and taken Constantinople, that pivotal and long-desired junction between the two continents. The city's fall was perhaps of more symbolic than strategic importance; still, it gave the Ottomans a new and splendid capital, the jewel in the sultan's turban, and they were poised to take unopposed control of the major east–west traffic of the Old – and still, just, the Only – World. And then, in less than a lifetime, the whole overland trade between east and west collapsed with the Portuguese rounding of the Cape, that back door to the wealth of the Indies . . . just as, far to the west, two whole continents in one rose unsuspected from the Circumambient Ocean. From the trade of the Americas the Ottomans were excluded – except as consumers, consoling themselves with its tobacco.

They may have been left high and dry by the changing currents of world trade, but the Ottomans were still suffering from the imperial itch. Yet now they too seemed stuck, as Arabs had so often been, between two growing lions – the increasingly wealthy and powerful European states to the west, and a newly nationalist Safavid Persia to the east. There was therefore only one way they could head to satisfy the itch: into the ruins of the old Arab empire. The old seats of Arab power fell into Ottoman hands in rapid succession: Damascus in 1516; Cairo and its Arabian dependencies, Medina and Mecca, in 1517; Baghdad in 1534. And not only the old capitals, but almost the furthest wings of the Arabic world: Algiers, which handed itself over soon after the fall of Cairo; Yemen, where every pass had to be fought for. Already for the last 600 years, distant Turkic cousins of the Ottomans had been displacing Arabs from the most important of these seats, slipping into them in a long-running game of musical thrones. This was different. Now Turks had their own throne on the Bosporus: they were no longer cuckoos in Arab nests, but fully fledged imperial eagles.

The latest forms of firepower accelerated the conquests. The Mamluk historian Ibn Ilyas evoked the way the Turks had suddenly loomed over Cairo, 'coming up from every direction like clouds . . . the noise of their musketry deafening, and their attack furious'. In just a few months, the Ottomans ended the 250-year dominance of the Mamluks in Egypt and Syria. Soon, too, an even longer era was to end. The Mamluks still had an Abbasid puppet caliph in residence, al-Mutawakkil III (they had long ago run out of new throne-names); the conquerors took him to Constantinople, now more usually called Istanbul, 'and the caliphate and the swearing of allegiance to it were cut off'. In the Ottoman capital, al-Mutawakkil was at first treated with due respect; later, however, he was accused of embezzling religious trust-funds, and was sent back in disgrace to Cairo, where he died in 1543. It was 800 years since the revolution in Khurasan had put his ancestors on the throne; but it was 600 years since that throne had meant serious rule, and 300 since it had been anything but a joke. Dynasties do not always provide the best lens through which to view the past. But the Abbasid family saga seems to sum up the whole middle period of Arab history: two centuries of power followed by three of pathos, then three more of bathos.

Turks had been instrumental in the beginning of the long-drawn Abbasid decline, and now Turks had brought about its conclusion. It was therefore appropriate that the Ottoman sultans adopted the title of caliph. They did so somewhat gingerly: you might be sultan, *padishah*, the Master of the World, the Second Alexander, but 'caliph' was not a title to be taken on lightly. It was heavy with history and, despite everything, with Arab mana.

Now, however, even those last numinous associations seemed to have dissipated.

ALIEN BROTHERS

Ottoman relations with their Arabic-speaking subjects are hard to summarize. The territory, from the western Mediterranean to the south of the Red Sea, was too various for generalization, the period too long – three, in places four centuries, largely of mutual tolerance or indifference but punctuated by occasional fits of passion. Arabs and Turks shared a religion, and a script, and many words; but never a language, either literal or metaphorical. Like those earlier Turks, the Saljuqs, the Ottomans had been persianized along their journey from the east before they were arabicized; unlike the Saljuqs and the many others who had already ruled Arabs, they now ruled them from outside the old Arab empire, from a capital inherited, ultimately, from Rome.

To most Arabs the Ottomans were nominal brothers-in-Islam, but always aliens – to be collaborated with, suffered or rebelled against as the case might be. Often the Turks were only effectively in control of the towns, and then only with the connivance of local elites. When Arab chieftains saw a weakness in the occupiers, they might ignite a local wheel of fire. But in general the alleged saying of Muhammad still applied: 'Leave the Turks alone as long as they leave you alone.' Individual Turks, and the Circassians, Albanians and others in their service, occasionally settled in imperial outposts and were absorbed by their arabophone neighbours. But the Ottoman empire as a whole was much too big and too heterogeneous ever to succumb to the power of Arabic culture, as had, for example, Berber rulers in the west or the Kurdish rulers in Egypt and the Levant. Besides, by 1500 the power of Arabic culture was at its lowest level ever as, just before the Ottoman takeover, al-Suyuti had illustrated so memorably with his image of the ancient caravan of Arabic knowledge reduced to a single plodding camel with a meagre load of second-rate books. And while Arabs might work with or for the Turks, the only way into the alien heart of Ottomandom was by being enslaved – a legal impossibility for most Arabs, as their rulers were fellow Muslims. The way to a top job in the Ottoman military or civil service was open to, say, a Bulgarian Christian enslaved in the *devshirme*, the 'levy of boys' recruited from non-Muslim subjects. To most Arabs, that route was firmly closed.

For 300 years and more, Arabs lived and died grumbling about Ottoman tax-collectors, paying lip-service in Friday prayers for their absentee sultan-caliph within his Sublime Porte on the Bosporus, but never sparing a thought for other Arabs in other lands, let alone for any ideas of unity with them.

Indeed, most Arabs would never have thought of themselves as Arabs: they were Muslims or Christians or Jews; they were people of Fez or Damascus or Muscat, or of country regions dependent on towns; and they were subjects of the Porte. It was not quite as one authority has put it, that 'The Arabs fell into a lethargy and ceased to be aware of their Arabness'. They spoke and wrote in forms of Arabic, and the intellectual few who thought about such matters were thus conscious of being *'arab* as opposed to *'ajam*, arabophones as opposed to non-arabophones. But in common usage *'arab* as such were, once more, those people who lived beyond the limits of civilization, herding flocks and raiding the God-fearing sons of Adam. A recent historian of Arabs under the Ottomans says of the Turkish conquest of Egypt, 'it was too early to speak of a distinct Arab identity that would object to "foreign" rule'. Looking only forwards from that time, he is right. But, looking backwards as well, it was too *late* to speak of that identity – an identity that had begun to form before the Christian era, had coalesced under the Lakhmid and Ghassanid kings, had solidified with Islam and reached its firmest form under the Umayyads and earlier Abbasids, but then had weakened and decayed around the time of the death of the last 'real' caliph in the mid-tenth century. What had happened since then was that Arab identity had reverted to its herding-raiding beginnings. The idea of *'urubah*, arabness, had been almost as mobile and various across time as the peoples and tribes to whom it attached; under the Ottomans, it entered a 300-year dip in the road, and became invisible.

There was one thing, however, that kept up the momentum of arabness throughout that trough. It was common to the people of Fez and Muscat, to the God-fearing townspeople and the apparently godless bedouin, to Jewish Yemenis and Christian Syrians: they all spoke Arabic of a sort, and if they could write, the Muslims among them at least tried to write the old high Arabic. In stark contrast to the way in which their language had colonized the subject-peoples of their own empire, less than 1 per cent of Arabic-speakers in the Ottoman empire would ever learn Turkish.

THE IRONIES OF EMPIRE

After that first shock of the Portuguese doubling the Cape, old momentums also built up again in the Indian Ocean. The organic patterns of migration and trafficking had been disturbed and distorted by European expansion, but Arabs soon acclimatized to the new currents, and began to swim with them: if arabness was in a trough in the old imperial heartlands, in the ocean it rode another crest. The pioneers of the new wave were few in number and limited in origin, but were as mobile and adventurous as their seventh- and fourteenth-century forerunners. In one case they would take their cue from the European empire-builders when, at the end of the seventeenth century, the rulers of Oman invested in naval power and staked out a new Arab mini-empire on the East African coast. Later centred on Zanzibar, it recapitulated the littoral state of Kilwa, founded 400 years earlier, and would last into the 1960s; its economic base was the export not of gold but of slaves and, later, cloves.

Elsewhere, the informal cultural empire resumed its expansion. Especially prominent in the revived growth were *sayyid*s – descendants of Muhammad – from Hadramawt in the Arabian south. Their shared ancestor had arrived there in the tenth century; they had multiplied and become locally important as mediators and power brokers. Now, in the relative calm after the stormy Portuguese arrival in the Indian Ocean, they rode its new currents as merchants, but also founded their own micro-empires as religious and sometimes political leaders. The al-Jufri family were, and in places still are, particularly successful. In the eighteenth century they established themselves on the Malabar coast of India and soon became prominent in the native Muslim community (thus reviving an old connection: Arabs had been 'masters of the coast' here in the time of Pliny). Further east and into the nineteenth century, Sayyid Muhsin al-Jufri would become one of the great tycoons of nascent Singapore, with agents scattered around the ocean arc from Suez to Surabaya; Joseph Conrad served on a Jufri (or 'Joofree') ship, and portrayed the family in his novels. Members of the clan are still to be found as far away as north-eastern Borneo, where they live in settlements with names like 'Kampong Arab', and trade in rattans and precious aloeswood – those same oceanic products that were listed in the earliest account of Arab travel. Other Hadrami *sayyid* families ended up at various different points around the arc: Kaffs and Saqqafs at both extremes, on the Swahili coast as well as in Singapore; Aydids in Mogadishu; Aydaruses in Ahmadabad and Kerala; Ba Faqihs in Calicut and Colombo.

Also in the eighteenth century, Hadrami missionaries continued to shine the lamp of Islam into ever further corners of the East Indies, for example among the seaborne Bugis of Sulawesi and surrounding regions. Southern Yemeni tribal warriors, meanwhile, began to forsake their lean ancestral land for richer pickings as mercenaries, particularly in the wealthy Indian state of Hyderabad. Sometimes Arabs became independent rulers abroad: a rare adventurer from the north, Sayyid Muhammad Shams al-Din of Hamah in Syria, made it to the Maldives at the end of the seventeenth century and married his way on to the throne of the island sultanate. He died before he could found a dynasty, but other expatriate sultanates would last longer. Among them were those of the Hadrami *sayyid* family surnamed Jamal al-Layl, 'Camel of the Night', because their ancestor would piously hump water around in the dark to fill mosque ablution-pools. Various branches of the Night Camels have been rulers of the Comoros, of Aceh in Sumatra (where, just like that wandering Abbasid, a few miles along the coast in Samudra-Pasai and 300 years earlier, they married into the local ruling family) and of the Malaysian state of Perlis, where they still rule today as rajas.

Numbers were never huge in the oceanic diaspora: in 1905, Hadramis in Indonesia, for example, numbered 30,000. But the southern Arabian lands from which nearly all the emigrants came were themselves sparsely populated, the range of destinations vast, and the power, economic, spiritual and at times temporal, of these Arab expatriates was far out of proportion to the census figures. And, creolized though many of them became, their identity remained Arab at heart. It was not the irruption of the Portuguese into the Indian Ocean that ended the informal oceanic empire, but the post-Second World War division of imperial territories, formal and informal, into nation-states. One could no longer be a creole, a citizen of the ocean shore: one had to have a nationality. Arab blood, however much diluted, had always been thicker than water; in the end the passport would prove more solid than either.

For three centuries and more, these geographically vast but often unnoticed Arab migrations extended a pattern of mobility that had begun in the post-Mongol thirteenth century, and further shaped today's Islamic world. This time, however, the migrations took place in the shadow of other peoples' empires – those of the Portuguese, closely followed by a scrum of other Europeans, from which the British emerged paramount in India and the Dutch in the East Indies. Among the resulting imperial ironies was the one that would make the British royal house of Windsor – if only for a few years from the end of 1917, when it controlled Cairo, Jerusalem, Damascus, Baghdad and India – the greatest 'Islamic' dynasty in history, at least in terms of numbers of Muslim subjects.

And there was another irony of empire in these centuries: the high point of Arab unity – in terms of the greatest population under a single rule over the longest time and the widest geographical extent – was achieved under the Ottomans. Arab unity was purchased at the expense of Arab independence, and in many ways also of Arab identity. That identity seems, sometimes, almost too potent: a self-consuming fire that forges an alloy, a unity – then vaporizes it. The Arab word, the Arabic world, was most effectively and durably gathered when, perhaps *because*, it was least audible. As millennia of dictators have known, argument and disunity can only come about when one can raise one's voice.

But the new world of these times contained yet another empire. It was not shown on any map, but it was as important as continents. In it, not only Arabs but also their Ottoman masters and all those who used the Arabic script were almost totally silenced.

PRINT-UNFRIENDLY

This new realm was the empire of the printed word. Developments in typography and geography were sudden and simultaneous. Gutenberg's Bible came out in 1455, two years after Constantinople fell to the Turks. By the time of the Portuguese rounding of the Cape in 1488, swiftly followed by the fall of Granada and Columbus's landfall in the New World in 1492, printing had spread across Europe; Latin movable type and European maritime imperialism got moving together. Arabic, the first conqueror, had preceded the Europeans to the limits of the Old World – in the Qur'an, on gravestones, as the script for non-Arab languages, even to the land of Urduja the pugilistic princess – but it didn't make the next vital stage of the journey: into print.

From the start, there was opposition to print from users of Arabic script. Under pressure from religious scholars, the Ottomans banned printing in Arabic as early as 1485, and confirmed the ban repeatedly thereafter. Naturally this delighted the copyists, who in Constantinople alone are said to have numbered tens of thousands. But apart from arguments about their jobs, or about the innate sacredness of Arabic letters as the medium of God's message, printed Arabic was an aesthetic and technical disaster. The basic problem was simple: cursive script and movable type don't go together. Add to that the difficulty of showing vowels that are not separate letters, but are written above or below their consonants, and it meant that complete Arabic fonts contained 900-plus different characters. A standard compositor's type case for English contains about a tenth of that.

To give a random example, the single Arabic letter *sad*, with its possible ligatures and vowels, has dozens of forms:

ص صَ صُ صِ صْ صً صٌ صٍ صَّ صُّ صّ صٌّ صِّ ـص ـصَ ـصُ ـصِ ـصْ
ـصً ـصٌ ـصٍ ـصَّ ـصُّ ـصِّ ـصٌّ ـصّ ـصـ ـصُـ ـصِـ ـصْـ ـصَّـ ـصُّـ ـصِّـ

The letter *mim*, one of the most frequently used, and on its own an unassuming tadpole

م

appears in as many as seventy-three different guises; the Latin equivalent of *mim* has just two, *m* and *M*. Latin inherited its detached characters and separate vowel letters from the Greek alphabet, which had itself taken shape by the mid-eighth century BC. In turn, Greek characters derived, as ultimately did Arabic, from vowelless Phoenician; but some bright Greek spark had the idea of adapting some characters from the parent script and using them to slip sounds into the consonantal line – just five extra letters, but they suddenly gave texts a voice. Coping with unvowelled Semitic scripts, meanwhile, remained that bit harder, the equivalent of lip-reading rather than hearing. It is another example of chaos theory at work in history: a brainwave in the Aegean in the time of Homer had far-reaching consequences when movable-type printing appeared more than 2,000 years later; perhaps, as we shall see, even further-reaching ones in the 500 years thereafter.

Lithography, enabling multiple copies to be printed from the same hand-written plate, would have avoided the technical problems of Arabic typesetting – and saved scribes' jobs – but it was invented too late, in 1798. And 1798 was exactly when letterpress printing finally established itself in the Arabic world – with Napoleon fly-posting Cairo. Then again, when printing did finally take off, the printed texts usually skimped on vowels and were thus harder to read than the manuscripts: contrarily, they aimed at a wider distribution, but they made the reading of Arabic an even more 'undemocratic' process than it had been. My modest library contains many multi-volume printed works where vowels are seldom, if ever, shown. By losing their vowels, they have lost their inflections, their 'logic'; reading them is that bit harder, a cryptic puzzle rather than the 'quick' one it would have been in the vowelled manuscript equivalent. As for typewritten Arabic, it would be even more horrible to look at and read, the disjointed tracks of crippled beetles. It lacked even the steampunk charm of Latin typewriting, and it was the very devil to do.

A couple of attempts in the nineteenth and twentieth centuries to make Arabic more print-friendly, by using only the separate forms of characters, got nowhere. Nor did attempts to invent the equivalent of capital letters, which help so much in navigating Latin texts (glance at this page: you can find a proper name like 'Arabic' almost instantly, because of its signpost capital). The 1928 Turkish solution, to scrap Arabic script and adopt Latin, provoked outrage in some quarters of the Arabic world. It was worse than vandalism: in an aniconic culture, it was the nearest thing to iconoclasm. 'Arabic script,' fumed one of its distinguished practitioners at the time,

> had committed no sin against them [i.e. the Turks]. It was just their way of going along with spurious 'civilization' . . . The decision did not result from sound theory or from logical reasoning . . . It was nothing but an intoxicating notion that fermented in the heads of their great leaders.

Atatürk would have begged to differ: the Turkish leader's reason was no less than the cultural re-orientation of post-Ottoman Turkey away from the Arabic-Islamic world, and its temporal re-orientation from the fourteenth century AH to the twentieth century AD. Whether his theory was sound may still be too early to tell.

Since Atatürk, however, there has been another revolution, and it has finally put paid to the scribes – but also to doubts about the viability of Arabic script in the contemporary world. Only twenty years ago, wanting the Arabic epigraphs of my first book to look good, I used the services not of a typographer but of a calligrapher. All this has changed with word-processing: now we can all be calligraphers, and we can print in an instant, with vowels, ligatures, frills, furbelows and all,

But for a full 500 years from Gutenberg to Microsoft, the problem was that essential print-unfriendliness of Arabic.

There were other problems too, quite apart from the technical or aesthetic ones. Arabic moveable type took a good two-thirds of those 500 years even to get moving in its homeland. The oldest surviving Arabic printed book, a volume of Christian prayers, was printed in Italy in 1514; from then on, Orientalists would print Arabic texts in Europe. As for the Arabic lands themselves, Christians in Lebanon experimented with printing a hundred years later, and in Aleppo another hundred years on, but in neither case did the technology spread to the Muslim majority. The first press in Constantinople was founded in 1722, but was not seen in the Arabic world, apart from those two abortive attempts, until Napoleon's Egyptian adventure of 1798 and the appearance of propaganda posters on calligraphic Cairo's walls:

> The *Amir* of the Army, BŪNĀBĀRTAH [Bonaparte] . . . is a man perfect in reason, merciful and kind to the Muslims, loving to the poor and needy!

This was followed by Muhammad Ali Pasha's establishment of a full-scale government-run press in the city in 1822. Only then did typography gain a permanent foothold in Arabic lands. Thus, for around 350 years after its spread to every corner of Europe, most Arabic users were utterly deprived of print. It is hard to quantify the effects; but there is no doubt that the time-lag put a powerful brake on progress, scientific and technological. Moreover, the brake may not only have slowed down the dissemination of new ideas. It has been argued that the European print revolution underlay the new concept of the fact as proof, as opposed to the 'proof' of rhetoric and of divine or human authorities; this new concept, in turn, underpinned the whole scientific revolution. If this is true, then it is something the Arabic world missed out on.

Both Bacon and Carlyle numbered printing along with gunpowder – and, respectively, the compass and Protestantism – as the three great discoveries of modern times. Elsewhere, Carlyle wrote,

> He who first shortened the labour of copyists by device of *Movable Types* was disbanding hired armies, and cashiering most Kings and senates, and creating a whole new democratic world: he had invented the art of printing.

For a sizeable section of humanity that whole new world was postponed, and for users of Arabic the reason was not only the conservatism of copyists and kings, but also their exquisitely beautiful but print-unfriendly script. Imagine the equivalent if, say, Arabic users were to have been prevented from using the internet for a third of a millennium.

That of course did not happen. Arabs are enthusiastic users of the internet, especially since the appearance of smartphones. And in this is another twist to the ramifications from that Greek invention of vowels, the best part of three millennia ago. For it may also be true to say that much of the Arabic world has vaulted over print and landed straight in the world of information technology – or perhaps of *mis*information technology, since, again, multiple versions of the 'truth' are simultaneously available, versions that rely once more on rhetoric and human or divine authority as much as on empirical fact. Many Arabs may thus have leapt straight from 'pre-truth' to 'post-truth' without going through the intervening stage.

THE WICKEDEST OF RACES

If those 300-odd years from the coming of the Ottomans seemed to retard scientific progress in the arabophone world, they seemed no better for Arab identity. Before the beginning of the Ottoman trough, Ibn Battutah (genetic Berber, cultural Arab) had referred to 'Arabs' in his rambling travel book (nearly a thousand pages in the full English translation) only about a score of times, despite the span of thirty-three years and around 120,000 kilometres of wandering, including all the Arabic-speaking lands. The references divide roughly into thirds: a third of them use 'Arab' as an ethnic-linguistic or cultural marker, as in, '*faqir*s [Sufi ascetics] of the Arabs, Persians, Turks and Anatolians'; a third refer to Arabs as desert guards and guides, marginal to the mainly civilized world in which Ibn Battutah travelled, for example those in the Eastern Desert of Egypt; and a third refer to Arabs as a danger, like the marauding Arab tribesmen he found besieging Tunis.

By the end of the 300-year trough, in the early nineteenth century, the best-known Arabic historian of the times – the Egyptian al-Jabarti (genetic Ethiopian, cultural Arab) – refers to Arabs in his nearly 2,000-page chronicle of Egypt more often than Ibn Battutah, but seldom in their 'cultural' or even linguistic role. Almost always they are Gog and Magog, the peril beyond the pale. 'Those accursed *a'rab*,' for example, 'are the wickedest of races, and the greatest evil that besets people.' To ignite panic and set off a stampede in which women were trampled to death, it was enough for the rumour-mongers of Cairo to go about shouting, 'O people! The *'arab* have fallen upon you!'

But all that was set to change. A new Arab identity was about to awaken, one that would embrace diverse peoples and tribes from the Indian Ocean to the Atlantic – and would fail, as ever, to unite them.

RE-EMERGENCE

1800—now

CHAPTER THIRTEEN

IDENTITY REDISCOVERED

AWAKENINGS

THE HANDSOME ONE WITH THE HANGING CLOAK

'In this age of ours,' wrote Abd al-Rahman al-Jabarti towards the end of the eighteenth century, in the introduction to his chronicle, 'people have abandoned the writing of history.' Al-Jabarti, who – as we have just seen – considered tribal Arabs 'the wickedest of races', was no less gloomy about history itself:

> For the times are running contrary; the shadow of the age has shrunk . . . No proper tally of events is kept or recorded in books; indeed, to employ one's hours in so useless a pursuit is but to squander it. What's over and done with cannot be brought back.

This age of oblivion had been going on, he said, for the past fifty years or so. The glory was gone, and now history too was trapped, like literature, in its own downward spiral – one in which wicked *badw* raided helpless *hadar* and plundered the Mecca pilgrim caravans, as they had done time out of mind; in which Mamluks still lorded it over Cairo, as they had done for over half a millennium, including 300 years of Ottoman rule.

Before the eighteenth century closed, however, the times had done an about-turn and taken off headlong into an unsettling future. Bedouins descending on Cairo caused panic; yet at least they were the *jinni*s you knew, as the saying goes – better than the humans you didn't know. For when, in July 1798, another horde descended on Egypt, it was not the familiar fiends but a species of raiding humans unknown for more than five centuries, since Crusading Franks had last invaded the Delta. Then, they had been repulsed. This time the contest was less equal: the Mamluks were blown to bits by superior artillery, the townspeople of Cairo had nothing with which to oppose this new breed of Frank but prayers and sticks, and Napoleon marched in.

His aim was not only to satisfy the imperial itch for expansion, but to disrupt Britain's communications in the eastern Mediterranean, and particularly the short but vital overland leg, through Egypt, on the way to her growing Indian empire. Al-Jabarti observed the latter-day Franks with an anthropologist's fascination. With stereoptypical Frenchness, one of the first things they did was to open restaurants providing a table d'hôte service and *prix fixe* menus:

> Each dining-room has a sign with the amount of *dirham*s the diner must pay . . . and when they finish their meal they pay this sum, neither less nor more.

'Neither less nor more . . . ': it was a small first in the metropolis of haggling. Observing both dining-room and bedroom, al-Jabarti noted that the French were not tardy in forming liaisons with the concubines of defunct Mamluks, 'white, black and Abyssinian . . . most of whom adopted the dress of the Frankish women'. In matters of dress, the revolutionary occupiers were less successful when they tried to get the three big religious shaykhs to change their traditional subfusc *taylasan*s, a sort of academic hood, to revolutionary tricolour versions.

They did, however, manage to launch a small tricolour Montgolfier. It turned out to be an over-hyped flop, as it was not manned – fortunately, as it fell apart in mid-air. Far from being, as al-Jabarti had expected, a means 'for people to travel to distant lands . . . it seemed more like those kites that the servants make for festivals and weddings'. Nor was he edified by the spectacle of the few hard-riding Frenchwomen who had come with the expeditionary force, dressed in their Paris fashions and 'shrieking with laughter and joking with the donkey-boys and the common yobs'. But some Frankish innovations did impress him. They included that brilliant invention, the wheelbarrow, and in particular the public library which the French opened. Al-Jabarti spent many hours there, noting that it was popular even among 'the lower ranks of the soldiery'. He also enjoyed visiting an interactive exhibition, where one could observe scientific experiments at close quarters, and even experience shocks from an electrostatic generator: 'One's body is immediately convulsed with a rapid quivering, and one feels as if the joints in one's shoulders and arms are being cracked.'

Apart from the new technologies and new fashions that he brought, Napoleon wielded a new broom in this land where the dust of the past lay so thick. Having demolished the gates that separated the quarters of Cairo, he had the streets swept and lit, and the city's properties registered. He began to sweep away some mental cobwebs too. The Cairene legal establishment, whose schools of jurisprudence had been formed the best part of a thousand years before, were surprised to find that French court procedure was based not on religion, but on reason. Napoleon also introduced new political ideas, including elections by ballot and a chamber of representatives. And in an attempt to keep newly opening minds under control, he also instituted the Arabic world's first printed propaganda, in the form of those posters proclaiming himself the friend of Islam. The friendship was not always apparent: registration of property led, of course, to plans for a property tax, which led in turn to a popular uprising, and the French tit-for-tat desecration of the hallowed mosque of al-Azhar.

Despite such provocations, al-Jabarti maintained a detached and non-judgemental view of the French. He seems to have regarded them as an unparalleled curiosity, as a scoop for his chronicle (they had, after all, kicked moribund history back to life) and as agents of divine retribution: 'Your Lord,' he writes more than once, quoting from the Qur'an,

> would never destroy towns unjustly as long as their people were doers of good.

The French, in other words, were the human equivalent of those natural disasters with which God had chastised the erring peoples of the distant past – Ad, Thamud and Saba. Some less philosophical Cairenes regarded the French as 'infidel dogs'; others, however, welcomed them. There was even a popular song that celebrated Napoleon, his trouncing of the unpopular Mamluks (the 'Ghuzz' – the Turks) and his subsequent suppression of the bedouin raiders (here, *'urban* – ironically, given the look of the transliteration, another plural of the far-from-urban *'arab*):

We longed for you, O General,
O you handsome one with the hanging cloak,
Your sword in Egypt made havoc
Of the Ghuzz and the *'urban.*

But more havoc was on its way: another species of Frank, hot on the heels of the first. Only a month after Napoleon had swept into Cairo, Nelson sailed into Aboukir Bay and destroyed the French expeditionary fleet in the Battle of the Nile. Napoleon was now cut off. The handsome general himself managed to slip away the following year; but the French position was untenable, and a combined Ottoman and British force squeezed them out of Egypt in the summer of 1801.

Once again, as in the distant pre-Islamic past when they had been 'stuck on top of a rock between two lions', and as so often since then, Arabs were caught between other peoples' empires. This time they were trapped between three: the Sublime but now crumbling Porte of the Ottomans and, more fatefully, those feisty foes Britannia and Marianne – the one intent on keeping open her short but vital land bridge through Egypt on the route to India, the other intent on blocking it. It had once helped Arabs to be middle-men, mediating between the two great zones of Old World trade, the Mediterranean and the Indian Ocean. Now, with two European powers both wanting to control both zones at the same time, Arabs found themselves in the way, pickle in the middle. (Nor would it be the last time: Caesar and Hulagu, as the two contending empires of the Cold War would be characterized by its greatest Arabic poet, had always prowled about the Middle East, and always would.)

PEOPLES, TRIBES AND EMPIRES

Once again, imperial pressures would remould Arab identity. The coming of the French to Egypt is usually seen as the turn of an era, the Arab turning point towards a modern, Western world. It was certainly the closest encounter with post-Renaissance Europe so far, but it wasn't the first. Already, the Omani overseas empire had been inspired and shaped for over a century by growing European maritime power. More recently, in the last quarter of the eighteeenth century, the burgeoning British empire had been sending warships to the Gulf: their mission was to protect British India-bound merchantmen from raids by Arab vessels based in what is now the United Arab Emirates. Whether the raiders were pirates, jihadists or freedom-fighters is a question of taste; what is not in question is that British naval operations were a foretaste of Western interventions in the Gulf down to our own time.

These earlier encounters, however, had been side-shows on the fringes of the Arabic world. The forces that had descended on Egypt were on a different scale: Napoleon's army arrived on a roll from a stunning Italian campaign; Britain's Mediterranean navy ruled the western waves. And Egypt itself, far from being at the fringe, had been the cultural heart of the Arabic world since the fall of Baghdad to the Mongols more than five centuries before. It sat across the joint between Mashriq and Maghrib, between two continents, and was home to the biggest Arabic-speaking population in all the lands of the Ottoman empire. That said, in 1798 the cultural heart was beating faintly at best, and Egypt's conscious arabness lay dormant. The time was long past when intellectual innovators like Ibn Khaldun had come to teach in the soaring new *madrasah*s of Cairo, those intellectual powerhouses of four hundred years and more before, or the great Egyptian synthesizers of knowledge, like the encyclopaedist al-Qalqashandi or the literary historian al-Suyuti, had compiled their vast data-banks of Arabic learning. Now in this Ottoman twilight, as al-Jabarti had noted, there seemed to be nothing worth adding to the past. Worse, the past was being lost: what was left of the great old *madrasah* libraries was being steadily filched or sold off, al-Jabarti lamented. The very stuff of Arab history and identity was being stolen.

Now, though, in the pre-dawn of what came to be called *al-Nahdah*, 'the Awakening', France, then Britain, had planted the first rough kisses that would rouse Arabs from their long sleep. Later in the nineteenth century the Ottoman empire, for long a hands-off ruler of most of its Arab domains, would put its own pressures on Arabs – and then those fractured peoples and tribes would begin to see themselves once more as a distinct group, joined by language and history. Arabs in all their diversity would be gathered again, not this time 'on the word of Islam', as Ibn Khaldun had put it, but on a new word: *qawmiyyah*, nationalism. Just as Germans, Italians and other disparate groups in Europe had been rediscovering (or reinventing) their roots at this time, and finding that they were nations with shared ancient languages and traditions, so too would Arabs. But while for Arabs the word 'nationalism' would be new, the idea was ancient: Islam had also tried to bring together settled peoples and mobile tribes, and to synthesize them into an *ummah*, a 'nation' in the sense of a great inclusive community. In the same way, Arab nationalism would have as its basis the idea of an *ummah 'arabiyyah*, a united Arab 'nation'. And even before Islam, a shared language had defined its users as a 'national' group in one sense, *'arab* as opposed to *'ajam*. So if the nineteenth-century Awakening 'planted the seed of an idea . . . that the Arabs were a nation, defined by a common language, culture and history', it was not for the first time. The seed had already been planted in pre-Islamic times, replanted in the early Islamic centuries, and nurtured during the early Abbasid age, when common language, culture and history were first fixed in writing.

Those older plantings had withered. At first, the nineteenth-century seed would grow into a new *'asabiyyah*, a sense of solidarity that would be stronger than in any age since the beginning of Islam. In time, in the middle of the twentieth century, the solidarity would fuel a wheel of fire that centred on Egypt but reignited on a pan-Arab scale. And, once more, Arabs would find unity elusive: the fire would only have itself to consume.

THE HOUSE OF TONGUES

In early nineteenth-century Egypt, all this was as yet unimagined. Egyptians were still reeling from the sudden twist in history brought about by Napoleon. But if a European visitor of 1806 can be believed, the brief encounter with the French had already acted as a wake-up call:

> The expedition of the French . . . produced a happy change in the ideas of the people. The immense advantages of civilization, of military tactics, of the political organization, of the arts and sciences of the nations of Europe, which they have had an opportunity of remarking; the philanthropic ideas common to all classes of society, which they have had time to appreciate; have inspired them with a respect for the nations which

> possess such great advantages over the Arabs and Turks, whose inferiority in regard to the Europeans they candidly acknowledge.

This might be no more than Eurocentrism, had we not the implicit corroboration of that local observer, al-Jabarti, and, more important, the explicit evidence of the coming decades of Egypt's history under the remarkable Muhammad Ali Pasha. He and his successors would import a plethora of advantages, sciences and ideas, and naturalize them to Egypt.

If the French had left a sense of inferiority, they also left a sense of egyptianness and of nation. From the first, Napoleon's proclamations had claimed to support 'the people of Egypt . . . the whole *ummah*' against the 'imported' Mamluks. This was something new. Egypt was a palimpsest of peoples and princes; the Mamluks were just the latest and longest in a series of imported, superimposed rulers. Then again, the Mamluks had kept power so long by *not* integrating, as had all the others. Muhammad Ali, the Ottoman viceroy of Egypt, would be different. He and his successors would tackle the sense of inferiority, turning away from Istanbul and looking for inspiration from modern, Western Europe. But the new stance would not be a mere reorientation (or reoccidentation); instead, it would firmly establish that idea of Egypt as a nation – a 'whole *ummah*', as Napoleon's declaration had put it – not a possession of the Porte. Inevitably, too, it would reawaken Egypt's arabness.

Muhammad Ali was himself an 'import', a Macedonian-born Albanian who had risen through the Ottoman military ranks. But like those of the alien dynasts of a thousand years before, the Tulunids, Ikhshidids and others, his offspring would be arabized by Egypt: 'the sun of Egypt changed my blood and made it all Arab,' declared his eldest son, Ibrahim Pasha. More important, they re-arabicized Egypt itself, by replacing Turkish with Arabic as the official language. This re-established Arabic on solid, middle ground, after it had for so long existed only at the extremes – the high liturgical language on the one hand, and the low patois of the common people on the other. Before, low Arabic had meant low prestige: Napoleon had been compelled to use Turks to keep order, as arabophones couldn't command enough respect to do so. The policies of Muhammad Ali and his successors restored that respect by giving Arabic back its official, public voice. The pasha also raised the profile of Arabic by reviving an innovation of the French. Napoleon had plastered the suq with printed posters; for a brief period in 1800, his second successor Menou had published *Al-tanbih*, *The Announcement* – the first Arabic newspaper. In 1828, Muhammad Ali took up the idea with his own newspaper, *Al-waqa'i' al-misriyyah*, *Egyptian Events*. The title was not quite a declaration of independence from Istanbul; but it was a powerful assertion of selfhood.

Muhammad Ali also ended the Ottoman centuries of isolation from further Europe. Notably, in 1826 he sent a group of young Egyptian men to study in Paris. Their spiritual bear-leader, a bright graduate of al-Azhar named al-Tahtawi, expressed his mixed feelings about the French city in verse:

> Does Paris have on earth a peer in which
> the suns of learning, like hers, never set?
> Or where – no less remarkable – the night
> of irreligion has no morrow yet?

It seemed impossible to him that such clever people as the Parisians had not become Muslims. All the same, he returned to Cairo with an admiration not just for French learning, but also for French political freedoms, and the realization that 'justice is the foundation of a flourishing civilization', as in Islamic theory – if not, he implied, in practice. Al-Tahtawi also came back an accomplished linguist, and was appointed founding director of the House of Tongues, set up by Muhammad Ali in 1835 to translate European books. It was a new edition of the Abbasid Caliph al-Ma'mun's House of Wisdom, founded in Baghdad almost precisely a thousand years before, in 832.

Under Muhammad Ali Pasha's successors, the translation process continued. But it went both ways, and took in not just books but the city itself, the culture and communications of the country, and even the geography of east–west commerce. The pasha's immediate heirs brought steam to Egypt, and Robert Stephenson (son of George 'Rocket' Stephenson) to design the lines and the rolling stock. In the 1860s, Muhammad Ali's grandson Isma'il Haussmannized Cairo, transforming it into a city of boulevards and avenues, and built that ultimate symbol of openness to other (European) traditions, an opera house. In the meantime, work was progressing on that most literal opening between east and west, the Suez Canal. Its inauguration in 1869 proved that, whatever Kipling would think, the twain *could* meet – at least for a brief time at the opening ceremony, in

> a mad carmagnole . . . with Kaisers and Dervishes, Emperors and Almey girls, Patriarchs and buffons, Emirs and engineers, Mussulman high priests and Italian sailors all mixed up helter skelter . . .

A fleet of steam yachts made the first passage of the Canal, including Isma'il's enormous *El Mahrousa* – much modified since but still, amazingly, the Egyptian presidential yacht. But it all came at a price: Ismail had bankrupted the Egyptian state, and in so doing he opened the way to another less welcome aspect of Western Europe, that most dogged of debt-collectors, the British bailiff.

A TURN OF THE HOURGLASS

Meanwhile, across the Red Sea from Egypt, another Arab awakening had been going on, but one that led in a diametrically opposite direction: into the past, and into itself. To the Wahhabi tribesmen of the Arabian Peninsula, a House of Tongues would have been a tower of Babel, and an opera house the boudoir of the Whore of Babylon; for them, all *bid'ah*, innovation, was heresy. And yet their movement was, like the events that had been set in motion in Egypt, a sort of precursor to the general Arab Awakening.

The Wahhabis' beginnings went back to the mid-eighteenth century, but it was only in 1798, the year in which the French invaded Egypt, that the Ottomans woke up to this other, home-brewed threat to their domains. Disturbed by increasingly organized bedouin incursions into the settled lands of Iraq – that old sign, from way back before Islam, of trouble fermenting in the Arab 'Island' – the Turks sent a 10,000-strong army into the peninsula. It surrendered ignominiously to a rabble of bedouin warriors.

What looked like a rabble was in fact an irregular but surprisingly disciplined tribal army. It was also unexpectedly large, for it had been mustering for a generation. We can probably dismiss the idea, mooted by an Ottoman writer in the 1880s, that Wahhabism was implanted in Arabia by an eighteenth-century British agent called 'Mister Hempher'. Rather, the movement took its inspiration and its most common name from a cleric from the bracing uplands of Najd in central Arabia, Muhammad ibn Abd al-Wahhab. Born in about 1720, he went travelling in his youth and was appalled by what he saw as the saint-worship and other forms of 'corruption' that had infected Islam in the sultry climes beyond his native plateau. Further inspired by the writings of a notorious fourteenth-century puritan, Ibn Taymiyyah, he began a mission to disinfect the faith. The mission was multiply rooted in the past: in the ideas of Ibn Taymiyyah, but also – as the Wahhabis' official name, 'al-Muwahhidun' or Unitarians, reveals – in that seminal message of the Qur'an: *tawhid*, the doctrine of divine unity that strips the deity bare of all associates and intermediaries. The Arabian Muwahhiddun thus shared a name and an aim with the Berber al-Muwahhidun, the 'Almohads' of twelfth-century North Africa and Spain. But they would prove to be a new and even more rigorous edition, and one that is still in circulation today.

Like that of other similar idealists before and since, the Wahhabis' Unitarianism would be both theological and political: once more, saying 'Yes' to the earthly ruler was tantamount to saying 'Amen' to the heavenly Creator. Like those others, too, the Wahhabi neo-neo-Unitarians found that even if God was One, a spirit named Legion held sway on earth. The growing movement began its struggle against both divine will and human nature by forging a super-tribal, pan-Arabian unity. If the story sounds familiar, that is because the Wahhabis were consciously replaying the beginning of the Islamic state of Medina; like the first Muslims, they even referred to their life before Wahhabism as al-Jahiliyyah, 'the Ignorance'. And by searching for purity they were also looking back to an Arab-only version of Islam, stripped of its foreign accretions and corruptions. Yet again, Arab identity was being shaped in reflex to outsiders: not only the degenerate Ottoman overlords of Arabia and the irredeemably Shi'i Persians, who were once again encroaching on the east of the peninsula as they had before Islam; but also that whole world beyond, wallowing in saint-worship, idolatry and innovation.

It would have been lonely for Muhammad ibn Abd al-Wahhab up on the rocky plateau of Najd, surrounded by threats imperial and theological. But he found a vital early convert in Muhammad ibn Sa'ud, leader of a prominent Najdi family. Ibn Sa'ud saw his chance: rather as the Quraysh *ancien régime* had harnessed the word gathered by the Prophet Muhammad ibn Abd Allah in order to hold on to and extend their own rule, so would the Al Sa'ud with the followers gathered by the reformer Muhammad ibn Abd al-Wahhab. With temporal support from the Al Sa'ud and an increasing stream of tribesmen joining the cause, the reformist mission soon turned into a rampage. Wahhabi raiders unleashed a wave of righteous vandalism across the peninsula, destroying anything that hinted of *shirk*, 'polytheism'. In particular, tombs that stood more than a handspan high were flattened, lest they tempt visitors down the slippery slope from respect via intercession to saint-worship. During the Wahhabi occupation of Medina (1805–12), much of the identifiable, visitable past was simply wiped out: the long-revered resting places of the Prophet's companions were reduced to anonymous piles of rubble. Even the Prophet did not escape unscathed: treasures donated over the centuries to his tomb were looted, and the dome above it threatened with destruction. All this was relatively restrained, however, compared with their earlier spree of violence in southern Iraq in 1802. There, in Shi'i Karbala, the Wahhabis had smashed the venerated tomb of Muhammad's martyred grandson, al-Husayn. And, not content with destroying the dead, they had also massacred the living townsfolk.

For many centuries, the fatal hourglass, that cursed, recursive history of conflict that went back to the first decades of Islam, had been gathering dust. The Wahhabis had turned it, setting the old clashes in motion once more, and their heirs – and, in turn, the heirs' antagonists – have been turning it again and again ever since.

With the Wahhabis in striking distance of Baghdad, the Ottomans clearly had to do something; but that defeat of 1798 inflicted on their army by Wahhabi tribesmen had shown that this imperial lion for one was, in reality, a paper tiger. The Porte eventually appealed for help to its viceroy in now French-free Egypt, Muhammad Ali Pasha. And in so doing it gave an extra nudge to Egyptian self-assertion – and also set in motion a new sort of clash, between a new kind of people, beginning to feel its way towards a future nationhood, and a newly united species of super-tribe, trying to complete what it saw as the unfinished work of history; a clash, in short, between progress and reaction, between an uncertain future and an imagined past.

This time it was the future that won, in 1818, after a grim five-year Arabian campaign by Muhammad Ali's forces. The captured Wahhabi leaders were executed in Istanbul; the corpses were displayed for three days, then thrown into the sea. (Did the Americans know that when they committed the Wahhabis' spiritual descendant Usamah Bin Ladin to the deep 200 years later?) It seemed the Wahhabis had met their Waterloo. But the influence of the rebarbative raiders was much harder to eradicate:

> An epidemical enthusiasm, compounded of sullen scrupulousness and warlike ferocity, which, in a people resigned to their own thoughts, and

> who, conversing only with each other, suffered no dilution of their zeal from the gradual influx of new opinions, was long transmitted in its full strength from the old to the young.

That is Samuel Johnson writing in 1775 on the Scots Calvinists; but he might as well have been writing of the Wahhabis of his time and later. In the last third of the nineteenth century, Egypt was conversing with Europe, and never more chattily than in the steam-powered decades of Muhammad Ali's successors. But five years after *Aida* premiered at the Cairo opera house in 1871, the English traveller Doughty found that 'The sour Wahaby fanaticism has in these days cruddled the hearts of the nomads'. Some hearts would remain cruddled (a Doughty archaism for 'curdled'), and would inspire movements to come – the revived twentieth-century Ikhwan ('the Brethren'), al-Qa'idah, the 'Islamic State', and others yet to be named.

All are *muwahhidun*, seekers after unity, God's and man's. But the unity they search for is never free of that other shade of meaning: *wahdah* is oneness, but it is also lone-ness, introversion, isolation. It may just be hindsight, but it is hard to imagine the Wahhabi awakening happening anywhere in the Arabic world other than in that remote upland heart of the peninsula, almost an island within the Arabs' 'Island'. In contrast, Egypt's awakening – to itself and to its arabness, but also to a wider world – took place where the great river of Africa opens the fan of its delta to the Mediterranean.

BORN AGAIN

Like Wahhabi ideology, the secular nationalism that developed with the nineteenth century also sought to create unity. It aimed, however, not at pristine Arab Muslim isolation but at pan-Arab integration; not at unison but at polyphony, with all Arabic voices in harmony. Such vast and motley choruses might work in *Aida*. In real life they would prove harder to orchestrate.

Under Muhammad Ali Pasha and his heirs, Egypt had been reclaiming its identity and proving its *de facto* independence from the Ottomans. In particular, that successful war against the Wahhabis had shown that Muhammad Ali was no cat's paw, but a strong-armed ruler in his own right. Since then, he and his successors had also given Egypt back its Arabic voice, reinstating Arabic as the official language and founding an Arabic press. The voice began to resonate next door, too, in the Levant – and in that denominationally diverse region, it was a call to unity. Egypt, of course, had a big minority of Coptic Christians. But while the Copts had been arabicized, they had never quite been arabized: they were still seen as aliens, conquered natives. In contrast, in Greater Syria, most of the many Christians were, or at least claimed to be, Arabs *ab ovo*, some of them tracing their descent back to the pre-Islamic Ghassanid kings. It was among them that the idea of a newly gathered word took shape – of a new pan-Arab union, an *ummah* based not on religion but on language. After all, that first unifier had proved superbly resilient: a thousand years of rule by others, mostly Turks, had not succeeded in turkifying Arabs or depriving them of their ancient tongue.

One of those at the forefront of the revival was Ibrahim al-Yaziji, a Lebanese Maronite Christian from a family of scholars. For him, Arabic was not just a force unifying the *ummah*; rather, 'Language *is* the *ummah* itself.' Arabic, in other words, was the essence and substance of the Arab nation. The language, he believed, held Arabs together far more surely than bonds of blood, religion and custom; it transcended geography, class and politics. And this was more than just academic theory: as in ancient times, activists like al-Yaziji would use poetry to transform ideas into deeds. By the 1860s Egypt had divorced itself from the Ottomans, at least with a decree *nisi*; but the fragmented Levant was still bound to Istanbul, and the Ottoman 'Sick Man of Europe' was already a dead weight on Arab progress. So when al-Yaziji's great ode of 1868 boomed out,

> Awake, O Arabs, and arise!

it was a call not just to rise and shine, but to buck up, buck the Turks off their back and reclaim a whole lost identity:

> The Turks stole what was yours by right of birth;
> in Turkish eyes you're men devoid of worth.
> Deprived of being, of title and of name,
> your honour lies forgotten, and your fame.

Nearly a thousand years earlier, Turks like Bajkam, with their outlandish names and manners, had pushed Arabs off the coinage and off the throne. Here at last was a passionate plea to restore the Arab name, the Arab face.

Other Christian Arab thinkers would energize the nationalist cause over the coming century of its existence. For them there was no conflict with the Islamic current that ran through the latter half of Arab history. On the contrary, to nationalists like Michel Aflaq, founder of the Ba'th movement in the early 1940s, Islam was, 'a great historical experience . . . [which] belonged not only to all Arab Muslims, but to all Arabs'. In a sense, his holistic vision was right: Islam is a creed, a confession, but with Muhammad's move to Medina it also became a political denomination that could embrace Arabs of other faiths. The Wahhabis were trying to reconstruct early Islam according to their own tunnel vision of what it should have been; Arab nationalism, inspired though it was in part by European models, in part by a renascent Egypt, sought instead to recapitulate something more like the Abbasid golden age. In that age, in a great outpouring of ink, a version of Arab identity, history and language was preserved on paper against the depredations of Persian Shu'ubis and other cultural independence movements. Now, in the belated age of Arabic printing, writers could at last celebrate arabness once more, and flaunt it in the face of other national identities. With print, the language gained new life, and literature sprang up again after the barren centuries in which this chapter began. The Wahhabis had confronted the Turks with born-again Islam; the nationalists were doing it with born-again Arabic, and their conversions were linguistic ones. Sometimes they verged on the miraculous: Sati' al-Husri, for example, hailing from Aleppo but educated solely in Turkish in Istanbul and long employed as an Ottoman official in the Balkans, renounced the Ottomans' language and embraced Arabic in his fortieth year; he went on to become one of the great theorists of Arab nationalism.

Once again, a new technology of letters had launched a new stage of Arab history. Early writing had influenced and preserved the Qur'an; Umayyad book-keeping had arabicized the empire; paper had defined and recorded Arab identity when the empire was falling apart. Now, long-delayed printing had helped to revive that identity. At the same time, the course of history had a circularity to it. As one observer of Arab civilization wrote, 'With Arab nationalism we are back at our starting point'. It is a starting point that precedes Islam and dates to a time when diverse peoples and tribes were searching for a unified identity for themselves. Now, once again, *'arabiyyah*, the old high Arabic, would be the core of *'asabiyyah*, solidarity. As the European Renaissance had rediscovered a classical past, the

Nahdah was an Awakening to the existence of the vast treasure of Arabic. It was as if Arabs had hit upon that treasure of ancient odes, buried by the king of al-Hirah, and were investing it in a greater future for themselves.

THE FORKED TONGUE

To begin with, however, the Arab Awakening was largely the Intellectual Christian Levantine Arab Awakening. Most Arabs, the genetically diverse speakers of a loose family of widely differing dialects, inhabiting a hugely varied territory from the Atlantic to the Gulf, slept on. A revived sense of arabness would dawn across the region, but very slowly. My adoptive land of Yemen, for example, was virtually untouched by it until almost a century after al-Yaziji's ode of 1868; now, another fifty years on, Yemen seems to be sinking back into its old and troubled coma. In the 1980s, the Moroccan cultural historian Muhammad al-Jabiri wrote that 'the Arab Awakening of modern times . . . has yet to become a reality'. Today, the reality sometimes seems even further off.

Part of the problem was that the modern revival movement was grounded so deeply in that very old, and very difficult, high language. The European Renaissance began just as people were beginning to write widely and creatively in their vernaculars; the later rise of Protestantism and the translation of scripture ensured that, in writing as well as speech, those vernaculars would eventually prevail over Latin and Greek. In contrast, the Arab renaissance, which sought common ground for all Arabs, ensured the victory of the old high language as the sole written medium. The European equivalent would have been for the continent to have rediscovered Virgil, but never to have had a Dante or a Chaucer; for the Latin Vulgate Bible to have had no rivals, and for Luther and Wycliffe never to have been born. Except for those in the Jewish, Christian and other non-Muslim Arab communities who had not studied the high language and wrote in the vernacular (but in Hebrew, Syriac and other characters, not Arabic script), most Arabs had never even thought of writing in dialect. And in more recent centuries – particularly in the historical and literary nadir of the eighteenth century that al-Jabarti described – people had given up writing altogether, or at least writing anything fresh; they simply rehashed. Now, with the Awakening, creative literature took off again – but still in the old language and idiom. Al-Yaziji's ode, for example, would have raised neither objections nor eyebrows among poets like Abu Tammam, who lived more than a thousand years earlier; the English equivalent would be Byron, say, still writing in the style and even the language of *Beowulf*. It was all part of that 'retreat from modernity', as a poet and critic of our times, Adonis, has called it. The Awakening, in other words, awakened nothing new; it simply 'returned the present to the past'.

This past idiom is essentially what most Arabs attempt to use today, at least when they are writing formal prose or speaking formally in public. Foreign learners of it are told that they are being taught something called 'Modern Standard Arabic'. It sounds as if it should be something new and shiny, but in reality it is to classical high Arabic rather as medieval Latin is to Latin of the golden age: a bit dumbed down syntactically; clunkier stylistically; broader lexically, yes; but in essence the same. Even a modern poet who may not use the old metres and rhymes still uses the ancient language:

> Whoever today can read Nizar Qabbani [died 1998] can read al-Abbas ibn al-Ahnaf [died *c.* 803] . . . This is a strange and amazing phenomenon, rarely encountered in other cultures.

Indeed it is, and it is part of the knotty nexus of what makes Arabs distinctive, and what holds them together, not just over space but also over time; even if part of the togetherness is being at each other's throats.

When Arabs write or speechify, therefore, they are using a language which is not exactly 'foreign', but which certainly is non-native. The distance from everyday speech to written Arabic, at its greatest – in Casablanca, say – can be as wide as that between Petrarch and Petronius, Romance and Latin. Getting the wording right is usually the first concern; content tends to be secondary. (The grammar of numbers is so easy to get wrong that a whole minting of tens of millions of coins was in circulation in my adoptive country before anyone noticed the small but dreadful error: they read *'ishruna riyalin*, 'twenty *riyal*s [genitive]' instead of *'ishruna riyalan*, 'twenty *riyal*s [accusative]'. The devil is in the detail.) Stuck on the horns of a diglossic dilemma, there are plenty of educated Arabs who take the easy way down, by speaking in Arabic but writing in other languages. Almost all scientific research is written up in English or other non-Arabic languages. The double problem of getting the Arabic right and finding the vocabulary is too daunting.

Does the linguistic duality really matter? It might do, if a danger some observers have warned of is real – that so forked a tongue as Arabic enables users to think with a forked mind. One critic has written of the 'ideal self' expressed, and believed, in 'the loftiest moral tone' of high Arabic, contrasting with the 'lower stratum of moral behavior' expressed in colloquial speech. I know what he means. I have listened, for example, to an acquaintance lambasting the *fasad*, the (high) 'corruption', of government ministers, and immediately going on to praise the ability of his wife, a ministry employee, to get *haqq Abi Hadi*, a (low) 'bit on the side'. That said, linguistic double standards are found in other languages; only a lot of hard research could establish whether Arabic was a special case.

There is a greater, and undoubted, danger. Even today, when official literacy figures are much higher than as little as a generation ago, very few Arabs feel comfortable writing their own 'national' language, and even fewer are comfortable speaking it. Over time, in fact, most Arabs have been scared speechless by the language that bears their name, deprived of their individual voices. Again and again they are silenced by *dictators* – in the word's most etymological sense, 'those who speak out loud all the time'. As one analyst has put it, most Arabs are excluded from their own language: 'In the language, *I* am not present – not as a person giving expression to my individual self.'

Social media, in which Arabs tend to write in colloquial form, may bring about change; but it would be change in the direction of diversity, not unity. It is too early to tell: most tweeting is in dialect, but most propaganda is still in high Arabic. And the propaganda has power: the old sacred tongue, the 'dead language that refuses to die', as Paul Bowles called it, still bewitches, mystifies and silences the masses as it did in the mouths of pre-Islamic poets and seers. It still has a weight and a volume that mutes the twittering. And it remains the most potent symbol of a long-elusive unity: 'We do not live in a land, but in a language.' Do away with that one shared territory, that almost impossibly difficult language, and you do away with the only aspect of unity that is not a mirage.

THE LAGGING LEXICON

In the nineteenth century, it was all very well for movers of the Awakening to reinvigorate Arabic letters and hope that language, the old catalyst of unity, would bring Arabs together in a new age. But there was a problem with the basic stuff of language – words: it was a long time since the Arabic Adam, like his Hebrew self in Genesis, had been taught the names of everything in creation. The Arabic dictionary was by now desperately far behind the needs of the age. For al-Jabarti, the greatest literary product of recent times was his teacher al-Zabidi's thumping great lexicon, finished in 1767 and forty volumes long in the edition I have. It was an expanded version of the already massive late fourteenth-century *Qamus*, the 'Oceanus' of words – expanded, but only with new citations and definitions, not with new entries. Anything post-classical was not 'chaste', and was excluded from the dictionary like a trollop from a nunnery.

The lexicon had ceased to reflect real life in the age of steam and opera. In practice, Arabic was adapting old words, coining new ones and absorbing many from European languages; but it was doing so organically. From the middle of the nineteenth century, however, the pioneering nationalist intellectuals in the Levant tried to drag the dictionary up to date and to standardize recent coinages: they realized that to unify Arabic's new vocabulary – to gather the words – would help to 'gather the word' of its users and bring pan-Arab political unity an important step nearer. But in the vast and still largely printless clime from the Strait of Gibraltar to the Strait of Hormuz, in which any education other than Qur'an schools was patchy at best, and travel was often as slow as it had been in the time of that first known Arab, the ninth-century BC camel-owning Gindibu (Damascus to Baghdad still took three weeks by camel in the early twentieth century), the reformers' best intentions were doomed.

The supposedly unifying language thus developed a disunited new vocabulary. 'Pendulum', for example, is *bandul* (French *pendule*) in Egypt, *raqqas* ('dancer') in Iraq and *nawwas* ('swinger, dangler') in Syria. 'Tyre' is often *tayr* (from the English), sometimes *dulab* (really 'wheel'), sometimes *kafar* (supposedly from English 'cover', although the root sense is the same in Arabic); in 'standard' Arabic it is *itar* ('rim') and in Egypt *kawitsh* ('rubber', French *caoutchouc*, ultimately from Quechua). Sometimes there were successes, like *hatif* for 'telephone', originally a disembodied voice crying in the wilderness, or coming from the entrails of a calf sacrificed to an idol; it ousted the less appealing *irziz* ('tremor, thunder'). *Qitar* ('train of camels') was an obvious choice for mechanical trains, but *jammaz* ('trotting camel, frisking ass') for 'tram' soon gave way to the loan *taramway*. 'Revolution' began as *fitnah* ('burning, trial, temptation, discord, slaughter, madness') and ended as the less coloured *thawrah*, 'an excitement'.

Sometimes, however, when a word was a straight loan but the thing named was abstract and complex, the whole idea was lost in transliteration; *dimuqratiyah* has been a notable example. But in translation, too, and usage, there are many losses. 'Republic', which began in Napoleonic Egypt, rather strangely, as *mashyakhah* ('shaykhdom'), but by the 1870s had become *jumhuriyyah* or '[rule-]of-the-mass', is a word that appears in the official names of many Arab countries; its sense has almost never been even the shadow of a reality on the ground. 'Citizens', to take another example, started as *ra'iyyah* ('subjects' – originally 'flocks, herds'), then became the more appropriate *sha'b* (that ancient word for a 'people' in contrast to a tribe), but has ended up as the bland *muwatinun*, 'fellow countrymen'. But in any case citizens – as civil legal entities in a reciprocal relationship with the state they live in, bound by rights and duties on both sides – are still an almost unknown species; they are like those mousy early mammals, waiting for the extinction of *Tyrannosaurus rex*. Politically, the Arabic world is one big Jurassic Park: it is one of the most pronounced features of that ever-present past. In practice, even 'republics' have subjects, not citizens. 'When will we learn our rights and responsibilities?' asked the Lebanese writer Faris al-Shidyaq, a leader of the literary and national revival and a coiner of new words, in 1867. As to many such questions the answer 150 years on is, 'Not yet.' Given the intimate and causal connexion between word, thought and deed, Arabic lexicography is not just a record of the language. It is also political activism, history-in-the-making.

It was not only the lexicon that had lagged; so had newspapers. Muhammad Ali Pasha's *Egyptian Events* of 1828 onwards was a lone voice until it was joined thirty years later by the Syrian *Garden of News*: two newspapers in the whole Arabic world compared with 3,000 in the USA alone at the same time. The number increased steadily in the second half of the nineteenth century, but the style of the journalism was hardly cutting-edge. One newspaper, for example, was written in verse, and even into the twentieth century, 'No self-respecting writer would publish a political article in anything but rhymed prose'.

But at least Arabs were starting make their voices heard through the press. And then another sort of silence descended on them: for no sooner did vocabulary expand and newspapers multiply than the Ottoman authorities imposed strict censorship; from the beginning of the last quarter of the nineteenth century, expressions like 'revolution', 'freedom' and 'Arab awakening' were banned in the Arabic press. The Porte was beginning to see its semi-conscious, increasingly articulate subjects, both Arab and others, as a threat. In a further response, the Ottomans started to use their own language as a tool of imperial control. It all came to a head with the Turks' own burgeoning nationalism and the revolution by the Young Turks in 1908. Under them, Istanbul began to impose its language on its Arab domains; what natural linguistic selection had not achieved over a thousand years of mostly Turkic rule, the Young Turks would now try to do by force. As a result, Arabic was banned in schools, except as a 'foreign' language. Just as Abbasid Arabism had found itself head to head with a powerful Persian Shu'ubi movement, a youthful Arab nationalism was confronted by its young and aggressive Turkish counterpart. But the Ottomans were not alone in their repression of Arabic, that core element of Arab identity.

THE OTHER GREAT GAME

In the later nineteenth century, the so-called 'Great Game' had entered its final phase, pitting Britain and Russia against each other to the north of the Indian subcontinent. But while the sahibs defended the Central Asian marches of their Raj, a hardly less important second eleven was playing against another side further west. It was a new round of the contest that had begun with Napoleon. This time it might have seemed more like a 'friendly' match; but the British aim was no less important than that of securing the borders of India – for in this second-division encounter they were securing the way there. When your two imperial capitals, London and Calcutta, are 16,000 kilometres apart by sea, even with the short cut at Suez, you need to make sure you can travel freely between them.

Britain's Napoleonic rivals in the Near Eastern game had been disappointed of Egypt in 1801. But the French imperial urge did not abate; a generation later, in 1830, they took advantage of a commercial and diplomatic spat to begin moving into Algeria, like Egypt a nominal vassal of the Ottomans. So large a territory needed time to be absorbed, but the French eventually followed on into Tunisia in 1883 and added a protectorate over large parts of Morocco in 1912. The French sphere of influence in the Arabic world would be rounded out after the Great War with a mandate over Syria, including Lebanon, in 1920.

The British, meanwhile, had gained a small but important toehold in southern Arabia by taking Aden in 1839. It was the first Victorian addition to the empire, and the first steam-driven event in the region: the British were looking for a coaling station for the nascent generation of India-bound steamships, and Aden, with its superb natural harbour just round the corner from the mouth of the Red Sea, was strategically perfect; as long as one didn't mind the absence of fresh water, the burning heat, and a volcanic backdrop that made it look to Kipling

like a barrick-stove
That no one's lit for years an' years.

For generations of British it would be the perfect dump in both senses, coal-hole and hell-hole.

In time, however, Aden grew on the British, particularly when, thirty years after they took the port, the Suez Canal transformed the Red Sea from a dead end into a live issue and a major seaway. Nor was it long before they got another toe in that new and highly convenient back door to India. Because of all those debts incurred in digging the canal – not to mention boulevardizing Cairo, hosting the Empress Eugénie and the Emperor of Austria-Hungary, hiring Stephenson, Verdi and a firmament of grand opera stars, and converting the Mamluk-era military into a model army – Egypt was bankrupt. The creditors were European and, from 1876, a posse of European powers imposed their own financial control over the country. It was also now that the cultivation of Egypt's independence and arabness, started by Muhammad Ali, began to bear bitter fruit for his heirs. Nationalist opposition to both the Europeans and the still dominant Turkic elite surged, and culminated in 1881 in native Egyptian army officers imposing their own will on the old pasha's great-grandson, Tawfiq. As trouble increased in the following year and turned to violence, Britain moved in at the behest of the Porte, shouldering the white man's burden with a dutiful sigh – but in fact delighted to keep the Frogs out once again, and to be in charge of that spanking new canal. Gibraltar, the Bab al-Mandab Strait at the mouth of the Red Sea, and now Suez: the British controlled all the bottlenecks on the long sea-road to India.

The top burden-bearer in Egypt, Evelyn Baring, might on paper have been the anglicized, distantly German-origin controller of finance for the arabized, distantly Albanian-origin vassal (with a Persian title, khedive, or 'prince') of the Turkish caliph-sultan in Istanbul; but he soon earned both promotion to the post of Britain's consul general – and the nickname, 'Over-Baring' – and as the real new ruler he joined a line of foreign pharaoh-functionaries going back to Kafur, the black eunuch slave and master of Egypt 900 years before. And not only of Egypt, for the British also found themselves in charge of Egypt's own vast imperial back yard, the Sudan. For form's sake, they adopted the fancy dress of rule *alla turca*, such as tasselled fezzes and titles like 'Bey' and 'Bimbashi'. As for the growing national aspirations of the Arab majority of the population, the new *de facto* rulers sent a clear message by condemning to death the rebellious officers' leader, Ahmad Urabi – whom, in a small but perhaps Freudian misnomer, they often referred to as Ahmad *Arabi*.

In the end, Urabi's sentence was commuted to exile. The British were also lenient towards less obviously threatening manifestations of Arab identity. Cairo continued to be the capital of the Arabic press; numbers of newspapers and periodicals increased, several of them launched by incomers seeking the freedom of expression not to be found in regions under direct Ottoman rule. These new Arabic vocal organs were of all political hues, including distinctly nationalist. Further west, however, the French wielded the language weapon as bluntly as their Ottoman counterparts. In their North African possessions, they discouraged the setting up of new Qur'an schools; in Algeria in particular, they attempted to ban the teaching of high Arabic, and promoted the use of dialect instead. By such measures, the French did their best to cut off the Maghrib from the increasingly politicized nationalists of the rest of the Arabic world. As well as attacking high Arabic, they promoted the Berber languages and cultures of the region. And in one case – that of northern Algeria – they detached the whole region administratively in 1881 and joined it to Metropolitan France. Linguistically, culturally, politically they were trying to de-arabize the thick end of Africa.

In the case of language they were especially successful. The struggles against France in the Maghrib would be among the bitterest of all wars of decolonization; but, rather as Persian Shu'ubis had resisted Arab dominance in Arabic, the main weapon on the North African language front was the imperial power's own tongue, French. After independence, it is said that even the staff of the Moroccan bureaux of re-arabicization used French to speak to each other in the office. But it was in Algeria – where, with its sparse cities, vast rural hinterland and many Berber speakers, high Arabic had never had much of a presence – that the effects of the French campaign against the language went deepest. Alone in the Arabic world, Algerian radio broadcasting was mostly in the colloquial language; Ben Bella, the first prime minister of independent Algeria, had to have an Arabic tutor; and the Algerian National Assembly of 1963 found it could only do business in French.

Meanwhile in Egypt and the Mashriq, the Arabic lands to the east, Arabs had rediscovered their own voice and were raising it ever louder. A nationalist movement that had begun as a cultural and linguistic one became ever more overtly political. As early as in the incipient turkicization of the 1880s, banners and placards had appeared in Ottoman-ruled Syria calling for both recognition of Arabic as an official language and that other demand (still to be granted today), freedom of speech. Two decades later, when the Young Turks muzzled their Arabic-speaking subjects even more tightly by banning their language in government schools, the Cairo press grew more outspoken in response. And along with placards and the press, poetry – still in the metres and monorhymes that originated before Islam – played an increasingly emotive part in politics. It could provoke draconian reactions: the Egyptian poet Ahmad Shawqi, for example, attacked British policy in verse, and was silenced by them in 1914 by being exiled to Barcelona. Later, in the anti-British uprising in 1920s Iraq, populist political poets would recite from the roofs of cars: echoes of the mounted poets and camel-back preachers of the pre-Islamic past.

The French might have imposed an angry silence on their North African possessions; further east, the Arab word was gathering itself in a crescendo of protest.

LANGUAGE AND LAND

Arab intellectuals had adapted ideas about language and nationhood from Fichte, Herder and other European theorists, but Arabs had had their own sort of linguistic 'nationalism' long before these European latecomers. There was, however, a difference: the national awareness that grew before and with Islam focused on language and cult; now, in the twilight of the Ottoman territorial empire, the sense of nationhood focused, in European style, on language and land.

There were problems with this focus. There was a unifying language; but no one spoke it as their mother-tongue and, with widespread illiteracy, few could read it well and even fewer write it. Conceivably, education could change that. There was little, however, that could be done to change the other ingredient of modern nationalism, land. The Arab territory was not a neat, discrete area like most of the nation-states of Europe, bordered by rivers, mountain ranges or gulfs. It was bigger than the whole of Europe together and, like its people, too disparate, not least economically. And there was a third problem: one of the forces that might have been expected to hold the territory together, Islam, seemed instead to undermine the whole notion of nation-states. 'The nation-state,' one recent commentator has said, 'was an entirely alien concept in Islamic theory and practice.' This is because 'Islamic constitutional theory is concerned only with community and not with territory'. 'Islamic constitutional theory' is not cast in bronze; it is hard enough to put down on paper. But the fact is that the ideas of Muslim scholars about the nature of rule have generally been about people not land, chaps rather than maps. It is hardly surprising, therefore, that many of the movers behind modern territorial nationalism were non-Muslim Arabs.

Perhaps, too, the problems that seem inherent in the idea of Arab nation-states are another aspect of the unfinished debate between *qabilah* and *sha'b*, mobile tribe and settled people. A state is, after all, cognate with stasis, not mobility: it is static. It would be very misleading to claim that the ancient South Arabian *sha'b* was anything like a modern nation-state; far from it, as far as we know (which is still not very far). But *sha'b*s did have a strongly territorial aspect, and their economies were based on cooperation rather than competition, on mutual aid not mutual raid. Bedouin mobility may be useful in the initial stages of empire-building; it is not so good at consolidating a territorial state. Borders, which define such a state, mean nothing to bedouins. But a territorial state without borders is a contradiction in terms. And yet the danger is that, if you do have borders that are effective, the bedouins – or the bedouin-minded – will be tempted to raid their own state.

For Arabs, then, the prospects for such a state or states did not look hopeful. But as the twentieth century was drawn towards its first great conflict, they were getting ever nearer the time when, like it or not, they would see their world defined in territorial terms, by lines on maps: lines laid down not by themselves but by those seemingly inescapable Others.

HIJRAHS OF STEAM

The decades before the Great War, however, would be another age of migration in a still – just – uncircumscribed world. There was a steady diaspora of Arabs, another *hijrah*; and as in the legends of the Marib Dam and the history of the first Muslims, *hijrah* would again be a catalyst, a mobilizer of change. Now, with the power of steam, a world of new destinations opened up, wider even than the Indian Ocean arc.

Although it was in a sense the next stage in a history of migration that had begun in the prehistoric past, the Arab age of the *babur* (from French *vapeur*, 'steamer') had modern-looking beginnings: from the 1870s there was a silk boom in Lebanon, and farmers and traders in their thousands would go to spend their summer holidays in France. But by 1890 the boom, and the holidays, were over. Instead, Levantine Arabs went to seek their fortunes as traders, pedlars and labourers in Europe and beyond, particularly West Africa and the Americas. Other Arabs travelled too: Yemenis, the pioneers of Arab settlement in the monsoon lands, now headed north from Aden's Steamer Point through the Suez Canal to found the first Arab communities in Britain – this time as stokers and stevedores rather than merchants and missionaries. But it was the eastern Mediterranean ports that shipped the most émigrés. By the early twentieth century, *hijrah* had become 'a virtual epidemic' in the Levant, and particularly in Lebanon. Estimates of how many Lebanese emigrated range from 'perhaps one-quarter of the total population' to 'almost half'; another authority puts the total of Lebanese migrants to the Americas at 300,000 by 1914. Whatever the exact figures, they are the reason why, in the United States, a Syrian-Lebanese quarter sprouted in what its inhabitants called 'Nayy Yark'; why, more recently, Salman Rushdie could find 'Egyptian' (in fact Lebanese) shops in Matagalpa, Nicaragua, run by the likes of Armando Mustafa and Manolo Saleh; and why on a visit to Dakar my breakfasts comprised Franco-Levantine *pain au chocolat*, Turkish coffee and Lebanese ladies with hairdos and Marlboros. They are also the reason why Argentina has had an Arab-origin president (Carlos Menem), Brazil another (Michel Temer), followed, in 2018, by an Arab-orign presidential runner-up (Fernando Haddad), and why Brazil's Arab-origin citizens now number twelve million, making it the ninth biggest Arab country by population – bigger than Lebanon. They went forth, multiplied and left the old country behind in every way.

These *hijrah*s of steam are also how, at last, modernity entered the Arab awakening of letters: not from imitation of the forms of other literary cultures, but rather from the sheer liberation of throwing off old muzzles and moving somewhere new. One of those who was moved to write was the Lebanese-born Jubran Khalil Jubran, who arrived in New York in 1912. Later famous in the West as a misty mystic and the author of *The Prophet*, he was also a founder of poetic modernism in Arabic. By leaving his old home, he and other emigrants seemed to free themselves from the passive past: not only from the centuries of Ottoman insulation, but also from the powerful poetic force field of ancient Arabia. With *hijrah*, as ever, came activity, creativity. Jubran addressed his fellow poets, stuck in the old style, and by implication his fellow Arabs left behind in the old country:

> You are neighbours to yesterday; we have inclined towards
> a day whose dawn is shot through with the hidden.
> You have sought remembrance and its ghosts,
> while we pursue the ghost of hope.
> You have roamed the earth to its edges;
> our journey rolls within itself the vault of space.

If those 'neighbours to yesterday' go anywhere, Jubran wrote elsewhere in prose, they only 'go from place to place along a track already beaten by a thousand and one caravans, never diverging from it for fear of getting lost in the wilderness'. It may be the safe route, but it is also the shortest one between 'the cradle of thought and its grave'.

RULERS WITH RULERS

In contrast to today's border-beset age – in which Syrian passports, even with valid visas, even accompanied by Green Cards, do not necessarily admit their bearers into 'Nayy Yark' – travellers into and out of Syria in 1876 did not need to worry much about documentation. 'The traveller's passport,' Baedeker's *Palestine and Syria* noted, 'is sometimes asked for, but an ordinary visiting-card will answer the purpose equally well.' The Ottomans and (more surprisingly) the British were similarly nonchalant when, in 1849, they found themselves imperial next-door neighbours in southern Arabia; it took fifty years for them to get round to drawing a boundary between the Aden Protectorate and Ottoman Yemen, re-occupied after a 200-year absence. A joint commission worked for a couple of years (1902–4), and the line wiggled slowly inland and upland from Bab al-Mandab. On the far side of the more populous highlands, however, they gave up and used a ruler to draw a straight line across the thinly peopled steppe – and then just carried it on into the Empty Quarter, aiming north-east towards the Gulf through 1,000 kilometres of Arabia. The line was not to apportion sovereignty, but to suggest 'spheres of influence'. A few months after it was ratified in 1914, the two powers went to war. But the south-western section would last until 1990 as the border between the northern and southern parts of a divided Yemen. Now, less than thirty years on from that date, that line seems to be reimposing itself. Imperial rulers, both the people and their straight edges, thus have a lot to answer for. But not everything to answer for: in the end it was oil, above all, that would turn borders into barriers and spheres into sovereignties. In the interim, however, the great powers' Great War helped to solidify the lines on the map.

Over the nineteenth century, Arab identity had been remoulded once again by contact with outside powers. When those powers went to war, they courted Arab potentates, just as Assyrians, Persians, Romans and others had done before them. This time round, however, the latter-day powers, Britain, France and Ottoman Turkey, had been joined by a fourth suitor – Germany, full of its own new-found nationalism and carried along by its own *Drang nach Osten*, or 'Thrust to the East'. As part of the push, Kaiser Wilhelm II had already persuaded the Ottomans, in 1898, to agree to extending their existing Anatolian railway in the direction of the Gulf. The idea was to have a continuous Berlin–Baghdad line, Germany's own short-cut to palm-fringed shores – and perhaps a palmy imperial future. In the event, work and funding were intermittent, and the first direct Istanbul–Baghdad train would not run until 1940. It was not followed by many more: post-Second World War events would chop the line into sections that eventually withered. The Ottomans were more immediately successful in building their own line, the Hijaz Railway, funded by donations from around the Muslim world and designed to carry pilgrims – and, of course, troops – from Damascus to Medina. Announced in 1900 and finished in 1908, it was the first improvement in Arabian overland travel since the Queen of Sheba; indeed, since the domestication of the camel.

From pack-camel to pilgrim express had taken three millennia; the Hijaz Railway would run for less than nine years. As the Great War ground into action, Britain decided both to derail the Turks' thrust to the south by destroying their shiny new Arabian train set and, more importantly, to side-track them from the conflict in the Fertile Crescent by provoking an Arabian tribal uprising that would be known as the Arab Revolt. To this end, they communicated with the local Arab potentate through whose Hijazi lands much of the line passed, Sharif Husayn ibn Ali, the Ottoman-groomed Amir of Mecca – already known from clandestine approaches to the British as the owner of a second, anti-Ottoman face. Displaying their own other face, the British now egged Husayn on in the very terms of the new nationalism they had recently tried to stamp out in Egypt – throwing off the Turkish yoke and gaining Arab independence. The rewards of rebellion would be the time-honoured ones of gold and arms, naturally, but also recognition of Husayn as King of the Hijaz, the north-western part of the peninsula. As in the days of Sasanian Persia and imperial Rome, an empire was buying an alliance with an Arab chief by the promise of client-kingship. Nor did the resonances from the past end there. That early client-king of the Persians (or the Romans, or both; as we have seen, he too seems to have had more than one face), Imru' al-Qays ibn Amr, had aggrandized himself as 'King of the Arabs' in that first great monument inscribed in the Arabic language, the al-Namarah inscription of AD 328. Now, in AD 1916, Husayn, too, upgraded himself to 'King of the Arabs'; although at times, as if to align himself with the new, territorial nationalism, he used the style, 'King of the Arab Lands'. And there was yet another echo from another persistent past. As his courtesy title of *al-sharif*, 'the noble', showed, Husayn belonged to Muhammad's Hashimi clan of Quraysh; moreover, as Amir of Mecca, the Qurashi ancestral city, he could with some justice claim to be head of the tribe that had provided the two great dynasties of Arab caliphs, the Umayyads and the Abbasids . . . and, sure enough, in time, he would claim the title 'caliph' too. For the moment, however, his dreams did not go beyond ruling a united Arab kingdom that took in all Arabic-speaking lands and populations east of Suez: merely the entire Mashriq.

The British High Commission in Cairo chewed their briars and reamed their dottle. Their responses to Husayn were mealy-mouthed and ambiguous. They had been looking for guerrilla back-up in the peninsula, that side-show to the Great War; they now found themselves contemplating Arabdom resurgent in the overweening person of Husayn. For the time being, they left his dreams intact. At its crucial moment, therefore – with the thousand-year preponderance of Turks over Arabs hanging in the balance – the Arab Awakening looked as if it was turning, in politics as in poetics, into a 'retreat from modernity': Husayn seemed like the past personified, a whole history of kings and caliphs, of Qurashis and Hashimis, boiled down into one man.

In the short term, Husayn's hopes would be dashed. In the longer, the British would indeed collude in 'returning the present to the past', by handing out Arab thrones to his sons. To raise the scions of Quraysh even to client-kingship might have looked like stability, continuity. But it would all complicate the web of opposing forces – stasis and mobility, tradition and adaptation, then and now – in which the Arab future would be caught.

The web would be even more cruel and complex, for it was warped to duplicity. Even while they were wooing their Arabian kinglet, the British were cheating on him. By the beginning of 1916, Husayn believed his crown as King of the Arabs was in the bag; a few months later, Britain came to an arrangement with her old rival, France, to carve up the Ottoman empire between themselves, once they had defeated it. As the Arab Revolt, ably commanded by Husayn's son Faysal, scored successes, in November 1917 there came an extra twist of the carving-knife – the Balfour Declaration, in which:

> H.M. Government view with favour the establishment in Palestine of a national home for the Jewish people . . . it being clearly understood that nothing shall be done to prejudice the civil and religious rights of other non-Jewish communities in Palestine . . .

As the fortunes of the Great War turned to the advantage of Britain and her allies, it seemed that Jews were on their way to achieving what Arabs were still wondering how to do: to take a diverse collection of humanity, encompassing in the Jewish case Rothschild barons in Mayfair and barefoot goatherds in Yemen, linked by little more than devotion for an ancient text (in the Arab case, devotion for the language of an ancient text), and to translate them into a 'people' who, in the terms of modern European nationalism, had a claim on a territorial nation-state. Many Jews, at least at the Mayfair end of the scale, agreed with Balfour's (Jewish) cabinet colleague, Edwin Montagu, in branding Zionism '"a mischievous political creed" that would promote anti-Semitism'. His words may have been more prophetic than he could have known. But in any case, various elements of the European nationalist model were missing from Zionism, like shared language, customs, history (at least for the most recent couple of thousand years or so) . . . but all that could be dealt with in time; and for the moment, it could be finessed with that idea of a Promised Land. Rather, the problem was the second part of the declaration, 'it being clearly understood . . . ' The Balfour Declaration was an insoluble equation, a logical impossibility. It was like saying you would build a new reservoir without prejudicing the people of the villages that would be flooded.

Arabic calls the Balfour Declaration *Wa'd Balfur*, literally 'the Balfour Promise' (although *wa'd* has a hint of 'threat' as well). Whether the land was promised by God or by Balfour didn't matter: 'a promise', an Arabic saying goes, 'is the sound of thunder; its fulfilment is the fall of rain'. And in this case, the thunder was ominous, telling of the flood to come. The omens were correct: the deluge came. That second part of the declaration was doomed not to work, and a hundred years on it most patently hasn't. It would have been impossible in any of the other places mooted as a Jewish national home, which included even the Yemeni island of Socotra. The only place it might have worked is Antarctica.

THE CHAFF OF DREAMS

In the aftermath of the Great War in the Near East, the winners got down to the real business of victors – dividing the spoils, in this case the lands of the Ottoman empire. Those non-committal mumblings to Sharif Husayn about Arab independence were quietly forgotten while Britannia and Marianne shaped not just Arab identity, but the map of the Arab world. Some commentators have argued that their pact, known after its negotiators as the Sykes–Picot Agreement, can be interpreted to demonstrate

> Britain's championing of Arab independence and unity over French opposition. In other words, the Sykes–Picot agreement was a tool of unification rather than the divisive instrument it is now commonly thought to have been.

That is sophistry. The agreement did, in fact, accept the *principle* of eventual Arab independence; but on condition of the two powers having permanent influence. A prisoner is not free just because he is under house-arrest, instead of in gaol.

By now it was clear that Sharif Husayn's vision of himself as sole and unencumbered hegemon of Arab Asia was, like Pharaoh's visions in the Qur'an, 'the chaff of dreams'. Husayn's son Faysal, however, who had spent most of his formative years in Istanbul and had led the Arab Revolt on the ground, had a greater grasp on realpolitik than his father. He also acknowledged the ever-growing importance of modern-style Arab nationalism, and wrote to the Paris peace conference that the aim of the movement was 'to unite the Arabs eventually into one nation'. Because of the vast discrepancies across the region, he admitted that this would be impossible in the short term. But, he summed up, 'If our independence be conceded, and our local competence be established, the natural influences of race, language, and interest will soon draw us into one people.' It was a noble sentiment. And even if 'race' had always been a genealogists' construct, and 'interest' had more often divided Arabs than drawn them together, there might yet be hope in that ever-powerful unifier, language. Faysal's case did not fall on deaf ears; but it fell on ears whose hearing had been rendered selective by the tumult of victory. In 1922, the League of Nations granted provisional independence to the Arab lands – but subject to the mandates already given to Britain and France. Borders that had been pencilled in were now gone over in indelible ink; nebulous 'spheres of influence' solidified into hard-edged blocks of imperial tutelage.

Faysal's comrade from the Arab Revolt, Colonel T.E. Lawrence – the boy from north Oxford who saw himself as a Byron in Arab costume, and had graduated from digging up Hittite ruins to blowing up the Hijaz Railway – was utterly disillusioned by British duplicity; or by some aspects of it. He had sketched out his own ideal map of the post-Ottoman region. In it, a vast area of the northern peninsula, inland Iraq and Transjordan is marked 'ARABS: Feisal'. Small areas are shown on the Mediterranean seaboard as 'SINAI', 'PALESTINE' (unZionized, of course), 'LEBANON' and, interestingly, surrounding the Gulf of Alexandretta, 'ARMENIANS'. But the Kurdish-majority regions of Anatolia and northern Iraq are labelled only with '??', and a large chunk of upper Mesopotamia is given to Faysal's younger brother under the designation 'ARABS: Zeid (under British Influence)'. Faysal's elder brother, meanwhile, got most of Iraq – 'IRAK: Abdullah (under Direct British Administration)'. As for the vast rest of the peninsula south of Faysal's patch, Lawrence wrote along its northern border, '*No Foreign Power other than Great Britain to be allowed any share in the Government of the country south of this line*'. Even the loyal Lawrence, then, like the duplicitous British desk-wallahs, believed that many of his Arab friends needed the strict regime of nanny Britannia. As for the French stake in Lawrence's spin on the map . . . *rien ne va plus*.

Neither Husayn's vision of a Mashriqi mega-monarchy nor Lawrence's of a map sans French, sans Zionists stood a chance. But the younger *sharif*s did get their nursery thrones. Faysal was installed as king of Syria; in the gap between nannies, he assembled a General Congress and was declared king also of Lebanon and Palestine. Then the French arrived with a force of North African troops and promptly expelled him. The British therefore shifted him sideways in 1921 to the throne of Iraq, where their original attempts to rule on their own had been stymied by a widespread tribal revolt. Faysal's brother Abd Allah, meanwhile, was made king of Transjordan in the same year. Their father, Sharif Husayn, stewed away in righteous bitterness on his Hijazi throne. The Hashimi (or 'Hashimite') family had not done badly, with three kingdoms; but the fact was that they were client-kings, just as the Lakhmids and Ghassanids had been clients of the Persians and the Romans 1,400 years and more before. Again, Arabs were caught on their rock between predatory powers – and the powers were now up on the rock too, in the person of British and French officials, dispensing 'advice' that was mandatory, deposing and enthroning as they saw fit.

The presence of Europeans hardened borders. It also widened them, in the sense that geographically adjacent territories might become strikingly different from one another. There had always been that *hadar–badw* disconnect between settled peoples and tribes; but dividing-lines had never been clear. Now, places that were 'Westernizing', however superficially, became even more alien than they had been to the tribal inhabitants of the surrounding, and often unchanging, country. An extreme case in every way, but one which points to other disunities created by imperial rule, was that of Aden, down at the far end of the peninsula. 'British colonial rule,' admitted one of its last dispensers there, High Commissioner Sir Kennedy Trevaskis, 'had converted Aden into an island which might have been separated by a hundred miles of ocean from the South Arabian mainland.' Aden, itself a miniature peninsula with ancient cosmopolitan connections, had never been more than loosely moored to Yemen and the peninsula as a whole. But by administering it from Bombay for a century, the British had floated it in the direction of India. (The resulting developmental – not to say mental – gulf between it and the rest of the country has contributed to the mess outside my window now. When the Adenis found themselves ruled from 1990 by a tribal-military clique from the inland mountains, 'Vikings' was one of the kinder epithets they gave them; it was not a propitious start to the union.) To a lesser degree, the same sort of dislocations would affect other semi-detached places, like Bahrain and Kuwait.

Borders have not only been a political and social impediment to integration. They have continually been the pretext for confrontations, sometimes bloodless, like that in which a British-officered force from Oman and Abu Dhabi threw the American-backed Saudis out of the oasis of al-Buraymi in 1955; but sometimes shockingly bloody, as when Saddam Husayn was bombed out of Kuwait in 1991 along the 'Highway of Death'. All Arab borders are fractures, not sutures – all the way from the one between Yemen and Saudi Arabia, an open wound, to the frontier between Morocco and Algeria, shut tight since 1994 while the two countries trade accusations of terrorism and war-mongering like crazy neighbours yelling over a fence. 'If a man hates at all,' as Samuel Johnson realized, 'he will hate his next neighbour.' And sometimes, today, all the borders and the hatreds seem to radiate out from that mother of all divides, the Israeli Separation Wall.

Nor do borders only keep out, and apart. As the Syrian writer Khalil al-Nu'aymi knows, they also imprison and entomb: 'Those who condemn us not to travel . . . condemn us to a slow death in a spacious grave.'

WEDGES AND SPLITS

It all begs the question: if borders were imposed by wicked scheming imperialists, why did Arabs not simply erase them when they did eventually gain real independence? Why did they not enter into that longed-for unity? After all, nothing reignited the rhetoric of that unity like the double dishonour of Balfour and Sykes–Picot, that dark alliance of perfidious Albion and fraudulent Gaul.

The answer, of course, should by now be clear. It was not lines on maps that prevented unity. They didn't help; but there had always been enough forces pushing Arabs apart from the inside. Blame it as they might on other peoples' empires, Arabs had never been a happy family: not since the division of the spoils of Islam; not since the pre-Islamic War of al-Basus, that forty-year super-squabble over grazing rights. They had never really been a family at all, except in tribal fictions of shared descent. If empires were to blame, it was as much as anything for inspiring, by reflex, the myths and mirages of unattainable union. Imperialists certainly divided and ruled, but more often than not they were driving their wedges into old splits. As the pro-independence activist Muhammad Ali Jawhar said to the British rulers of 1920s India, 'We divide and you rule.' And by the reverse of the same token – *You divide and we rule* – post-imperial, post-nationalist Arab rulers have found it easier to try to keep control within the more manageable areas delineated by the old imperial borders.

We may now be getting enough distance on imperialism to look back at some of its features with greater clarity. One of those features is the wickedness of it all, and the legacy of hatred and division that it left. Imperialism undoubtedly had a wicked side. What could be more wicked, for example, than the Dinshaway Incident of 1906? A peaceful hamlet in the Nile Delta; the villagers' pigeons cooing in their dove-cote, others twinkling on the wing over the nearby fields . . . suddenly a party of boorish twelve-bored British officers breeze in and start shooting the flying birds. Jolly good sport! The village men rush out – shouts – fists – blows with gun-butts and *nabbut*s . . . one too heavy, on a British skull; an effendi dies. There is a round-up, a trial, a lesson for the fractious fellaheen: four villagers are sentenced to hang, two others to life with hard labour, others to lesser imprisonments and lashings. It was an over-reaction, and undeniably wicked. But wickedness ought to be quantifiable by the amount of suffering it causes, and if the British in Palestine were measurably wickeder than the British in Egypt, and the French in Algeria wickeder than both, then so too are the Egyptians in Egypt today, where the current regime can imprison a young man for two years for wearing a 'No Torture' T-shirt, and can sentence islamist opponents to death by the hundred. Iraqi Saddam Husayn was wickeder still, gassing – for example – at least 3,000 Iraqi Kurds to death in the village of Halabjah in one fell swoop. So too is Syrian Bashshar al-Asad, in whose Syrian gaols alone 18,000 are said to have died over the first five years of civil war, while his armed forces and militia were allegedly responsible for the violent deaths of between 92,000 and 187,000 Syrian civilians alone during the same period.

Al-Hajjaj ibn Yusuf, the Umayyad viceroy and mass-murderer, is alive and well and as wicked as ever; and as admired, by some Arabs: 'He is strong!'

they say. Logically, the fact that he and Bashshar al-Asad are Arabs killing Arabs whereas the hanging judge of Dinshaway was a Brit killing Arabs shouldn't come into the calculation of relative wickedness. But it does. Where civil liberties do not exist, the void where they should be is often occupied by national pride. And wounds to national pride – wounds inflicted by outsiders – can be made to hurt out of all proportion to the deaths they cause.

KINGS AND CARPET-BAGGERS

Following their successes in the earlier scramble for Africa, Britain and France had now emerged as joint winners in the scrummage for the Near East. This did not mean the end of Arab nationalism; on the contrary, it energized the movement. Throughout the 1920s and 1930s protests and revolts fizzed and rumbled against the imperial occupiers, at times violently. In Morocco, where Spain also claimed protectorates over areas of the northern coast and south-western desert regions (the latter called 'Spanish Sahara'), a bloody war was waged between 1921 and 1926 by the Berbers of the northern Rif Mountains against both the Spanish and the French colonialists; it failed, however, to ignite the rest of the population, and was put down by the two European powers working in tandem. At the Levantine end of the Mediterranean, however, another highland enclave, the Mountain of the Druze in Syria, was hotting up and would become a further flashpoint. In 1925, armed rebellion broke out there against the French; the uprising spread to other regions of Syria, and was quelled only in 1927, when French forces were brought in from the now cooling battlefields of Morocco.

For the British, Palestine would prove the biggest headache, as we shall see, from the later 1930s on. Iraq, meanwhile, following the violent anti-British tribal revolt of 1920, remained in a state of suspended confrontation. Egypt provided occasional shocks, like the assassination in 1924 of Sir Lee Stack, governor-general of the Anglo-Egyptian Sudan. But the anti-colonial opposition could wield charm as well as arms, and there was cooperation towards independence – albeit with strings attached – as well as struggle. The most promising progress at this time was made in Egypt, which in 1923 became a constitutional monarchy in which political parties multiplied; one, the Wafd, was dominant, but others often held the balance of power. Admittedly the king and the British threw their weight about too; but there was genuine debate and pluralism.

As a whole in these inter-war years, the Arabosphere was looking kaleidoscopically plural: if the colonial powers at times mirrored each other, they were opposed by a plethora of local forces that constantly rearranged themselves. Advocates of a greater Arab unity, the beautiful simple vision inspired by the Awakening, were lost in the increasing complexity of the picture. Besides, the king-making and -breaking that had followed the Great War had also reminded pan-Arab nationalists of a problem that was perennial: even if Arabs could shape some sort of unity for themselves, who would lead it?

The one keen candidate for leadership, Sharif Husayn, had already been disabused of that extra title he had adopted, 'King of the Arabs'. Soon, however, he went one better: when in 1924 the now empireless Ottoman ex-sultan, Abd al-Majid II, was stripped of his caliphal title and banished from Turkey, Husayn leaped at the vacant caliphate. A thousand years after al-Radi, 'the last real caliph', it was not certain what a caliph's job description was, except that it implied some kind of vague spiritual suzerainty over the world's Muslims, or at least the Sunni ones; but in the event, no one recognized the *sharif*'s claim. Husayn might have saved himself this added disappointment if he had heeded earlier protests by Indian Muslims, the most numerous in the world, when the defeated Ottoman caliph-sultan had been made to cede sovereignty of Mecca to him in 1920. The Indian reaction had highlighted a change that had passed many Arabs by. Husayn was not any old Arab: he was a Qurashi, a Hashimi, a descendant of the Prophet. In his own and some other eyes, his descent gave him the highest degree of nobility, and the strongest claim to rule the holy city. But Islam had long outgrown its Arab past: since Mamluk times, Mecca had been an international enclave, a true world-navel; for the great majority of Muslims, Islam was not a family firm but a global corporation. To restore Mecca to local rule was like handing the Vatican over to the Municipality of Rome. For Husayn now to lay claim, on top of this, to the title of caliph was an act of vaunting pride that could only invite a fall. And, sure enough, nemesis was on its way from next-door Najd.

Already, Husayn's promotion from Amir of Mecca to King of the Hijaz had excited envy elsewhere in the peninsula. Not to be outdone, his southern neighbour and distant cousin-*sharif* Yahya, the imam of Yemen, had in 1920 upped his imamate to a kingdom. Now, with Husayn's 1924 bid for the caliphate, another neighbour weighed into the title fight. He was no *sharif*, but a member of the Al Sa'ud clan of chieftains in the dour uplands of Najd, and he was a bruiser: tall and craggy in physique, Abd al-Aziz ibn Abd al-Rahman, often known simply as Ibn Sa'ud, was backed by the Wahhabi tribes who had long been allies of his family. The alliance's ambitions had been crushed by Muhammad Ali Pasha a century earlier. Now they were revitalized by the Ottoman collapse, and by the charisma and military prowess of Ibn Sa'ud himself. They had already captured all of Najd; next they fell on the Hijaz and the hapless Husayn. The *sharif* fled to Cyprus while Ibn Sa'ud took his land, his title as king of the Hijaz and, over the coming few years, more and more Arabian territory. Admittedly, other than the Hijazi pilgrim cities, the more useful parts of the Arab Island – in particular Yemen and Oman – were still not his; Ibn Sa'ud was king of a wilderness with few resources and no name. And although he had united much of the peninsula for the first time since early Islam, he had done it by brute sectarian force, and by alienating not only the Hashimites but also much of the Arabic-speaking world. When in 1932, therefore, he named his land after his own family, 'the Kingdom of Saudi Arabia', it seemed another ultimate act of pride.

This time, however, pride was followed not by a fall, but by petroleum. Inspired by recent discoveries in the other lands around the Gulf, Ibn Sa'ud gave the first exploration concession to Standard Oil of California in 1933. It took five years for them to strike commercial quantities of oil, at Dhahran on the shore of the Gulf, but from then on there was no looking back. Ibn Sa'ud's unpromising realm would prove to contain the biggest reserves of petroleum in the world and, via the American firms that now crowded in, he had a direct route into what would soon be the biggest market for the stuff.

It may not have seemed so from their recent expansion into the Levant, but the grand old European powers, the product of ocean trade and coal-fired industry, were running out of steam. In the imperial relay, the baton was passing to a new world power, an automobile empire that would run on internal combustion and conspicuous consumption. The gas-guzzling United States, despite its well-known aversion to absolute monarchies, would snuggle up to Ibn Sa'ud when it found out what lay beneath his kingdom. And with the strange embrace of oil-fired absolutism and the Land of the Free, there began a new chapter in the relationship between tribes and empires. British-Indian influence in the peninsula gave way to

American, box-wallahs to carpet-baggers and to the portmanteau world, bulging with petro*riyal*s, of Aramco – the Arabian American Oil Company, a giant post-Second World War consortium. In 1939, the relative British and American shares in Middle Eastern oil production were 13 per cent against 60 per cent. In 1954 they were 65 per cent to 30 per cent.

The US–Saudi affair was, and is, an exceedingly peculiar relationship. A photograph in Richard Halliburton's 1936 travel book, *Seven League Boots*, seems to foreshadow something of its nature. Captioned 'The king posing with the author' (shouldn't it be the other way round?), it shows an Ozymandias-like Ibn Sa'ud in his beetling headgear and a cheeky Yankee in a natty white suit, but both somehow at ease in each other's company: Saturn and Mercury, planets apart but orbiting in the same system.

The coming together brought about an equally peculiar mix of change and stasis in the peninsula. In the conquests of the 1920s, Ibn Sa'ud's Wahhabi raiders had been the last of their kind to use the ancient but still devastating camel+horse combination. In the 1930s, with the promise of oil, cash coming in already, and courtier-concessionaires like St John Philby flogging Fords to them, they entered the mechanized age. According to one authority, 'the age of tribal raiding came to an end'. But 2,000 years of the raiding habit were not so quickly erased; raiding as an institution lived on and thrived in other forms. The Al Sa'ud have therefore always ruled in their own web of tensions, between themselves and the Americans, but also with their own tribal warriors; at times the latter relationship has resembled that between Muhammad's state of Medina and its own dangerous but indispensable bedouin raiders. There was no doubt about the threat the warriors posed: in 1921, for example, extremist Wahhabi tribesmen had pillaged and massacred the main Yemeni pilgrim caravan on its way to Mecca. Re-enacting the history of the early Islamic state, as Ibn Sa'ud's authority grew, he tried to collectivize and settle his more unruly nomads, placing them in communities which he called *hijrah*s – that same word denoting Muhammad's migration to a new life. And just as the earliest caliphs had failed to mix tribes when settling their own *muhajirun* – '*hijrah* migrants' – in the new garrison towns, so too did Ibn Sa'ud. Tribal ties remained as strong as ever, and in 1929–30 several of the most extreme Wahhabi tribes, the Ikhwan or 'Brethren', revolted against the king and had to be bloodily suppressed. From Ibn Sa'ud's point of view, some of the *a'rab* were living up to their description in the Qur'an as 'the worst in unbelief and hypocrisy'.

As for the new kingdom's *a'rab* in general, they might be induced in the twentieth century as in the seventh to give up their wandering lifestyle – the nomad population of Saudi Arabia went down from 40 per cent in the 1950s to less than 5 per cent in 1998 – but not all of them were converted into good bourgeois citizens. The unpredictable, volatile spirit of the Brethren lives on, channelled where possible into the National Guard and the Committee for the Commandment of Virtue and the Suppression of Vice – the 'morality' police – but at times inspiring new manifestations of extremism, of which al-Qa'idah was only the first.

To the south, the British had similar problems with tribesmen when, in the 1930s, they at last got round to doing something about the seemingly endemic anarchy in the vast hinterland of Aden. In Hadramawt, the situation might have been better described as polyarchy gone mad: Harold Ingrams, sent in to deal with it, reported that there were about 2,000 separate 'governments' in the province, some as small as a hamlet or even a single household, each of which claimed not to owe allegiance to any higher authority. Working with traditional local power-brokers – as so often, descendants of Muhammad – Ingrams hammered out a peace treaty that halted chronic fighting between the larger factions. The bedouin tribesmen, however, proved the most troublesome element: they still lived as herders, hauliers and raiders, and the British had to bomb them into renouncing that third immemorial means of livelihood.

As with their tribal equivalents to the Saudi north, however, there was no way even British-governed and British-bombed *badw* would change overnight into law-abiding *hadar*. Hadrami *badw* terms for their non-tribal neighbours go some way to explaining why: settled folk are *masakin*, from the root *sakana*, like *hadara* 'to be sedentary, quiescent', but also meaning 'unfortunate, miserable ones'; they are also *hirthan*, 'ploughmen', from the root *haratha*, 'to cultivate, plough', but also in its basic sense 'to work for one's living'. Tribesmen do not work for a living – at least, they do not work the land; they herd, they transport, they raid, and they look down on 'trade' as haughtily as any antique European aristocrat. (In a latter-day state system, tribesmen may well draw pay as nominal government employees, preferably of the army or police, but usually without the bother of actual square-bashing or pounding the beat: doing nothing and getting paid is a kind of raid, too, on the state coffers.) For traditional *badw* in Hadramawt and elsewhere, to replace your string of camels with a Bedford lorry was acceptable. But to beat your sword or rifle into a ploughshare has always been anathema; it is to cease to be armigerous, arms-bearing, honourable. Peace, passivity, settlement, quiescence, cultivation, following the furrow, living by the sweat of one's brow, mean the end of history in the Fukuyaman sense.

And yet, for a couple of decades, it did seem that the old time was over. Of the Hadrami *badw* in the decades of British-brokered peace, one observer who thought he knew them well said, 'They are dead'. The announcement was premature; time was only on pause.

THE MUDDLED EAST

As the last of the Ottomans lived out his Parisian exile, arranging his butterfly collection, many Arabs regretted the end of the slow, simple centuries in the penumbra of the Sublime Porte. Now they were in the full glare of the twentieth century, and the Middle East, as it was becoming in Western eyes, was rapidly becoming the Muddled East. A second great mechanized war was cranking into action, and there was both excitement and fear about the future. Would more empires be swept to their doom? And if so, would the competing rhetoricians of Arab unity finally get their word together? The second possibility seemed unlikely. The Arabic-speaking world was as fragmented as it had ever been, and over the third and fourth decades of the century its inherently complex social and political map had taken on an almost vorticist twist:

... with its mixture of foreign-backed monarchies and colonial intervention – sometimes gentle, as in Hadramawt, where Ingrams made peace in sandals, a loincloth and silver bangles and the RAF dropped polite warning notes before they dropped bombs; sometimes jackboot, as in Mussolini's nine-year war to get his own chunk of Arab world in Libya; sometimes an increasingly insistent foot in the door, as with the growing influx of foreign Jews into Palestine;

... with its strange juxtapositions, of fanatical *badw* raiders and American oilmen at the Saudi court, of chintzy memsahibs and indigo-painted tribesman in Aden, of Freya Stark's cameleers borrowing her 'Miss Lethbridge's' Bond Street facecream to polish their daggers;

... with Ibn Sa'ud against the Hashimites, the Hashimites sometimes against each other, and everyone always against the Hashimite Abd Allah of

Transjordan, seen as a British and Zionist stooge who had his own imperial eye on a Greater Syria;

... with the French using troops from the Maghrib against insurgents in the Mashriq, battered by Berbers in the one and by Druze in the other, and with the British in Palestine battered by Arabs and Jews simultaneously as Balfour's contradiction in logic turned inevitably into confrontation on the ground;

... with Egypt, her post-Ottoman khedive now a king with another British client-crown, his anti-British government following their own Nilotic current of nationalism – 'If you add one zero to another, and then to another,' Prime Minister Sa'd Zaghlul is supposed to have said, despairing of the idea of a united Arab world, 'what sum will you get?'

... with all this, prospects for Arab unity were receding ever further.

THE THIEF OF FIRE

If political unity seemed a broken dream, at least the Arab *Kulturnation* – revived by the 'Awakening' – seemed to have benefited from its centuries-long beauty sleep, with newly creative writers and poets giving Arab identity life and cohesion. But, here too, splits were appearing. Intellectual as well as political doubts were radiating from the land at the centre of the Arabic world, Egypt, and they were threatening to undermine the whole cultural basis of nationalism.

Like the man often billed as the most recent great Arabic poet, the eleventh-century AD Syrian al-Ma'arri, the Egyptian scholar Taha Husayn was blind but disturbingly visionary. During the First World War he had studied in France and married a Frenchwoman, and he believed that Egypt should both re-espouse Hellenic-European civilization and be open, as it had been over history, to the influences of all 'civilized peoples in the east and west'. This chimed with what many other Egyptian intellectuals of the time believed. But Taha Husayn, while he acknowledged that Arabic was 'mingled with [our] life in a way that has formed it and shaped its personality', was not afraid to examine its founding texts critically – not the sacrosanct Qur'an, but the even deeper underpinnings of Arabic heritage, Muslim and non-Muslim, and of the language that had given voice to the whole Arab Awakening. His 1926 book *On Pre-Islamic Poetry* goes straight for its subject's jugular:

> The overwhelming majority of what we call pre-Islamic poetry is not pre-Islamic at all. It was fabricated and falsely attributed after the appearance of Islam.

The golden treasury of odes – the gold standard of the language, the ancient downpayment for a new future as a nation – was, as he showed in argument piled on argument, almost all dross; the early Islamic transmitters of ancient poetry were Chattertons, the ancient poets Ossians. The Arab past, and thus Arab identity, were not merely reshaped in the Umayyad and Abbasid eras, but were faked up wholesale in their poetry 'factories'. He had arrived at this conviction by examining the evidence of the poems, internal and external, and by what he called 'Cartesian detachment' – by 'forgetting' his nationality and religion; such detachment, he explained, was 'the distinguishing mark of the modern age'. Modern it was; but in a culture in which words are almost the sole material of art, and poems the ultimate cultural product, what Taha Husayn did was like taking a sledgehammer to the Elgin Marbles. Or worse: the icons he had trashed were ancestral portraits, not cold marble, but flesh and blood that came to life afresh with every recitation.

In a sense it doesn't matter whether Taha Husayn was right or not. There is no question that some poetry was fabricated, and probably much else was restored and repolished in Islamic times. Many critics, however, feel that he was wrong to dismiss 'the overwhelming majority' of pre-Islamic poetry. But the deed was done. And along with the poetic baby and its bathwater, the book threw out some disconcerting questions. While he did not apply his Cartesian detachment directly to scripture, Taha Husayn did interrogate a number of long-cherished stories that had filled in dots in the Qur'an's elliptical text. These included the traditional accounts of the people of Ad, of the Marib damburst, and of much else in the apocryphal Arab Genesis. His book was banned on the grounds that it threatened public order by calling aspects of the Qur'an and the Prophet into question, and in 1927 he was summoned to appear in court on a charge of heresy. Among other complaints from the Shaykh al-Azhar, the highest Muslim authority, he was accused of 'belittling' Muhammad's ancestry – something 'no infidel or polytheist has ever dared' to do – and of implying that the original Arab faith had not been Abrahamic monotheism. A lot of the case hinged on the historicity and role of Abraham/Ibrahim and his son Ishmael/Isma'il, so important in the forging of a united Arab identity from Umayyad times onward. But 'forging' in which sense: 'hammering out' or 'faking'?

Taha Husayn himself was literally in two minds. In the court hearing, he asserted that,

> as a Muslim he did not doubt the existence of Ibrahim and Isma'il, or of any Qur'anic material connected with them. But as a scholar he was compelled to submit to methods of academic research, and therefore could not accept the existence of Ibrahim and Isma'il as a fact of scholarly history.

It was the old pitfall, between faith and reason, rhetorical truth and empirical fact. And there was Taha Husayn, down in the pit but looking bravely up. The trial might have been the Arab-Muslim world's long-delayed 'Galileo moment'.

He was by no means the first Muslim thinker caught in the binary trap. But most had turned a blind eye to their predicament, like the tenth-century logician al-Sijistani who simply stated that the Qur'an was exempt from logic. That the physically blind Taha Husayn could admit to that stereoscopic vision was indeed a 'modern' viewpoint, and deeply subverting. Moreover, it peered into a dark chamber in the heart of being Arab: 'Dualism,' wrote a more recent and equally shrewd observer, Muhammad al-Jabiri, 'constitutes the essence of being Arab in all its domains.'

One must beware of cod psychology. But this sort of dualism – the ability to look at phenomena simultaneously from two opposite viewpoints, in two contrasting lights – might go towards explaining a number of apparent anomalies: how, for example, a whole mass of Arabic words can mean one thing and its opposite (*jawn* = black/white, *jalal* = great/small); how people can adore a political leader while admitting that he is blatantly corrupt, and can speak of him without irony as *sariq watani*, 'a patriotic thief', or even – as we have seen – *sariq 'adil*, 'a just thief'. The perspective is Cubist, the 'doublethink' Orwellian. And apart from points of view, there are the great and undeniable dualities: peoples/tribes, spiritual Mecca/temporal Medina, *hajj/hijrah*, *haram/halal*, unclean sinister left hand/clean dexter right hand, quietist Sufis/militant Wahhabis, *'arab/'ajam*, high Arabic/Arabic dialect . . . a perpetual dialectic in society, religion, language, in which the world is a series of conflicting opposites, thesis and antithesis. Cod psychology or good red herring, some considerable Arab thinkers have fished the subject. Adonis, too, netted a whole catch of double-headed dichotomies that concluded with '. . . country/city, Arabs/Greeks, Arabs/West, prophecy/technology'. All these, he said, are 'opposing dualities that paralyse creative movement', as if Arabs are in the position of Buridan's ass, who couldn't choose between the two mangers on either side of him and died of starvation . . . not just stuck on a rock between lions, then, but also stuck in a stable, stalled between stalls.

It is nice and neat to see everything in such Manichaean terms, but ultimately simplistic. All the same, Muhammad al-Jabiri may have been right when he guessed that a specific dualism lay at the core of what this present book is about, the problem of Arab unity. Of the pairing 'unity/particularity' he observes how

> regional idiosyncrasies compete with the pan-national whole – but without either the parts or the whole seeking to cancel or negate each other. Such a negation would be a self-defeating act, because the existence of one is dependent and conditional on that of the other.

Like the ancient Arabian duality of *hajj* and *hijrah*, Mecca and migration, then, the idea of Arab unity works as both magnet and centrifuge: it attracts, but inevitably repels. Pilgrims travel hopefully, arrive – but must always leave. Womblike Mecca cannot hold them all for ever; even holy migrants turn into madding masses. Unitarians are pilgrims, too, in perpetuity, filled with hope on the road but always fleeing the crowd for reality and home.

The judge in Taha Husayn's trial was scholarly and open-minded, and the case was dismissed. The book, however, was punished: it was permitted to be reissued, but with the offending passages bowdlerized. The bigger questions, about bipolarity, dichotomy, detachment, remained and still do so, glaringly; Galileo has yet to be freed. In fact, Taha Husayn's message is even more disturbing nowadays. The more distant political unity seems, the more reassuring are those ancient poetic foundations of Arab cultural solidarity; the more Islam is pulled apart by its own opposing extremists, the more important is that stable, unquestionable core, the Prophet and the Qur'an.

And yet Taha Husayn sparked off ideas that still smoulder. The poet Nizar Qabbani remembered him as 'the Thief of Fire' and longed for him to return. Would he be acquitted today?

A PLURALITY OF UNITIES

Around the time of Taha Husayn's trial, T.E. Lawrence, who had once been the advocate for a united Arab east, came to that realization already mentioned, that 'Arab unity . . . is a madman's notion'. It is a realization all romantics arrive at if we live long enough in the real Arab world. If it could be conjured into existence, Arab unity would not be the Egyptocentric Sa'd Zaghlul's nihilistic sum of zeros; neither would it be some neat binary chimaera, a pushmi-pullyu. Rather, going by attempts to achieve it in the 1930s and 1940s, it would be a many-headed monster, a hydra with a multiply-split personality.

From 1936 onwards, King Abd al-Aziz Ibn Sa'ud was mooting a pan-Arab federation, with himself as head. At the same time and until his assassination in 1951, King Abd Allah of Transjordan was lobbying for union with Syria, eventually to incorporate Palestine and Iraq, with himself as head. Later, the Iraqi Prime Minister Nuri al-Sa'id was trying to persuade the British to work towards a union – again with Syria, Palestine and Transjordan, but with Iraq at its head. Not unexpectedly, nothing came of these ideas. More surprising was that Egypt abandoned its sphinx-like aloofness and proposed what, in 1945, became the Arab League. The founder members were Egypt itself, together with the reluctant quadrille of Syria, Iraq, Transjordan and Palestine; also Lebanon, Saudi Arabia and Yemen. More surprising still is that, other than in the aftermath of its Camp David Accords with Israel, when Egypt was ostracized and from 1979 to 1990 the League was chaired by a Tunisian, every one of its secretaries-general has been an Egyptian.

Needless to say, the other members would never have agreed to a virtual Egyptian monopoly if the League had ever been anything more than a toothless talking-shop, a diplomatic Drones Club in which the members always 'agree to disagree'. They did, however, agree at the start on some aims that were diffident enough to satisy the most paranoid sovereign:

> To strengthen the ties between the participant states, to co-ordinate their political programme in such a way as to effect real collaboration between them, to preserve their independence and sovereignty, and to consider in general the affairs and interests of the Arab countries.

The League has expanded and now has twenty-two members. The criterion for membership is having Arabic as an official language; this brings together some strange bedfellows, including Somalia and the Comoros. As for the League's answer to the old question of who or what an Arab is, it is someone whose language is Arabic and who lives in an Arabic-speaking country (which would seem to exclude actual Somalis and Comorans), and who 'sympathizes with the aspirations of the Arabic-speaking peoples'. What these aspirations are, and how sympathy for them should be expressed, is not clear. A woolly mammoth as well as a tuskless one, the League exhibits few vital signs, and has been branded as 'still-born from the inception', and 'an institution of the dying age of tyranny'. But reports of its death, either before its birth or in the future, are probably exaggerated, and it may have done slightly more good than harm.

In any case, like all the best gully-gully men, the Egyptians had something much more surprising up their sleeve. Egypt had been home to the first stirrings of the Arab Awakening, and had given birth to the Thief of Fire. But in the 1950s it brought forth the Knight of Dreams – a man who for a brief, bright decade would ignite the biggest Arab wheel of fire since Muhammad.

CHAPTER FOURTEEN

THE AGE OF HOPE

NASSERISM, BA'THISM, LIBERATION, OIL

THE EMPTY THRONE

Early in the summer of 1952, a plump and pampered camel processed around Cairo, accompanied by a guard of honour and a brass band. Atop its hump, rocking to the music, rose an elaborate litter with a pyramidal roof. Enclosed by superbly embroidered panels of cloth and decorated with silver-gilt finials, the litter, or palanquin, resembled a small but gorgeous pavilion. The *mahmal* or 'bearer', as it is called in Arabic, was empty, but full of symbolism – it was a cipher of sovereignty, mobility, pilgrimage and, in its calligraphic covering, of the power and beauty of the Arabic language. It was in effect a travelling throne-room in miniature, and in former times it had gone to Mecca to pay the Egyptian ruler's homage to the House of Allah – an armchair pilgrimage in which the chair itself did the travelling.

The *mahmal* was also full of history. It may have originated as early as in Umayyad times, but it became a regular institution in the thirteenth century under the first Mamluks of Egypt. Soon, other regions began sending *mahmal*s to Mecca – Yemen, Syria and, later, Ottoman Turkey – each paying its allegiance to the unity symbolized by the ancient Arabian city, the navel of the world, but each also expressing its independence. Like the rest of the pilgrim caravan, the *mahmal* came home after the pilgrimage, and its journey to and from Mecca was powered by the pull and push that held the Arab world together and yet kept it apart.

The *mahmal*'s travels were as much about local politics as about pilgrimage. In his brief role as infidel defender of the faith, Napoleon had a new *mahmal* made and sent to Mecca. The Franco-Egyptian procession that saw it off from Cairo seemed to the historian al-Jabarti

> a wonder of wonders, with its variety of forms, diversity of shapes and mingling of denominations. In it the hoi polloi were raised high, the riff-raff multiplied, and the marvels of creation came together in a conjunction of opposites and a total contrast to tradition.

Tradition, however, soon re-established itself after the French had gone. Some of it was strange enough in itself. For instance, the *mahmal* was customarily followed by an old man called 'the Shaykh of the Camel', who had long hair but no other covering than a pair of pyjama bottoms –

> He was mounted on a camel, and was incessantly rolling his head . . . all assert that he rolls his head during the whole of the journey.

At times, the old man was himself followed on another camel by a scantily clad old woman called 'the Mother of Cats', half a dozen of which shared her saddle to Mecca and back. Such picturesque characters, however, would have no place in the modernized Egypt of the later nineteenth century. From 1884 the Egyptian *mahmal* travelled by train to Suez, in its own private carriage, then by steamer down the Red Sea to Jeddah; there it was hoisted on to the traditional dromedary. Such adaptations perhaps helped the Egyptian *mahmal* to survive; the Yemeni *mahmal* had disappeared in the seventeenth century, and the Turkish-Syrian one would fall victim to the Great War. But the Egyptian *mahmal* was doomed as well. In 1926 Ibn Sa'ud's Wahhabi Ikhwan, the new protectors of Mecca, stoned it, beat up its bandsmen and clashed with its guard: for the puritan tribesmen it was a *bid'ah*, a heretical innovation, even if the 'innovation' was 600, or perhaps 1,200, years old. Since then, for a generation, it had only paraded around Cairo, all dressed up and nowhere to go.

The parade of 1952, however, was its last. Later that summer, a group of army officers overthrew the British-backed king of Egypt; the past and its superannuated symbols, including the *mahmal*, were consigned to the lumber-room of history. Besides, since 1926 the camel and its empty palanquin had been a reminder of a bitter present. Travel was easier, camel trains had been replaced by steam trains and steamships, and the Arab world should have come closer together in the face of imperialism and its new and wayward step-daughter, Zionism. But the last remaining symbol of the old connectedness had been rejected by the new masters of Mecca. Now the new masters of Egypt rejected it too: for them it was the opposite of an innovation – an anachronism. The symbolism of the empty palanquin was now itself empty; emptier even than the rhetoric in that other, newer symbol of Arab connectedness in Cairo, the Arab League.

If anything, Egypt, sitting between the Maghribi and Mashriqi wings of the Arabic world but belonging to neither, had just distanced itself a little more from its fellow Arab states. The revolution was following a current that had been released by Napoleon's propaganda of liberation and had strengthened ever since: Egypt was pursuing its own national course into the uncertain future, and the nationalism was Egyptian, not Arab. It had, everyone pointed out, its first truly Egyptian rulers since the pharaohs; although what 'truly Egyptian' meant, in a land that had been the confluence of humanity from three continents and for at least as many thousand years, was not clear. It certainly did not mean that the revolutionary officers were Copts, whose name comes from that of the country; etymologically, a Copt is a 'Gypt'. Rather, it meant that the new leaders were not any of the relatively recent arrivals – Mamluks, Ottomans, Albanians or, God help us, British. Like that revolutionary of seventy years earlier, Ahmad Urabi, they came from Arab or arabized settler stock and, in this land of the *longue durée*, 1,300 years were deemed long enough to have turned Arab invaders into indigenous Egyptians.

In the event, four years after the 1952 revolution Egypt's new Egyptian rulers would change tack, and not just assert their arabness but assume the leadership of Arabs everywhere. Arabness, as so often, was something to be forgotten and rediscovered, cast off then reassumed, to be recollected and reshaped. It was something that ebbed and flowed according to the phases of the times and their political mood, and it was about to have a spring tide.

THE DAGGER IN THE MAP

Four years before the 1952 revolution, arabness and Arab unity had, in contrast, been at one of their lowest ebbs ever. Zionism had waved the wand of religion over colonialism . . . and magicked it into territorial nationalism. The transformation had taken place against a background of events both foreseeable and unpredictable.

Among the foreseeable events was the utter unworkability of the Balfour Declaration. Between the two world wars, uncontrollable Jewish immigration and land purchase in Palestine ignited inter-communal violence; predictably, the Palestinians revolted against the British mandatory power, which in return inflicted brutal collective punishments. What had happened to the 'sweet, just, boyish master' of the world, as George Santayana had described imperial Britain only a decade earlier? Later came the turn of the Jews to revolt, when the British tried to stem the influx of immigrants. Most violent were the extremist Zionist groups, the Irgun and the Stern Gang:

> By using terror tactics to achieve political objectives they . . . set a dangerous precedent in Middle Eastern history – one that plagues the region down to the present day.

The *locus classicus* of terror was the King David Hotel in Jerusalem, the 1946 bombing of which by the Irgun killed nearly a hundred. The explosion reverberates down the decades, from the Holy City to Beirut to Baghdad to Manhattan. The Israelis, meanwhile, have graduated from planting or throwing bombs to the more civilized method of dropping them.

Other unforeseen events, however, eased the transformation from Zionist colony to Israeli nation-state. What none but a prophet could have predicted was the suffering inflicted by Nazism on the Jews of Europe. As if silenced and blinded by its enormity, the rest of the post-war world affected not to notice the suffering of Palestine. Arabs were only too aware of it. But their perceptions of Palestine were skewed, variously, by their own self-interests. When the show-down came in 1948 – the war between the Zionists and their neighbours, Egypt, Transjordan, Syria, Lebanon and Iraq – the Arab allies were thus fatally divided. The most notable unity they achieved was when four of them ganged up to stop Abd Allah, the Hashimite king of Transjordan, enlarging his realm by grabbing Palestinian Arab territory. The fear was well founded: Abd Allah had already been in contact with the Zionists, trying to get guarantees to this very end. As one contemporary observer put it, apart from this joint attempt to contain Abd Allah's ambitions, 'the Arab states' campaign was crippled by lack of unity . . . [and]

mutual distrust'. It was this mistrust that was the 'something false and rotten' in the Arab ranks, and it was as tragic a flaw for the Five Against Zion as anything in the Aeschylean drama of *Seven Against Thebes*; as destructive as those divided ranks when, at the time of the first appearance of the Crusaders in the Levant, 'The sultans were at loggerheads with each other, and this enabled the Franks to occupy the country'.

The Israeli victory caused major Arab migrations, including those of tens of thousands of Jewish Arabs to Palestine. But the contrary migrations of Palestinians, both Muslim and Christian, were a flight, an expulsion. Hagar and Isma'il were in exile once again, but on a vast scale: after the 1948 war, there were 750,000 Palestinian refugees in the neighbouring lands and beyond. The mythical medieval figure of the Wandering Jew was replaced by the modern, and all too real, Wandering Palestinian.

The *Nakbah* or 'Disaster' of 1948 is living, moving history, and will continue to be so as long as Palestinians are excluded from their homeland. As the Palestinian lawyer and writer Raja Shehadeh admits,

> We continue to be bewildered and wonder how it could have happened, why it happened, how it can be explained and understood. We can never have enough of it.
>
> Is it like the Holocaust to those Jews who were touched by it?

If we include those for whom the touch is indirect, there could be few Jews, even at a distance of over seventy years, whom the Holocaust has not touched. Similarly, few Arabs have not shared the pain inflicted on Palestine. The State of Israel, as it now became, felt like a wound in the north of the Arabian subcontinent. On the map it is the shape of some ancient dagger, its hilt lying along the Mediterranean coast, its point striking the head of the Red Sea, its wedge-shaped blade driven between Egypt and the Levant. The wound was small, but it was deep. It has never healed, and as long as it does not, the pain will be felt.

BEWARE THE AMERICANS BEARING GIFTS

In the aftermath of the Second World War, the old European empires had begun to go the way of Nineveh and Tyre. The British had handed back India, hacked bloodily in two with Partition; now they divested themselves of the mess of a divided Palestine. Elsewhere in the Arab world, they had already granted Iraq formal independence in 1930, but thanks to its reasonably tame Hashimite king had kept effective control of the country's foreign policy and also retained some useful air bases. The French, meanwhile, had withdrawn from Syria and Lebanon by the end of 1945, but still clung on to their North African possessions.

In Egypt, where the client-king Faruq reigned, British forces were withdrawn after 1945; but not from the Canal Zone, on which Britain exerted a military stranglehold. This continued presence rankled with many in the Egyptian army, and in particular with the middle-ranking officers drawn from the 'yeomanry' – men who felt an allegiance to the physical land of Egypt which the urban upper classes did not necessarily share. The Disaster of 1948 had further fuelled the officers' anger at the ineptitude and corruption of the king and the ruling Wafd party. Discontent was also simmering among the urban poor, and in January 1952 it boiled over in riots in which British and other foreigners in Cairo were attacked and their property torched. The army were called in to contain the mayhem. That they did so swiftly and efficiently only increased the self-confidence of the anti-regime officers: under their command, they had an effective tool for political action – and for rule. On the night of 22–23 July 1952, the Free Officers, as they called themselves, moved on the royal palace. Faruq was deposed and shipped out on *El Mahrousa* – the royal yacht that, more than eighty years before, had led the way along the new Suez Canal. To pull the punch of the coup, the king's baby son was elevated to the throne *in absentia*, with the junta's elder frontman General Neguib as his prime minister; a year later, the royal fiction was abandoned and Egypt became a republic with Neguib as president. In the fashion of *The Thousand and One Nights*, however, the fiction contained another fiction: there was yet another power behind the republican throne, smiling over the general's shoulder.

There was also a new generation of world empires in the wings, and it was not long before an envoy came from one of them. In May 1953 US Secretary of State Dulles arrived in Cairo bearing a gift from General Eisenhower to General Neguib – a nickel-plated Colt revolver engraved with a presentation inscription. If it had a meaning, a Colt in the Cold War could hardly but be loaded with a *double entendre*: defend American interests, or do the honourable thing. But when Dulles went on to meet the prime mover of the revolution and the real power in the land, Colonel Jamal Abd al-Nasir, there were no hidden meanings. Nasser, as he became known in the non-Arabic world, wanted bigger guns, and tanks and warplanes. Of course the Americans would supply them, Dulles told him – provided Egypt joined a defence pact with the US and UK against the USSR, and agreed to guarantee the British presence in the Canal Zone. For Nasser and the revolution, that would indeed have been political suicide; he refused the deal, point-blank. Instead, Egypt turned to the Eastern bloc and got its arms, no strings attached, from the Soviets. The Americans retorted with an offer of funding for the Aswan High Dam, the revolution's ambitious but exorbitantly costly project to supply Egypt with dependable irrigation and industrial power. But there was another condition: stop buying Soviet arms.

The old European powers might have begun to bow, reluctantly, out of the region. But Egypt and its Arab neighbours were still up on their same rock, and new empires had already stepped into the old power game, supporting and opposing, dangling loans and arms, then snatching them away. Was it better to be a US puppet or a Soviet Pinocchio? Choosing between Eastern and Western blocs would always be a gamble, Russian roulette with an American revolver.

And so it would go on, the most outspoken Arab poet of the age knew, as long as

> we are still those shattered, scattered tribes
> That feed on buried malice and blood-feuds
> . . .
> For in the east is Hulagu, and in the west is Caesar.

It is poetic licence to concertina chronology and call the two twentieth-century Cold Warriors by the names of a thirteenth-century Mongol and a first-century BC Roman. But that is the point. Time can be an hourglass; but it is also a squeezebox, and one that plays variations on very old themes.

THE MUSLIN CURTAIN

Those lines of Nizar Qabbani just quoted come from a birthday ode addressed to Nasser in 1971. The ode was an elegy, not a celebration, for by that time the poet's 'Knight of Dreams' was dead; disappointment had killed the dreams and the man, well before his grand climacteric. But, like some secular Hidden Imam, the deceased leader whose followers believe him to be merely in a state of miraculous concealment, something of him seemed to survive the dissolution of the body. Was it just the smile? (Nasser's smiling, front-page face is my own earliest memory of Arab history.)

It was the smile of a Cheshire Cat, but also of a matinée idol. Nasser, who had planned and headed the coup of 1952, could not bear to be anything other than the male lead. In March 1954, at the age of thirty-six, he had removed General Neguib from office, put him under house arrest and assumed the presidency himself. That, however, was only a start. Exactly when Nasser began to see himself as the leader not just of Egypt but of all Arabdom is not clear. It has been said that, before 1956, he 'never spoke of himself as anything but Egyptian'. But the idea of a bigger role was probably there from the beginning, for he said in a broadcast only three months after taking power that 'The aim of the Revolution Government is for the Arabs to become one Nation with all its sons collaborating for the common welfare'. For the time being, however, he was too busy at home to pursue that wider aim – busy using his charm to disarm his own people (they had liked the fatherly General Neguib), arming himself against the Israelis, looking for finance for the Aswan Dam, and mucking out the Augean stable of corruption that was Cairo. What would change everything, giving Nasser an intercontinental audience and inspiring him to gather the word of Arabs everywhere, was Suez.

In July 1956 the Americans, true to their threat, withdrew the offer of funding for the Aswan Dam. A week later Nasser nationalized the Suez Canal Company, on the grounds that its takings would go towards making up the shortfall of $200 million for the dam. At this, Britain, France and Israel got together and did a secret deal. As a result, in October the Israelis advanced on the Canal. Egyptian forces, as expected, moved into the Canal Zone to oppose them. Now Britain and France – in their role as joint shareholders of the Canal Company – warned both sides to pull out. As the plan had assumed, the Egyptians dug in. At this point the French and British sent in their own forces, which attacked and occupied parts of the Canal Zone. So far so Machiavellian. And it was all more than faintly reminiscent of the successful operation of 1882, when a joint Anglo-French naval squadron had descended on Egypt during the Urabi revolution and Britain had ended up taking the country over. But that was when they were the superpowers. Now, seventy years on, there was a contingency that their plan – a combination of gunboat imperialism, gung-ho adventure and gangster heist – had overlooked: the possibility that the new superpowers might not take kindly to their predecessors meddling in the Middle East. For the region, whatever else it had been called, was and always had been in the middle; Arabs were still middle-men, as they were when they mediated between the two spheres of Old World trade, the Mediterranean and the Indian Ocean. Now, in the 1950s, the Arab lands were no less central, no less sensitive – particularly as no Iron Curtain divided them but only a diaphanous veil, a shifting muslin curtain between the eastern and western wings of the Cold War world. And so the superpowers entered the fray. The USSR threatened to march in militarily on the Egyptian side; the USA threatened to sell off its British currency bonds and destroy the UK economy in a meltdown of the pound sterling. The Suez escapade was abandoned: the British bulldog slunk off, tail between legs; the Gallic cockerel crowed its crestfallen last. The Israelis stayed on to fight another day, but having placed themselves in the middle of the middle they had no choice.

For France and Britain it was a disaster. The British prime minister fell, his French counterpart teetered; national souls were searched. And their action, doomed as it was, produced another reaction, the old habitual reflex of Arabs uniting under pressure. The Suez Canal joined the Med to the Red; the Suez Crisis would join Arabs from the Atlantic to the Gulf.

A TRANSISTORIZED ORGASM

If Suez was the death-rattle of those two moribund powers, among Arabs it set off a frisson of surprise mixed with what Arabic calls *shamatah*, and English – which coyly professes not to know the feeling – calls by the borrowed name of *Schadenfreude*. An eye-witness in Britain's last Arab possession, the journalist David Holden, put it in plainer terms: 'the thrill of an Arab victory ran like an orgasm through the back streets of Aden.' It was Nasser who brought on the climax. Although it was actually superpower pressure that had defeated the aggressors of Suez, he worked up the defeat into his own triumph. As an experienced officer who had inspired and led a coup, he already had a way with words. He now also took upon himself the mantle of a long rhetorical tradition. Ancient Arabs had been led by charismatic *kahin*s, poets and prophets. Now they had a charismatic Egyptian president who, with his rhetorical spin on Suez, was creating a powerful new *'asabiyyah*, a wheel of fire much wider than Egypt – and he was doing so with the help of another element, air.

Print had prepared the ground for a new Arab unity. Print, however, was earthbound and could be contained. In their rebellious North African possessions, the French had put a strict ban on Egyptian magazines, with their dangerously alluring pictures of Nasser's soldiers

> demonstrating to students the technique of throwing hand grenades . . . marching through the magnificent streets of Cairo in their khaki shorts. Everyone looked happy and healthy; the women and girls waved from the windows of the apartment houses.

But you couldn't ban the oxygen of the airwaves. Moreover, 1954, when Nasser became president, was exactly when the small but powerful offspring of the old valve wireless set, the transistor radio, was first produced commercially; 1956, the year of Suez, was when it became widely and cheaply available. Under the colonial nose from the Interzone of Tangier to the Free Zone of Aden, these small but insistent organs of disembodied speech insinuated themselves into the Arabic world, and spoke in Nasser's voice. Yet again, a new development in communications was unlocking a new phase of Arab history: the growth of the unifying high language, the writing of the Qur'an, Umayyad book-keeping, Abbasid paper-making, nineteenth-century printing, and now the twentieth-century transistor – all opened chapters in the long Arab story.

Cairo's radio transmitting power rose from 73 kilowatts at the time of the 1952 revolution to nearly 6,000 kilowatts in 1966. At its height, Egypt was broadcasting 589 hours of radio a week, not far short of the BBC's 663 hours at the same time. By then, broadcasts included many in non-Arabic languages, especially African ones; Nasser's mission was gaining new dimensions. But Arabic was always the focus. In the Nasserist view – as also for the Arab League, the Arab Awakening, and in the ancient division of humanity into *'arab* and *'ajam* – an Arab was defined above all by language. And the great thing about radio waves was that they respected no other definitions: they vaulted sectarian dividing-lines and imperial lines on the map, and united the linguistic homeland.

Radio broadcasting revived the ancient power of spoken Arabic, and gathered the Arab word on a huge scale; as a call to unity, it was comparable to the slogans of early Islam. It was the ideal medium: listeners couldn't answer back; they could always switch off, but the message was too novel, too exciting, and it was right there in your house, in your stall in the suq. Nasser's audience would number millions, but he had an enviable knack – not so much the common touch as the individual reach. Add to this, genuine heroic cool: on 26 October 1954 a bungling would-be assassin from the Muslim Brotherhood fired eight shots at Nasser while he was making a speech. They all missed; but where many a president would be bundled off, Nasser stood his ground, paused briefly, then ad-libbed:

> I will live for your sake and die for the sake of your freedom and honor. Let them kill me; it does not concern me so long as I have instilled pride, honor, and freedom in you. If Jamal Abd al-Nasir should die, each of you shall be Jamal Abd al-Nasir!

It was pan-Arab, populist, but intensely personal. And it came direct from the man himself. Combining good looks, bedroom eyes, a mellifluous tongue and a magical message, he was the ultimate political crooner. Men hero-worshipped, women swooned. The word had regained its ancient sorcery; almost its divinity. In his posthumous birthday ode to his 'Knight of Dreams', Nizar Qabbani spoke on behalf of the man in the pan-Arab suq of the one

> on whose love we were drunk, like a Sufi drunk on God . . .

It is all but blasphemous, and that is the point.

Love pumped out over the airwaves at ever increasing kilowattages. Across the independent Arabic world, leaders upgraded their own transmission power. Would-be leaders, too, recognized the supreme importance of broadcasting. From now on, one of the first calls in any coup, like the one that overthrew the monarchy in Iraq in 1958, would be 'Seize the radio station!' In societies in which facts are subservient to human or divine authority, to have control of rhetorical truth was even more important than controlling the palace.

In time, the strategic weapon of choice for coup-mongers would be the satellite TV channel. But even in Nasser's era there was a visual side to his message, for Arab – which at the time meant, effectively, Egyptian – cinema began to flourish. However, as well as ideas of pan-Arab unity, Egyptian movies disseminated images of multiplicity. Arabs began to see other aspects of themselves – not just reasonably recognizable robed fellaheen in bucolic settings, but also women in perms and cocktail dresses, living in *gemütlich* Cairene interiors. In addition, they heard *en masse* for the first time just how differently their Egyptian cousins spoke in real life. When one reflects that the expression for 'No' in the San'ani dialect that I speak is *mashi*, and that *mashi* in Cairene dialect means 'OK, yes', one will realize that the potential for misunderstanding is high.

BECOMING ARAB

Nasser himself would exploit Arabic's slippery diglossia. In his speeches for Egyptian consumption, he would begin and end in high Arabic, but would switch between one and the other in the middle. These linguistic gear-changes were a way of making points about 'local [Egyptian] nationalism versus pan-Arabism'. In his speeches to the wider Arabic world, however, he would use the high language alone. And if one high theme ran through nearly all of them, it was that of the threat of imperialism, and the need for Arabs to achieve unity in order to confront it. A full 2,500 years after Assyria and Babylon, other peoples' empires were still lions on the prowl. But now the rock of *'urubah*, arabness, was firmly planted in Egypt. Nasser was playing, consummately, the part of the lion-tamer, and himself being lionized by the Non-Aligned Movement. To the blocs that formed this movement he was now adding another – a pan-Arab world with Egypt and himself at its centre.

Not everyone was happy with Egypt being the great Arab monolith, and some of the dissenters were themselves Egyptian. Taha Husayn had questioned the authenticity of ancient poetry, and had championed the diversity of Egypt's heritage; but he had always celebrated high Arabic, and as one of its great modern stylists had confirmed Egypt's place at the heart of modern Arabic letters. In the 1940s and 1950s, however, there appeared a number of extreme dissidents like the Egyptian-nationalist enfant terrible Luwis Awad. A Copt, a Cambridge man and a natural stirrer, he launched in his book *Plutoland* a virulent attack on the 'occupation' of Egypt by Arabs and Arabic. The attitude was reminiscent of the Shu'ubi literary attacks against Arabs in the heyday of their empire; as then, Awad's polemic provoked vicious counter-attacks. He was branded, for example, a 'wicked charlatan, impostor, transgressor, puppet, trash, insane, odious, rotten, depraved, useless thing, missionary errand boy . . . ' A few neo-Shu'ubis, like Awad's fellow Copt Salamah Musa, were for cutting out the unifying high Arabic tongue altogether. Musa argued that Egyptians should write in Egyptian dialect, not in the pan-Arab high language – and yet he preached but did not practise, for he himself wrote in that same high Arabic. Given such intellectual hemlock-drinking, and the number of poison pens wielded by the defenders of Arab culture, Egypt's *'urubah* won.

It was not surprising. Egypt had become the centre of Arabic culture after the fall of Baghdad 700 years earlier. Following the long sleep of Ottoman times, the land had been central to the nineteenth-century Arab Awakening. Now Nasser had placed Egypt at the political centre of the Arabic world, and if his speeches provided its slogans, then the songs of the great diva Umm Kulthum were its cultural theme tunes. Her magnificent voice billowed out on the airwaves, often as a warm-up act to Nasser, whose speeches would be broadcast after her radio concerts. It almost seemed as if she was addressing him, the idol, personally, on behalf of each one of the millions of individuals drunk on love of him:

> I'll not forget you, you who swept me from my feet
> with words so soft that came from lips so sweet.
> I'll not forget you, you whose hand stretched out to save
> me, drowning, deep from in the swelling wave.
> . . .
> Has love known such as us, so drunk on ecstasy?
> We built about us walls of fantasy!

For the first time since the seventh century, Arabs everywhere rode a wave of unity. The ride was ecstatic; but it was also, in the most literal sense, fantastic.

At home, meanwhile, with the high Arabic magic of Umm Kulthum and the pan-Arab mission of Nasser, Egyptians questioned their arabness at their peril. But there would always be rebels. One was the young Leila Ahmed who in a later memoir, in a chapter entitled 'On Becoming an Arab', recalled an irate teacher correcting her high Arabic reading at school in the 1950s:

> 'You're an Arab!' she finally screamed at me. 'An Arab! And you don't know your own language!'

'I'm not an Arab!' I said, suddenly furious myself. 'I am Egyptian! And anyway we don't speak like this!' And I banged my book shut.

A VERY TEMPORARY MARRIAGE

The Balfour Declaration; mandates and military bases; client-kings, fat-cat courts and cabinets; the British in Palestine; the French in Algeria, where a bloody war for independence had begun in 1954; Britain, France and Israel in cahoots at Suez in 1956 . . . It was all a crescendo of broken promises, a catalogue of duplicity and dashed hopes, and it left Arabs both suspicious of outsiders' intentions towards their world and unconvinced – as they still are, a lifetime later – that the Westerners' solution of supposedly harmonious multiplicity could work for them. Thus the continuing pursuit of the mirage of unity, whether led by a living hero like Nasser or, as more recently, by the long-dead Prophet of Islam. The mirage had always eluded them; but at least it was their own dream, not someone else's hallucination.

Nasser, however, was not alone among the living in claiming to champion pan-Arabism. A decade before his rise to power, the Ba'th movement had formed in Syria and Iraq. Its beginnings sound like the start of a joke: 'There were these three Syrians, a Christian, a Sunni and an Alawi . . . ' But the three – Michel Aflaq, Salah al-Din al-Bitar and Zaki al-Arsuzi – were serious. *Ba'th* is 'resurrection', and in its founders' minds, the movement promised a sort of apocalyptic Arab Awakening, a secular End Time in which Arabs would rise as one and enter a state of blissful unity. The mark of the elect was that most ancient one of all: for the Ba'th, as for Nasserists and proto-nationalists, an Arab was defined above all by language. Defined, and led: 'Our language,' said a Ba'thist academic in 1956, 'is like the flag behind which soldiers march.' As well as a flag, however, the rather cerebral Ba'thists needed a populist flag-bearer. Nasser, covered with the borrowed laurels of Suez and basking in stardom, was perfect.

On 12 January 1958, a group of high-ranking army officers, including Ba'thists, flew from Damascus to Cairo to put the idea of bringing Syria and Egypt closer together politically. Nasser sent them home with stars in their eyes and an agreement for a full union with Egypt in their pocket – with, of course, Nasser in control. The politicians back in Damascus were presented with a *fait accompli*. Syria, independent for little more than a dozen years, was independent no longer: it was part of the United Arab Republic (UAR). And if the politicians didn't like it, they could lump it, in gaol.

Extraordinarily, the reactionary, absolute and highly eccentric king-imam of Yemen, Ahmad, immediately took his country into a federation with the UAR; the new and kinky *ménage à trois* was called the United Arab States (UAS). Perhaps on reflection, however, Yemen's joining was not altogether strange. Like his father, Imam Yahya, Ahmad had always harped on the theme of throwing the British out of Aden and its Protectorates and forming a reunited Greater Yemen – with, of course, himself as king. To this end, arms and advisers now flowed into the country from Egypt. So too did rhetoric, and Yemen's radio, which had also modestly upped its wattage, crowed in the tones of Cairo, 'The Arab giant will drive imperialism into the pit. The claws of death have clutched at the imperialists.'

With not just one but two unions – the UAR and the UAS – orbiting around Nasser, the two remaining Hashimite monarchies, Jordan and Iraq, formed their own union. For a historical split second, the Arab world seemed to be heading not for unity but for yet another duality; perhaps for its own Cold War. Time, though, did not tell. In July 1958, belatedly inspired by the 1952 Egyptian revolution but with that extra dash of gore that always seems to have been to local taste, a coup by army officers in Baghdad killed the young king and most of the royal family. While the blood was still fresh, Ba'thist officers considered taking Iraq into the UAR; the coup leader, Brigadier Abd al-Karim Qasim, however, feared that Egypt and Syria would gang up on him and quashed the idea. In this world of alpha males, some were more alpha than others, and they all knew that one, Nasser, was alpha-double-plus.

In the event, both the UAR and UAS were doomed. Theoretical Arabs might have been led by the flag of a standard language; real-life Arabs marched to the cross-rhythms and disharmonies of different dialects, both linguistic and political. Theirs was never a simple Sousa melody ('Keeping Step With The Union'?) but the fantastic complexities of Charles Ives. The cross-purposes soon revealed themselves in Syria, where Nasser's functionaries had brushed the Ba'thists aside, nationalized the holdings of astonished landowners, and tormented the populace with red tape (Egypt, having invented papyrus, has always been inordinately fond of paperwork). On 28 September 1961, less than four years after they invited them in, Syrian army officers rose up and gave the Egyptians the boot. Yemen's Imam

Ahmad, who had had second thoughts about the UAS from the start, cut his own ties with the UAR (as Egypt continued to call itself, alone and wistful, until 1971). A pre-modern monarch if ever there was one in modern times, he did so by attacking Nasser's socialism with the ancient edged weapon of verse:

To grab all property and 'nationalize',
and, in the name of 'justice', equalize
The inequality of rich and poor –
both acts are crimes against God's holy law.

The Egyptians counter-attacked, most memorably in a feature film that portrayed the imam as a concubine-fondling tyrant who kept a lion chained next to his throne.

Nasser's dream of union was over. But worse, much worse, was to come. The two main Ba'th parties, of Syria and Iraq, would follow a forked path and end up fighting each other: the Ba'th dissolved in bathos, and battles. 'Nothing was resurrected with us,' said Sami al-Jundi, an early member of the 'Resurrection' Party, 'but the age of the Mamluks.' In Iraq, under the Ba'thist Saddam Husayn, it would be more like the age of the Umayyad bogeyman al-Hajjaj ibn Yusuf. As for the current state of the Syrian Ba'th, it is the final punch-line, the tail-end of the shaggy dog story that began with those three founders and their good intentions; its slogan, 'Unity, Freedom and Socialism', would be more accurate if changed to 'Disunity, Tyranny and Fascism'. The irony, again, is that calls for union, both Nasserist and Ba'thist, could lead to such division. It was as if Arab nationalist leaders were magnets attracting popular support – until the leaders tried to come together, and found that like poles repel.

Some leaders, however, did not need to come together to feel that mutual repulsion. In 1958, rumour (in the form of Syrian intelligence) had it that King Sa'ud of Saudi Arabia, the son and successor of Abd al-Aziz, had offered $2 million for Nasser's murder. True or not, the hatred came horribly into the open in Yemen. There, as in Iraq, Nasser-inspired army officers had overthrown the monarchy in September 1962. It was third time lucky, as there had been attempted republican coups against the old imam-king, Ahmad, in 1955 and 1961; the second time, he had taken three revolvers-full of bullets and lived. The 1962 coup, seven days after Ahmad's death from 'natural' causes (though what could be more 'natural' for rulers than assassination?), was at first successful; but when the Saudis began backing the deposed imam-of-a-week, Muhammad al-Badr, Nasser marched in to support the republicans. It has been said that, for the Egyptian leader, this new embroilment was 'a confusion between rhetoric and *realpolitik*'. The point might be made about almost any war. That conflicts are rhetorical in origin had been acknowledged long before by the last Umayyad governor in Khurasan:

> Fire's kindled with two firesticks,
> war with words . . .

The war in Yemen soon blazed up into Egypt's Vietnam, napalm and all. If Nasser had a way with words, he didn't have a way with wars.

A SPARROW AMONG RAINDROPS

So much for Arab unity in the time of Nasser. In contrast, the other element of Nasser's theme, the anti-imperial one, was proving more successful in this age of worldwide decolonization. The French granted independence to Tunisia and Morocco in 1956, in both cases following popular resistance that had surged following the 1952 Egyptian revolution. Algeria, however, their first Arab possession, they held on to at huge cost in blood. Both sides committed terrorist atrocities against civilians, but probably the worst were those inflicted by French settlers on their Arab neighbours. The colonial authorities freely used torture and internment without trial as weapons, and at the height of the conflict had half a million troops on the ground.

A result of the horrors was that, perhaps for the first time, Arabs everywhere – in both Maghrib and Mashriq – began to feel a genuine solidarity, a mass sympathy with their fellows in Algeria. It was a unity of spirit that leapt borders and ignored the personality clashes of their leaders. Again, radio broadcasting was vital in forming this awareness. But, unlike Suez, the long and bitter Algerian war needed no Nasserite spin: its heroes and heroines were inspiration enough. The most celebrated was Jamilah Bu Hayrad, a woman in her early twenties who delivered bombs and other messages for the resistance, and whose capture and torture in 1957 made her a secular martyr across the Arab world:

Jamilah among their bullets,
A sparrow among raindrops.
A shock of volts shakes her wine-dark body,
Burns on her left breast
On her nipple . . .
On . . . on . . . the shame of it . . .
. . .
Revolutionary from the Atlas
Remembered by lilac and narcissus
Remembered by citron flowers.
How small is France's Jeanne d'Arc
Beside my country's Jeanne d'Arc!

France had tried to make Algeria her own; by turning Jamilah Bu Hayrad into Joan of Arc, the Arab poetic imagination had colonized the colonizers' own national epic. The Maid of Algiers was condemned to the guillotine, but her sentence was commuted to life imprisonment. After the French left Algeria in 1962, worn down by the war and by public opinion at home, Jamilah – in her own remake not of Joan of Arc but of the frog prince – married her French defence lawyer. Now, *that* is independence.

Meanwhile at the far end of the Arab world, Aden, Britain's first Arab possession (if we except Tangier, Catherine of Braganza's dowry to Charles II in 1662, abandoned in 1684), taken like Algiers in the 1830s, was also proving to be its last. The British withdrew in 1967, bombed out by the local resistance, but also budgeted out by Prime Minister Harold Wilson's defence cuts at home. Abandoning a royal flush of client-rulers, they slipped away, as the military commander Brigadier Lunt put it, 'like thieves in the night'.

Across the peninsula, the British redeemed themselves, to some extent, in their last spheres of Arabian influence. The now withered hand of empire had already helped to machinate in 1966 the succession of Shaykh Zayid as ruler of Abu Dhabi; now, in 1970, it eased that of Sultan Qabus in Oman. The millennial history of imperial kingmaking had life in it yet. The stability of the resulting states – the United Arab Emirates, formed of Abu Dhabi and its six smaller neighbours, and the Sultanate of Oman – was by no means guaranteed: over time, Oman had never been any more united than next-door Yemen; of Zayid's fifteen predecessors at Abu Dhabi, eight had been murdered and five deposed. But small populations and oil-filled coffers have helped.

There was, however, one other late manifestation of colonialism that would prove more baleful. That the sins of Balfour and Sykes–Picot had been amply expiated, in many international eyes, by the sacrifice of Jews in the Holocaust, was not obvious to Arabs. They saw the simple fact of outsiders coming and settling on land where their own people had lived time out of mind. At the same time, the Zionist intrusion still had the potential to form the core of a new Arab solidarity. Arabs had lost the 1948 war with the Zionists because of that 'something false and rotten' in themselves; but perhaps the State of Israel would prove to be something unexpectedly beneficial, like the grit in the oyster.

THE CATASTROPHE

In June 1967, while Nasser still had a third of his forces in Yemen, he suddenly found himself up against a foe much nearer home. He had built up his aggressive capability with Soviet-supplied tanks and warplanes, the camelry and cavalry of the Cold War. Recently, he had signed military agreements with Syria and Jordan. All wanted vengeance for the defeat of 1948, and it seemed that Arabs were poised on the edge of another moment of unity, perhaps of greatness. The Israelis, however, had also been building up their military muscles, and especially their air power. On 5 June they struck first, wiping out the Egyptian air force on the ground, and in a few short days seizing not only Egypt's Sinai Peninsula as far as the Suez Canal, but also the Jawlan or Golan Heights of southern Syria and, most fatefully, the remaining Arab parts of Palestine – the Gaza Strip and Jordanian-run East Jerusalem and the West Bank. Even more disastrously than in the long slow debacle of the Yemen war, Nasser had been the victim of his own dreams, his own rhetoric. He had learned that rhetoric is to truth as dreams are to realities.

The calamity generated much elegy, and – that rare thing – much honesty. There was no way a loss of this magnitude could be alchemized into anything other than defeat. Poetry became confession. In particular, it was recognized that while words might start wars, they were no match in the actual fighting for modern weaponry well used. In 1798 the Egyptians had opposed Napoleon with words and their rhetorical adjuncts, sticks. Similarly, in 1967,

If we lost the war, no wonder,
For we go to war
With all the speechifying talent that an Oriental has,
With the Lays of Antar that never killed a fly . . .

If verses about ancient warriors like Antar couldn't kill flies, what could they do against Israeli Mirage jets? As Nizar Qabbani went on to explain in this most bitter ode, 'Marginalia in the Notebook of the *Naksah*' – the 'Catastrophe', the Disaster Mark II – the speechifying had drowned out genuine speech, the expression of people's real thoughts, hopes and fears:

O my master . . . O my master the sultan
You have lost the war twice
Because half our people have no tongue . . .

As so often, the gathering of the word had meant the silencing of the crowd.

Writing over twelve years before the 1967 war, Edward Atiyah had noted how Arabs were well aware that the power of the unwelcome presence in their midst might be

> great enough, perhaps, to enable the Israelis (if the Arab states were unable to defend themselves adequately) to snatch another piece of Arab territory – in Jordan or the Gaza region – with impunity.

Such sober prophecies had been forgotten in the euphoria of the moment, of armament, and of Nasser's grandiloquent stage presence. Now the worst had happened; or worse than the worst, for the Israelis had snatched both those two territories and a lot more besides. It was a defeat that put Arab time and motion back on pause. The only movement was that of the new flood of refugees, some of them double refugees, driven from their old homes in 1948 and now in 1967 from their temporary homes. As for the prime mover himself, the Knight of Dreams, he now became, according to his vice-president and successor Anwar al-Sadat, 'a living corpse'. For his later biographer, Said Aburish, Nasser was *The Last Arab*. Hyperbolic though the title is, the hundred million and more Arabs who were left had indeed lost something huge: Nasser had made them feel like a people, '*the* Arabs'; now the definite article was in doubt again, perhaps even the capital

A. It was all a new Arab awakening, and a harsh one. Umm Kulthum's songs now seemed to be about this cruel morning after:

> But time dispelled the wine; day dawned, and we awoke –
> O to delay the sober day that broke
> And, breaking, killed our dreams. Thus did our slumber end;
> night turned its back on us – dear night, our friend . . .

Night, and the Knight.

No dream, however noble, could survive so many cold dawnings – the collapse of the UAR and the UAS, the Yemen war, and now this comprehensive defeat. And yet the pan-Arab ideal, like its great champion, was to have a zombie-like existence in the service of the next generation of would-be idols. On Nasser's actual death in 1970 the young and oil-rich Mu'ammar al-Qadhdhafi, who in the previous year had dethroned the British-installed king of Libya, offered Egypt $500 million for the Leader's body. It might seem that inflation had set in since King Sa'ud's alleged offer of a measly $2 million for Nasser's head, but al-Qadhdhafi's intention was to build a shrine in Libya for Arabdom's greatest secular saint. Pan-Arabism might have been down the pan, but al-Qadhdhafi claimed Nasser had designated him his successor as the 'trustee' of the movement. The new young Knight of Dreams, as he saw himself, would turn in time into an aged Knight of Nightmares; but for the moment he looked like a groovy new model of Nasser, a youthful Mick Jagger to the old matinée idol.

In Cairo, even after the Catastrophe, a Qasr al-'Urubah or 'Palace of Arabness' would be opened in the suburb of Heliopolis for the reception of Arab delegations. Poets, however – those inveterate truth-speakers – knew that *'urubah* was no dream-palace but a collection of warring camps:

> Fall and scatter
> Like dry leaves, you tribes of *'urubah.*
> Fight among yourselves
> And feud
> And kill yourselves,
> You second edition
> Of the biography of Andalus the Conquered.

Again, the accordion chronology, squeezing together the fifteenth and twentieth centuries. But the fighting and feuding are not poetic licence: in the so-called Black September of 1970, blood flowed in the streets of Amman as the Hashimite king of Jordan fought a civil war with his radically politicized Palestinian guest-population.

THE PILGRIMAGE OF OIL

The 1967 war, however, was itself to have a second edition. In the war of 1973, Arabs would have a new weapon more powerful than words, more devastating than MiGs or Mirages. The new weapon was oil, and to wield it Arabs would act together – 'for once', said Muhammad Hasanayn Haykal, ghostwriter to the late President Nasser. The Age of Hope was not dead, yet.

In October 1973, Egypt and Syria launched a simultaneous assault on Israel, the Egyptians crossing the Suez Canal and the Syrians attacking in the occupied Golan. The suddenness of the assault won it initial success, but the Israelis drove it back and the USA and USSR intervened to stop the fighting. There were no real winners or losers; but Arab honour had been restored, in part. More important, however, than the immediate raid and its repulsion were its indirect yet massive and long-term effects on the world economy. As well as the two-pronged military attack, Arab oil exporters had cut production and threatened to keep it down as long as Israel remained, in flagrant breach of international law and UN resolutions, in the Arab territories it had occupied in 1967. For a time, also, Saudi Arabia went further and suspended all oil exports to the United States and to the Netherlands, which it considered to be the most pro-Israeli state in Europe. By the end of the year, oil prices had risen by more than 50 per cent, from a 1972 price of less than $2 per barrel to nearly $3. This was only the beginning. The apparent ease of the initial rise suggested that prices could go higher still: OPEC, the Organization of Petroleum Exporting Countries, saw that – to put it bluntly – they had been getting a bum deal from the world's wealthy buyers, and set out to see just how high they could go. The result was that by 1974 a barrel of oil cost $10.41. By this stage the economic pips were squeaking in the consumer countries, my school homework and *Monty Python* were interrupted by power cuts, and OPEC took off the pressure; but they were now squeezing more than five times more cash out of their customers than they had been just two years before. This was to have an indelible effect, not only on the world economy but also on the world 'order', and not least on that of its Arabic-speaking part. As recently as 1967, a commentator could remark of the oil-producing Arab states that 'even those that have money are simply backwaters too small to exert much influence'. All that had now changed. The Arab petrocrats of Saudi Arabia, Kuwait and elsewhere suddenly had a lot more money, and money could buy them out of the backwaters and into the mainstream.

Moneyed Arabs suddenly became mobile, and internationally visible. Veils, headscarves and hubble-bubbles appeared on London's Edgware Road; the Saudi oil minister Ahmed Zaki Yamani held forth, impish and bearded, on TV screens. Images of jet-setting bedouins were touched by caricature – oil shaykhs stuffing the cleavages of belly-dancers on Cairo's Pyramids Road with hundred-dollar bills, Harrods or Saks Fifth Avenue opening out of hours for the convenience of petro-potentates leading their hawk-masked harems. But other images gave Arabs, or some of them, a more solid presence abroad than they had ever had. From being the object of enmity in the Crusades, of myth in later ages, and most recently either a cinematic romance (thanks to David Lean and Omar Sharif) or a dashed nuisance (hijacking canals and, latterly, airliners), Arabs were now people in foreign eyes – perhaps even *a* people – with a proper history and culture, as events like London's 1976 World of Islam Festival demonstrated. Nasser had not been The Last Arab. Arabs were back on the world stage, and with a bigger role than they had played for over a thousand years.

At home, and almost overnight, the oilier parts of Arabia became a building site. Petroleum installations, palaces, government offices, schools, housing mushroomed. Foreigners went to work in 'Saudi' – which, innocent of the pharyngeal twang of the Arabic name, they pronounced to rhyme with 'Howdy!', or even 'Lordy!' – when they wanted to pay off the mortage. Within the wider Arabic world, too, oil meant mobility and mutual rediscovery. From its more populous and better-educated lands, labourers, clerks, teachers and other workers flocked to the oil-rich peninsula. It all stirred up a new sense of shared arabness, as if the great diaspora of the seventh century had at last gone into reverse. For most Arabs, it was the first time – apart from, for a few, in the sacralized setting of the Mecca pilgrimage – that they had got to meet their distant cousins in the flesh since that great early parting. The oil migrations were thus a kind of secular *hajj*, in which the oil wells of Dhahran took the place of the holy well of Zamzam, and the whole point was to lay up treasures upon earth.

The pilgrimage of oil involved huge numbers: in the 1975 census, 1.23 million North Yemenis were abroad, nearly all of them in the neighbouring oil states, mainly Saudi Arabia. That was 19 per cent of the total population; but it was probably nearer half of the adult male population, who were the only ones who went abroad to work. If there was a greater sense of solidarity, therefore, it was that of men on campaign, in the oil field rather than the battlefield. Families were left fatherless for years on end; but the migrants remitted money home, and eventually came themselves, sporting sparkly watches and, often, the title of '*hājj*' from the sacred pilgrimage too. Recalling his father, a pre-oil migrant to Argentina who had returned home to Syria and to his old job as a weaver of goat-hair tents, the sculptor and writer Asim al-Basha said,

> My father would express his amazement at the 'riches' that building workers in Saudi Arabia and the Gulf states could acquire in just a few years. He would compare the results of their labours with those of his twenty-eight long years spent at the end of the earth.

To a degree, oil money lubricated grating economic disparities, both between the diverse parts of the Arabic world and, as remittances went via local agents to the family in the village, between governments and governed, town and country. By the end of the 1970s, 'the Arab world [was] more closely linked socioeconomically . . . than at any time in its modern history', probably, in fact, since early Abbasid times, more than 1,100 years before.

At the same time, as with Egyptian movies, the more Arabs saw of each other the more they realized how diverse they were. Many, too, found that sudden riches had not done much to promote ideas of equality and cousinly love. The Mecca pilgrimage, with its Gandhiesque uniform of unsewn white cloth, imposes at least a simulacrum of equality. Oil pilgrims, however, were a new version of the ancient tribal *mawla*s or *halif*s, the affiliated clients or allies. In the countries where they worked, they often had no independent personal status; rather, they had to attach themselves to a *kafil*, a 'sponsor' or 'guarantor', either an individual or a company, and since the arrangement was temporary, they probably had fewer rights than the old tribal affiliates and allies. This hurt, and in particular because many of the migrants came from what they themselves saw as more civilized societies. Another Syrian could say of building work in the Gulf, 'Why should we go and lay tile by tile by tile, just so that camels can stand around on them?' His compatriot, the poet Nizar Qabbani, was pessimistic about the levelling effect of oil:

> The Arab world stores its oil
> In its bollocks . . . and your Lord is the Gracious Bestower!
> While the people, whether Before Petroleum or Anno Petrolei,
> Are drained dry just the same, beasts bled by their masters.

Sometimes the anger boiled over:

> If I had a whip in my hand
> I'd strip those desert emperors of the robes of civilization
> . . .
> I'd grind into the dust their patent-leather shoes
> And gold watches . . .
> And give them back their camel's milk . . .

It is all *de haut en bas*; or, more precisely, as it was a heated continuation of the old dialogue between civilized peoples and uncivilized tribes, *de hadar en badw*.

THE DARK PEARL

The 1973 war filled many Arab hearts with pride and, in the longer term, at least some Arab pockets with cash. And yet it was followed by capitulation. In the new sober dawn after the Catastrophe, it had been a realistic war rather than a rhetorical one. Since 1967 and the death of pan-Arabism, hotheads may still have raved about driving the Zionists into the sea, but Anwar al-Sadat was more modest in his strategic aims:

> For Sadat, the war of 1973 had not been fought to achieve military victory, but in order to give a shock to the superpowers, so that they would take the lead in negotiating some settlement of the problems between Israel and the Arabs.

The problem was that the hint went unheeded. So in 1977 al-Sadat himself went to Jerusalem for direct talks. The visit was more shocking than the war: it was a breaking of the ranks, of the rules – for even if they were at each other tooth and claw behind it, Arabs tried to present at least a facade of unity in the face of Zionism. But Egypt had a long habit of going its own unaccountable way. If Nasser had been the smiling sun-god who had shone abroad and then set, then al-Sadat was a creature of the shadowed side of Egypt: a sphinx, an enigma.

The Jerusalem visit led to the American-hosted summit at Camp David in the following year, in which Egypt got Sinai back from the Israelis. However, the central question about the future of the occupied West Bank and Gaza Strip was disastrously fudged. The Israelis spoke vaguely of the eventual self-rule of the regions, but would not be tied to details. The Americans had got the all-important handshake for the cameras; now, like Rome's special representative in Palestine, Pontius Pilate, they could wash their own hands of the mucky business.

Al-Sadat's treaty with Israel was 'a cold peace', and it sent shivers of disgust through the Arabic world. Nizar Qabbani wrote, despairing of the future,

> They've given us the Pill
> That stops our history having children . . .

Egypt was cold-shouldered by its fellow Arab states. Even the Arab League roused itself from its clubbish torpor and removed itself from Cairo to Tunis. The Palestine Liberation Organization (PLO), founded in 1959, and other groups continuing the armed struggle on behalf of the Palestinians, reaped popularity at home and upped their profile abroad. The Egyptians were left to simmer in their own treachery.

Al-Sadat's assassination in 1981 at the hands of newly active Islamic militants – even though it might well have sent another sort of shiver through the Arabic world – probably atoned for some of Egypt's sins. Time also did its own healing. But as bad as Camp David, or worse, was to come in 1993 with the Oslo Accords between the Palestinians and Israel, in which the latter finally condescended to grant 'autonomy' to the occupied territories of Palestine. The Israelis duly withdrew, leaving limited local rule in Palestinian hands. The vital questions, however – Israeli settlements in the West Bank, borders, return of refugees, Jerusalem – were put off again. The question of settlements has been the most contentious of all. 'Under the Oslo Agreements,' explained Raja Shehadeh – who as a Palestinian lawyer knows much about land disputes – the PLO, now representing the Palestinian people,

> agreed to keep an area equal to about a third of the West Bank, referred to as Area C, outside the jurisdiction of the Palestinian Authority . . . Israel presented this to its public as tacit recognition by the PLO that the land, most of which Israel had already registered in the same Land Authority where Israeli state land is registered, would remain with Israel. This gave the settlement project a great boost.

The Oslo Accords were thus 'the worst surrender document in our history'. On this point, if nothing else, moderate Palestinians and extremist Israelis saw eye to angry eye. For Yigal Amir, an Israeli of Yemeni background, Prime Minister Rabin's concession to the Palestinians of even the most parochial rule was surrender of the most treacherous sort, and in 1995 Amir shot Rabin dead. A flash of symmetry, across the long hall of mirrors that is history, with the sacrifice of al-Sadat.

Accords, agreements always imply some surrender by both sides. That the greater surrender was that of the Palestinians has only become evident with time. Today, more than twenty years after Oslo and forty years on from Camp David, the occupied territories have become the besieged territories. The Gaza Strip is the third most densely populated territory on earth, after Singapore and Hong Kong. Access is rigorously controlled from without, and for most inhabitants – or inmates – to leave is impossible; tunnelling out is one of the easier options. Gaza is thus a concentration camp in its most literal meaning, and on an industrial scale. The West Bank, meanwhile, where it is not disfigured and dismembered by the Israelis' Separation Wall, is blotched with an ever-spreading rash of Israeli settlements. The autonomy of the Palestinian authorities there is that of a living head that may be able to think autonomously, but whose body is the object of amputations and infestations: a paralytic who is free to feel pain but not to do anything about it.

The pain radiates out from Palestine across the Arabic world. As long as Israel remains such an aggressive and provocative neighbour, it is a gift for Arab dictators. The 'Zionist Entity', that intrusive grit, has grown into a black pearl of great price, an almost transcendental foe whose existence is the subject of endless rhetoric and the occasional symbolic act. Saddam Husayn, for example, letting off Scud missiles at Israel early in 1991, reaped the adulation of many Arabs. His bombastic barrages caused some material damage and, directly, the deaths of two Israelis (others died from heart attacks and similar causes); the deaths of tens of thousands of Iraqis slaughtered by Saddam at home were forgiven, if noticed, by the Man in the Suq. In Syria the Asads, father and son, have been happy to confront Israel – which occupies the Golan, the ancestral camping-grounds of the Ghassanid kings – with fighting words while, as we shall see, they have turned their heavy weapons on their opponents at home: weapons of mass destruction camouflaged by words of mass distraction. In my adoptive land, the head of the rebels' Revolutionary Council has said that the school curriculum needs rewriting, 'because it was planned by America and Israel', which no doubt comes as a surprise to former Yemeni ministers of education. More recently, adding to the pick-'n'-mix bag of bogeymen, the rebel-appointed minister of education has also said that the curriculum was planned by the so-called Islamic State.

It is all a strange, dark symbiosis: the continued presence of an aggressive Israel, behaving with grotesque injustice towards the people of the territories it occupies in the face of international law, merely prolongs the life of *Tyrannosaurus rex arabicus* – also aggressive, also unjust, and towards his own countrymen.

'Death to America! Death to Israel!' the little children chant, down in the square below my house. But do the people who teach them that rallying-cry know that if those two foes ever actually died, so too would they themselves? The still greater irony, Catch-22 cubed, is that only if the dinosaurs die out and Arabs become truly free will they be able to confront Israeli injustice from a position of real strength, moral not military, and that all such moves to freedom are in themselves branded by the dictators as an Israeli plot. 'The Arab Spring', as we shall see, would thus be successfully billed by the forces of reaction as 'the Zionist Arab Spring'.

It is all a great conundrum, but also part of a great continuum: that of alien empires shaping Arab identity and history since the days of Assyria and Babylon. The difference is that the Israeli mini-empire, the dark pearl, the dagger twisting in the map, has been doing the shaping from the inside. Then again, so too has the black and liquid wealth that lies beneath the

Arabs' 'Island', and most copiously under the infertile parenthesis between the northern and southern fertile crescents. It has redressed the ancient imbalance of felicity between Arabias Deserta and Felix; but it has also fuelled new levels of avarice and new forms of rule, especially since that leap in revenues in 1973, in which tribal shaykhs have become monarchs as absolute as any in human history.

In the early 1980s, a decade or so after the death of Nasser and pan-Arabism, it seemed that, between them, dictators and monarchs of one shade or another had the Arabic world tied up. There were exceptions: a fragmented and imploding Lebanon; a South Yemen where Islamic jurisprudence had been ditched for Marxist dialectic and tribalism re-expressed as Stalinist/Maoist factionalism. But, as so often, the region as a whole seemed to be suspended in a multiple cat's cradle of tensions, in which the power-holders could by its very nature never join hands.

And then, all of a sudden, unity was back on the agenda, and about to prove more divisive than ever before.

CHAPTER FIFTEEN

THE AGE OF DISAPPOINTMENT
AUTOCRATS, ISLAMOCRATS, ANACHARCHS

GUERNICA-ON-THE-ORONTES

About twenty years ago I visited the Syrian city of Hamah, a sleepy place on the Orontes interspersed with tangled orchards and with the groans and gull-cries of giant wooden wheels that raise water from the deep-sunk river. I particularly wanted to find a venerable riverside mansion, Bayt al-Kaylani, that I had seen in an old photograph. The house had its own enormous waterwheel attached and was wonderfully strange, half palazzo, half paddle-steamer. But it had vanished: its site and the surrounding area were a public park planted with giant plastic toadstools.

My quest for the strange was more successful in the Great Mosque. The first thing that caught my eye in the prayer hall was a fine ancient inscription – of, unaccountably, the first words of the *Odyssey* . . .

> ΑΝΔΡΑΜΟΙΕΝΝΕΠΕ . . .
> Tell me of the man . . .

After that it was not Homer, and not about Odysseus but someone called Elias; more than that my rusty Greek would not tell me. It was a double dislocation: Greek in a mosque, and Homer that was not Homer. Looking around, everything else was wrong, too. I knew the Great Mosque of Hamah was an Umayyad foundation, 1,300 years old, and yet it had none of the patina of an ancient building; much of it might have been built yesterday. There were jarring details, including an aluminium door that said 'PUSH' on the handle. This led into the tomb-chamber of a local thirteenth-century potentate, a member of Saladin's family. The chamber too seemed to have been recently and hastily rebuilt. The prince's original cenotaph had gone, and was replaced by a jerry-built thing little better than a packing case.

'I wasn't expecting to find that so much had been . . . restored,' I said to the mosque-goers who were showing me around.

They said nothing.

Most of the Great Mosque, all of Bayt al-Kaylani and much else in Hamah had been destroyed fifteen years before my visit, in February 1982, by aerial bombardment followed up by tanks and artillery: as an example of modern mechanized slaughter, Hamah was an Arab Guernica. The many dead were members of the Muslim Brotherhood, adherents of a newly militant Islam who had seized the city four days earlier; those killed included, of course, their families, neighbours and anyone else who happened to be in the way. The man responsible for the destruction was Hafiz al-Asad, one of a new – but in some ways very old – breed of autocrats. He himself had seized Syria in 1970, and had never bowed to the increasing demands of Islamic hard-liners. In Hamah, the intersection of hard lines cost between 8,000 and 25,000 lives – at least five Guernicas'-worth and at most more than the London Blitz; no one is sure. History is often founded on such variables, even when it happened in living memory. Not that many outside Syria remember Hamah: the Syrian victims had no Picasso to memorialize them, no Churchill to give heart to the survivors. Within the country, silence was their monument, and the newly empty spaces and hastily built antiquities in Hamah itself.

It is all very well to run a tight ship (or to keep a tidy shop: Hafiz al-Asad's omnipresent portrait made him look to my eyes less like a tyrannous captain of state than a friendly neighbourhood grocer). But clearly something is wrong if you feel you have to kill 8,000 or more of your fellow countrymen in one go. Apart from the Black Death and the Mongols, these are the sort of figures for sudden extermination that we have not had since al-Hajjaj ibn Yusuf, who was massacring opponents in Iraq at the time when the Great Mosque of Hamah was first built. It may be conducive to short-term unity, in that you have terrified your opponents into silence; but it is only likely to make things worse in the long run. And, with the death-toll in the current Syrian war waged by Hafiz al-Asad's son now standing at perhaps half a million, it has.

AFTER ORPHEUS

Looking back to the mid-1960s, just a few years before al-Asad *père* grabbed power, the Palestinian writer Samir Kassir wrote that the Arabic world was 'largely optimistic: the Arabs seemed as if they were on the move'. Arabs were still in the active, transitive mood that had returned with their Awakening. Unless you were an old-fashioned tyrant, a male supremacist or a dispossessed Palestinian, the middle decades of the twentieth century had seemed in many ways an age of hope. 'During the interwar years,' Eugene Rogan has pointed out, 'Egypt achieved the highest degree of multiparty democracy in the modern history of the Arab world.' Women in Syria, Kassir noted, got the vote before women in France. In the mid-1950s, Iraq seemed to have a hugely promising future, perhaps as 'a kind of Oriental Canada'. Kuwait looked set for liberal democracy. Nasser, flawed as he was, had radiated hope. Admittedly the Catastrophe – the 1967 war with Israel – had severely damaged the optimism, but in the 1970s the revolution in oil prices and the pilgrimage of petroleum had mobilized Arabs anew and given them fresh hope. Even my adoptive land, seemingly locked in mountains and the past, could have a book written about it in the early 1980s entitled *Yemen Enters the Modern World*. Arabs everywhere talked of *al-taqaddum*, 'progress'.

And then, in the 1980s, as the Islamic calendar edged into its fifteenth century, the forward motion stalled. It wasn't just that there was a fork in the path, a hesitation; for many, there was a complete about-turn. It was as if Arabs had begun to sense that the path of progress was leading them into alien territory – into the 'Modern World', but also out of their own Arab world. That, at least, has been the warning to them put out by a remarkable reactionary double-act of new-wave autocrats and islamocrats. Both have been empowered by the swelling wealth of the region, by the machinations of superpowers, and most recently by that other ancient leaven of Arab history, developments in information technology. Both have been able to use old rhetorics in ever more creative and persuasive ways.

New-wave though they might be, they are also inheritors of a very old legacy of power that had been in danger of slipping from their hands. In

1970, in the Afterword to the tenth edition of his *History of the Arabs* that he had been updating for a third of a century, Philip Hitti wrote that

> Reconstructing Arab society on a democratic political basis and reconciling Islam and the modern world remain the greatest tasks confronting the contemporary generation.

They had been the greatest tasks for several editions of the *History*; in fact, the business of reform had already exercised half a dozen generations of thinking Arabs, since the beginnings of the Awakening in the first half of the nineteenth century. In 1980, it was a process that still needed more time and forward motion. Over the four decades or so since then, however, autocrats and islamocrats have blocked social reconstruction and Islamic reconciliation at every step. It is what one would expect: the last thing they want is to lose power. What is more surprising is that most Arabs have gone along with them, silently, obediently backwards.

Meanwhile the vision of unity, that shimmering phantom to which Arabs had reached out in the time of Nasser – their knight, their Orpheus, their charmer – receded too, lost perhaps for ever.

PEOPLE OF THE CAVE

Along with that fleeing phantom, many Arabs after Nasser seemed to have lost the thread of their own arabness: to have lost that definition he had given them as a people, *the* Arabs. But in the labyrinth of the modern world – to evoke another subterranean myth – there was another thread for them to follow: 'Hold fast,' the Qur'an says,

> all of you together, to the *habl* of Allah, and do not be divided among yourselves.

As we have seen, *habl* is 'a cord, a rope'; but it is also 'a binding covenant, a treaty', and evidently it is the same term used in the most ancient inscriptions for treaties, made under the auspices of a patron deity, that bound the pre-Islamic unitary states of South Arabia. Could Islam now provide the thread of unity once more? The idea was alluring; the reality was more complex. The bond that held the Islamic state of Medina together had unravelled within a generation of Muhammad's death; since then it had frayed still further. With multiple sectarian claimants now insisting that they held the one and only true end of the thread, it was impossible to know which one to follow into an increasingly Daedalian future. The alternative, of course, was to do what Almohads and Wahhabis – both '*Muwahhidun*', Unitarians – had tried to do, and head the other way, back to the brief but glorious unity of Muhammad's Medina. This retrogressive trend was to become so widespread in Islam over the closing decades of the twentieth century that terms like 'Wahhabi' and 'Salafi' (that is, following the example of the *salaf*, the pious fathers of the faith) seem too constricting, too particular for it. One solution might be that, just as secular politics is conveniently if simplistically seen in terms of left and right, the politics of religion should be thought of as orientated forward or in reverse.

The reverse-leaning militants of Hamah, who dreamed of turning Syria into an Islamic state, sometimes look like the Arab vanguard of a new political Islam; but that is partly because they stand in such sharp contrast to the secular setting of Ba'thist Syria and the recent nationalist past of the region. Islam has been political ever since Muhammad moved to Yathrib and it became Medina, his *madinah*, his *polis*. Subsequent Arab leaders have always used Islam for political ends – from Abu Bakr al-Siddiq, defeating the 'apostate' (in other words, opposition) tribes of Arabia in the 630s, to Abd al-Aziz Ibn Sa'ud occupying most of the peninsula in the earlier twentieth century with his raiding Wahhabi tribesmen. Or were they using politics for Islamic ends? It is hard for mortals to distinguish.

There is, however, something new and different about political Islam in its current global form. It is a creature of contemporary globalization, and a by-product of secular pan-Arabism's failure. That is why it seemed new to an observer like Ali Allawi, who can say, 'I don't recall ever coming across the word *jihad* in any contemporary context', when growing up in 1950s Iraq. Yet, even at that time, the movement was germinating. It took an American novelist in a far corner of the Arabic world to notice it with clarity. Paul Bowles, writing of a cell in the independence movement in Morocco in 1954, knew that the majority were orientated to Nasser's Egypt; but one, Benani, had other ideas:

> They dreamed of Cairo with its autonomous government, its army, its newspapers and its cinema, while he [Benani], facing in the same

> direction, dreamed just a little beyond Cairo . . . to Mecca. They thought in terms of grievances, censorship, petitions and reforms; he . . . in terms of destiny and divine justice . . . They saw factories and power plants rising from the fields; he saw skies of flame, the wings of avenging angels, and total destruction.

In the lurid light of September 2001 and the attacks on New York, that is a chillingly prophetic vision. Soon after, astute political observers were also beginning to predict the growth of a new political Islam. In 1955, for example, Edward Atiyah wrote, 'if Western democracy and reformist military dictatorship failed, the alternative would be the forces of revivalist, theocratic Islam'. Before then, political Islam had seemed the precise opposite of contemporary and global – anachronistic and parochial. Islam's most recent major political and military success, those conquests of the Saudi–Wahhabi alliance, was confined to a still-tribal, pre-petroleum Arabia where society had changed relatively little since the early seventh century. The new political Islam, however, would be far from parochial: its Promised Land is the whole world. It is a logical development. Muhammad had achieved *tawhid*, unification both political and theological, in the Arabs' 'Island'. His immediate successors had extended it over the Arabian subcontinent. The subsequent conquests had tried to impose it on a wider Old World. Now, in a more or less globalized world, the ideal is even bigger. So too is the sense of failure and anger when the ideal collides with the reality of a planet that, even if interconnected, is immensely and irreversibly (we presume) various.

Three major factors, more recent than the Saudi conquests, and all of them originating outside the Arab arena, energized political Islam. The first was those crushing but instructive victories of political and military Judaism, in 1948 and 1967. The next was the Islamic Revolution of January 1979 in Iran. Here was an Islam that was not uniting and empowering impoverished tribesmen, but taking over a wealthy state whose regime was backed by one of the two latest 'lions', the United States. The fight against old-fashioned colonialism had already been won, in the decades immediately following the Second World War; the fight against the new cultural and economic imperialism of the Cold War could triumph too – with the blessing of Allah (or at least, in His name, of Ayatollah Khomeini), rather than of Nasser or Che Guevara. The third factor came into operation when, at the end of that same year, 1979, the second, Soviet, lion pounced on Afghanistan. From 1983, this time with the blessing of the United States as well as of Allah, Arab fighters went to join the Afghan resistance. Afghan and 'Afghan-Arab' mujahideen were the toast of the West; 'jihadists', the cognate with the darker connotations, had yet to be coined.

In all three cases, pressures exerted by foreign empires – the US, the USSR, and that third, implanted empire-in-miniature, Israel – were shaping the region and moulding Arab identity. Or rather, they were remoulding it as Muslim identity, and not just for the relatively few young Arab men who made it to Afghanistan. In 1981, *Middle East* magazine ran a survey in which Arab respondents spoke of the ideal of Arab unity. They felt it had been shown up as a myth; yet they also still felt strongly Arab – even if they could not explain why, except in terms of 'vague, though intense feelings'. The findings revealed, however, that Arab identity was under threat: 'Being an Arab today on a personal or even a national level means being in crisis in perhaps a more acute form than had ever been the case in the last 50 years.' The survey was small; its conclusions were themselves vague and impressionistic. But they did seem to confirm that the Arab thread was dangling, if not already lost.

By the new AD millennium, the crisis of Arab identity was rapidly coming to a head. In a 2005 poll conducted in six Arab countries, almost half of the participants identified themselves as Muslims first, only a third as Arabs first, and an even smaller minority as nationals of a particular country; it seemed that being Arab was going out of fashion. Subsequent surveys revealed as many as 79 per cent of respondents giving their first identity as Muslim (in Egypt) and as few as 10 per cent or less giving their first identity as Arab (in Egypt, Jordan, Saudi Arabia, Morocco, Iraq and Algeria). Nasser may not have been The Last Arab; but since his death and burial, arabness too had been buried under a revived – and in some aspects a new – Islamic identity.

It probably helped the obsequies that one of the Cold War lions had itself expired in 1991, partly as a result of exhaustion from its Afghan adventure. It was then that the world's geo-political GPS seemed to go awry, and the path of 'progress' and 'modernity' to look ever more misleading. Left and right lost their definition: Communist Party bosses in ex-Soviet states held on to power but swerved off to the 'right'; China was technically communist but, looping the loop, was going rampantly capitalist. At the same time, the forward–reverse axis came into play: the American religious 'right' swung round towards their puritan past and turned their backs on the 'permissive' post-war decades; Russian traditionalists emerged from the woods and called for the canonization of the Romanovs. Caught in the middle of this global gyre, which direction would Arabs take? And would they go as a body? It certainly seemed that a newly invigorated, retrogressive Islam might succeed in forging Arab solidarity where secular pan-Arabism had failed. In its new ideological guise, signalled by a suffix – Islam*ism*, like Arabism – that solidarity is what it has been trying to achieve ever since, as part of its mission of worldwide unity.

However, the attempt to replay the Arabian seventh century on a global twenty-first-century scale has faced many challenges. First time round, Islam and Arabs had a 'fit': Islam was, after all, born of Arabia and of ancient Arabian beliefs and customs. But Islam itself went global long ago, far beyond its Arabian origins. And – quite apart from the obvious fact that not all Arabs are Muslims – Arabs themselves, diverse enough to begin with, have become even more so over the diaspora of continents, centuries and manners. In an early chapter I mentioned two eighth-century brothers who ended up as governors in Sind and North Africa. Today there are further dimensions of distance: I might mention two brothers I know, of whom one is a fine-dining golfer and the other an al-Qa'idah sympathizer. One size does not fit all.

Latter-day political islamists therefore find that, while you can flip the hourglass and re-enact the battles and the martyrdoms, even with Allah on your side it is hard to make time run backwards to the imagined uniformity of the Medinan utopia. Islamism's more extreme proponents – the 'Islamic State' for example – have thus come to resemble the People of the Cave, a story the Qur'an shares with Christianity. The Seven Sleepers of Ephesus, as they are known in the Christian version, were persecuted for their monotheistic beliefs under the third-century Roman emperor Decius. Taking shelter in a cave, God put them into a state of hibernation – for 309 years in the Qur'anic version, although to the sleepers it seemed no more than a day – and only caused them to wake under the safely monotheistic emperor Theodosius II. The point of the comparison is this: the nineteenth-century Arab Awakening was a secular movement in its most basic sense, in that it recognized the passing of *saecula*, 'ages', during the long sleep, and the need to adapt to change; in contrast, recently awakened islamists find themselves out of synch with an altered world (in their own view, of course, the world is out of synch with them). Their solution is to ignore change; to deny the basic laws of *al-kawn wa-'l-fasad*, generation and corruption, that govern the universe; to deny history and time.

It has been said that 'a sense of history is a sense of loss'. It is also a sense of change. Contemporary political islamists, in rejecting history, thus deny the organic life and flexile strength of Islam, which has constantly renewed itself in a changing world, adapting to complexity, maturing. The idea that Islam is 'an evolving culture-bound dynamic of belief and behavior' is not only an opinion of historians and anthropologists. If it had ever been a monolith, it would have crumbled soon after the first cracks appeared.

The Wahhabis recapitulated the beginning of Islam on an Arabian peninsular scale. Arab nationalism recapitulated *'asr al-tadwin*, the Abbasid 'age of setting down' in which an Arab ethos was fixed in ink. Both the Wahhabis and the nationalists were standing up, in different ways, to the Shu'ubiyyahs – the non-Arab cultural alternatives – of the Ottomans and the European empires. More recently, political Islam has been attempting to recapitulate the lot, but on an even grander scale: in effect, contemporary political islamists are fighting against the Shu'ubiyyah of the whole messy, modern, multicultural, complex, confused, tangled, tied-up, hung-up, interconnected world. They are fighting for one version of a heavenly ideal versus a multifarious earthly reality. The fight appeals to some precisely because it promises simplicity instead of complexity, monism as against pluralism; but it is also a struggle for totalitarianism versus individualism. In that last respect, it can resemble other recent totalitarianisms. We had the Brownshirts and the Blackshirts; for the moment we have the Longblackshirts (though not *too* long – long enough to cover the knee, but not to pick up ritual impurities from the ground). But fashions change, and so do uniforms, and contemporary political Islamism will soon be yesterday's trend.

There will always be other trends. Another one that has taken off in my adoptive country, and zoomed into reverse gear, is that of the neo-Zaydi Hashimi-supremacist Huthis. Their leader has actually been known to sleep in a cave, safe from Saudi missiles and from the progressing world.

NOT GOOD NEIGHBOURS

In parallel with the new Islamism, deeper patterns of Arab identity were re-emerging. With the demise of that other overarching -ism, pan-Arabism, many Arabs now seemed to return to old habits of fragmentation and mutual raiding, sometimes with outside help. The extreme case would be Lebanon where, from 1975 on, everyone – Sunni, Shi'i, Maronite, Druze, Palestinian – fell bloodily out. Israel would also weigh into the fight in 1978 and 1982, the second time especially murderously as its own clients from the Maronite Phalanges massacred Palestinians in the camps of Sabra and Shatila.

The raiding was not only mutual. In 1980 the ancient phenomenon of Arabs raiding Persians updated itself as an Iraqi raid into Iran. The difference was that the old Arab target of the eastern Sawad – the 'Black Country', so called from its dense dark groves of date palms – was now the Black Country of the Iranian oil industry. The new Iraqi dictator, Saddam Husayn, was also understandably worried about Iran's Shi'i Islamic Revolution spreading to Iraqi Shi'is, who made up the majority of his subjects. In his adventure he was supported by an outside empire – the United States, who were happy for him to wreak proxy revenge on the revolutionary Iranians who had overthrown their client-shah. The initial mobility of the raid, however, was soon bogged down in a trench war. By its inconclusive end in 1988 there were no winners, but up to a million dead.

The Americans were not so happy about their Iraqi client's next raid, on Kuwait in 1990. One might argue, and of course Saddam did, that Kuwait as a sovereign state was a creation of British imperial lobbying that only became an Arab League member in 1961, and that it was historically often a dependency of Iraq. But Iraq itself as a sovereign state – rather than an ill-defined geographical region, the lowlands where two great rivers oozed together into the Gulf (geographers pointed out that the common noun *'iraq* is 'the bottom of a waterskin') – was also the creation of British cartographic doodling. The British may have been over-imaginative with their pencils; but during the previous seventy years oil had solidified boundaries and imposed its own new realities. Saddam was trying to reunite a notional, 'natural' Iraq; in doing so he only succeeded in disuniting Arabs as a whole. A majority of Arab governments opposed him and sided with the American-led coalition that threw him out of Kuwait in 1991; the rest were vehemently against the intervention. But in the pro-coalition states there were deep splits between governments and governed: the Iraqi hard-man was supported by a majority of Men in the Suq. It is hard to quantify such things, but Saddam's Kuwait escapade was probably as divisive as any other event in Arab history since the fateful seventh-century war between the old and new regimes of Quraysh under Mu'awiyah and Ali. It also led eventually to what was by far the biggest physical superpower intervention in the region since the days of Byzantium and Sasanian Persia: in the anti-Saddam coalition force of nearly a million, US forces alone numbered 650,000.

A numerically smaller but ultimately more fateful intervention was to come in the 2003 American-led invasion of Iraq, which aimed to remove the now intractable Saddam from power. In this it was successful. What came next was not part of the plan: there was no plan. US President George W. Bush, who with his neo-conservative advisers masterminded the blank blueprint, had wished to remove a ruler whom he branded, spuriously, a threat to the West. He also wanted to liberate Iraqis from a dictator who was a proven threat to many of his own people. Laudable though the second aim sounds, Bush might have done better by keeping in mind James Baldwin's dictum: 'Freedom is not something that anybody can be given; freedom is something people take and people are as free as they want to be.' In the case of Iraq, it was not that Iraqis did not want to be 'free'. But, for most of them, freedom meant something different from what it meant in the mind of Bush. For Iraqis, as for many other Arabs, 'freedom' was the right to be controlled by someone of your own kind – whether tribe, sect, denomination or dialect group – or, failing that, a guarantee of protection by someone of a different group. 'Freedom' does not yet have the same nuances in the Arabic world as it does elsewhere, the same resonances of individualism; and while it is easy for a superpower to implement 'regime change', it is much harder for it to bring about dictionary change.

It is still too soon to know what the long-term ramifications of the 2003 invasion will be. In the short term, however (unlike the divisive events of 1990–1, which began with that inter-Arab raid on Kuwait), superpower pressure had the time-honoured effect of forcing Arabs together: this time, governments and people united in condemnation. The invasion of Iraq also showed – in the US claims, dutifully chorused by its allies, about the military 'threat' posed by Saddam Husayn to the West – that Arabs and Arabic have no monopoly on rhetorical 'truth'.

Elsewhere, conflicts bubbled or raged on through this increasingly fractious and depressing post-pan-Arab age with little or no outside help. Scanning the scene from west to east, Morocco and Algeria have been particularly bad neighbours because of Algeria's backing for the Polisario Front, a movement which since 1975 has sought to throw off Moroccan control of the old Spanish colony of Western Sahara. In Algeria itself, meanwhile, islamists won the first round of national elections at the end of 1991, upon which the ruling party cancelled the second round, setting off a civil war that may have killed 100,000 or more. Next door, Libya's thespian dictator Mu'ammar al-Qadhdhafi would survive in power long enough – over four decades – to stage a one-man show of the entire Age of Disappointment: he played the Nasserist, the post-Nasserist, the islamist, the tribal neo-nomad and, ultimately, the ageing and isolated autocrat. During that time, he managed to land himself in conflicts with most of his neighbours, as well as with others in Africa and further afield.

Those next, anomalous neighbours to the east, Egypt and Israel, had exchanged handshakes and olive branches; otherwise, the Israeli mini-empire-within continued to destabilize the region. As talk of 'autonomy' in the territories it had occupied in 1967 was revealed as mere temporizing, their Palestinian inhabitants rose up against their tormentor from 1987 to 1993, and again from 2000 to 2005; in so doing they gave a new Arabic word to the English dictionary – *intifadah*, meaning in Arabic 'a shaking off'. The Israelis responded with excessive force, bullets against pebbles. But the pebbles themselves would turn into something more deadly. As the inmates of the giant concentration camp of Gaza grew more crowded and more angry, their newly elected islamist rulers, Hamas, began firing rockets across the border into Israel. The reaction from Gaza's gaolers was again one of overkill. In the 2014 campaign, for example, Palestinian to Israeli dead numbered more than 2,100, mostly civilians, to 73, of whom 7 were civilians. The Palestinian number has been debated. But even in figures from Israeli sources, the disproportion is clear enough: over all, between 2000 and the middle of 2018, 9,456 Palestinians have been killed by Israeli security forces, compared with 1,237 Israelis killed by Palestinians – almost 8:1.

In the 'autonomous' West Bank, meanwhile, Israeli policy would make nineteenth-century European colonialism and twentieth-century apartheid seem liberal by comparison. For example, an Israeli property law causes any land which is not actually lived on by its owner to revert to the 'original' possessors – that is, the Israeli state. Since the State of Israel dates back only to 1948, the use of 'original' seems strange; it is, of course, an allusion to the Jewish presence in Palestine in ancient times, and to the modern Zionist-colonial interpretation of ancient references to a sacred 'Promised Land'. The equivalent thinking applied to England would result in absentee land-owners forfeiting their property to a foreign-based sect of revivalist Druids, on the grounds that the land was sacred to them before Julius Caesar's invasion. As a tunnel vision of history, a denial of time, the State of Israel's viewpoint is even more astonishing than anything the so-called Islamic State has come up with.

TRIBES TRIUMPHANT

During these increasingly disturbed decades, an island of relative calm was the 'Island' of the Arabs, the Arabian Peninsula. There too, however, border wars flared on and off through the 1970s between the two parts of a divided Yemen, while a major insurgency in Oman's south-western Dhofar province threatened the new unity of the sultanate. These conflicts were not minor, yet they were peripheral. But the occupation in November 1979 of the Meccan Haram – the great pilgrimage complex centring on the Ka'bah – by militant islamists, and a bloody siege to eject them, brought the dangerous energy of a newly re-politicized Islam to its navel.

Islam and politics were converging again; at the same time, even the most secular-seeming politics could not rid itself of religious associations. The heady scientific socialism that developed in the 1970s in the People's Democratic Republic of Yemen (PDRY), the southern part of the divided land, now has an air of unreality: the nationalization of bicycles was mooted; acrobatics and ballet were taught; women joined the army. But there were threads of connection to the past. Traditional Muslim clerics were persecuted, but several of the main proponents of scientific socialism were from Hashimi families belonging to the old religio-political elite, while the

> Chief Politburo exegete was Abd al-Fattah Isma'il, an expert on Socialist doctrine who was known, wrily, as *al-Faqih* (literally, the scholar of holy writ). Under his guidance, the early caliphs of Islam were classified according to their rightist or leftist tendencies.

But if Yemen was a land divided, so was the Party in the PDRY. Pulled every which way by its own leftist, rightist, traditionalist and reformist wings, 'splittism' became rife and internal conflict ever more aggressive, leading to a crescendo of violence in 1986 in which thousands were killed.

As with much 'religious' sectarian conflict, struggles between the various doctrinal sects of Socialism were a metaphor for old tribal differences that were bubbling up afresh. Pan-Arab unity had failed, and now – whatever the lines on the map proclaimed – many of the lesser unities, the territorial nation-states, were also beginning to fall apart, almost as soon as they had been cobbled together. It had often been relatively easy for colonial powers to sketch in borders, even to disarm tribal warriors; but it had been much harder to implant the institutions that nation-states need to survive. Writing of Aden, British government minister Richard Crossman admitted to his diary in 1967 that 'Chaos will rule after we've gone, and there'll be one major commitment out – thank God'. The 'chaos' was not confined to Aden. It ruled much of the Arabic world, in the form of a lot of people vying for power and influence and, unconstrained by strong institutions, doing so with the millennially tried and tested vehicles of kinship and tribe, raid and feud; in other words, creating new wheels of fire. Poets, still often the only speakers of truth nearly 1,500 years on from Imru' al-Qays and al-Shanfara, told it like it was. In 1980 Nizar Qabbani summed up the scene:

> From the Gulf to the Atlantic, tribes
> Running rampant, devoid of thought and culture . . .

Qabbani's tirade thundered on, a long and bitter attack on Arab pretensions to unity and civilization – recited not to some coterie of intellectuals, but to the Arab League at its thirty-fifth birthday party. Only a poet could have got away with it.

Sometimes the perimeter of a wheel of fire did coincide with the lines on the map. This was true in some of the Gulf statelets, small and rich enough to maintain their integrity. It was also true at the far end of the Arabic world in Morocco, where a critical mass of shared history – a 300-year Hashimi dynasty, and the recent shared struggle against the French – had brought rulers and ruled together. But, just as often, state boundaries were wildly at variance with the demographies of loyalty. This was the case, for example, in Iraq and Syria, where numerical majorities – of Kurds and Shi'is in the one, of Sunnis in the other – were only kept in check by the arms and the terror of the ruling cliques. Whether states were successful or not, however, what was clear was that 'tribes', sometimes overt, sometimes disguised as sects that were religious, political, or both together, were still part of the narrative. The old debate between *hadar* and *badw*, peoples and tribes, was continuing with new vigour.

Most often, the *hadar–badw* debate has continued as a dispute between weak institutions and strong men, the latter ruling through a web of bloodlines, business deals and military loyalty. From 1980 or so, the strong men were winning the debate, and getting ever stronger. This was true even in Egypt, a land that had previously attained high levels of statehood, and had enjoyed more stable institutions than anywhere else in the Arabic world. Under President Husni Mubarak, the fact that the ruler was a military man with control of an expanding arsenal and economy, and – particularly – that he would rule for thirty years, had predictable consequences: institutions withered, and the warp and weft of patronage and corruption grew ever tighter.

Other than in an absolute hereditary monarchy, probably the most important act of the leader of a well-run state is to leave his or her job quietly, and to leave the country in good order. In poorly-run states, it is more likely that leaders will have to be thrown out or otherwise disposed of, if they do not conveniently die in office; this was the case with post-colonial Arab states for several decades. But over time, with security apparatuses growing more technologically advanced and effective, this healthy turnover-by-coup decreased. By the turn of the AD millennium, nearly all of the Arabic world found itself controlled by either absolute monarchies or long-lived dictatorships, and in all of them what mattered to the ruled was not so much one's relationship as a citizen with an impersonal state as one's connection to the network of a personal leader. Whether these connections were overtly tribal or not differed from country to country; but even where they were not, ties of blood and other forms of loyalty – *wala'* – were mattering more and more again, just as they had mattered for ancient tribes with their supposed blood-links and affiliated *mawla*s, those joined by *wala'*. States were becoming little more than *wala'*-webs, centring on hungry and insatiable spiders.

DEMONARCHIES

Of the Arab states that are not overt hereditary monarchies, all but one include the term *jumhuriyyah*, 'republic', in their official names. Nominally, then, rule is by the *jumhur*, 'the mass of people'. (The exception has been Libya, which until the fall of Mu'ammar al-Qadhdhafi was a *jamahiriyyah*, from the plural, 'masses' – maybe a case of *horror vacui* in a big country with a small population. Now it seems to be simply 'the State of Libya'.) A wry but more honest term, however, has been coined recently, and applies to many of these *faux* republics: *jumlakiyyah*, an amalgamation of *jumhuriyyah* and *malikiyyah*, 'monarchy' – perhaps in English 'rexpublic', or even, to retain the alleged democratic element, 'demonarchy'. An example is my adoptive country. If I now focus on it for two or three pages, it is because I am an eye-witness of its recent history, and in any case it lies, like the troubled lands of the northern Fertile Crescent, on a major fault line between peoples and tribes. It is a case study in the surprising survival of those tribes.

Until 1990 Yemen was divided in two: the post-British, Soviet-backed People's Democratic Republic of Yemen (PDRY, South Yemen), and the richer, more populous and vaguely non-aligned Yemen Arab Republic (YAR, North Yemen). The British had left South Yemen in 'chaos'; but with the fall of the USSR a short generation later and the loss of its new backer, the country found itself even less viable than it had been, and united with the YAR in May 1990 to form the Republic of Yemen (RoY). The unification, or reunification, seemed right and proper: unlike the modern state of Iraq, say, *al-Yaman*, 'the South' of the Arabs' Island, feels like a natural whole, geographically, culturally, historically. It was home to the ancient South Arabian settled states and has been politically united on and off – admittedly much more off than on – at various times over the past couple of thousand years and more.

The equation of this latest reunification

(PDRY – USSR) + YAR = RoY

sums up a lot of Arab history. The combined pressure exerted by two superpowers in opposition was off, and Arab identity softened. With pan-Arabism removed from the sum as well, the resulting state became visibly, nominally, less Arab: the 'Arab' of the old Yemen Arab Republic was dropped. Were Arabs set to 'disappear' once more, lost in new nation-states? It seemed not: Egypt is still the Arab Republic of Egypt; Syria is still the Syrian Arab Republic; the Emirates are still the United Arab Emirates (although perhaps, like the Kingdom of Saudi Arabia, they should really be the United *Arabian* Emirates; the word is ambiguous in Arabic). School exercise books in Yemen still have a map of *al-Watan al-'Arabi*, 'the Arab Homeland', on one pair of endpapers. Equally, on the other pair of endpapers they have a world map that still shows Yugoslavia and the USSR. Perhaps it is just that no one has bothered to do away with the old names.

Soon after Yemen's unification, there was a short and oxymoronic 'War of Unity' in 1994, in which some of the old PDRY bosses led an attempt to secede. The union was preserved, but at a cost: the war set the seal on the dominance of the old YAR and its leader, Ali Abd Allah Salih. Then, as another element was added to the equation – time – the freedoms contracted. Salih at first exercised a tolerably benign dictatorship. But in the world of change and decay, of generation and corruption, dictators, however benign to begin with, have fairly short half-lives; as they age they tend to become progressively more unstable and less benign. A soldier from a tribal background, Salih had earlier been nicknamed *tays al-dubbat*, 'the billy-goat in the officers' mess': thick-skulled, head down, butting his way to the front. His caprine, capricious side found it less constricting to run things via personal, informal links with tribal leaders. 'The state,' he had said in 1986, 'is part of the tribes, and our Yemeni people is a collection of tribes.' This was, strictly, a contradiction in terms – or at least in ancient Arabian and Qur'anic terms, in which *sha'b*s and *qabilah*s, peoples and tribes, are two distinct creatures, sheep and goats. Or was it another attempt finally to reconcile the two?

It wasn't. Increasingly, after 1990, society was intentionally re-tribalized. This happened even in the former South, which had been nominally *de*-tribalized. There, the British and then the Socialists had tried to disarm the tribes, turning them into citizens without arms (and, in their own view, without 'honour'); but the tribesmen had never deigned to take up ploughshares, and after 1990 they re-armed themselves with a vengeance. Apologists saw no anachronism; on the contrary, wrote one, with an eloquently unfortunate choice of phrase, those who warn of the dangers of old-fashioned tribalism in the modern state 'might as well look for camel-trains at metro stations!' – and get knocked over by the other sort of train while looking . . . Tribes, too, like trains, are mechanized these days, and even more dangerous than they used to be.

Democracy withered – though not Salih's popularity, for as the press became less free again, the word became more gathered. Eventually even the 'Republic' was lost from the equation in all but name: the country became a *jumlakiyyah*, a demonarchy, with Salih grooming his son Ahmad to succeed. Posters of the two, in uniforms and mirrored aviator shades, began to proliferate and to swell in size; a later version included a third generation, Ahmad's small son, out of nappies and into fatigues. And the demonarchy took on an ever more 'tribal' aspect, with the president as paterfamilias: '*But he is my father!*' a friend of mine protested when I criticized the leader. At times, the relationship was more complicated: 'Ali [Abd Allah Salih], you are my brother, my son, my father!' one poster exclaimed. Society under such a leader is founded not on a constitution or laws or even shared faith but, like tribal society, on the multiply impossible fantasy of a blood-relationship. As for the 1,000 years of ancient South Arabian civil history in this same land – of *sha'b*s, peoples united not by claims of blood but by divine covenants – and the 1,400 years of Islamic history that followed and built on it across continents – it might all never have happened.

Salih, preferring swords to ploughshares, indulged in an orgy of arming himself, and put his nearest and dearest in charge of the arsenal. He, naturally, was commander-in-chief; his son Ahmad was in charge of the elite Republican Guard; his brother ran the air force; and so on. Arms, and loyal lieutenants to bear them, are the marks of honour of the tribesman, and Salih was becoming a super-tribesman. The civil state was entirely hollowed out. Even school uniforms were changed to military green. Across the turn of the millennium, similar processes were under way across the Arabic world. With the distracting rise of al-Qa'idah, foreign observers of the region spoke much of an international clash of civilizations; they overlooked the internal clash of cultures – peoples versus tribes, agriculture versus armiculture – in which tribes and arms were winning hands down.

Yemen is a poor country, but shocking amounts of its money were spent on weaponry. To the north, the Saudis were doing exactly the same (but, being immeasurably richer, on an immeasurably bigger scale). When in 2015 they destroyed just one of Salih's Scud missile silos, housed in a mountain 7 kilometres away, a seismic shock-wave made my house sway three times. They then destroyed another, nearer mountain arsenal, and we were showered with rockets – smaller ones minus, thank heaven, their warheads. It was apocalyptic, like the great earthquake at the end of time when 'the earth disgorges its burdens'.

It may be assumed that most if not all arms deals produced rich kickbacks. Corruption ruled, literally. It was not just that the system was corrupt: rather, corruption *was* the system. Seen from another angle, however, it is all a version of the old raiding economy updated for the age of the nation-state, in which the chief raids the state he rules, and retains his quarter or fifth of the booty. Seen from yet another, slightly different angle, the state income does not belong to the people; it belongs to the dominant tribe or loyalty-group, and effectively to its patriarch, who happens to have the misleading title of 'president'. All this became apparent when, early in 2015, the UN publicly alleged that, over his third of a century ruling the YAR and the RoY, the billy-goat had acquired something between $30 *billion* and $62 *billion* from oil and gas contracts and from corruption in general. He laughed this off: as if he had that sort of money in the bank! Of course, he hadn't. A lot of it had been ploughed back (at last, a ploughshare) into the economy to buy support; a lot went to buy yet more weapons. (Naturally, the neighbouring oil monarchies do exactly the same, but they don't pretend to be 'republics' so they can do it blatantly. They can also generally afford to do it without beggaring most of their subjects.) In Yemen, few seemed to be aware of the allegations of theft. Of those who were, few believed them in principle – they came from untrustworthy foreigners. Even fewer seemed particularly bothered; an Arab ruler enriching himself is not news. The poor, who are most noticeably deprived of their share, have no voice with which to complain.

Looked at with bleak detachment, a plundering-redistributing demonarchy is doing something similar to a tax-collecting state. The main difference is that, in the first case, there are no checks and balances; only cheque-books and bank-balances, held ultimately by one man. But, if nothing else, the system has the imprimatur of long usage. As the scribe of the Almoravid leader Yusuf ibn Tashfin advised his master before he set out to annex Spain in the late eleventh century,

Man jāda sād, / wa-man sāda qād, / wa-man qāda malak al-bilād.

An open hand gives you the upper hand; / an upper hand leads the band; / lead the band, and you'll rule the land.

TO RUIN OR TO RULE

Similar narratives played out across the Arab world in other countries where a mask of republicanism was in place. In the big lands of the northern Fertile Crescent, Iraq and Syria, and in its western extension, Egypt, other presidential sons were groomed to succeed their fathers. They were emboldened by the US presidential election victory in 2000 of George W. Bush, son of President George Bush: if Americans did it, why shouldn't Arabs? It was a fair point. Whatever he meant to do for liberal democracy by invading Iraq, George Bush II had already undone it by simply being who he was, the son of his father, Būsh ibn Būsh ('Nonsense son of Nonsense' in some Arabic dialects, from a Turkish word that also gives English 'bosh').

By a very glazed or indulgent eye, the pseudo-republics may be seen as a 'dynamic political order . . . an alternative notion of democracy' created by the 'stalemate . . . [between] liberalism, republicanism and Islamism'. But, shorn as they are of a free press, an impartial judiciary, and any popular understanding of what *dimuqratiyah* really means, they are the wispiest phantoms of alternative notions of democracy. It would be more accurate to look on *dimuqratiyah* as an alternative name for what has been going on in the Arabic world since time out of mind. It is 'gathering the word' in a new guise, but in the same old sense: in Arabic, 'voices' and 'votes' are the same word, *aswat*, and the massive election majorities claimed for leaders, with percentage shares in the 90s, are the evidence for the continued search for unanimity. For example, in the 2014 election that gave the first *imprimatur* to Egypt's current president, al-Sisi, a year after he seized power, the coup leader gained 97 per cent of the vote; those who had voted freely and fairly for his overthrown predecessor, al-Mursi, remained necessarily silent, for they had no one to vote for. *Dimuqratiyah* is thus closer to monarchy in instalments – like that of Napoleon (elected emperor with a 99 per cent majority) and of the Roman emperors (Augustus, for example, was unanimously voted monarchical privileges for periods of five or ten years). It is a whole semantic world away from *demo-kratia*, 'people-power', in its most ancient sense, and from democracy in its usual modern sense. The notional 'peoples' have the power to 'elect' their leaders; they do not yet have the power – or perhaps the vision – *not* to elect them.

It would be more honest to ditch the alien word *dimuqratiyah* and revert to the old Arabic term, *mubaya'ah*, usually translated as 'giving allegiance'. The word is from a root that means 'to sell or buy, to do a deal', and the particular derivative suggests that the deal is reciprocal, a social contract: you sell your political freedom, and in return you are paid with justice and with as safe and prosperous an existence as circumstances allow. In practice, however, *mubaya'ah* comes to mean 'selling out'. As the lexicon puts it,

> *Baya' al-amir*: He promised, or swore, allegiance to the prince; making a covenant with him to submit to him the judgement of his own case and . . . not to dispute with him in respect of anything thereof, but to obey him in whatever command he might impose upon him, pleasing and displeasing.

Inevitably, as power corrupts over time, the displeasing preponderates. The prince gets more princely and more puissant and does not keep to his side of the bargain; he takes freedom, but does not dispense justice. He ignores his people, but he also begins to ignore his advisers, and to engage in rash acts to remove his opponents. He reverts to his autocratic, usually military self, and rules by command and cunning, not by consensus and planning. His sycophants multiply and praise his 'wisdom' – and as Bacon said, 'Nothing doth more hurt in a state than that cunning men pass for wise'. With rule ever more autocratic and arbitrary, such institutions as there might have been wither too; not least the law. The leader becomes a sort of lid on lawlessness and can say – as did Ali Abd Allah Salih – with increasing truth but zero honesty, 'Without me, the country will become a second Somalia'.

That statement sounds like a warning, but it is actually a threat. Such leaders are perfectly aware of the dangers they more or less contain. They need the fears – of sectarian extremism, of tribal raiders, the collapse of society, the coming deluge – to maintain their own control. They are not chairmen running an ordered system, but ringmasters of mayhem or, to coin a word, anarcharchs. Their philosophy might be that of Milton's fallen Satan,

> better to reign in hell than serve in heaven;

their policy is that of Dryden's Achitophel, 'born a shapeless lump, like anarchy',

> In friendship false, implacable in hate:
> Resolved to ruin or to rule the state.

A HISTORY OF ASHES

By the new AD millennium, the Arab age of hope seemed a distant memory. Extreme militant islamists were becoming ever more audacious, striking in

2001 at the secular navel of the world, the World Trade Center in New York and its twin stretch-Ka'bahs of capital. At home, oil monarchs and anarcharchs tightened their grip, and began increasingly to resemble both each other and Sindbad's Old Man of the Sea, the persuasive parasite who wheedles his way on to an unsuspecting wanderer's back, then wraps his legs around the victim's throat and uses him as a riding-beast and a cherry-picker to pluck the choicest fruit. And there were those new generations being groomed to inherit, Young Men of the Sea. The American experiment of 2003 in Iraq – 'regime change' – removed one Old Man from his subjects' backs; but it also lifted the lid on the underlying anarchy. Across the Arabic world, the sages of the suqs shook their heads and said, as ever, 'Iraq needs a Saddam, a Hajjaj ibn Yusuf. It needs the stick.' The grip, the lid, the stick have all been there so long that they seem normal, and necessary. They seem to be what holds things together.

Arabs were – are – in an age of disappointment, 'a history of ashes,' as the poet and political commentator Adonis called it. Because belief in a before-life is as comforting as belief in an afterlife, they looked back to supposed golden ages. Some, as we have seen, found perfection in early seventh-century Medina, splendid to aspire to but impossible to return to. Others found it in al-Hajjaj ibn Yusuf's bloody late seventh-century Iraqi police state, all too easy to recreate with modern surveillance and weaponry. That other golden age, the early Abbasid period of cultural and intellectual synthesis celebrated by Arabs of the nineteenth- and twentieth-century Awakening, seemed to have receded with the end of the pan-Arab dream. Its afterglow – the glory that was – only mocked the tarnished present. Even nostalgia wasn't what it used to be.

The escape-route of education was blocked by obstacles too. Across the Arabic world, more young people were getting higher qualifications; society, however, had not yet grown to accommodate their new skills and aspirations. In a system composed of impenetrable layers of patronage, for most new graduates the ceilings were not of glass, but of granite. In December 2010, for example, I hitched a ride on a motorcycle taxi – and found myself discussing, in fluent English, the metaphysics of Eliot's *Waste Land* with the driver. He was the top graduate of his year, but had found no other job than this. I wished him better luck. He shrugged. 'Here in Yemen I feel I'm in prison.'

That young man and the millions like him would soon be as important to the Arab history of our times as the demonarchs and dictators. For it was just then that people like my metaphysical biker began to look the other way, out of prison, out of the past, to a golden age in the future. Why, after all, should one be at the mercy of the toss of a coin in which heads are autocrats and tails islamocrats, with only the free fall of anarchy to decide between the two? One submits, of course, because the autocrats and islamocrats hold all the weapons, a fearsome arsenal of gunfire and hellfire. But, as the earliest Arab poets and orators knew, and as the Qur'an proved most eloquently of all, words can be weapons too.

THE SPRING THAT HAD NO SUMMER

More than forty years ago, the Moroccan writer Abdallah Laroui was already calling this age of disappointment 'the long winter of the Arabs'. It felt long then, but it had only just begun. The events of the new millennium – the al-Qa'idah attacks on the United States, the Americans' 'war on terror', their destabilization of Iraq – would plunge the winter into its dark solstice. Seasons, however, eventually turn, and at the end of 2010 it looked at last as though the time had come.

As if in some rite of spring, a sacrifice was needed. The story has often been told of Muhammad Bu Azizi, the young Tunisian street-vendor persecuted by the police, who set himself on fire in protest and died in January 2011. Anger at his death spread across the country, then through much of the Arabic world. It was a mass uprising against the tyranny, corruption and arbitrary rule of authoritarian regimes, and it spread spontaneously. But the spontaneity was given form and direction by those two perennial tools of revolution – language and technology. Old-style slogans combined with brand-new social media to drive what soon became known, prematurely as it turned out, as the Arab Spring. ('*Since to look at things in bloom / Fifty springs are little room . . .*')

Of course, the potential for protest had always been there, lying dormant but shooting up from time to time and place to place; spring had been a seasonal, regional occurrence. What was different about this one was its geographical reach, from Morocco to Oman, and its sudden simultaneity. Both were due to new technologies, and especially satellite television and the internet. Despite the new speed and scope of the revolution, however, there were constants in play. One of them was the central position, between Maghrib and Mashriq, of Egypt. It had always been a fertile land for protest.

Going backwards in time, there had been violent bread riots in Egypt in 1977. In 1968, following the defeat in the war with Israel, 'a generation that had been systematically lied to', as Fouad Ajami called them, demonstrated against what they saw as the hypocrisy of Nasser's regime. Further back, during the uprising of Ahmad Urabi in 1881–2, anti-regime soldiers defending the people against the ruler occupied Abdin Square, the central urban space of its day. Further back again, groups belonging to an underclass called (by the chroniclers) *zu''ar*, 'hooligans', staged periodic uprisings against the Ottoman and Mamluk authorities; in early Mamluk times, their predecessors the *harafish*, or 'rascals', had demonstrated openly and vociferously against the periodic excesses of the long-reigning sultan, al-Nasir. The difference in 2011, of course, was the speed with which the spores of discontent born in Tunisia and bred in the Egyptian hotbed would spread abroad: television viewers and internet users across the Arabic world could follow those seminal protests as they developed. Most, as ever, would remain unmoved, inert. A few, however, would be inspired; enough for the movement to spread.

The use of new technologies to communicate protest is also a constant. If it was Facebook pages that mobilized protesters in Cairo in 2011, it was the political pages of the new Cairo newspapers that had activated their ancestors in the Urabi uprising. (And there is that great prototype – the use of the new writing to spread the original Islamic revolution of the seventh century.) But the technologies of 2011 were remarkable for a reach that was both geographical and social. One of the major motive factors in the Arab Spring was 'the meeting of minds' – and of hairstyles: in Cairo's Tahrir Square, an islamist protester could admit to his new leftist comrade-in-protest, 'the secular and shaggy-haired Adam',

> 'I would never have imagined I would be talking to someone with hair as long as yours.' To which Adam responded, 'Nor did I ever imagine befriending someone with a beard as long as yours.'

Lefties and fundies were coming together. So too were words and freedom. The new information technologies were uncontrollable, uncensorable, and so were the crowds. 'We are all here together,' the Egyptian writer Ahdaf Soueif noted in Tahrir Square, 'all doing what we've not been able to do for decades: each and every one is speaking, acting, expressing themselves'. A lot of that self-expression articulated alternative truths to those of the traditional rulers. In contrast, 'This [Egyptian] regime lies as naturally as it breathes'. All regimes did. Everywhere, regime media put out the tired old lie that the protesters were 'foreign agents'. At times, misinformation was more precise. When more than fifty protesters were shot dead by rooftop snipers in the Yemeni capital San'a on 18 March 2011, a day the protest movement had dubbed 'the Friday of Dignity', Salih's regime put it about that the marksmen were local householders annoyed at the disturbance to their lives.

As in all the best revolutions from Islam on, slogans were vital. The feisty Cairenes, with centuries of protest behind them, were adepts in the art of the political haiku. A typical chanted demand was for

'Aysh!
Hurriyyah!
Karamah insaniyyah!

Daily bread!
Liberty!
And our human dignity!

Again, the call for dignity. Perhaps, though, it lacks the strange piquancy of the pro-Ottoman chant in the time of Napoleon's occupation of Cairo:

God save the Sultan!
God ruin Fart al-Rumman!

Fart al-Rumman, 'Surfeit of Pomegranates' (or maybe 'of Breasts', for which they are the poetic metaphor), being a nonsensical distortion of 'Bartalamin', the name of a prominent local Christian in the French service. As for the 'rascals' of the fourteenth century, their brazen slogan – chanted beneath the walls of the Cairo Citadel by thousands – had been a demand to the sultan, chronically lame in one foot, to release their patron: 'Luckless Limper, let him go!' The man was set free; when he was later re-arrested, protests by the massed orphans of Cairo secured his release.

To return to 2011, the slogan raised in every country touched by the Arab Spring was the simple but rhythmic:

Al-sha'b
Yurid
Isqat al-nizam.

The people
Demand
The fall of the regime.

At first sight it is the same sort of demand that has felled dictators in Latin America and toppled thrones in Europe. But to a historian of their region if not to themselves, *al-sha'b*, 'the people', is a word with other resonances, faint but clear: from those ancient South Arabian inscriptions in which the *sha'b* is the settled, plural, non-tribal society; from the Shu'ubiyyah, the pluralist 'peoples' movements' of the eighth century on, in which the diverse peoples of the Arab empire sought equality with their imperial ruling elite. It is thus a slogan freighted with past meaning. But it is also fraught with present danger. That last word, *nizam*, is a calque on the French *régime*, and in Arabic it is 'bipolar': in its imported sense it means '(bad) regime, rule'; but in its traditional sense it means '(good) order, law-and-order'. Come the counter-revolution, it would not be hard for traditional, reactionary rulers to spread the word that the youth of the Spring had actually been calling for anarchy . . . The protesters may not have been 'foreign agents'; but was the language they were using in itself foreign, a sort of semantic fifth column? Then again, if protesters import meaning, dictators distort it: their 'good' *nizam* is often a facade fronting anarchy; disorder is the order of their day.

Semantics apart, the mere act of speech was liberating. And the voices raised were not just those of angry young men. An older woman at the Tahrir Square protest in Cairo saw Ahdaf Soueif taking notes, and said to her,

> Write, write that my son is in there with the *shabab* [the young men]. That we're fed up with what's been done to our country. Write that this regime divides Muslim from Christian and rich from poor. That it's become a country for the corrupt. That it's brought hunger to our door.

'Everybody,' Soueif realized, 'everybody here has become an orator. We have found our voice.'

This was the word ungathered. The monopoly on speech of the dictator – in that most basic meaning, 'he who speaks constantly' – was broken. Individuals were expressing themselves in the open again, like those earliest audible Arab voices in graffiti carved on desert stones; like the *su'luk*s, those early poets-errant and freelancers of the truth; like al-Hallaj, protomartyr of free speech. Everybody was an orator, and everywhere in the populous demonarchies people were calling – not in the obedient unison that dictators love, but in their own ragged polyphony – for a civil state in which all would be equal under the law, a civilian state not ruled by army men barking orders. Their word for 'civil/civilian' was *madani*, from *madinah*, 'city'. They might equally have used another word with more ancient resonances, *hadari*: for the Arab Spring was a new variation of a very old theme – the debate between *hadar* and *badw*, between those who wanted to build society and those who wanted to raid it; between peoples and tribes.

Hope sprang everywhere. As late as May 2013 one Panglossian optimist, an Egyptian poet, was seen on television predicting a united Arab world 'by 2017'. ('How I admired him!' said the viewer, Raja Shehadeh, Candide to Pangloss.) But much of the hope was guarded, and the majority – the actual Man in the Suq – remained, as ever, silent and static, looking on but not taking part, often not even taking in what the protests were really about.

In the end, what the Arab Spring proved to be about was superficial change. Adonis, who knew as a poet that Arabs were

> stalled between seasons,

diagnosed in prose the nature of the Arab impasse as long ago as 1980, the start of the present long winter:

> The current Arab regimes, however many they may be, are in fact one regime . . . a regime founded essentially on repression. This regime must be utterly rejected and fought at every level. But fighting the regime and defeating it does not in itself necessarily guarantee the advent of democratic rule. That is because social and economic infrastructure is itself repressive . . . and needs to be deconstructed from the foundations . . . The political level of revolution is the shallowest level . . . Attaining power should come as the crowning act of a vast process of dismantlement. Without this process, gaining power changes nothing.

As the original revolutionaries of Islam knew, 'Allah will change nothing for a people unless they change what is in themselves'.

Today, those individual voices that were raised have been silenced again. Another spring has had no summer; like so many revolutions, Muhammad's included, it was begun by those who were hungry for justice, but was hijacked by those who were hungry for power. In several cases, notably that of Egypt, it was a double hijacking: first by the self-styled proponents of the *ancienne révolution*, the islamists – for the straggly beards soon ousted the shaggy heads – and then by the *anciens régimes* themselves, the insatiable tyrannosaurs.

It might be said that Arab history is a series of stolen revolutions.

THE TYRANNOSAURS FIGHT BACK

In Egypt, a year after the Muslim Brotherhood gained power in national elections, the old rulers, the army men, staged a coup. All opposition, islamist or independent, was silenced; many were imprisoned, and hundreds were condemned to death. In Syria, Bashshar al-Asad, the second-generation demonarch, began mercilessly to exterminate opponents, and ignited a civil war that has killed around half a million. In Bahrain, a rising by the Shi'i population, the majority, had already been swiftly crushed with the help of Saudi tanks. Fainter rustlings of Spring in other overt monarchies had been stamped out or hushed up. Tunis, where the Spring began, has been its only success story, perhaps; we shall return to it later.

There was another initial 'success story', in Yemen. It soon turned into a failure of fabulous proportions, the causes of which are rooted in several very ancient pasts; I have watched the failure happening and, like everyone else in the country, suffered from it. At first, Ali Abd Allah Salih, the now long-toothed billy-goat and long-term demonarch, stepped down in a deal in which he was replaced by his vice-president. Unlike the ex-dictator of Tunisia, however, he did not head into platinum-plated exile. He stayed at home under a guarantee of immunity from prosecution, and – always cunning, never wise – plotted revenge: he wanted, as the Arabic phrase has it, 'to wash his liver'. His co-conspirators were a militant neo-imamist movement influenced by Iranian Shi'ism, who call themselves 'the Helpers of Allah'. They are more commonly known as the Huthis after the surname of several of their main leaders, all related and belonging, like most of the group's upper echelons, to the Hashimi clan of Quraysh, and in particular to the line that descends from Muhammad via his daughter and her husband, his cousin Ali ibn Abi Talib. Over the previous decade, Salih had squandered Yemeni lives and resources by fighting no fewer than six wars against these very same Huthis; after losing power, he performed a sudden about-turn – goats, even old ones, are agile – and joined forces with them to unseat the post-Spring consensus government by force of arms. He would have agreed with Lord Beaverbrook's maxim: 'What I want is power. Kiss 'em one day and kick 'em the next.' Now Yemen is divided once more. It is at war, both with itself and – in the case of the Huthis – with all its peninsular neighbours (except Oman, which has remained neutral) and with an even wider Arab coalition. The result of all this is that the economy is ruined, poverty and disease are rampant, the innocent die in droves, alternative truths are not permitted and to engage in debate is to promote *fitnah*, 'heresy', diversity and unity are dead. ('Screw unity!' exclaimed an old friend of mine, now a Huthi sympathizer. It may not be the official line; it came from the heart.)

In all these events, there are three repercussions from a long Arab past. When army units still loyal to the deposed Salih allowed the Huthis' tribal warriors – some, knee-high to a Kalashnikov, as young as ten or eleven years old – to take over the capital and much of the country, some older townspeople had a sense of *déjà vu*: in 1948, the ruling imam invited in tribesmen to sack the capital in punishment for the assassination there of his father. But the playing of the tribal trump is much older still. As long ago as the decline of pre-Islamic Saba, failed rulers had wielded marauding tribesmen in their vendettas against those who had ousted them. In the event, Salih was to be the victim of his own plot, as many of the tribesmen had no inherent loyalty to him; loyalty is a commodity that goes to the highest bidder, and in this case the Huthis outbid him. And here is a second repercussion from a distant past: in the person of the Huthis, the Hashimi branch of the Meccan tribe of Quraysh is still proving its resilience 1,400 years after its first revolution. Salih had set himself up as the super-tribesman; but the Qurashis, including their Umayyad and Abbasid lines, have proved themselves time and again to be the super-*tribe*. The third ancient theme is reprised in the vehemence of the Arab coalition's reaction to the Huthis, for Yemen's peninsular neighbours view the Iranian-inspired movement as agents of a millennial struggle by Persia to dominate the Arabian subcontinent. Nor is this third theme much varied: nearly 1,400 years after their ancestors began to adopt Islam, the cruder sort of Gulf propaganda still calls the Huthis' Iranian backers '*Majus*' – 'Magians', or Zoroastrians, as if they still adhered to the state religion of the ancient Persian shahs . . . One does not have to be a novelist to see history, as did Lawrence Durrell, as 'that vast complex of analogies'.

The reunification of Yemen, less than twenty-four years before these calamitous events, had been an event to be celebrated in the long Arab winter. But if the country has now torn itself apart again, then it is only following a fashion. Nearly everywhere in the Arabic world, disunity rules. There is an unspoken disunity in Egypt, where the opposition is judicially gagged or with its neck in the noose. Elsewhere there is open disunity: in Libya, split like Yemen into areas controlled by legitimate government, militia, and armed gangs who do not even merit the latter term; in Lebanon, with its Hizb Allah state-within-a-state; in Palestine, where the Israeli dagger divides a Hamas-run Gaza from a Fatah-run West Bank, often themselves at daggers drawn; in Syria, which makes Pandora's Box seem a mere can of worms, and where not only the current superpower, the United States, but *three* ex-superpowers – Turkey, Persia and Russia – are all stirring like mad; in the hornets' nest of Iraq, poked into venomous life by that first superpower. Sudan has split, though more understandably, into Arab and non-Arab parts. Things could be worse in Algeria; but probably only because they were so bad in the 1990s, with the civil war dead reaching six figures, that Algerians lost the will to kill each other. Only the absolute monarchies seem to work at all, a system most of the rest of the world has abandoned. So perhaps the soothsayers of the suqs are right: Arabs *are* different – they need to be ruled by al-Hajjaj, by Saddam, with the stick, and talk of freedom and truth and Spring is so much Western eyewash. And if the stick is hereditary, a sceptre – well, it saves a lot of bloodshed when it passes on.

But there is, so far, an exception: Tunisia, the only country where the Arab Spring has had a reasonably successful outcome. The country is not without problems, including sporadic acts of islamist terrorism; but as yet there seems to be an underlying stability. Why there and not elsewhere? Partly, perhaps, because it had the first Spring revolution, and the old dictator cut his losses and ran before he could be edified by the example of his fellow-tyrannosaurs fighting back. Partly because of enlightened leadership: Munsif al-Marzuqi had been admired as an Arab confrère of Sakharov and Solzhenitsyn more than twenty years before he became Tunisia's first post-Spring president. Probably also, to be honest, because of the preponderance in Tunisia of *hadarah* over *badawah*, settled civilization over tribal nomadism, since ancient times. The Phoenicians made the Tunisian coastland a settled hub of trade in the first millennium BC. It was the wealthy Roman province of 'Africa', exporting grain and olive oil to Italy. With the Arab takeover and the founding of the garrison and trading city of al-Qayrawan, it became the administrative centre of the Maghrib. It survived the eleventh-century migrations and depradations of Banu Hilal and other Arab tribes better than elsewhere. French colonialism treated it more lightly than the rest of the region – the *mission civilisatrice* had already been accomplished, in ancient times – and the divorce from France was far less violent than in neighbouring Algeria. On independence, it had a progressive leader in Habib Bourguiba, who spent a quarter of the national budget on education, encouraged the emancipation of women and even tried, unsuccessfully, to bring in laws to stop the working population fasting in Ramadan. It lacks the sprawling and underdeveloped tribal hinterlands that form the mass of most Arab countries. And, finally, unlike most Arab countries today it is, and always has been, geographically and culturally outward-looking: it wears its heart on its coast.

So maybe the exception, Tunisia, is a riposte to those suq soothsayers and casbah Cassandras. For a start, their premiss – that 'the Arabs' are different from everyone else – is wrong. Arabs are too diverse, too different from each other, too deeply mingled too long ago with the peoples of a vast and various empire, to be lumped together or even to be a 'the'. What *has* been different is their historical environment, and particularly that formative setting of the Arabian subcontinent. It gave rise to the yin and yang of *hadar* and *badw*, conjoined twins constantly arguing but necessarily coexisting, in which settled civilization has never achieved the decisive victory it has won across most of the world. The present wars are hardest fought at the perennial points of greatest contact and conflict between the two types of society: here in Yemen, in our smaller, southern Fertile Crescent, and in the greater crescent in the north, the lands of Syria and Iraq. The conflict has been less bitter where settled civilization and openness have predominated over time.

Of course, the bigger, fuller picture is never as stark as 'nomad' versus 'settled', tribes versus peoples. It never has been. But the dichotomy does seem to lie at the heart of history, and to influence a present in which a derived form of *badawah* is dominant. Its derivation is not obvious, for latter-day '*badw*' do not generally ride camels or live in hair tents. If, for example, Hafiz al-Asad resembled a grocer, his son Bashshar looks like the eye-doctor he trained in London to become. And yet they and their fellow autocrats are no less raiders and herders than the raw desert dynasts of Ibn Khaldun's classic theory. Their power is taken and held by raiding; their people – their *ra'iyyah*, 'subjects', or in its first meaning, 'private flock' – are controlled by herding, a herding of minds.

2020/1441

The herding – with words, in the form of rhetoric and propaganda – has recently become even more effective. With advances in information technology, a ruler's folk, his flock, graze contentedly in a land of literal make-believe: they believe what he makes them believe. But how is this possible, in a world permeated with alternative sources of information? Even the most repressive Arab regimes have not banned satellite TV and the internet. Surely these technologies should, like those before them, usher in a new stage of Arab history. In particular, by revealing the freedoms enjoyed by the world's liberal democracies, they ought to inspire long-oppressed Arabdom to want the same. That, anyway, was the expectation of the Arab Spring.

In the first place, alternative truths have come up against a firewall of inertia. Within the firewall, another metaphor applies: many, perhaps most Arabs are subject to what might be called a Mass Stockholm Syndrome. It is a 'coping mechanism': if you are in the thrall of all-powerful men, rather than admitting that you yourself are weak and powerless and thus losing your self-respect, your 'honour', you begin instead to declare that your masters are good. Over time it becomes a rhetorical truth, however much the empirical evidence contradicts it. Much of Arab public life is lived in this way, in a willing suspension of reality. The suspension is also usually conscious: 'We know he's bad, but we still love him!' The notion of 'unfitness for public office' does not exist: however high people's moral standards are in private life, public life is *expected* to be amoral. The bemerded shoes are shed at the door; inside, all is purity. It is one of the great bipolarities of Arab existence.

Of course, most of humanity for most of history has had to put up with authority, however bad; it has been a simple matter of survival. However, the fact that Arabs still tend to do so is not only due to their repressive rulers or to their own coping mechanisms. It is also due to the form Islam often takes among them, in which religious belief and politics are so deliberately entangled. Just as there is, and always has been, 'political Islam', there is also '"islamic" politics' – from *islam* not in any spiritual, moral or doctrinal sense, but in its most basic meaning, of 'submission'. There is an illustration outside my window. Banners of loyalty to the Huthi leader bear the words,

> *Labbayka Ya Qa'id Al-Thawrah!*
> At Your Service, O Leader Of The Revolution!

That first word, *labbayka*, is far from being an everyday Arabic term; it is rare even in high Arabic. It is usually used only in two settings: by a *Thousand and One Nights* genie appearing from a magic lamp or ring to serve his summoner; and by a pilgrim approaching Mecca, addressing Allah. Both the genie and the pilgrim are in a state of submission and servitude.

Enthusiastic foreigners assume that Arabs want or ought to want 'freedom' from their tyrants. Quite a few do, but they are the ones who already talk the foreigners' talk. The vast inert mute apathetic majority collude and collaborate with the tyrannosaurs. They are accomplices: as Samuel Johnson put it, 'Cunning has effect from the credulity of others.' And the credulity works both ways: 'The Emperor's New Clothes' might have been written for an Arab audience today.

Arab free-thinkers – poets, in other words – have long observed the effects of the Mass Stockholm Syndrome. In the sixth century, Imru' al-Qays reviled his father's killers as the servile dupes of their leaders, 'slaves of the stick'. A later poet said, bitterly:

> If Time enthrones some lowly bum
> and ruler's robes his shoulders drape,
> Then to Time's power you must succumb,
> and bend and nod and bow and scrape.
> . . .
> If lions are gone, and apes are come –
> then dance to the time of the ape!

In the thirteenth century of Ibn Khallikan, who quotes the verse, the last line was proverbial. The proverb is long overdue for a revival.

Whether Arabs will ever break free of the baton and out of the rhythm, this hypnotizing dance to the music of time, is a question that has been asked regularly for nearly 200 years, ever since the start of the nineteenth-century Awakening. The break may not be inevitable; or it may need centuries of

Springs. 'Give me five hundred years,' the new Syrian leader Husni al-Za'im famously said in 1949, 'and I will make Syria as prosperous and enlightened as Switzerland.' He may be right. Perhaps one cannot hurry history. Perhaps different sorts of progress run by different clocks, and while in the present (AD 2020/AH 1441) most Arabs are in AD 2020 as far as their smartphones go, almost all might be in about *AD* 1441 in terms of comparative sociopolitical development: before, that is, Gutenberg, Reformations, Enlightenments, French and Russian Revolutions, World Wars, Springs (at least, successful ones). The comparison is not meant to be invidious. It is simply that different sorts of history flow at different rates in different environments – as they do within the Arabic world itself. (In Dubai I have been the guest of princes in the world's tallest skyscraper; on the Yemeni island of Socotra, I have feasted with cavemen on raw goats' kidneys, and the welcome there was princely too.) There can also be eddies, where the flow goes into reverse; that is what may have happened in the Arabic world over the last few decades. Looked at as a proportion of human history as a whole, that 600-odd-year gap is almost nothing; even as a proportion of political and intellectual history – if we place its beginning at the time people began to talk, between 100,000 and 50,000 years ago – it is a difference of around 1 per cent or less. At the same time, these last 600 years have been a kind of historical *accelerando*. For Europe, they were a political adolescence. The Arab Spring was part of the delayed and now re-postponed onset of that adolescence, the beginning of the loss of faith in 'paternalistic' rule (*'He is my father!'*); but only for some. For the rest, the former state continues, an increasingly disturbing innocence, like that of Peter Pan.

Of course, change doesn't have to take half a millennium. Many countries in Eastern Europe and South America have recently swapped dictatorships for tolerably workable democracies in the space of a few years; Spain did so almost overnight on the death of Franco. But it is in the interests of the tyrannosaurs that change does take a long time: it gives them a stay of extinction. They may sleep peacefully for the time being; or with just one eye open, for they have each other to fear more than their own peoples.

THE BONFIRE OF THE VERITIES

There is another answer to that question of how repressive regimes deal with multiple sources of information, another reason why the tyrannosaurs may sleep peacefully, and that is that they themselves have adapted extraordinarily well to the changing information environment. This adaptation is the most recent development in a history of Arabic information technology – and of political control – that began with the unified high Arabic language, and took off with Arabic script. The Arab Spring may have been a 'Facebook revolution', but it would soon be the victim of its own facilitating technology. In 2011, the relatively few Arabs who used social media were often the same sort of people who would espouse the freedoms that the Spring was meant to promote. Many more Arabs use social media today; but the dinosaurs are now on Facebook too, and on everything else, and are avid *mufasbikun*, 'Facebookers', and *mugharridun*, 'chirpers', that is, 'Twitterers'. They are the ones who have always known best how to gather the word; now they have the perfect tools with which to do it, and to insert that word instantly into as many minds as are connected to smartphones. 'Words,' said Nizar Qabbani,

> are shots of morphine,
> Dope for rulers drugging masses
> Ever since the seventh century.

Now the words are mass-mainlined even more directly to the brain. Such misinformation streams might be called 'lie-fi'. They speed their users ever deeper into the territory of Benedict Anderson's *Imagined Communities* and Martin Nowak's *Supercooperators*; of Wittgenstein's 'bewitchment of our intelligence by means of language'. The end product is a programmed proletariat, not the Great Unwashed but the Great Brainwashed.

Older methods of word-gathering, or dissension-silencing, still exist. The ruling house of Qatar, for example, who founded that state-of-the-art media outfit, Al Jazeera, can also resort to 'cutting the tongue' of a poet who piques them. When mildly critical verses by the Qatari poet Muhammad al-Ajami came to their attention, he was put on trial and given a fifteen-year gaol sentence. He was pardoned after serving three years, but his story shows how the ancient sorcery of poetry still scares the holders of more prosaic power. Eastwards along the Gulf in Dubai, meanwhile, there is an example of the poetry of power: around one of the famous artificial archipelagos in the shape of palm trees is an outer ring of man-made islets spelling out a verse by the ruler. As it says (or will do when it is finished),

> It takes a man of vision to write on water . . .

A thousand years after Sultan Qabus of Jurjan was suspended in a crystal coffin in his calligraphic tower-tomb, conspicuous constructions with grand inscriptions can still project the might of princes and the sinuous, sinewy magic of Arabic characters. Latin script writ large would simply never work: it would always smack of the HOLLYWOOD sign.

As for Arabic rhetoric in general, its power is undiminished, and its role even more important than ever, given the plethora of truths competing in the ether. No less than in the time of Tarifah, the legendary pre-Islamic seeress, telling the truth is like telling a joke: it's the *way* you tell it that matters. An old verse about the art of spin sums it all up:

> Call it 'sweet nectar of the honey-bee',
> or call it 'stinging insects' vomit':
> It's art that tells your hearers what to see,
> takes darkness and spins daylight from it.

Admittedly, the art does not have to be very high. I have heard recently on San'a radio:

> Presenter [*in a tone of quizzical donnish detachment*]: Contrary to what most people believe, the USA is not a Christian state. It is in fact a Jewish state.

A pandemic of proclamations, in metre-high letters and fine calligraphy, covers walls in public places. A recent one, during a massive cholera outbreak in Yemen in 2017, read:

> CHOLERA IS THE GIFT OF AMERICA.

Such 'facts' gain their own surreal currency by repetition, especially when no one is allowed to question them publicly. Gathering the word of the media is thus the key, then pumping out the vomit and the nectar as loudly and as often as possible – and if you have seized the radio and TV stations, and if you can afford a satellite channel or two and the technology to reach millions of smartphones, you can pump it out very loudly indeed. The consequences are terrifying. For example, the conflict in my adoptive land is a civil war in which the neighbours have become involved. It emerges, however, from interviews with captured anti-Coalition fighters, that many have been convinced that they are battling not fellow Arabs and Muslims but 'Americans and Israelis'. No wonder Arab unity has been so hard to achieve.

In the 1950s, Claude Lévi-Strauss could write about people's vulnerability to 'lies propagated in printed documents. No doubt, there can be no turning back now'. There certainly has been no turning back. The controllers of truth have forged on with the transistor radio and the television, the internet and the smartphone, proliferating their own verities and messaging them ever more directly and instantly into people's minds. Whether viewed from 2020 or from 1441, *Nineteen Eighty-Four* seems a long time ago.

A FLIGHT TO NOWHERE

One can resist, silently, and live in a sort of internal, unspeaking exile; or one can speak out, utter alternative truths, and suffer the consequences. Most people take an easier route: they both say and think nothing. It is better than losing one's mind, or one's life. Ignorance, feigned or real, may not be bliss, but at least it is survival.

There is, however, another escape route, the old physical one of *hijrah*. Just before the desprung Arab Spring, one of those who took the path, the Paris-based writer Khalil al-Nu'aymi, could recall the provincial ennui of his Syrian childhood and contrast it with his present mobility and creativity:

> Here I am, going far . . . and back on the furthest horizon I see the scenes of my earliest childhood . . . I see al-Tawilah with its red hill sitting proudly on the plain. Directly beneath it flows the Khabur River, its red water full of mud and weeds and the last stalks of the cotton that we had gathered in a few days before. The cotton would travel to Aleppo and its giant caravanserais, and on beyond, elsewhere – while we stayed where we were, prostrate, like unclaimed corpses.
>
> And now here I am, getting my revenge on all that uncreative inertia with this far travel of mine . . .
>
> Go! Go far! The past will rejoice in you, for it is that which has transported you to this place.

He is riding the same wave that carried his countrymen like Jubran Khalil Jubran to Europe and the Americas a century earlier.

Now, only a few years on, travel for many Syrians and others is not a flight of creativity, but a flight from doom. Their past is broken and lost; far from rejoicing, it weeps blood. Contemplating his own downfall, Mu'ammar al-Qadhdhafi threatened to swamp Europe with migrants. The threat turned out to be a prophecy, but on a scale even the Libyan anarcharch had not foreseen. From Syria alone more than five million have fled – nearly a third of the population. It almost seems as if Arab history is spiralling into a grim parody of its own beginnings: the ancient sporadic waves of exodus from the northern Fertile Crescent are now a relentless human flood; this time round, the sufferings of Isma'il, the Qur'anic child-migrant and legendary Arab progenitor, are relived by millions. Europe and America are closing their doors, for the new diaspora has sown fears, further cultivated by populist, anti-liberal politicians in France, in the Netherlands, in a Britain which is in its own flight from Europe, in the United States of the Trump era. Indirectly, then, the reaction to the Arab Spring by Arab demagogues and their obedient *demoi* has globalized itself: the dinosaurs have by no means had their day, and perhaps not just in the Arabic world. Nothing is safe: not Western liberal democracy; not the life of a single Syrian or Yemeni child.

For those of us left in the Arabic world, and especially in those eventful regions, the Fertile Crescents both northern and southern, the Age of Disappointment now verges on an Age of Despair. The oldest places seem the most hotly contested, ancient centres of civilization on the margins of tribal territory: in Yemen San'a and Ta'izz, in Iraq Mosul, in Syria al-Raqqah and Aleppo. In that last city, for example, fought over by everyone from the Akkadians on, many of the giant caravanserais to which al-Nu'aymi's childhood cotton travelled are now battered beyond recognition. Its citadel, al-Shahba', 'the Iron-Grey', where the poet al-Mutanabbi was loaded with gold by his tenth-century Hamdanid patrons, and which later withstood a siege by Hulagu's Mongols,

> Lo! on her grim and massy rock
> That laughs to scorn the foeman's shock,

has been left gap-grinned by twenty-first-century artillery. And the sort of destruction inflicted on the Hamah mosque by the father, Hafiz al-Asad, the Grocer, has been visited on its Aleppan counterpart in the time of the son, Bashshar the Eye-doctor (though by which of the several sides is disputed).

On my antiquarian Syrian jaunt twenty years ago, the deep melancholy that had shadowed me from Hamah was dispelled by that second mosque, a place rife with light and time. Before the Umayyads built on it, the site had been the garden of the Byzantine cathedral; before that, the Hellenistic agora. I had come looking for fourteenth-century features seen by the traveller Ibn Battutah, in what he called 'one of the most splendid buildings of its kind'. In particular I wanted to see its 'pavement of vast extent, and its pulpit of exquisite workmanship, inlaid with ivory and ebony'. Two-thirds of a millennium on, the pavement, overlooked by a soaring, script-bound Saljuq minaret, was as my predecessor saw it. It was laid in rectangles of light and dark stone, like giant polished prayer carpets, on which elderly Aleppan gentlemen took the sun in chairs or read. The *minbar*, or pulpit, a gift from the Mamluk ruler al-Nasir, was brand-new in Ibn Battutah's time – and there it stood, still, a wooden stairway to a preaching platform, a flight to nowhere but high-flown words:

> Its surface was an interlocking mass of marquetry polygons in fruitwoods, set off by deep-cut ivory trefoils and miniature screen-work of criss-crossing ebony balusters with tiny ivory knobs at the nodes. A few bits of inlay had gone missing; otherwise, it was as crisp and fresh as when Ibn Battutah had seen it. The workmanship was indeed exquisite. With its interplay of polychromatic parts, it was a Bach fugue for the eyes.

And there I was, looking at it through Ibn Battutah's eyes: our sight-line, our time-line was unbroken. For a moment, I was in a geometry that might have extended for ever.

Now, two further decades on and seven years into a civil war, the Aleppo mosque, too, is in ruins. The calligraphic minaret was felled in 2013; the stone-carpeted courtyard and the prayer hall have been wrecked. As for the pulpit, it has gone. It may have been 'dismantled and transferred to an unknown location', but no one is sure.

Perhaps when the wars are over and the eye-doctor, the billy-goat, the 'Islamic State', the 'Helpers of Allah' and all the rest of them are one with the Umayyads and Gindibu the Arab, perhaps then the survivors of Aleppo will steal back, and begin to reassemble their lives and their city. Perhaps their pulpit, too, with its interplay of ivory and ebony. I hope so. It is the word made geometry, a harmonious dialogue of dark and light.

AFTERWORD

IN THE STATION OF HISTORY

Had I written this book ten years ago, it would have turned out differently. Recent events have made it darker than it might have been.

The Age of Disappointment may prove to be shorter than it feels when you're in it. But on it drags. I began with an image of Arab time, Nizar Qabbani's hourglass. In a poem of his called 'Waiting for Ghudu' – the Arabic 'Godot' – there are other measures of time:

> We're waiting for the train
> Waiting for a traveller unknowable as Fate
> To come out of the cloak of years
> To come out of Badr
> Out of al-Yarmuk
> Of Hittin
> To come from the sword of Saladin

The past is calibrated in battles and heroes. As for the present,

> We're waiting for the train
> Broken, since we came, is the clock of the years
> Time does not pass

> . . .
> Come, Ghudu,
> Save us from tyrants and their tyranny
> For we are imprisoned like sheep in the station of history.

It sounds like the constant present that, for St Augustine, was the eternal, infernal timeline of hell. But it is really that ever-present past – Max Weber's 'eternal yesterday', the relentless authority of tradition. It is no paradox that, in Arabic, the word *hadith* means both 'a tradition' and 'modern'.

Today, an Arab Spring on from that poem, the clock is still broken; but the hourglass turns and the squeezebox plays the same old tunes. The latest-issue octogenarian king in Saudi Arabia has been busy 'gathering the word' – that is, silencing opposition – by appointing his son Crown Prince and sanctioning the detention of royal cousins on suspicion of corruption. At the same time, the Saudis and their allies have been ganging up on their neighbour, Qatar, for 'splitting the stick', that is, diverging from the jointly gathered word of the club of Gulf regimes.

A particular bane to them has been Qatar's independent media voice, Al Jazeera Arabic. Rather than reporting that the ruler has sent a telegram of congratulation to the president of Ruritania on the occasion of his amicable country's national day, Al Jazeera has jazzed up the Arabic media with innovations like investigative journalism. The neighbouring regimes see the network as having fanned the poisonous breezes of the Arab Spring. They also see Qatar as having crossed the old red line by reaching out to the millennial foe, Iran. Some of them have brought in laws against 'showing sympathy for Qatar'. Egypt's President al-Sisi has said that he would 'cut the tongue' of Al Jazeera – that ancient threat wielded by pre-Islamic tyrants against turbulent poets. As I put the finishing touches to my text (or rather, prepare to let it go; books are never really finished, histories least of all), the royal court in Riyadh is admitting that one of its critics, Jamal Khashoggi, himself a Saudi national, was murdered on a visit to his country's consulate in Istanbul. It seems that perhaps rather more than his tongue was cut: the Turkish authorities claim that he was dismembered and the parts dissolved in acid. Arab allies of the Saudis have condemned international criticism of the killing as an infringement of the kingdom's sovereignty and *'urubah*, arabness ... All those sticks, tightly bound: symbols of authority, tools of execution. To eyes that have regarded the European past, they cannot fail to look like *fasces*.

Words are still the sharpest weapons; language remains at the core of identity, community and continuity. The Israeli government knows this as well as any Arab leader, and in July 2018 inflicted its own mass tongue-cutting by demoting Arabic from the status of an official language of the State of Israel. For the Arab 17.5 per cent of Israeli citizens, who live in a language as well as a land, it is not the final solution – that would be an imperial Ottoman-style ban on the teaching of Arabic – but perhaps it is the penultimate solution.

In much if not most of the Arabic world, the clock seems not just to be broken but to be going backwards. Even Tunisia, the lone land where the revolutions of 2011 appeared to have achieved anything lasting, is faltering in its forward progress: the revolution there has not magicked an ailing economy back to health, and autocrats, islamocrats, tyrannosaurs and terrorists are by no means extinct. In Syria, the Eye-doctor, Bashshar al-Asad, appears to have clung on to power – with the backing of those two old empires-in-abeyance, Russia and Iran. The Aleppo mosque, victim of the war that has prolonged his rule (and probably victim of his own artillery), is being rebuilt with Chechen cash. The whereabouts of its glorious pulpit are still a mystery.

In my own corner of the Arab world, the former Arabia Felix, Fortunate Arabia, I have watched the people of a reasonably united Yemen sleepwalk – or be led, sleeping – into the ultimate nightmare, civil war. I have lain listening to the missiles and wondered if they were the last sounds I would hear. It has all been tragic in its most literal sense, and as this book neared its end, so too did our tragic hero-anti-hero: Ali Abd Allah Salih, the 'billy-goat in the officers' mess' who had ruled for a third of a century. In 2014 he had wreaked revenge on the people who had dethroned him by siding with that even more inexorable force, the Huthis. Together, in a massive raid on the capital, they had overthrown Yemen's new rulers. Not surprisingly the Huthis, the *soi-disant* 'Helpers of Allah', did not wish to be the Helpers of Ali: he had fought six wars against them. And yet this most impossible of unions lasted three years before it exploded in recriminations, then all-out violence. The shelling reached a crescendo on the night of 3–4 December 2017; next day, news dawned that the old billy-goat was dead. (I said it was literally tragic: was not *tragōidia* originally performed at the sacrifice of a *tragos*, a goat?)

More recently, however, Ali had been better known for his association with another creature. Well before that unnatural and doomed alliance was revealed, I had written,

> Ali Abd Allah Salih, who is supposed to have compared ruling Yemen to 'dancing on the heads of snakes', should have kept a much older Yemeni saying in mind – 'In the end, the snake always gets the charmer.'

It wasn't a hard prophecy to make. The snake-charmer ended up in the squamous and multiplex coils of his own creation, like Laocoön – the old Trojan whose punishment, in one account, was for contracting an unholy marriage. Both of them died grappling with an overwhelming fate that they themselves had loosed. Yet Ali's end was not squalid: he resisted, and died like the soldier he never ceased to be. His corpse lies, we think, in a freezer up the road: history unburied; the past on ice.

He has probably united more people in death than he did in his lifetime. Meanwhile, with power-centres in at least three places, the body politic of the unified Republic of Yemen seems beyond preservation. Unity, as always, is that mirage briefly grasped.

Or as almost always, for there are exceptions. The United Arab Emirates still lives up to its name, as well as to the rhetorical past. Just as the ruler of Dubai launches the arrows of his verse in battle against the millennial threat from over the Gulf, so does his son gather the word of the land in lines like these, part of a long ode recited by him in a slickly produced and very popular video:

> Already when we unified in 'seventy-one, we were one folk:
> The hearts united first, and then the homes.
> United we remain – within the minds of men, true Arabs,
> In our bloodlines that endure and never die.
> . . .
> May God for ever keep our peoples strong! (All say, '*Amen!*')
> May God preserve our unity as long as ages run!

Amid the skyscrapers and shopping malls, a new generation of leaders is picking up the old thread of language, spinning out the eternal word-magic.

Nearly everywhere, however, words and resulting deeds have blown societies apart, not unified them. It is painful to watch all this happening to a land

I love, and to see a wider Arabic world suffering from so much self-harm. But is the pain made worse by my own heritage, by the feeling that things might be better if – to be honest – they were ordered more like they are in the land where I was born and formed? Half a century ago, the wise Doreen Ingrams, who was both the last and greatest of Arabian imperial lady travellers and a pioneer post-imperialist, wrote after the British withdrawal from Aden,

> The assumption that the 'natives' must prefer the order and justice of our administration to the disorder and injustice of their own was one of the more astonishing aspects of the British attitude towards their colonial subjects.

Fifty years on, not all the Arab world is disordered; but probably half of it is, going by population, and nearly all of it is unjust – outrageously unjust, by the standards of liberal democracies. But is it a form of intellectual colonialism even to apply those liberal standards, and to hope Arabs will do so themselves? Maybe Samuel Huntington *was* right about the clash of civilizations. That is certainly what the dictators and 'Islamic State' and our own Huthis say, and it is all part of how they keep their grip on power.

But if Doreen, whom I knew a little and remember with great fondness, was wise, so was Taha Husayn, writing a little earlier in the twilight of Western imperialism:

> We live in an age . . . in which freedom and independence are not an end to which people and nations strive, but a means to ends higher, more permanent and more comprehensive in their benefits.

Those higher ends include, presumably, order and justice in those free and independent societies.

They are both right, of course. Taha Husayn, however, is an ambiguous figure to Arabs who still know of him: he was wise and eloquent, but he was a cosmopolite who believed in a Hellenic-Islamic civilization. He was an Arab, but he was also an Egyptian, and one who was married to Europe literally and figuratively. He believed in clinches, not clashes. He had also written, 'As time goes by, [our Arab mentality] strives towards change, accelerating in its contact with Westerners.' But he wrote that more than ninety years ago, and in recent decades the acceleration has gone into reverse. There is that fear of homogenization, of the global blur, the loss of *ethos*. And ethos – not just as some woolly manner of thinking, some nebulous 'Arab mentality', but in its original sense of 'character', that of a group, its genius, its daemon and its fate – is a power more elemental than organized religion.

It is partly fear of its loss that causes those temporal confusions. People, an old Arabic saying goes, resemble the times they live in, much more than they resemble their fathers. But, often, people *want* to resemble their fathers, to retain the ethos. Thus, temporal dislocation: they fight against the times and maintain that ever-present past, the eternal yesterday; they do not want to fix the broken clock. They know that to become part of the present continuous, the blur, would be to enter the biggest super-*hadarah* ever, to become more like everyone else on earth. And a recurring characteristic of being *'arab*, or Arab, right from the start, has been that of being marginal, independent, *not* like everyone else. To the extent that one enters *hadarah*, civilization, one ceases to be 'Arab' in one of the word's oldest senses. Arabs, after all, sparked off the then biggest super-*hadarah* ever with Islam, and ended up on its margins.

What now if they came back in from the margins, and took an active place in the current, wider *hadarah* of civil societies that try to be truly democratic, free from tyrannosaurs and from incessant conflict, with working constitutions, equality under the law, with liberty of speech and religion, and Baskin Robbins thirty-one flavours of ice-cream everywhere (admittedly, they are almost everywhere now – including, I'm told, at one of the gates of the sacred temenos of the Ka'bah)? Would they become merely 'West Asians' and 'North Africans'? They would have nothing left but their shared language and history – in short, their culture. Would that be enough? Only they can know.

Then again, no *hadarah*, however super, lasts for ever. Nor is the extinction of tyrannosaurs inevitable. And while they are still at large, to remain flock-like, even if it means being raided, herded, penned in the station of history and periodically slaughtered, offers quite a lot of Arabs a modicum of security for a majority of the time, as it has for most people over most of human history.

But the clock need not stay broken. It can be made to work, and can be set to Arab time. It can run in parallel with the rest of a world in which Arabs have so often been not just stuck on a rock, but also the essential middlemen, the central cog in the global clockwork.

The fact that recent centuries have run largely on Western time has left the world out of kilter. This bias to a hemisphere (really a hemi-demisphere, the north-west) has left its neighbours looking at it askance. For many Arabs, in particular, the West is ambiguous: if not a Gorgon with a gaze that destroys, it is at best a Siren that both enchants and endangers. Arabs might do better to look away, towards themselves, and to listen to their own voices. They certainly do not have to submit to 'the gaze of the Western Other – a gaze that . . . foredooms all your hopes', or to reject apparently 'Western' and 'cosmopolitan' ideas as a 'crusade' against the Muslim mind, as Muhammad Jalal Kishk, a founder of modern political Islam, put it. What matters is the idea itself – not where it comes from. This is what al-Kindi, the ninth-century 'Philosopher of the Arabs', knew: he pursued truth, 'wherever it may come from – even if it comes from races who are distant from us and societies quite different from our own'. It is what the great thirteenth-century Sufi divine, Ibn al-Arabi, knew:

> He sees the lightning to the east, and for the east he longs;
> And if it flickers westward, to the west he'll lean.
> 'My love,' he says, 'is not for places or for lands.
> My only passion's for the lightning-flash.'

If they look, Arabs will see flashes in the mirror of their own history – their whole history, not just that blinding flash of greatness in the middle of it. They will find that individualism, liberalism, cosmopolitanism, inclusiveness, civil society, objective truth are not part of some 'Western crusade', but are part of their own past. They will see, for example:

… the search for freedom and independence of those original diverse pioneers who left the northern fertile crescent for the wild south of the peninsula – the likely first *'arab*;

… the settled, productive, non-tribal pre-Islamic societies of that other fertile crescent in South Arabia;

... the cosmopolitan networks of trade and culture that centred on great caravan cities like Palmyra, Qaryat and Mecca, meeting-places of *badw* and *hadar*;

... the eloquent individualism of the pre-Islamic 'vagabond' poets like al-Shanfara, seekers and speakers of truth beyond tribal boundaries;

... the all-embracing heaven of the earlier Qur'anic revelations –

> Those who believe and those who are Jews and Christians and Sabians [a gnostic sect in Mesopotamia], whoever believes in Allah and the Last Day and acts righteously, they shall have their reward with their Lord;

... the inclusiveness of Muhammad's first Constitution of Medina, and of his Farewell Sermon, the crystallization of his mission;

... the brief but marvellous openness of Abbasid society at its height, particularly under the philosopher-caliph, al-Ma'mun (before he became infallible);

... the 'cultured, sophisticated, broad-minded' contemporary caliphate of Cordova, where life was 'something glorious in itself, to be ennobled by learning and enlivened by every kind of pleasure';

... the liberating theologies of Sufism;

... the adaptability and spiritual depth of Islam in the expansive, oceanic fourteenth and fifteenth centuries and after;

... the intellectual, intercredal movers of the nineteenth-century Awakening;

... the twentieth-century advocates of cultural collaboration, like Taha Husayn, married to Europe as he was;

... the truth-seeking poets of the exodus in our own times, spiritual descendants of the 'vagabonds';

... the seekers of liberty, dignity and daily bread now and to come.

For Arabs to reconsider their past is long overdue. The foremost 'vagabond' of recent years put the challenge forcefully:

> We want a generation who are angry . . .
> Who will wrench up history from the roots.

The history is human and live. Some of it will come up shrieking like a mandrake, and as deadly to its discoverers. But to get at the truth of their past, to allow it to have its own *intifadah*, its shaking-off of dust, and then to re-examine the roots, to share as common property what has been buried in the celebration of a brief imperial greatness and the long mourning of its loss – for Arabs, all this would be more than just preserving heritage and culture.

Truth, despite the old saying, will not always out. Some of it is just too deeply buried. But as well as al-Yarmuk and Hittin and all the victories over Byzantines and Persians and Franks, Arab schoolchildren must learn about those inglorious Arab–Arab battles: the seventy severed hands and the 7,000 dead of the Day of the Camel, that fight between Muhammad's son-in-law and his favourite wife; the 70,000 dead of Siffin, the battle between the old and new regimes of Muhammad's tribe; all the other inter-Arab battles since, with their concatenating zeros of dead. It would be to reclaim the past not as a theme-park for the present, but as ground for a better future.

It would be a way of being true to themselves, without having to be antagonistic to a Siren-Gorgon 'West'. Selfhood is still often imagined, sometimes expressed (in both senses, 'articulated' and 'forced out'), by opposition. 'Allah is great,' say the slogans beneath my window,

Death to America
Death to Israel
The curse of Allah on the Jews
Victory to Islam.

It is still identity moulded in negative, in opposition to the big empire without and the little empire within (and the irony is that this version of the old mould itself comes from one of the oldest of the moulding empires, Iran: it was the slogan of Khomeini's revolution). Allah's own book advocates not opposition but apposition, parallel coexistence: 'To you,' Muhammad was told to say to those who did not believe in his mission, 'be your religion, and to me mine.' More loosely, we can each have our own ethos.

Reclaiming history by the roots might even suggest ways to reconcile the debate between peoples and tribes. *Badawah* and *hadarah* can coexist, as do the malady and the remedy, according to that alleged saying of Muhammad, in the two wings of a fly. The secret is not to let the curse overcome the cure, not to let that 'something rotten' take over. As for all the internecine hatreds of the present, reconciliation can only be approached – as it has been elsewhere in recent history – via truth: the problems of the present can only be given decent burial when the realities of the past have been unearthed and examined. No one but Arabs can do this. And they cannot afford the time to wait for others to unearth history, like those villagers of my Foreword who waited 2,000 years for the British to dig out a well that the Romans had filled in.

I for one am done with digging. But I trust that my own history has qualified me to archaeologize. My earliest Arab memories being those of Nasser's smiling face and, more vaguely, of the Brits getting the bum's rush in Aden on a flickering black-and-white TV screen, I am inevitably a post-imperialist. Arabist and historian by education but Arabian by experience – living in a land, not a library, in peace as well as war in my tower on its *tell*; living in a present built on a many-layered past – I am also a post-Orientalist: the 'Orient' is my home, not just my subject of study (or, God forbid, object of domination). Because of all this, while I look around and see disorder, injustice and, nowadays, the faces of dead youth smiling down from their martyrs' posters, smiles blown up in both senses – while I see all this, I know that there can be no justification for imperialism, territorial or cultural, 'Western' or whatever. Those days are long over.

But there is another imperialism that is alive and well. The best (perhaps the only) answers to present Arab questions will emerge from the Arab past. That past, however, is and always has been invaded, colonized and exploited by homegrown power-raiders and power-wielders, in order to justify their continued grip on the present; and not just on the present. As Orwell knew, control the past and you control the future. Physical Arab lands have been reclaimed from the old occupying empires; the Arab past is still under occupation, from within.

New generations must know that this past is their country, too; that it is waiting to be liberated and then explored, with open eyes and minds. Only then can anyone think of building a better future on it.

CHRONOLOGY

TIME	EVENTS	LANGUAGE, CULTURE, SOCIETY, IDENTITY
2 million years BP?	hominids leave Africa via Sinai and Bab al-Mandab Strait	
125,000+ years BP?	modern humans leave Africa via Sinai and Bab al-Mandab Strait	
8th–5th millennia BC	most recent 'major wet period' in Arabia	
6th millennium BC	people in S Arabia are herding cattle	
5th millennium BC		Arabic-like features branch off from a Semitic root language
4th millennium BC	people in S Arabia are starting to grow crops and develop irrigation systems	
	people are settling the Arabian coastline, using mangroves for building and shellfish for food	
3rd millennium BC	camels domesticated for milking, probably in SE Arabia	
	people living by the Arabian/Persian Gulf begin to export pearls	
by 2000 BC	horse-drawn chariots used in N Arabia	
2nd millennium BC	camels begin to be used as pack- and riding-animals	
	pioneer nomads moving from Fertile Crescent into Arabian Peninsula?	

CHRONOLOGY

	proto-Sabaeans leave Syria-Palestine, make their way to S Arabia	
by 1000 BC	camel transport used across much of Arabia	
		camel culture enhances *badawah*, mobile society
	in S Arabia, large-scale irrigation projects have begun	
		irrigation necessary for food crops leads to development of *hadarah*, settled society
1st millennium BC	Saba (Sheba) becomes the major power in S Arabia	
	the Marib Dam, perhaps pre-Sabaean in origin, is enlarged	
10th century BC	biblical visit of S Arabian Queen of Sheba (Saba) to Solomon	
853 BC		earliest known inscription (Assyrian) mentioning Arabs
	Gindibu the Arab provides camels for an anti-Assyrian force	
by 800 BC	Sabaeans trading with the Fertile Crescent	
750 BC on	Qedar, perhaps a tribal confederation, active in N Arabia	
730s BC	the Assyrians defeat Shamsi, 'queen of the Arabs'	
7th century BC	the Assyrians impose a puppet 'queen', Tabua, on Qedar	
		confederations in S Arabia united by loyalty to a single deity
5th century BC	Persians employ Arabs to defend their borders against Egypt	
4th century BC?	horses begin to be used for riding in Arabia	
3rd century BC on	Arabophone Nabataeans trade out of Petra	
2nd century BC	S Arabian Minaeans trade with Egypt and the Aegean	
1st century BC on	Arabophone Palmyrenes trade out of Tadmur (Palmyra)	
26 BC on	a Roman expeditionary force briefly penetrates S Arabia	
by 0 AD	camel saddles have been improved, enabling extended travel	
		proto-Arabic graffiti proliferate in N Arabia
	Arabs are used widely as mercenaries by S Arabian powers	
		a distinct Arab identity has begun to form

CHRONOLOGY

1st century		earliest known Arabic text, embedded in an Aramaic text in Negev
	Himyaris become a major power in S Arabia	
106	Rome annexes Nabataean territories	
2nd century	W Arabian Thamud tribe sends levies to the Romans	
2nd century on	horse+camel combination: unique mobility and raiding power	
		Arabs and Arabic become prominent in S Arabia
3rd century on	Kindah nomads develop Qaryat (C Arabia) as their emporium	Sabaic etc. still written, but Arabic takes over S Arabian speech
	in traditional accounts, Khuza'ah tribe are in control of Mecca	
		Mecca already a sacred centre
226	Sasanian dynasty established in Persia	
244	Philip the Arab, born in Damascus, becomes Roman emperor	
267		earliest fully Arabic text, an inscription at Mada'in Salih (Saudi Arabia)
272	Rome absorbs Palmyrene territories	
late 3rd century	Hadramawt falls to Himyari-dominated state of Saba	
	S Arabia united under the Himyari-Sabaean state	
	the Lakhm tribe form a Persian client-dynasty at al-Hirah (Iraq)	Lakhmids have become a nucleus around which Arab identity solidifies
early 4th century	Persians extend influence over E Arabia	
		Arabophones infiltrate the Aramaic-speaking Fertile Crescent
	Kindah and Madhhij tribes migrate from C to S Arabia	
	the Himyaris send expeditions N and E across Arabia	
328	in his epitaph, the Lakhmid Imru' al-Qays is 'king of all the Arabs'	
before 400?		a 'high' form of Arabic speech develops
		Arabic script begins to develop from Nabataean

CHRONOLOGY

5th century on		high Arabic poetry becomes a pan-Arabian cultural product
	introduction of the horse stirrup enhances Arab fighting power	
	increasing infiltration of S Arabia by nomad Arab tribes	
	Azd and its sub-tribe, Ghassan, migrate N and E from Marib	
5th century	Qusayy, ancestor of Muhammad's Quraysh tribe, arrives in Mecca	
	Quraysh begin to control Arabian trade routes	
c. 490	a branch of Ghassan forms a Byzantine client-dynasty in Syria	
		Ghassanids and Lakhmids are rival patrons of poetry
		Arabic culture and identity empowered by inter-dynastic rivalry
	the ailing Himyari state promotes its own Arab client-king from Kindah	
490s–530s	intermittent tribal 'War of al-Basus' in N Arabia	
early 6th century	the Byzantines entitle their client-ruler 'king of the Arabs'	
	fighting between Himyari- and Persian-backed client-kings	
6th century	frequent tribal wars flare up across Arabia	
		oldest extant high Arabic poems, by Kindah poets
		prominence of *su'luk*s – ex-tribal 'vagabond' leaders and poets
	Christianity widely adopted in Ghassanid and Lakhmid areas	
	monotheism (Christian, Jewish, indigenous) spreads in S Arabia	
early 6th century	the Himyari king espouses Judaism	
c. 518	massacre by Himyaris of Christians at Najran	
525	the Christian Ethiopians conquer the Himyari-Sabaean state	
mid-6th century	the Kindah poet-leader Imru' al-Qays courts Byzantium	
	wars between the Ghassanids and Lakhmids	

		prestige of high Arabic promotes Arab cultural self-awareness
	Meccan leaders use joint capital to expand caravan trade	
570	traditional dating of Ethiopian-led attack on Mecca	
	traditional dating of Muhammad's birth	
c. 575	Persians establish rule over S Arabia	
c. 582	in tradition, the boy Muhammad is recognized as a prophet	
late 6th century		Arabic script reaches Mecca
		Mecca gains wide popularity as a pilgrimage destination
		charismatic preacher Quss ibn Sa'idah, admired by Muhammad
		by now, a firm sense of Arabs as a pan-Arabian cultural group
	Byzantium and Persia both dispense with their Arab client-kings	
early 7th century	Muhammad begins his contemplative retreats	
	final collapse of the Marib Dam	
602	the Persians kill their last Lakhmid client-king	
604	Arab tribes defeat a Persian force at Dhu Qar	
c. 608	the Ka'bah in Mecca is rebuilt after a flood	
	Muhammad mediates in a dispute over the rebuilding	
c. 610 on		Muhammad's revelations begin
	Persians occupy Byzantine territory in Syria and, briefly, Egypt	
616?	some of Muhammad's followers seek refuge in Ethiopia	
619?	death of Khadijah, Muhammad's first wife	
before 620		the Qur'an, the first Arabic book, begins to take shape
620s	Byzantines regain territory from Persians	
622	Muhammad and followers move from Mecca to Yathrib (Medina)	
		their *hijrah*, migration, is the start of the Islamic calendar
624	Muhammad raids a Meccan caravan at Badr	
		Muhammad changes prayer direction from Jerusalem to Mecca

625	Medinans defeated by Meccans at Uhud	
626	the Jewish tribe Banu al-Nadir are expelled from Medina	
627	the Meccans besiege Medina	
	many Medinan Jews are killed for allegedly backing the Meccans	
	Persian colonists in Yemen submit to Medinan rule	
628	truce between Medina and Mecca	
630	Muhammad takes over Mecca	
630–1	Arabian tribal leaders pledge allegiance to Muhammad	
631	Medinans besiege the town of al-Ta'if	
	'false prophets' Musaylimah (E Arabia) and al-Aswad (Yemen)	
632	Muhammad's 'Farewell Pilgrimage' to Mecca and last sermon	
	death of Muhammad	
	Abu Bakr elected *khalifah*, caliph or 'successor', to Muhammad	
		Abu Bakr gathers the disparate parts of the Qur'an
	most Arabian tribes 'apostasize', i.e. cut ties with state of Medina	
	'false prophets' proliferate	
633–4	Musaylimah is defeated by a force from Medina	
	al-Aswad is assassinated	
	other 'false prophets' capitulate	
	the Arabia-wide 'apostasy' is put down by force and diplomacy	
	the peninsula is united, in theory, under the rule of Medina	
634	death of Abu Bakr, succession of Umar as caliph	
635–*c.* 750	Arabs conquer an empire from W Europe to C Asia	
	major migrations of population from Arabia (mostly 635–44)	
		all Arabians are united, in theory, by scripture and empire
636	Arab defeat of Byzantines at al-Yarmuk (Syria–Jordan)	
636/7/8	Arab defeat of Persians at al-Qadisiyyah (Iraq)	

638	foundation of al-Basrah, garrison city in Iraq	
638 or after	foundation of al-Kufah, garrison city in Iraq	
639	Arabs begin incursions into Egypt	
641	Arabs take the Egyptian fortress of Babylon (Old Cairo)	
	foundation of al-Fustat, garrison city in Egypt	
642	battle of Nihawand opens E Persian empire to Arabs	
644	death of Caliph Umar, Uthman nominated as successor	
644 on		a committee produces a canonical written Qur'an
		non-canonical oral variations of the Qur'an persist
656	some Arab troops in the provinces mutiny and march to Medina	
	Uthman killed by the mutineers	
	Ali, Muhammad's cousin and son-in-law, becomes caliph	
	'Battle of the Camel' between Ali and the 'pro-Uthman' faction	
657 on	Ali and the old regime of Quraysh fight at Siffin (Syria)	
	fighting is ended, rival claims are put to inconclusive arbitration	
661	Ali assassinated by disaffected supporters of his *shi'ah*, 'party'	
	Mu'awiyah, of Meccan old regime, widely accepted as caliph	
	Mu'awiyah first of the Umayyad dynasty of caliphs	
	his capital, Damascus, becomes that of the Arab empire	
670	foundation of al-Qayrawan, garrison city in Tunisia	
680	death of Mu'awiyah	
	al-Husayn b. Ali revolts against Umayyad rule and is killed	
	he becomes the first great martyr of the *shi'ah*, the party of Ali	
680s	Arab-led forces reach the Atlantic shore of N Africa	

	Abd Allah b. al-Zubayr establishes anti-caliphate in Mecca	
	a 'N–S split' has re-emerged in those of peninsular origin	
	Ibn al-Zubayr courts 'Northerners', wins territory even in Syria	
691		Dome of the Rock completed in Jerusalem
692	Meccan anti-caliphate of Abd Allah b. al-Zubayr defeated	
	peninsular Arabia sidelined politically	
		peninsular Arabia sidelined culturally
694 on	al-Hajjaj tries to exterminate anti-Umayyad opposition in Iraq	
by late 7th century	population of al-Basrah, Iraq, reaches 200,000	
		spoken Arabic begins to 'mongrelize'
		large numbers of non-Arabs are affiliated to Arab tribes
c. 700		an Arabic-inscribed coinage is introduced
		high Arabic is made the language of imperial administration
		an upsurge in writing brings about improvements in Arabic script
		the use of high Arabic spreads rapidly among non-Arabs
		linguistic sciences (grammar, philology, etc.) begin to develop
early 8th century	Arab-led forces established in C Asian Transoxania	
	Arabs establish limited rule in Sind (Pakistan)	
711	Tariq b. Ziyad leads mainly Berber forces into Spain	
715		the Umayyad Mosque of Damascus is completed
by *c.* 720		construction of N Arab lines of descent from Isma'il
		construction of S Arab lines of descent from Qahtan
		all Arabs now united in theory by genetics, if not by politics

732	Arab-led forces clash with Carolingian force near Poitiers	
747	Abbasid revolution launched in Khurasan (E Persia)	
	fellow revolutionaries include supporters of the *shi'ah* of Ali	
750	Abbasid forces defeat and exterminate Umayyads	
	al-Saffah becomes first Abbasid caliph	
	Abbasids start eliminating fellow revolutionaries	
751	Arab-led forces clash with Chinese, E of the Syr Darya River	
754	al-Mansur succeeds al-Saffah as Abbasid caliph	
mid-8th century on		paper-making spreads through the Arabic world
		written Arabic proliferates because of the cheapness of paper
		smoothness of paper promotes further improvements to script
		Islamic legal and moral systems begin to be synthesized
756	an Umayyad survivor, Abd al-Rahman, founds Spanish dynasty	
	Arab migration to Spain increases	
762	al-Mansur founds Baghdad	
762 on	al-Mansur eliminates opposition within Abbasid family	
	he eliminates potential opposition from Abbasid revolutionary elite	
	he begins a trend by relying on non-Arab slaves as soldiers	
774		King Offa of Mercia, England, imitates Abbasid coinage
788	a descendant of Ali founds the Idrisid dynasty in Morocco	
late 8th century on		beginning of 'the age of setting down'
		during this age, Arab cultural legacy and identity are enshrined for posterity
		a 'bedouin' past is promoted (actual bedouins are now marginal)

		Persians, then many others, resuscitate their own cultures their 'Shu'ubi' movements challenge Arab cultural hegemony
809	death of Caliph al-Rashid the empire is divided between three of al-Rashid's sons two of the sons, al-Ma'mun and al-Amin, fight each other	
813 on	al-Ma'mun is victorious, establishes rule over all the empire al-Ma'mun imports Transoxanian troops into Baghdad	
early 9th century		intellectual openness under the caliph al-Ma'mun the Mu'tazilah promote theological debate written Arabic prose at last becomes a medium of expression
816	al-Ma'mun designates the Shi'i imam al-Rida as his heir	
818	al-Rida dies; reconciliation with the Shi'ah is shelved	
832		al-Ma'mun founds the House of Wisdom
833	al-Mu'tasim becomes caliph, imports Turkish and other troops the troops cause havoc in Baghdad	
836	al-Mu'tasim moves non-Arab troops to a new capital, Samarra'	
9th century		al-Baladhuri records Arab conquests al-Jahiz analyses arabness, rebuffs the Shu'ubis islamization accelerates, belatedly, across the empire 'being Arab' now matters less: the empire is cosmopolitan Byzantines and Chinese imitate Arab clothing fashions Spanish Christians become completely arabicized
mid 9th century		under Caliph al-Mutawakkil, theological speculation is banned

861	al-Mutawakkil killed in plot by son and Turkish guards	
	real power in hands of Turkic military commanders	
868	Persian Saffarid dynasty independent of Baghdad in the E	
	Egypt breaks away from Baghdad under C Asian Tulunids	
869–83	rebellion in Iraq of the Zanj (plantation slaves from E Africa)	
890 on	rebellion in Iraq and beyond of peasants under Hamdan Qarmat	
	the rebellion allies itself to the Isma'ilis, a Shi'i splinter-group	
late 9th century	Samarra' abandoned	
early 10th century	from now, political power of Baghdad caliphate only covers Iraq	
10th century	the Arab empire fragments irreparably	
		but in the C and the W culture is still Arabic, patrons proliferate
		multi-volume anthologies and histories enshrine Arab heritage
	Arab Hamdanid dynasty prominent in N Iraq and N Syria	
910	Fatimid dynasty (of dubiously Arab origin) established in N Africa	
	Fatimids adopt the title 'caliph'	
922	execution of the nonconformist visionary al-Hallaj	
929	Abd al-Rahman III (Spanish Umayyad) claims the title 'caliph'	
930	Qarmati rebels raid Mecca and remove the sacred Black Stone	
938	Bajkam, Turkish generalissimo, effective ruler in Baghdad	
940	death of al-Radi, 'the last real caliph' (even if powerless)	
	now there are three rival titular caliphates: Baghdad, Cairo, Cordova	
		the idea of Arab unity is at a low, 300 years after its high point
945	Iranian Buwayhids take power in Baghdad	
mid 10th century		Cordova now a great centre of Arabic culture

966–8	the eunuch slave Kafur holds power in Egypt	
968	Fatimids enter Egypt	
969	Cairo founded as new Fatimid capital	
c. 970	Turkic Saljuqs begin takeover of caliphal territory	
later 10th century		the Qarmati-Isma'ili 'intellectual wing' synthesizes scientific lore
1031	the Umayyad caliphate in Spain fragments	
	the 'Party Kings' rule numerous small Iberian states	
1055	Saljuqs take Baghdad	
mid-11th century	Banu Hilal and other big Arab tribes are moved W from Egypt	
		belated arabization of rural N Africa
1061 on	Normans take over Arab-ruled Sicily	
later 11th century	Saljuqs control the entire E wing of the old Arab empire	
		Saljuqs have adopted Persian as their cultural language
		Saljuq Vizier Nizam al-Mulk encourages *madrasah*s and Arabic studies
1085	Christian Spanish retake Toledo	
		Christian Spanish maintain traditions of Arabic learning
1086 on	Berber Almoravids stop Christian advance and take over S Spain	
		Almoravids claim Arabian ancestry
1099	Crusaders take Jerusalem, massacre inhabitants	
1130s		court of Roger II, Norman king of Sicily, largely Arabic in culture
12th century		the Crusades channel Arabic words and ideas to Europe
		Arabic learning spreads into Europe via Sicily and S Italy
mid-12th century	Berber Almohad alliance takes over S Spain	
	Almohad leader is first avowed non-Arab to adopt the title 'caliph'	

		Almohads embrace urban Arabic culture
1169	Kurdish Ayyubids established in Cairo	
1171	Ayyubid Salah al-Din (Saladin) abolishes Fatimate caliphate	
	Saladin re-establishes nominal suzerainty of Abbasid caliphs	
1219	Crusaders take Damietta (Egypt)	
	Mongols appear in Islamic lands	
	Mongols perpetrate urban massacres, cause rural devastation	
13th century		Ibn Khallikan's biographical dictionary, *Notable Deaths*
1248	Christian Spanish retake Seville	
1250	Turkic Mamluk slave-soldiers take over in Egypt and Syria	
1258	Mongols under Hulagu take Baghdad, kill Caliph al-Musta'sim	
		any last pretense of Arab unity ends
		social breakdown: tribal Arabs raid settled lands
	Mamluks host Abbasid puppet caliphate in Egypt	
1260	Mamluks halt Mongol advance at Ayn Jalut (Palestine)	
late 13th century	Arabs found sultanate of Kilwa Kisiwani (Tanzania)	
		W Mongols adopt Islam and Persian culture
	most Crusaders have left the Levant	
early 14th century	Arab tribes switch loyalties from Mamluks to Mongols and back	
14th century	Pax Mongolica: hemiglobal trade and travel flourish	
	Egypt-based Karim merchants active from Atlantic to Pacific	
		Arabic culture and Islam spread between W Africa and E Indies
		Arabic script used for many languages, Africa to Asia
	start of 250-year diaspora of Arabs around Indian Ocean rim	
		Moroccan Ibn Battutah travels in three continents

		Cairo is the biggest city outside China and the capital of Arabic culture
		Arabic culture also flourishes in Granada, Spain
1343	Sultanate of Delhi a nominal vassal to Abbasid puppet caliph	
1340s on	plague destroys a third of humanity from China to Europe	
1375–9		Ibn Khaldun works on his *History*
c. 1400	Mongol leader Timur Lang (Tamerlane) devastates Levant etc.	
15th century	Arab al-Ma'qil tribe begin to penetrate Mauritania	
		belated arabization from this last major migration
1453	Ottoman Turks take Constantinople	
1485		Ottomans ban printing in Arabic
1488	Portuguese round the Cape of Good Hope	
	start of European attempts to monopolize Indian Ocean trade	
1492	Granada falls to Christian forces from Castile	
1516	Ottomans take Damascus	
1517	Ottomans take Cairo and its dependencies, Medina and Mecca	
	Ottomans remove Abbasid puppet caliph to Constantinople	
1519	Algiers submits to Ottoman suzerainty	
1520s	Ottomans established in Yemen	
1534	Ottomans take Baghdad	
16th century on	much of Arabic world Ottoman-ruled for most of the next 300 years	
	Arabs are united politically, but at the cost of their independence	
		any sense of widely-shared Arab identity enters a trough
1543	last Abbasid puppet caliph dies	
	in time, Ottoman sultans assume the title 'caliph'	
early 17th century		Lebanese Christian Arabs experiment with Arabic printing
		the experiment does not spread
1630s on	opposition to Ottoman rule in Yemen	

	Ottomans withdraw from Yemen	
1662–84	English control Tangier (Morocco)	
late 17th century	Omanis expand naval power, found E African coastal empire	
c. 1720	birth of Muhammad b. Abd al-Wahhab, puritan reformer	
1722		first Arabic printing press in Constantinople
18th century	renewed diaspora of Arabs around Indian Ocean rim	
	S Arabian oceanic emigrants lead commerce, religion, politics	
mid-18th century	Persian encroachment in E Arabia	
	rise of Wahhabi puritan movement, C Arabia	
	Wahhabi alliance with Muhammad b. Sa'ud	
late 18th century	British navy protects merchantmen in Gulf from Arab raids	
1783	Bedouin raiders conquer Bahrain	
1798	Wahhabis defeat an Ottoman army sent to subdue them	
	French under Napoleon invade Egypt, defeat Mamluks	
		French introduce Arabic printing to Egypt
1800		French in Cairo print the first, short-lived Arabic newspaper
1801	Ottoman-British forces expel French from Egypt	
1802	Wahhabis devastate Shi'i sites in S Iraq	
1805–12	Wahhabis occupy Mecca	
1812	Muhammad Ali Pasha exterminates Mamluk remnants in Egypt	
1813–18	Muhammad Ali defeats Wahhabis in Arabian Peninsula	
19th century		Muhammad Ali re-orientates Egypt intellectually towards Europe
		Arabic replaces Turkish as official language in Egypt
		printing begins to spread slowly through the Arabic world
		the 'Awakening': a renewal of Arab identity

		reinvigoration, among intellectuals, of written high Arabic
		idea of an Arab 'nation', part-inspired by European nationalisms
1822		government press founded in Cairo
1826		a group of young Egyptians is sent to study in Paris
1828		the first enduring government newspaper is established in Cairo
1830	French begin takeover of Algeria	
1835		Cairo 'House of Tongues' founded to translate European books
1839	British take Aden	
mid-19th century	Ottomans re-occupy parts of Yemen	
	the steam railway introduced to Egypt	
		first Arabic newspapers outside Egypt
1860s		Cairo gets a Parisian-style street-plan and an opera house
1869	opening of the Suez Canal	
1870s on	British-ruled Aden flourishes with increased sea traffic	
		Ottomans impose strict censorship on burgeoning Arabic press
1876	Egypt bankrupt: European powers impose financial control	
1881	revolt of Egyptian army officers under Ahmad Urabi	
1881 on	N Algeria brought under metropolitan French administration	
		French suppress use of high Arabic, especially in Algeria
1882	British enter Egypt at Ottoman behest, assume administration	
1883	French take Tunisia	
1890s on	Levantine Arabs migrate to Europe, W Africa, the Americas	
	Yemenis found first Arab communities in Britain	

	Germans woo Ottomans to gain presence in Arab lands	
1908	Hijaz Railway (Damascus–Medina) completed	
	revolution of the nationalist 'Young Turks'	
		Turkish enforced as sole official language of Arab lands
1912	French protectorate over much of Morocco	
	Spanish protectorates in N and SW Morocco	
1916	British recognize Sharif Husayn as King of the Hijaz	
	Sharif Husayn promotes himself to 'King of the Arabs'	
	Husayn's British-backed 'Arab Revolt' against Ottomans	
	France and Britain agree to divide Ottoman-ruled Arab lands	
1917	Balfour Declaration, promoting Jewish settlement in Palestine	
1918 on	the victorious powers divide the Ottoman empire	
1920	French mandate over Syria, including Lebanon	
	British mandate over Palestine, Transjordan, Iraq	
	Faysal b. Husayn made king of Syria	
1920s	anti-British uprising in Iraq	
	foreign Jewish immigration to Palestine increases	
	oil discoveries begin in the Gulf region	
1921	Faysal expelled from Syria by French	
	Faysal made king of Iraq by British	
	Abd Allah b. Husayn made king of Transjordan by British	
	Wahhabi tribesmen raid and massacre Yemeni pilgrims	
1921–6	Moroccan Berbers fight French and Spanish colonialists	
1922	League of Nations grants provisional Arab independence	
	the independence is subject to British and French mandates	

1923	Egypt a constitutional monarchy with political pluralism	
1924	Ottoman ex-sultan stripped of title 'caliph'	
	Sharif Husayn makes unsuccessful claim on caliphal title	
	Abd al-Aziz Ibn Sa'ud invades Hijaz, deposes Husayn	
1925–7	Druze and wider Syrian rebellion against French	
1926		Taha Husayn questions authenticity of pre-Islamic poetry
	Wahhabis attack Egyptian pilgrim procession at Mecca	
1928		post-Ottoman Turkey drops Arabic script, adopts Latin
1929–30	Ibn Sa'ud suppresses extremist Wahhabi 'Ikhwan'	
1930	British grant formal independence to Iraq	
1930s	British try to pacify Aden hinterland	
1932	Ibn Sa'ud names his Arabian realm 'Kingdom of Saudi Arabia'	
1934	Italians establish colony of Libya	
1936 on	British in Palestine in conflict with Palestinians, then with Zionists	
	Ibn Sa'ud moots Arab unity with himself at head	
	Abd Allah (Transjordan) moots Arab unity with himself at head	
	Iraqis moot Arab unity with themselves at head	
1938	commercial quantities of oil found at Dhahran, Saudi Arabia	
early 1940s	Ba'th ('Resurrection') Party founded, Syria	
1945	Arab League founded at Egyptian instigation	
	French have withdrawn from Syria and Lebanon	
	British forces leave Egypt but stay in Suez Canal Zone	
1946	King David Hotel, Jerusalem, bombed by extremist Zionists	

CHRONOLOGY

1948	war between Zionists and Arab neighbours	
	the war sets 750,000 Palestinian refugees in motion	
1952	anti-British riots in Cairo	
	revolution of Free Officers in Egypt topples British-backed king	
1953	King Abd al-Aziz Ibn Sa'ud dies	
1954	Nasser assumes presidency of Egypt	
	failed assassination attempt on Nasser by Muslim Brotherhood	
	war of liberation begins in Algeria	
1955	Saudis expelled from al-Buraymi (Oman–Abu Dhabi border)	
1956	Nasser nationalizes Suez Canal	
	Britain, France and Israel confront Egypt in Canal Zone	
	USSR and USA force Britain, France and Israel to withdraw	
	French grant independence to Tunisia and Morocco	
1956 on		cheap transistor radios become widely available
		Arab leaders begin to espouse radio broadcasting
		Egypt the political and cultural centre of the Arabic world
1958	Egypt and Syria form the United Arab Republic (UAR)	
	Yemen joins the UAR to form the United Arab States (UAS)	
	Jordan and Iraq briefly form their own union	
	Nasser-inspired revolution in Iraq overthrows the monarchy	
1959	Palestine Liberation Organization (PLO) founded	
1961	the UAR and UAS dissolve	
1962	French rule ends in Algeria	
	Nasser-inspired revolution in Yemen overthrows the monarchy	
1962 on	civil war in Yemen	
	in the war, Egypt backs republicans, Saudi Arabia monarchists	

1967	pre-emptive attack by Israel on Arab neighbours
	Israel seizes Sinai, Golan, Gaza, E Jerusalem, W Bank
	Britain withdraws from Aden and dependencies
1969	S Yemen leadership espouse far-left Socialist politics
1970	Nasser dies
	war in Jordan between government and Palestinian population
	Hafiz al-Asad seizes power in Syria
1970s	border conflicts between N and S Yemen
	insurgency in Dhofar province of Oman
1973	simultaneous attack by Egypt and Syria on Israel
	Arab oil exporters cut production: oil price rises
	USA and USSR intervene, Arab–Israel war ends in stalemate
by 1974	oil price has risen by more than 500% in two years
mid-1970s	influx of workers into now oil-rich Arabian Peninsula
1975 on	civil war in Lebanon
1977	Egyptian President al-Sadat goes to Israel for direct talks
1979	'Islamic Revolution' overthrows monarchy in Iran
	Camp David Accords between Egypt and Israel
	militant islamists occupy Meccan mosque, are bloodily ejected
	USSR invades Afghanistan
1979–90	Egypt ostracized from Arab League
1979	Islamist movements gain prominence
1980–8	Iraq invades Iran, Iran–Iraq War
1981	islamist militants assassinate al-Sadat in Cairo
1982	Hafiz al-Asad crushes islamist revolt in Hamah
	Israel invades Lebanon
1983 on	Arab fighters join anti-USSR resistance in Afghanistan

1980s	the modern Marib Dam is built	
1985	Islamic reformer Mahmud Muhammad Taha executed in Sudan	
1986	brief but bloody civil war in S Yemen	
1987–93	first Palestinian *intifadah* against Israeli occupiers	
1990	N and S Yemen unify	
	Iraq invades and occupies Kuwait	
1991	Saddam Husayn expelled from Kuwait by US-led coalition	
	islamists win elections in Algeria but are prevented from ruling	
	Algerian civil war begins	
1990s on		word-processing simplifies Arabic printing and typing
		satellite television becomes widespread
1993	Oslo Accords between Palestine and Israel	
1994	former S Yemen attempts to secede: 'War of Unity'	
1994 on	Moroccan–Algerian frontier closed	
1995	Israeli prime minister Rabin assassinated by Zionist extremist	
2000–5	second Palestinian *intifadah* against Israeli occupiers	
2001	attacks on USA inspired by Saudi extremist Usamah Bin Ladin	
2003	US-led invasion of Iraq	
2007–8	Israeli campaign against Gaza militants	
early 21st century		new social media lay ground for popular movements
2011	demonstrations in Tunisia topple its authoritarian president	
	popular movements against dictatorships (the 'Arab Spring')	
	Bahrain, with Saudi help, crushes Shi'i opposition	
	start of Syrian civil war	
	S Sudan becomes an independent state	
		Arab regimes espouse social media as a tool of control
	post-'Spring' unrest increases migration to Europe and beyond	

2012	Muslim Brotherhood win elections in Egypt	
2013	Egyptian military coup ends Muslim Brotherhood rule	
2014	Israeli campaign against Gaza militants	
	'Islamic State' takes over areas of Iraq and Syria	
	Huthi rebels and ex-president Salih take over western Yemen	
2015 on	civil war in Yemen	
2017	Gulf states impose embargo on their fellow state, Qatar	
	most territory regained from 'Islamic State'	
	Yemeni ex-president Salih killed by Huthi former allies	
2018		Israel demotes Arabic from status of official language
	Syrian regime appears to survive civil war with military help from Russia and Iran	
	Saudi regime implements limited social reform but silences dissent ever more rigorously	

NOTES

FOREWORD THE WHEEL AND THE HOURGLASS

If Yemen were to be united . . . strengthened: Ibn Fadl Allah al-Umari quoted in Tim Mackintosh-Smith's introduction to Searight and Taylor, p. 12.

a recent United Nations report . . . 'battle-related deaths': *UNDP Arab Human Development Report 2016*, quoted in the *Guardian*, 2 January 2017.

The Arabs would have won . . . rotten in themselves: Atiyah, p. 185.

Shaʿb . . . family of mankind: Lane, *Arabic-English Lexicon*, s.v. *shʿb*.

that wisdom descended . . . the tongues of the Arabs: Jahiz, quoted in Ibn Khallikan III, p. 163.

The first known ancient inscription . . . dates from 853 BC: Hoyland, p. 59.

A distinguished historian . . . Albert Hourani: Albert Hourani, p. xiii.

words and ideas . . . like cream into a churn: Ibn Khaldun, *Muqadimmah*, pp. viii-ix; Arabic in Ibn Khaldun, *Rihlah*, p. 266.

O mankind . . . that you may know one another: Qur'an, 49:13.

civilization . . . where the Bedouins took over: Ibn Khaldun, *Muqadimmah*, p. 119.

even cannibals . . . have their own rationalities: Montaigne quoted on cannibals in Rennie, p. 52; Sahlins on cannibals in the *London Review of Books*, 9 May 2013, p. 29.

what Jorge Luis Borges . . . called 'the Zahir': Borges, p. 189.

This is a country . . . is ever present: Harold Ingrams, *Yemen*, p. 36.

to make the past ever present: Adonis, *Thabit* I, p. 19.

an antique autocracy: Morris, *Sultan*, p. 23.

Time present and time past . . . contained in time past: T.S. Eliot, *Four Quartets*, 'Burnt Norton', part 1.

a village shaykh . . . species of 'Frank': Harold Ingrams, *Yemen*, p. 36.

the hourglass that swallows you / Night and day: Qabbani, p. 760.

INTRODUCTION GATHERING THE WORD

The main function . . . is to gather the word of all: Dresch, *Tribes*, p. 100.

Before sunrise on a winter's day . . . : the story of Abu Sufyan in Yathrib/Medina appears in Baladhuri, p. 47.

The captive . . . called Abu Sufyan. Some sources assert that Abu Sufyan was not a captive, but was in Yathrib/Medina to negotiate with Muhammad. Cf. *EI*², s.v. 'Muᶜāwiya'.
noble messenger: Qur'an, 69:40.
This community will split into seventy-three sects: quoted in the *hadith* collections of Abu Dawud, Ibn Majah and al-Tirmidhi.
By the night . . . to different ends: Qur'an, 92:1–4.
We have sent it down . . . that you may understand: Qur'an, 12:2.
The *a'rab* are the worst . . . to His messenger: Qur'an, 9:97.
Of the *a'rab* . . . and the Last Day: Qur'an, 9:99.
a unifying national ideology . . . an Arab national hero: cf. the views of al-Arsuzi in Suleiman, p. 157.
the third stage in the series of conquests: Hitti, p. 361.
someone who has found . . . a precious necklace: Mas'udi IV, p. 386.
deepest strand of 'being Arab': cf. p. xxiii, above.
'asabiyyah, 'group solidarity': cf. p. xix, above.
mystical tongue . . . recitation of poetry: Retsö, p. 40.
the most deadly force . . . draw blood: Whitman, p. 334.
A poet . . . to lead them to that world: Johann Gottfried von Herder quoted in Ascherson, p. 205.
To walk . . . was to become incomprehensible: Robb, p. 14.
morally and spiritually a nation long before Muhammad: Nicholson, p. 72.
Muhammad 'gathered . . . the word of Islam': Ibn Khaldun, *Rihlah*, p. 391.
how language . . . can win dominance: cf. the ideas of Martin Nowak in *Supercooperators*.
faster . . . than could religious dogma: cf. Versteegh, *Arabic Language*, p. 93.
Awake, O Arabs . . . your knees: al-Yaziji, *Diwan*, quoted in Antonius, epigraph.
'Arabiyyah . . . of the Arab world: Versteegh, *Arabic Language*, p. 196.
there are four different dialect words . . . and *nāy*: cf. Munsif al-Marzuqi, 'What language will the Arabs speak in the next century?', article on aljazeera.net, 6 November 2011.
the 'Baharnah' . . . a 'bedouin' one: cf. Owens, *Handbook*, pp. 434 and 437.
Fear the reed . . . and theriac: Kurdi, p. 431.
to split the stick: cf. Lane, *Arabic-English Lexicon*, s.v. *ᶜṣw*.
Both poetry and prose . . . secondary to the words: Ibn Khaldun, *Muqaddimah*, p. 450.
organic relationship . . . blasphemy: Adonis, *Poetics*, pp. 83–4.
To understand . . . understanding Arab history: Adonis, *Thabit* I, p. 31.
saying 'Yes' . . . to God's commands: cf. Adonis, *Thabit* IV, p. 233.
the management and training of horses, camels etc.: Lane, *Arabic-English Lexicon*, s.v. *sws*. *Siyasah* also went through a long period meaning, additionally, 'non-canonical punishments inflicted by a ruler to maintain his authority': *EI*², s.v. *Siyāsa*.
Everybody . . . found our voice: Soueif, pp. 145–6.
An anecdote from early ninth-century al-Kufah . . . two come together and unite: Ibn al-A'rabi's biography, including this story, is in Ibn Khallikan II, pp. 375–6.

CHAPTER 1 VOICES FROM THE WILDERNESS

Other comparisons . . . to the rest of Eurasia: cf. the comparison between India and Europe in Keay, pp. xxii–xxiii.
an arena of more fitful empires . . . into nation-states: cf. once more Keay, p. xxiii.
around 160 million: figures are the approximate ones for 2015.
A 'wave theory' . . . the Nile: e.g. Hitti, pp. 11–12.
This, the most recent 'major wet period' . . . the monsoon: Hoyland, p. 10, and Parker and Rose, pp. 29 and 33.
The early tenth-century geographer . . . most minimal of landscapes: Hamdani, *Sifah*, pp. 270–1.
In the green garden . . . eighty dams: Hamdani, *Iklil* VIII, p. 29.
the locations . . . are still known in the area: *Mawsu'ah*, s.v. 'Yaḥṣub'.
a catchment area of 10,000 square kilometres: Daum, p. 58.
a parable for societal . . . the Qur'an: Qur'an, 34.
The wormwood has put forth leaves . . . sprung forth: Jahiz, part 1, p. 229.

There is a plausible theory . . . 'camel herd': Hess, pp. 24–5.
madar wa-wabar . . . udder[-milking]: e.g. in Jahiz, part 1, p. 174.
O mankind . . . that you may know one another: Qur'an, 49:13.
some scholars argue . . . anachronistic: e.g. Piotrovsky, p. 136, and Iryani, p. 311.
the tribes of Asir . . . Nizari descent: Hamdani, *Sifah*, p. 230.
two major sections . . . 'brothering': Dresch, *Tribes*, pp. 329f.
A pedigree . . . resulting connection: Ibn Khaldun, *Muqaddimah*, p. 99.
that [they] may know one another: Qur'an, 49:13.
a background shade . . . tell one other apart: cf. Jahiz, part 2, p. 37.
Ernest Gellner . . . criticized for it: e.g. by Varisco, p. 65. See also Zubaida, pp. 34–8 and 65.
in Arabian history . . . a 'dialogue' between *badw* and *hadar*: cf. Abd Allah, pp. 260–1.
Recent studies . . . changes in climate: see in particular the work of Rémy Crassard.
People were herding . . . irrigation systems: see Harrower, *passim*.
The sixth-century poet . . . legendary capital of Ad: Imru' al-Qays, p. 161.
Have you not seen . . . Ad?: Qur'an, 89:6.
What He did ... with a thunderbolt: Qur'an, 41:15.
or a 'barren' wind: Qur'an, 51:41.
It is tempting . . . major wet period: cf. Mackintosh-Smith, *Yemen*, p. 192. All references are to the original 1997 edition unless otherwise stated.
the earliest surviving Arabic history . . . their destruction: Abid, p. 344.
when at last the destructive wind . . . impart the news: Abid, pp. 353–4.
Those who discuss . . . reporting it: Abu 'l-Fida', *Mukhtasar* part 1, p. 98.
maintained links . . . with levies: Macdonald, *Development*, p. 19.
knowing their own nemesis . . . ready-carved tombs: Abid, p. 401.
Aribi . . . who know neither overseers nor officials: Hoyland, p. 8.
that first known Arab, Gindibu: see pp. xxi–xxii, above.
the oldest . . . a thousand of them: Hoyland, p. 59. Hoyland gives an excellent summary of the earliest references to Arabs, pp. 59ff.
Robert Hoyland . . . called themselves: Hoyland, pp. 5–8.
remarkably coy . . . first Assyrian mention: in the al-Namarah inscription, on which see below, pp. 66–7.
named . . . enemies in mind: Tha'alibi, p. 257.
Waki' . . . 'Desert Rat son of Colcynth': Baladhuri, p. 408. Waki' was passed over for the post of governor in Khurasan because he was 'too rough and desert-Arab': Baladhuri, p. 410.
Others that appear in the Assyrian texts . . . 'Hamdanu': *EI*[2] I, p. 562.
the 30,000 the king claims to have seized: Hoyland, p. 60.
Within my land one bought a camel . . . for a few pence: Hoyland, p. 61.
The most powerful . . . called Qedar: Macdonald, *Development*, p. 14.
the Assyrians imposed . . . Tabua: Hoyland, p. 134.
A reference in Herodotus . . . in the fifth century BC: Hoyland, p. 63.
The people in Arabia asked . . . Assurbanipal: Hoyland, p. 62.
To begin with, Arabs . . . of the southern kingdoms: there is a lone appearance of *a'rab* in a single Sabaean inscription of the seventh or sixth century BC: Hoyland, p. 230.
it is clear . . . typical [South Arabian] culture: Beeston, 'Kingship', p. 257.
linguistic and cultural . . . conversion: cf. Versteegh, *Arabic Language*, p. 93.
All Arabs are one . . . and their language is one: Jahiz, part 3, p. 112.
From Sam . . . and the Sabaeans: Ibn Khaldun, *Rihlah*, p. 389.
It may be useful . . . hard to achieve: Keall, p. 98.
scores of thousands of graffiti: Macdonald, *Development*, p. 16.
the word 'Arab' doesn't appear in them: Macdonald, 'Nomads', p. 371, n. 435.
far away . . . neither overseers nor officials: cf. p. 30, above.
have their own writing . . . for amusement: Macdonald, *Development*, p. 7.
About 18,000 Safaitic graffiti are known: Macdonald, 'Nomads', p. 304.
where with luck . . . consistent: Macdonald, 'Nomads', p. 384.
spent the [early spring] . . . and fed on truffles: Macdonald, 'Seasons', p. 3.

S^{1}lm . . . distressed, overshadowed': Macdonald, 'Nomads', p. 366.
he was very love-sick . . . and had joyous sex with her: Hoyland, p. 207.
graffiti-writers add 'something rude': Macdonald, *Development*, p. 16.
does the verb *'tm* . . . fuck?: Winnett, p. 239.
this is his camping place year after year: Hoyland, p. 206.
a torrent made him flee . . . trust not the torrent-bed: Macdonald, 'Seasons', p. 2, with my rhyming version of the rhyming original.
clearly played . . . culture and economy: *EI*^{2} VIII, pp. 761–2.
the camel was created from the *rimth* bush: Jahiz, part 1, p. 232.
The history of the camel has been much written about: most interestingly by Bulliet.
it was domesticated . . . in the third millennium BC: e.g. Diamond, p. 167.
probably in the south-east of the Arabian Peninsula: e.g. Hoyland, p. 90.
that first datable mention of Arabs – 853 BC: see pp. xxi–xxii, above.
a riding camel . . . buried with its owner: Mas'udi III, p. 149; Lane, *Arabic-English Lexicon*, s.v. *blw*.
bearers of men, stanchers of blood, buyers of women: Suyuti II, p. 455.
the second caliph . . . reach by camel: quoted in Lewis, *Arabs in History*, p. 126.
[Arabs] own the land . . . owning all of it: Mas'udi II, p. 121.
[Arabs] weighed up . . . reason and perception: Mas'udi II, p. 120.
their origins . . . of the settled populations: cf. *EI*^{2} I, p. 872.
[disparate people] joined or mixed together: cf. Lane, *Arabic-English Lexicon*, s.v. *ʿrb*.
many other long-enduring names . . . 'to come together, gather': cf. Hamdani, *Sifah*, p. 197.
Sabaic *hmr*, a 'type of pact, alliance between communities': Beeston *et al.*, s.v. ḤMR II.
'arab originally meant 'desert people, nomads': e.g. Dunlop, pp. 5–6; Hitti, p. 41; Lewis, *Arabs in History*, pp. 2–3.
Some scholars . . . well into the Islamic period: e.g. Retsö, p. 51.
'arab could conceivably mean 'from the west': Retsö, pp. 52–3.
those who entered . . . or his property: Retsö, p. 598 and passim.
we are 'in utter confusion' over the meaning: Husayn, p. 27.
It is doubtful whether the term . . . ethnic sense: Romila Thapar quoted in Keay, p. 19.
both are mobile, migrating . . . eventually fossilizes: on *arya*, see Keay, pp. 20, 24, 34–6, 59, 132, 151 and 153.
perhaps that Semitic root . . . a wider, 'Afroasiatic' family: for different views see Owens, *Handbook*, pp. 15–16.
two verb paradigms . . . recorded in AD 2005: Owens, *Linguistic History*, pp. 29–30.
Greek *kalam*^{os} . . . Arabic *sayf*, 'sword': cf. Gelder, p. 400, n. 717.
a pre-Semitic 'Mediterranean substratum': Giovanni Garbini in Daum, p. 105.
a 'dialect bundle' . . . North Arabian: Macdonald, *Development*, pp. 16–17.
The distinguishing feature . . . '*al-*' definite article: Hoyland, p. 201.
Herodotus, who says that 'Alilat' . . . deity of the Arabs: Hoyland, p. 607.
the graffito of the grieving S^{1}lm: p. 36, above.
Even the Prophet Muhammad . . . those who used it: an example is preserved in the *hadith*, *Laysa mina 'm-birri 'm-ṣiyāmu fi 'm-safar*, 'It is not part of piety to fast while travelling.' Hibshi, p. 22.
a tomb inscription of AD 267 . . . with Nabataean touches: Healey and Smith, *passim*, Macdonald, *Development*, p. 19.
the oldest known Arabic . . . an otherwise Aramaic text: Versteegh, *Arabic Language*, p. 32.
some very old . . . features: e.g. Versteegh, *Arabic Language*, pp. 18–21 and 24.
after the debacle at Babel . . . across the land: Mas'udi II, pp. 132–6.
80 for 'honey': Suyuti I, pp. 320–1.
200 for 'beard', 500 for 'lion': Suyuti I, p. 257.
800 for 'sword': Chejne, p. 10.
1,000 for 'camel': Hitti, p. 22.
an old saw amongst Arabists . . . is not entirely untrue: e.g. *rāsh*, 'to eat much, to eat little, a camel with hairy ears'. Hava, s.v. *rwsh*.
the droppings of bustards . . . by loudness: Tha'alibi, pp. 92–3.
the sound of locusts eating: Tha'alibi, p. 152.

the spaces between the fingers: Tha'alibi, p. 66.
no fewer than fifty Arabic dialects . . . Qur'anic vocabulary: al-Wasiti cited in Rabin, *Ancient West-Arabian*, chapter 3. Cf. Suyuti I, pp. 209–12.
The Arab tongue . . . that person be a prophet: Suyuti I, p. 53.
no one can know . . . what was and what shall be: Jahiz, part 2, pp. 11–12.
Robert Hoyland sees language . . . first millennium BC: Hoyland, p. 230.
the most important condition of *'arab* identity: Hoyland, p. 254, n. 1.
An improved type of camel saddle was developed: Versteegh, *Arabic Language*, p. 24.
the graffiti . . . in what is now Lebanon: Hoyland, p. 65.
on a corridor wall . . . in Roman Pompeii: Gysens, *passim*.

CHAPTER 2 PEOPLES AND TRIBES

It was the seat . . . '*thib*' means 'be seated': Yaqut, s.v. Ẓafār.
If a Tamimi [Arab] comes . . . in his father's loins: Abu Nuwas, pp. 510–11.
the islamized Himyari . . . pious king concludes: Mas'udi II, p. 305.
the proto-Sabaeans . . . well after 2000 BC: Knauf, p. 84.
is the survivor . . . around 1200 BC: Knauf, p. 79.
Other analyses . . . in the Fertile Crescent: e.g. Walter W. Müller in Daum, p. 49.
some scholars . . . beginnings of South Arabian civilization: e.g. Maigret, pp. 220–4.
these peoples formed . . . in South Arabia: cf. Beeston, *Descriptive Grammar*, p. 1.
The virtuous circle . . . touched on: pp. 24–5, above.
the earliest Sabaic inscriptions . . . for rain: Daum, p. 49.
the last Sabaic inscriptions . . . occupying the south: *Mawsu'ah*, s.v. Abrahah.
give as an offering . . . of their villages: Iryani, p. 287.
its 'two gardens' mentioned in the Qur'an: Qur'an, 34:15.
The depth of the deposits . . . work of irrigation: *EI*[2] VI, p. 559.
the two gardens covered 9,600 hectares . . . expanse: *EI*[2] VI, p. 563.
They came in . . . the summer rains: Hoyland, pp. 137 and 161.
The conditions . . . in other pilgrimages across Arabia: Hoyland, p. 161.
the House of Ilmaqah: Iryani, p. 339.
he may have been . . . of vegetation: Giovanni Garbini in *EI*[2] VIII, p. 665.
one scholar has seen . . . sun deity: Jacques Ryckmans in Daum, p. 107.
The Sabaeans . . . 'worship the sun': Qur'an, 27:24.
the Sabaic verb *wqh*, 'to command': Beeston *et al.*, s.v. WQH.
represents . . . the collective will of the *sha'b*: Beeston, 'Kingship', p. 262.
The Sabaeans were . . . 'children' of Ilmaqah: Beeston, 'Kingship', p. 267.
Sam'ay's own patron . . . pilgrimage to Marib: Robin, p. 96; Ghul, p. 147.
Ta'lab also reminds . . . on each of two days: Ghul, p. 148.
Ta'lab even tells . . . several centuries later: Ghul, p. 152.
al-Hamdani . . . pre-Islamic struggles: cf. Wilson p. 23.
over a hundred places . . . South Arabian inscriptions: Abd Allah, p. 341.
sanctuaries . . . define group unities: Iryani, p. 447.
the title *mkrb* . . . as 'unifier': Iryani, p. 330.
the role . . . as head of the Commonwealth: Beeston, 'Kingship', pp. 264–5, cf. Beeston in *EI*[2] IV, p. 747.
he established every . . . alliance: Serjeant, *South Arabian Hunt*, p. 109, n. 358.
and hold fast . . . divided among yourselves: Qur'an, 3:103.
the Muslim community . . . as its basis: Hitti, p. 120.
Pliny the Elder . . . merchant's expenses: Mackintosh-Smith, *Yemen*, p. 39.
finds of Sabaean products . . . as early as 800 BC: Hoyland, pp. 38–9.
an altar to the god . . . in the second century BC: Dunlop, p. 7.
mummified, . . . to his home country: *EI*[2] I, p. 887.
the compiler of the Greek *Periplus* . . . Red Sea: Mackintosh-Smith, *Yemen*, p. 143.
an Arabian 'nation far off' . . . the Sabaeans: Joel, 3:8.
the Nabataeans . . . spoke a form of Arabic: Macdonald, 'Nomads', p. 381; Macdonald, *Development*, p. 19.

prince Wahballat . . . 'Caesar Wahballat Augustus': Hoyland, pp. 1930–4.
claiming descent from Cleopatra: Hoyland, p. 75–6.
Iam pridem Syrus . . . and ways of life: Juvenal, *Satires*, no. 3, l. 62.
The Nabataean realm was annexed by Rome in AD 106: Hoyland, p. 73.
Palmyra . . . took it over in AD 272: Hoyland, pp. 74–5 and 76.
They should have pondered . . . who disturbed it: Ibn Khallikan II, p. 73.
In time, *nabat* . . . an antonym to *'arab*: *EI*[2] VII, p. 836; Jahiz, part 1, p. 227.
clashes between *rm* . . . (Philippus): Macdonald, 'Nomads', pp. 341–2.
its importance . . . emerged in the 1970s: Abd Allah, p. 266.
Ijl ibn Sa'd al-Lat . . . Athtar Shariqan: Hoyland, p. 232.
that oldest known Arabic . . . rhythm: Hoyland, pp. 211-12; pp. 42–3, above.
a Greek history . . . *odai*, 'popular songs': *EI*[2] IX, pp. 225–6.
the archive of . . . their nobility: Ibn Khaldun, *Muqaddimah*, p. 330.
Turbans . . . are their archives: Suyuti I, p. 273. The 'girdles' are shawls or belts bound about the loins by a person squatting, so he can maintain his squatting position.
One theory . . . a mystical, oracular tongue: Retsö, p. 40.
the original meaning . . . that which others cannot: Suyuti II, p. 416.
'Go!' urged al-Shanfara . . . flees by night: Irwin, p. 19.
mutual borrowing . . . in Najd: Versteegh, *Arabic Language*, p. 39.
to use the terms . . . *Kulturnation* was forming: cf. Grunebaum, p. 5.
Mecca . . . best of all in Arab speech: Suyuti I, p. 166.
the *a'rab* . . . and its *hjr*-people [townspeople]: Abd Allah, p. 286.
the third century AD . . . a purely epigraphic language: *EI*[2] VIII, p. 663.
the learned Yemeni . . . Sabaic features: Rabin, *Ancient West-Arabian*, chapter 5.
South Arabians were forbidden . . . script: Ibn Khallikan II, p. 163–4.
he shall be a wild ass . . . against him: Genesis, 16:12.
The Assyrians . . . fondness of Arabs for raiding: *EI*[2] I, p. 525.
Arab Banksys . . . prayers for booty: *EI*[2] VII, pp. 761–2.
usually a quarter . . . of any particularly desirable items: *EI*[2] II, p. 1005.
the Sanskrit word for 'cow' . . . that for 'war': Keay, p. 25.
Fertility . . . to eat up anyone weaker: Jahiz, part 1, p. 232.
You may criticize me . . . dearer far to me than old: Shaykhu, p. 769.
Urwah ibn al-Ward . . . raiding to support themselves: Shaykhu, pp. 892–906.
an eleventh-century Arab . . . no notice of them: Ibn Khallikan III, p. 135.
the man who . . . ruled my adoptive country: see pp. 504–6, below.
His hands filled . . . the Arabs fell under his sway: Shaykhu, p. 144.
Allah, when He wished . . . borne home on your back: Mas'udi II, p. 227.
Recently discovered . . . major wet period: Harrigan, pp. 2–11.
Undoubted horses . . . perhaps to 2000 BC: Harrigan, pp. 7–9.
Horses for riding . . . of the last millennium BC: *EI*[2] I, p. 884.
a period . . . fourth to second centuries BC: Hoyland, p. 188.
like camels . . . with deceased warriors: Hoyland, p. 175; cf. p. 37, above.
a passing mention . . . in Bahrain: Baladhuri, p. 85.
By the running horses . . . to the dawn raid: Qur'an, 100: 1–3.
charging, fleet-fleeing . . . high by the torrent: quoted in Irwin, p. 10.
some tribes could field . . . the Horseman or Cavalier: *EI*[2] IV, p. 1144.
The combination . . . second to fourth centuries AD: *EI*[2] I, p. 884.
South Arabian states . . . fielded only footsoldiers: Iryani, p. 242.
On clouded nights . . . smiling all the way: Ibn Khallikan III, p. 216.
the invention . . . of the saddlebow: Versteegh, *Arabic Language*, p. 24.
to begin with . . . made of wood: Jahiz, part 2, p. 9.
one of the best aids for . . . striking with a sword: Jahiz, part 2, p. 7.
the fall of Petra . . . disturbed peninsular trade: cf. Piotrovsky, pp. 158–9.
The Arabs were always . . . power to the Age: Rogan, p. 8.
a developed form . . . becoming Arabic: Bellamy, p. 33.

The Namarah epitaph is . . . standard, unified Arabic: Abd Allah, p. 293; Owens, *Linguistic History*, pp. 20–1.
'This', it begins . . . the seventh day of Kislul: quoted in Hoyland, p. 79.
Later Arab historians . . . in Persian-dominated Iraq: e.g. Mas'udi II, p. 98.
a Persian inscription . . . of the Sasanian empire: Hoyland, p. 79.
he and at least part . . . had 'gone over' to Rome: EI^2 V, p. 632.
one Arab historian . . . become a Christian: al-Tabari in Hoyland, p. 79.
he appointed as viceroys . . . Romans: after Bellamy, in Versteegh, *Arabic Language*, p. 31.
Procopius . . . leaders in this period: Sizgorich, p. 1012.
the British promoted . . . Sharif Husayn of Mecca: Atiyah, p. 133.
stuck . . . between two lions, Persia and Rome: Qatadah quoted in Kister, p. 143.

CHAPTER 3 SCATTERED FAR AND WIDE

this might well be . . . Imru' al-Qays's epitaph: Abd Allah, p. 275.
Shammar . . . far north and east into Arabia: *Mawsu'ah*, s.v. Shammār.
the Himyari . . . 'Shammar destroyed it': e.g. Ibn Khallikan II, p. 262.
he had led Himyaris to Tibet: Mackintosh-Smith, *Yemen*, pp. 33 and 46.
Along the way . . . called Madhhij: Hoyland, p. 79.
Madhhij . . . moved south en masse: Abd Allah, p. 276.
King of Saba . . . Arabs of the Highlands and Lowlands: Daum, p. 52.
to pursue vendettas . . . was destruction: Iryani, p. 329.
Ibn Khaldun observed . . . North Africa: Ibn Khaldun, *Muqaddimah*, p. 119.
The Sabaeans . . . word was gathered: Mas'udi II, p. 181.
the trouble began . . . fifty men could not have rolled: Mas'udi II, p. 186–7.
There was for Saba . . . far and wide: Qur'an, 34:15–16 and 19.
final, irreparable breach . . . in the seventh century: EI^2 VI, pp. 563–4.
the infiltration . . . over the two preceding centuries: EI^2 VI, p. 564.
'these human rats' . . . its last [independent] state: Iryani, p. 329.
a great diaspora . . . pre-Islamic damburst: EI^2 VI, p. 564.
The kings . . . both *badw* and *hadar* dwell: Hamdani, *Sifah*, p. 325.
Tarifah . . . led the migration of her people, Ghassan: Abid, part 2, p. 287. Tarifah appears in some sources, with a letter-dot, as Zarifah.
the unveiling of meaning: Jahiz, part 1, p. 35.
By the truth of . . . what is recited by me: Abid, part 2, p. 290.
the story of the Marib Dam . . . Arab 'national' epic: Hoyland, p. 233.
nations . . . getting history wrong: quoted in Suleiman, p. 27.
there were large-scale tribal movements across Arabia: EI^2 I, p. 528.
tribes recognizable . . . Strabo and Pliny: Hoyland, pp. 26 and 231.
if they strap . . . on their horses: quoted in Jahiz, part 1, pp. 203–4.
You shall be fugitives . . . children's land: quoted in Ajami, *Dream Palace*, p. 70.
the Assyrians' *Aribi* . . . 'neither overseers nor officials': p. 30, above.
Most of Ghassan . . . freedom and poverty: Abid, part 2, pp. 294–7.
beginning with . . . the exalted title *basileus*, 'king': Hoyland, p. 81.
Most of them . . . differed from imperial orthodoxy: EI^2 II, pp. 1020–1.
they led a semi-mobile life . . . fixed capital: Nicholson, pp. 53–4.
al-Jabiyah . . . included a monastery: EI^2 II, p. 360.
they maintained . . . Aramaic for writing: Hitti, p. 78.
they wrote in Nabataean . . . of the region: Hoyland, pp. 241–2.
the later Ghassanid . . . performed in '*rumiyyah*': EI^2 IV, p. 820.
Eugene Rogan's insight . . . empowering Arabs: p. 66, above.
from the Syriac . . . 'encampment': EI^2 II, p. 360.
Byzantine influence . . . many of their people: EI^2 III, p. 462.
an aged sage . . . arabized Nabataeans: Jahiz, part 1, p. 227.
In about 544 . . . put him to death in revenge: Hitti, p. 79.

the Lakhmid rulers . . . stop the incursions: Kister, p. 153.
The Lakhmids . . . raiding with trading: Kister, pp. 155–6, 161–2 and 167.
speaking Arabic but writing in Syriac: Hitti, p. 84.
they used the Nabataean script: Hoyland, pp. 241–2.
used by Adam to write on clay tablets: Suyuti II, p. 293.
the 'Preserved Tablet': Qur'an, 85:22.
The more down-to-earth . . . Iraq: Kurdi, pp. 18–19 and 41.
they grew . . . out of Nabataean script: Macdonald, *Development*, pp. 20–1.
with influences from other . . . writing systems: Jones, Review of Beatrice Gruendler, p. 429.
very few graffiti . . . earlier than the fifth century: Versteegh, *Arabic Language*, p. 33.
it reached Mecca 'a little before Islam': Ibn Khallikan II, pp. 163–4.
fewer than a score of Meccans could write: Baladhuri, p. 453.
An experiment by . . . Hisham: Jahiz, part 1, p. 299.
marked by relics dim . . . on ancient stone: Nicholson, p. 120.
it helps to know . . . to read it: cf. Haeri, p. 74, and Shouby, p. 297.
unvowelled and undotted . . . read in 300 ways: 300 sounds a lot, but the first stalk could represent five possible consonants, each with three possible short vowels, the second pair of stalks another five consonants and three vowels plus the no-vowel sign, and (5 × 3) × (5 × 4) = 300.
written Arabic is . . . a 'foreign' language: cf. Ibn Khaldun, *Muqaddimah*, pp. 439–41.
This may have been going on since . . . Amr ibn Adi: *EI*² IX, p. 450.
the evolving 'high' language . . . in central Arabia: p. 60, above.
healthy competition . . . in 'collecting' poets: *EI*² IX, p. 226.
the later part of the sixth century was its high point: cf. *EI*² VIII, p. 119.
al-Nabighah's description . . . let it be thus: Mas'udi II, pp. 99–100.
one of the kings of al-Hirah . . . when in *wudu'*: Shaykhu, p. 417.
gave orders . . . those of al-Basrah: Suyuti I, p. 197.
the elusive original sense . . . different origins: pp. 38–9, above.
linguistic 'nationalism' . . . century onwards: e.g. Suleiman, p. 32.
Arabs love their language . . . in a way less human: Jabiri, p. 75.
Thinking . . . employed by Arabs: Ibn Khaldun, *Muqaddimah*, pp. 419–20.
Abu Hayyan . . . the syntax of reason: quoted in Jabiri, p. 258.
I think in Arabic . . . therefore I am an Arab: quoted in Suleiman, p. 121.
I'm an Arab . . . I'm no good at foreign gabble!: Jahiz, part 1, p. 207.
big blocs . . . Byzantines or Persians: cf. Hoyland, p. 240.
the now ailing Himyari . . . 'king of the Arabs': *EI*² I, p. 526.
When the *'arab* became one . . . cast in one instant: slightly adapted from the quotation in Retsö, pp. 21–2.

CHAPTER 4 ON THE EDGE OF GREATNESS

to track a tribe like Anazah . . . cousins still live: *EI*² I, pp. 482–3.
who we sense are still here . . . never once fallen: Jabiri, pp. 38–9.
the Himyari King Yusuf . . . in about the year 518: Daum, p. 53.
the event is commemorated . . . in the Qur'an: Qur'an, 85:4–10.
raids by *'arab* tribes . . . had been increasing: e.g. Iryani, pp. 136–8.
central state rulers relied . . . for protection: Iryani, p. 46.
a late Himyari inscription . . . in a united kingdom: Iryani, pp. 324 and 345.
King Yusuf . . . into the waves: Mackintosh-Smith, *Yemen*, p. 42.
One of these is recorded . . . the year 552: Hoyland, p. 55. Other dates are proposed, e.g. 547 in Daum, p. 53.
'Chapter of the Elephant' . . . armed with pebbles: Qur'an, 105.
he reigned 260 years or . . . rather less than that: Mas'udi II, p. 78.
Aren't the cattle of al-Sawad . . . a vile abomination: Mas'udi II, pp. 100–1.
A people's fortunes . . . kings are Persians: quoted in Suleiman, p. 236.
There is even an idea . . . Persian presence in Arabia: Retsö, p. 17.

a hereditary line . . . West Africa: cf. Jahiz, part 1, p. 147.
the role of the poet . . . their emulators for cash: Jahiz, part 1, pp. 105–6.
The force was . . . supernatural inspiration: cf. Nicholson, p. 73.
captured poets . . . being slaughtered: Shaykhu, p. 79.
enemy orators . . . wrecking their enunciation: Jahiz, part 1, p. 134.
deadlier . . . in the dark of night: Jahiz, part 1, p. 117.
We have cut off his hand . . . Khusraw's battle-banners!: Shaykh Muhammad bin Rashid Al Maktum, ode beginning *Usūd al-jazīrah ḥimāt al-diyār*, 2015. baraqish.net accessed 7 November 2015.
The title . . . of the ancient Hebrew *kōhēn*: *EI*[2] IV, p. 421.
their ability to divine . . . 'rolled up like a gown': Mas'udi II, p. 179.
prophets connect . . . falsehood: Ibn Khaldun, *Muqaddimah*, p. 80.
a 'word-gathering' role: cf. Rabin, *Ancient West-Arabian*, chapter 11, n. 6; Lane, *Arabic-English Lexicon*, s.v. *zʿm*.
their own raiding and plundering increased: e.g. Iryani, p. 151.
the total dead . . . for three years of hostilities: Shaykhu, p. 526.
a clumsy-hoofed she-camel called . . . 'Mirage': Lane, *Arabic-English Lexicon*, s.v. *srb*.
But now such folk . . . to tear!: Nicholson's translation, Nicholson, p. 57.
'War! *War!* . . . filled with its roar!: Shaykhu, p. 241; Nicholson's translation, Nicholson, p. 60.
The forty-year roar . . . intervention of the Lakhmid king: Hitti, p. 90.
much of the account . . . Islamic-era squabbles: Husayn, p. 240.
the War of Dahis . . . cheating in a horse race: Nicholson, p. 61.
You have sundered . . . what you've done: Shaykhu, p. 155.
a list of towns . . . two opposing factions: Hamdani, *Sifah*, p. 237.
he had appointed . . . killed a third brother: Shaykhu, pp. 1–6.
an old-fashioned . . . tribal poet-lord: *EI*[2] IX, pp. 115 and 226.
the Servant of [the sky-god] Qays: cf. *EI*[2] IV, pp. 803–4.
breastbone burnished . . . hairpins stray: translation in Mackintosh-Smith, 'Interpreter of Treasures: A Portrait Gallery', p. 39.
Imru' al-Qays is the forerunner . . . made it flow: Suyuti II, p. 405.
the last ruler . . . before Islam: Abd Allah, p. 296.
a lot of Imru' al-Qays's biography . . . ibn al-Ash'ath: Husayn, pp. 206–7.
from Hadramawt to Asia Minor to Bahrain: cf. Imru' al-Qays, pp. 55–60.
Have I not worn out . . . glittering of mirage?: Imru' al-Qays, p. 43.
The young Imru' al-Qays . . . 'vagabonds': Imru' al-Qays, p. 5.
poetry . . . is free from ideology: Adonis, *Poetics*, p. 72.
the most notable . . . that of Sufism: Adonis, *Thabit IV*, p. 163.
rode to the place . . . gnawed at his flesh: translated in Mackintosh-Smith, 'Interpreter of Treasures: Food and Drink', p. 40.
a sayer of words . . . to the farthest bounds: Irwin, p. 19.
Sons of my mother . . . jackal with long hair: Irwin, p. 19.
the absolute individualism . . . all around it: Dunlop, p. 28.
the case of Urwah ibn al-Ward: pp. 62–3, above.
All those wealthy chiefs . . . in my hand before I ask: Shaykhu, p. 906.
eternity in men and women: Whitman, p. 335.
was so revered . . . young and old, could recite it: Shaykhu, p. 203.
Arab unity is a madman's notion . . . a fair parallel: quoted in Karsh, p. 8.
metrical units . . . 'tent, room, house': cf. Adonis, *Poetics*, pp. 25–6.
the Persians left . . . those who came before them: Pellat, p. 132.
A line of poetry . . . uninhabited is no good: Gelder, p. 278.
A few critics . . . the entire canon: cf. Husayn, *passim*.
the descriptions . . . are most admirable: Lane, *Arabic-English Lexicon* I, p. x.
one hungry chilly dusk . . . in the fold: Imru' al-Qays, p. 81.
those who, like the clan . . . protection in his wanderings: Imru' al-Qays, p. 141.
Himyari . . . itching from the crupper: Imru' al-Qays, p. 80.

the parallel idea of *hasab* . . . future generations: cf. *EI*^{2} III, p. 239.
the obligation to follow . . . one's ancestors: Grunebaum, p. 15.
Buddhist *dharma* . . . society on track: cf. Keay, pp. 97 and 149.
Quraysh . . . ancestors in the pre-Islamic Ka'bah: Mas'udi II, p. 278.
You can deny God . . . the Prophet: quoted in *EI*^{2} VII, p. 377.
a love and a lodging . . . the trace is obliterated?: Irwin, p. 7.
many of the Safaitic graffiti . . . loved ones: *EI*^{2} VIII, p. 762.
al-A'sha . . . advertisements for plainer girls: Shaykhu, pp. 360–1.
Contestants . . . duelled in verse: *EI*^{2} IX, p. 226.
Where now are Thamud . . . this din of yours: Jahiz, part 1, p. 131.
his super-tribal importance . . . Sage of the Arabs: Mas'udi I, p. 69.
It was the Prophet . . . without exception: Jahiz, part 1, pp. 25–6.
There is on the face of the earth . . . to protect you: Gelder, p. 111. Here *din* is translated as 'religion'.
founded a collective memory: Hoyland, pp. 242–3.
a large part . . . wellspring of our imagination: Adonis, *Poetics*, p. 32.
supra-tribal . . . ethno-cultural group: Versteegh, *Arabic Language*, p. 37.
a mythical land . . . we all agreed to dream: Rushdie, pp. 129–30.
When their descendants . . . exterminated each other: Hamdani, *Sifah*, p. 331.
70,000 youths . . . ruined them for evermore: Shaykhu, pp. 625–39.
I've wept for Zayd . . . how fearful: Abu 'l-Fida', *Mukhtasar* part 1, p. 100.
Both the Byzantines . . . from their own people: Kennedy, pp. 368–9.
Your rule . . . is the pride of every Yemeni: Mas'udi II, p. 108.
personal animosity . . . denunciation: cf. *EI*^{2}, s.v. al-Nuʿmān b. al-Mundhir.
Today the *'arab* have demanded . . . and have won: Shaykhu, p. 136.

CHAPTER 5 REVELATION, REVOLUTION

When Quraysh rebuilt . . . his wisdom: Mas'udi II, pp. 278–9.
Because . . . that had been the Prophet's custom: *EI*^{2} IV, p. 320.
istalama . . . 'gaining security with a deity': Beeston *et al.*, s.v. S^{1}LM.
unworked stones . . . at Bethel in Genesis: Genesis, 28:11–19.
they would select . . . around the Ka'bah: Ibn al-Kalbi, pp. 28–9.
The most binding oaths . . . on sacred stones: e.g. Ibn al-Kalbi, p. 15.
an alliance of Qurashi clans . . . the making of vows: *EI*^{2} III, p. 389.
Abraham's son . . . during the building of the Ka'bah: Hitti, p. 100.
originally white . . . 'Age of Ignorance': *EI*^{2} IV, p. 321.
Muhammad returned . . . once more the Black Stone: Baladhuri, p. 49.
the Islamic-period story . . . divine inspiration: for all these stories, see Mas'udi II, pp. 46–9.
Abd al-Muttalib . . . digging the well out: Mas'udi II, p. 127.
'Macoraba' . . . the site of Mecca: Hitti, p. 103.
a Sabaic word . . . 'temple': Beeston *et al.*, s.v. KRB.
an Arabian toponym . . . between hills: e.g. Piamenta, s.v. *ghrb*.
In the traditional histories . . . fought for control: Mas'udi II, pp. 49–51.
possibly no later than . . . Mudar and Iyad: *EI*^{2}, s.v. Iyād.
it was Khuza'ah . . . the One God: Mas'udi II, p. 56; Ibn Khallikan II, p. 286.
Amr ibn Luhayy . . . from Syria: Mas'udi II, p. 238.
Hubal ('spirit, vapour' in Aramaic): Hitti, p. 100.
something imaginary . . . resulting connection: Ibn Khaldun quoted on p. 26, above.
taqarrasha, 'to gather people together': cf. p. 39, above.
qarsh, 'making money': Ibn Khallikan III, p. 135.
The following verses . . . slither of snakes: Suyuti I, pp. 273–4.
seedy Khuza'i . . . skinful of wine: Mas'udi II, p. 58.
the position of Quraysh . . . Lakhmids and Himyaris: Mas'udi II, pp. 59–60.
they were able to gain . . . routes in general: Ibrahim, p. 344.

Byzantine–Persian hostilities . . . dominated by Mecca: *EI*[2] X, p. 789; Lewis, *Arabs In History*, pp. 29–30.
The network . . . covered much of the peninsula: Serjeant, *South Arabian Hunt*, p. 62.
the new – for Meccans . . . merchant ventures: Kurdi, pp. 59–60.
mudarabah . . . trading ever further away: Ibrahim, p. 344.
winter and summer journeys: Qur'an, 106:2.
Ma'in . . . close relations with Gaza: Mackintosh-Smith, *Yemen*, p. 39.
Muhammad's uncle . . . during the pilgrimage: Lecker, p. 349.
Amr ibn al-As . . . rich land of the Nile: cf. Kennedy, p. 73.
Abu Sufyan . . . in what is now Lebanon: Baladhuri, p. 131.
The old everyday dialect . . . far from high Arabic: cf. Ferguson.
as late as . . . South Arabian tongues: Rabin, *Ancient West-Arabian*, chapter. 1.
selected . . . innate linguistic ability: Ibn Faris quoted in Suyuti I, p. 166.
rain on parched earth: Gelder, p. 199.
15,000–20,000 by the early seventh century: Atiyah, p. 21.
its Qur'anic title of *umm al-qura*: e.g. Qur'an, 6:92.
the Ethiopians . . . on the Day of the Elephant: see p. 90, above.
the mountain of Arafat . . . local side-show: *EI*[2] III, pp. 31–2.
tribal groups . . . totemic animal: Ibn al-Kalbi, pp. 4-6; *EI*[2] IX, p. 424.
One interpretation . . . the area around Mount Arafat: *EI*[2] XI, p. 441.
the pilgrimage fell in . . . a three-month truce: *EI*[2] III, pp. 31–2.
Muslim geographers . . . 'the navel of the earth': Yaqut, s.v. al-Ka[c]bah.
the same term . . . sacred stone: Hornblower and Spawforth, s.v. omphalos.
a womb that expands . . . numbers of pilgrims: e.g. Ibn Jubayr, p. 148.
at a cost of 100 *dirhams* . . . the arrows drawn: *EI*[2] IV, pp. 263–4.
Qusayy . . . al-Lat, Manat and al-Uzza: *EI*[2] V, p. 692.
a pair of statues . . . turned to stone: Ibn al-Kalbi, p. 8.
the Ka'bah . . . gallery of Quraysh ancestors: Mas'udi II, p. 278; see p. 104, above.
the meeting-houses . . . all the clans together: Mas'udi II, p. 277.
an image of Jesus and Mary . . . paraphernalia: Harawi, p. 85.
Ka'bah of Najran . . . Christian victims: *EI*[2] VII, p. 872.
Ka'bah of Sindad . . . seems to be known: Ibn al-Kalbi, pp. 38–9.
We've been the family of Allah . . . long past: Mas'udi II, p. 129.
The 'Comforter' . . . to console the world: New Testament, John, 14:16.
is interpreted . . . as Muhammad: cf. Qur'an, 61:6.
Muhammad is supposed . . . signs of divine grace: Mas'udi I, p. 75.
Abu Bakr . . . declared his prophethood: Ibn Khallikan II, p. 32.
Satih, the supposedly boneless seer: p. 93, above.
a Persian nobleman's . . . birth is nigh: Ibshihi, pp. 467–8.
the later the sources . . . the life of the Prophet: *EI*[2] IX, p. 662.
Collectors of *hadiths* . . . 5,000 are supposed to be reliable: the figure of a million is ascribed to Ahmad ibn Hanbal (Ibn Khallikan I, p. 40). Al-Bukhari is said to have collected a slightly more credible 600,000 (Ibn Khallikan II, p. 324). Abu Dawud weeded out his own half million and came up with 4,800 'sound' *hadiths* (Ibn Khallikan I, p. 383).
Muhammad himself forbade . . . that far: Mas'udi II, p. 270.
beyond Ma'add . . . the record was unreliable: Mas'udi II, p. 274.
'Genealogists,' he said bluntly, 'tell lies': Mas'udi II, p. 270.
from a poorer clan of Quraysh: *EI*[2] VI, p. 146.
the two grandsons . . . cut bloodily apart with a sword: *EI*[2] X, p. 841.
the Umayyad line . . . free-for-all: Ibrahim, p. 347.
the Umayyads . . . the ruling elite of Quraysh: Ibrahim, p. 353.
By some accounts, he spoke Ethiopic: *EI*[2] VII, p. 862.
Muhammad was sent . . . Sa'd ibn Bakr: Lane, *Arabic-English Lexicon* I, p. vii.
late Sabaic inscription . . . wet-nursed by nomadic *a'rab*: Iryani, p. 138.
Caliph Abd al-Malik . . . to the *badiyah*: Jahiz, part 1, p. 251.

as late as the 1920s . . . *badiyah* boarding school: EI^2 VI, p. 160.
They are not *a'rab* . . . people of their *qariyah*: quoted in Abd Allah, p. 294.
It has been claimed . . . their nomad neighbours: e.g. EI^2 VI, pp. 145–6.
the elect wear silk . . . youthful cupbearers: e.g. Qur'an, 76:12–21.
Its gardens are watered . . . underground: e.g. Qur'an, 61:12.
he had named one of them Abd Manaf . . . Abu Talib: EI^2 VII, p. 362.
he sacrificed . . . to the goddess al-Uzza: Ibn al-Kalbi, pp. 16–17.
Muhammad began emulating . . . overlooking Mecca: EI^2 X, p. 98.
he told his wife . . . that he was turning into a *kahin*: Karsh, p. 11.
the diagnosis of . . . Umar: EI^2 VIII, p. 93.
His *shaytan* . . . is keeping him waiting!: EI^2 IX, p. 407.
iqra' . . . revealed by Gabriel to Muhammad: Qur'an, 96:1.
I am no reciter: Kilito, pp. xix–xx.
according to Ibn Hisham's biography . . . both senses: EI^2 VIII, p. 96.
the hymnist Caedmon . . . 'I cannot sing': James Sutherland (ed.), *The Oxford Book of Literary Anecdotes*, Oxford, 1975, p. 1.
compared to Isaiah's angel . . . with a burning coal: EI^2 IX, p. 450.
it is enough to compare . . . birds in the air: quoted in Jones, 'Qur'an'.
By the sun . . . veiling it: Qur'an, 91:1–10.
Muhammad would . . . distance himself from them: Jahiz, part 1, pp. 123 and 124.
There can be no *kahin*hood after prophethood: EI^2 V 99.
This is indeed the word . . . how little you reflect!: Qur'an, 69:40–2.
Do you not see . . . that they would never do?: Qur'an, 26:225–6.
Lines attributed . . . like the Day of the Elephant: Shaykhu, pp. 219–31.
On the Day of Resurrection . . . false: Shaykhu, p. 219.
So set your face towards religion . . . people do not know: Qur'an, 30:30.
he was . . . an opponent of Muhammad: Mas'udi I, pp. 70–1.
elegies on those killed in Muhammad's raids: Shaykhu, pp. 222–5.
Orientalists . . . tried to show the opposite: Husayn, pp. 147–52.
that there might well be some authentic material: EI^2 X, p. 839.
I have submitted . . . mountains firm upon it: Shaykhu, pp. 621–2.
Zayd would go . . . to the One God, Allah: EI^2 XI, pp. 474–5.
'Islam' . . . after the move to Medina: EI^2 III, p. 165.
With an alphabet . . . sets out upon a journey: Ascherson, p. 204.
the influences . . . the longest and bloodiest war: Whitman, p. 400.
printed and electronic . . . oral tradition: EI^2 V, p. 426.
Recite! . . . Who has taught by the pen: Qur'an, 96:1–4.
South Arabia . . . priestly scribes: cf. p. 61, above.
By the pen and what they write: Qur'an, 68:1.
the written symbol . . . indicated by it: Ibn Khaldun, *Muqaddimah*, p. 31.
script that fills the ears of him that sees it: quoted in Ibn Khallikan II, p. 51.
seems in itself a form of oratory . . . the visible: Byron, p. 271.
The pen is a second tongue: Jahiz, part 1, p. 37.
The revelations . . . imported papyrus: Rabin, 'Beginnings', p. 28, n. 2.
Umar . . . happened to find in his sister's house: EI^2 VIII, p. 835.
a form of aide-mémoire . . . Muhammad's followers: Schoeler, p. 430.
the scribes of the revelation: Baladhuri, pp. 453–4.
a verse . . . to prompt him: al-Zamakhshari cited in Jones, 'Word Made Visible', pp. 7–8.
one of the scribes . . . descended to criticize him: Baladhuri, pp. 454–5.
earlier ones . . . 'writing, book': Versteegh, *Arabic Language*, p. 55.
Or do you have . . . telling the truth!: Qur'an, 37:156–7.
Muhammad was from . . . a scripture: EI^2 V, p. 403.
the story mentioned . . . predicting his prophethood: p. 124, above.
Abu Bakr's first reaction . . . to write at all: Ibn Khallikan II, p. 32.

Stories . . . some ability to write: e.g. Jones, 'Word Made Visible', pp. 5–6.
Benedict Anderson argues . . . language: Anderson, *passim*.
I could not help . . . knowing how to use it: Lévi-Strauss, p. 300.
It had . . . raised commerce to new levels: cf. Kurdi, pp. 59–60.
by which you . . . ancient script of Himyar: Suyuti II, p. 297.
seventeen Qurashis . . . to include women: Baladhuri, pp. 453–4.
five of them acted as his secretaries: Kurdi, p. 60.
If all the trees . . . would not be exhausted: Qur'an, 31:27.
the commentator . . . doesn't surprise: Jahiz, part 1, p. 153.
Edward Said . . . an Orientalist cliché: cf. Rippin, p. 42.
In it are verses . . . from our Lord: Qur'an, 3:7.
magoi . . . tradition in Media: Hornblower and Spawforth, s.v. magus.
Muhammad compared . . . clang of a bell: Ibn Khaldun, *Muqaddimah*, p. 70.
the ideas . . . are secondary to the words: see p. 12, above.
has denied Muhammad . . . original authors: Gelder, p. xxvii.
is not merely a carrier . . . itself is content: quoted in Kaye, p. 447.
I saw the Almighty . . . without understanding: quoted in Chejne, p. 12.
Ibn Qutaybah . . . speech of the Qur'an: quoted in Adonis, *Thabit* II, p. 172.
The proof . . . together by belief in it: Ibn Khaldun, *Muqaddimah*, pp. 73–4.
If you [Muhammad] had spent . . . Allah has united them: Qur'an, 8:63.
challenged . . . and disabled their minds: Mas'udi II, p. 299.
the first conquest: cf. pp. 5–6, above.
was built on a magical foundation . . . dying: quoted in Adonis, *Thabit* IV, p. 114.
Muhammad . . . on the verge of disappearing: Retsö, p. 626.
'arab . . . guardians of local cults: cf. p. 39, above.
The Qur'an . . . to the Arabic language: quoted in Adonis, *Thabit* IV, p. 114.
the Qur'an is the equivalent . . . of Christ, the Logos: *EI*[2] V, p. 427.
Our [Arab] community . . . lives in a language: al-Marzuqi (aljazeera.net).
The Hijaz . . . in the Mediterranean-Arabian world: cf. *EI*[2] VIII, p. 155.
a tentative early monotheism . . . the God of Heaven: Iryani, p. 412.
a new indigenous monotheism . . . 'the Merciful': Iryani, pp. 395–6.
several Meccan Christians are known by name: e.g. Ubayd Allah b. Jahsh (*EI*[2] VII, pp. 862–3), Adi b. Hatim (Ibn al-Kalbi, p. 52) and Waraqah b.Nawfal (Shaykhu, pp. 616–18).
The *hanif* . . . chapter of the Qur'an: Mas'udi I, pp. 67-8; Mas'udi II, pp. 226–7.
Say, 'He is Allah, One . . . ': Qur'an, 112.
the poet Imru' al-Qays . . . snapped them: Imru' al-Qays, p. 12.
Banu Hanifah had an idol . . . they ate him: Ibshihi, p. 463.
an oath . . . the Christian God: Ibn al-Kalbi, pp. 30–1.
By al-Lat . . . Allah, verily He is greater than both: Ibn al-Kalbi, p. 15.
And if you ask . . . they will surely say, 'Allah': Qur'an, 43:87.
And if you were to ask . . . surely answer, 'Allah': Qur'an, 29:63.
Muhammad's father . . . a hundred camels: *EI*[2] I, p. 42.
most people felt happier . . . via intermediaries: cf. Mas'udi II, p. 126.
The old South Arabians . . . shared deity: cf. pp. 53–4, above.
habl Allah, Allah's uniting and binding covenant: Qur'an, 3:103.
the Sabaean term . . . *hbl*: Serjeant, *South Arabian Hunt*, p. 109, n. 358.
the shared concept . . . his grandson Muhammad put it: for Abd al-Muttalib's words, see p. 124, above. Muhammad's phrase is in Hamdani, *Sifah*, p. 41. Cf. Abu Bakr quoted in Jahiz, part 3, p. 114.
Muhammad began . . . two years into the revelations: *EI*[2] V, p. 411.
Say . . . the Most Beautiful Names: Qur'an, 17:110.
In the name of Allah, al-Rahman, al-Rahim: Qur'an, 1:1.
'Al-Bari' . . . attributes of the One God: Iryani, p. 414.
they, too, were increasingly . . . Zoroastrian: cf. Hoyland, p. 27.
To understand . . . the key to Arab history: cf. pp. 12–13, above.

And if your Lord . . . will not cease to disagree: Qur'an, 11:118.
they would spend . . . the night awake in prayer vigils: *EI*^{2} X, p. 97.
Woe to every slanderer . . . cast into the crushing Fire!: Qur'an, 104:1–4.
Ibn Hisham tells . . . the community: quoted in Adonis, *Thabit* II, p. 170.
a whole chapter . . . of hellfire: Qur'an, 111.
a son of Abu Bakr . . . in the coming Raid of Badr: *EI*^{2} I, p. 110.

CHAPTER 6 GOD AND CAESAR

Abu Sufyan . . . with their braided locks!: cf. p. 2, above.
But I have never seen . . . his sputum: Ma'arri, p. 37.
O Allah . . . the ties of blood!: al-Tabari quoted in Nicholson, p. 158.
'severance' is what it meant to the Meccans: *EI*^{2}, s.v. Hidjra.
some early activists . . . almost as apostasy: Crone, *passim*.
Muhammad had first . . . fallen through: Nicholson, p. 158.
his father's father . . . his own Yathribi mother's house: *EI*^{2} I, p. 80.
a sort of loose garden city . . . shelter from attack: *EI*^{2} V, p. 994.
legend sees . . . Nebuchadnezzar's campaigns: Baladhuri, p. 25.
Medina was conquered by the Qur'an: Baladhuri, p. 17.
One of his first acts . . . tax-free zone: Baladhuri, p. 24.
the traditional market-day . . . congregational prayers: *EI*^{2} VII, p. 368.
The simple mosque . . . palm-frond awnings: Baladhuri, p. 16.
much of its shape . . . Jewish scripture: see on this e.g. Hitti, pp. 125–6.
it confirms the book of Moses in the Arabic tongue: Qur'an, 46:12.
Muhammad's message . . . a true religion: Carmichael, p. 53.
Ritual ablutions . . . at Marib and elsewhere: Doe, pp. 163 and 166f.
it seems the southerners . . . to Yathrib: cf. Qur'an, 9:108; Baladhuri, p. 14.
The usual 'Orientalist' take . . . Muhammad: *EI*^{2} VII, p. 368; cf. Hitti, p. 118.
The new polity . . . taking decisions: cf. *EI*^{2} V, pp. 995–6.
most such alliances . . . performed around fire: *EI*^{2} III, pp. 388–9.
Abd al-Muttalib . . . hung it up in the Ka'bah: Schoeler, p. 425.
The pagan Meccans . . . 'the family of Allah': p. 124, above.
the new community is fathered . . . the first monotheist: Qur'an, 22:78.
Muhammad's own wives . . . 'mothers' of the community: Qur'an, 33:6.
closer to the believers than their own selves: Qur'an, 33:6.
these dissidents . . . adopted Christianity: Baladhuri, pp. 13–14.
Muhammad's original Constitution . . . its polytheists: *EI*^{2} VII, p. 367.
Kulayb . . . set off the War of the Camel's Udder: pp. 94–5, above.
the traditional tribal grazing-grounds . . . the *ummah*: *EI*^{2} XII, p. 694.
submitted their faces . . . the Meccan Ka'bah: cf. the verses by Zayd ibn Amr, p. 132, above.
O you who believe . . . surely he is one of them: Qur'an, 5:51.
the expulsion in 626 . . . the survivors were expelled: Hitti, p. 117.
Qur'anic verses descended in justification: cf. e.g. Baladhuri, p. 28.
The latter are clearly historical . . . to modern conditions: Allawi, p. 130.
when they could work . . . north of Medina: Baladhuri, p. 43.
overlook . . . with gracious forgiveness: Qur'an, 15:85.
Anthropology . . . as violent and uncivil: Varisco, p. 10.
never . . . so impressive as this: Burton, closing words of chapter XXXI.
Whatsoever . . . your Lord will remain: Qur'an, 55:26–7.
There were almost thirty . . . a third of them: Mas'udi II, pp. 287–8.
they belong to . . . the 'Days of the Arabs': cf. *EI*^{2} IX, p. 661.
a son of Abu Bakr . . . on the pagan Meccan side: p. 146, above.
So did al-Abbas . . . dynasty of caliphs: *EI*^{2} I, p. 9.
We are the Tariq girls . . . love you: quoted in Gelder, p. 94.
another uncle . . . gnawed his liver: *EI*^{2} VII, p. 264.

the angel Gabriel . . . an outmoded *jinni*: Husayn, p. 116.
Hassan eulogizing . . . fine wine and kisses: Ma'arri, p. 167.
Throw dust in the faces of the panegyrists: Mas'udi II, p. 300.
A'sha Qays . . . life of Medina: Shaykhu, pp. 365–6.
the only prophet . . . made licit: Jahiz, part 3, p. 114.
its chapter called 'The Spoils of War': Qur'an, 8. See e.g. 8:41.
warnings of hellfire . . . no one cheated: Qur'an, 3:162.
those whose hearts are reconciled: Qur'an, 9:60.
Do prophets come with a sword?: cf. the title of David Sizgorich in *American Historical Review*.
hijrah would come . . . garrison towns: Hoyland, p. 102; Crone, p. 367.
One authority bluntly glosses *hijrah* . . . as 'military service': EI^2 II, p. 1006.
an aim of 'de-islamizing' Arab history: p. 5, above.
in Samir Kassir's opinion . . . its current malaise: Kassir, pp. 34 and 92.
Islam . . . 'unseparated Siamese twins': Pintak, p. 202.
Banu Shaybah . . . sacristans of the goddess al-Uzza: Ibshihi, p. 464.
were granted the keys . . . to the Ka'bah today: EI^2 IV, p. 320.
The Shaybah clan . . . opening the Ka'bah: EI^2 IX, p. 389.
in the case of al-Taif . . . to invest the town in 631: Baladhuri, p. 63.
Muhammad's Qurashi ancestors . . . the peninsula: cf. Serjeant, *South Arabian Hunt*, p. 62.
The only phenomenon . . . a political system: Lévi-Strauss, p. 299.
public announcements . . . fixed to the wall of the Ka'bah: EI^2 VIII, p. 835.
Medina also had a recent tradition of literacy: Kurdi, pp. 60–1.
he gave orders . . . how to write: Kurdi, p. 61.
a *hadith* . . . dictated to his cousin and son-in-law Ali: Mas'udi IV, p. 171.
a land-grant written on . . . a palm-branch: Baladhuri, p. 23.
demands for tribute from . . . Dumah: Baladhuri, pp. 67–9.
a letter to the Hadramis . . . to Medina: Jahiz, part 1, p. 181.
the Yemenis . . . by the time of Islam: Ibn Khallikan, pp. 163–4.
I have sent you a scribe: quoted in Adonis, *Thabit* IV, 22.
Medina was 'conquered' by it: Baladhuri, p. 17.
stunned their hearing and disabled their minds: p. 139, above.
4,000 loudspeakers . . . 9 kilometres away: BBC, 'News From Elsewhere', 14 July 2014.
How often have tribes . . . got to submit: quoted in Chejne, p. 14.
Martin Nowak's . . . insertion of ideas: Nowak, *Supercooperators*, *passim*.
Christian Arabs . . . from north-eastern Arabia: EI^2 XI, p. 219.
the Byzantine emperor . . . Abyssinian highlands: Ibn Khallikan II, p. 377.
numerous marriages: eleven according to Rogerson, p. 109.
Does royalty give itself to trade?: Lecker, p. 353.
he employed nomad tribes . . . as persuaders: EI^2 XI, pp. 219–20.
a response to Persian encroachment . . . subcontinent: Retsö, p. 17.
Khalid ibn Sinan al-Absi . . . last prophet before himself: p. 141.
saved Arabia from . . . fire-temples: Mas'udi I, p. 67–8.
Muslims will rejoice at . . . the Byzantines: Qur'an, 30:4.
Abu Bakr . . . his Arab opponent, al-Aswad: Baladhuri, p. 110.
I have never heard . . . unless it be Antarah: Shaykhu, p. 797.
the origin of the Arabs and the material of Islam: Jahiz, part 1, p. 188.
the worst in unbelief and hypocrisy: Qur'an, 9:97; cf. p. 4, above.
The *a'rab* say . . . belief has not yet entered your hearts: Qur'an, 49:14.
Between us, Lord . . . with no begetter!: Serjeant, *South Arabian Hunt*, p. 12.
It is very doubtful . . . as a universal religion: EI^2 VII, p. 372.
a social and political . . . spiritual experience: EI^2 IX, p. 452.
believing without belonging: Davie, *passim*.
its doctrine of total . . . unitarianism: cf. Adonis, quoted on pp. 12–13, above.
I do not know if shall meet you . . . except in piety: Jahiz, part 1, pp. 183–4.
nor is black superior to white: e.g. the version quoted in Rogerson, p. 208.

he was a fan . . . with fully open mouth: Jahiz, part 1, p. 182.
an old woman asked . . . nubile virgins!: Ibn Khallikan II, p. 9.
was once spotted . . . a fine camel you've got!: *hadith* on the authority of Jabir.
Suggestions as to his age . . . sixty-five lunar years: Mas'udi II, pp. 290–1.
doubts about the dating of the Day of the Elephant: p. 90, above.
Muhammad rarely appeared in public unveiled: Jahiz, part 3, p. 40.
the concept of *'arab* . . . disappearing altogether: Retsö, p. 626.
gathered the Arabs together upon the word of Islam: p. 9, above.
Muhammad . . . the fall of Ghassan and Kindah: Jahiz, part 1, p. 181.
Arabs . . . kingship through prophecy: quoted in Adonis, *Thabit* I, p. 29.
mosaics and columns . . . in the Meccan Ka'bah: Mas'udi III, p. 92.
The mosque also incorporated . . . the Sabaeans: Razi, p. 254.

CHAPTER 7 CRESCADERS

Islamic historians . . . have been Jewish: Baladhuri, pp. 106–7.
the others . . . accusation of harlotry: Beeston, 'So-Called Harlots', pp. 20–1.
the 'harlots' . . . front teeth knocked out: Beeston, 'So-Called Harlots', p. 19.
an old punishment for subversive orators: Jahiz, part 1, p. 134.
Azerbaijan . . . for a time as governor: Lecker, *passim*.
a pretty spouse . . . 'Hail to our lord!': Jahiz, part 1, p. 237.
Abu Bakr's 'election' . . . as arbiter, not autocrat: cf. Lewis, 'Concept', p. 6.
Abu Bakr took over . . . a rubber-stamp: cf. Lewis, 'Concept', p. 7.
Ali and other members . . . six months: Mas'udi II, pp. 307–8; EI^2 IX, p. 420.
within a week or two . . . began to fall apart: Mas'udi II, p. 306.
This world . . . worship it as they were wont to do: Ibn al-Kalbi, p. 32.
the goddess al-Uzza . . . ashes before his eyes: Ibn al-Kalbi, pp. 21–2.
you snapped . . . as the poet Imru' al-Qays had done: pp. 141–2, above.
you the called them bastards . . . in their rain hymn: p. 167, above.
Malik ibn Nuwayrah . . . described in chapter 2: p. 65, above.
Different versions of the story exist: EI^2 VI, pp. 267–8.
Malik had been one of the delegates . . . alienated: Ibn Khallikan III, pp. 215–16.
Other tribes went on praying but not paying: Baladhuri, p. 99.
like Muhammad . . . to call his followers to prayer: Baladhuri, p. 96.
Frog, daughter of two frogs! . . . a hostile lot: Gelder, p. 112.
Musaylimah, who suggested . . . from Muhammad: Baladhuri, pp. 93–4.
Musaylimah was killed . . . different accounts: Baladhuri, p. 98.
Sajah may have been Christian . . . defeat: Baladhuri, p. 104; EI^2 VIII, p. 738.
So too did Tulayhah . . . on his own defeat: Baladhuri, pp. 101–2.
You are better . . . defend them!: Gelder, pp. 112–13.
Tulayhah's prophetic pretences . . . camels to Medina: EI^2 X, p. 603.
Islamic polemic . . . prostrated itself to him: Baladhuri, p. 109.
who captivated . . . by his discourse: Abu 'l-Fida', *Mukhtasar*, part 1, p. 155.
he expelled the Muslim . . . readily accepted Islam: Baladhuri, pp. 109–10.
the Marxist ideologues . . . nationalist: Mackintosh-Smith, *Yemen*, p. 44.
We left Shurayh . . . overwhelmed with vultures: Baladhuri, pp. 90–1.
Abu Bakr . . . people to fight the Byzantines: Baladhuri, p. 111.
Today you live . . . so too will the further lands: Jahiz, part 1, pp. 187–8.
Umar . . . designated before his death: Lewis, 'Concept', p. 7.
the Persian Threat . . . unprovable theory: cf. pp. 165–6, above.
the first campaigns . . . to unify arabophones: cf. Versteegh, *Arabic Language*, p. 93.
Abu Sufyan . . . bought estates in Byzantine territory: cf. p. 121, above.
the emperor Heraclius . . . lost Byzantine territory: Hitti, pp. 147–8.
a force of 24,000: Baladhuri, p. 112.
Most of the scattered . . . to the Muslim side: Baladhuri, pp. 119–20.

prostration . . . in the Syrian Orthodox Church: cf. William Dalrymple, *From The Holy Mountain*, HarperCollins, 1997, p. 105.
In Damascus . . . seventy years: Baladhuri, p. 133; cf. Kennedy, p. 86.
Muslims and Christians . . . to reach their mosque: Ibn Shakir quoted in *EI*[2] I, s.v. Architecture.
a prince . . . medicine and alchemy: Ibn Khallikan I, p. 300.
As for the Jews . . . another Byzantine governor: Baladhuri, p. 139.
the '100,000' troops guarding its walls: Baladhuri, p. 144.
an Arab woman . . . killed seven Byzantine soldiers: Baladhuri, p. 121.
Named after a river . . . in the Yarmuk gorges: cf. Kennedy, pp. 83–5.
Go on! Prune the Foreskinned Ones with your swords!: Baladhuri, p. 137.
the Byzantine side relied on . . . other tribes: Baladhuri, pp. 136 and 164.
Jabalah is said . . . implications of Islam: Baladhuri, pp. 137–8.
al-Mughirah parleying . . . on his throne: Baladhuri, p. 253; Kennedy, p. 113.
the West of the East . . . described Islam: Lévi-Strauss, p. 405.
Yazdgard III . . . thrown into a central Asian river: Kennedy, pp. 190–1.
the Persian capital . . . Asia Minor: cf. Ibn Khaldun, *Muqaddimah*, p. 129.
it fell at some time between 636 and 638: Kennedy, p. 109.
Arab forces . . . may have numbered 12,000: Kennedy, p. 108.
a Persian army . . . 120,000 by some accounts: Baladhuri, p. 252.
Spindles! Spindles! . . . chain-mail that we wore: Baladhuri, p. 256.
there was a single palm-tree . . . at the Sawad yet?: Mas'udi II, p. 326.
the captured Persian . . . honeycombs: Mas'udi II, pp. 320–1.
the last of the thirty . . . to goggling Arabs: Baladhuri, p. 282.
Huraqah . . . the Arab victor of al-Qadisiyyah: Mas'udi II, pp. 102–4.
Hind . . . an expert on ancient Arabia: Mas'udi III, pp. 33–4.
home only to owls . . . from the skulls of the dead: Mas'udi II, pp. 102–5.
It was demolished . . . third successor, Uthman: *Mawsūʿah*, s.v. Ghumdān.
the aged warrior-hero, Durayd ibn al-Simmah: cf. p. 62, above.
The youth tried to kill . . . your ancestresses: Shaykhu, pp. 772–3.
the pre-Islamic belief . . . never complete his journey: Ibshihi, p. 466.
Khalid ibn al-Walid . . . juices in their stomachs: Kennedy, p. 75.
The leaders . . . had to expand or collapse: Kennedy, pp. 56–7.
it was . . . exceptional and miraculous: Ibn Khaldun, *Muqaddimah*, p. 255.
they would send out *saraya* . . . in charge: e.g. Baladhuri, p. 224.
Arab warrior's kit . . . and his horse: Baladhuri, p. 310. 'Broadsword' is tentative, reading *mikhfaq* for the *mkhff* (vowels uncertain) of the edition I have to hand.
Caliph Umar . . . to leave with his family: Baladhuri, p. 434.
If you travel . . . down among your nether bits: Jahiz, part 3, p. 121.
The second decisive showdown ... to Arab forces: Kennedy, pp. 171–2.
he scraped together . . . newly conquered Iraq: Baladhuri, p. 296.
A single generation of Arabs . . . nicely put it: Hitti, p. 259.
one 'very tentative' estimate . . . of the conquests: Atiyah, p. 35.
Ibn Khaldun gives . . . time of Muhammad: Ibn Khaldun, *Muqaddimah*, p. 140.
Umar managed to field . . . battle of Nihawand: Kennedy, p. 171.
five of Muhammad's first cousins . . . Samarqand: Ibn Khallikan II, p. 31.
How far between his birth and his death . . . Qutham: Baladhuri, p. 398.
in AH 200 al-Abbas's descendants . . . number 33,000: Mas'udi IV, p. 28.
the same very unusual . . . migrations: the feature is an intrusive syllable between participles and pronominal suffixes. Owens, *Linguistic History*, pp. 160–2.
Caliph Umar . . . could not be reached by camel: cf. p. 37, above.
Umar was not pleased . . . 'ticks on sticks': Baladhuri, p. 416.
it would be taken . . . in the eighth century: Keay, p. 183.
An Arab army . . . south of the Caspian: Baladhuri, p. 326.
You fought the foe . . . you drew your prick: Baladhuri, p. 412.
O Lord . . . fighting the unbelievers!: Kennedy, p. 214.

as big as or bigger than the Roman: cf. Dunlop, 18.
that vigorous, vegetal ataurique . . . the Old World: cf. pp. 13–14, above.
Never since . . . won in any city: Mathews, p. 41.
what might be called . . . the 'Crescades': I was pleased to coin this, and then discovered that others had done so already. The trouble with the internet is that one can find out very quickly that one isn't as original as one thought.
In the Name of Allah . . . sufficient as a witness: Baladhuri, p. 174. The last sentence is Qur'an, 13:43.
Exactly the same tax . . . in 2014: *Daily Telegraph*, 27 February 2014.
To withhold tax . . . termed *kafara*: e.g. Baladhuri, pp. 176 and 379.
the Mardaite Christians . . . excused the poll-tax: Baladhuri, pp. 161–2.
the Christian Arab . . . barbarians: Baladhuri, pp. 181–3; Suleiman, pp. 56–7.
the value of masonry . . . tax-deductible: Baladhuri, p. 280.
40,000 . . . were massacred: Baladhuri, p. 378; Kennedy, p. 184.
half a million peasant farmers: Baladhuri, p. 266.
I fear . . . smash each other's faces in: Baladhuri, pp. 261–4.
the annual revenue . . . at the end of the seventh century: Baladhuri, p. 266. Such comparisons are exceedingly difficult to make, but the *dirham* might be thought of as being worth about couple of US dollars, or perhaps a little more.
the people of al-Ruha . . . at the [main] gate: Baladhuri, p. 174.
he offered . . . the right to despoil the corpse: Baladhuri, pp. 250–1.
al-Mughirah . . . and are humbled: Baladhuri, p. 253. The Qur'anic quotation is Qur'an, 9:29.
'40,000 head' of slaves . . . region of Sistan: Baladhuri, p. 382.
We have cooled . . . Dahir's head: Baladhuri, p. 423.
Al-Hajjaj . . . dissuaded Sawad peasants from converting: EI^2 VII, p. 971.
he even expelled . . . the poll-tax of the unbeliever: Ibn Khallikan III, p. 355.
Umar ibn Abd al-Aziz . . . in post-conquest Sind: Baladhuri, pp. 425–6.
among the Berbers of North Africa: Baladhuri, pp. 228–9.
by AD 750 . . . embraced Islam: Karsh, p. 43.
they were not just a *fath* . . . of those lands: Jabiri, p. 141.
three daughters . . . captured Persian women: Ibn Khallikan II, pp. 127–8.
such offspring had been . . . socially inferior: Lewis, 'Crows', p. 89.
the chaste Arabic . . . interloping mother-tongue: Jahiz, part 1, pp. 10–11.
When Umar saw . . . keep yourselves rough: Jahiz, part 3, p. 9.
an affiliate of an Arab tribe: EI^2 X, p. 846.
Arabs . . . between ten and twenty *mawla* followers: Ibn Khallikan I, p. 208.
a group of Shaybani . . . refused to mix: Jahiz, part 3, p. 24.
the tribes disappeared: Ibn Khaldun, *Muqaddimah*, p. 100.
the arrant faking . . . al-Muktafi: Ibn Khallikan III, pp. 315–16.
the poet Abu Nuwas . . . in the country: Abu Nuwas, pp. 524 and 571.
the grammarian . . . to avoid seeing him: Ibn Khallikan III, p. 397.
al-Farra' himself was of . . . Daylamite origin: Ibn Khallikan III, p. 290.
the Persian . . . king of al-Hirah: p. 91, above.
The term for the opposite union is *iqraf*: e.g. Ibn Khallikan II, p. 47.
loathsome infection: Hava, s.v. *qrf*.
the uncircumcised ones will penetrate us!: Baladhuri, p. 334.
And Allah has made . . . broad roads: Qur'an, 71:19–20.
hijrah was keenly . . . apostasy: p. 148, above.
Muhammad had cursed . . . after *hijrah*: Crone, p. 356.
You moved . . . to your new *dar hijrah*, 'migratory home': Crone, p. 363.
Arabs already there . . . to settled areas: Baladhuri, p. 151.
Our thickets . . . the earth beneath us is gold: Jahiz, part 1, p. 205.
It was *de rigueur* to teach . . . horsemanship: Jahiz, part 1, p. 239.
you and they . . . to die in sweaty Sind: Ibn Khallikan III, pp. 249–50.
in 671, 50,000 men were moved . . . to Merv: Kennedy, p. 237.
Bernard Lewis . . . relied on 'desert-power': Lewis, *Arabs in History*, p. 54.

the developed Islamic usage . . . not 'severance', but 'town': cf. Crone, p. 375; p. 53, above.
misr is an ancient Semitic . . . 'border(-town)' there: cf. *EI*[2], s.v. Miṣr.
its public buildings . . . on extended raids: Baladhuri, pp. 337–8.
later in the seventh century . . . they were expelled: Baladhuri, pp. 362–5.
al-Basrah had a population . . . 120,000 dependants: Baladhuri, pp. 340–1.
captives . . . built a mosque 'in the Kabul style': Baladhuri, p. 384.
our teak and ivory . . . and our rolling river: Jahiz, part 1, p. 150.
when famine struck . . . in the steppelands: Ibn Khallikan III, p. 249.
ordered the commanders . . . stay in their midst: Baladhuri, p. 113.
the smallest tribes grouped . . . under a joint flag: Ibn Khallikan II, p. 63.
in al-Kufah . . . each tribe having its own mosque: Baladhuri, pp. 270–3.
Adnanis . . . each had their own *'asabiyyah*: Husayn, p. 130.
in all the *amsar* of Islam . . . 'Ignorance': Husayn, p. 120.
We know no other . . . never-ending eloquence: quoted in Kurdi, p. 53.
The Arabs have . . . in these two cities: quoted in Suyuti II, p. 353.
I spent a long time . . . forgeries: quoted in Suyuti II, p. 353.
Scholarship . . . never came back to you: quoted in Jahiz, part 1, p. 142.
The souls of the ambitious . . . stay at home: quoted in Rosenthal, p. 51.
the inhabitants of tombs: quoted in Ibn Khallikan III, p. 193.
The amounts . . . were heritable: *EI*[2] I, s.v. ʿAṭā'.
Umar was warned . . . 'That is inevitable': Baladhuri, p. 440.
His vision . . . included child-support payments: Baladhuri, p. 441.
his economic innovations . . . camel-hide *dirhams*: Baladhuri, p. 452.
by investing . . . the strong eat up the weak: Jahiz, part 1, pp. 188–9. The Qur'anic quotation is Qur'an, 59:7.
Arabs would only remain great . . . as a vice: Jahiz, part 1, pp. 203–4. Cf. p. 77, above.
Treasure in conquered lands was 'de-thesaurized': cf. Kennedy, p. 173.
150,000 [gold] dinars . . . was more than that: Mas'udi II, pp. 341–3; translation from Ibn Khaldun, *Muqaddimah*, p. 163.
he spent sixteen dinars . . . extravagant: Mas'udi II, p. 343.
a ninth-century judge . . . sour milk and dates: Ibn Khallikan III, p. 393; cf. Mas'udi III p. 351.
'Hail, great *amir*!' . . . to sit upon a throne!: Jahiz, part 3, p. 167. Poet and *amir* are unidentified, although Zayd can be the Arabic equivalent of 'Joe Bloggs'. In some accounts, the verses are aimed at an eighth-century governor, Ma'n ibn Za'idah.
Umar was killed . . . by a slave: e.g. Baladhuri, p. 370.
the murdered caliph . . . nominate a successor: Lewis, 'Concept', p. 7.
Abu Bakr . . . 'gathered the Qur'an between boards': Ibn Khallikan II, p. 33.
The Qur'an was many . . . abandoned all but one: al-Tabari, quoted in Schoeler, p. 431.
secondary copies . . . by in-house scribes: Kurdi, p. 446.
Arabic was beginning . . . Medina: Jahiz, part 1, pp. 10–11; cf. p. 201, above.
Qur'an and Sunnah . . . preserved the Arabic language: Ibn Khaldun, *Muqaddimah*, p. 295.
the legendary . . . Abd Shams and Hashim: cf. pp. 125–6, above.
'Who is my son shouting at?' . . . humbled others: Mas'udi II, p. 306.
he had alienated . . . fifth share of booty: *EI*[2] IX, p. 420.
his loss at this time . . . down a well: *EI*[2], s.v. ʿUthmān.
exiled whistleblowers: e.g. Abu 'l-Dharr: *EI*[2] I, p. 382.
Dismissed as governor . . . milked her: Baladhuri, p. 221.
The killing . . . was utterly in the wrong: Adonis, *Thabit* I, pp. 316–17.
he also reversed land-grants . . . to his cronies: Mas'udi II, p. 362.
How far . . . *A day's journey for the sun*: Jahiz, part 3, p. 106.
rare and remote . . . city of the philosophers: Ibn Khaldun, *Muqaddimah*, p. 257.
Two of those . . . amassed fortunes: p. 212, above.
in the tradition of pre-Islamic seeresses: cf. Carmichael, p. 91.
on a camel . . . covered with chain-mail: Mas'udi II, pp. 370–1.
seventy men's hands . . . looked like a porcupine: Mas'udi II, pp. 375–6.

News of the battle . . . carried by a vulture: Ibn Khallikan II, p. 10.
7,000 dead – a 'conservative' estimate: Mas'udi II, p. 360.
By Allah . . . A'ishah laughed and rode away: Ibn Khallikan II, p. 9.
duped by the woman . . . Commander of the Faithful: Mas'udi II, p. 379.
The battle of Siffin . . . across from al-Raqqah: Mas'udi II, p. 384.
Where's that Mu'awiyah? . . . to Hell!: Mas'udi II, p. 396.
There was such fighting . . . on top of Ubayd Allah: Mas'udi II, p. 397.
Ali . . . in a day and a night: Mas'udi II, p. 399.
Dawn broke . . . no longer knew the times of prayer: Mas'udi II, p. 399.
Places . . . inclined to happiness, others to grief: Maqrizi I, p. 348, translation from Mackintosh-Smith, *Tangerine*, p. 226.
Every man on Mu'awiyah's side . . . raised it high: Mas'udi II, p. 400.
They are not people of religion and the Qur'an: Mas'udi II, p. 401.
But his men were set . . . and Ali deferred to them: Mas'udi II, pp. 400–1.
70,000 . . . 25,000 on Ali's: Mas'udi II, p. 361.
Some authorities . . . over half as much again: Mas'udi II, p. 404.
it was the climax . . . the opponents: Mas'udi II, p. 361.
Ali, under pressure . . . should be caliph: Mas'udi II, pp. 402–3.
The arbiters . . . agreed on nothing: *EI*[2] VII, p. 265.
Muhammad . . . seventy-three sects: cf. p. 3, above.
a lost ninth-century ode . . . of sects and sectarians: Mas'udi IV, p. 40.
Quraysh liked me . . . more than Ali: Jahiz, part 1, p. 215.
heritage . . . is a sociopolitical problem: Adonis, *Thabit* IV, p. 207.

CHAPTER 8 THE KINGDOM OF DAMASCUS

Abd al-Malik noticed . . . the hall be destroyed: Mas'udi III, p. 117.
That year, 661 . . . the Year of Unity: *EI*[2] VII, p. 265.
you would promote . . . ibn Abi Balta'ah: Jahiz, part 3, p. 185.
It was the same argument . . . between cousins: cf. pp. 125–6, above.
V.S. Naipaul's Durkheimian notion . . . come and go: Naipaul, p. 63. In Durkheim's terms, changing (Islamic) civilization 'articulates' essential (Arab) culture. Cf. Zubaida, p. 124.
After me . . . a king or kings: Ibn Khallikan I, p. 225; Ibn Khaldun, *Muqaddimah*, p. 281.
a legend about Mu'awiyah's mother . . . birth to a king: Ibshihi, p. 468.
he fathered a line . . . the emperor Nicephorus I: Hitti, p. 300.
Caliph al-Walid . . . including his penis: Mas'udi III, pp. 227–8.
he allegedly shot darts . . . a charlatan: Mas'udi III, pp. 228–9.
Abd al-Malik – seen above . . . prematurely grey: Jahiz, part 1, p. 60.
He slept little . . . *hilm*: Mas'udi III, pp. 39–41.
to a Christian monk . . . from our grandfathers: *EI*[2] VII, p. 267.
impious deviation from an established tradition: Crone, p. 387.
Mu'awiyah . . . was also *anf al-'arab*: Jahiz, part 1, 221.
Al-Jabiyah . . . an Umayyad power-base too: *EI*[2] II, p. 360.
the same . . . fought for the Ghassanids: *EI*[2] VII, p. 267.
In these, too . . . anticipated by the Ghassanids: *EI*[2] II, p. 1021.
its mural paintings . . . the Visigoths in Spain: Hitti, p. 271.
Muhammad . . . in its fleshpots: Mackintosh-Smith, *Tangerine*, p. 166.
By the figs and the olives . . . without end: Qur'an, 95:1 and 4–6.
We'll fight for . . . the fruits and rivers of Paradise: Mas'udi II, p. 395.
I will never give up . . . 'Bait your hook with Egypt': Mas'udi II, p. 363. The word *tu'mah*, at least to later readers, has a nice extra meaning – as well as 'bait', it can also mean 'a percentage of taxes'. Lecker, p. 338.
I have subdued . . . hidden treasure: Ibn Khallikan III, p. 379.
I found him . . . in her right hand a pitcher: Ibn Khallikan I, p. 294.
the hard-drinking . . . court poet to Abd al-Malik: *EI*[2] s.v. al-Akhtal.

He could compose . . . 'dizzy and effeminate': Ibn Khallikan I, p. 472; cf. Suyuti I, p. 459.
Umar ibn Abd al-Aziz . . . and North Africa: p. 200, above.
Their leader . . . I have seen otherwise: Yaqut quoted in Mackintosh-Smith, *Tangerine*, p. 144.
the iconoclast emperor . . . direct from Damascus: Mathews, p. 58.
an Islamic layer . . . a Byzantine imperial gloss: Adonis, *Thabit* I, p. 317.
news reached the emperor . . . among evil men: Mas'udi III, p. 195.
Observing him deliver . . . twelve *dirhams*: Ibn Khallikan I, p. 336.
the Abbasid Caliph . . . their kidneys: Ibn Khallikan II, p. 83; Mas'udi III, pp. 184–6.
Listening to a richly embroidered account . . . it is ours: Abid, p. 484.
the earliest sense . . . 'a mixed people': pp. 38–9, above.
They discovered him . . . in a foreign land: cf. Husayn, p. 91.
Augustus claimed descent from Aeneas: Hornblower and Spawforth, s.v. Aeneas.
Hagar herself . . . 'the Mother of the Arabs': Ibn Khallikan I, p. 39; Yaqut, s.v. Umm al-ᶜArab.
We have already seen . . . community of southerners: p. 118, above.
their major prophet . . . his more distant ancestry: p. 125, above.
at some time around . . . Umar ibn Abd al-Aziz: Retsö p. 33; Serjeant, review of René Dagorn, p. 52.
That there are at least three . . . inspires confidence: Mas'udi II, p. 273.
His original tongue . . . blew from Babel: Suyuti I, pp. 29–30.
the southerners, too, got . . . prophetic honour: cf. *EI*[2] IV, p. 448.
a unifying 'ethnic' identity . . . had not existed before: Macdonald, *Development*, p. 22.
O mankind . . . you may know one another: Qur'an, 49:13.
the first Caliph Umar . . . aware of the shortfall: pp. 193–4, above.
Were it not for the swords . . . *Allahu akbar*!: quoted in Akwa', p. 103.
In the year 700: Baladhuri, p. 192.
The reason was . . . change the records [to Arabic]: Baladhuri, pp. 192–3.
there is no event . . . causes and effects: Borges, pp. 196–7. English version by Alberto Manguel, *A Reader on Reading*, Yale University Press, New Haven and London, 2011, p. 56.
People turned . . . sophistication of literacy: Ibn Khaldun, *Muqaddimah*, p. 199.
both reined in . . . civilization and science: Jabiri, p. 68.
it troubled him . . . deprived you of this profession: Baladhuri, p. 193. Sergius was the father of the future saint, John of Damascus; Sergius's own father had been in charge of taxes under the Byzantines.
Hassan al-Tanukhi . . . scribe and translator: Ibn Khallikan I, p. 287.
The older, more angular . . . Nabataean parent: Kurdi, p. 111.
the sudden need . . . of cursive script: Versteegh, *Arabic Language*, p. 57.
It can be written . . . in other scripts: Kurdi, p. 160.
diacritical marks . . . papyrus of AH 22/AD 643: Jones, 'Word Made Visible', p. 15; Macdonald, *Development*, p. 1.
Grammar, syntax and philology . . . Arab sciences: cf. Jabiri, p. 76.
the beginnings . . . from Anaximander on: cf. Hornblower and Spawforth, s.v. Anaximander.
because eloquent words . . . congenial to the Arabs: Ibn Khaldun, *Muqaddimah*, p. 217.
Say, 'He is Allah, One . . . ': Qur'an, 112.
In retaliation . . . to mint his own: Baladhuri, pp. 237–8.
Islam . . . never had a Pentecost: for this phrase I thank in turn Professor Kamal Abdel Malek.
Hammad . . . for each letter of the alphabet: Ibn Khallikan I, p. 293.
non-Arabs further developed . . . a cultural whole: cf. Drory, p. 42.
Abu Ata . . . patronized by the later Umayyad caliphs: Huart, p. 57.
Some are raised . . . my poems are my lineage: Lewis, 'Crows', p. 95 (translation slightly modified).
topography and climate . . . and *shu'ub*, peoples: cf. pp. 25–6, above.
What are you Yemenis? . . . a hoopoe told them about it: Jahiz, part 1, p. 143; Mas'udi II, p. 183; cf. Mackintosh-Smith, *Yemen*, p. 5 and footnote.
We can't abide . . . while we walk the walk: Jahiz, part 1, p. 165. The last phrase goes, more literally, 'They must do the speaking while we must do the doing.'
he had shown the Qurashis' Allah . . . to be one God: cf. pp. 143–4, above.
the Ansar had been excluded . . . exclusion rankled: cf. *EI*[2] I, p. 545.

al-Farazdaq . . . clients of Quraysh: Ibn Khallikan III, pp. 395–6.
late pre-Islamic *qwls* . . . in Umayyad Syria: Piotrovsky, pp. 304–5. On *qwls*, see p. 94, above.
later in ninth-century India: Baladhuri, p. 428.
in eighteenth-century Lebanon: Hitti, p. 281.
in twentieth-century Oman: e.g. EI^2, s.v. Hinā.
Al-Husayn's friends . . . a small force of followers: Mas'udi III, pp. 64–6.
Hearts are with you . . . Victory is in heaven: Jahiz, part 1, p. 243.
We cleave the heads . . . against that mouth to kiss it: Mas'udi III, pp. 70–1.
They saw that they . . . had not gone to help him: Mas'udi III, p. 100.
Iranian pilgrims in the Umayyad Mosque: Mackintosh-Smith, *Tangerine*, p. 144.
Abd Allah ibn al-Zubayr . . . won their backing: Hitti, pp. 280–1.
Tell Yazid from me . . . chop him up limb from limb: Jahiz, part 1, p. 221.
the *dabb*, is a lizard . . . a painful weapon: Freya Stark had a live *Uromastyx*, 'a charming pet and very tame, and answers to the name of Himyar'. Freya Stark, *Seen in the Hadhramaut*, John Murray, 1938, p. 116.
Mu'awiyah had already sent . . . Ka'bah precinct: Mas'udi III, p. 85.
Yazid . . . died in rapid succession: Mas'udi III, pp. 81–2.
the anti-caliph rebuilt the focal shrine of Islam: Mas'udi III, p. 92.
it was rumoured that he died . . . from the succession: Mas'udi III, pp. 97–8.
navel of the earth: cf. p. 123, above.
in one year . . . a Khariji group that reviled it: EI^2 I, p. 55.
Abd al-Malik . . . built the Dome of the Rock: Ibn Khallikan II, p. 35.
the head of Abd Allah . . . made its way to Damascus: Hitti, p. 193.
The year of the anti-caliph's defeat . . . 'Year of Unity': EI^2 X, p. 842.
at the end of 694, Abd al-Malik sent him to . . . Iraq: Hitti, p. 207.
I am the son . . . turbans and beards: Jahiz, part 1, pp. 289–90.
Often he would begin . . . corners of the mosque: Ibn Khallikan I, p. 213.
He could be . . . quite justified: Jahiz, part 1, p. 163.
That enemy of Allah . . . worse than the Antichrist: Jahiz, part 1, p. 164.
putting to death . . . killed in fighting: Mas'udi III, pp. 175–6.
I am iron-hearted . . . cruel and jealous: Jahiz, part 3, p. 99.
the thirteen-page entry . . . one of the longest: Ibn Khallikan I, pp. 206–19.
How can you sit . . . he pawed at the ground with his feet: Mas'udi III, pp. 167–9; Ibn Khallikan I, p. 214.
'I do,' said the astrologer . . . used to call me: Ibn Khallikan I, p. 217.
but thereafter . . . the beginning of his life: Mas'udi III, p. 132.
the *amsar* . . . forbidden to non-arabophones: Ibn Khallikan III, p. 355.
Al-Hajjaj is a fool . . . not to enter it!: Jahiz, part 3, p. 153.
in the vast eastern province . . . Arabs spoke Persian: EI^2 I, p. 530.
the Persian mother . . . said Ziyad: Jahiz, part 1, pp. 34 and 254. As well as the 'Membrum virile', as Hava's dictionary terms it, *ayr* (without the twang) can also mean 'the north wind' and 'the east wind'. Sailors must have terrible problems.
The first I hear . . . masculines that feminize: Jahiz, part 1, p. 34.
Al-Walid . . . bedouin 'finishing school': p. 126, above.
His lapses . . . undermined his dignity: Jahiz, part 1, p. 251.
his most famous *faux-pas* . . . 'Who circumcised you?': Suleiman, p. 54.
becoming a Muslim . . . as a *mawla*: p. 201, above.
By Allah, if this lad . . . character and eloquence: Ibn Khallikan III, p. 378.
sayyid al-kalam . . . was making masters of its people: Abid, p. 43.
Muhammad's famous declaration . . . except in piety: Jahiz, part 1, p. 183, cf. p. 169, above.
Berbers and Slavs . . . and the dregs of humanity: Jahiz, part 1, p. 125. Jarmaqis come from an oasis in the great desert of central Iran; Jarjumis are the Mardaite Christians of northern Syria.
Khalid ibn al-Walid . . . an Arab Christian called Nusayr: Baladhuri, p. 244.
The latter became . . . *mawla* of the Umayyad clan: Baladhuri, p. 228.
Men, where can you fly . . . penetration will delight: Ibn Khallikan III, p. 161.

Arabs in Khurasan . . . piled up from its conquest: Jahiz, part 1, p. 285.
al-Muhallab . . . sub-tribe, the Mahalibah: Ibn Khallikan III, pp. 177 and 178.
'*A'rab*,' Qutaybah called them . . . pile up its booty!: Jahiz, part 1, p. 221. Abarkawan, today called Qishm, is an island just inside the Strait of Hormuz.
he wrote . . . to send an army against him: Ibn Khallikan III, p. 348.
But none of his men . . . killed in 715: Kennedy, pp. 274 and 275.
Defeated in 720 . . . bid for the caliphate itself: Ibn Khallikan III, pp. 351–4.
It is unclear . . . perhaps Kurdish origin: Ibn Khallikan II, p. 74.
he was bilingual in Arabic and Persian: Ibn Khallikan II, p. 71.
I have achieved . . . the lion does the shepherding: Ibn Khallikan II, p. 73. 'Marwan's line' are the later Umayyads, descended from Marwan ibn al-Hakam.
Among the ashes . . . come to wake and rise!: Ibn Khallikan II, pp. 71–2.
in their vanguard . . . when time has run its course?: Mas'udi III, p. 265.
One of the few survivors . . . what was happening: Mas'udi III, p. 241.
Egypt, where he tried . . . and so was he: Mas'udi III, p. 265.
They were the mother-lode . . . as proper Arabs: Jahiz, part 3, p. 138.
The Abbasid dynasty . . . Arab and bedouin-Arab: Jahiz, part 3, p. 139.
A more poignant image . . . by the wildest poet: Johnson and Shehadeh, p. 36.
In Lebanon and Palestine . . . part of the eighteenth century: Hitti, p. 281.

CHAPTER 9 THE EMPIRE OF BAGHDAD

How are all the kings . . . this king of ours: al-Sirafi and Ibn Fadlan, pp. 79–81.
the wise infidel . . . literary character: al-Sirafi and Ibn Fadlan, p. 11.
the Christian king . . . their irreligiosity: Ma'sudi III, pp. 296–7.
the old Classical age had finally ended: cf. Henri Pirenne's view in Dunlop, pp. 18–19.
Fire's kindled . . . of corpses and of heads: cf. p. 258, above.
al-Abbas's sons . . . to Central Asia: cf. pp. 194–5, above.
Hisham's own corpse . . . burnt: Mas'udi III, pp. 219–25; Ibn Khallikan III, p. 260.
50,000 workmen laboured . . . to build it: Mas'udi III, p. 318.
al-Mansur soon commanded . . . Karkh: Baladhuri, p. 289.
over each one al-Mansur built . . . pavilion: Mas'udi III, pp. 299–300.
Here is the Tigris . . . China: Ya'qubi quoted in George Hourani, p. 64.
He made a bid . . . it was accidental: Mas'udi III, pp. 302 and 315–16.
Al-Mansur had him killed . . . Abbasid Trotsky's name: Mas'udi III, pp. 303–6.
The leaders . . . of course decapitated: Mas'udi III, pp. 307–11; Hitti, p. 290.
two brothers . . . the known world: Ibn Khallikan I, pp. 337–8.
to travel express . . . more than 1,500 kilometres: Mas'udi III, p. 397.
myrobalans . . . arrive fresh: Baladhuri, p. 415.
Surviving dissident descendants . . . Atlantic: Mas'udi III, pp. 307–8.
the ancestral Mauritanian stronghold . . . Baghdad: Mackintosh-Smith, *Landfalls*, pp. 252–4.
most Persians . . . were still Zoroastrian: *EI*[2] X, p. 226.
Drink . . . from a kindly Lord: Mas'udi IV, pp. 337–8.
the late ninth-century Baghdad comedian . . . grammarians: Mas'udi IV, p. 253.
the camp-followers of the caliph's army: Suyuti II, p. 354.
The most important stage . . . from those times: Adonis, *Thabit* III, p. 149.
the Mu'tazilah . . . his ethical responsibilities: *EI*[2] I, p. 326.
The reason why books . . . there is no more 'then': quoted in Jabiri, p. 222.
that hypothetical city of the philosophers: cf. Ibn Khaldun, *Muqaddimah*, p. 257, and p. 217, above.
wrote to the Byzantine . . . initial reluctance: quoted in Jabiri, p. 222.
Al-Mamun was fascinated . . . QED: Ibn Khallikan III, pp. 83–4.
the ancient metrologists . . . into that of practice: Ibn Khallikan III, p. 83.
the sciences of the non-Arabs . . . 'traditional sciences': Chejne, p. 72; Jabiri, p. 135.
al-Qasim ibn Sallam . . . time of al-Ma'mun: Ibn Khallikan II, pp. 265–6.
he had been schooled . . . as a youth: *EI*[2], s.v. al-Ma'mūn.

in 816 al-Ma'mun . . . his daughter in marriage: Mas'udi IV, pp. 28–9.
a niggling rumour . . . swapped the two bodies: Qazwini, p. 392.
Shi'i pilgrims . . . curse, triply, al-Rashid's grave: *EI*[2] XII, p. 605.
an ecumenical body . . . fizzle out and die: *EI*[2] X, pp. 139–40.
at a fork in the path of pilgrimage: cf. p. 185, above.
Allah taught Adam . . . all things in creation: Qur'an, 2:31.
Arabic versions . . . for an enthusiastic Umayyad prince: Jabiri, p. 194.
the sum paid . . . 500 gold dinars a month: Ibn al-Nadim quoted in Nicholson, p. 359, n. 2.
the pay . . . was twenty dirhams a month: Ibn Khallikan III, p. 124. On the translation movement in general, see for example Mas'udi IV, pp. 314–15, Carmichael, pp. 167–70, Nicholson, pp. 358–60.
Ibn al-Nadim . . . in Umayyad times: Kurdi, p. 92.
al-Rashid . . . 'cooking of the books': *EI*[2] IV 419.
the oldest known . . . about 800: Bloom, p. 17.
The smoothness . . . cursive Arabic scripts: Bloom, p. 22.
the kiss-curl of the beloved is the letter *waw*: Ibn Khallikan I, p. 351.
the lovers entwined are a *lam-alif*: Ibn Khallikan I, p. 326.
Perfume the literature . . . ink their precious scent: Kurdi, p. 421.
A scholar of Nishapur . . . take down his words: Ibn Khallikan I, p. 398.
the *wazir* Ibn al-Furat . . . the bursting email inbox: Ibn Khallikan II, p. 201.
an official with loose bowels . . . too late: Ibn Khallikan III, pp. 256–7.
Abu Tammam . . . poring over pre-Islamic verse: Ibn Khallikan II, p. 42.
al-Sahib ibn Abbad . . . 400 camels to transport it: Ibn Khallikan I, p. 124.
he grew up in Baghdad . . . lands of the Levant: Mas'udi I, pp. 7 and 10.
the salon of the poet . . . extremes of empire: Ibn Khallikan II, p. 375; cf. pp. 194–5, above.
I was reciting . . . reached both East and West: Ibn Khallikan II, p. 92.
The caravan . . . will surely always follow you: quoted in Gelder, p. 280.
Al-Kindi . . . in the name of religion: cf. *EI*[2] V, p. 122.
It is right and proper . . . different from our own: quoted in Jabiri, p. 240.
the emperor Theophilus . . . turbans and kaftans: Mathews, pp. 77 and 91.
Tang-era Guangzhou . . . in fashion: Whitfield, pp. 89 and107.
The last Umayyad . . . Abbasid revolution: cf. pp. 258 and 264, above.
to Islam and to the Arabs – farewell!: Mas'udi III, p. 255.
'ajamiyyah khurasaniyyah, non-Arab and Khurasani: p. 260, above.
Al-Mughirah . . . the viceregal throne: p. 189, above.
'ornamentalism': cf. David Cannadine's *Ornamentalism*, Oxford University Press, 2002.
al-Saffah . . . in public audience: Mas'udi III, p. 279.
some of the Umayyads had done so too: Mas'udi I, p. 247.
a turban adorned with gems: *EI*[2] X, p. 57.
court astrologers . . . of the 'Magi': Ibn Khallikan III, p. 246; *EI*[2] X, pp. 226–7.
al-Mansur's assassination . . . Sasanian shahs: Jahiz, part 3, pp. 140–1.
a story about the third Abbasid . . . close companions: Mas'udi III, pp. 321–2.
al-Mu'tasim . . . meaning of the word *kala'*: Ibn Khallikan III, pp. 48–9.
the children of slaves . . . unacknowledged: cf. the story of the poet Antarah, e.g. in Nicholson, p. 115.
The other mothers were . . . Abyssinian: cf. Hitti, p. 332.
The world has intermingled . . . Samarkand: quoted in Baerlein, p. 105.
'Barmak' is Sanskrit . . . monastery: Mas'udi II, pp. 238-9; *EI*[2] I, p. 1033.
al-Rashid . . . poking out of individual collars: Ibn Khallikan I, p. 170.
the old taboo – as old as the pre-Islamic Lakhmid kings: p. 91, above.
al-Rashid married . . . a son born: Ibn Khallikan I, pp. 170–1; Mas'udi III, pp. 385–91.
How could she . . . with a Persian client?: Ibn Khaldun, *Muqaddimah*, p. 19.
the Barmak . . . against al-Rashid: Ibn Khaldun, *Muqaddimah*, pp. 19–21.
When you were . . . bereft of husband, and of child: Mas'udi III, p. 391.
The fall of the house of Barmak has never been explained: *EI*[2] I, p. 17.
Vicious court rivalries . . . al-Fadl ibn al-Rabi': Ibn Khallikan II, p. 256.

He was the last . . . to renew that ancient link: Ibn Jubayr, p. 152.
When Allah . . . provides reasons for it: Ibn Khallikan II, p. 256.
united and flourished . . . disunited and perished: Ibn Khallikan II, p. 200.
united to destroy . . . themselves: quoted in Keay, p. 243.
al-Kisa'i was visiting . . . they had not been born: Mas'udi III, pp. 360–1.
gem-studded boots: Mas'udi IV, p. 318.
her growing son . . . *ghulamiyyat*, 'gamines': Mas'udi IV, p. 318.
the Sarah versus Hagar . . . syndrome: cf. al-Mas'udi III, p. 400.
al-Mu'tamin . . . in charge of the Byzantine marches: *EI*^{2} III, p. 234.
an act of great symbolism . . . in the Ka'bah at Mecca: cf. p. 151, above.
the proclamation . . . fell down: Mas'udi III, p. 364.
Most astonishing . . . to wipe his nose!: Mas'udi III, pp. 404–6.
interior decoration . . . gold gill-rings: Mas'udi III, p. 403.
Brother fought brother . . . goods looted: Mas'udi III, p. 409.
Severed . . . tales told to others near and far: Mas'udi III, pp. 409–10.
the ancient people . . . 'as tales once told': Qur'an, 34:19; cf. p. 73, above.
Al-Amin said . . . It is barren: Mas'udi III, p. 421.
'Muhammad ibn Zubaydah': e.g. Baladhuri, p. 304.
al-Mansur . . . in preference to Arabs: Mas'udi IV, p. 315.
al-Ma'mun . . . on the official payroll: Baladhuri, pp. 415–16.
The result . . . Hellenistic civilization: e.g. Carmichael, pp. 58 and 154.
the questions . . . a genitive case: Jahiz, part 1, pp. 256–7.
How long . . . your beard's going grey?: Ibn Khallikan III, p. 530.
One lexicographer benefited . . . a bedouin tribe: Lane, *Arabic-English Lexicon* I, p. xxxiv.
Some researchers paid . . . for their information: Suyuti II, p. 431.
some informants moved . . . to sell their knowledge: Jabiri, p. 84.
how often do grammarians . . . defend her?: Ma'arri, p. 321.
a two-year war . . . time of al-Rashid: Abu 'l-Fida', *Mukhtasar*, part 2, p. 13.
raiding the Mecca pilgrim caravans . . . in 898: Mas'udi IV, pp. 261–5.
Arab personality began to be conscious of itself: Jabiri, p. 192.
you haven't a Tamimi hair . . . drink ostrich piss: Ibn Khallikan I, p. 363.
anyone with literary . . . pre-Islamic tribes: Ibn Khallikan III, p. 316.
al-Isfahani's . . . 1,700 of them: *EI*^{2}, s.v. Abū 'l-Faradj.
the emigrant . . . in twentieth-century São Paulo: *EI*^{2} V, pp. 1256–7.
It may not be an exaggeration . . . foundation of the state: Jabiri, pp. 88–9.
strange to the culture: Ajami, *Dream Palace*, p. 128. It is coincidental that Ajami's surname means 'non-Arab': his ancestors moved to Lebanon from Iran (Ajami, *Dream Palace*, p. 14).
I am exhausted by my Arabness . . . a punishment?: Qabbani, p. 857.
'gigantic bluff': the phrase is from Philip Ziegler, *Soldiers*, Plume/Penguin, 2003, p. 324.
the non-Arab *mawali* . . . for the Arab community: Drory, p. 42.
Ibn Khaldun agreed . . . scholarship by non-Arabs: Ibn Khaldun, *Muqaddimah*, pp. 428–30.
Two [bedouin] men differed . . . It's *ẓaqr*: Suyuti I, p. 207. Cf. the English 'saker'.
the philologists' policy . . . only acceptable one: Ibn Khallikan II, pp. 223 and 232; Suyuti I, p. 146.
grammar, syntax . . . the first formal Arab sciences: cf. p. 238, above.
The rules of grammar . . . its whole thought-world: Jabiri, pp. 124–7.
empirical Arabic minds . . . at the margins: cf. Jabiri, pp. 344–5.
Abd al-Samad ibn al-Fadl . . . not in the observation: Jahiz, part 1, p. 131.
from the period . . . 4,000 grammarians: Versteegh, *Arabic Language*, p. 74.
al-Sahib ibn Abbad's 400-camel-load library: p. 278, above.
sixty camel-loads . . . on Arabic philology: Suyuti I, p. 74.
By Abbasid times . . . without an enormous effort: Mas'udi IV, p. 239.
in polite court circles . . . about the year 900: *EI*^{2} I, p. 570.
a philologist . . . speaking 'Indian': Ibn Khallikan II, p. 232.
a poet . . . casting a spell on the river: Ibn Khallikan I, p. 58.
a grammarian . . . parodying the Qur'an: Mas'udi IV, pp. 239–40.

the scholars were . . . distinguished by their dress: Ibn Khallikan III, p. 389.
Nazar and *ra'y* . . . suspicion of heresy: Mas'udi IV, pp. 86 and 319.
To shut the gate . . . to shut down thought: Adonis, *Thabit* III, p. 218.
He who interprets . . . happens to be right: Adonis, *Thabit* I, p. 16.
Guide us to the straight way . . . who went astray: Qur'an, 1:6–7.
Guide us to the Straight Way . . . (such as the Christians): version in *Translation of the Meanings of the Noble Qur'an in the English Language*, Medina, AH 1417, 1:6–7.
the 'Preserved Tablet' mentioned in the Qur'an: Qur'an, 85:22.
members . . . of the [Arabic] alphabet: quoted in Jabiri, p. 226.
Born in Fars . . . Buddhist and Hindu societies: *EI*[2] III, pp. 82–102.
He advocated . . . clothing thirty orphans: Ibn Khallikan I, p. 262; Abu 'l-Fida', part 2, pp. 70–1.
the most ancient pre-Islamic pilgrimages . . . to Marib: pp. 51–2, above.
subversion of the most dangerous sort: Ibn Khallikan I, p. 262.
views differed . . . as they did over Jesus: Ibn Khallikan I, p. 261.
One day I took him his plate . . . was disbelieved: Ibn Khallikan I, p. 261.
al-Hallaj moved his hand . . . dirhams were scattered: Ma'arri, p. 23.
the pre-Islamic *su'luks*, or 'vagabond' poets: pp. 99–101, above.
the Sudanese visionary Mahmud Muhammad Taha: p. 154, above.

CHAPTER 10 COUNTER-CULTURES, COUNTER-CALIPHS

I went by boat . . . say nothing in reply: Mas'udi IV, p. 337.
It means in Turkic, 'Horsetail' or 'Yaktail': *EI*[2], s.v. Badjkam.
to be *akhzar* . . . as un-Arab as possible: Ibn Khallikan I, p. 167.
until the time . . . like hammered shields: Ibn Khallikan II, p. 131.
utruku 'l-turka . . . they leave you alone: Lane, *Arabic-English Lexicon*, s.v. *trk*.
the caliph's tutor tried . . . shindig along the Tigris: Mas'udi IV, pp. 337–8.
And so . . . their rank was lost: Mas'udi IV, p. 315.
Revenues from agriculture . . . under the Umayyads: cf. p. 199, above.
supposedly conservative . . . true figures: Mas'udi IV, pp. 207–8.
one of these Arab *sharifahs* . . . your *mawla* now!: Mas'udi IV, p. 208.
There are mills . . . the wages of the millers: Khusraw, p. 143.
a raid on Mecca in 930 . . . from the Ka'bah: Ibn Khallikan I, pp. 264–5.
In philosophy . . . Mithraism have been detected too: *EI*[2] III, pp. 1075–6.
the three captured Persian princesses . . . nobility: cf. pp. 200–1, above.
The story of Harun . . . consummate the union: cf. pp. 283–4, above.
Nor is any Arab superior . . . except in piety?: p. 169, above.
My father never urged . . . disdainful sovereignty: van Gelder, pp. 35–6.
Ahl al-Taswiyyah, the Levellers: Jahiz, part 3, p. 3.
created you . . . the most pious: Qur'an, 49:13.
You were herdsmen . . . addressing the deaf: Jahiz, part 3, p. 6.
Al-Jahiz believed . . . the empire and Islam: cf. *EI*[2] IX, pp. 514–15.
The Book of the Stick, has already been mentioned: pp. 11–12, above.
pre-Islamic reliefs . . . later centuries BC: Serjeant, *South Arabian Hunt*, pp. 66 and 104.
camel-riders of the ninth century BC: Hoyland, p. 92.
an extension of the orator's hand . . . his gestures: Jahiz, part 3, p. 46.
Orators are to be found . . . of inspiration: Jahiz, part 3, p. 11.
He and other defenders . . . lost political control: cf. Husayn, p. 183.
He who speaks Arabic is an Arab: Adonis, *Thabit* II, pp. 182–3.
the 'splitting of the stick': p. 12, above.
he dislikes foreigners knowing his language: Kilito, p. 87.
and feels they have 'robbed' him of it: Kilito, p. 91.
Do not speak Arabic in the house of the Moor: quoted in Patrick O'Brian, *HMS Surprise*, HarperCollins, 1993, p. 89.
In Egypt and North Africa . . . Copt and Berber Shu'ubis: Suleiman, p. 60.

Non-Arab Muslims . . . short-lived statelets: EI^2 VII, pp. 807–8.
By the eleventh century . . . movement in the East: EI^2 IX, p. 515.
Abu Nuwas . . . laying into backward bedouins: cf. p. 47, above.
the old macho bedouin . . . drooling over pretty boys: Abu Nuwas, p. 559.
the poet spent a long spell . . . Harun al-Rashid: Husayn, p. 176.
the 'North–South split' . . . of Umayyad times: cf. pp. 241–3, above.
Urban lampoons . . . would persist for centuries: e.g. Gelder, pp. 107–8.
Ottoman nationalists: EI^2 IX, p. 515.
opponents of Arab Nationalism: Suleiman, p. 238.
even Marxists: EI^2 IX, p. 515.
Saddam Husayn's . . . war of the 1980s: Suleiman, p. 63.
likened to the Qarmatis: by the Grand Mufti of Iraq, quoted in baraqish.net, December 2016.
and to . . . Abrahah the Ethiopian: by a Yemeni shaykh of the al-Shayif clan, quoted in baraqish.net, December 2016.
al-Mansur . . . power-base in Khurasan: Baladhuri, pp. 415–16.
Turks . . . are the bedouins of the non-Arabs: Jahiz quoted in Pellat, p. 97.
The Turk has two . . . at the back of his head: Jahiz quoted in Pellat, p. 93.
his mother was herself a Turkic slave-concubine: Hitti, p. 466.
Al-Mu'tasim founded . . . foreign troops to it: Mas'udi IV, pp. 53–4.
Samarra' has been likened to Versailles: Nicholson, p. 263.
al-Mu'tasim's jester . . . po-faced courtiers: Mas'udi IV, pp. 49–50.
they were divided . . . scale model of the empire: Mas'udi IV, pp. 54–5.
six variant ways of writing the name in Arabic: Ibn Khallikan I, p. 29.
Sword tells more truth . . . lights of heaven: quoted in Irwin, p. 132.
The poet . . . moral foundation of the Islamic state: Suzanne Pinckney Stetkevych, p. 64.
ancient Arab heroism . . . by an army of Turks: Mas'udi IV, p. 60.
al-Abbas ibn al-Ma'mun . . . on Constantinople: Mas'udi IV, p. 60.
He was exceedingly drunk . . . buried together: Mas'udi IV, pp. 120–1.
he died of a chill . . . and a poisoned scalpel: Mas'udi IV, pp. 133–4.
Mother, give up . . . two shirts instead of one: Ibn Khallikan I, p. 494.
Bugha and Wasif . . . A polly-parrot's squawk: Mas'udi IV, p. 145.
the Turks eventually . . . beheaded him: Mas'udi IV, pp. 164–5.
How marvellous . . . their guest in his own caliphate: Mas'udi IV, p. 169.
Moving quickly . . . in a poisoned bedsheet: Mas'udi IV, p. 176.
swoop down on him . . . in gaol a few days later: Mas'udi IV, p. 177.
to whitewash over . . . his own business: Mas'udi IV, pp. 189–90.
some of his more sybaritic subjects . . . Turkish guard: Mas'udi IV, p. 183.
a complex power-struggle . . . Turkish factions: EI^2, s.v. al-Muhtadī.
killed by a drunken Turk . . . his victim's blood: Mas'udi IV, p. 186.
He replied . . . as quickly as possible: Mas'udi IV, p. 186.
Another glass! . . . Harem warder of stars: quoted in Irwin, p. 145.
he lasted less than . . . partisans of his nephew: EI^2, s.v. Ibn al-Mu^{c}tazz.
Ibn al-Mu'tazz had himself . . . the caliphate's decadence: Irwin, p. 143.
Let's chuck this age in . . . to the fiery pit: Mas'udi IV, p. 298.
Our alien *amir* . . . took off, alas!: Mas'udi IV, p. 299.
al-Radi, faded away of dropsy at the age of thirty-one: EI^2, s.v. al-Rāḍī.
he was blinded . . . to drown his screams: Mas'udi IV, pp. 342–3.
'That,' said his uncle . . . Now we need a third: Mas'udi IV, p. 343.
al-Mustakfi was dethroned . . . band of Iranian hillmen: Mas'udi IV, p. 371.
their father, Buwayh . . . buried treasure: Ibn Khallikan II, pp. 190–1.
serving in the armies . . . greater power themselves: EI^2, s.v. Buwayhids.
the Hamdanids . . . generally pro-Shi'ah: EI^2, s.v. Ḥamdānids.
'Al-Muti' . . . with no power to command or forbid: Mas'udi IV, pp. 371–2.
Mu'izz al-Dawlah the Daylamite spoke no Arabic: Karsh, p. 64.
an 'Iranian intermezzo': Minorsky quoted in EI^2, s.v. Buwayhids.

Adud al-Dawlah . . . verses in praise of wine: Ibn Khallikan II, p. 264.
Tughril . . . could only speak to the caliph via an interpreter: Hitti, p. 474.
Tughril . . . marriage with the caliph's daughter: Ibn Khallikan III, p. 34.
Alp Arslan . . . after his uncle's death: *EI*[2], s.v. Alp Arslān.
the first Turk to cross the Euphrates: Ibn Khallikan III, p. 36.
ruled an empire . . . emperor of the world: Ibn Khallikan III, p. 143.
nothing but his title: Ibn Khallikan III, p. 145.
the killing in 1138 . . . by Ghiyath al-Din: Ibn Khallikan III, p. 102.
to crown Saljuq princes . . . ceremonial armlets: Ibn Khallikan III, p. 38.
The non-Arab rulers . . . destruction of Arabness: Ibn Khaldun, *Muqaddimah*, p. 166.
Arabs turned in on themselves: Ibn Khaldun, *Rihlah*, p. 394.
I wish . . . peace and blessings be upon him: Ibn Khallikan I, p. 255.
The best marksmen . . . all the wealth in the world: Ibn Khallikan III, p. 145.
The *madrasah*'s origins . . . further than Nizam al-Mulk: Albert Hourani, p. 163.
the eponymous Nizamiyyah . . . basis of all learning: cf. Hitti, p. 410.
later *madrasah*s ... including Sufism: Albert Hourani, p. 163.
some aspects . . . imitated from the *madrasah*: Hitti, p. 410.
You've built fine colleges . . . from perdition: Maqrizi II, p. 375.
The university student . . . late Abbasid *madrasah*: Rabin, 'Beginnings', p. 19.
*madrasah*s . . . continuity of the old Arab empire: cf. Hodgson II, p. 48.
*madrasah*s were pro-Sunni, anti-Shi'ah: cf. *EI*[2] I, p. 20.
the former in the southern . . . other non-Arabs: Ibn Khaldun, *Rihlah*, p. 386.
al-Muttaqi . . . his Turkish protectors/persecutors: Mas'udi IV, p. 340.
Sayf al-Dawlah . . . raids into Byzantine territory: Ibn Khallikan II, p. 193.
To petticoats . . . multicoloured underlapping train: Ibn Khallikan II, p. 191.
the meeting-place of writers . . . their palace gates: Ibn Khallikan II, p. 191.
with an amount of cash . . . about his guests: Ibn Khallikan I, p. 454.
descendants of Arab tribesmen . . . Persian-speakers: cf. p. 250, above.
a Persian version of the Qur'an: Kennedy, pp. 261–2.
Ya'qub . . . made of silver: Ibn Khallikan III, p. 402.
he took an army deep into . . . Persia and Iraq: Mas'udi IV, pp. 200–2.
the lieutenant-governor . . . from the caliph: Hitti, pp. 452–3.
Ahmad ibn Tulun's father . . . on Iraqi home ground: Mas'udi IV, pp. 210–13.
the Abbasids . . . in the middle of things: cf. p. 263, above.
the caliph reasserted himself over Egypt and Syria: Hitti, p. 455.
a common name . . . because camphor is so white: Ibn Khallikan II, p. 449.
He had been bought for . . . eighteen dinars: Ibn Khallikan II, p. 283.
You think the earth of Egypt . . . made it belly-dance: Ibn Khallikan, p. 285.
A well-hung . . . with no balls?: Ibn Khallikan II, p. 284.
The sun of Egypt . . . made it all Arab: quoted in Suleiman, p. 80.
His immovability . . . a wry nickname, 'the Black Stone': *EI*[2], s.v. Kāfūr.
their ancestor . . . his actual father was a Jew: Maqrizi I, pp. 348–9.
When he was securely . . . 'We hear and obey!': Ibn Khallikan II, p. 40.
the full caliphal look . . . with jewelled turban: Ibn Khallikan III, p. 187.
variously into books . . . and downright sadism: Ibn Khallikan, s.v. individual Fatimid caliphs.
an Armenian . . . Sayf al-Islam, 'the Sword of Islam': *EI*[2], s.v. Fāṭimids.
they had roamed . . . points further west: *EI*[2], s.v. Hilāl; Kennedy, p. 205.
still almost entirely Berber . . . Arab-founded towns: cf. Owens, 'Dialect History', p. 732.
The Arabs outnumbered . . . most of their lands: Ibn Khaldun, *Muqaddimah*, pp. 29–30.
the mass migrations numbered a . . . million: cf. Versteegh, *Arabic Language*, p. 96.
the Berber languages . . . highland areas: Versteegh, *Arabic Language*, p. 96.
Formerly, the whole region . . . in ruin: Ibn Khaldun, *Muqaddimah*, p. 119.
the traveller . . . death at the hands of malefactors: al-Abdari quoted in Mackintosh-Smith, *Tangerine*, p. 52.
the Mediterranean . . . thus cursed by Allah: Maqdisi, p. 28.

Ibn Khaldun . . . his wife and five daughters were drowned: Ibn Khaldun, *Rihlah*, p. 295 and n. 1364.
Al-Ma'qil . . . the great Arabian grouping called Madhhij: EI^2, s.v. al-Ma^{c}qil.
Sir: You know who we are . . . Greetings: Ibn Khallikan III, p. 185.
in 929 Abd al-Rahman III . . . hallowed office: EI^2, s.v. ^{c}Abd al-Raḥmān III.
in the shape of a bird . . . its finest part is its tail: Ibn Khallikan III, p. 162.
Tariq ibn Ziyad's largely Berber incursion: cf. p. 254, above.
followed by a wave of Arab settlers: Kennedy, pp. 309–10.
al-Azd, al-Aws . . . Arabic letters of one such list: Maqqari VIII, pp. 231–5.
His distant ancestor . . . shifted to North Africa: Ibn Khaldun, *Rihlah*, pp. 50–8.
Abd al-Rahman II . . . at the conservatoire in Medina: EI^2 IV, p. 822.
al-Qali . . . the old Arabian homeland: Ibn Khallikan I, p. 122, III, p. 522.
the caliph of Cordova commissioned . . . two capitals: Ibn Khallikan II, p. 146.
al-Hakam, ordered . . . *De materia medica*: Mathews, p. 91.
he had agents . . . illuminators were to be seen: Jabiri, p. 302.
Al-Hakam's library . . . contained 400,000 volumes: EI^2 VI, p. 198.
Cordova, a city with . . . seventy libraries: Atiyah, p. 71.
competition . . . levels of literary patronage: cf. Ibn Khallikan II, p. 158.
every individual . . . follow accepted authority: Jabiri, p. 309.
Ibn Rushd . . . into the European Renaissance: Jabiri, pp. 322–3 and 344.
O Palm . . . have my old friends forgot: Nicholson, p. 418.
letters addressed . . . at Medina: e.g. Ibn Khaldun, *Rihlah*, p. 286.
King Offa's Arabic coinage: pp. 263–4, above.
In Nomine Domini: Non Deus Nisi Deus Solus: Kennedy, pp. 316–17.
intoxicated . . . with Arab eloquence: Hitti, pp. 515–16.
studying alongside Muslims in . . . Cordova: Hitti, pp. 530–1.
an Arabic Bible for the Christian 'Mozarab' population: Lewis, *Arabs in History*, 134.
musta'rib . . . of that other peninsula, Arabia: cf. p. 30, above.
about 4,000 . . . Arabic loan words in Spanish: Versteegh, *Arabic Language*, p. 228.
the Abbasid caliph al-Qa'im . . . ibn Qabban: Ibn Khallikan I, p. 105.
the Arab *Staatsnation* . . . to being a *Kulturnation*: Grunebaum, p. 8.
culture . . . when they have lost all else: quoted in Jabiri, p. 38. The original goes, 'La culture, c'est ce qui demeure dans l'homme lorsqu'il a tout oublié.'
Arabs had . . . fallen: cf. p. 307, above.
nations and fictional characters . . . run out of steam: Rushdie, p. 391.
poems were engraved . . . sleeves of robes: e.g. Ibn Khallikan I, pp. 119 and 482–3.
Such lines of descent . . . back 1,500 years: e.g. the twentieth-century author's own line in Kurdi, pp. 211–16.
al-Sahib ibn Abbad . . . library of manuscripts: p. 278, above.
Is this the hand of Qabus . . . *tawus* [a peacock]?: Ibn Khallikan II, p. 275.
extraordinary momentum . . . buildings of the world: Byron, pp. 198–9.
Arab historians call him 'the last real caliph': Hitti, pp. 469–70.

CHAPTER 11 THE GENIUS IN THE BOTTLE

low humour, sharp satire and touches of smut: cf. EI^2, s.v. Khayāl al-Ẓill.
al-Radi was 'the last real caliph': cf. p. 347, above.
Such as I / live when we die . . . flatulence: Abu 'l-Fida', *Mukhtasar* part 4, p. 132. The translation, somewhat loose but very much in the spirit of the original, is from Mackintosh-Smith, *Thousand Columns*, p. 53.
he and his family . . . had to sell their clothes: Ibn Hajar II, p. 142.
Crusaders shared . . . baronial wars: Atiyah, p. 44.
against the pagans . . . among the Christians: Fulcher of Chartres quoted in Karsh, p. 73.
the navel of the world . . . of their treasures: Fulcher of Chartres quoted in Karsh, pp. 73–4.
European chroniclers . . . even cannibalism: Maalouf, pp. 39–40.
The slaughter of Muslims . . . 360 years earlier: Maalouf, pp. 50–1.

The sultans were at loggerheads . . . the country: Ibn al-Athir quoted in Karsh, p. 77.
in 1111, another plea arrived . . . to expel them: Maalouf, p. 83.
the Saljuq sultan mobilized . . . refused to join it: Karsh, p. 77.
The men of war . . . went to the winner: Ibn Jubayr, pp. 260–1.
in expiation . . . to drink alcohol: Maqqari II, pp. 385–6.
reciprocal alms-giving: Ibn Jubayr, p. 259.
al-Harawi . . . his Muslim pilgrim-guide: Harawi, p. 31.
They have the qualities . . . in carrying loads: Usamah, p. 132.
a few of the older Frankish hands . . . polish: Usamah, pp. 134 and 140.
would address me as 'my brother' . . . do not disobey her: Usamah, p. 132; translation in Mackintosh-Smith, 'Interpreter of Treasures: Encounters', p. 38.
Benedict . . . or perhaps 'of the Ape': Usamah, pp. 40 and 41.
the Frankish lord of al-Shaqif . . . of Muhammad: Ibn Khallikan III, p. 506.
Dikiz (de Guise), Shanbur (Chambord): Maalouf, p. 276.
Franjieh . . . and Bardawil (Baldwin): Hitti, p. 670.
the Abbadid mini-dynasty . . . of al-Hirah: Ibn Khallikan III, p. 12.
The Franks . . . busy fighting each other: Ibn Khallikan III, p. 16.
It is better . . . swine of the Franks: Ibn Khallikan III, p. 469.
according to a German . . . Muslim subjects in line: Suchem, p. 8.
his young grandson . . . keep the family alive: Ibn Khallikan III, pp. 20–1.
the ancient Lakhmid ruler . . . 'king of all the Arabs': pp. 67–8, above.
Arab rule dwindled . . . faded away: Ibn Khaldun, *Rihlah*, p. 56.
that Arab fall in the east: cf. p. 307, above.
the daughter of al-Andalus: Ibn Jubayr, p. 297.
The meadow-land . . . for all the rest's a wilderness: Maqqari I, p. 210.
Yusuf ibn Tashfin . . . 'al-Himyari' in the traditional histories: Norris, p. 35.
Ibn Khaldun would dismiss the claims: Ibn Khaldun, *Muqaddimah*, pp. 14–15.
the myth . . . is still alive: e.g. in Muḥammad Ḥusayn al-Faraḥ, *ʿUrūbat al-barbar*, San'a, 2004.
Muhammad ibn Tumart forged . . . the Prophet: cf. *EI*[2] III, p. 1064.
Yusuf ibn Abd al-Mu'min . . . minds of the day: Ibn Khallikan III, pp. 477–9.
Ah, the wonders of the world . . . Kumyah: Ibn Khallikan III, p. 480; the Qur'anic quotation is Qur'an, 36:78.
there were attempts . . . dismissed them: Ibn Khallikan III, pp. 481–2.
The great commander . . . quote poetry: Ibn Khallikan III, pp. 507 and 513.
his younger brother composed . . . Arabic verses: Ibn Khallikan I, p. 152.
Saladin exhumed . . . for reburial in Medina: Ibn Khallikan I, pp. 137–8.
corpses . . . Meccan rites before burial: e.g. Ibn Khallikan I, p. 180.
the Egyptians had fought . . . home town, Medina: Ibn Khallikan III, p. 211.
Turanshah . . . punishing posting: Ibn Khallikan I, p. 160.
Another Ayyubid . . . lost his mind: Ibn Khallikan I, pp. 436–7.
turned in on themselves: p. 328, above.
England's Black Prince . . . on his bed-curtains: Tuchman, p. 294.
Boccaccio embroidered . . . in the *Decameron*: Boccaccio, *Decameron*, Oxford University Press, 1993, pp. 652–68.
He has the longest entry . . . Arab origin: Ibn Khallikan III, pp. 481–519.
Spanish uses . . . 4,000 Arabic loan words: p. 344, above.
Sicilian dialect . . . terms used by farmers: Carmichael, p. 256.
Piazza Ballarò . . . Indian monarch, Balhara: Yule I, p. 241. 'Balhara' itself is from a Prakrit title meaning 'well-beloved king'.
military and associated innovations . . . dyestuffs: Hitti, pp. 663–8.
English . . . 2,000 Arabic-origin words: Cannon, *passim*.
a cheque . . . a quarter of Baghdad: the examples are from Cannon. One or two are disputed by the *Oxford English Dictionary*.
up the Amazon . . . *mamalucos* (*mamluks*, slaves): cf. Elizabeth Bishop and Robert Lowell, *Words in Air*, Farrar, Straus, Giroux, New York, 2008, p. 317. In the French Caribbean colonies in the

eighteenth century, a *mamélouc* was specifically a person with one black great-great-grandparent. Patrick Leigh Fermor, *The Traveller's Tree*, Penguin, London, 1984, p. 243.
Chile's Robinson Crusoe Island . . . an *aldea*: cf. Gavin Young, *Slow Boats Home*, Penguin, London, 1986, pp. 322–4.
Alfonso VI . . . called himself 'King of the Two Faiths': Atiyah, p. 66.
a scholar of high lineage . . . with great favour: Ibn al-Khatib III, p. 48.
their students were known as *arabizantes*: Versteegh, *Arabic Language*, pp. 1–2.
We [Italians] . . . extinguished genius of Italy!: quoted in Kilito, p. 2.
he would refuse . . . medications with Arabic names: Kilito, p. 38.
the old Graeco-Italian wind rose . . . Souróko for the south-east wind: Patrick Leigh Fermor, *Mani*, Penguin, London, 1984, pp. 275–6.
The Island of Anqiltarrah . . . It always rains there: Idrisi II, p. 944.
Hastinkash (Hastings) . . . Aghrimas (Grimsby): Idrisi II, p. 880.
Rujar al-Mu'tazz bi 'llah . . . [the Pope] of Rome: Idrisi I, pp. 3–4. To pick a nit, he was in fact the Strengthener of the Antipope Anacletus II.
William II . . . including his head chef: Ibn Jubayr, pp. 297–300.
lofty palaces . . . from such temptation: Ibn Jubayr, p. 298.
Of this ancient city . . . its famous name: Ibn Jubayr, pp. 193–4.
polymaths like the Syrian Ibn Wasil: Abu 'l-Fida', *Mukhtasar*, part 4, pp. 38–9.
poets like the Egyptian Ibn al-Qalaqis: Ibn Khallikan III, p. 310.
it is as if they do not believe . . . God's earth: Ibn Jubayr, pp. 193–4.
a young man . . . to go about incognito: Ibn Jubayr, pp. 203–4.
Fi 'l-harakah barakah . . . pain can lead to gain: Ibn Khallikan III, p. 270.
that made me forget home . . . greediest glutton: Ibn Khallikan III, p. 270.
spent the last part . . . outside Aleppo: Ibn Khallikan III, p. 268.
he longed to translate himself . . . never took root: Ibn Khallikan III, p. 273.
the greatest calamity of all: Abu 'l-Fida', *Mukhtasar*, part 3, p. 122.
Khwarizm Shah . . . let the Mongols in: Baghdadi, pp. 126–7.
al-Nasir . . . Khwarizmian invasion of Iraq: Abu 'l-Fida', *Mukhtasar*, part 3, p. 136.
the Khwarizmian generals . . . let them in: Abu 'l-Fida', *Mukhtasar*, part 3, p. 128.
The news of the Tatars . . . forget all histories: Baghdadi, p. 136.
Probably not until the end . . . seen again: quoted in Maalouf, p. 235.
that whitens the hair . . . of the godless Tatars: Ibn Khallikan III, p. 271.
The same traveller . . . raids by the Khafajah tribe: Ibn Jubayr, p. 187.
Baghdadi townsfolk . . . battling each other: Serjeant, *South Arabian Hunt*, pp. 23–5.
the vizier . . . raid on a Shi'i town: Abu 'l-Fida', *Mukhtasar*, part 3, pp. 193–4.
The fate of al-Musta'sim . . . kicked to death: Abu 'l-Fida', *Mukhtasar*, part 3, p. 194.
is said to have made complete forecasts . . . into the Tigris: Ibn Khaldun, *Muqaddimah*, p. 261. It is known (Dunlop, p. 178) that al-Kindi predicted a slightly later date for the destruction – AH 693/ AD 1293. His margin of error is thus a creditable 7 per cent.
Only in war . . . divination too will perish then: Osip Mandelstam, 'Tristia', 1922, translated by C.M. Bowra.
tribal Arabs . . . raid into the settled heartland of Iraq: Carmichael, p. 246.
[There were] Ad and Thamud . . . desert origins: Ibn Khaldun, *Muqaddimah*, pp. 121–2.
Al-Radi . . . the last to preach at Friday prayers: p. 347, above.
the imams descended from . . . Quraysh: p. 363, above.
Abu Sufyan . . . discipline never seen among Arabs: p. 2, above.
masters . . . fending off the tyrannous and aggressive: Maqrizi II, p. 214.
al-Nasir . . . a great-grandson reigned after him: cf. Hitti, p. 673.
boundless in multitude . . . scarce contain them: Ibn Battutah I, p. 41.
on a rock between two lions: p. 69, above.
he went about playing . . . to the Mamluk fold: Ibn Hajar, s.v. Muhannā.
Fayyad . . . badly behaved: Ibn Hajar, s.v. Fayyāḍ.
they adopted Persian . . . cultural first language: cf. Chejne, p. 81.
Arabic was further diminished: cf. Nicholson, pp. 446–7.

Ah, woe to him on whom it calls! . . . cringed and crumpled: Ibn al-Wardi in Abu 'l-Fida', *Mukhtasar*, part 4, p. 152. The translation is from Mackintosh-Smith, *Tangerine*, p. 163.
the all-consuming plague . . . upon it: Ibn Khaldun, *Rihlah*, p. 74.
Ibn Khaldun was in the city . . . Mongolian: Ibn Khaldun, *Rihlah*, p. 408.
writing to the Berber sultan . . . his hordes: Ibn Khaldun, *Rihlah*, p. 416.
an Abbasid chancer . . . puppet-caliph: Ibn Khaldun, *Rihlah*, pp. 409–10.
was plundered . . . naked in the wilderness: Ibn Khaldun, *Rihlah*, p. 413.
the arabness . . . stressed by local historians: e.g. Ibn al-Khatib I, p. 36.
a [Berber] Masmudi client of . . . Banu Makhzum: Ibn al-Khatib III, p. 231.
Ibn Battutah . . . immigrants from West Africa and India: cf. Arié, p. 303.
an uncle and a nephew were battling . . . the sultanate: Hitti, p. 553.
Fortune desires . . . busy looms of Yemen: quoted in Irwin, pp. 306–7.
there was little or nothing . . . 1058: e.g. Baerlein, p. 17; Huart, p. 98.
If I were asked . . . I would be at a loss to answer: Kilito, p. 8.
could not outrun its own shadow: Jaroslav Stetkevych, p. 9.
'asr al-taraju', the Age of Retrogression: e.g. Jabiri, p. 328.
It was an age of condensations . . . of commentaries on all these: Ibn Shaqrun, p. 104; translation from Mackintosh-Smith, *Tangerine*, p. 43.
Ibn Khaldun's 'turning in': cf. p. 328, above.
al-Sahib ibn Abbad's . . . Arabic philology alone: p. 296, above.
Most books disappeared . . . a load for a single camel: Suyuti I, p. 74.
the Arabic world . . . since the fall of Baghdad: Adonis, *Poetics*, p. 77.
it has been ruled . . . 'the resigned mind': Jabiri, p. 328.
Half our verses . . . when the building's falling down?: Qabbani, p. 785.
imitators in Persian and even Hebrew: *EI*[2], s.v. Maḳāmāt.

CHAPTER 12 MASTERS OF THE MONSOON

I do not know . . . either of them: Ibn Battutah III, p. 683.
the Mamluks' shadow-puppet caliph in Egypt: cf. pp. 348–9, above.
two pages . . . about the man's avarice: Ibn Battutah III, pp. 683–5.
The Arabic inscription . . . to Caliph al-Mustansir: Hurgronje, pp. 101–2.
the neighbouring grave . . . of the sultan's daughter: Lambourn, p. 235.
By God . . . from such a state of things!: Ibn Battutah III, pp. 684–5.
Cambay memorials have been found . . . in Java: Mackintosh-Smith, *Landfalls*, p. 34; Lambourn, *passim*.
the ogival tops . . . hanging in a niche: e.g. Daum, pp. 249–51.
Allah is the Light . . . whomever He wishes: Qur'an, 24:35.
a quotation from a Persian poem by Sa'di: Lambourn, pp. 229–30.
particularly from Jain temples: Lambourn, p. 233.
Two hungers . . . worldly things: quoted in Mackintosh-Smith, *Landfalls*, p. 339.
he landed at a place . . . resolutely virgin: Ibn Battutah IV, pp. 884–7.
that island in al-Hariri's tales . . . and a sphinx: p. 377, above.
Dawah wa-batak . . . the Compassionate: Ibn Battutah IV, p. 886.
Arabic had begun . . . the script of Old Malay: *EI*[2] IV, p. 1128.
Majapahit coins . . . the messenger of Allah: http://masterpieces.asemus.museum/masterpiece/detail.nhn?objectId=11280 (accessed 1 November 2018). The glorious syncretism has lived on. Writing of those shadow-puppet deities in the mid-twentieth century, Anthony Burgess described a puppet-master calling, before a performance, 'on many gods and devils ... not to take offence at the crude representation of their acts ... he abased himself before their greatness. And he remembered the one true religion, invoking the protection of the four archangels of the Koran'. See Anthony Burgess, *The Malayan Trilogy*, Vintage, London, 2000, p. 346.
the spiteful Mediterranean . . . precious products: Maqdisi, p. 28; cf. p. 339, above.
the Sea of India . . . many are its blessings: Sirafi and Ibn Fadlan, p. 125.
His own verses . . . found in Sumatra: p. 384, above.

in a song . . . in the Chinese city of Hangzhou: Ibn Battutah IV, p. 903.
I shall take Persian sulphur . . . I shall give up trading: Sa'di, p. 131.
the Mongol ravages . . . 'energized' ocean trade: cf. Ho, p. 100.
a hemispheric trade network . . . to the Pacific: Abu-Lughod, pp. 228–30; EI^2 IV, p. 641.
they were expatriate Arabs . . . Hashimi clan: Levtzion and Pouwels, p. 255.
merchants from Sumatra . . . to attract trade: Ho, p. 102.
Local histories . . . direct from Mecca to Sumatra: EI^2, s.v. Indonesia.
The flow increased . . . the thirteenth century: cf. Hardy, p. 33.
Muhammad Shah sent fleets . . . to recruit Arabs: Dunn, p. 226.
They gathered . . . moths around a candle: Isami quoted in Dunn, p. 183.
Ghiyath al-Din had . . . a gold bath: Ibn Battutah III, p. 681.
the buttons . . . were pearls as big as hazelnuts: Ibn Battutah III, p. 683.
addressed them all as 'my lord': Ibn Battutah III, pp. 745–6.
Muhanna ibn Isa, the *amir* of the Arabs in Syria: cf. p. 370, above.
Muhammad Shah assigned . . . of the season: Ibn Battutah III, pp. 686–9.
The sultan showed . . . in the sultan's gaol: Ibn Battutah III, pp. 689–90.
learned good manners and refinement: Ibn Battutah III, p. 692.
The sultan would share . . . with no one else: Ibn Battutah III, p. 680.
the part of Delhi . . . the Abode of the Caliphate: Ibn Battutah III, p. 619.
Muhammad Shah lay . . . on the sultanic neck: Ibn Battutah III, pp. 682–3.
the Mamluk's puppet-caliph al-Mustakfi Sulayman: pp. 348–9, above.
by the time . . . his son and successor: Jackson, p. 272.
My father prevented . . . to become an idolator: Husain, pp. 173–4.
in Delhi and then again . . . own birthplace: Ibn Battutah IV, pp. 899–900.
he stayed with al-Bushri's brother . . . the Sahara: Ibn Battutah IV, p. 946.
How far apart they were!: Ibn Battutah IV, p. 900.
the five sons . . . from Tunisia to Samarqand: p. 194, above.
the brother governors in Tunisia and Sind: p. 267, above.
the distinguished Granadan . . . in Timbuktu: Ibn Battutah IV, p. 969.
names on the surviving . . . Persians and Turks: Mackintosh-Smith, *Landfalls*, p. 199; cf. Chen and Kalus I, *passim*.
the richest city under the heavens: Chen and Kalus I, p. 28.
twelve of the twenty-two . . . were Muslims: Chen and Kalus I, p. 33.
Ibn Battutah met a Jew . . . unremarkable: Ibn Battutah II, p. 480.
Abraham ibn Yiju . . . in the India trade: Ghosh, *passim*.
Abu Zikri ha-Kohen . . . in Sudanese Sawakin: Chaudhuri, p. 59.
when the preacher rose . . . science of grammar: Ibn Battutah II, p. 277.
the first extant Old Malay text . . . as early as 1326: EI^2 IV, p. 1128.
The list of languages . . . in the Balkans: e.g. Macdonald, *Development*, p. 22, n. 47; EI^2 IV, p. 1113; Kurdi, pp. 47–53.
certain 'secret' languages . . . Madagascar: Versteegh, *Arabic Language*, p. 232.
Persian *nasta'liq* . . . *ducks*: Kurdi, pp. 363–4.
In post-Ottoman Turkish . . . still 26 per cent: Versteegh, 'Linguistic Contacts…', p. 495.
attempts to persianize . . . in the nineteenth century: Versteegh, 'Linguistic Contacts…', p. 491.
at least 30 per cent of the vocabulary remains Arabic: Chejne, p. 4.
Sikh *khalsa* . . . *khalisah* is 'pure': Yule and Burnell, s.v. Khalsa.
'Blighty' . . . especially Europe/Britain: Cannon, s.v. Blighty; Yule and Burnell, s.v. Bilayut.
Bangladeshi Bengali . . . of Arabic origin: Versteegh, *Arabic Language*, p. 237.
Arabic has bequeathed . . . 3,000 loan words: Versteegh, *Arabic Language*, 238.
Elcho Island . . . Allah, exalted is He: *BBC Magazine* (accessed 25 June 2014).
Banu Hilal . . . arabicized the lowlands: pp. 338–9, above.
Berber languages . . . now Arabic: Versteegh, 'Linguistic Contacts…', p. 482.
Bornu . . . inhabitants of Arab origin: Versteegh, 'Linguistic Contacts…', p. 483.

Arabic has loaned it . . . half of its vocabulary: <40 per cent according to Versteegh, 'Linguistic Contacts...', p. 487; <50 per cent according to Versteegh, *Arabic Language*, p. 231.
saikolojia . . . the science of the soul: Versteegh, *Arabic Language*, p. 230.
Nafisah's in Cairo has been mentioned: p. 358, above.
that of Qutham . . . in Samarqand: pp. 194–5, above.
a real live Abbasid . . . en route to Delhi: Ibn Battutah, p. 679.
buried and venerated in . . . Tamil Nadu: Hussein, p. 472.
the sacred house . . . Vestibule of the Ka'bah: Mackintosh-Smith, *Landfalls*, p. 276.
Nizam al-Din . . . on a flying camel: Rizvi, pp. 9–10.
Daftar Jaylani . . . 5,000 kilometres away: Mackintosh-Smith, *Landfalls*, pp. 156–7.
The great number . . . through custom: Ibn Khaldun, *Muqaddimah*, pp. 414–15.
are Arabs . . . there is no need for translations: Haeri, p. 75.
cave eremism . . . from their Buddhist peers: Rizvi, p. 88.
pranayama . . . from yogis: Rizvi, pp. 95–6 and 189.
Muslim penitents . . . at Khajuraho: Ibn Battutah IV, p. 790.
Haydari dervishes . . . penis-piercing: Ibn Battutah III, p. 583.
from Naga *sanyasis*: Rizvi, p. 307.
he converted a Hindu temple . . . with the building: Lawrence, p. 123.
Isma'ili missionaries . . . Ali of Vishnu: Rizvi, p. 110.
Mecca was still . . . the navel of the world: p. 123, above.
Receptive now my heart is . . . my faith: Lings, p. 62.
metamorphic masks . . . Muhammad's uncle is cursed: Levtzion and Pouwels, p. 499, ill. 500; the chapter is Qur'an, 111; cf. p. 146, above.
came here and brought Islam . . . their own beliefs as well: Mackintosh-Smith, *Landfalls*, pp. 278–9.
Sulayman al-Mahri . . . Good Hope: Tibbetts, p. 43.
The Ming revolution . . . foreign traffic: cf. Abu-Lughod, p. 259.
coming up from every direction . . . attack furious: quoted in Rogan, p. 21.
and the caliphate . . . were cut off: Jabarti I, p. 37.
the Ottoman sultans adopted the . . . somewhat gingerly: cf. Hitti, p. 705.
Leave the Turks alone as long as they leave you alone: p. 306, above.
al-Suyuti had illustrated . . . second-rate books: p. 375, above.
The way to a top job . . . non-Muslim subjects: Rogan, p. 31.
The Arabs fell into a lethargy . . . aware of their Arabness: Chejne, p. 83.
the intellectual few . . . non-arabophones: e.g. Jabarti I, p. 462.
it was too early to speak . . . to 'foreign' rule: Rogan, p. 24.
less than 1 per cent . . . would ever learn Turkish: Versteegh, *Arabic Language*, p. 175.
Arabs had been 'masters of the coast' . . . the time of Pliny: Cherian, p. 1.
they live in settlements . . . like 'Kampong Arab': Young, p. 269.
trade in rattans and precious aloes-wood: Young, p. 244.
those same oceanic products . . . of Arab travel: p. 386, above.
Kaffs and Saqqafs . . . and Colombo: Mackintosh-Smith, *Thousand Columns*, p. 287.
Hadrami missionaries . . . seaborne Bugis: Ho, pp. 162–8.
Sayyid Muhammad . . . could found a dynasty: Taj al-Din, pp. 34 and 45–6.
rulers of the Comoros . . . today as rajas: Ho, p. 168 and n. 15.
in 1905, Hadramis . . . numbered 30,000: Versteegh, 'Linguistic Contacts...', p. 499.
the British royal house . . . 'Islamic' dynasty: cf. Mather, p. 240.
Under pressure . . . repeatedly thereafter: EI^2 VI, p. 795.
in Constantinople alone . . . tens of thousands: EI^2 VI, p. 795.
complete Arabic fonts . . . 900-plus different characters: Abu-Absi, p. 340.
The letter *mim* . . . seventy-three different guises: Abu-Absi, p. 340.
the Greek alphabet . . . mid-eighth century BC: Hornblower and Spawforth, s.v. Alphabet; cf. p. 83, above.
using only the separate forms of characters: Kurdi, pp. 128–9.
attempts to invent the equivalent of capital letters: Kurdi, pp. 109–10.
Arabic script . . . of their great leaders: Kurdi, pp. 72 and 160.

The oldest surviving Arabic printed book . . . in 1514: *EI*^{2} VI, p. 795.
Christians in Lebanon . . . a hundred years later: *EI*^{2} VI, p. 796.
in Aleppo another hundred years on: Hitti, p. 747.
The first press in Constantinople . . . in 1722: *EI*^{2} VI, p. 795.
The *Amir* of the Army . . . to the poor and needy!: Jabarti II, pp. 226–7.
Muhammad Ali Pasha's . . . in 1822: *EI*^{2} VI, p. 797–8; Carmichael, p. 287.
the European print revolution . . . scientific revolution: e.g. in Wootton, *passim*.
Bacon and Carlyle . . . discoveries of modern times: Francis Bacon, *Novum Organum* I, Aphorism 129; Thomas Carlyle, *Critical and Miscellaneous Essays*, 'The State of German Literature'.
He who first shortened . . . the art of printing: Thomas Carlyle, *Sartor Resartus* I, chapter 5.
faqirs . . . Persians, Turks and Anatolians: Ibn Battutah II, p. 479.
those in the Eastern Desert of Egypt: Ibn Battutah I, p. 68.
the marauding Arab . . . besieging Tunis: Ibn Battutah IV, p. 922.
Those accursed *a'rab* . . . that besets people: Jabarti II, p. 350.
O people! The *'arab* have fallen upon you!: Jabarti II, p. 257.

CHAPTER 13 IDENTITY REDISCOVERED

In this age of ours . . . cannot be brought back: Jabarti I, p. 9.
the wickedest of races: pp. 408–9, above.
age of oblivion . . . fifty years or so: Jabarti I, p. 12.
plundered the Mecca pilgrim caravans: e.g. Jabarti I, pp. 309–10.
the townspeople of Cairo . . . prayers and sticks: Jabarti II, p. 186.
Each dining-room . . . neither less nor more: Jabarti II, p. 196.
white, black and Abyssinian . . . Frankish women: Jabarti II, p. 251.
they tried to get the three . . . tricolour versions: Jabarti II, pp. 203–4.
for people to travel . . . festivals and weddings: Jabarti II, p. 230.
shrieking with laughter . . . the common yobs: Jabarti II, pp. 436–7.
the wheelbarrow: Jabarti II, p. 232.
the public library . . . lower ranks of the soldiery: Jabarti II, p. 233.
One's body . . . being cracked: Jabarti II, pp. 234–6.
Having demolished . . . properties registered: Jabarti II, pp. 206–10.
French court procedure was based . . . on reason: Jabarti II, p. 359.
elections by ballot: Jabarti II, p. 215.
a chamber of representatives: Jabarti II, p. 238.
the Arabic world's . . . friend of Islam: Jabarti II, pp. 226-7; cf. p. 407, above.
plans for a property tax . . . mosque of al-Azhar: Jabarti II, pp. 219–21.
Your Lord . . . doers of good: e.g. Jabarti II, p. 351; Qur'an, 11:117.
Some less philosophical . . . infidel dogs: Jabarti II, p. 318.
We longed for you . . . Ghuzz and the *'urban*: quoted in Pryce-Jones, p. 63.
stuck on top of a rock between two lions: p. 69, above.
Caesar and Hulagu . . . its greatest Arabic poet: Qabbani, p. 782.
The Omani overseas empire . . . maritime power: cf. p. 402, above.
the burgeoning British . . . Arab Emirates: Parry, p. 35.
what was left . . . filched or sold off: Jabarti I, p. 11.
the idea of an *ummah* . . . a united Arab 'nation': *EI*^{2}, s.v. Ḳawmiyyah.
planted the seed . . . language, culture and history: Rogan, p. 171.
The expedition of the French . . . acknowledge: Ali Bey I, pp. 311–12.
the people of Egypt . . . the 'imported' Mamluks: Jabarti II, pp. 182–3.
the sun of Egypt . . . made it all Arab: quoted in Suleiman, p. 80; cf. p. 336, above.
they re-arabicized Egypt . . . as the official language: Chejne, p. 102.
Napoleon had been compelled . . . respect to do so: Carmichael, p. 250.
in 1800 . . . Menou had published *Al-tanbih*: *EI*^{2} II, p. 465.
in 1826 he sent . . . men to study in Paris: Adonis, *Thabit* IV, pp. 29–34.
Does Paris have on earth . . . no morrow yet?: Adonis, *Thabit* IV, p. 34.

justice is the foundation of a flourishing civilization: Adonis, *Thabit* IV, pp. 32–3; Rogan, pp. 105–6.
was appointed . . . to translate European books: Suleiman, pp. 169–70.
The pasha's immediate heirs . . . rolling stock: Searight, p. 110.
a mad carmagnole . . . all mixed up helter skelter: the *Spectator* on the opening celebrations for the Canal, quoted in Searight, pp. 117–18.
their movement . . . to the general Arab Awakening: cf. EI^2 I, p. 554.
the Turks sent a 10,000-strong army . . . bedouin warriors: Rogan, p. 70.
he went travelling . . . beyond his native plateau: cf. Nicholson, p. 466.
tawhid . . . associates and intermediaries: cf. p. 3, above.
the 'Almohads' of . . . North Africa and Spain: p. 356, above.
saying 'Yes' to the earthly ruler . . . the heavenly Creator: cf. Adonis, *Thabit* I, p. 31.
they even referred to their life . . . as al-Jahiliyyah: EI^2 III, p. 1064.
Persians . . . as they had before Islam: EI^2 I, p. 554; Parry, p. 35; and cf. p. 70, above.
Muhammad ibn Sa'ud: strictly, the name should be vowelled 'Su'ud'. 'Al Sa'ud' are 'the family/house of Sa'ud'.
treasures donated . . . threatened with destruction: EI^2, s.v. Wahhābiyyah.
in Shi'i Karbala, the Wahhabis . . . massacred the living townsfolk: Nicholson, p. 466. Nicholson gives the number killed as 5,000.
The captured Wahhabi leaders . . . thrown into the sea: Rogan, p. 87.
An epidemical enthusiasm . . . from the old to the young: Johnson and Boswell, *A Journey to the Western Islands*, Penguin Classics, London, 1984, p. 37.
The sour Wahaby fanaticism . . . of the nomads: quoted in Tidrick, p. 151.
Ikhwan ('the Brethren'): the Egyptian-based al-Ikhwan al-Muslimun, 'the Muslim Brotherhood', share a name and Wahhabi leanings with the Saudi Ikhwan, but usually not the latter's mad-eyed scariness.
Language *is* the *ummah* . . . class and politics: Suleiman, pp. 99–100.
al-Yaziji's great ode . . . and your fame: cf. p. 10, above.
Turks like Bajkam . . . off the throne: pp. 305–6, above.
a great historical experience . . . all Arabs: quoted in Albert Hourani, pp. 404–5.
Sati' al-Husri . . . theorists of Arab nationalism: Suleiman, pp. 127–32.
With Arab nationalism we are back at our starting point: Dunlop, p. 25.
that treasure . . . buried by the king of al-Hirah: pp. 84–5, above.
the Arab Awakening . . . has yet to become a reality: Jabiri, p. 347.
retreat from modernity: Adonis, *Poetics*, p. 77; cf. p. 375, above.
returned the present to the past: Adonis, *Thabit* I, p. 41.
Whoever today can read Nizar Qabbani . . . in other cultures: Kilito, p. 10.
When Arabs write . . . non-native: Ibn Khaldun, *Muqaddimah*, pp. 439–41.
The distance . . . to written Arabic: on the distance between dialects themselves, Versteegh says it 'is as large as that between the Germanic languages and the Romance languages . . . if not larger.' Versteegh, *Arabic Language*, p. 98. I feel this is an exaggeration.
the 'ideal self' . . . expressed in colloquial: Shouby, pp. 301–2.
In the language . . . to my individual self: Adonis, *Thabit* III, pp. 220–1.
dead language that refuses to die: Bowles, p. 294.
We do not live in a land, but in a language: al-Marzuqi (aljazeera.net).
the Arabic Adam . . . everything in creation: Qur'an, 2:31.
the greatest literary product . . . finished in 1767: Jabarti II, pp. 105–8.
Anything post-classical . . . excluded from the dictionary: cf. EI^2 X, p. 240.
Damascus to Baghdad . . . in the early twentieth century: Atiyah, p. 89.
'Pendulum' . . . in Syria: Chejne, p. 157.
it ousted . . . *irẓiẓ* ('tremor, thunder'): Versteegh, *Arabic Language*, p. 181.
jammaẓ . . . gave way to the loan *taramway*: Versteegh, *Arabic Language*, p. 181; Chejne, p. 152.
'Revolution' began as *fitnah*: Versteegh, *Arabic Language*, p. 174.
'Republic' . . . as *mashyakhah* ('shaykhdom'): EI^2 VI, pp. 725–6.

'Citizens' . . . 'fellow-countrymen': cf. Versteegh, *Arabic Language*, p. 174.
In practice, even 'republics' have subjects, not citizens: cf. Kassir, p. 26.
When will we learn our rights and responsibilities?: quoted in Kilito, p. 68.
the Syrian *Garden of News*: Abu-Absi, p. 347, n. 3.
3,000 in the USA alone at the same time: Whitman, p. 355. The figure of 3,000 was for 1856.
One newspaper . . . was written in verse: Suleiman, p. 89.
No self-respecting writer . . . rhymed prose: Huart, pp. 444–5.
expressions like 'revolution' . . . in the Arabic press: Cioeta, *passim*.
Istanbul began to impose its language on its Arab domains: Carmichael, pp. 304–5; Rogan, pp. 182–3.
Arabic was banned . . . except as a 'foreign' language: Suleiman, pp. 79 and 85–8.
Abbasid Arabism . . . Turkish counterpart: cf. Suleiman, p. 91.
several of them launched . . . direct Ottoman rule: cf. Ajami, *Dream Palace*, p. 297; Atiyah, p. 84.
These new Arabic vocal organs . . . all political hues: *EI*[2] II, pp. 466–7.
they discouraged . . . new Qur'an schools: Haeri, p. 70.
they attempted to ban . . . dialect instead: Versteegh, *Arabic Language*, p. 132.
they promoted the Berber . . . cultures of the region: Atiyah, pp. 137–8.
rather as Persian . . . dominance in Arabic: cf. Versteegh, *Arabic Language*, p. 198.
the staff of the Moroccan bureaux . . . the office: Versteegh, *Arabic Language*, p. 200.
Algerian radio . . . was mostly in the colloquial: Atiyah, p. 204.
Ben Bella . . . had to have an Arabic tutor: Chejne, p. 109.
the Algerian National Assembly . . . in French: Versteegh, *Arabic Language*, pp. 200–1.
banners and placards . . . freedom of speech: Suleiman, p. 83.
Ahmad Shawqi . . . exiled to Barcelona: *EI*[2] IX, p. 229.
in the anti-British uprising . . . the roofs of cars: *EI*[2] IX, p. 230.
The nation-state . . . in Islamic theory and practice: Allawi, p. 46.
Islamic constitutional theory . . . not with territory: *EI*[2] X, p. 127.
from the 1870s . . . holidays in France: Ajami, *Dream Palace*, pp. 35–6.
'a virtual epidemic' . . . particularly in Lebanon: *EI*[2] V, p. 1253.
perhaps one-quarter of the total population: Rogan, p. 265.
Estimates of how many ... 'almost half': *EI*[2] V, p. 1253.
the total of Lebanese migrants . . . by 1914: Albert Hourani, p. 294.
a Syrian-Lebanese quarter sprouted in . . . 'Nayy Yark': Rawaa Talass, 'Nayy Yark' (unpublished dissertation), Dubai, 2014.
'Egyptian' (in fact Lebanese) . . . Manolo Saleh: Salman Rushdie, *The Jaguar Smile: A Nicaraguan Journey*, Picador, London, 1987, p. 75.
Jubran Khalil Jubran: often spelled, including by himself, 'Gibran Kahlil Gibran'.
a founder of poetic modernism in Arabic: cf. Adonis, *Thabit* IV, pp. 140–2.
You are neighbours . . . vault of space: quoted in Adonis, *Thabit* IV, p. 146.
go from place to place . . . its grave: quoted in Adonis, *Thabit* IV, p. 187.
today's border-beset age . . . into 'Nayy Yark': almost the first of Donald Trump's acts as president was to ban all visitors from seven Muslim-majority countries entering the United States.
The traveller's passport . . . equally well: Baedeker, *Palestine and Syria*, 1876, 'Passports and Custom House'.
A joint commission . . . of a divided Yemen: Dresch, *History of Modern Yemen*, pp. 10–11.
Kaiser Wilhelm II . . . Berlin–Baghdad line: Carmichael, p. 302.
post-Second World War . . . eventually withered: Searight, pp. 249–50.
clandestine approaches . . . anti-Ottoman face: Atiyah, pp. 91–2.
in AD 1916, Husayn . . . 'King of the Arabs': Carmichael, p. 319.
he used the style, 'King of the Arab Lands': *EI*[2] III, p. 263.
Their responses to Husayn were . . . ambiguous: cf. Atiyah, pp. 92–4.
H.M. Government view . . . in Palestine: quoted in Atiyah, pp. 102–3.
a mischievous political creed . . . anti-Semitism: quoted in Gilmour, p. 481.
the Yemeni island of Socotra: Doreen Ingrams IX, pp. 737–8; Mackintosh-Smith, *Yemen*, p. 239.
Britain's championing . . . commonly thought to have been: Karsh, p. 193.

The agreement . . . having permanent influence: Albert Hourani, p. 318.
the chaff of dreams: Qur'an, 12:44.
to unite the Arabs . . . draw us into one people: quoted in Rogan, p. 195.
his own ideal map . . . *country south of this line*: the map was shown at the exhibition, 'Lawrence of Arabia: the Life, the Legend', Imperial War Museum, London, 2005.
the French arrived . . . and promptly expelled him: Rogan, p. 202.
had converted Aden . . . the South Arabian mainland: Trevaskis, p. 94.
If a man hates . . . he will hate his next neighbour: James Boswell, *The Life of Samuel Johnso*n, London, 1992, p. 238.
Those who condemn us . . . in a spacious grave: quoted in Jarrah, p. 290.
nothing reignited the rhetoric . . . Sykes–Picot: cf. Atiyah, p. 124.
We divide and you rule: quoted in Keay, p. 464.
the Dinshaway Incident . . . lashings: cf. Rogan, pp. 180–1.
in Egypt today . . . a 'No Torture' T-shirt: BBC report, 25 January 2017.
Bashshar al-Asad . . . of civil war: Amnesty International quoted in BBC report, August 2016.
his armed forces . . . during the same period: *Guardian*, 12 October 2016.
the last real caliph: p. 347, above.
no one recognized the *sharif*'s claim: Atiyah, p. 133.
protests by Indian Muslims . . . in 1920: Keay, p. 479.
In 1939 . . . 65 per cent to 30 per cent: Morris, p. 36.
Ibn Sa'ud's Wahhabi raiders . . . camel+horse combination: *EI*^{2} I, p. 885.
the age of tribal raiding came to an end: *EI*^{2} III, p. 1068.
the latter relationship . . . bedouin raiders: cf. pp. 4–5 and 166–7, above.
in 1921 . . . on its way to Mecca: Arashi, p. 93. This source claims that the number killed was 3,000.
he tried to collectivize . . . *hijrahs*: *EI*^{2} III, p. 361; Atiyah, p. 133.
the earliest caliphs had failed . . . so too did Ibn Sa'ud: cf. *EI*^{2} III, p. 361.
in 1929–30 . . . bloodily suppressed: *EI*^{2} III, pp. 1067–8.
the worst in . . . hypocrisy: Qur'an, 9:97; cf. pp. 4 and 167, above.
the nomad population . . . 5 per cent in 1998: *EI*^{2} XII, p. 465.
Harold Ingrams . . . any higher authority: Harold Ingrams, *Arabia*, p. 25.
Hadrami *badw* terms . . . 'to work for one's living': Bujra, *passim*.
They are dead: Abu Bakr ibn Shaykh al-Kaff quoted in Ingrams, *Arabia*, p. 36.
Freya Stark's cameleers . . . polish their daggers: Stark, p. ix.
Abd Allah of Transjordan . . . stooge: Atiyah, pp. 135–6.
his own imperial eye on a Greater Syria: Carmichael, p. 335.
the French using troops . . . insurgents in the Mashriq: Rogan, p. 202.
If you add . . . what sum will you get?: quoted in Karsh, p. 149.
civilized peoples in the east and west: quoted in Albert Hourani, p. 341.
mingled with [our] life . . . its personality: quoted in Albert Hourani p. 341.
The overwhelming majority . . . appearance of Islam: Husayn, pp. 70–1.
faked up wholesale in their poetry 'factories': Husayn, pp. 162–3.
Cartesian detachment . . . mark of the modern age: Husayn, pp. 74–5.
he did not apply . . . directly to scripture: Husayn, p. 79.
accounts of the people of Ad . . . Arab Genesis: e.g. Husayn, p. 171.
in 1927 he was summoned . . . on a charge of heresy: Husayn, pp. 254–5.
he was accused of . . . Abrahamic monotheism: Husayn, pp. 257–8.
the historicity and role . . . his son Ishmael/Isma'il: e.g. Husayn, pp. 89–91.
so important in . . . Umayyad times onward: cf. pp. 233-6, above.
as a Muslim . . . a fact of scholarly history: Husayn, pp. 289–90.
al-Sijistani . . . the Qur'an was exempt from logic: Jabiri, p. 261.
constitutes the essence of being Arab in all its domains: Jabiri, p. 52.
jawn = black/white: Suyuti I, p. 305.
jalal = great/small: Suyuti I, p. 306.
sariq 'adil, 'a just thief': p. 63, above.

country/city . . . creative movement: Adonis, *Thabit* IV, pp. 139–40.
regional idiosyncrasies . . . conditional on that of the other: Jabiri, p. 52.
Nizar Qabbani . . . longed for him to return: Qabbani, p. 808.
Arab unity . . . is a madman's notion: cf. p. 102, above.
From 1936 onwards . . . with Iraq at its head: cf. *EI*[2] VIII, p. 246.
other than in the aftermath . . . has been an Egyptian: *EI*[2] XII, pp. 240–1.
the members always 'agree to disagree': *EI*[2] VIII, p. 246.
To strengthen the ties . . . of the Arab countries: quoted in Atiyah, p. 169.
The criterion . . . as an official language: Kassir, p. 68.
still-born from the inception: Pryce-Jones, p. 223.
an institution of the dying age of tyranny: al-Marzuqi (aljazeera.net).

CHAPTER 14 THE AGE OF HOPE

Enclosed . . . small but gorgeous pavilion: cf. the illustrations in Chekhab-Abudaya and Bresc, pp. 104–19.
it became a regular institution . . . Mamluks of Egypt: Hitti, pp. 135–6.
Napoleon had a new *mahmal* made and sent to Mecca: Jabarti II, p. 203.
a wonder of wonders . . . total contrast to tradition: Jabarti II, p. 259.
He was mounted . . . the whole of the journey: Lane, *Account of the Manners*, p. 440.
a scantily clad old woman . . . to Mecca and back: Lane, *Account of the Manners*, p. 441.
the Turkish-Syrian one . . . the Great War: *EI*[2] VI, pp. 44–6.
In 1926 Ibn Sa'ud's Wahhabi . . . clashed with its guard: *EI*[2] III, p. 1067.
uncontrollable Jewish immigration . . . violence: cf. Rogan, pp. 247–8.
the Palestinians revolted . . . punishments: cf. Rogan, pp. 256–7.
sweet, just, boyish master: quoted in Mackintosh-Smith, *Yemen*, p. 152.
By using terror tactics . . . down to the present day: Rogan, p. 318.
the 1946 bombing . . . killed nearly a hundred: Rogan, pp. 314–15.
Abd Allah had already been . . . to this very end: cf. Rogan, pp. 332–3.
the Arab states' campaign . . . mutual distrust: Atiyah, p. 180.
something false and rotten: Atiyah, p. 185; cf. p. xiii, above.
The sultans were at loggerheads . . . occupy the country: Ibn al-Athir quoted in Karsh, p. 77; cf. p. 351, above.
after the 1948 war . . . 750,000 Palestinian refugees: Rogan, p. 338.
We continue to be bewildered . . . by it?: Shehadeh, *Diaries*, p. 74.
they had already granted Iraq . . . useful air bases: Albert Hourani, p. 329.
the officers' anger . . . the ruling Wafd party: Atiyah, p. 190.
a nickel-plated Colt revolver: cf. George Lyttelton and Rupert Hart-Davis, *The Lyttelton Hart-Davis Letters 1955–62: A Selection*, John Murray, London, 2001, p. 18.
Of course the Americans . . . presence in the Canal Zone: Rogan, p. 364.
another condition: stop buying Soviet arms: Rogan, p. 376.
we are still those shattered, scattered tribes . . . Caesar: Qabbani, p. 782; cf. p. 416, above.
never spoke of himself as anything but Egyptian: Carmichael, p. 351.
The aim of the Revolution . . . common welfare: quoted in Karsh, p. 155.
mucking out the Augean stable of corruption: cf. Atiyah, p. 193.
a joint Anglo-French . . . Urabi revolution: Rogan, pp. 159–60.
the thrill of an Arab victory . . . the back streets of Aden: Holden, p. 23.
he worked up the defeat into his own triumph: cf. Rogan, pp. 382–3.
demonstrating to students . . . apartment houses: Bowles, p. 375.
Cairo's radio transmitting . . . 663 hours at the same time: *EI*[2] III, pp. 1014–15.
In the Nasserist view . . . by language: Suleiman, p. 125.
I will live for your sake . . . Jamal Abd al-Nasir: cf. Rogan, p. 363.
on whose love we were drunk, like a Sufi drunk on God: Qabbani, p. 780.
like the one that overthrew . . . Iraq in 1958: Rogan, p. 394.
In his speeches . . . end in high Arabic: Versteegh, *Arabic Language*, p. 196.

local . . . nationalism versus pan-Arabism: Clive Holes cited in Owens, 'Arabic Sociolinguistics', p. 442.

In his speeches . . . the high language alone: Versteegh, *Arabic Language*, p. 196.

Taha Husayn had questioned . . . Egypt's heritage: pp. 453–6, above.

he launched in his book . . . Arabs and Arabic: Suleiman, p. 198.

Shu'ubi literary attacks . . . heyday of their empire: pp. 310–15, above.

wicked charlatan . . . errand boy: quoted in Suleiman, p. 248, n. 15.

he himself wrote in that same high Arabic: Suleiman, p. 182.

I'll not forget you . . . walls of fantasy!: from the ode by Ibrahim Naji, '*Al-Atlal*'. http://lyrics.wikia.com/wiki/أم_كلثوم:الأطلال accessed 14 November 2018.

'You're an Arab!' . . . And I banged my book shut: Leila Ahmed, *A Border Passage*, quoted in Haeri, p. 79.

for the Ba'th . . . defined above all by language: Suleiman, p. 125.

Our language . . . which soldiers march: Ajlani quoted in Chejne, p. 21.

On 12 January 1958 . . . they could lump it, in gaol: cf. Rogan, pp. 386–8.

The Arab giant . . . at the imperialists: quoted in Dresch, *History of Modern Yemen*, p. 82.

the two remaining . . . formed their own union: Albert Hourani, p. 368.

Ba'thist officers considered taking Iraq into the UAR: Pryce-Jones, p. 246.

Brigadier Abd al-Karim . . . quashed the idea: Pryce-Jones, p. 342; Rogan, p. 399.

On 28 September 1961 . . . gave the Egyptians the boot: Rogan, pp. 402–3.

To grab all property . . . against God's holy law: adapted from the version quoted in Dresch, *History of Modern Yemen*, p. 86.

a feature film . . . next to his throne: '*Thawrat al-yaman*', *c.* late 1960s.

Nothing was resurrected . . . but the age of the Mamluks: quoted in Ajami, *Arab Predicament*, p. 42.

Unity, Freedom and Socialism: Ajami, *Arab Predicament*, p. 180.

In 1958, rumour . . . offered $2 million for Nasser's murder: Pryce-Jones, p. 278.

a confusion between rhetoric and *realpolitik*: Rogan, p. 417.

Fire's kindled with two firesticks, war with words: Ibn Khallikan II, pp. 71–2; cf. p. 258, above.

Jamilah among their bullets . . . country's Jeanne d'Arc: Qabbani, p. 695.

Jamilah . . . her French defence lawyer: Wikipedia, s.v. Djamila Bouhired.

like thieves in the night: quoted in Mackintosh-Smith, *Yemen*, p. 158.

of Zayid's fifteen predecessors . . . five deposed: Morris, pp. 123–4.

he had signed . . . with Syria and Jordan: Albert Hourani, p. 413.

The Israelis . . . especially their air power: Albert Hourani, p. 413.

In 1798 the Egyptians had opposed . . . sticks: cf. p. 414, above.

If we lost the war . . . never killed a fly: Qabbani, p. 699.

O my master . . . half our people have no tongue: Qabbani, p. 703.

great enough, perhaps . . . Gaza region – with impunity: Atiyah, p. 235.

a living corpse: quoted in Karsh, p. 171.

Nasser was *The Last Arab*: the title of Said Aburish's biography is *Nasser: The Last Arab*, St. Martin's/Dunne Books, New York, 2004.

But time dispelled the wine . . . dear night, our friend: from the ode by Ibrahim Naji, '*Al-Atlal*'. http://lyrics.wikia.com/wiki/أم_كلثوم:الأطلال accessed 14 November 2018.

Mu'ammar al-Qadhdhafi . . . the Leader's body: Ajami, *Arab Predicament*, p. 14.

al-Qadhdhafi claimed . . . 'trustee' of the movement: Ajami, *Arab Predicament*, p. 93.

Fall and scatter . . . Andalus the Conquered: Qabbani, p. 762.

'for once', said Muhammad Hasanayn Haykal: quoted in Rogan, p. 468.

oil prices had risen . . . $10.41: *EI*[2] VII, pp. 886ff.; cf. Albert Hourani, pp. 418–19.

even those that have money . . . much influence: Carmichael, p. 357.

The oil migrations were thus a kind of secular *hajj*: cf. Rogan, p. 496.

in the 1975 census . . . the total population: Swanson, p. 55.

My father . . . at the end of the earth: Basha, p. 160.

the Arab world [was] more closely linked . . . in its modern history: Sa'd al-Din Ibrahim quoted in Rogan, p. 496.

Why should we go and lay tile by tile . . . around on them?: Basha, p. 160.

The Arab world stores . . . beasts bled by their masters: Qabbani, p. 858.
If I had a whip . . . their camel's milk: Qabbani, pp. 738–9.
For Sadat, the war . . . Israel and the Arabs: Albert Hourani, p. 419.
The Israelis . . . would not be tied to details: cf. Hourani, pp. 419–20.
They've given us the Pill . . . having children: Qabbani, p. 813.
agreed to keep . . . a great boost: Shehadeh, *Walks*, pp. 109–45.
the worst surrender document in our history: Shehadeh, *Diaries*, p. 160.
His bombastic barrages . . . and similar causes: figures from the Jewish Virtual Library website.
because it was planned by America and Israel: report in baraqish.net, 14 September 2016.
the curriculum was planned by the so-called Islamic State: report in baraqish.net, February 2017.
a position of real strength, moral not military: cf. Abdallah Laroui quoted in Pryce-Jones, p. 214.

CHAPTER 15 THE AGE OF DISAPPOINTMENT

a fine ancient inscription . . . someone called Elias: The inscription is the base of a missing statue commemorating a man who built a public bath, possibly around the fifth century AD. R. Mouterde and C. Mondésert, 'Deux inscriptions grecques de Hama', *Syria* 34, 1957, pp. 284–7.
destroyed . . . by tanks and artillery: Rogan, p. 513.
between 8,000 and 25,000 lives: Haag, p. 153.
largely optimistic . . . on the move: Kassir, p. 32.
During the interwar years . . . history of the Arab world: Rogan, p. 238.
Women in Syria . . . before women in France: Kassir, p. 63.
Iraq seemed to have . . . liberal democracy: Atiyah, pp. 222–4.
a kind of Oriental Canada: Morris, p. 83.
Yemen Enters the Modern World: I. Rashid, *Yemen Enters the Modern World*, Chapel Hill, 1984.
Reconstructing Arab society . . . contemporary generation: Hitti, p. 755.
Hold fast . . . and do not be divided among yourselves: Qur'an, 3:103.
habl is 'a cord, a rope' . . . states of South Arabia: cf. pp. 53–4, above.
I don't recall . . . any contemporary context: Allawi, p. ix.
They dreamed of Cairo . . . and total destruction: Bowles, p. 104.
if Western democracy . . . revivalist, theocratic Islam: Atiyah, p. 240.
those crushing . . . in 1948 and 1967: cf. Ajami, *Arab Predicament*, pp. 69–70.
vague, though intense feelings . . . in the last 50 years: quoted in Pryce-Jones, p. 373.
In a 2005 poll . . . Morocco, Iraq and Algeria: Pintak, p. 196.
Nasser may not have been The Last Arab: cf. p. 478, above.
two eighth-century brothers . . . in Sind and North Africa: p. 267, above.
the People of the Cave: Qur'an, 18:9–26.
for 309 years in the Qur'anic version: In the Christian version, from Decius to Theodosius II would be a mere two centuries at most.
a sense of history is a sense of loss: Naipaul, p. 177.
an evolving culture-bound dynamic . . . behavior: Varisco, p. 125.
Saddam Husayn . . . the majority of his subjects: cf. Albert Hourani, p. 432.
up to a million dead: Rogan, p. 518.
in the pro-coalition states . . . and governed: cf. Rogan, pp. 565–71.
US forces alone numbered 650,000: Rogan, p. 567.
Freedom is not something . . . as free as they want to be: James Baldwin, *Nobody Knows My Name*, 'Notes for a Hypothetical Novel', Dial Press, New York, 1961.
governments and people united in condemnation: cf. Rogan, p. 614.
a civil war that may have killed 100,000 or more: Albert Hourani, p. 465.
In the 2014 campaign . . . seven were civilians: BBC report, 1 September 2014, quoting UN figures.
between 2000 and the middle of 2018 . . . almost 8:1: figures from the Israeli human rights organization B'Tselem, quoted in the *Guardian*, 14 August 2018.
an Israeli property law . . . the Israeli state: Shehadeh, *Walks*, p. 13.
the nationalization of bicycles . . . women joined the army: Mackintosh-Smith, *Yemen*, p. 165.
Chief Politburo exegete . . . tendencies: Mackintosh-Smith, *Yemen*, p. 165.

Chaos will rule . . . thank God: Mackintosh-Smith, *Yemen*, p. 158.
From the Gulf to the Atlantic . . . thought and culture: Qabbani, p. 857.
to the Arab League at its thirty-fifth birthday party: Qabbani, p. 853.
the billy-goat in the officers' mess: the nickname is attributed to his assassinated predecessor-but-one as president of North Yemen, Ibrahim al Hamdi.
The state . . . is a collection of tribes: quoted in Dresch, *Tribes*, p. 7.
might as well look for camel-trains at metro stations: Mu'allimi, p. 37.
the earth disgorges its burdens: Qur'an, 99:2.
the chief . . . retains his quarter or fifth of the booty: cf. pp. 61–2, above.
early in 2015 . . . corruption in general: BBC report, 26 February 2015.
Man jāda sād . . . and you'll rule the land: Ibn Khallikan III, p. 469.
dynamic political order . . . republicanism and Islamism: Volpi, p. 1061.
in the 2014 election . . . 97 per cent of the vote: *Guardian* report, 20 March 2018.
Baya' al-amir . . . pleasing and displeasing: Lane, *Arabic-English Lexicon*, s.v. *by*^{c}.
Nothing doth more hurt . . . cunning men pass for wise: Francis Bacon, *Essays*, 'Of Cunning'.
better to reign in hell than serve in heaven: John Milton, *Paradise Lost*, book 1, line 261; cf. Ajami, *Dream Palace*, p. 142.
In friendship false . . . to rule the state: John Dryden, *Absalom and Achitophel*, part 1, line 173.
a history of ashes: Adonis, *Thabit* III, p. 229.
the long winter of the Arabs: quoted in Pryce-Jones, p. 14.
The story . . . of Muhammad Bu Azizi: e.g. Rogan, pp. 626–31.
a generation . . . systematically lied to: Ajami, *Arab Predicament*, p. 88.
the uprising of Ahmad Urabi in 1881–2: p. 433, above.
zu''ar, 'hooligans', staged periodic uprisings: *EI*^{2}, s.v. Zu^{cc}ār.
the *harafish*, or 'rascals' . . . al-Nasir: Ibn Battutah I, p. 54.
Facebook pages . . . protesters in Cairo in 2011: e.g. Soueif, p. 155.
the political pages . . . in the Urabi uprising: cf. Zubaida, p. 168.
the meeting of minds: Shehadeh, *Diaries*, p. 112.
the secular and shaggy-haired . . . as yours: Shehadeh, *Diaries*, p. 116.
We are all here together . . . expressing themselves: Soueif, p. 56.
This [Egyptian] regime lies as naturally as it breathes: Soueif, p. 133.
the protesters were 'foreign agents': Soueif, p. 144.
'Aysh! . . . And our human dignity!: adapted from Soueif, p. 18.
God save the Sultan! / God ruin Fart al-Rumman!: Jabarti II, p. 326.
Luckless Limper, let him go!: Ibn Battutah I, p. 54.
Write, write . . . We have found our voice: Soueif, pp. 145–6.
an Egyptian poet . . . 'How I admired him!': Shehadeh, *Diaries*, p. 133.
stalled between seasons: quoted in Ajami, *Arab Predicament*, p. 1.
The current Arab regimes . . . changes nothing: Adonis, *Thabit* III, p. 165.
Allah will change . . . what is in themselves: Qur'an, 13:11.
What I want is power . . . kick 'em the next: quoted in *Kipling Journal*, vol. 38, no. 180, 1971, p. 6.
failed rulers had wielded . . . who had ousted them: cf. Iryani, p. 329.
that vast complex of analogies: Lawrence Durrell, *Reflections on a Marine Venus*, Faber & Faber, London, 1953, p. 80.
Munsif al-Marzuqi . . . and Solzhenitsyn: Pryce-Jones, p. 401.
Habib Bourguiba . . . fasting in Ramadan: *EI*^{2}, s.v. Tunisia.
their *ra'iyyah* . . . private flock: cf. p. 431, above.
Cunning has effect from the credulity of others: Johnson and Boswell, *A Journey to the Western Islands*, Penguin Classics, London, 1984, p. 288.
slaves of the stick: Imru' al-Qays, p. 134.
If Time enthrones . . . the time of the ape!: quoted in Ibn Khallikan III, pp. 236–7, and sometimes attributed to Imam al-Shafi'i.
Give me five hundred years . . . Switzerland: quoted in Pryce-Jones, p. 4.
the time people began to talk . . . 50,000 years ago: Diamond, p. 40.
Words . . . Since the seventh century: Qabbani, p. 759.

Benedict Anderson's *Imagined Communities*: cf. p. 135, above.
Martin Nowak's *Supercooperators*: cf. ideas on language and dominance, pp. 9 and 163, above.
bewitchment of our intelligence by means of language: Ludwig Wittgenstein, *Philosophische Untersuchungen*, part 1, section 109.
the Qatari poet . . . a fifteen-year gaol sentence: BBC reports, 30 November 2012 and 22 October 2013.
Qabus of Jurjan . . . his calligraphic tower-tomb: cf. pp. 346–7, above.
Call it 'sweet nectar' . . . daylight from it: quoted in Ibn Khallikan I, pp. 24–5.
Contrary to what most people believe . . . a Jewish state: San'a Radio, February 2017.
many have been convinced . . . 'Americans and Israelis': report in baraqish.net, April 2017.
lies propagated . . . no turning back now: Lévi-Strauss, p. 300.
Here I am, going far . . . to this place: Jarrah, pp. 290–1.
From Syria . . . five million have fled: UN figure in the *Guardian*, 31 March 2017.
Lo! on her grim and massy rock . . . foeman's shock: Gibb's translation in Ibn Battutah I, p. 96.
one of the most splendid . . . ivory and ebony: Ibn Battutah I, pp. 97–8.
Its surface . . . fugue for the eyes: Mackintosh-Smith, *Tangerine*, p. 188.
dismantled . . . an unknown location: www.unesco.org/ne/en/safeguarding-syrian-cultural-heritage, accessed June 2018.

AFTERWORD IN THE STATION OF HISTORY

We're waiting . . . in the station of history: Qabbani, pp. 754–7.
the constant present . . . the timeline of Hell: cf. Alberto Manguel, *The Library at Night*, Yale University Press, New Haven and London, 2009, p. 331, n. 23.
Max Weber's 'eternal yesterday': Max Weber, *Gesammelte politische Schriften*, Drei Masken Vlg, 1921, p. 507.
the royal court . . . Istanbul: BBC and *Guardian* reports, 20 October 2018.
Arab allies . . . *'urubah*, arabness: e.g. statements by the legitimate Yemeni government quoted on sahafah.net, *c.* 16 October 2018.
in July 2018 . . . language of the State of Israel: *Guardian* report, 19 July 2018.
The Aleppo mosque . . . Chechen cash: Reuters report, January 2018.
Ali Abd Allah Salih . . . the charmer: Mackintosh-Smith, *Yemen* (2014 edition), 'Afterword'.
Already when we unified . . . as ages run!: from Shaykh Hamdan bin Muhammad Al Maktum's ode, 'Al-Jār li 'l-Jār', https://lyrics-on.net/en/1096426-el-jar-lil-jar-lyrics.html, accessed 14 November 2018.
The assumption . . . their colonial subjects: Doreen Ingrams, p. 153.
We live in an age . . . in their benefits: quoted in Suleiman, p. 191.
As time goes by . . . contact with Westerners: Husayn, p. 109.
People . . . resemble their fathers: Jahiz, part 3, p. 113.
the gaze . . . foredooms all your hopes: Kassir, p. 2.
apparently 'Western' . . . the Muslim mind: Ajami, *Arab Predicament*, pp. 52–3.
wherever it may come from . . . different from our own: cf. p. 280, above.
He sees the lightning . . . the lightning-flash: Jarrah, p. 41. I thank Dr Khaldun al-Sham'ah for first reciting these verses to me.
Those who believe . . . have their reward with their Lord: Qur'an, 2:62.
something glorious . . . every kind of pleasure: Jan Morris, *Spain*, Penguin, London, 1982, p. 14.
We want a generation . . . history from the roots: Qabbani, p. 703.
To you . . . be your religion, and to me mine: Qur'an, 109:6.
something rotten: cf. p. xiii, above.
those villagers . . . that the Romans had filled in: cf. p. xxv, above.

BIBLIOGRAPHY

[c]Abd Allāh, Yūsuf Muḥammad, *Awrāq fī tārīkh al-yaman wa-āthārihi*, Beirut, 1990.

[c]Abīd ([c]Ubayd) b. Sharyah al-Jurhumī, *Akhbār*, in Wahb b. Munabbih al-Yamānī, *Kitāb al-tījān fī mulūk ḥimyar*, Hyderabad, 1928, reprinted San'a, 1979.

Abu-Absi, Samir, 'The Modernization of Arabic: Problems and Prospects', *Anthropological Linguistics* 28, 1986.

Abu 'l-Fidā', [c]Imād al-Dīn Ismā[c]īl, *Al-mukhtaṣar fī akhbār al-bashar*, Cairo, n.d.

Abu-Lughod, Janet L., *Before European Hegemony: The World System AD 1250–1350*, Oxford University Press USA, New York, 1991.

Abū Nuwās, al-Ḥasan b. Hāni', *Dīwān*, ed. Aḥmad [c]Abd al-Majīd al-Ghazālī, Beirut, 1984.

Adonis [[c]Alī Aḥmad Sa[c]īd Isbir], *An Introduction to Arab Poetics*, Saqi Books, London, 2003.

Adonis [[c]Alī Aḥmad Sa[c]īd Isbir], *Al-thābit wa-'l-mutaḥawwil*, Beirut, 2011.

Ajami, Fouad, *The Arab Predicament*, Cambridge University Press, Cambridge, 1981.

Ajami, Fouad, *The Dream Palace of the Arabs: A Generation's Odyssey*, Pantheon, New York, 1998.

al-Akwa[c], Muḥammad b. [c]Alī, *Al-yaman al-khaḍrā' mahd al-ḥaḍārah*, San'a, 1982.

Ali Bey, *Travels of Ali Bey*, Garnet Publishing, Reading, 1993.

Allawi, Ali A., *The Crisis of Islamic Civilization*, Yale University Press, New Haven and London, 2009.

Anderson, Benedict, *Imagined Communities*, Verso Books, London and New York, 1983.

Antonius, George, *The Arab Awakening: The Story of the Arab National Movement*, Routledge, London, 1938.

al-[c]Arashī, Ḥusayn b. Aḥmad, *Bulūgh al-marām fī sharḥ misk al-khitām*, ed. and continued by Anastase-Marie al-Kirmilī, Cairo, 1939.

Arié, Rachel, *L'Espagne musulmane au temps des Nasrides (1232-1492)*, Editions de Boccard, Paris, 1973.

Ascherson, Neal, *Black Sea: The Birthplace of Civilisation and Barbarism*, Farrar, Straus and Giroux, London, 1996.

Atiyah, Edward, *The Arabs*, Penguin, Harmondsworth, 1955.

Baerlein, Henry, *The Singing Caravan: Some Echoes of Arabian Poetry*, John Murray, London, 1910.

al-Baghdādī, [c]Abd al-Laṭīf b. Yūsuf, *Kitāb al-ifādah wa-'l-i[c]tibār* (Appendix 1), ed. Aḥmad Ghassān Sabānū, Damascus, 1983.

BIBLIOGRAPHY

al-Balādhurī, Aḥmad b. Yaḥyā, *Futūḥ al-buldān*, Beirut, 1983.

al-Bāshā, ʿĀṣim, *Al-shāmī al-akhīr fī gharnāṭah*, Abu Dhabi, 2011.

Beeston, A.F.L., *A Descriptive Grammar of Epigraphic South Arabian*, Luzac, London, 1962.

Beeston, A.F.L., 'Kingship in Ancient South Arabia', *Journal of the Economic and Social History of the Orient* 15, 1972.

Beeston, A.F.L., 'The So-Called Harlots of Ḥaḍramawt', *Oriens* 5, 1952.

Beeston, A.F.L., *et al.* (eds), *Sabaic Dictionary*, Peeters, Beirut and Louvain-la-Neuve, 1982.

Bellamy, James A., 'A New Reading of the Namārah Inscription', *Journal of the American Oriental Society* 105, 1981.

Bloom, Jonathan M., 'The Introduction of Paper to the Islamic Lands and the Development of the Illustrated Manuscript', *Muqarnas* 17, 2000.

Borges, Jorge Luis, 'The Zahir', *Labyrinths*, Penguin, London, 1970.

Bowles, Paul, *The Spider's House*, Random House, New York, 1955.

Bujra, Abdalla S., *The Politics of Stratification*, Oxford University Press, Oxford, 1971.

Bulliet, Richard W., *The Camel and the Wheel*, Harvard University Press, New York, 1975.

Burton, Richard F., *Personal Narrative of a Pilgrimage to al-Madinah and Meccah*, Tylston and Edwards, London, 1893.

Byron, Robert, *The Road to Oxiana*, Picador, London, 1981.

Cannon, Garland, *The Arabic Contribution to the English Language: An Historical Dictionary*, Harrassowitz Verlag, Wiesbaden, 1994.

Carmichael, Joel, *The Shaping of the Arabs: A Study in Ethnic Identity*, Allen and Unwin, London, 1969.

Chaudhuri, K.N., *Trade and Civilisation in the Indian Ocean*, Cambridge University Press, Cambridge, 1985.

Chejne, Anwar G., *The Arabic Language: Its Role in History*, University of Minnesota Press, Minneapolis, 1969.

Chekhab-Abudaya, Mounia and Cécile Bresc, *Hajj: The Journey Through Art*, Skira, Milan, 2013.

Chen Da-sheng and Ludvik Kalus, *Corpus d'inscriptions arabes et persanes en Chine* I *(Province de Fu-Jian)*, Geuthner, Paris, 1991.

Cherian, A., 'The Genesis of Islam in Malabar', *Indica* 6, 1969.

Cioeta, Donald J., 'Ottoman Censorship in Lebanon and Syria, 1876–1908', *International Journal of Middle East Studies* 10, 1979.

Crone, Patricia, 'The First-Century Concept of "Hiğra" ', *Arabica* 41, 1994.

Daum, Werner (ed.), *Yemen: 3000 Years of Art and Civilisation in Arabia Felix*, Pinguin Verlag, Innsbruck and Frankfurt/Main, n.d. [*c.* 1988].

Davie, Grace, *Religion in Britain Since 1945: Believing without Belonging*, John Wiley, Hoboken, 1994.

Diamond, Jared, *Guns, Germs and Steel*, Vintage, London, 2005.

Doe, Brian, *Southern Arabia*, Thames & Hudson London, 1971.

Dresch, Paul, *A History of Modern Yemen*, Cambridge University Press, Cambridge, 2000.

Dresch, Paul, *Tribes, Government and History in Yemen*, Clarendon Press, Oxford, 1989.

Drory, Rina, 'The Abbasid Construction of the Jahiliyya: Cultural Authority in the Making', *Studia Islamica* 83, 1996.

Dunlop, D.M., *Arab Civilization to AD 1500*, Longman, London and Beirut, 1971.

Dunn, Ross E., *The Adventures of Ibn Battuta: A Muslim Traveler of the 14th Century*, University of California Pres, Berkeley and Los Angeles, 1989.

EI[2] = *The Encyclopaedia of Islam*, 2nd edition, Brill, Leiden, 1960–2005.

Ferguson, Charles, review of Anwar Chejne, *American Anthropologist* 75, 1973.

Gelder, Geert Jan van (ed. and trans.), *Classical Arabic Literature: A Library of Arabic Literature Anthology*, New York University Press, New York and London, 2013.

Ghosh, Amitav, *In an Antique Land*, Vintage, London, 1994.

Ghul, M.A., 'The Pilgrimage at Itwat', *Proceedings of the Society for Arabian Studies: A.F.L. Beeston at the Arabian Seminar*, 2005.

Gilmour, David, *Curzon*, Macmillan, London, 1994.

Grunebaum, G.E. von, 'The Nature of Arab Unity Before Islam', *Arabica* 10, 1963.

Gysens, J. Calzini, 'Safaitic Graffiti from Pompeii', *Proceedings of the Society for Arabian Studies* 20, 1990.

Haag, Michael, *Syria and Lebanon* (Cadogan Guides series), Cadogan, London, 1995.

Haeri, Niloofar, 'Form and Ideology: Arabic Sociolinguistics and Beyond', *Annual Review of Anthropology* 29, 2000.

al-Hamdānī, al-Ḥasan b. Aḥmad, *Kitāb al-iklīl* VIII, ed. Nabīh Amīn Fāris, Princeton, 1940, reprinted Beirut and San'a, n.d.

al-Hamdānī, al-Ḥasan b. Aḥmad, *Ṣifat jazīrat al-ᶜarab*, ed. Muḥammad b. ᶜAlī al-Akwaᶜ, San'a, 1983.

al-Harawī, ᶜAlī b. Abū Bakr, *Al-ishārāt ilā maᶜrifat al-ziyārāt*, ed. Janine Sourdel-Thomine, Damascus, 1953.

Hardy, Peter, *Historians of Medieval India: Studies in Indo-Muslim Historical Writing*, Munshiram Manoharlal Publishers, New Delhi, 1997.

Harrigan, Peter, 'Discovery at al-Magar', *Saudi Aramco World*, May/June 2012.

Harrower, Michael, *Water Histories and Spatial Archaeology: Ancient Yemen and the American West*, Cambridge University Press, Cambridge, 2016.

Hava, J.G., *Al-farā'id al-durriyah: Arabic-English Dictionary for the Use of Students*, Beirut, 1915.

Healey, John F., and G.R. Smith, 'Jaussen Savignac 17: The Earliest Dated Arabic Document', *Atlal* 12, 1989.

Hess, Richard S., *Studies in the Personal Names of Genesis 1–11*, Butzon & Bercker, Neukirchener, 1993.

al-Ḥibshī, ᶜAbd Allāh Muḥammad (ed.), *Al-yaman fī lisān al-ᶜarab*, San'a, 1990.

Hitti, Philip K., *History of the Arabs*, 10th edition, St Martin's Press, London, 1970.

Ho, Engseng, *The Graves of Tarim: Genealogy and Mobility across the Indian Ocean*, University of California Press, Berkeley and Los Angeles, 2006.

Hodgson, Marshall G.S., *The Venture of Islam* 2, University of Chicago Press, Chicago, 1977.

Holden, David, *Farewell to Arabia*, Faber & Faber, London, 1966.

Hornblower, Simon, and Antony Spawforth (eds), *The Oxford Classical Dictionary*, 3rd edition, Oxford University Press, Oxford, 2003.

Hourani, Albert, *A History of the Arab Peoples* (with Afterword by Malise Ruthven), Faber & Faber, London, 2002.

Hourani, George F., *Arab Seafaring in the Indian Ocean in Ancient and Early Medieval Times*, revised and expanded by John Carswell, Princeton University Press, Princeton, 1995.

Hoyland, Robert G., *Arabia and the Arabs: From the Bronze Age to the Coming of Islam*, Taylor & Francis, London, 2001.

Huart, Clément, *A History of Arabic Literature*, William Heinemann, London, 1903.

Hurgronje, C. Snouck, *Verspreide Geschriften* IV, Brill, Bonn and Leipzig,1924.

Husain, Agha Mahdi, *The Rise and Fall of Muḥammad bin Tughluq*, Luzac, London, 1938.

Ḥusayn, Ṭāhā, *Fi 'l-shiᶜr al-jāhilī*, Cairo, 2007.

Hussein, Asiff, *Sarandib: An Ethnological Study of the Muslims of Sri Lanka*, Neptune Publications, Dehiwala, 2007.

Ibn Baṭṭūṭah, Muḥammad b. ᶜAbd Allāh, *The Travels of Ibn Baṭṭūṭa*, trans. H.A.R. Gibb and C.F. Beckingham, Hakluyt Society, London, 1958–94.

Ibn Ḥajar al-ᶜAsqalānī, Aḥmad b. ᶜAlī, *Al-durar al-kāminah fi aᶜyān al-mi'ah al-thāminah*, Beirut, 1993.

Ibn Jubayr, Muḥammad b. Aḥmad, *Riḥlat ibn jubayr*, Beirut, 1980.

Ibn al-Kalbī, Hishām, *The Book of Idols*, trans. Nabih Amin Faris, Princeton University Press, Princeton, 1952.

Ibn Khaldūn, ᶜAbd al-Raḥmān b. Muḥammad, *The Muqadimmah: An Introduction to History*, trans. Franz Rosenthal, ed. and abridged N.J. Dawood, Princeton University Press, Princeton, 1989.

Ibn Khaldūn, ᶜAbd al-Raḥmān b. Muḥammad, *Riḥlat ibn khaldūn*, ed. Muḥammad Ibn Tāwīt al-Ṭanjī and Nūrī al-Jarrāḥ, Abu Dhabi and Beirut, 2003.

Ibn Khallikān, Aḥmad b. Muḥammad, *Wafayāt al-aᶜyān*, Beirut, 1997.

Ibn al-Khaṭīb, Lisān al-Dīn, *Al-iḥāṭah fi akhbār gharnāṭah*, Beirut, 2003.

Ibn Shaqrūn, Muḥammad b. Aḥmad, *Maẓāhir al-thaqāfah al-maghribiyyah: dirāsah fi 'l-adab al-maghribī fi 'l-ᶜaṣr al-marīnī*, Casablanca, 1985.

Ibrahim, Mahmood, 'Social and Economic Conditions in Pre-Islamic Mecca', *International Journal of Middle East Studies* 14, 1982.

al-Ibshīhī, Muḥammad b. Aḥmad, *Al-mustaṭraf fi kull fann mustaẓraf*, ed. Muḥammad Ḥalabī, Beirut, 1998.

al-Idrīsī, Muḥammad b. Muḥammad, *Kitāb nuzhat al-mushtāq*, Cairo, n.d.

Imru' al-Qays, Ḥunduj b. Ḥujr, *Dīwān*, Beirut, 1983.

Ingrams, Doreen, *A Time in Arabia*, John Murray, London, 1970.

Ingrams, Doreen and Leila (eds), *Records of Yemen*, Archive Editions, Neuchâtel, 1993.

Ingrams, Harold, *Arabia and the Isles*, 3rd edition, John Murray, London, 1966.

Ingrams, Harold, *The Yemen: Imams, Rulers and Revolutions*, John Murray, London, 1963.

Irwin, Robert, *Night, Horses and the Desert: The Penguin Anthology of Classical Arabic Literature*, Penguin, London, 2000.

al-Iryānī, Muṭahhar ʿAlī, *Nuqūsh musnadiyyah wa-taʿlīqāt*, 2nd edition, San'a, 1990.

al-Jabartī, ʿAbd al-Raḥmān, *ʿAjā'ib al-āthār fi 'l-tarājim wa-'l-akhbār*, Beirut, n.d.

al-Jābirī, Muḥammad, *Takwīn al-ʿaql al-ʿarabī*, Beirut, 2011.

Jackson, Peter, *The Delhi Sultanate: A Political and Military History*, Cambridge University Press, Cambridge, 1998.

al-Jāḥiẓ, ʿAmr b. Baḥr, *Kitāb al-bayān wa-'l-tabyīn*, Beirut, 2009.

al-Jarrāḥ, Nūrī (ed.), *Arḍ al-taʿāruf: ṣūrat ūrubbā, al-ḥajj, al-riḥlah al-muʿāṣirah*, Abu Dhabi, 2011.

Johnson, Penny, and Raja Shehadeh (eds), *Seeking Palestine*, Olive Branch Press, Northampton, Mass., 2013.

Jones, Alan, 'The Qur'an in the Light of Earlier Arabic Prose', in Alan Jones (ed.), *University Lectures in Islamic Studies* I, Al-Tajir World of Islam Trust, London, 1997.

Jones, Alan, 'The Word Made Visible: Arabic Script and the Committing of the Qur'an to Writing', in C.F. Robinson (ed.), *Texts, Documents and Artefacts*, Brill, Leiden, 2003.

Jones, Alan, review of Beatrice Gruendler, *Vetus Testamentum* 44, 1994.

Karsh, Efraim, *Islamic Imperialism: A History*, 2nd edition, Yale University Press, New Haven and London, 2007.

Kassir, Samir, *Being Arab*, Verso Books, London, 2013.

Kaye, Alan S., review of Yasir Suleiman, *Journal of the American Oriental Society* 125, 2005.

Keall, Edward J., review of Jan Retsö, *Bulletin of the American Schools of Oriental Research* 330, 2003.

Keay, John, *India: A History*, Harper Collins, London, 2004.

Kennedy, Hugh, *The Great Arab Conquests*, Orion Publishing, London, 2008.

Khusraw, Nāṣir, *Safarnāmah*, trans. (into Arabic) Yaḥyā al-Khashshāb, Beirut, 1983.

Kilito, Abdelfattah, *Thou Shalt Not Speak My Language*, Syracuse University Press, New York, 2008.

Kister, M.J., 'Al-Ḥīra: Some Notes on Its Relations with Arabia', *Arabica* 15, 1968.

Knauf, Ernst Axel, 'The Migration of the Script, and the Formation of the State in South Arabia', *Proceedings of the Society for Arabian Studies* 19, 1989.

al-Kurdī, Muḥammad Ṭāhir b. ʿAbd al-Qādir, *Tārīkh al-khaṭṭ al-ʿarabī wa-ādābihi*, n.p., 1939.

Lambourn, Elizabeth, 'From Cambay to Samudera-Pasai: The Export of Gujarati Grave Memorials to Sumatra and Java in the Fifteenth Century CE', *Indonesia and the Malay World* 31, 2003.

Lane, Edward William, *An Account of the Manners and Customs of the Modern Egyptians*, with Introduction by Jason Thompson, American University, Cairo, 2003.

Lane, Edward William, *Madd al-qāmūs: An Arabic-English Lexicon*, Williams and Norgate, London, 1863–93.

Lawrence, Bruce B., 'Early Indo-Muslim Saints and Conversion', *Islam in Asia* I, ed. Yohanan Friedmann, Magnes Press, Jerusalem, 1984.

Lecker, Michael, 'Kinda on the Eve of Islam and during the "Ridda"', *Journal of the Royal Asiatic Society* 4, 1994.

Lévi-Strauss, Claude, *Tristes Tropiques*, Penguin USA, New York, 1992.

Levtzion, Nehemia, and Randall L. Pouwels (eds), *The History of Islam in Africa*, Ohio University Press, Athens, Ohio, 2000.

Lewis, Bernard, *The Arabs in History*, 6th edition, Oxford University Press, Oxford, 1993.

Lewis, Bernard, 'The Concept of an Islamic Republic', *Die Welt des Islams* 4, 1956.

Lewis, Bernard, 'The Crows of the Arabs', *Critical Inquiry* 12, 1985.

Lings, Martin, *Sufi Poems: A Mediaeval Anthology*, Islamic Texts Society, Cambridge, 2004.

Maalouf, Amin, *The Crusades Through Arab Eyes*, Saqi Books, London, 1984.

al-Maᶜarrī, Abu 'l-ᶜAlā', *The Epistle of Forgiveness* I, ed. and trans. Geert Jan van Gelder and Gregor Schoeler, New York University Press, New York and London, 2013.

Macdonald, M.C.A. (ed.), *The Development of Arabic as a Written Language*, Oxford University Press, Oxford, 2010.

Macdonald, M.C.A., 'Nomads and the Ḥawrān in the Late Hellenistic and Roman Periods: A Reassessment of the Epigraphic Evidence', *Syria* 70, 1993.

Macdonald, M.C.A., 'The Seasons and Transhumance in Safaitic Inscriptions', *Journal of the Royal Asiatic Society* 2, 1992.

Mackintosh-Smith, Tim, *The Hall of a Thousand Columns: Hindustan to Malabar with Ibn Battutah*, John Murray, London, 2005.

Mackintosh-Smith, Tim, 'Interpreter of Treasures: Encounters', *Saudi Aramco World*, March/April 2013.

Mackintosh-Smith, Tim, 'Interpreter of Treasures: Food and Drink', *Saudi Aramco World*, May/June 2013.

Mackintosh-Smith, Tim, 'Interpreter of Treasures: A Portrait Gallery', *Saudi Aramco World*, September/October 2013.

Mackintosh-Smith, *Landfalls: On the Edge of Islam with Ibn Battutah*, John Murray, London, 2010.

Mackintosh-Smith, Tim, *Travels with a Tangerine: A Journey in the Footnotes of Ibn Battutah*, John Murray, London, 2001.

Mackintosh-Smith, Tim, *Yemen: Travels in Dictionary Land*, John Murray, London, 1997.

Mackintosh-Smith, Tim, *Yemen: The Unknown Arabia*, revised edition, The Overlook Press, New York, 2014.

Maigret, Alessandro de, 'The Arab Nomadic People and the Cultural Interface between the "Fertile Crescent" and "Arabia Felix"', *Arabian Archaeology and Epigraphy* 10, 1999.

al-Maqdisī (al-Muqaddasī), Shams al-Dīn, *Aḥsan al-taqāsīm fī maᶜrifat al-aqālīm*, ed. M.J. de Goeje, Brill, Leiden, 1967.

al-Maqqarī, Aḥmad b. Muḥammad, *Nafḥ al-ṭīb min ghuṣn al-andalus al-raṭīb*, ed. Iḥsān ᶜAbbās, Beirut, 1988.

al-Maqrīzī, Aḥmad b. ᶜAlī, *Kitāb al-mawāᶜiẓ wa-'l-iᶜtibār bi-dhikr al-khiṭaṭ wa-'l-āthār*, Cairo, n.d.

al-Marzūqī, Muḥammad Munṣif, 'Ayyu lughah sa-yatakallam al-ᶜarab al-qarn al-muqbil?', aljazeera.net, 6 November 2011.

al-Masᶜūdī, ᶜAlī b. al-Ḥusayn, *Murūj al-dhahab wa-maᶜādin al-jawhar*, ed. Muḥammad Muḥyi 'l-Dīn Ḥamīd, Beirut, n.d.

Mather, James, *Pashas: Traders and Travellers in the Islamic World*, Yale University Press, New Haven and London, 2009.

Mathews, Thomas, *Byzantium: From Antiquity to the Renaissance*, Yale University Press, New Haven and London, 1998.

Al-mawsūᶜah al-yamaniyyah, ed. Aḥmad Jābir ᶜAfīf *et al.*, San'a, 1992.

Morris, Jan, *Sultan in Oman*, Eland Books, London, 2000.

al-Muᶜallimī, Aḥmad ᶜAbd al-Raḥmān, *Kitābah ᶜalā ṣarḥ al-waḥdah al-yamaniyyah*, n.p. [San'a], n.d. [1994].

Naipaul, V.S., *An Area of Darkness*, Picador, London, 1995.

Nicholson, Reynold, *A Literary History of the Arabs*, Cambridge University Press, Cambridge, 1930.

Norris, H.T., *Saharan Myth and Saga*, Oxford University Press, Oxford, 1972.

Nowak, Martin, *Supercooperators*, Free Press, New York, 2011.

Owens, Jonathan, 'Arabic Dialect History and Historical Linguistic Mythology', *Journal of the American Oriental Society* 123, 2003.

Owens, Jonathan, 'Arabic Sociolinguistics', *Arabica* 48, 2001.

Owens, Jonathan, *A Linguistic History of Arabic*, Oxford University Press, Oxford, 2006.

Owens, Jonathan (ed.), *The Oxford Handbook of Arabic Linguistics*, Oxford University Press, Oxford, 2013.

Parker, A.G., and J.I. Rose, 'Climate Change and Human Origins in Southern Arabia', *Proceedings of the Society for Arabian Studies* 39, 2009.

Parry, James, 'The Pearl Emporium of Al Zubarah', *Saudi Aramco World*, November/December 2013.

Pellat, Charles, ed. and trans. (into French), *The Life and Works of Jāḥiẓ*, trans. (into English) D.M. Hawke, Routledge & Kegan Paul, London, 1969.
Piamenta, Moshe, *Dictionary of Post-Classical Yemeni Arabic*, Brill, Leiden, 1990.
Pintak, Lawrence, 'Border Guards of the "Imagined" *Watan*: Arab Journalists and the New Arab Consciousness', *Middle East Journal* 63, 2009.
Piotrovsky, M., *Al-yaman qabl al-islām*, trans. Muḥammad al-Shuᶜaybī, Beirut, 1987.
Pryce-Jones, David, *The Closed Circle: An Interpretation of the Arabs*, Weidenfeld & Nicolson, London, 1989.
Qabbānī, Nizār, *Al-aᶜmāl al-shiᶜriyyah wa-'l-siyāsiyyah al-kāmilah*, Beirut and Paris, 2007.
al-Qazwīnī, Zakariyyā' b. Muḥammad, *Āthār al-bilād wa-akhbār al-ᶜibād*, Beirut, n.d.
Rabin, Chaim, *Ancient West-Arabian*, Taylor's Foreign Press, London, 1951.
Rabin, Chaim, 'The Beginnings of Classical Arabic', *Studia Islamica* 4, 1955.
al-Rāzī, Aḥmad b. ᶜAbd Allāh, *Tārīkh madīnat ṣanᶜā'*, ed. Ḥusayn ᶜAbd Allāh al-ᶜAmrī and ᶜAbd al-Jabbār Zakkār, Damascus, 1974.
Rennie, Neil, *Far-Fetched Facts: The Literature of Travel and the Idea of the South Seas*, Clarendon Press, Oxford, 1995.
Retsö, Jan, *The Arabs in Antiquity: Their History from the Assyrians to the Umayyads*, Routledge/Curzon, London, 2002.
Rippin, A., 'The Qur'ān as Literature: Perils, Pitfalls and Prospects', *Bulletin of the British Society for Middle Eastern Studies* 10, 1983.
Rizvi, Saiyid Athar Abbas, *A History of Sufism in India* I, Munshiram Manoharlal Publishers, New Delhi, 1997.
Robb, Graham, *The Discovery of France*, Picador, London, 2007.
Robin, Christian, *Les Hautes-Terres du Nord-Yémen avant l'Islam* I, Nederlands Historisch-Archaeologisch Institut, Istanbul, 1982.
Rogan, Eugene, *The Arabs: A History*, Penguin, London, 2011.
Rogerson, Barnaby, *The Prophet Muhammad: A Biography*, Abacus, London, 2004.
Rosenthal, Franz, 'The Stranger in Medieval Islam', *Arabica* 44, 1997.
Rushdie, Salman, *Midnight's Children*, Penguin USA, New York, 1991.
Sa'di, *The Rose-Garden*, trans. Edward B. Eastwick, Octagon Press, London, 1979.
Schoeler, Gregor, 'Writing and Publishing: On the Use and Function of Writing in the First Centuries of Islam', *Arabica* 44, 1997.
Searight, Sarah, *Steaming East*, Bodley Head, London, 1991.
Searight, Sarah, and Jane Taylor, *Yemen: Land and People*, Pallas Athene, London, 2003.
Serjeant, R.B., *South Arabian Hunt*, Luzac, London, 1976.
Serjeant, R.B., review of René Dagorn, *Journal of the Royal Asiatic Society* 2, 1982.
Shaykhū, Luwīs, *Shuᶜarā' al-naṣrāniyyah fī 'l-jāhiliyyah*, Cairo, 1982.
Shehadeh, Raja, *Occupation Diaries*, Profile Books, London, 2012.
Shehadeh, Raja, *Palestinian Walks: Notes on a Vanishing Landscape*, Profile Books, London, 2008.
Shouby, E., 'The Influence of the Arabic Language on the Psychology of the Arabs', *Middle East Journal* 5, 1951.
al-Sīrāfī, Abū Zayd, and Ibn Faḍlān, *Two Arabic Travel Books*, ed. and trans. Tim Mackintosh-Smith and James E. Montgomery, New York University Press, New York and London, 2014.
Sizgorich, Thomas, '"Do Prophets Come with a Sword?": Conquest, Empire, and Historical Narrative in the Early Islamic World', *American Historical Review* 112, 2007.
Soueif, Ahdaf, *Cairo: My City, Our Revolution*, Bloomsbury, London, 2012.
Stark, Freya, *The Southern Gates of Arabia: A Journey in the Hadhramaut*, John Murray, London, 2003.
Stetkevych, Jaroslav, 'Some Observations on Arabic Poetry', *Journal of Near Eastern Studies* 26, 1967.
Stetkevych, Suzanne Pinckney, 'The ᶜAbbasid Poet Interprets History: Three Qaṣīdahs by Abū Tammām', *Journal of Arabic Literature* 10, 1979.
Suchem, Ludolph von, *Description of the Holy Land and the Way Thither*, trans. Aubrey Stewart, Palestine Pilgrims' Text Society, London, 1895.
Suleiman, Yasir, *The Arabic Language and National Identity: A Study in Ideology*, Edinburgh University Press, Edinburgh, 2003.
al-Suyūṭī, ᶜAbd al-Raḥmān b. Abū Bakr, *Al-muzhir fī ᶜulūm al-lughah al-ᶜarabiyyah*, Beirut, 2009.

Swanson, Jon C., *Emigration and Economic Development*, Westview Press, Boulder, 1979.

Tāj al-Dīn, Ḥasan, *The Islamic History of the Maldives Islands*, ed. Hikoichi Yajima, Tokyo, 1984.

al-Thaʿālibī, ʿAbd al-Malik b. Muḥammad, *Fiqh al-lughah wa-sirr al-ʿarabiyyah*, ed. ʿAbd al-Razzāq al-Mahdī, Beirut, 2010.

Tibbetts, G.R., *Arab Navigation in the Indian Ocean Before the Coming of the Portuguese*, Royal Asiatic Society, London, 1971.

Tidrick, Kathryn, *Heart-beguiling Araby: The English Romance with Arabia*, revised edition, Tauris & Co., London, 1989.

Trevaskis, Kennedy, *Shades of Amber*, Hutchinson, London, 1968.

Tuchman, Barbara W., *A Distant Mirror: The Calamitous 14th Century*, Macmillan, London, 1979.

Usāmah Ibn Munqidh, *Kitāb al-iʿtibār*, ed. Philip Hitti, Princeton University Press, Princeton, 1930.

Varisco, Daniel Martin, *Islam Obscured: The Rhetoric of Anthropological Representation*, Palgrave Macmillan, New York and Basingstoke, 2005.

Versteegh, Kees, *The Arabic Language*, Edinburgh University Press, Edinburgh, 2013.

Versteegh, Kees, 'Linguistic Contacts Between Arabic and Other Languages', *Arabica* 48, 2001.

Volpi, Frédéric, 'Pseudo-Democracy in the Muslim World', *Third World Quarterly* 25, 2004.

Whitfield, Susan, *Life Along the Silk Road*, John Murray, London, 2000.

Whitman, Walt, *The Portable Walt Whitman*, ed. Michael Warner, Penguin USA, New York, 2004.

Wilson, Robert T.O., *Gazetteer of Historical North-West Yemen*, G. Olms, Hildesheim, 1989.

Winnett, F.V., 'Studies in Ancient North Arabian', *Journal of the American Oriental Society* 107, 1987.

Wootton, David, *The Invention of Science: A New History of the Scientific Revolution*, Harper Collins, London, 2015.

Yāqūt al-Ḥamawī, *Muʿjam al-buldān*, ed. Farīd ʿAbd al-ʿAzīz al-Jundī, Beirut, n.d.

Young, Gavin, *In Search of Conrad*, Penguin, London, 1992.

Yule, Henry, *Cathay and the Way Thither*, 2nd edition, revised by Henri Cordier, Hakluyt Society, London, 1916.

Yule, Henry, and A.C. Burnell, *Hobson-Jobson: The Anglo-Indian Dictionary*, 2nd edition, ed. W. Crooke, John Murray, London, 1903.

Zubaida, Sami, *Beyond Islam: A New Understanding of the Middle East*, Tauris & Co., London, 2011.

INDEX